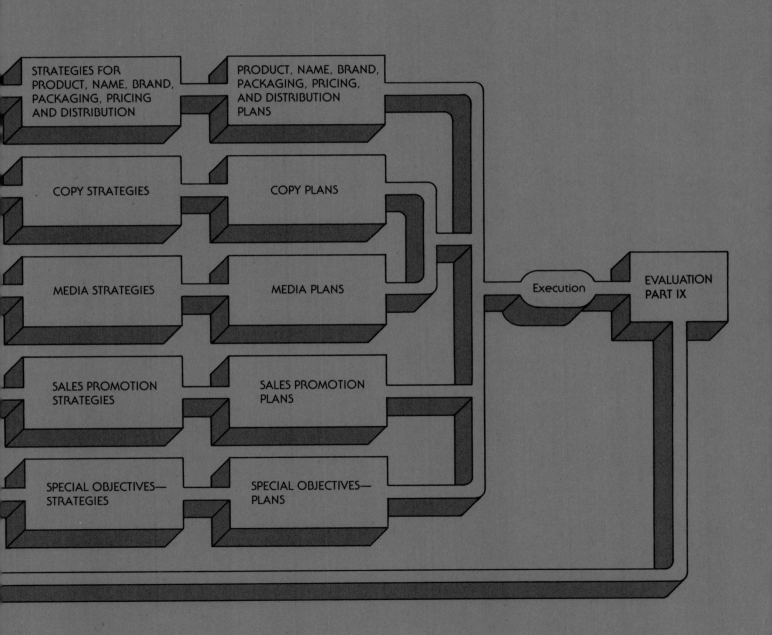

ADVERTISING

and the
Practice of Marketing

Kenneth E. Runyon

Northern Arizona University

Charles E. Merrill Publishing Company

A Bell & Howell Company

Columbus   Toronto   London   Sydney

This book is dedicated to the Lord, under Whom it was possible, and to my wife, Janie, and our children, Cynthia, Katherine, and Michael.

Additional credits: Page 14, Fig. 1–7, reprinted from JOURNAL OF MARKETING, Feb. 1971, vol. 8, Richard Johnson's "Market Segmentation," p. 16, published by the American Marketing Association. Color insert across from p. 91, Plate 5–5, reprinted with permission of General Wine and Spirits Co. Quotes from Mayer on pp. 187 and 215 are reprinted by permission of Curtis Brown, Ltd. Copyright © 1958 by Martin Mayer.

Photos: Celia Drake, p.157, Fig. 1–9; p. 158, Fig. 9–3; p. 159, Fig. 9–5; p.357, Fig. 19–8; p.368, Fig. 20–2; Picture desk of Newark, N.J. and Transit Advertising Association of Washington, D.C., p. 348, Fig. 19–4; Foster and Kleiser, p. 345, Figs. 19–1 & 19–2.

Published by
Charles E. Merrill Publishing Company
A Bell and Howell Company
Columbus, Ohio 43216

This book was set in English Times and Serif Gothic.
The production editor was Sharon Keck Thomason.
The cover was prepared by Will Chenoweth.
Cover photo: Four by Five.

Library of Congress Catalog Card Number: 78-70068
International Standard Book Number: 0-675-0-8311-7

Printed in the United States of America
2 3 4 5 6 7 8 9 10 / 85 84 83 82 81 80 79

Contents

Preface

There are a number of excellent books on advertising. Most of them are comprehensive, but few are developed within a systematic framework that enables one to conceptualize the planning process or visualize how a mass communications program should actually be developed. That is the purpose of this book.

One of the problems of advertising is that the communications plan for a modern marketer is extremely complex, involving a myriad of activities, all of which must be coordinated in order to be mutually supportive. The way in which the various elements of the marketing mix are manipulated will always depend upon the particular situation with which the marketer must deal. Such variables as whether industrial or consumer goods are being marketed; the nature of competition; the type of distribution employed; prevailing practices in the industry; the roles of advertising, sales promotion, price, packaging, and the product itself make up the situation. All of these variables must be isolated, evaluated, manipulated, and finally integrated into a unified, comprehensive, and persuasive marketing plan.

There is a temptation to try to include everything relating to marketing in a book on advertising because, surely, all of the various marketing elements are intertwined. But to do so would result in an encyclopedia of marketing and advertising—not a one semester text. So, choices have to be made; elements have to be eliminated; and those elements retained must be related to one another within a meaningful framework. I have chosen to do this through the device of the marketing plan, the basic document that underlies the execution of the final communications program.

Further, because this book is a book about "mass" communications, discussions of the sales force and its management have been eliminated. This is not meant to derogate the work of the sales force, which is a central ingredient in most marketing programs. The work of the sales force is not mass communication, however; it is "personal" communication. And, to do justice to the importance of personal selling requires a book in itself. Further, in most companies, the sales plan is a separate document from the marketing plan. In a mass production society, the marketing plan itself is basically a document for mass communications. At the same time, however, the marketing plan deals with more than advertising. Advertising does not stand by itself; it is an integral part of the marketing plan and is firmly rooted in strategic marketing considerations.

The marketing plan in a modern, sophisticated company is a coherent document that deals with all aspects of mass communications—the product and its position, packaging, price, distribution, advertising, sales promotion, and public relations. All of these are tools of mass communications. The whole process starts with a market review or situational analysis and culminates in an evaluation of whether or not the program has been successful. This evaluation, then, becomes a central part of the marketing review for the marketing plan for the next period of time. (The diagram on the inside front and back covers of this book illustrates the organization of a sample marketing plan. Part numbers are given to indicate the section of the text in which each section of the plan is discussed.)

For the successful company, marketing planning never ceases. While one plan is being executed, the next planning cycle begins. Plan follows plan, the consequences of each providing imput for its successor.

Marketing and advertising are demanding disciplines. They require many talents—analytical, judgmental, and creative. It is my hope that this book will provide the student of marketing and advertising with both an understanding and a "feel" for the planning process.

In preparing this book, I am indebted to many people. Specificially, I acknowledge my indebtedness to four former presidents of the Gardner Advertising Company with whom I worked over a period of twenty years. To Elmer Marshutz, who brought a sense of humanity and compassion to the practice of advertising. To Charlie Claggett, whose toleration of my idiosyncrasies taught me patience and forbearance. To Champ Humphrey, who helped me understand the meaning of personal integrity. And to Warren Kratky, from whom I learned the value of analysis and systematic thinking. And there are others who made significant contributions to my education: Bea Adams, a great copywriter; Rudy Czufin, Executive Art Director; John Davidson, an Account Supervisor; Bill Spencer, Executive Director of the Creative Department; and many, many others. On the client side, I am particularly indebted to Bob Piggott, Director of Advertising for Pet, Inc. a good friend. These debts can never be repaid.

Introduction

The first two chapters of this book serve as an introduction to, and an organizational framework for that which will follow.

Chapter 1 characterizes the nature of the economy within which marketing and marketing communications are a dominant force. It also defines a number of basic marketing terms, identifies the role of marketing communications, and briefly characterizes the marketing process.

Chapter 2 deals with the nature and structure of the marketing industry, comments on the ways in which advertising agencies are compensated, looks briefly at forms of organization characteristic of advertisers and advertising agencies, and introduces the subject of marketing budgets.

All in all, the purpose of this first section is to give the student a broad perspective and general understanding of the marketing system and of the organizations and processes which characterize it.

The Marketing Process

Volkswagen

Or the Magic Transformation of the Beetle: in which a Jewish Advertising Agency turns a Nazi automobile into the Sixth-Largest-Selling Car in the United States, as William Bernbach, Helmut Krone, and Julian Koenig take a Small, Cheap, Ugly, Slow, Imported German Car, and without laying Hand to Fender change it into a Popular, Desirable, Lovable, Attractive Staple of American Life; Or, THANK GOD FOR THE SECOND WORLD WAR: IT BROUGHT US ALL CLOSER TOGETHER.[1]

Thus, Robert Glatzer begins the story of Volkswagen, a marketing phenomenon of the 1960s. All of us have our favorite Volkswagen headlines: "Lemon," "Think Small," "How does the man who drives the snow plow get to work?" or, the commercial storyboard shown in figure 1–1: "Got a lot to carry? Get a Box."

When we think of Volkswagen's success, we think of advertising. But, that's not where it started. Volkswagen had sold tens of thousands of automobiles in

the United States before its national advertising began. It was a marketing success *before* it started advertising. Advertising only helped it to become a greater success. There is often a tendency to overemphasize the role of advertising in the success or failure of a product or service, to assume that increased sales are the inevitable result of sound advertising, and faltering sales the dependable consequence of weak advertising. We sometimes forget that other factors in the marketing mix can sabotage an outstanding advertising campaign or camouflage the shortcomings of a weak one.

Rosser Reeves, an outstanding advertising practitioner, speaks to this point with the following observations:

A famous razor-blade manufacturer had been running a brilliant campaign. Sales had been forging ahead. Then, by accident, millions of blades with defective steel were let loose on the market. Sales shot down, and the brand was almost crippled, but—the decline was not the fault of advertising.

A great laxative had been running a strong campaign. For years it had produced a steady increase in sales. Then, an accident of chemistry made thousands of

---

1. Robert Glatzer, *The New Advertising* (New York: The Citadel Press, 1970), p. 19.

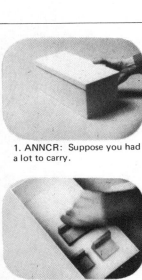

1. ANNCR: Suppose you had a lot to carry.

2. You get a box.

3. And suppose you wanted to carry lots of people too.

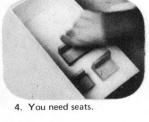

4. You need seats.

5. And maybe you'd work it so you can walk to the back . . .

6. to change a diaper or squash a rebellion.

7. And windows ...

8. 23 at least.

9. And why not a hole in the roof . . .

10. to let the sun in.

11. Doors ... of course. Two in front.

12. Two big ones here ...

13. and one here. In the back.

14. Paint it up real pretty. Put it on wheels. (SFX)

15. And you've got the whole idea behind the Volkswagen station wagon.

Figure 1–1. (Volkswagen of America)

bottles highly toxic. The brand almost disappeared from the market, but again—the decline was not the fault of advertising.

A food product, on the other hand, had been running a very poor campaign. Competitors were moving steadily ahead. Then, a change in product made the brand almost a household sensation, and sales shot up—with no change in advertising.

One of America's richest companies decided to enter the dentifrice field. Within a period of three years this company introduced not one, but two major brands—spending over $50,000,000 in powerful advertising, sampling, and promotion. The share of market of many of the older brands, naturally, dipped down. It would be folly, however, to equate this decline with their advertising campaigns. . . .

Recently a group of marketing men, almost idly, at a luncheon table, listed thirty-seven different factors, any or all of which could cause the total sales of a brand to move up or down.

Advertising was only one of these.

The product may be wrong. Price may be at fault. Distribution may be poor. The sales force may not be adequate. Budgets may be too low. A better product may be sweeping the market. A competitor may be outwitting you with strong deals. There are many variables.

And when a wheel has many spokes, who can say which spoke is supporting the wheel.?[2]

A great advertising program does not stand alone. It is firmly rooted in sound marketing strategies and coordinated with other marketing activities. Volkswagen is a case in point. The indomitable Beetle or Bug burst on the American scene at a propitious time. American cars were getting bigger, flashier, and more expensive—both to buy and to operate. Planned obsolescence, a marketing strategy based on annual design changes, turned last year's dream into an antique. Americans were becoming more affluent, and a second car was becoming a psychological "must" in a society dominated by suburban living, widely dispersed shopping centers, and almost nonexistent public transportation. The American housewife was becoming a prisoner in her suburban castle. But, even increased affluence was hard pressed to accommodate two or more standard sized American cars plus all of the other attractive consumer goods that were inundating the market place. Volkswagen was an answer to this problem. It was a small, inexpensive car that could be parked on a dime and turned on a nickel, a car designed for short trips and overcrowded parking lots.

An ideal complement to the "monsters" that filled American garages.

Another time, another place, another competitive situation, another consumer psychology, and the Volkswagen advertising campaign might have been unheeded; the Bug would have been another also ran. After all, the Baby Austin of the 1930s and the Crosley of the 1940s were small cars that didn't really make a ripple in the marketing pond. And in the 1970s, the Rabbit, the Scirocco, and the Dasher—also Volkswagen built—are not living up to the legacy handed down by the Bug.[3]

ADVERTISING—THE TIP OF THE ICEBERG

In a sense, advertising is only the tip of the iceberg. True, it is an expensive tip—over $37 billion in 1977. But $37 billion is too large a sum for most of us to grasp—its magnitude makes it an empty number. The true magnitude of advertising is better comprehended through the following quotation from *Advertising Age.*

Every day 4.2 billion advertising messages pour forth from 1,754 daily newspapers, millions of others from 8,151 weeklies, and 1.4 billion more each day from 4,147 magazines and periodicals. There are 3,895 AM and 1,136 FM radio stations broadcasting an average of 730,000 commercials a day, and 770 television stations broadcast 100,000 commercials a day. Every day millions of people are confronted with 330,000 outdoor billboards, with 2,500,000 cards and posters in busses, subways and commuter trains, with 51,300,000 direct mail pieces and leaflets, and with billions of display and promotion items.[4]

Despite its magnitude, advertising is still only the tip of the iceberg because it is the most visible portion of the entire marketing effort. Behind every commercial that is broadcast by radio or television and behind every print ad that appears in magazines or newspapers, are thousands of hours spent in research and development, data analysis, strategic planning, plan preparation, creative conceptualization, mechanical production, and all of the record keeping and clerical functions that accompany these activities. In order to understand advertising, we must understand its genesis—how it is developed, and the thinking upon which it is based. This means that we must briefly examine the marketing economy and define some key marketing terms.

2. Rosser Reeves, *Reality in Advertising* (New York: Alfred A. Knopf, 1961), pp. 3–5.

3. "Volkswagen's Herr Fix-It," *Time* (May 16, 1977): 66–67.
4. Leo Bogart, *Strategy in Advertising* (New York: Harcourt, Brace, & Jovanovich, 1967), as reported in "The Ads Pour Forth," *Advertising Age* (November 21, 1973): 7.

THE MARKETING ECONOMY

Throughout history, organized societies have faced the problem of applying *distributive justice*. Distributive justice refers to the way in which an organized society distributes its benefits and burdens among its members. [5]

The problem of administering distributive justice arises because each member of society has a variety of needs and, in the aggregate, these needs are infinite. At the same time, the resources required to meet these needs are finite, and not all needs of all members of society can be met. This problem became particularly acute in the United States in 1973 when a shortage of petroleum products resulted in many service stations closing because of inadequate supplies of gasoline, and those stations remaining open were beset by long lines of frantic, impatient, and sometimes angry motorists. The severe winter of 1977 created a shortage of natural gas and other heating fuels that resulted in both the closing of schools and manufacturing plants and an appeal from the President of the United States for consumers to reduce their thermostats to 65 degrees during the day, and even lower at night. A coffee shortage in 1977 drove coffee prices sky high, and the shift of consumers to tea drove up the price of this commodity. The President of the United States warned of an energy crisis on prime-time television, and consumers started becoming aware that the future promised world-wide shortages of energy, food, and other basic commodities.

The shortages referred to above are often described as crises because their sudden onset worked hardships on a public accustomed to an ample supply of the commodities in question. Short of a crisis, however, all organized societies have had to deal with a disparity between human needs and the resources to meet these needs. In an industrialized society such as the United States, this disparity gives rise to such pragmatic questions as

1. Who shall have an education?
2. Who shall have an automobile?
3. Who shall have a refrigerator?
4. Who shall own a home?
5. Who shall have medical treatment?
6. Who shall eat steak?

The ultimate questions become how much of a particular product or service shall be produced, and whom within society shall benefit from this production?

Every society, if it is to survive, must find some way of reconciling the disparity between supply and demand, between limited resources and unlimited needs. Practically, for an industrial society, there are two possibilities: an *authoritarian society,* which defines needs and allocates resources in terms of consciously determined societal goals, and a *marketing society,* sometimes called a *capitalistic, price,* or *enterprise* economy, which lets price control the supply and demand of products that consumers want. [6]

The Authoritarian Society

On the surface, an authoritarian society appears to offer the simplest solution to the disparities between supply and demand. Someone in society—a central committee or government agency—determines society's needs and allocates resources to meet these needs within a specified period of time. Unfortunately, the authoritarian system is not as simple as it sounds. Failure to identify consumer needs properly, conflicts in priorities among planners, inability to coordinate and control the execution of the plan, and the rigidity and unresponsiveness of the entire process lead to misallocation of resources, chronic shortages, shoddy merchandise, and turn what appears to be a rational process of allocation into an exercise in frustration, bureaucratic bungling, and corruption. [7]

The Marketing Society

A marketing economy differs from an authoritarian economy in that it appears to operate without conscious planning since there is no central committee or government agency to determine society's needs and to allocate resources to meet them. However, planning does exist. In the marketing economy, planning is done primarily at the level of the individual firm, within broad constraints established by the government.

The marketing economy was first described by Adam Smith in the *Wealth of Nations* in 1776. The basic assumption underlying the marketing economy is that each member of society is best able to determine his own needs, and should be left free to pursue his own self-interest without government interference.

5. Norman E. Bowie, *Towards a New Theory of Distributive Justice* (Amherst, Massachusetts: The University of Massachusetts Press, 1971), p. 4.

6. Kenneth E. Runyon, *Consumer Behavior and the Practice of Marketing* (Columbus, Ohio: Charles E. Merrill Publishing Co., 1977), p. 5.

7. For a popular account of problems of allocation in an authoritarian society, see: Hedrick Smith, *The Russians* (New York: Quadrangle/The New York Times Book Co., 1976).

Supply and demand are regulated by the price mechanism. Those products are produced that the consumer is willing to pay for, and the consumer will pay for those products desired. The consumers' "votes," as measured in dollars of purchasing power, determine resource allocation automatically.

Each producer is free to make whatever product it chooses in the quantity it is willing to produce. The only restriction on a producer's actions is its ability to induce consumers to purchase the product. If the producer sells all or most of what is produced at a price that is greater than the costs, there will be a profit. If the producer is unable to sell the total production at a satisfactory price, it will suffer loss and, in extreme cases, be forced out of business. Failure in one business does not preclude shifting to another, provided the capital required to start the new enterprise is available. [8]

The overriding mechanism that makes the whole system work is disarmingly simple; it is *competition.* Adam Smith referred to competition as the *invisible hand* that guided the system in such a way that both society and the individual benefitted from its operation.

Each producer competes with every other producer for the consumers' dollars. Those who compete effectively succeed, and those who compete ineffectively fail. Since consumers, acting out of self-interest, buy only what they want, the pressure is on producers to provide products and services that meet consumers' needs.

The marketing system is not perfect. Fraud, misrepresentation, abuse of power, greed, collusion, and the promotion of patently harmful products have marred its operation and forced government intervention to protect both individual consumers and society itself. Critics have castigated the marketing system for being wasteful and for promoting personal consumption over societal benefit; they have condemned it for manufacturing demand and misallocating resources. Despite its imperfections, the marketing system has produced an unequalled abundance of consumer goods and an immeasurable array of consumer choice; it has elevated consumption to a national pastime in the United States.

Marketing in the United States

The United States is a leading exponent of the marketing system. Competition among producers is a national policy of the United States government. The sanctity of competition has been protected by the Sherman Antitrust Act (1890), the Federal Trade Commission Act and the Clayton Act (1914), the Robinson-Patman Act (1936), and the Anti-Merger

Act (1950). Taken together, these acts discourage contracts, combinations, or conspiracies in restraint of trade; prohibit unfair methods of competition; define price discrimination as unlawful (subject to certain defenses); and prevent intercorporate acquisitions which may have an adverse effect on competition. As a consequence, competition is a way of life for producers. Competition exists in all areas, and in many it is intense. The success of a business enterprise depends upon its ability to persuade consumers to buy its products.

Nor has the consumer been neglected. Beginning with the Pure Food and Drug Act and the Meat Inspection Act of 1906 (the purposes of which were to protect consumers from dangerous drugs and adulterated foods) Congress and state legislatures have passed consumer protection legislation in ever increasing quantities. The Wheeler-Lea Amendment (1938) prohibits deceptive packaging, deceptive pricing, and deceptive advertising; the Flammable Fabrics Act (1955), the Automobile Information Disclosure Act (1958), the Cigarette Labeling and Advertising Act (1967), and a host of other legislation are designed for the benefit of the consumer. Many critics of consumer protection legislation believe that the government has exceeded good judgment in this area and has erected unreasonable barriers against free competition. They are probably right. Although some of the consumer protection legislation is clearly desirable, some is disputable or even absurd. As a case in point, the FTC challenged Wonder Bread in the mid-1970s for using the copy line "Wonder Bread helps build strong bodies 12 ways." Wonder Bread was brought to court, not because their claim was untrue, but because it was not unique; the FTC contended that other enriched breads provided the same benefit. The courts ruled in favor of Wonder Bread, establishing a precedent that truthful claims are not unlawful despite the opinion of a government bureaucracy. Cranapple, a combination apple and cranberry juice drink, was enjoined by the FTC to run corrective advertising to clarify the company's claim that Cranapple was higher in food value than competitive beverages. Again, the issue was not that the statement was untrue, but that it was misleading. *Food value* means calories, a fact that the FTC contended was unknown by most consumers.

One effect of marketing legislation has been to place producers on the defensive, and cause them to carefully scrutinize their marketing and advertising programs to avoid unintentional violations of the law. Advertising copy must be carefully checked for legal compliance; packaging and labeling are thoroughly reviewed by company attorneys; and contests, promotions, and point-of-sale materials are surrounded by legal restrictions.

---

8. Runyon, *Consumer Behavior,* p. 8.

SOME KEY MARKETING CONCEPTS

Before we turn to the role of advertising and other forms of mass communications in marketing products and services, we need to define a few marketing terms that are central to the entire process. In this section, I will define *marketing, the market,* the *marketing concept, product differentiation, market segmentation, product space, product positioning, product concept,* and *product image.*[9]

Marketing

According to Peter Drucker, a leading management consultant, the only valid purpose of a business is to create a customer.

> Because its purpose is to create a customer, the business enterprise has two—and only these two—basic functions: marketing and innovation. Marketing and innovation produce results; all the rest are "costs."
>
> Marketing is the distinguishing, unique function of the business. A business is set apart from all other human organizations by the fact that it markets a product or a service. Neither church, nor army, nor school, nor state does that. Any organization that fulfills itself through marketing a product or a service is a business. Any organization in which marketing is either absent or incidental is not a business and should never be managed as if it were one.[10]

Drucker emphasizes marketing in terms of its relationship to a business, or profit-making enterprise. Since the early 1970s, there has been a strong movement to extend the definition of marketing to include nonbusiness organizations as well—organizations such as churches, charities, government, and so forth.[11] Those who support this extended definition of marketing argue that many marketing activities can be used in support of causes and organizations for which economic profit is not a major objective. They are quite right, of course. Many of the tools of marketing—objective and systematic thinking, identification of target groups for persuasion, paid communications (advertising), and so forth—can be applied to other areas of human activity. However, they go beyond this point. They say, in effect, marketing involves exchange—the exchange of money for goods or services. Therefore, marketing is exchange. Other organiza-

tions also involve exchange—the exchange of a charitable contribution for a feeling of philanthropy; the exchange of a vote for a political promise; the exchange of membership in a church for personal salvation. Thus, since marketing is exchange, all exchange is marketing.

Critics of this point of view strongly disagree. They insist that to say that "marketing is exchange, therefore all exchange is marketing" is like saying "A dog is an animal, therefore all animals are dogs"—obviously a logical fallacy. They agree that many marketing activities can be applied to nonprofit organizations and causes. However, they insist that marketing is more than a "bundle of techniques"; it also involves a system of ethics and an economic philosophy that may not be applicable to charitable foundations, churches, politics, and other similar nonprofit endeavors.

I will not try to resolve this conflict in this text. The disagreements have been characterized by emotional arguments rather than by thoughtful analysis. For the purposes of this text, marketing will be treated as it applies to business, always recognizing that some of the marketing tools we discuss may be useful in other situations.

In keeping with this approach, we will define marketing as *the performance of business activities that direct the flow of goods and services from producer to consumer or user.*[12] This definition of marketing may be referred to as *micromarketing* since it deals with the activities of individual firms. By contrast, the term *macromarketing* is used to refer to the aggregate activity of business, or the total of the economic activities of a society. Although our focus throughout this book will be on micromarketing, we must recognize that micromarketing is carried out within the framework of the philosophy and constraints of the macroeconomic system.

Markets

The term *market* is a somewhat ambiguous concept that is used in a variety of ways, depending upon the context of its use. Generically, the market is a group of people with purchasing power who are willing to spend money to satisfy their needs. Three aspects of this definition should be noted: people, purchasing power, and willingness to spend.

People. All products and services are acquired by people, and these people are the object of all market-

9. The following discussion of marketing definitions is, with minor modifications, taken from Runyon, *Consumer Behavior,* pp. 9–22.
10. Peter Drucker, *Management* (New York: Harper & Row, Publishers, 1974), pp. 61–62.
11. Philip Kotler and Sindey J. Levy, "Broadening the Concept of Marketing," *Journal of Marketing* (January, 1969): 10–15.
12. R.I. Alexander and The Committee on Definitions of the American Marketing Association, *Marketing Definitions* (Chicago: American Marketing Association, 1960), p. 15.

ing activity. This is true whether we are speaking of a pet owner buying food for the family pet, an industrial buyer making a purchase for a company, a housewife buying for other members of her family, or an individual making a purchase for himself.

Purchasing power. The second element in the concept of a market is purchasing power. Without purchasing power, there is no market in the business sense. Most people, for example are not a part of the market for a Rolls-Royce simply because they do not have the $43,200 or so that is required to buy the economy model.

Willingness to spend. The third element in the concept of market is willingness to spend. People must be willing to spend their purchasing power for a product before they can be considered a part of its market. People spend their money in satisfaction of their needs. Or, as Peter Drucker has pointed out: "It is the customer alone whose willingness to pay for a good or for a service converts resources into wealth." [13]

These three elements—people, purchasing power, and willingness to spend—constitute our basic definition of a market. *Market* may be used in other ways also; for example, we may speak of a city as a market, or we may speak of the automobile market (meaning all people who want and are able to purchase an automobile). But in all cases the use will imply or assume these three elements.

The Marketing Concept

The marketing concept is the central theory in marketing. It has emerged over time as the response of business to changes in the economic environment. During its history as a nation, the United States has grown from an undeveloped economy to a highly developed one, from an agricultural society with few manufacturing facilities to an industrial society that produces an almost infinite variety of manufactured goods in an constant stream. The growth of its manufacturing capabilities, along with the development of an extensive system of distribution, became so great that consumers began demanding choice in the things they purchased. They were no longer willing to buy what business wanted to produce. It was no longer sufficient to produce a product, distribute it, and high pressure consumers into buying it. Consumers became particular. They demanded products that were tailored to their specific needs.

The marketing concept is the sellers' response to the demands of consumers. Instead of manufacturing a product and then trying to sell it, the business enterprise operating under the marketing concept first finds out what the consumer wants and then produces that product. The approach sounds simple, but it is often difficult to implement. The sellers' preoccupation with what the consumer wants is referred to as *consumer orientation.*

Consumer orientation alone is not enough to operate a successful business. It is possible to give consumers what they want and still fail to make a profit. We would all be delighted to buy a new Chrysler Cordoba for $1,200, but Chrysler could not afford to charge this price and avoid bankruptcy. So, the second element of the marketing concept is *profit.* Business must please the consumer, but it must also make a profit.

There is still a third element in the marketing concept. A business is a complex organization, and communication and coordination within the enterprise are difficult to bring about. Decisions at one level or in one division of a business operation may be cancelled out, unconsciously or intentionally, by the activities at another level or in another sector. The product designed with the consumer in mind may be sabotaged by a cost-conscious production department. The effort of a salesperson to build warm customer relations may be erased by the thoughtless decision of a credit manager. To avoid such errors, a consumer orientation must permeate the entire enterprise, and the company must be organized for the service of the consumer. Lack of such coordination may lead to the humorous situation depicted in the cartoon in figure 1–2.

To summarize, the marketing concept is made up of three parts:

1. *Consumer orientation.* The products of the firm must be created with consumer needs in mind.
2. *Profit.* In serving the consumer, the enterprise must make a profit. Consumer orientation is a strategy to attain that end.
3. *Internal organization.* The entire company must be organized and coordinated in the service of the consumer.

The marketing concept has certain clear implications for the manufacturer who adopts it as a philosophy of business. First, there must be a basic understanding of consumer needs and of the psychological and social factors that influence consumer behavior. Second, the manufacturer must keep in constant touch with consumers through marketing research, so that at all times the product will reflect those attributes that are important to consumers.

13. Drucker, *Management,* p. 61.

As marketing requested it   As sales order it   As engineering designed it

As plant manufactured it   As field service installed   What the customer wanted!!!

Figure 1-2. Internal Communication

Product Differentiation and Market Segmentation

Product differentiation and market segmentation are the two basic strategies that a seller may use in approaching a given market. In product differentiation, the marketer goes after the whole market but attempts to differentiate the company's brand from competitive brands through unique product features or on the basis of advertising claims alone. In market segmentation, on the other hand, the marketer does not try to appeal to the entire market, but chooses to isolate a part or segment of the market and direct the marketing effort toward this segment alone.[14]

Product differentiation. In many markets, a number of similar products compete for consumer sales. For all practical purposes, the products are identical in function, and may be used interchangeably. The consumer has no real basis for choosing one product over the other. A firm faced with this kind of competitive situation may attempt to create consumer preference for its brand by making unique advertising claims or by modifying the brand in some insignificant way so that is *appears* different and can be distinguished from competitive brands. Styling differences in the automotive industry are examples of product differentiation. Pall Mall's gold package is an

attempt to impute quality to the brand and differentiate it from other brands of cigarettes. "Green Power," an advertising claim for a brand of lawn and garden fertilizer, is an effort to achieve the same end. Wonder Bread's use of the headline "Helps build strong bodies 12 ways," is an example of product differentiation. Applied effectively, product differentiation may be successful in creating sales and increasing market share. This is particularly true when the differentiated claim makes sense to consumers and is consistent with what they believe to be important in terms of product performance. In product differentiation, however, the marketer continues to direct marketing efforts toward the entire market for the product type. The Quasar television advertisement (figure 1-3) is an excellent example of product differentiation.

Market segmentation. Few markets are entirely homogeneous. The market for a particular product type is often composed of several submarkets of consumers, each with somewhat different product expectations and needs. Market segmentation is the development of a different marketing approach for each identifiable market segment. Philip Kotler has defined market segmentation in the following way:

> Market segmentation is the subdividing the market into homogeneous subsets of customers, where any subset may conceivably be selected as a market target to be reached with a distinct marketing mix.[15]

14. W. R. Smith, "Product Differentiation and Market Segmentation as Alternative Marketing Strategies," *Journal of Marketing*, **21** (July, 1956): 3–8.

15. Philip Kotler, *Marketing Management* (Englewood Cliffs, New Jersey: Prentice-Hall, Inc., 1972), p. 166.

When it comes to buying a color TV, the last thing to trust is your luck.

The problem with the good luck method of buying a TV, is you never know how long your luck will hold out. Which is why it pays to depend on Quasar.

We challenge any other TV maker to make this statement.

In the first 8 months, our records show that during the warranty period, 97% of the new Quasar® 13" and 15" diagonal sets with the Service Miser™ Chassis, required no repairs. And we challenge any other television maker to match that.
Ask your Quasar dealer for his facts. Then ask him to show you a Quasar.
That way, when you buy your next TV, you'll finally have a choice. **You can trust the facts.** Or trust your luck.

you can depend on
Quasar

Quasar Electronics Company 9401 W. Grand Ave., Franklin Park, IL 60131

Figure 1-3.   (Quasar Electronics Co.)

Markets may be segmented in a variety of ways. They may be segmented in terms of age, income, sex, occupation, family size, or other demographic characteristics. They may be segmented on the basis of psychological factors, sociological dimensions, quantities purchased, or other usage patterns. A classical example of market segmentation is the strategy of economic segmentation recommended by a policy committee of General Motors in the early 1920s. This committee recommended that General Motors market six different automobiles, falling into the following price ranges:[16]

1. $450 - $600
2. $600 - $900
3. $900 - $1,200
4. $1,200 - $1,700
5. $1,700 - $2,500
6. $2,500 - $3,500

The automobile industry has changed in the past fifty years—all prices have increased, and in some cases price distinctions have become blurred. Nonetheless, the segmentation strategy behind this initial

16. Alfred P. Sloan, *My Years with General Motors* (New York: McFadden Books, 1965), p. 67.

pricing recommendation can be seen in the comparative price ranges of the Cadillac, the Oldsmobile, and the Chevrolet.

Much of the marketing segmentation that exists takes place on the basis of geographic or demographic dimensions. In addition, however, markets may be segmented in terms of psychological or social characteristics. The cigarette market is segmented in terms of filter and nonfilter cigarettes, the presumed difference in consumers being their concern for "mildness," or fear of lung cancer or other respiratory ailments. Within the filter market, cigarettes are segmented even further. Some cigarettes, such as Bensen & Hedges' Multi-Filter, are designed for the "sophisticated"; others, such as Marlboro, are "down to earth." Some emphasize fun; others emphasize independence, femininity, masculinity, or sex. An outstanding example of segmentation is represented by Virginia Slims and Eve. Both are directed at the women's segment of the cigarette market. But within this segment, they are clearly directed toward different kinds of women. The Virginia Slims package is plain, almost masculine in its simplicity, enhanced only by the product name and edged on one side by a series of straight lines. The advertising is impudent and self-assertive. The model wears masculine clothes, exudes confidence, and is attractively audacious. The copy and illustration compare the traditional role of women with today's liberated woman and sums up the comparison with the headline, "You've come a long way, baby."

And then there is Eve—pretty Eve. The package is delicate and feminine, covered with frills and interwoven vines and leaves. The advertising carries out the feminine theme, characterizing femininity as soft, desirable, dependent, and unique. The choice is clear. Virginia Slims is for the liberated woman; Eve is for the woman who likes things the way they were. Virginia Slims and Eve represent two different kinds of women, dramatically different in personality.

Not all products can be segmented in the same way. The particular form of segmentation depends upon the needs and interests of the consuming groups involved. Furthermore, successful segmentation generally requires three conditions. The market being identified for segmentaion should be measurable, sizable, and reachable.

Measurable.   A market segment should be subject to both definition and measurement. If it cannot be defined, it cannot be measured; and if it cannot be measured, its potential for sales cannot be estimated. Segmentation based on psychological or behavioral characteristics is more difficult to measure than segmentation made along standard demographic or geographic dimensions.

Sizable. The market segment must be large enough to support an independent marketing effort. There are many market segments that are too small to justify the cost of developing a product to serve their needs. Frequently, a segment may be so small that it will not produce sufficient revenue to permit the product to be advertised or promoted. The marketing system does not guarantee that all consumer needs will be served. It only serves those needs that can be served at a profit.

Reachable. It is not enough for a market segment to be measurable and sizable. It also must be reachable with advertising and promotion. Often, special-media exist, which make it possible to reach particular markets. The baby market, a segment of the family market, may be reached through magazines and gift packs distributed in the maternity wards of hospitals. Sports car buffs, a segment of the automotive market, may be reached through magazines edited with their specialized interests in mind. In some instances, a market segment may be large enough to justify the use of general media. The market for blond hair rinses, a segment of the cosmetic market, is an example.

Although market segmentation is a widely used marketing strategy, it is often difficult to identify viable market segments. Thus, a survey of marketing executives found that "recognizing, defining, understanding, and segmenting markets" is one of their most worrisome problems.[17]

One way to approach the problem of market segmentation is to consider the concepts of product space, product position, and product concept.

Product Space, Product Position, and Product Concept

Every product has a variety of dimensions or attributes that are distinguishable by consumers. These attributes include price, size, texture, taste (in food products), method of distribution, hardness, quality, convenience, and so forth. *A product space is an abstract space bounded by relevant product attributes.* Thus, we can construct a product space on the basis of one or more of these attributes. Figure 1–4 shows a linear product space—a product space based on a single attribute. In this instance, the product category chosen is automobiles; the single product attribute is price.

Different brands of automobiles may be *positioned* on this line in terms of their price; the Chevette at one end of the line, for example, with Rolls-Royce at the other. Other automobile brands may be positioned in

17. C. N. Waldo, "What's Bothering Marketing Chiefs Most? Segmenting," *Advertising Age* (June 4, 1973): 77.

Chevette	Rolls-Royce
Under $3,000	Over $40,000

Figure 1–4. Linear product space for automobiles based on price

their appropriate places between these two extremes. A Plymouth Fury at a price of $7,000 represents a possible product position on the price dimension. The position of a product in this product space determines the market segment for which it has been developed, and to which its advertising and promotion is addressed. This can be clearly seen in the differences in the advertising for the Chevy Chevette and the Rolls-Royce (see plates 1–1 and 1–2 in insert following p. 26). The Chevy Chevette advertisement is clearly based on economy; the Rolls-Royce advertisement, on luxury.

Figure 1–5 shows a two-dimensional product space for a candy product, with intensity of chocolate flavor and amount of sweetness as the product attributes upon which the product space is built. Product A represents a position for a product that has a slightly sweet and weak chocolate taste; position B is for a product that is slightly sweet with a strong chocolate flavor; position C, very sweet with a weak chocolate flavor; and position D, very sweet with a strong chocolate flavor. Other positions may be located in various intermediate points in the product space. Different consumers have different taste preferences for intensity of flavor and for degree of sweetness. No one position in the product space satisfies all consumers equally well.

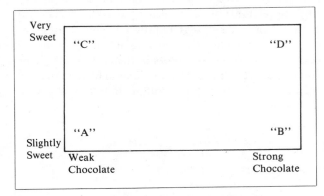

Figure 1–5. Two dimensional product space based on sweetness and flavor

In the 1960s when Sego and Metracal were battling for domination of the liquid diet-food market, Sego used the product dimensions of flavor and sweetness to gain a competitive share advantage. Both brands were developing and introducing new flavors as fast as possible in an effort to increase their market share. Most new flavors were standard offerings such as vanilla, chocolate, dark chocolate, pineapple, strawberry, cherry, coconut, and so forth. As the number of flavors grew, it became difficult to think of a flavor that one of the two brands did not have. Furthermore, as new flavors became more esoteric and bizarre, they generated fewer sales.

Sego broke the stalemate through product positioning research conducted by the Arthur D. Little Company. Professional taste testers employed by Arthur D. Little found: (1) all of the flavors for both Sego and Metracal occupied an intermediate position in a product space bounded by intensity of flavor and degree of sweetness; and (2) a substantial body of consumers preferred a flavor that was very sweet and very intense. Sego capitalized on this research by introducing a new line of Very flavors—Very Sweet and Very Rich (see figure 1–6). By doing so, it captured market leadership.

Figure 1–7 shows consumers' perceptions of the product positions for several well-known beers in a two dimensional product space constructed on the product attributes of mildness and lightness. The closer the position of brands in the product space, the more similar they appear to consumers.

Budweiser and Schlitz are seen as similar; they are

Figure 1–6. (Pet, Inc.)

both perceived as mild and a little on the heavy side. By contrast, Blatz and Budweiser are seen as quite different, particularly on the mildness dimension. Miller occupies a unique position in the product space, and is not directly competitive with any of the other brands shown.

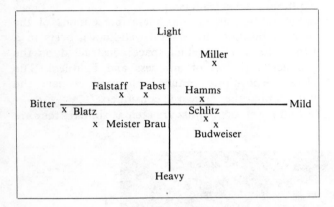

Figure 1–7. Consumer perceptions of beer brands on dimensions of mildness and lightness

Figure 1–8 shows a three-dimensional product space for a paper towel product based on three attributes: softness, absorbency, and general utility. Many positions can be located in this product space. Thus, the consumer market for paper towels can be segmented in a variety of ways, some viable as commercial enterprises and some not viable.

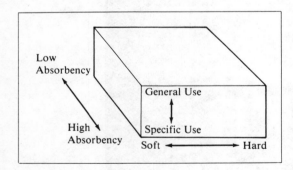

Figure 1–8. Three-dimensional product space based on softness, absorbency and general utility

A product space may be linear, two dimensional, three dimensional, or multidimensional, depending upon the number of product attributes used in its construction. Not all product attributes are equally important to consumers; neither do all product positions appeal to enough consumers to justify an inde-

pendent marketing effort. As a consequence, marketing research and imagination should be used to identify relevant product attributes and to measure the relative attractiveness of different positions in the product space. The goal of the marketer is to locate a position in the product space that appeals to a large number of consumers and is relatively free of competition.

The analysis of existing and potential product positions in a relevant product space enables the marketer to determine how the company's product should be positioned. The marketer then develops a *product or brand concept*, which defines the characteristics of the brand in terms of the attributes appropriate to the product position selected. This, of course, requires a thorough knowledge of the product category and competition as well as an understanding of consumer needs. Assuming that an adequate product concept has been developed, the task of the marketer then becomes one of clearly communicating this concept to consumers.

MARKETING COMMUNICATIONS

Marketing communications is the process through which the product concept is presented to consumers. But, communications is more than the words we say and the symbols we use in an advertisement. Marketing communications encompasses *all* of the marketer's activities that are visible to the consumer.

Traditionally, the term *promotion* has been used to refer to the marketing communications process. Traditionally, *advertising, sales promotion, personal selling,* and *publicity* have been considered the tools of promotion. It is a thesis of this book, however, that the traditional view of promotion is inadequate and represents a *restricted* view of marketing communications. A more realistic approach to marketing communications takes an *extended* view of promotion. The extended view considers promotion as *all of the activities undertaken by the marketer that are visible to consumers and may have an effect on their buying behavior.* This point of view accepts the traditional promotional activities as a part of marketing communications. But it also includes the product itself, the brand name, packaging, pricing, and the method of distribution as communication variables because, surely, these activities are also important avenues for communicating with consumers.

The Brand Image

The purpose of marketing communications is to translate the product concept into an appealing *brand image* because it is a fundamental marketing principle that consumers make their purchasing decisions on the basis of the images they form of the different brands offered to them on retail shelves.[18] Thus, the brand image—the picture or likeness of the brand that exists in the consumer's mind—is the major motivating factor in determining brand preference. This brand image, while existing only in the mind, is as real as any other psychological phenomenon. It is created in response to certain stimuli to which the consumer is exposed, and it constitutes the sum of the consumer's reactions to the brand.

The stimuli which together give rise to the brand image are in part physical and in part psychological. They include purely physical stimuli, like the product's actual physical nature. They also include purely psychological stimuli, like the brand name. Between these two extremes, they embrace other stimuli (such as the product package) which are both physical and psychological in nature. These stimuli provoke in the consumer both rational and emotional responses. The rational responses typically are judgments concerning the actual performance of the brand in relation to its price. The emotional responses likewise tend to be judgmental and related to product performance, but they are shaped primarily by the psychological overtones which have become attached to the brand in the consumer's mind. These two kinds of responses, rational and emotional, blend together in the consumer's mind to form an image of the brand. By this image the brand is known and identified. The degree to which the brand is accepted or rejected is governed by the strength and nature of the brand image.

The manufacturer can, of course, shape and manipulate the brand image by virtue of control over all the major physical stimuli and most of the psychological stimuli that determine the product's ultimate image. The image itself exists in the consumer's mind, but it is what the manufacturer does or fails to do that shapes it. Properly shaped, it is an important marketing tool with which to create widespread consumer acceptance of a brand.

Building the Brand Image

Generally, there are six means which a manufacturer can use to shape the image of the brand that exists in the consumer's mind.

1. The *product* itself and the specific physical and performance characteristics which it possesses.
2. The product *package*, which combines both physical attributes (size, shape, and convenience) and

psychological overtones (conveyed primarily by label design and colors).
3. The brand *name* with its psychological significance.
4. The brand *price*, which also has psychological implications.
5. The *method of distribution*, since the outlets in which a product is sold often carry connotations of quality, dependability, and value.
6. *Advertising and sales promotion*, which carry the burden of disseminating news of the brand and its features, as well as surrounding the brand with the psychological overtones and symbols which make its image appealing to consumers.

By each of these means, a manufacturer can implement and reinforce the product's brand image. With careful and coordinated use of all six of these means, there is every prospect that the manufactuer will succeed in implanting in the consumer's minds the desired brand image.

If, however, the manufacturer neglects to make use of these six means, or if the means are not carefully coordinated so they can work together reinforcing one another, the opportunity to shape an appealing brand image for the product will be lost. In this event, chance will largely determine achievement of a strong, clear, and appealing brand image for the product that will make it stand out in consumers' minds and motivate consumers to select it over competition. But prudent marketers do not rely on chance to insure their position in the market place.

The Value of the Brand Image

The role of the brand image in marketing products is well recognized among marketing professionals. It is a truism in the brewing industry, for example, that consumers do not drink beer—they drink their *image* of a beer. Support for this observation is found in the strong brand preferences that exist among beer consumers despite evidence from repeated tests that most beer drinkers cannot distinguish one beer from another on the basis of taste. W. A. Evans, lecturer in marketing at the Cranfield School of Management in England, has observed: "It is a product's . . . image which differentiates it from competing products in the market place, and once an image has been strongly established it is difficult, if not impossible, to change."[19] Irving White, in commenting on the brand image as a source of meaning, says

The image of the brand appears to be a relatively stable organization of percepts about a product. Once estab-

18. Kenneth E. Runyon, "A Touch of Magic," in *New Directions in Marketing*, F. E. Webster, Jr., ed. (Chicago: American Marketing Association, 1965), pp. 773–79.

19. W. A. Evans, *Advertising Today and Tomorrow* (London: George Allen & Unwin Ltd., 1974), p. 47.

lished, a brand image lends the consistency and predictability in the consumer's relationship with the product which allow him to select and experience those aspects of the product he values. Schweppes quinine water must indeed be a different experience to those who have responded to its image than is that of several brands. The senses have become attuned differently, and the social value in the product-consumer interaction are different from brand to brand.[20]

Mass Communications and the Brand Image

Not all marketing communications are mass communications. The activities of the sales force, essential ingredients in marketing success, are personal communications. This is true whether we are talking about the contact of a salesperson with a chain store or an industrial buyer, about a retail sales clerk in a department store, or about the in-home calls of a Tupperware, the Avon, or the Fuller Brush representative.

This book is primarily concerned with mass communications—the nonpersonal communications of advertising, the package, the brand name, the price, and other mass communications variables. In a mass consumption society, it is these variables that are crucial in the formation of the brand image and in the success of the brand. Warren Kratky, former president of the Gardner Advertising Company and one of the most competent marketing executives I have known, has observed:

> Modern marketing has become *primarily a matter of mass communications.*
>
> Once marketing was primarily a matter of mass production. Later it was primarily a matter of mass distribution. Then primarily a matter of mass selling. Now I maintain, marketing has become primarily a matter of mass communications.
>
> Today in most major businesses, it is mass communications that exert the major, decisive influence upon *how* the business is viewed by its customers.[21]

Further, the marketing plan, around which this book is organized, is primarily a mass communications document. In most companies, the sales plan is a separate document from the marketing plan and is devised to detail the personal contact activities of the sales force. To do justice to the work of the company sales force would require a book in itself. As a consequence, while the importance of the sales force in marketing success is explicitly recognized, these activities will not be dealt with in this text.

20. I. S. White, "The Functions of Advertising in Our Culture," *Journal of Marketing*, **24** (July, 1959): p. 12.
21. Warren J. Kratky, remarks before a marketing conference in St. Louis, April, 1967.

THE PROCESS OF MARKETING

Marketing is a complex process. The development of an effective program of mass communications requires the participation of many organizations and diverse talents. The entire process must be supervised and coordinated so that all parts of the marketing mix work together.

The Participants

The participants in the marketing effort include the manufacturer of a product or service, often referred to as the *client* or the *advertiser*, advertising agencies, package design shops, photographic studios, broadcast producers, media organizations, and many others. Each participating organization has a unique role, and each employs a variety of specialists who contribute only a part of the entire organization's effort. There are many ways in which these specialists can be organized, many ways in which they are used, and many ways in which they are compensated for their services. Chapter 2 will deal specifically with the organizations of two of the major participants in the marketing process, the advertiser and the advertising agency.

The Tasks

Earlier, it was pointed out that advertising is the tip of the iceberg. That, behind the commercial that is broadcast and behind the advertisement that appears in print media are thousands of hours of work. This work requires analytical skill, business judgment, organizational talent, executional ability, and creative inspiration. Markets must be analyzed, product concepts defined, products developed, packages designed, brand names selected, copy written, illustrations conceived and rendered, material produced, sales forecast, budgets set, media selected, and the entire program executed.

Throughout, innovation and creativity are essential to the marketing process, and to marketing communications. Not only is the idea behind the communication essential, but the form of expression is often critical. The right idea and the right words or symbols are the essence of creative expression. The creativity required by marketing communications is not the creativity of the artist or poet, however. "Art for the sake of art" is not the theme of marketing. Marketing creativity has a problem-solving character; it is a controlled creativity designed to persuade and convince. Charlie Brower, an outstanding advertising practitioner of recent years, has written:

> Creativity is the ability to have worthwhile ideas. Ideas alone are a dime a dozen. But the ability to have

selling ideas within the restrictions of the market—and good selling ideas at that—is not easy. Writing is not enough. Art is not enough. Production is not enough. The ideas are the thing, and the people who have them seem to be more scarce every year. [22]

The history of marketing is the history of ideas. "The Kodak Camera. You push the button, we do the rest" is a selling idea that first appeared as the headline in an advertisement in 1890 and has helped Eastman Kodak to become a $6 billion company. "Always a bridesmaid but never a bride" is a marketing classic that introduced Listerine and launched a multimillion dollar product field. AT&T's "Let your fingers do the walking in the yellow pages"; Clairol's "Does she . . . or doesn't she"; Alka-Seltzer's "I can't believe I ate the whole thing"; Avis's "We're number two, so we try harder"; Purina Dog Chow's "So complete all you add is love"; Crest's "Look Mom! No cavities"; Virginia Slims' "You've come a long way, baby" are all expressions of selling ideas that have lifted products from obscurity to success. And, to produce these ideas, and to present them to the consuming public requires an enormous amount of planning and coordination.

Coordination

Truly complex tasks can only be accomplished by breaking them down into their component parts and working on each part separately. This is the key to the success of the modern business organization. It is the key to mass production. But, when the parts are reassembled they will not fit together properly unless they have been constructed according to a single, overall design. In the manufacture of a physical object, such as an automobile, this problem is solved through the use of engineering plans that specify how each component is to be constructed· and the magnitude of the tolerances that will be allowed.

Marketing is a complex task. It, too, must be broken down into component parts, and each part constructed according to a single, overall design. The instrument that provides the unity of design for the marketing effort is the marketing plan. The marketing plan will be discussed in detail in chapter 3, and the rest of the book will be organized around the component parts of the marketing plan.

Conflicts

In a process as complex as that of marketing, interpersonal conflicts and disagreements inevitably arise.

Some of these conflicts arise because different participants have different convictions about how a product should be positioned, how a package should be designed, or how a particular product or service should be advertised. These conflicts are both desirable and necessary because they stimulate thinking, spark new ideas, and encourage creativity. The person who is uncomfortable in the face of conflict, and unable to deal with it, will probably not be happy in the profession of marketing.

There is another kind of conflict that arises in the development of a marketing program that is less desirable, however. This is the conflict that arises from a lack of appreciation and understanding on the part of some participants for the problems and contributions of others. The marketing analyst and planner, for example, who is often business trained and profit oriented, may neither appreciate nor sympathize with the problems faced by the creative people who write advertisements, design packages, and produce commercials. He may see them as undisciplined, irresponsible, and unconcerned about the business requirements of the enterprise.

Creative people, on the other hand, often exhibit a similar disregard for the contributions of the business oriented analyst and planner. To them, such people often appear unimaginative, unreasonable, unduly restrictive, unappreciative, and unconcerned about that portion of the marketing effort that is truly important—the advertising.

Such conflicts are unfortunate because these two groups of people need each other. Neither can devise an effective marketing program alone. Yet, their differences are often difficult to resolve because they appear to be rooted in different temperaments, different ways of thinking, different ways of approaching problems, and different value structures. They represent, in short, two different ways of looking at the world. These two different world views have been characterized in a variety of ways: Dionysian versus Apollinian; cosmic versus rational; or intuitive versus rational. Manifestations of these two different ways of thinking have been reflected in literature (Pirsig's *Zen and the Art of Motorcycle Maintenance* is one of the more recent examples [23]), in marketing (a series of articles by Jack Trout and Al Ries appeared in *Advertising Age* [24]), and in the psychological literature (which suggests that these differences in thinking are

22. Charlie Brower, *Me and Other Advertising Geniuses* (Garden City, New York: Doubleday & Company, Inc. 1974), p. 196.

23. Robert M. Pirsig, *Zen and the Art of Motorcycle Maintenance* (West Caldwell, New Jersey: Morrow, William & Co., Inc., 1972).

24. Jack Trout and Al Ries, "The Positioning Era Cometh," *Advertising Age* (April 24, 1972): 35–38; "Positioning Cuts Through Chaos in Marketplace," *Advertising Age* (May 1, 1972): 51–54; "How to Position Your Product," *Advertising Age* (May 8, 1972): 114–16.

rooted in neural physiology, and related to dominance by the left versus the right cerebral hemisphere[25]).

Regardless of the cause, lack of understanding and failure to appreciate the point of view of coworkers is the result. One purpose of this book is to relate the planning and creative portions of marketing in such a way that their interdependence will become apparent.

SUMMARY

Great advertising does not stand alone. It is firmly rooted in sound marketing strategies and influenced by other marketing activities. And, in order to understand advertising and marketing, we must examine the economic system within which it operates.

Every society must face the question of how much of various products will be produced and whom within society will benefit from this production. For an industrial society, two alternatives—an authoritarian economy and a marketing economy—represent polar responses to this question. Neither system is without fault. The authoritarian system tends toward rigidity, failure to meet consumer needs, shoddy merchandise,

25. Robert E. Ornstein, "Right and Left Thinking," *Psychology Today*, **6** (May, 1973): 86 ff; Paul Bakan, "The Right Brain Is the Dreamer," *Psychology Today*, **10** (November 1976); Andrew Weil, *The Natural Mind* (Boston, Massachusetts: Houghton-Mifflin, 1972).

and bureaucratic inefficiency. The marketing economy has been criticized for being wasteful, promoting personal consumption over societal needs, and misallocating resources.

The United States is a leading exponent of the marketing system. This system has produced an unprecedented abundance of consumer goods and an immeasurable array of consumer choice. However, federal legislation has been required to prevent consumer exploitation and societal abuses. One effect of marketing legislation has been to place producers on the defensive, causing them to subject their marketing and advertising programs to careful scrutiny to avoid unintentional violation of the law.

A number of key marketing terms are defined in this chapter—*marketing, markets, the marketing concept, product differentiation, market segmentation, product space, product position, product concept,* and the *product or brand image*—and *marketing communications* is defined as the process through which product concepts are presented to consumers.

Marketing is a complex process involving a number of participants and a variety of tasks. The process is often characterized by conflict and requires a high degree of coordination. The instrument that is used to coordinate this process, and minimize conflicts among participants, is the marketing plan.

QUESTIONS

1. Explain what is meant by the statement "Advertising is the tip of the iceberg." What does this have to do with the effectiveness of advertising?
2. What is meant by *distributive justice?* What does it have to do with marketing?
3. In the text, marketing is treated as a business activity. Since the early 1970s, there has been a movement to expand the term *marketing* to apply to nonprofit organizations such as charities, churches, government, and so forth. What are the implications of the *marketing concept* in terms of nonprofit organizations?
4. Identify the three components of the generic definition of a *market*. What are some of the specific ways in which the term *market* is used? How do these uses relate to the generic definition?
5. Explain what is meant by *the marketing concept*. What are the implications of this concept for the producer of consumer goods?
6. Distinguish between product differentiation and market segmentation. How may each be used as a marketing strategy?
7. Distinguish between product space, product position, and product concept. Identify a product space for a man's after-shave lotion. Position a product in this space. What advertising appeals might be used to translate this product concept into a product image?
8. Distinguish between a limited and extended view of marketing communications? How does this relate to the ways in which a manufacturer may control the product image?

9. Explain how "distribution" can be a channel of communication about a product. Give some specific examples.
10. Why is marketing considered a complex process? What does this have to do with the marketing plan?

PROBLEM

Bob Cole, product manager for a toiletries company, had been given the assignment of defining a product position for a new brand of deodorant/antiperspirant. An analysis of the four leading brands (A, B, C, and D) indicated the following characteristics, rated on a scale of 1 to ten:

Brand ratings

	A	B	C	D
Effective antiperspirant (10, high)	8	5	5	4
Effective deodorant (10, high)	8	5	5	4
Astringent (stings when applied)	7	4	3	1
Amount of scent (10 = strong)	6	4	4	2
Wet (10 = wet)	7	4	4	4
Masculine/feminine (10 = masculine)	9	3	3	1

The company's research and development department had reported that they could develop any combination of these characteristics. However, as products became more effective as antiperspirants and deodorants, they would also become more astringent. That is, they would sting more when applied. The stinging sensation was temporary, however, and normally would not cause skin irritation. It was possible to reduce the astringent effect by using a semimoist powder spray rather than a liquid spray. With a semimoist powder, the astringency rating could be reduced substantially. For example, a product with a rating of 10 for deodorant and antiperspirant effectiveness would have an astringency rating of about 4.

Consumer research indicated the following preference ratings for the leading brands among consumers, with 10 being the most preferred, and 1 being the least preferred:

Brand prefererence rating

Consumer groups	A	B	C	D
Women	3	5	7	9
Men	8	4	3	2

Brands C and D were advertised to women, whereas the advertising of brands A and B was directed to the entire family. Research also indicated that 80 percent of all deodorants were purchased by women, and 20 percent were purchased by men. Brand shares held by the leading brands were:

Brand A	25%
Brand B	22%
Brand C	18%
Brand D	14%
All other	21%

Bob Cole was pondering how the new brand should be positioned in the market in terms of product characteristics and perceptions and in terms of the target market.

Assignment

1. Define the position the product should have in terms of the attributes discussed.
2. Identify the target market.
3. Suggest a product name.
4. Should any further research be done?

2

Structure and Organization in Marketing

As we enter this chapter, there are three closely inter-related terms that need to be clarified: *marketing, marketing communications,* and *advertising.*

Marketing   The parent discipline. As pointed out in chapter 1, it is the performance of business activities that direct the flow of goods and services from producer to consumer or user. The process of marketing involves clients (producers), advertising agencies, media, and a host of collateral suppliers.

Marketing communications   That *part* of marketing that communicates product messages to channels of distribution and to consumers. It includes all *visible* marketing variables: the product, the product name, package, price, type of retail outlets used, advertising, sales promotion, personal selling, publicity, and so forth.

Advertising   A *part,* albeit an important part, of marketing communications. It consists of paid media advertising, whether in trade publications or consumer media.

Throughout this book, these distinctions should be kept in mind.

Lennon and Newell

In 1970, Lennon and Newell was the sixteenth largest advertising agency in the world and the thirteenth largest in the United States. It had billings of $160 million, employed over a thousand people, represented a galaxy of blue-chip accounts, and appeared to have a brilliant future. In 1971, Lennon and Newell billed less than $90 million, and street rumors had it that, by year's end, its current billings were less than $25 million. In February, 1972, Lennon and Newell filed a petition for bankruptcy, and soon thereafter it ceased to exist. In less than a year and a half, a major advertising agency became a suite of empty rooms. It has been said that the demise of Lennon and Newell was brought about by an arrogant and paternalistic chief executive who planned poorly, organized badly, managed autocratically, and invested unwisely. Thus, the mighty fall.

Managing an Advertising Agency

David Ogilvy, in *Confessions of an Advertising Man,* makes the following observations about managing an advertising agency.

Running an agency takes vitality, and sufficient resilience to pick oneself up after defeats. Affection for one's henchmen, and tolerance for their foibles. A genius for composing sibling rivalries. An unerring eye for the main chance. And morality—people who work in advertising agencies can suffer serious blows to their *esprit de corps* if they catch their leader in acts of unprincipled opportunism.

Above all, the head of an agency must know how to delegate . . . the act of delegation often results in interposing a foreman between the agency boss and his staff. When this happens, the employees feel like children whose mother turns them over to the tender mercies of a nanny. But they become reconciled to the separation when they discover that the nannies are more patient, more accessible, and more expert than I am.[1]

Crumbling Structures

A number of changes in the traditional structure of the marketing communications industry have been made in the past decade. This point is emphasized by W.A. Evans in his book, *Advertising Today and Tomorrow.*

The traditional structure of advertising is already showing signs of incipient collapse. True, the edifice will stand for a few years yet, but the rot is in the foundations, and there is a limit to the length of the time that they can continue to support what is above them. Let us therefore examine in detail how these changes are coming about.

The single most important aspect of the transformation is the development of creative consultancies. These are quite separate from the agencies, and are being formed at a fast pace by agency creative men and women who are not only disenchanted by the conditions which have been described but also recognize the opportunities which exist in an independent unit. Sometimes labelled "hot shops" by the agencies they have foresaken, they are concentrating singlemindedly on the provision of a straight creative service to the industry. Their terms of reference are quite simple: to give clients what they want.[2]

These three examples reflect different dimensions of organization in marketing. The Lennon and Newell example demonstrates how poor management can destroy a successful advertising agency; Ogilvy emphasizes the need for delegation in an advertising enterprise; and Evans points out current changes in the traditional marketing structure.

---

1. From *Confessions of an Advertising Man* by David Ogilvy, p. 16. Copyright © 1963 by David Ogilvy Trustee. Reprinted by permission of Atheneum Publishers.
2. W.A. Evans, *Advertising Today and Tomorrow* (London: George Allen & Unwin Ltd., 1974), p. 166.

In order to understand the operation of marketing as an industry, it is helpful to look at it from different perspectives. In this chapter, we will examine five of its more important dimensions: (1) the nature of the industry, (2) the structure of the industry, (3) advertising agency compensation, (4) organizational structures for advertisers and advertising agencies, and (5) marketing budgets.

THE NATURE OF THE INDUSTRY

Assemble five marketing practitioners in one room, and there will probably be five different opinions on almost any subject that is broached. However, on one subject they will all agree: marketing is a "people" business. Its operation is heavily dependent on interpersonal relationships, and business is often gained or lost on the basis of confidence. It was a crisis of confidence that precipitated the bankruptcy of Lennon and Newell. Poor management weakened the agency financially and led to the loss of one or two major clients. Other clients became concerned about the competence of the agency; rumors became rampant; clients started panicking; and Lennon and Newell went down the tubes.

The following, fictitious story is told by Robert Glatzer in *The New Advertising.*

Once upon a time, in the bad old days, the president of Procter & Gamble came to New York from his headquarters in Cincinnati to pay a visit to his advertising agencies. He stopped first at 347 Madison Avenue, headquarters of Dancer-Fitzgerald-Sample, where he indirectly controlled the careers of 112 people working to promote Oxydol, Dreft and Thrill detergents—all Procter & Gamble products. He told them he was not very satisfied with their work.

Then he walked down the street to 285 Madison Avenue to visit Young & Rubicam, where he met sixty-three people devoting their lives to advertising Cheer—another Procter & Gamble detergent. He told them he was not very satisfied with *their* work either.

That afternoon, he stopped in at Grey Advertising, over on Third Avenue, where he listened to reports on Top Job, Joy and Duz—all of them P&G detergents. Joy was outselling Thrill, but Dreft was beating Duz. He said he was pleased with Joy, but unhappy about the others.

Back on Madison Avenue, he visited Compton Advertising, where 217 people worked on P&G's Dash, Tide and Ivory Liquid detergents. He learned that Tide was beating Oxydol, but that Cheer was outselling Dash, Tide and Ivory Liquid. He told Compton that he might have to take the account away and give it to Young & Rubicam.

Early the next morning, he caught the company jet to Chicago, where he dropped in on Tatham-Laird & Kudner, to check up on Bold and Mr. Clean. He was told that Mr. Clean was holding his own, but that Bold was losing out to Dash, though still ahead of Cheer, Tide, Oxydol, Joy and Duz. He told them to dig in and get creative, or else.

The next day he went home to Cincinnati, gave the Thrill account to Compton, the Tide account to Grey, the Tob Job and Bold accounts to Young & Rubicam, and the Dreft account to Tatham-Laird. Then he rested from his labors.

Ninety-four people were fired as the result of his trip, not counting media buyers and secretaries, and sixty-one were hired from other agencies to bring new "creative" blood to the accounts. Most of the ninety-four found jobs sooner or later at other agencies, but a few gave up entirely, retiring as "failures" from the business.[3]

Although this story is fictitious, it is, at worst, a mild exaggeration. Every issue of *Advertising Age* reports a number of account changes. Each year, usually in March, the publication devotes an issue to advertising agencies. This issue gives brief profiles of over six-hundred U.S. advertising agencies, listing among other things the clients each has gained and lost. These profiles read like a game of musical chairs, and the reasons behind many of the agency switches are arbitrary, political, and capricious.

The problem is, of course, that marketing is a highly competitive business. Large sums of money are at stake. The field is filled with ambitious people. Personal reputations are on the line, and there are no sure answers. The reason that products succeed or fail is often obscure, and the role of advertising in their success and failure is not always clear. Most advertisers are looking for miracles. When a miracle is not forthcoming, they sometimes seek a scapegoat. That scapegoat is usually the advertising agency.

THE STRUCTURE OF THE INDUSTRY

The marketing industry is composed of four groups of participants: advertisers, advertising agencies, media, and collateral services. These participants, in various combinations, carry out the numerous tasks involved in marketing. Edmund McGarry has analyzed and classified these tasks as—

1. *Contractual*—the searching out of buyers and sellers.
2. *Merchandising*—the fitting of goods to market requirements.

3. *Pricing*—the selection of a price high enough to make production possible and low enough to induce users to accept the goods.
4. *Propaganda*—the conditioning of the buyers or of the sellers to a favorable attitude toward the product or its sponsors.
5. *Physical distribution*—the transporting and storing of goods.
6. *Termination*—the consummation of the marketing process.[4]

The advertiser is intimately involved in all of these activities. The advertising agency may be involved, to a greater or lesser extent, in the first four. Media suppliers are generally involved only in the propaganda function, although they often undertake collateral activities such as research and merchandising in order to attract the attention and interest of advertisers and advertising agencies. Collateral services have specialized and limited tasks in one or more of the functional areas.

The direction and control of the marketing effort lies first with the advertiser and second with the advertising agency. The other two participants fulfill supportive, but critical roles. For this reason, the primary focus of this book is on the advertiser and advertising agency. The other participants will be dealt with only to the extent that a knowledge of their functions is important to those who exert direction and control over the entire process.

The Advertiser

Statistical Abstracts defines a business firm as *a business organization under a single management which may include one or more plants or outlets.*[5] Thus, a giant retailer such as Sears is a single business firm, as is a "mom and pop" grocery outlet. Exxon, with receipts of over $54 billion is a single business firm, as is a small independent gasoline station operated by a man and his wife. Under this definition, there are over 13 million business firms in the United States, all of which are engaged in marketing products or services. Sixty-six percent of these business have receipts of under $25 thousand and account for only 2 percent of total business receipts. By contrast, 1.9 percent of these business firms account for 77.4 percent of total U.S. business receipts.[6] Although any business can benefit from a systematic approach to its marketing

3. Robert Glatzer, *The New Advertising* (New York: The Citadel Press, 1970), p. 9.

4. Edmund D. McGarry, "Some Functions of Marketing Reconsidered," in *Theory in Marketing,* Reavis Cox and Wroe Alderson, eds. (Homewood, Illinois: Richard D. Irwin, Inc., 1950), pp. 269–73.
5. U.S. Statistical Abstracts: 1976, p. 505.
6. U.S. Statistical Abstracts: 1976, p. 508.

activities, very few of them bother. Only a minute percentage employ an advertising agency, and only a fraction of these develop a formal marketing plan. Yet, it is with this tiny group that we are most concerned because this miniscule is the dominant force in the U.S. economy.

Advertising Agencies

There are almost six thousand advertising agencies in the United States; many of them are one and two person shops that deal, primarily, with small retailers. Advertising agencies range in size from J. Walter Thompson—with billings of over a billion dollars and a gross income of $188.8 million in 1977—to small operations whose total billings were less than $50 thousand and whose gross incomes were barely able to cover their principals' meager salaries.

Table 2-1 summarizes *Advertising Age's* report on agency operations in 1977.[7] This report covers 583 advertising agencies which had a combined gross income of almost $2.9 billion, and an estimated billing of $19.4 billion. From table 2-1 it can be seen that less than 12 percent of the advertising agencies account for almost 82 percent of advertising agency income, pointing up the concentration of business that exists in the industry.[8]

Table 2-1. Size of advertising agencies in the U.S.

Size group, based on gross income	Advertising agencies		Gross income	
			Millions of	% of
	Number	% of total	dollars	total
$5,000,000 plus	67	11.5	$2,344.3	81.8
3-5,000,000	43	7.4	157.1	5.5
1-3,000,000	130	22.3	229.6	8.0
Under 1,000,000	343	58.8	134.5	4.7
Totals	583	100.0	$2,865.5	100.0

SOURCE: Adapted from James V. O'Gara, "583 Agencies Record $2.9 Billion Income," p. cover story. Reprinted with permission from the March 13, 1978 issue of *Advertising Age*. Copyright 1978 by Crain Communications, Inc.

Aside from size, advertising agencies differ in a variety of ways. For example, there are agencies that specialize in industrial products, in consumer products, or in fashion advertising. There are agencies,

generally the smaller ones, that specialize in retail accounts, or in real estate, or in financial advertising. In short, advertising agencies, by tradition or plan, sometimes carve out highly specialized niches for themselves. Most major agencies, however, handle a variety of accounts, cutting across the specialty spectrum.

Historically, the advertising agency industry has been a highly flexible one, adapting to the demands of advertisers and offering whatever array of services their clients required. Since the early 1960s, the industry has been in a turmoil because advertisers, in an effort to obtain better service and reduce costs, have insisted that agency services be tailored to their specific needs. In the following material, we will look briefly at the major types of advertising agencies that are currently serving the industry.

Full-Service Agencies. A full-service advertising agency is one that provides a broad, if not totally complete, range of marketing services. The development of the full-service agency was a process of evolution. Beginning in the early 1880s as space brokers—agents that bought newspaper and magazine space in bulk quantities from publishers and resold it to advertisers in individual units—advertising agencies gradually added additional services as competitive strategies to attract clients and facilitate growth. Today, a full-service agency is generally staffed to handle the entire gamut of marketing counsel for their clients with the exception of personal selling and public relations, although some full-service agencies also undertake public relations functions.

In addition to the necessary internal functions of any commercial organization such as management, finance, accounting, personnel, new business acquisition, and so forth full-service agencies generally provide all or most of the following functions.

Account service. Account service or account management is the liaison between the advertising agency and its clients. The function of the account manager, usually referred to as an account executive or account supervisor, is twofold: (1) she works with the client on a day-to-day basis, is responsible for understanding the client's business needs and for interpreting them to agency personnel; (2) she works closely with agency personnel in developing plans and recommendations and is responsible for presenting and obtaining client approval for agency recommendations. The account manager is the focal point of agency-client relations and coordinates and oversees internal agency activity.

In some agencies, the account manager is an experienced and knowledgeable marketer who carries the major responsibility for market planning on the cli-

7. James V. O'Gara, "583 Agencies Record $2.9 Billion Income," *Advertising Age* (March 13, 1978): 1.
8. Historically, *Advertising Age* has emphasized agency billings as their indicator of agency size. In 1977, however, emphasis was shifted to agency income as the most meaningful measure.

ent's product. She may write the client's marketing plan, working in close coordination with her contact in the client organization. In other agencies, the account manager does not bear the brunt of planning, but works closely with those who do in both the client and agency organizations.

Creative services. The creative services department of an advertising agency is responsible for the creation and execution of advertisement, commercials, and often for package design, point-of-sale material, and other forms of promotion. Creative services generally include four functional areas: copy, art, print production, and radio and television production. These four functional areas may exist as separate departments, although there is a trend to merge these groups into a single department in order to facilitate collective thinking and to provide a closer integration of these areas in the creative process. Regardless of how the various creative service functions are organized, they have the following responsibilities:

1. *Copy.* Copy writers are generally assigned to particular accounts and are responsible for conceiving ideas for advertisements and for writing the headlines, subheads, and body copy for advertisements; they also write copy for broadcast media. Copy writers may also prepare a rough visual layout for an advertisement or a television storyboard, even as an art director may contribute copy ideas. In any case, copy writers work closely with art directors and with those responsible for print and broadcast production.

2. *Art.* Artists in an advertising agency are responsible for the design of advertisements (the layout) and for its pictorial elements. In the case of television, the layout is known as a storyboard and depicts the sequence of action that makes up the commercial. In general, artists are responsible for the visualization of all artwork, the execution of layouts and storyboards, the preparation of mechanicals (detailed instructions for the production of advertisements), and type specification, although this latter function may be handled by specialists known as typecasters. Since little finished artwork is actually produced by advertising agencies, there is usually at least one art buyer who is responsible for locating and contracting with free-lance artists, independent art studios, and photographers for the finished work.

3. *Print production.* After copy, layout, artwork, and mechanical specifications have been completed and approved, advertisements must be produced. Since advertising agencies do not actually produce finished advertisements, the production group acts as a purchasing agent to select and oversee outside suppliers. A further function of the print production specialists is to work closely with copywriters and artists, counseling them on the limitations and flexibility of the various graphic art techniques.

4. *Television and radio production.* In the early days of radio and television, broadcast producers in advertising agencies often originated the format and content of programs. Today, this activity is largely handled by the networks, individual stations, or by independent producers. As a consequence, the primary responsibility of broadcast producers in an advertising agency is supervising the production of commercials. In this capacity, agency producers are responsible for selecting independent production studios. Using the storyboard as a blueprint, the agency producer will generally participate in and supervise casting, the selection of props and settings, editing, and the thousand-and-one details that go into the production of commercials. In the case of live commercials, where there is no filming or recording, agency producers simply supervise the commercial part of the program. Again, because there are no hard and fast lines separating the various stages of creating commercials, copy writers and art directors may participate in the production process.

Traffic. As agencies become larger, and more complex, coordination becomes a major problem. To insure coordination, a traffic department is established and given the responsibility for meeting schedules and closing dates. Closing dates are deadlines for submitting advertisements and commercials to media. The traffic department is sometimes a part of the creative services group, but it is sometimes set up as a separate department in the agency.

Media. Regardless of how good an advertisement or commercial is, it has no value to the advertiser until it appears in broadcast or print media. The job of the media department is to analyze, plan, select, and contract for the media that will be used in the advertiser's marketing program. It is a herculean task. Media departments employ both print and broadcast buyers who sift through and analyze an enormous amount of data concerning the various media and their audiences in making their final recommendations and in preparing schedules. The activities of the media department must be closely coordinated with the activities of the creative department and with the budget restrictions of the client. Often, media considerations—the ability of a medium to create a particlar mood, or portray some aspect of the product—have a major influence on the creative effort.

Marketing Research. The role of the marketing research department is to gather, analyze, and report information that will be helpful in preparing the marketing plan and in developing advertising. The activities of the agency research department range from consulting with the client organization, to preparing forecasts. It includes such activities as: analyzing sales data; conducting surveys and product tests; testing advertising concepts, headlines, layouts, and finished advertisements and commercials. Although most major clients have their own marketing research departments, the agency research department is an invaluable asset to the advertising agency and its management.

Other Functions. The foregoing functions are the central activities of most full-service agencies. Many large agencies are also organized to perform other marketing functions, depending upon the needs of their clients. For example, some advertising agencies have sales promotion (sometimes called *merchandising*) departments that specialize in designing point-of-sale material, product display racks, contests, retail presentations, and other promotional materials. Some have home economics departments that develop recipes for clients who market food ingredients. I was associated with an advertising agency that, for a number of years, maintained a home economics department equipped with both gas and electric kitchens, as well as a high-altitude kitchen in Utah. The function of the department was to develop and test recipes to be used on packages and in advertisements for the agency's food clients, work with the copy department in simplifying instructions for recipes and package directions, and supervise the preparation of food for photography and for live broadcast commercials. A number of agencies also have public relations and product publicity departments.

Earlier, it was pointed out that full-service agencies evolved as the result of inter-agency competition to attract clients. There was still another reason for their development. Advertising agencies are often judged by the success of their clients' products. Yet, marketing success depends on the entire marketing program—not just the advertising. As a consequence, advertising agencies sought to gain more control over the success or failure of their clients' marketing programs by involving themselves more deeply in all aspects of the effort—sales promotion, marketing re-

search, marketing strategy, pricing, product planning, and so forth. So, they developed the people, the departments, and the skills that qualified them to participate broadly in their clients' entire marketing programs. After developing these capabilities, advertising agencies provided these skills as a "packaged deal" to their clients, whether their clients wanted them or not.

The 1960s saw a rebellion on the part of advertisers who, in an effort to cut costs and improve service, wanted to dispense with some of these services and to shop around for others. For example, an advertiser might want to buy the creative service of one agency, the media expertise of another, the research capabilities of a third, and so forth. A number of major agencies refused to participate in this process and lost clients as a result. Other agencies yielded to these pressures. This resulted in the *modular* advertising agency.

Modular Advertising Agencies. A modular or a la carte advertising agency is, essentially, a full-service agency that sells its services on a piecemeal basis. Thus, an advertiser, for a fee, may commission the agency's creative department to develop an advertising campaign, while obtaining other agency services elsewhere. Or, an advertiser may hire the media department of an agency to plan and execute a media program for advertising that another agency has developed. In each case, a fee is charged for the service provided, with the size of the fee being negotiated in terms of the amount of work done.

In-house Agencies. The in-house agency is owned by the advertiser and operates under the advertiser's direct supervision and authority. It generally provides all of the media and creative functions of a full-service agency, but does so at a lesser cost because the profit normally retained by an independent advertising agency is pocketed by the advertiser. The primary purpose of the in-house agency is to save money for the advertiser, but it also stabilizes the people working on the account and gives the advertizer greater control over agency activities.

Critics of the in-house agency (and there are many) argue that the advertiser loses the benefit of the experience and "outside" point of view that an independent agency can bring to bear on her marketing problems, that creative groups grow stale working on the same product lines, and that in-house agencies are unable to attract the same quality creative personnel as the independent advertising agency. There is merit to these arguments, particularly in the loss of an independent, outside point of view. Anyone who has worked in or with an advertiser-controlled organization often finds that the people in the organization tend to become narrow in their thinking, and to focus their attention inward on internal problems and concerns rather than outward toward the consumer. Nonetheless, in-house agencies appear to be growing in popularity and are utilized by a number of advertisers, including J.B. Williams, Norton Simon, and General Electric.[9]

Boutiques. During the 1960s, increasing competition led to a renewed interest in advertising creativity. Some advertisers felt that full-service agencies were emphasizing other marketing services at the expense of creativity. Simultaneously, many members of agency creative departments felt that their creativity was being hampered by the management structure of the agency and some of their best ideas were not being presented to clients because of excessive caution on the part of account management. As a result, some of the "star" copy writers and art directors (often with covert arrangements with leading clients) left full-service agencies to set up their own shops which became known as *creative boutiques*. The creative boutique performs only the creative function, usually for a fee and/or an agreed upon percentage of the media expenditure.

Creative boutiques reached the peak of their popularity in the late 1960s but appeared to be on the wane by the mid-1970s. A major reason for their decline was that a number of clients, who were intrigued by the idea of a purely creative shop, found that they still wanted traditional agency services. As a consequence, many of the original boutiques themselves became full-service agencies as they found that a creative service alone was not enough, and as it became apparent that advertising must be coordinated with the rest of the marketing effort. At this point, the future of the creative boutique as an agency form is uncertain, although in any industry as volatile as the advertising business it is probable that they will continue as a viable alternative to full-service agencies at least for some advertisers and for some creative projects.

Media Organizations

The major media organizations in the advertising industry are newspapers, magazines, radio and televi-

sion networks, and individual radio and television stations. In addition, there are a number of minor media which include outdoor advertising (billboards), transit advertising (cards in subways and buses), movie theater films, programs for entertainment events (plays, baseball games, musical performances, etc.). (Each of the major media will be dealt with in later chapters of the book.) Along with advertisers and advertising agencies, media organizations dominate marketing and advertising in the United States.

Collateral Business

There are dozens of collateral businesses that are supported by advertisers, advertising agencies, and the major media. They include package design houses, sales promotion firms, premium shops, media buying services, research organizations, printing companies, production studios, program producers, consulting firms, free-lance artists and copywriters, photographers, recording studios, mailing list houses, coupon redemption centers. Each provides a highly specialized service which advertisers and their agencies use when the need arises. The marketing industry is a highly complex one; as the need for a particular service arises, companies emerge to meet this need. As needs are eclipsed, so are the companies that serve them. The entire industry is a prototype of the marketing economy.

ADVERTISING AGENCY COMPENSATION

The methods by which advertising agencies are compensated for their services has been a subject of controversy for years, and there is no evidence that suggests the controversy will diminish.

The Agency Commission System

Traditionally, advertising agencies have been paid a percentage of the gross billing charged by media and other suppliers. Also, traditionally, this commission has been 15 percent of gross billing (although outdoor advertisers generally give 16⅔ percent, and some trade publications offer 20 percent). Other commissions may be charged in some situations, but 15 percent is almost universal in the United States. Table 2–2 shows how the commission system works. Assume that an advertising agency spends $100,000 for an advertiser in television, magazines, or some other media offering the standard 15 percent commission. After the advertising has run, the media will bill the agency

9. John S. Wright, Daniel S. Warner, Willis L. Winter, Jr., and Sherilyn K. Ziegler, *Advertising,* 4th ed. (New York: McGraw-Hill Book Company, 1977), p. 171.

The $2999 Chevy Chevette

Read it again and brighten your day some more.

$2999.

Manufacturer's Suggested Retail Price for this 4-passenger Chevette Scooter including dealer preparation. Priced higher in California. Tax, license, destination charges and available equipment additional.

A surprising price for a car full of surprises: Over 38 inches of front seat head room. (More than many intermediate-size cars.) A cargo volume of 26.3 cu. ft. with the rear seat folded flat. Almost 6,000 Chevy dealers handy for parts and service just about everywhere.

And the highest EPA gas mileage numbers of any car made in America, when you order Chevette's available 1.6-litre engine and standard manual transmission—43 miles per gallon EPA highway, 31 miles per gallon city estimates. (EPA figures are estimates. Your mileage will vary depending on your type of driving, driving habits, car's condition and available equipment. In California, EPA figures are lower.)

Chevette: The highest EPA mileage figures of any car made in America.

Or: An MSRP of only $2999.

It's enough to make you think twice, isn't it?

It'll drive you happy.

Plate 1-1. The Chevy Chevette advertisement is clearly based on economy (Reprinted by permission of Chevrolet Motor Division, General Motors Corporation).

Rolls-Royce brings back a great name. Silver Wraith II.

The last of the Silver Wraiths was built in 1959. Or so it seemed at the time.

But the richest of Rolls-Royce memories have a way of living on in the newest of Rolls-Royce motor cars. And so it is with the Silver Wraith II of 1977.

The Timeless Pleasure

The long, sleek look of the Silver Wraith II reflects a time gone by.

You can sense it in the graceful lines, the contrasting top, the gleaming bright work, the tasteful craftsmanship and the roomy interior.

And, for the most up-to-date reasons, the Silver Wraith II is a new air of comfort, a new sense of quiet and a new feeling of command.

A new rack-and-pinion steering system makes the Silver Wraith II quick to respond and rewarding to drive, no matter how narrow the road or sudden the curve.

A unique automatic air-conditioning system maintains any temperature you desire at two levels of the interior. And, because the system creates a rarefied atmosphere all your own, its built-in sensors alert you to outside temperatures as well as icy roads.

The Silver Wraith II also offers you the sophistication of an advanced electrical system, the performance of a quiet V-8 engine, the security of a dual braking system and the sensitivity of a self-leveling suspension.

And, to name one of the many other subtle details you'll discover, the electronic odometer will contemplate recording the miles from 000000.0 to 999999.9.

The Priceless Asset

From the distinctive radiator grille to the matching walnut veneers, the Silver Wraith II is built almost entirely by hand.

In tribute to this enduring Rolls-Royce tradition, it is no coincidence that more than half of all the motor cars we have ever built remain very much on the road. And, in return for the purchase price of $49,000,* it is little wonder that a Silver Wraith II speaks so warmly of the past and so surely of the future.

◄◄ ◄◄ ◄◄

A collection of Rolls-Royce masterpieces is waiting at your nearest Authorized Rolls-Royce Dealership. For further information, call 800-325-6000 and give this ID number: 1000.

*Suggested U.S. Retail Price March 1, 1977. The names "Rolls-Royce" and "Silver Wraith" and the mascot, badge and radiator grille are all Rolls-Royce trademarks.
© Rolls-Royce Motors Inc. 1977.

The heart and soul of a masterpiece

Plate 1-2. The Rolls-Royce advertisement is based on luxury (Rolls-Royce Motors, Inc.).

$100,000 *less* 15 percent commission, *less* 2 percent cash discount if the bill is paid within ten days.

Table 2-2. Example of agency commission system

Media charges agency	$100,000
Less: agency commission of 15%	15,000
Equals: cost of media	85,000
Less: 2% cash discount for payment within ten days	1,700
Agency pays media	83,300
Agency charges advertiser	100,000
Less: 2% cash discount	1,700
Advertiser pays agency	98,300
Agency compensation	
Advertiser pays agency	98,300
Agency pays media	83,300
Agency compensation for work	$15,000

Agencies generally pass the 2 percent cash discount along to their clients. So, assuming that both the agency and the client pay promptly, the agency will bill the client $100,000 less the 2 percent cash discount on the net amount, or $98,300.

Historically, commissions from media provided about 65 percent of agency income, although the larger the agency, the higher the proportion of income accounted for by media commissions. Even among the largest agencies, however, 10–25 percent of income came from sources other than media.

In addition to income received from media, advertising agencies also receive direct payment from clients for materials and services such as finished art, comprehensive layouts, television storyboards, supervision of production for outside suppliers, research, design of point-of-sale material, package design. Generally, the smaller the agency (and the smaller the advertiser) the greater extra charges will be because media commissions are not sufficient to cover the costs of preparing advertising. In some cases, these additional charges are based on agency costs (cost of materials, for example), on a flat fee or hourly rate (for point-of-sale material or package design, for example), or a commission on outside services such as commercial production. The particular schedule of charges will vary agency by agency and will be spelled out in detail in the advertiser-advertising agency contract.

Qualification for Agency Commissions

The commission system is, in effect, a functional discount paid to advertising agencies for performing functions that benefit the media. From the standpoint of media, the agency performs the following functions: (1) they centralize the servicing of accounts and reduce billing costs; (2) they reduce credit risks by screening clients and guaranteeing payment; (3) they reduce the media's cost of publication by providing materials that meet the media's mechanical specifications; and (4) they promote advertising as a form of marketing communication.

Traditionally, media commissions were only granted to *recognized* agencies. To gain recognition, an advertising agency had to have acceptance by individual advertisers and their trade associations.[10] Acceptance was gained by meeting four general criteria: (1) the advertising agency must be a *bona fide* agency (it must not be owned or controlled by advertisers or media); (2) it must keep all commissions and not rebate to either media or advertiser; (3) the agency must have personnel with the experience and ability to service its clients and promote advertising; and (4) the agency must have the financial resources to meet the commitments it makes to media.[11]

Although media observance of these criteria was purely voluntary, trade association support of these standards carried considerable clout. One consequence was to make it difficult for in-house agencies to gain recognized status since they obviously rebated their commissions to the advertisers who owned them. This restriction did not eliminate in-house agencies, but it did introduce a certain amount of obscurity, deceit, and hypocrisy into the nature of their financial ownership.

Challenges to the Commission System

Despite its widespread use, a number of advertisers and advertising agencies believed that the commission system was inherently wrong because there was not necessarily a relationship between the amount of work done by an advertising agency and the compensation it received. For example, two advertising campaigns might require the same amount of agency work to create and produce. Yet, one of the campaigns would have $100 thousand spent behind it, generating $15 thousand in agency commissions, while the second campaign might have $3 million spent behind it,

10. The leading trade associations involved in recognizing advertising agencies were: American Newspaper Publishers Association (ANPA), for most newspapers; Periodical Publishers Association (PPA), for consumer magazines; American Business Press (ABP), for most trade and industrial publications; and Agricultural Publishers Association (APA), for most farm papers.

11. C.H. Sandage and Vernon Fryburger, *Advertising Theory and Practice,* 9th ed. (Homewood, Illinois: Richard D. Irwin, Inc., 1975), pp. 634–35.

thereby generating $450 thousand in agency commissions.

In 1955, the Department of Justice brought civil suit against the American Association of Advertising agencies (the 4 A's) and five leading media associations. The suit alleged that the defendants were violating the Sherman Anti-Trust Act in—(1) promulgating uniform standards for recognition of advertising agencies; (2) withholding commissions from agencies not recognized; (3) charging gross rates to advertisers, while charging only net rates to advertising agencies; and (4) fixing the commission at 15 percent of the gross rate. In 1956, a consent decree was entered in the U.S. District Court in New York City enjoining and restraining the 4 A's from engaging in the alleged practices. Similar consent decrees were later entered for the media associations involved in the suit. The Justice Department's suit dealt only with associations of advertising agencies and of media; it did not prevent individual media from establishing criteria for the recognition of advertising agencies. Nonetheless, the net result of the court action was to open up the field to advertisers and agencies to work out any compensation agreement they saw fit.

The consent decree on agency compensation was handed down in 1956. In 1971, some fifteen years later, it was reported that 45 percent of the leading advertisers were still using the commission system.[12] Current practices in the field involve a variety of compensation systems. Some advertisers still use the commission system; others negotiate a flat fee with their agencies; others use a cost plus system; and still others use a combination of commissions and fees. It is not unusual for a given advertising agency to have several different compensation systems with its various clients.

Fee and Cost-Plus Compensation Systems

Fee and cost plus systems are generally advantageous to the advertiser (client) when substantial sums are spent in relatively high cost media such as national consumer magazines and television and when the agency provides few other marketing services such as market planning, research, preparation of point-of-purchase (in-store) materials, and so forth. Such systems are advantageous to the advertising agency when consumer media expenditures are relatively low, and when substantial noncommissionable marketing services are required.

Fee Systems. In a fee system, the advertiser and its agency negotiate a flat sum to be paid to the agency

for all work done. Such an arrangement usually involves the advertising agency making an estimate of how much the job will cost (in terms of agency payroll and out-of-pocket costs) to serve the client during the coming year and adding in a desired profit margin. This total is submitted to the client who either accepts it or starts negotiating. During negotiations, some agency services (marketing research, for example) may be eliminated as an agency responsibility; or, perhaps, the client will agree to have fewer account executives assigned to the account. Negotiations continue until an agreement is reached.

One major advertiser was spending approximately $20 million in major media. Its agency was compensated 15 percent of this amount, or $3 million, through commissions. After negotiating a fee system, the client paid the agency a flat $2 million in fees, and all media commissions were rebated to the client, effecting a savings for the client of $1 million annually. The agency, in this particular instance, was able to negotiate a reduction in service in the areas of: (1) the account group; (2) marketing research; (3) development of sales aids for the sales force; and (4) reduced participation in developing sales promotion materials. As a result, agency costs were substantially reduced, so that agency profits on the account, while smaller than before, were still significant. This example points up one major advantage of a fee system: it forces both the client and the advertising agency to reexamine the services provided and to reach agreement on what role the advertising agency will play in the client's marketing effort. There are two major disadvantages in a fee system: *first,* it gives client management a critical look at the internal compensation and management practices of the agency, causing the agency to lose some of its operating independence; *second,* in the name of economy, it sometimes leads to the elimination of services that the client can ill afford to forego.

Cost-Plus Systems. Cost-plus systems are most often used when media billings are relatively low and a great deal of agency service is required. This happens most often with industrial accounts, on new products being prepared for marketing, and in other instances in which a disproportionate amount of agency help is needed in preparing brochures, catalogues, and other noncommissionable marketing activities.

In a cost-plus system, the client agrees to pay the agency the cost of its work (employee costs as well as out-of-pocket expenses) plus a certain percentage of this amount (often 25 percent) to cover agency overhead and profit. In practice, the agency and client estimate the amount of work that will be required during the coming year and estimate its cost, usually on a

---

12. *The Gallagher Report,* Vol. 19 (November, 1971).

quarter by quarter basis. The client then makes monthly payments against this estimate and periodically (usually quarterly) reviews the estimate with the agency to make sure that actual costs are in line with the estimate. In some cases, if necessary, the estimate will be revised upward or downward as the year progresses. Table 2–3 shows a simplified cost plus schedule of charges for an agricultural product account.

Table 2–3. Example of a cost plus system for an agricultural account

Agency Service		Cost
Corporate management (plans board)		2,250
Account service		94,256
Creative department		126,677
advertising	76,227	
collateral material	50,450	
Production		48,450
inside time	10,670	
out-of-pocket	37,780	
Media		21,367
Marketing research		5,490
Administrative services		9,236
Supplies		270
Communications (telephone)		2,260
Travel		21,090
Total		383,886
Plus 25% for unallocatable overhead and profit		95,972
Total charge		$479,858

NOTES:
1. Hourly charges for inside time include salary, fringe benefits, and payroll taxes. Time cards, with a minimum time interval of 15 minutes were kept by all agency personnel working on the account.
2. Administrative services include accounting, data processing, personnel, agency library, office services, local telephone charges, etc. Charges based on an hourly rate or agreed upon formula.
3. Travel is relatively high because the client was an ''out-of-town'' company, and weekly trips to the client's home office were required.

The advantages and disadvantages of a cost-plus system are similar to those of the fee system. On the positive side, it forces the client and agency to critically examine agency services in relation to client needs. On the negative side, the agency's independence is eroded as the client becomes privy to internal agency cost figures.

Regardless of how the agency is paid—by commissions, a flat fee, cost plus, or by some combination of these methods—the whole area of agency compensation is both sensitive and complex. The creative work of an advertising agency does not roll off of an assembly line like so many Barbie Dolls with a neat price tag affixed to each unit. A creative idea may take a week to develop, or it may take three months of intensive work. A marketing plan may pull together quickly, or take months of effort. Because of these variables,

mutual trust and respect are essential ingredients in the client-agency relationship. And, when the client starts to worry that the agency is making too much money, there is a good probability that mutual trust is turning sour and that the agency is in trouble.

ADVERTISER ORGANIZATION

There are any number of ways in which advertisers may organize their marketing effort. The particular form of organization used will depend upon the size of the company, the number of products it markets, the nature of the industry in which it is engaged, and the marketing philosophy of its management. Responsibilities may be divided by function, by geographic area, by end user (industrial products versus consumer products, for example), by media, or in a number of different ways. A number of different organizational patterns are often employed simultaneously, with some forms of organization superimposed over others. For example, an organization may be structured in terms of geographic divisions. Each division, however, may be organized along functional lines. General Motors is organized in terms of product divisions—Chevrolet, Pontiac, Buick, Cadillac. Each of these product divisions is organized along functional lines—accounting, manufacturing, marketing, personnel, design, etc. The sales force, which is a part of marketing, is organized on a geographic basis.

Instead of trying to describe all of the organizational variations that are possible, we will focus on the advertising manager and the major ways in which her role is integrated into the overall marketing organization. In the following material, three forms of organization for a multiple product advertiser are described. The first form is that of a company organized by function. The two succeeding forms represent forward steps in integrating the marketing effort and emphasizing the importance of the basic marketing function. Note that the role of the advertising manager or advertising director changes in each organizational form.

Organization by Function

Figure 2–1 shows a simplified organizational chart for the traditional form of organization.

Marketing activities are split along functional lines; advertising, sales promotion, and publicity activities fall within the domain of the advertisng manager. The advertising manager occupies an important position, although she is often subordinated to the sales manager insofar as many marketing decisions are concerned. The advertising manager is basically respon-

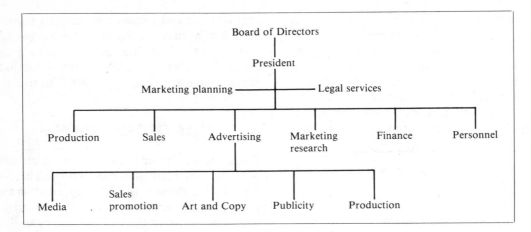

Figure 2-1. Advertiser organization by function

sible for all promotional activities except sales, works closely with the company's advertising agency or agencies, and develops the overall promotional budget for the company.

The problem with this structure is one of coordination and responsibility. Major marketing functions are split into different departments, and no one department is specifically responsible for the welfare of individual products. Decisions are centralized, and the entrepreneural spirit, so essential to successful marketing, is often lost.

Product Manager Organization

Figure 2-2 shows a simplified product manager form of organization. This approach is intended to accomplish three objectives: (1) to coordinate marketing activities by placing them under the overall supervision of a marketing director, (2) to decentralize decision making by assigning individual product managers to each product and charging them with the profit responsibility for the product, and (3) to introduce entrepreneurship into the organization by letting the product managers compete for company resources.

In this form of organization, the functions formerly associated with the advertising manager are transferred to the individual product managers, and product planning, insofar as it occurs, is delegated to the product management group. The advertising manager's role is decreased in importance, and her primary function is an advisory one, although she may have the authority to override product management decisions relating to creative work submitted by the company's advertising agency.

While the product manager form of organization accomplishes many of its objectives, it also exhibits some shortcomings. For example: (1) product managers often lack the knowledge and experience in ad-

vertising, sales promotion, media, production, and publicity to deal with these areas effectively; (2) short term planning and day-to-day problems of supervising and coordinating activities on individual products often preclude long range planning; and (3) the persuasiveness and effectiveness of individual product managers in competing for company resources may lead to a misallocation of company resources. Thus, a product with little long-range profit potential may receive more company resources than a product with a greater profit potential. These problems have led to the third form of organization, which is referred to as a *coordinated product manager system.*

Coordinated Product Manager System

The coordinated product manager system is diagrammed in figure 2-3. Although it retains most of the features of the product manager system, it is modified in two major respects: (1) planning is removed from the product group and installed as a staff function responsible to the marketing director; (2) the role of the advertising manager has been enlarged and staff specialists installed in an advisory capacity under her direction. In addition, an agency coordination function is added to the advertising manager's responsibilities. The purpose of this function is to coordinate the selection of media among various products and/or advertising agencies in order to obtain maximum media discounts where this can be done without losing quality.

The entire thrust of the organizational progression from a functional organization to a product manager system to a coordinated product manager approach is to increase marketing effectiveness. This is accomplished by first making individual product managers responsible for planning and coordinating all marketing activities for particular products. Then, staff spe-

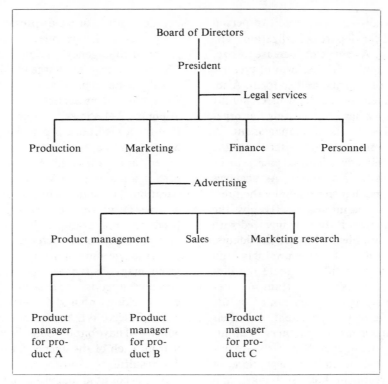

Figure 2-2. Product manager organization

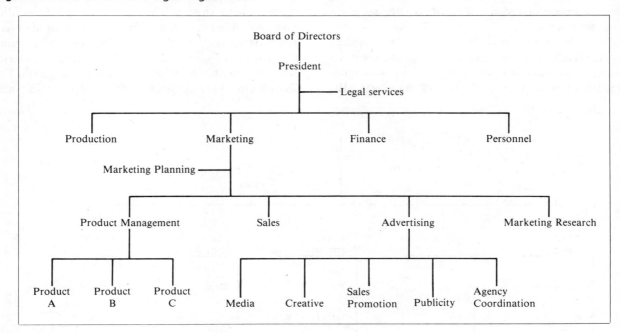

Figure 2-3. Coordinated product manager organization

cialists are installed under the advertising manager to counsel with and advise the product managers. At the same time, long range planning is taken away from the product managers and established as a separate function, removed from competition with the day-to-day activities of managing existing products.

ADVERTISING AGENCY ORGANIZATION

Like advertisers, advertising agencies may be organized in different ways, although there is a basic organizational structure that underlies most large agencies.

In the very small agency—the one- and two-person shop—there is no need for departmentalization. The principals do everything. As agencies increase in size, specialization starts to appear in the form of creative departments, media departments, and so forth. Also, hierarchies in management begin to form. Generally speaking, advertising agencies are relatively flat organizations—they have few levels of management. A major reason for this is that most advertisers want the top managements of their advertising agencies to be personally involved with their products. As agencies become larger, such intimate involvement by the president of the agency becomes impossible. To give the illusion that top management is directly involved with each account, agencies are filled with vice-presidents. The account supervisor on most major products (and many minor ones) carries this title to create the illusion, if not the fact, that she is an important member of management. Some agencies, embarrassed by the profligate use of the title of vice-president, call their key contact personnel *associates* or *partners* in an attempt to imply that they are agency principals. Advertising agencies are not alone in this deception, of course. Law firms, investment houses, banks, and other institutions in which personal contact with clients is a major ingredient of business success follow the same practice.

The widespread use of the title of vice-president among members of the client contact group creates a certain amount of unrest and dissatisfaction with mundane job titles throughout the rest of the agency. Ev-

eryone wants to be a vice-president. One of my former associates (a vice-president who was also creative director of the agency) claimed for himself the title of "Vice-president in Charge of All Creation." This was a real put-down because I was only "Vice-president in Charge of Client Service."

Figure 2–4 shows the typical functional organization for a medium sized to large advertising agency. Several comments need to be made about this form of organization. First, this diagram represents the *formal* organization for purposes of staffing and salary administration. The actual working arrangements consist of a series of informal groups organized around clients' products. For example, let us assume that account group *A* represents a detergent advertiser. Depending upon the size and importance of the client, the account group may consist of a single account executive or of an account supervisor with a number of account executives working with her. The account executive or supervisor will serve as the coordinator of an informal group, which will have one or more representatives assigned to it from each of the agency's functional departments. The resulting work group is diagrammed in figure 2–5.

The account manager has no formal authority over anyone in the group. It is a group of equals, each a specialist in her own area. This fact alone leads to conflict and tension in the agency. Since the account manager is ultimately responsible for coordination and "getting the work out," she often *assumes* a role of authority which is resented by other members of the group. For this reason, skill in democratic forms of leadership and

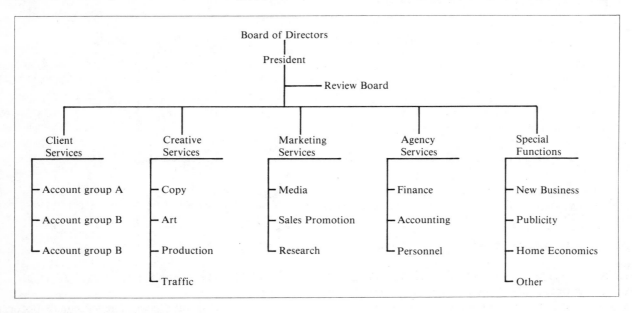

Figure 2–4. Typical agency organization

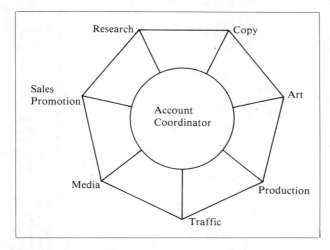

Figure 2-5. Agency work group

sensitivity to interpersonal relations are important ingredients that are sometimes lacking in the account service group.

Second, the creative service division may be organized in functional departments such as is implied by the formal organization chart in figure 2-5. There is a growing tendency, however, to abolish departments and organize creative service personnel into work groups that contain all of the creative functions.

Third, the review board, often called the *plans board,* generally consists of the agency president and the directors of client service, creative services, and marketing services. Its function is to review all major plans and creative material produced by the agency prior to its presentation to the client.

Fourth, since the agency works in informal groups, there is a great deal of flexibility in forming new groups as they are needed, and dissolving groups whose tasks have been completed.

Fifth, there are no hard and fast rules about who does what in an agency work group or how jobs get done. The emphasis is on performance with little regard to the niceties of organizational protocol. This, too, often gives rise to conflict and disagreement. It is no place for thin skins and easily bruised feelings. If conflicts and disagreements cannot be resolved in the work group (and that is where they should be resolved), they are taken to the directors of the agency divisions. If they can't be resolved there, they are taken to the plans board. In most agencies, anyone in the work group can appeal disagreements to a higher level for resolution. But personnel in the agency who consistently resort to this form of conflict resolution generally find that they have no future in the advertising agency business.

In summary, the advertising agency work group is a loose organization of experts, all doing their own jobs, tied together by a personal sense of responsibility for their own contributions and coordinated by the account manager and the strictures of the marketing plan. The group's work sounds casual, but it is not. It is demanding, backbreaking work, governed by performance and accountability.

THE MARKETING BUDGET

There are two groups of items that make up the marketing budget. One group consists of *fixed or semi-fixed* expenses such as salaries of marketing personnel, office space, utilities, warehousing, depreciation of office equipment, and so forth. These items are relatively stable from year to year and do not vary sharply with increases or decreases in marketing activity. A second group of items, such as advertising, sales promotion, marketing research, and so forth, are more *discretionary* in nature and are subject to special appropriations each year. We will be primarily concerned with this second group of items because they are the ones over which the marketing manager has the greatest control and because, for the most part, they represent planned expenditures designed to accomplish specific communications objectives.

In addition to those expenditures identified above, there are other company expenditures which are, properly speaking, marketing expenditures but which are not normally charged to the marketing budget. Packaging is a case in point. For consumer goods, packaging often serves several functions: (1) product protection, (2) display, and (3) dispensing. Frequently, marketing will require display and dispensing features for the package which substantially increase packaging costs. These increased costs are clearly marketing expenditures, although normally they are charged to the manufacturing department's budget as product costs. The one packaging expenditure that is generally recognized as a marketing expense is a new package design, when package redesign is required for marketing considerations. In this instance, design costs are usually treated as a marketing expense.

Within the marketing budget, there is still a problem of allocating expenses into various functional categories such as advertising, sales promotion, publicity, marketing research, package design, test marketing, and so forth. Unfortunately, there is no consistent pattern followed in making such allocations. Table 2-4, reprinted from *Printers' Ink,* identifies three lists

Table 2–4. "Printers' Ink" guide to allocation of advertising appropriations (sometimes called the "white, black, and gray list")

White list (these charges belong in the advertising account)

Space	Catalogs	Administration	Mechanical
(paid advertising in all recognized mediums, including:)	Package inserts (when used as advertising and not just as direction sheets)	Salaries of advertising department executives and employees	Artwork
Newspapers	House magazines to dealers or consumers	Office supplies and fixtures used solely by advertising department	Typography
Magazines	Motion pictures (including talking pictures) when used for advertising	Commissions and fees to advertising agencies, special writers or advisers	Engraving
Business papers	Slides	Expenses incurred by salesmen when on work for advertising department	Mats
Farm papers	Export advertising	Traveling expenses of department employees engaged in departmental business	Electros
Class journals	Dealer helps	(Note: In some companies these go into special "Administration" account)	Photographs
Car cards	Reprints of advertisements used in mail or for display		Radio & TV production
Theater programs	Radio		Package design (advertising aspects only)
Outdoor	Television		Etc.
Point of purchase	All other printed and lithographed material used directly for advertising purposes		Miscellaneous:
Novelties			Transportation of advertising material (to include postage and other carrying charges)
Booklets			Fees to window display installation services
Directories			Other miscellaneous expenses connected with items on the white list
Direct Advertising			
Cartons and labels (for advertising purposes, such as in window displays)			

Black list (these charges do not belong in the advertising account, although too frequently they are put there)

Free goods	Special rebates
Picnic and bazaar programs	Membership in trade associations
Charitable, religious, and fraternal donations	Entertaining customers or prospects
Other expenses for goodwill purposes	Annual reports
Cartons	Showrooms
Labels	Demonstration stores
Instruction sheets	Sales convention expenses
Package manufacture	Salesmen's samples (including photographs used in lieu of samples)
Press agentry	Welfare activities among employees
Stationery used outside advertising department	Such recreational activities as baseball teams, etc.
Price lists	Sales expenses at conventions
Salesmen's calling cards	Cost of salesmen's automobiles
Motion pictures for sales use only	Special editions which approach advertisers on goodwill basis
House magazines going to factory employees	
Bonuses to trade	

Gray list (these are borderline charges, sometimes belonging in the advertising accounts and sometimes in other accounts, depending on circumstances)

Samples	Premiums
Demonstrations	Membership in associations or other organizations devoted to advertising
Fairs	Testing bureaus
Canvassing	Advertising portfolios for salesmen
Rent	Contributions to special advertising funds of trade associations
Light	Display signs on the factory or office building
Heat	Salesmen's catalogs
Depreciation of equipment used by advertising department	Research and market investigations
Telephone and other overhead expenses, apportioned to advertising department	Advertising allowances to trade for cooperative effort
House magazines going to salesmen	
Advertising automobiles	

This chart is based on the principle that there are three types of expenses that generally are charged against the advertising appropriation.

The first charge is made up of expenses that are always justifiable under any scheme of accounting practice. These have been included in the white list of charges that belong in the advertising account.

A second type consists of those charges which cannot and should not under any system of accounting be justified as advertising expenses. These have been placed on the black list.

There is a third type of expense which can sometimes be justified under advertising and sometimes not. Frequently the justification for the charge depends upon the method used in carrying on a certain activity. These charges have been placed on a borderline gray list.

The chart is the result of the collaboration of the editors of *Printers' Ink* and several hundred advertisers. It has been revised for a third time with the aid of advertising and accounting men. It may be considered, therefore, to represent sound, standard practice.

of activities that are sometimes charged to advertising. The first list, referred to as the "white" list, clearly belongs in the advertising budget. The second list (the "grey" list) is made up of borderline items that sometimes belong in the advertising budget depending upon the circumstances. The third list (the "black" list) consists of items that should not appear in the advertising budget, but sometimes do.

All too frequently, the advertising budget becomes a catchall for expense items that more properly should be charged to other departments such as finance, personnel, or public relations. Of course, such misallocations distort advertising expenditures.

Obviously, the lack of standard practices in regard to allocation procedures makes it difficult to compare advertising expenditures between companies from the figures given in company operations statements.

A CONCLUDING NOTE

The complexity of the marketing process, the number of activities that must be performed, and the diversity of skills that must be enlisted in order to develop a marketing program point up the need for a control mechanism to coordinate the contributions of the participants.

That control mechanism is the marketing plan. It is the blueprint that enables the overall task to be broken down into its component parts, worked on independently, and then be reassembled into a unified, integrated course of action. The marketing plan is the subject of the next chapter.

SUMMARY

Marketing is a "people" business, heavily dependent upon interpersonal skills and based on confidence. It is also highly competitive, involves large sums of money, and is populated by competent and ambitious people.

Structurally, the industry consists of four groups of participants: advertisers (clients), advertising agencies, media, and collateral services. In various combinations, these participants carry out five broad functions. These functions are: (1) contractual—the searching out of buyers and sellers; (2) merchandising—the fitting of goods to market requirements; (3) pricing—determining optimal prices for products being sold; (4) propaganda—creating favorable consumer attitudes toward the products being offered for sale; and (5) termination—making the final sale. The advertiser or client is involved in all five of these functions. Advertising agencies are involved to a greater or lesser extent in the first four. Media are primarily involved in propaganda, and the collateral services have specialized and limited tasks in one or more of the functional areas.

The primary focus of this book is on the advertiser and advertising agency, with the other participants being dealt with only to the extent that a knowledge of their functions is important to the first two groups.

Each of the four participants have been briefly defined in terms of major functions, and methods of compensating advertising agencies were discussed.

Basic organizational forms for both advertisers and advertising agencies have been outlined, with an emphasis on organizational trends that have emerged to improve the coordination and integration of the marketing process.

Finally, reference has been made to the marketing budget and the types of expenditures it normally contains. In this discussion, it was pointed out that there is a certain amount of ambiguity about what is charged to the marketing budget and that the advertising portion of this budget, in particular, often ends up as a catchall for miscellaneous items that should properly be charged to other areas of the company.

QUESTIONS

1. Identify and explain the functions of the various participants in the marketing process.
2. Distinguish the various forms of advertising agencies and the forces which gave rise to these forms.
3. Identify and briefly describe the basic functions of a full-service advertising agency.
4. Identify and explain the major methods of compensating advertising agencies.
5. Explain the nature of the controversy over methods of compensating advertising agencies.
6. Trace the organizational development of client organizations in their attempts to integrate the marketing function.
7. What are the primary advantages and disadvantages of each of the organizational forms referred to in question 6?

8. Identify the typical organization of an advertising agency. What does it mean to say that agency organizations are relatively "flat?"
9. How does the formal structure of an advertising agency differ from the "working arrangements" that exist within a typical agency?
10. Distinguish between *fixed and semifixed* costs and *discretionary* expenditures in the marketing budget.

PROBLEM

Carson-Kelly is an old, established company that has achieved significant success in manufacturing a line of low-cost gasoline stoves and ovens that are used primarily for camping and in vacation homes. The leading product in the company's line is a two-burner stove that accounts for 60 percent of its volume, and 65 percent of its profits. For years, the company has operated with the following organization structure:

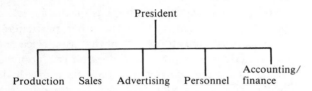

While the company is profitable, its sales have leveled during the past few years, and it has not been active in introducing new products. Its most recent new product, a deluxe version of its basic stove had not been particularly successful.

In an effort to revitalize the company, the president and granddaughter of the company's founder reorganized the company in line with a product-manager system she had read about in the *Harvard Business Review*. Myers, the sales manager, was named vice-president of marketing, and two regional sales managers were brought into the company as product managers. Jorge, formerly advertising manager, was named marketing research director, with the under-standing that, as the need arose, additional research personnel would be added to the staff. The new organization chart had the following form:

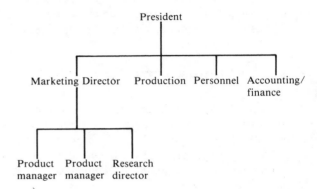

Two years after the reorganization, the president, in viewing the results, was frankly disappointed. There had been no appreciable activity in new product development, and sales of current products were beginning to weaken. She was also disappointed in recent advertising, and was developing severe doubts about the value of the product manager system.

Assignment

1. Evaluate the reorganization undertaken by Carson.
2. Should she abandon the product manager system?
3. Are there any changes she should make?

The Marketing Plan

The marketing plan is the control mechanism that gives coherence to the marketing and advertising effort. It is the central document that defines problems, evaluates opportunities, establishes objectives, determines strategy, gives guidance to and coordinates the various elements of the marketing program.

The marketing plan is not a long document, but it is a comprehensive one. It is the rationale and the blueprint that details the planned activity of a brand.

Sometimes the marketing plan is written by the advertising agency; sometimes by the client. But, regardless of who writes it, it is a joint activity in which both the agency and client should be deeply involved.

Chapter 3 not only describes the functions and context of the marketing plan, but it also gives a "practical guide on how to write one." The sections of the marketing plan are outlined; the context of each section is explained. Examples of typical statements appearing in each section are given.

Read this chapter for understanding.

Keep it as a reference.

Use it as a guide to write your own marketing plans.

The Marketing Plan

President Kennedy is reputed to have said, "Planning is everything." And, in the practice of marketing, this often seems to be the case. Unfortunately, not all plans are well conceived nor well executed, and even the best of plans can turn to ashes because of variables over which the marketer has no control. Yet, planning is a crucial element in marketing success. Successful products don't just happen. Neither do great advertisements. Products become successful through a careful assessment of marketing opportunities and the thoughtful use of company resources. Crest toothpaste and the Trac II razor are cases in point.

Crest

Crest toothpaste burst into the dental care field with all the subtlety of an atomic bomb. Spearheaded by massive door-to-door sampling, publicized by heavy consumer advertising extolling the benefits of fluoride, and supported by the endorsement of the American Dental Association, Crest made American consumers cavity conscious. "Look, Mom! No cavities" became a national byword. But it didn't happen by chance.

Proctor and Gamble had carefully identified cavities and expensive dental work as a major consumer concern. They had developed a product containing fluoride that was effective in inhibiting cavities; then they postponed the product introduction while they carefully amassed the clinical tests that were necessary to obtain the approval of the American Dental Association for their advertising claims. The success of Crest is an outstanding example of thorough planning.

Nor is Crest an exception in Procter and Gamble's stable of products. P&G brands rank first in detergents (Tide), potato chips (Pringles), shortening (Crisco), disposable diapers (Pampers), toilet paper (Charmin), and a number of other product areas. Success seems to be such a habit at Procter & Gamble that they must have a secret. *Fortune*, in an article titled "P&G's Secret Ingredient," states:

That secret, in a word, is thoroughness. Procter & Gamble manages every element of its business with a painstaking precision that most organizations fail to approach. Thoroughness extends to the careful and tenaceous recruitment of employees, the development of a much admired executive corps, the design of man-

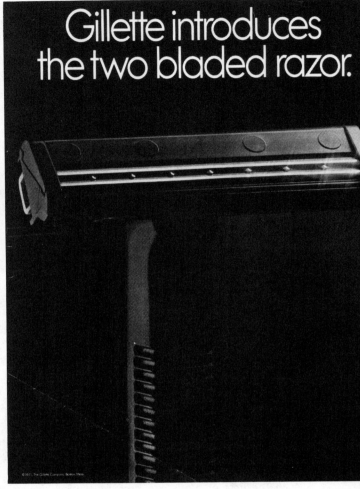

Figure 3-1. (The Gillette Company)

ufacturing facilities, and the creation and testing of products. By the time a product gets to the marketing stage, the thorough preparation through all the prior stages has already endowed it with an edge on competition.[1]

And every P&G product is backed up and guided through the marketplace by a thorough marketing plan.

Trac II

Early in 1971, Gillette North America launched a crash program to introduce the Trac II razor during the fall World Series telecasts. The company had been

___
1. Peter Vanderwicken, "P&G's Secret Ingredient," *Fortune* (July, 1974): 75 ff.

working on a twin-blade shaving system for several years and, now that it was approaching introduction, a monumental amount of work remained to be done. William G. Salatich, then president of Gillette North America, stated:

With only a few brief months remaining before World Series time, a great deal of work had to be done. We organized teams for development, manufacturing, purchasing, personnel, marketing, promotion, and so on. I asked Clif Eaton, who was president of our Safety Razor Division at that time, to assume the role of product development manager, and live with the project day and night through its development and production. We had to find an advertising agency and a name for the new system. Packaging and pricing work had to be done. We had to figure out what profit or loss draw this product would have on our other products.

Plans for advertising, promotion, dealer allowances, minimum stock requirements had to be made and events scheduled and executed on time. [2]

The deadline was met. Trac II commercials were shown fourteen times during the World Series. During the month of October alone, it was estimated that seven out of ten homes saw Trac II commercials. Advertisements also appeared in print media—*Life, Sports Illustrated,* and other magazines (see figure 3–1). A new product had been successfully launched. And, behind the success of Trac II, was a masterpiece of planning and coordination.

THE SCOPE OF PLANNING

Few topics have received as much attention as planning in the marketing and management literature. In most management texts, planning is treated as one of the primary functions of management. Yet, too frequently, the planning that is done is haphazard, and many so-called plans represent little more than the thoughtless perpetuation of past management errors. This point is dramatized in Theodore Levitt's well-known and often quoted essay, "Marketing Myopia." [3] Leon Winer has pointed out that "The biggest problem in marketing is *planning.* Many companies have a marketing 'plan,' yet few of these plans represent any real planning." [4] And, Philip Kotler has observed:

> Firms that do little formal planning may not make the best use of their opportunities and resources and may be vulnerable to changing markets . . . most American companies probably err more in underplanning than in over planning.
>
> Planning is regarded with some suspicion in the pragmatic setting of business. Some executives of the old school argue that "pluck and luck" count for more than careful planning and claim that their firms are too successful to take the time out for planning. Yet planning does yield positive benefits, and though it can be carried to excess, excess is usually not the problem. The problem is one of developing appropriate planning procedures together with companywide participation and competence in carrying them out. [5]

Much of the literature on marketing deals with top management decisions on the broad strategy that a company should follow in determining the fields in which it should compete and how the company should be organized and its resources utilized to insure survival and growth. Thus, Peter Drucker emphasizes the importance of determining what business a company is or should be in, [6] and Alfred P. Sloan, Jr., generally considered the architect of General Motor's success, is quoted as claiming he made only three important decisions in his years at General Motors: a decision on the organization of the company; a decision on financial controls; and a decision on product policy.

Yet, there is another side to marketing; a side that occupies most of the time and energies of those who engage in its practice. And that is the planning, the development, and the execution of marketing activities for existing products. It is in this planning activity that the advertising and other mass communication activities are rooted, and it is the result of this activity that determines the success or failure of the products that fill retail shelves. The document that gives direction to the day-to-day marketing activities that influence consumers in their buying practices is the company marketing plan with the objectives, strategies, and tactics that it contains.

THE MARKETING PLAN

William Lazer has pointed out that

> the central idea of marketing planning is very simple— it is that planned marketing activity is more effective than unplanned activity; that marketing factors, regardless of their variability and situational differences can be planned; and that a company to a considerable degree can help shape its own destiny—it can plan its marketing posture. Yet marketing is a relative late comer to the planning fraternity.
>
> Planning endeavors to foretell the future and prepare for it. Planning activity is based on three major assumptions:
>
> 1. That marketing executives can learn from past experience and observations and reach conclusions regarding future events in the market place and their impact on the firm.
> 2. That marketing executives need not merely take these events as given, but can also partially shape and mold them to meet the desires of the firm.

2. William G. Salatich, "Gillett's Trac II: The Steps to Success," in *Marketing Now,* R. F. Hoel, ed. (Glenview, Illinois: Scott, Foresman & Company, 1973), p. 190

3. Theodore Levitt, "Marketing Myopia," in *Modern Marketing Strategy,* E. C. Bursk and J. F. Chapman, eds. (Cambridge, Massachusetts: Harvard University Press, 1964), pp. 24–48.

4. Leon Winer, "Are You Really Planning Your Marketing," *Journal of Marketing,* **29,** no. 1 (January, 1965): 1-8.

5. Philip Kotler, *Marketing Management,* 2nd ed. (Englewood Cliffs, New Jersey: Prentice-Hall, Inc., 1972), p. 363.

6. Peter Drucker, *Management* (New York: Harper & Row, Publishers, 1974), pp. 86–91.

3. That thorough planning, proper strategies, decisions, and adjustments may be arrived at, and the effects of future events themselves may be changed to increase the profitability and effectiveness of the firm.

Marketing planning, therefore, is rooted in the past, has a perspective of the future, and provides the basic directional guidance for marketing activities. It refers to the planning of human action that molds events—goals that are reached as a result of marketing planning.[7]

Since the marketing plan as it is developed for most products is, essentially, a mass communications document, it is generally prepared or supervised by the marketing manager, although many people participate in its development. It seldom includes the sales plan which, as a separate document, details the activities of the sales force. Technically the sales plan is also a part of the company's marketing plan. One major reason why the two documents are prepared separately is that many companies market a number of products that are handled by the same sales force. Thus, there may be a number of marketing plans (one for each product) but only one sales plan, which allocates sales activity to the various products as needed. One consequence of this situation is that the marketing manager for a particular product may be competing with the marketing managers of other company products for sales force attention. Ultimately, if this competition becomes too severe and makes more demands on the sales force's time than it can accommodate, top management must decide how to best allocate sales force time. In a single product company, the sales plan may indeed be a part of the basic marketing document. However, since our primary concern is that of mass communications in support of specific products, the sales plan is not treated as a part of the marketing plan, a convention widely followed in marketing practice.

According to Lazer, the purpose of the marketing plan is to provide guidance for future marketing activities. Thus, it is primarily concerned with those variables over which the marketer has control. These variables are frequently referred to as the *4 P's*—Product, Place, Promotion, and Price[8]—and the way in which they are manipulated in support of a particular product is referred to as the *marketing mix*. The marketing plan systematically examines each of these marketing variables in order to determine how they can best be used and coordinated in order to reach a desired marketing goal.

The Time Frame

Marketing plans may be either long-range or short-term documents. Long-range plans often cover a period of five or more years; plans of less than five years are considered short range. The marketing plan as it is treated in this text is a short-range plan, usually covering a one-year period. Some marketing practitioners believe that the plan should cover at least a three-year period and be updated and extended on an annual basis. The arguments for this position are that it provides continuity for the marketing program; and by forcing the planner to look further ahead, it encourages a more careful consideration of marketing decisions. There is merit in this position because a new planning period always brings pressure for change, and successful advertising themes may be prematurely discarded. Most marketing practitioners, however, opt for a one-year plan. They argue that because marketing conditions change so rapidly, a three-year plan is futile and time consuming; plans that extend beyond one year tend to be inflexible and become difficult to change even though the marketing situation may require a redirection of effort.

I feel that it makes little difference whether the plan is for three years or for one year since no marketing plan is so good that it does not need constant reexamination to make sure that environmental changes have not made it obsolete. Further, the marketer who signals a basic strategy change simply because he is entering a new planning period, with little regard for competitive requirements, is hardly competent to put together an effective plan in the first place.

The Function of the Marketing Plan

While the purpose of the marketing plan is to provide guidance for future marketing activities, it also serves several other functions within the organization.

1. *Brings together in one place all of the important facts, conclusions, and operating decisions which bear on the marketing problem and its solution.*
2. *Provides a complete operating guide to all personnel working on the product,* both within the advertiser's organization and in other participating organizations, such as the company's advertising agency.
3. *Provides a summary of basic facts and conclusions for review* by new personnel, and by personnel who

7. William Lazer, *Marketing Management: A Systems Approach* (New York: John Wiley & Sons, Inc., 1971), pp. 76–77.
8. E. Jerome McCarthy, *Basic Marketing: A Managerial Approach,* rev. ed. (Homewood, Illinois: Richard D. Irwin, Inc., 1964) pp. 38–40.

are not directly or intimately involved in the preparation or implementation of the plan.

4. *Establishes benchmarks against which marketing and advertising accomplishments can be judged.*

In addition to these key functions, the preparation of a comprehensive marketing plan at least once each year offers these additional values. *It encourages clear and logical analysis of marketing problems,* bringing the various elements of the problems and their solutions into an orderly sequence from: (a) problem definition to (b) the setting of objectives, to (c) proposed solutions and the selection of means to achieve objectives. *It provides a framework for viewing problems objectively. It forces the author or authors of the plan to dig deeply into the product, its market, and the product's problems and opportunities. It helps identify gaps in available information,* or weak links in the chain of logic leading to recommended actions. Further, to the extent that the written plan is formally structured, it sets apart each major decision or judgment upon which the detailed plan is based. This format facilitates critical appraisal of each element of the plan and decreases the danger of continuing past activities without careful, periodic review.

The marketing plan is a basic document that serves as a control center for the effective management of all aspects of a company's marketing activities.

A Note on Terminology

There is no universally agreed upon terminology to describe the concepts used in a marketing plan. Instead, there is a profusion of terms that are used: goals, objectives, strategies, plans, tactics, copy platform, image, program, promotion, sales promotion, merchandising, etc. Some of these terms are used interchangeably, and some have unique, and sometimes highly idiosyncratic meanings. To avoid confusion, we will define some terms that will be used in the following material.

Objective The term *objective* is used to describe the end result that is to be achieved in a specific period of time. The statement of objectives at any level (that is, marketing objectives, media objectives, sales-promotion objectives, etc.) *always* identifies *what* is to be accomplished, *not how* it is to be accomplished. The terms *goal* and *objective* are often used synonymously.

Strategy The term *strategy* is used to describe a decision as to *how* the objectives are to be accomplished. Thus, strategy statements communicate the principles used in selecting and/or utilizing various marketing techniques or devices. Thus, we speak of marketing strategy, media strategy, copy strategy, and so forth.

Plan The term *plan* is used in two ways. When preceded by the word *marketing,* it refers to the entire document. When it is preceded by such words as *advertising, media, copy,* it refers to the detailed presentation of recommended action. This latter use of the word *plan* is synonymous with the term *tactics.* (Academicians tend to use the word *tactics,* while practitioners tend to use the word *plan.* Why? I don't know.)

Sales Promotion The term *sales promotion* is used to describe special incentives to consumers, to the trade, or to the sales force, or to other activity designed to stimulate action by one of these groups— *excluding* advertising, packaging, publicity, and normal pricing. Point-of-purchase material is considered sales promotion. By convention, advertising agencies often use the word *merchandising* when they mean sales promotion, but this is technically an improper use of the term. Technically, the term *merchandising* refers to the activities of *merchandise houses,* which is what *department stores* were originally called. Its original meaning referred to the selection, pricing, display, and promotion of the goods or merchandise offered by these stores. It is still used in this way in the retail trade. However, advertisers and advertising agencies have appropriated the word and use it as a synonym for sales promotion.

Advertising *Advertising* is defined to include only paid media advertising, including direct mail.

Publicity Publicity is a form of promotion. It differs from advertising in that it is not paid for at standard rates, and the sponsor is not identified. Usually, publicity appears (unidentified as such) in the editorial or news columns of printed media or in the noncommercial portion of radio or television programs. [9] There is another term, *public relations,* which will *not* be used in connection with the marketing of a product, but which is often used in describing the communications activities of a company. *Public relations* is a broader term than publicity and involves a variety of practices designed to build good relations between a company and the various publics with which it deals. Public relations may involve publicity, advertising, or a number of other techniques in accomplishing its objectives.

9. S.W. Dunn and A.M. Barban, *Advertising: Its Role in Modern Marketing* (Hinsdale, Illinois: The Dryden Press, 1974), p. 9.

There is a certain arbitrariness in the use of the above definitions. I have chosen to use them because I am comfortable with them; the way in which I have used them is a convention followed by many marketing practitioners; and by agreeing upon these terms and definitions, a great deal of confusion can be avoided.

A Note on Style

The main body or text of the marketing plan should be as concise as possible. It should be neither an outline of key points nor a written transcript of an oral presentation. Style and organization should be uniform throughout. Language should be clear and specific and should avoid clichés or jargon that are unique to advertising, marketing, or the particular field for which the plan is written. After all, it is a document of communication that should be comprehensible to readers who may not have the unique background or specialized knowledge of the author of the marketing plan.

The plan should *flow* smoothly from one section to the next and from one point to the next within a section. Formal structuring of the text, using subheads and titles, is usually the best way to achieve a clear progression of ideas without excessive wordiness at transition points.

Finally, the marketing plan is *not* a "sales-pitch." Its persuasiveness should arise from its real strengths—from knowledge, analysis, logic, incisiveness, and imagination—not from irresponsible one-sided enthusiasm.

CONTENT OF THE MARKETING PLAN

The marketing plan is a systematic document that proceeds from the general to the specific—from an assessment of the marketing environment (referred to as the *market review* or *situational analysis*) to a detailed summary of the marketing budget. Each step logically leads to the next, and each specific marketing recommendation is firmly rooted in the material that precedes it.

A marketing plan is not a long document. In most cases it does not exceed fifteen to twenty single-spaced, typewritten pages, including tables and exhibits. The main text of a relatively simple plan can usually be handled effectively in less than ten, single-spaced pages. This is so because the marketing plan represents a *distillation* of the *relevant* marketing facts and judgments that influence the marketing program. A great deal of data may be examined in order to distill

out that which is relevant, but only that material which bears directly on marketing decisions will find its way into the marketing plan itself. A single table, for example, may result from an analysis of many work sheets of basic data. These work sheets, while not a part of the marketing plan itself, are usually included in a back-up marketing facts book that serves as supportive data, should it be needed. This marketing facts book becomes a repository for the detailed history of the market and the product's performance in that market.

The marketing plan for an established product usually contains the following parts:

1. Market review.
2. Problems and opportunities.
3. Marketing objectives.
4. Marketing strategy.
5. Advertising objectives.
6. Advertising strategy.
7. Copy strategy.
8. Copy plan.
9. Media strategy.
10. Media plan.
11. Sales promotion strategy.
12. Sales promotion plan.
13. Special objectives, strategies, and plans.
14. Budget summary.
15. Schedule of activities.

The special objectives, strategies, and plans section (item 13) refers to marketing variables such as product, packaging, pricing, publicity, marketing research that *may not* be a part of the marketing plan for an *established* product. If the product is a new product, rather than an established one, then the marketing strategy section should be followed by sections devoted to product objectives, strategy, and plan or packaging objectives, strategy, and plan, and so forth. With an established product, these variables are usually givens; unless they are to be changed in some significant way, there is no need for objectives, strategies, and plans for them.

In the following material, each major section of the marketing plan will be described and clarified. This material, which is designed to show you how to write a marketing plan, should be approached in three ways. *First,* read it all the way through in order to get an impression of the various parts and how they fit together. *Second,* study each section of the market plan in order to understand its purpose and construction. *Third,* use this material as a guide for preparing a marketing plan of your own. The only way to learn to write marketing plans is to write them, again and again. A vice-president of a major consumer products company told me that one of the biggest problems his company has is teaching new product managers how to write a marketing plan.

Appendix 1 at the end of the book, shows a marketing plan for a fictitious product. From this example, you can see how the various parts of the plan fit together, and how the material flows from section to section.

THE MARKET REVIEW

The market review is the first section of the marketing plan. It provides the factual basis for the definition of problems and opportunities, for the marketing objectives, and for the marketing strategies that follow it. Its purpose is to summarize the *relevant* information that will shape marketing decisions.

The preparation of a marketing review is not simple and routine. This part of the marketing plan is critical, and its value depends wholly on the analyst's ability to select those facts that are important to an understanding of the current situation, be objective in selecting and reporting these facts, and report them in a manner that is concise, yet fully intelligible to a reader who is not intimately involved in marketing the product on a day-to-day basis.

It is difficult to generalize about the content of the marketing review section because the dynamics of individual markets vary widely for different products and because there are major differences in the kinds and amount of information available to the marketing analyst. For example, the analyst for a grocery or drug store product that has access to A.C. Nielsen data will have information on: (1) bimonthly national and regional sales for the industry and for selected competitors, (2) market share data nationally, by region, by county size, and by store type, (3) pricing, promotions, and retail inventories, and (4) special analyses such as the effect of shelf facings on market share. By contrast, the analyst who does not have access to the A.C. Nielsen service may have only company sales records, rough estimates of market share, and possibly local reports of product performance provided by media surveys of brand preferences in major markets. Similarly, the marketing planner who has recently completed a test market, a promotion test, or a major consumer survey will have relevant data to include in the market review section that will not be available to the planner who has not conducted such activities.

The first step in preparing the marketing review is often the development of a checklist from which information that appears to be important can be selected. Such a checklist, taken from an article appearing in *Advertising Agency* Magazine, is given in appendix 2.[10]

The purpose of the marketing review section is to describe the *current* marketing situation. To this end, historical data should be summarized and used only to the extent that it serves to explain or highlight the present market condition and its trends. For example, an analysis of historical data may show that the total market or the brand share for the product being examined is increasing or decreasing at a regular rate, at an accelerating, or at a decelerating rate. This fact, revealed by historical analysis, may have a profound effect on forecasts of the market and on brand performance. Generally, however, the marketing review concentrates on developments in the market *since* the last marketing plan. Thus, its focus is on developments of the past year.

The following outline shows the major areas of interest from which relevant facts are extracted in the preparation of the marketing review section.

The Market

1. Definition of the relevant market. For example, if the marketing plan is being prepared for a dog food product, it should make clear what part of the dog food market is considered relevant. Is it the *total* market for dog food, or a particular segment of the market such as canned, moist, or dry dog foods? If it is dry dog food, is the marketer primarily concerned with baked products, meals, kibbles, snacks, or some combination of these types?
2. Market size and growth trends.
3. Forecast of market growth.
4. Make-up of market by product type, brand, package size, price, and other relevant characteristics.
5. Distribution of the total market by region, season, city or county size, sales by outlet type, etc.
6. Significant trends or changes in any of the above areas.

Competitive Position

Frequently, key points can best be emphasized by contrasting the brand's strengths or weaknesses with that of competition. Relevant considerations are:
1. Product quality, both technical and as judged by consumer tests.
2. Pricing, sizes available, and packaging features.
3. Distribution of the product category in retail outlets as well as the distribution for individual brands and for the various package sizes that are offered.

---

10. Herbert West, *Advertising Agency Magazine* (May 10, 1957).

4. Brand shares of market and/or per capita consumption data. If possible, this information should be examined for the total market, by outlet type, by geographic regions, and so forth.
5. Trends or recent changes in any of the above areas.

The Consumer

1. The size of the consumer market in terms of persons, households, or families, whichever is the most relevant.
2. Frequency of purchase, usage rates, trial, repurchase rates, etc.
3. Definition of the consumer market by socioeconomic groups and by socio-psychological characteristics. This data, combined with usage rates, serves to identify target markets.
4. Consumers' knowledge and/or attitudes toward the product category and individual brands.
5. Consumer usage habits. This includes such things as the occasion of use, where the product is consumed, etc.
6. Factors influencing brand selection. Who within the family selects, purchases, and uses the product? What are the decision patterns for the brand?
7. Trends or recent changes in any of the above factors.

Dealers/Distributors/Brokers

1. Buying patterns, including such characteristics as "seasonal loading."
2. Attitudes toward the company, its product, pricing, advertising, and other aspects of the company's marketing program.
3. Mark-ups, promotional practices, and so forth.
4. Trends or new developments in the above areas.

Advertising History

This information should be obtained both for the company's brand as well as for competition.

1. Advertising expenditures, in total, per unit or case, and as a percent of sales. If possible, this information should be broken down by markets, regions, seasonal periods, package sizes and other relevant considerations such as flavor, models, etc.
2. Copy. An analysis and comparison should be made of basic appeals, claims, themes, and the mood or tone of presentation.
3. Media. An analysis should be made of the major media used, media mix, coverage, reach, frequency, scheduling, selectivity among primary target groups, and media efficiency.

4. Advertising results. Analysis should be made of any copy tests, media tests, research findings on awareness, registration of specific selling point, attitudes, and so forth.

Sales Promotion

Again, this information should be analyzed for the company's own brand as well as for competition, insofar as competitive information is available.

1. Types and amounts of sales promotion activity.
2. Estimated promotional expenditures in total, by item, by region, and by season.
3. Traceable results of past promotions in terms of trade and sales force comments, special pricing, displays, retail advertising, and consumer action.
4. Trade attitudes toward various forms of promotion for the product category.

The presentation of marketing facts in the review section should proceed from the general to the specific, starting with the market as a whole and ending with a discussion of individual brands. This procedure contributes to objectivity and facilitates understanding on the part of the reader. The point always to be kept in mind is that the presentation should be clear, concise, logical, and easily understandable.

Earlier, it was pointed out that the marketing review should be *objective*. This point is worth reemphasizing. The general tone of the marketing review should be responsible, analytical, logical, and professional. This is *not* the place to defend a recommended course of action or to be overly optimistic, enthusiastic, or persuasive.

PROBLEMS AND OPPORTUNITIES

This section of the marketing plan is linked directly to the marketing review section and consists of the conclusions derived from it. It appears as a separate section for two reasons: to highlight key findings by setting them apart from the background analysis from which they are derived, and to allow additional latitude for interpreting the meaning and implications of these key findings.

The problems and opportunities section provides the bases for the marketing objectives as well as for major points of marketing, advertising, copy, media, and promotion strategy. Points appearing in this section generally fall into one of the following three groups: (1) the identification of specific marketing *problems,* (2) the identification of specific marketing *opportunities,* and (3) basic conclusions or judgments that have a major bearing on the action which will be recommended in later sections.

This section of the report should be quite brief. All major points can usually be made concisely on a single page since these points have been mentioned in the marketing review section and represent key conclusions from the foregoing analysis.

Examples of the kinds of conclusions that might be drawn in this section are shown below in terms of: general marketing conclusions, advertising conclusions, and sales promotion conclusions.

General Marketing Conclusions

We conclude that investment spending in behalf of the product in 19xx is not warranted because of: (1) competitive weaknesses in the product itself, and (2) disappointing results of the heavy spending tests in Nashville and Tulsa last year,

Analysis of retail distribution indicates that there is an attractive profit opportunity in the introduction of a new package size in the 12–18 ounce range. This conclusion is augmented by the facts that: (1) 50 percent of consumer purchases are of multiple packages, and (2) a package in this size range introduced by a major competitor last year has achieved widespread distribution and currently accounts for 30 percent of their sales.

The results of the pricing test in Des Moines has, thus far, failed to provide evidence that increased distribution and market share will result from a permanent price reduction.

There is an opportunity to increase sales through investment spending in this market. This conclusion is based on the findings that: (1) only 25 percent of the target market has tried the product, (2) repeat purchases among those who have tried the product exceeds 50 percent, and (3) there is no strongly entrenched competitor in this field.

Advertising Conclusions

Results of an advertising awareness test conducted during October indicate that the new "moistness you can see" compaign has performed well above expectations in registering key selling points and increasing "intention to buy" attitudes among consumers.

An analysis of the audience of our television effort indicates a need to strengthen coverage in: (1)

the Southeastern Region, and (2) families with incomes over $12,000 in all areas.

Promotion Conclusions

The results of last year's national in-pack coupon effort fail to justify the use of this technique as a device for improving the repurchase rate.

A comparison of monthly sales figures and actual retail movement for the July-December period indicates that the free-case offer during July and August did stimulate trade loading, but did *not* have a measurable effect on brand share in the two test regions.

The conclusions section of the marketing plan is an excellent place to identify important gaps in marketing information. It is not the place, however, to develop a research proposal for gathering this information. If such a proposal is to be included in the marketing plan, it should be described briefly in the section for other objectives, strategies, and plans and the details of the proposal should appear in a separate document.

MARKETING OBJECTIVES

The marketing objectives section follows immediately after the conclusions section. The objectives section should be brief and spell out the commitment made to management in return for the allocation of resources that is requested. At a minimum, the objective section specifies sales for the marketing period for which the plan is being prepared and the amount of money that will be spent in obtaining the sales objective.

Other objectives, if relevant, may also be included in the objectives section. For example, the commitment to develop a new package, to introduce new flavors or a new model, to initiate product improvements or a major research project may appear in the objectives section.

Marketing objectives should always be *specific, actionable,* and *achievable.* If they do not meet these three criteria, they provide little guidance for marketing activity and no basis for evaluating the marketing program. Examples of marketing objectives are shown in the following material.

Market Share Objectives.

The objective for 19xx is to achieve an average market share of 22.5 percent, with an expenditure for advertising and sales promotion of $3,250,000.

The objective for 19xx is to achieve a market share of 23.5 percent by the end of the fiscal year with an expenditure for advertising and promotion that does not exceed $2,400,000.

Sales Volume Objective

The sales objective for 19xx is to invoice 1.2 million equivalent cases of 24's during the fiscal year with an expenditure for promotion of $800,000. (Note: the concept of equivalent cases is often used when more than one package size or more than one case size is being marketed. Thus, all units are converted to a single case size for analytical convenience.)

Size of Market as an Objective

A major objective for fiscal 19xx is to stimulate new trial and increased usage rates for the product category as a whole sufficient to increase industry sales from 10,300,000 equivalent cases of 24's to 10,920,000 cases, an increase of approximately 6 percent.

Introduction of New Flavors as an Objective

A major objective of the brand during fiscal 19xx is to introduce the new strawberry and lime flavors throughout the Eastern Region, as a first step toward national distribution of these items.

Research as an Objective

It will be an objective of the brand during fiscal 19xx to complete a national, random sample survey of consumers in order to develop more complete information on consumer demographics, product preferences, and usage patterns.

Note that each of these objectives is specific (so that it is subject to measurement) and actionable (there are specific activities that can be undertaken in order to achieve it). The *achievable* criterion of an objective simply means that, in terms of the company's resources and present marketing position, the objective appears reasonable. Earlier, it was pointed out that the marketing plan being presented is a short-term plan, limited to a year. A short-range plan will sometimes refer to a longer range plan that is in existence when the longer range plan has a direct bearing on strategy for the current period. In such cases, a longer-range objective is usually best handled as a lead-in thought

for a statement of an objective for the current period. For example: "In view of the long-range objective of completing national distribution by the end of 19xx, it will be a primary objective of the current fiscal year to introduce the three basic package sizes into at least 30 percent of the U.S."

MARKETING STRATEGY

The marketing strategy section stands at the heart of the marketing plan as the basic statement of *how* the various marketing variables will be used in order to achieve the marketing objectives. Strategy statements define the roles of advertising, sales promotion, pricing, packaging, distribution, and even personal selling.

Marketing strategy is the first real test of the competence of the marketing planner. To this point, he has analyzed the current situation and set objectives. The marketing strategy is the test; it brings together understanding, imagination, vision, and decisiveness to give direction to the entire marketing effort. If the marketing strategy is ill-conceived or ambiguous, there is little chance the plan will be successful. While it is also true that a well-conceived strategy can be sabotaged by inept execution, it is still at the strategy level that the key decisions are made that can spell the difference between a brilliant marketing program and just another mediocre one.

Marketing strategy provides the framework within which specific strategies and plans are developed for each area of marketing activity. An important part of this framework is the clarification of the interrelationships between the various elements in the marketing mix: between advertising and sales promotion, between distribution and pricing, between product and packaging. In the following material, several areas of strategy have been identified and examples of strategy statements given.

How total marketing resources will be allocated among various activities, especially the relative emphasis given to advertising versus sales promotion:

Sales promotion expense will be held to a maximum of 20 percent of the total marketing budget ($300 thousand) in view of the need to offset competitive claims with a strong advertising program.

Total marketing expenditures will be allocated between advertising and sales promotion in the ratio of 70 percent for advertising and 30 percent for sales promotion. This ratio is based on: (1)

general practices within the industry; and (2) the judgment that the brand cannot compete effectively with private label brands without strong advertising support.

During fiscal 19xx, 40 percent of the advertising-sales promotion budget will be spent in promotion. This is a departure from the normal promotional expenditure of 20 percent of the total budget because of the need for an extensive sampling program to induce consumer trial of the improved product.

How total marketing weight will be distributed in place, time, or among several target groups in order to achieve the marketing objectives:

Since historical patterns indicate peak competitive activity during the January-June period, 70 percent of the advertising and sales promotion budget will be spent during this period in order to dominate competitive activity.

It is recommended that total advertising and sales promotion weight be concentrated in the product's top twenty-five volume markets. These markets account for nearly 80 percent of total sales, yet they include less than 40 percent of the population in the entire distribution area. Thus, concentration of funds in these markets will: (1) make the most efficient use of media funds, and (2) permit an effective program within the constraints of a limited budget.

What the basic role(s) of advertising is to be in terms of what is to be advertised, to whom, and for what purpose:

Advertising will be employed as an important, but secondary technique for creating familiarity with the company and its product lines among the estimated two thousand key purchasing agents and management personnel who comprise the primary target group.

The major portion of the marketing budget will be devoted to consumer advertising directed to both current and prospective users. These users are housewives between the ages of 24 and 35, with family incomes of over $10 thousand, and with children under the age of six.

In view of the reduced profitability of the basic flavors, advertising and promotion support will be devoted to the three new flavors.

How a packaging change will be used to meet a specific objective:

In order to stimulate trade and consumer interest in the recent product improvement, basic marketing strategy for fiscal 19xx will be to introduce a completely redesigned line of packages by October 1.

During the first six months of the fiscal year, advertising will feature the advantages of the new, convenience package. During the second half of the year, advertising will revert to an emphasis on product claims, and the new package will be given a prominent, but secondary position in our advertising communications.

How pricing will be used to meet company objectives:

Average selling price will be increased approximately 10 percent in order to: (1) meet the company's profit objectives, and (2) generate marketing expenditures competitive to the case rate employed by competition.

Average selling price will be maintained at current levels, despite the 10 percent increase in ingredient costs, because of recent consumer resistance to price increases in the industry.

How sales promotion will be used in order to accomplish objectives such as increasing market share or increasing trade purchases:

The primary use of sales promotion during fiscal 19xx will be to obtain consumer trial of the improved product.

Sales promotion expenditures will be devoted primarily to obtaining retail distribution for the new, economy package size.

The preceding examples are general. They do not attempt to specify what media will be used, what specific sales promotion devices will be employed, or precisely how the advertising will be written. This is left to the experts in these fields. The strategy statements do place certain constraints on the experts, however. Boundaries are given for how much money may be spent for a particular activity, the kinds of people to be reached, the areas of the country in which media is to be used. Within these constraints, however, creative groups, sales promotion experts, and media buyers are free to exercise their imagination, judgment, and experience.

ADVERTISING OBJECTIVES

Advertising objectives are an extension of the general marketing strategy. The purpose of this section is to define further the role of advertising in the total marketing effort and to establish specific advertising goals for the current planning period. Advertising objectives should *not repeat* anything that has been stated in the marketing strategy. This leads to unnecessary redundancy. Instead, the advertising objectives section should add new dimensions to the advertising part of the marketing plan. Further, the statement of advertising objectives should provide the primary basis for future evaluations of advertising effectiveness.

Since advertising is only one of the controllable marketing variables that affect sales results, advertising objectives should usually be *communications* objectives. They should not be defined in terms of sales results or other direct consumer action such as product trial, product satisfaction, or purchase rates. The whole area of evaluating advertising is covered in chapter 22.

The advertising objectives section will ordinarily be quite brief. Since it is supported by separate copy and media strategies and plans, it should cover only those decisions which affect both copy and media. Normally, advertising objectives do two things. They define the target group or groups in terms of *who* they are, and *where* they are. If these definitions have been made in the marketing strategy section, and they sometimes are, they should *not* be repeated in this section. Second, advertising objectives provide specific, measurable communication goals such as awareness of the product or its advertising, knowledge of product attributes, or attitudes toward the product. Thus, effective advertising objectives are usually based on research measurements. The following examples of advertising objectives are those typically found in a marketing plan:

To increase awareness of product attribute X from its present level of 20 percent to 30 percent among U.S. urban housewives in the 20–45 year age group.

To create awareness of brand advertising among at least 50 percent of the primary target group, namely, adult males in the 40–65 year age group.

To increase favorable attitudes toward the product (as defined in the 19xx attitude study) from 50 percent to 60 percent among U.S. housewives in the 25–35 age group.

To direct consumer advertising to adult women who are full-time housewives in families of average or larger size since they constitute the primary purchase group for the product type.

The advertising objectives section should always make provisions for measuring the extent to which the proposed advertising accomplishes its objectives. Normally, this provision may be handled in either of two ways. It may be a prefatory paragraph introducing the section. For example, "Consumer research will be used to measure the extent to which the advertising program accomplishes its stated objectives." It may be treated as one of the advertising objectives, per se. For example, "The objective of the print advertising effort will be to achieve a Starch seen-associated score of 20 percent or higher."

Sources of information for evaluating advertising effectiveness may include such things as coupon returns, unsolicited consumer letters, press comment, trade comments, or response from the company's sales force. These are generally weak measures, however, and every effort should be made to develop more sophisticated techniques for measuring the advertising program, preferably periodic consumer studies.

The details of the techniques for measuring advertising effectiveness need not be spelled out in the objectives section. These details can be spelled out briefly in the "special objectives, strategies, and plans" section of the report.

ADVERTISING STRATEGY

The advertising strategy section is an optional section in the marketing plan for an established product. It is generally more appropriate in the case of a new product or where unusual conflicts between copy and media objectives need to be reconciled. The basic rule as to whether it should be included is the *rule of redundancy*. If it leads to redundancy, don't include it. Statements that might be reflected in the advertising strategy section are given in the following examples.

The way in which the advertising budget will be apportioned between two or more communication tasks or between two or more target groups.

The first priority in allocating the advertising budget will be given to consumer advertising. Insofar as funds are sufficient for this purpose, second priority will be given to influencing the retail trade through advertising directed to retail grocers.

Ways in which the total advertising effort will be distributed in place and time.

Advertising support will be sustained throughout as much of the year as possible in order to: (1) capitalize on the rapid growth of the market by reaching new users who will be coming into the market throughout the year, and (2) achieve initial trial by the large number of users who purchase products in this category infrequently.

The way in which advertising will be related to other marketing activities, since these relationships may either affect advertising timing or require a change in the copy approach.

Forty percent of the media and copy support will be concentrated during the final quarter of the year to support the consumer sampling program planned for September.

Further clarification of what is to be advertised in terms of such factors as the allocation of advertising among products in a line.

Advertising support will be apportioned within the product line according to individual product sales forecasts.

Advertising support will be concentrated on the deluxe model, with other models being referred to in body copy only.

Which of two considerations—media or copy—will govern the overall advertising program.

Thus, spectacular units might be used for advertising impact at the sacrifice of reach, frequency, or advertising continuity.

In order to achieve maximum concentration of advertising support during the four-week periods preceding Christmas and Mother's Day, media considerations of continuity will be subordinated to the need for major copy units such as multiple-page spreads or full program sponsorship in television.

COPY STRATEGY

A single marketing plan may contain two or more separate copy strategies. This will occur when the product is advertised to two or more groups. For example, a cereal product might be advertised to both children and mothers, using different appeals for the two groups; or, separate advertising campaigns might be directed to consumers and to the retail trade. Separate strategies may also be required when a product is being advertised for two or more uses. For example, a soap or detergent that is used for both laundry and dishes; or evaporated milk which is used for infant feeding, cooking, and in creaming coffee. In instances of multiple product use, the copy strategy should indicate the relative weight that will be given to each use.

The copy strategy should contain at least two elements: It should contain *what* will be presented, that is, the particular product claims that will be emphasized. Further, these claims should always be stated in competitive terms. For example, the claims should be expressed as "superior to" or "better than" competition. Failure to do this can lead to pale, washed-out, me-too copy. Second, the strategy should state *how* the product will be presented: the mood that will be employed, the role of product demonstrations, whether the product name will appear in the headline, whether price will be used in advertising, and so forth.

Examples of copy strategy points are given below. None of these statements represents a complete strategy for a single product.

What will be presented

Brand X evaporated milk will be presented to consumers in the following ways: (1) *for cooking* (60 percent of the weight)—as an ingredient item that is *superior* to competitive products in terms of richness, creaminess, and blending qualities; (2) *for infant feeding* (30 percent of the weight)—as a baby formula that is *superior* to competitive products because it contains all required vitamins and minerals, is easy to digest, easy to prepare, and economical; (3) *for table use* (10 percent of the weight)—as a *superior* creaming agent distinguished by extra richness, convenience, and economy.

Brand Y detergent will be advertised on the basis of its *greater* versatility and ability to get clothes whiter than competitive products.

Brand Z lawn mower will be sold on the basis that it is *easier* and *more economical* to use than competitive mowers because of exclusive feature "A," which guarantees easy starting and reduces maintenance costs.

How the product will be presented

Both print and broadcast copy will convey a general feeling of spontaneity, gaiety, and the fun of social participation in order to emphasize pleasure associated with product use.

The tone of the advertising for headache remedy O will be clinical, so as to associate it with the medical profession.

COPY PLAN

The copy plan explains how the copy strategy will be executed in a specific advertising campaign. It is a short-term document that records the decisions and rationale which have entered into the creation of a recommended copy unit. The copy plan is prepared *after* the copy itself has been written, so as to give maximum freedom to the creative groups to develop a persuasive copy approach. Thus, the chief role of the copy plan is to provide a coherent explanation as to *why* the copy was executed as it was. Copy that lacks this kind of logical support is usually highly vulnerable to attack and criticism. Another value of the copy plan is that it formalizes the creative approach and provides a pattern for the development of further commercials or advertisements. A separate copy plan is required for each creative strategy statement and for each medium employed, since the same plan can seldom be used for both magazines and television because the two media require different presentation techniques.

The copy plan typically covers the following areas, although these are not exhaustive.

The specific product claims (or facts) that are to be communicated

The phrase, "Gets clothes cleaner than ever before," will be featured in all copy as the articulation of the basic selling proposition. This claim will be supported by a testimonial from a "typical" user who will be featured in the advertising.

The relative degree of emphasis to be given to various claims that may be used

Primary emphasis will be given to "natural flavor," with secondary emphasis given to convenience of preparation and economy.

A specification of the media units to be employed along with a justification for the choice

All commercials will be 60 seconds because of the need for this commercial length to develop the basic copy story and to show consumer satisfaction.

Visual devices that will be used to communicate key ideas.

The solubility claim will be supported visually in the following ways: (1) in print copy, by a time-lapse photo sequence; (2) in television, by means of a continuous-action demonstration utilizing direct side-by-side comparisons with the leading competitive product which will be referred to as "brand X."

The way in which copy or action is used to capture attention or achieve believability. For a dog food commercial, the copy plan might state:

The dog(s) used in the feeding scenes on television will always be shown 'jumping eagerly' in anticipation of being fed.

Ways in which the "tone" or "mood" specified in the copy strategy will be achieved

Settings will be informal, featuring happy social groups at a barbecue or picnic.

The way in which the product itself will be presented, including such considerations as the model or package size that will be shown or how special problems in illustrating the product or package will be handled.

The large-sized package will be featured in all advertising because of its: (a) superior legibility, and (b) more favorable size impression relative to other visual elements.

The ways selective appeals will be used to increase copy effectiveness among specific subgroups of the target audience, or how a series of different appeals will be featured in a series of related ads or commercials

Real people rather than professional models will be used, and in successive ads, they will be chosen from different occupational groups and shown in a setting that will clearly identify their occupations.

If the copy plan is truly well written, a new creative group, with no previous experience with the product, could use the copy plan to develop advertising that would fit smoothly into the campaign.

MEDIA STRATEGY

The media strategy is subordinate to both the marketing and advertising strategies, which have already established general media constraints such as the amount of money available, definition of the target group or groups of consumers, the relative emphasis to be given to the various target groups, and when (during the year) advertising support is to be delivered. The basic function of the media strategy is to show how media will be selected and used to meet these general objectives.

The marketing and advertising strategies may not, however, provide a complete statement of the factors affecting the media plan. In such cases, the media strategy statement lists additional factors which will influence the final media plan. To avoid the redundancy that usually results from separate statements of media objectives and media strategy, these clarifying factors can usually be linked directly to a strategy statement. For example:

(1) Spot radio will be purchased on an alternate week basis to extend advertising support throughout the peak buying season; or (2) Local spot television will be employed to fill gaps in major-market network coverage; or (3) On judgment, it is believed that the media program must provide effective message reach among at least 50 percent of the primary male user-group in order to achieve the penetration specified under advertising objectives.

Media strategy statements generally cover the following areas:

The use of local versus regional versus national media and the reasons for these decisions

Media plans will use local media exclusively since: (1) local media satisfy the creative requirements of the advertising and (2) provide the flexibility required by marketing objectives.

The use of print versus broadcast media, and the reasons for this choice

Spot television will be used as the primary medium because it offers the optimum combination of mass coverage, cost efficiency, flexibility in both time and place, and meets the creative requirements.

The selection of a specific kind of media within the broad categories of radio, television, magazines, newspapers, and so forth

Black and Spanish-language radio and television will be used to bolster coverage of these target groups because basic coverage of these groups by magazines is deemed inadequate.

The way each medium selected will be used to meet requirements of reach, frequency, cost efficiency, or other factors influencing media scheduling.

Spot television will be scheduled in three, twelve-week flights spread over the entire year in order to provide year around coverage within the budget restrictions.

The particular time or space units that will be used

In print advertising, all ads will be full page, four-color, bleed units in order to meet creative requirements.

The way in which factors such as seasonality of sales, the timing of promotion, or the availability of copy will affect media scheduling.

Thirty percent of the budget will be spent in August and September in support of the "back-to-school" promotion.

The ways in which two or more media will be combined to meet specific marketing and advertising objectives.

Since magazines do not provide the depth of coverage required in the Southeastern Region, coverage in this area will be supplemented by local newspapers in major markets.

The ways in which specific broadcast time periods or space positions will be used to achieve advertising objectives.

News programming on network radio will be used during the 5:00 P.M. to 6:00 P.M. 'drive-time' periods in order to reach adult males.

The way in which the media plan compromises between optimum reach and frequency and the use of large space units.

Since the complexity of the advertising message requires relatively large space and time units, reach and frequency will be subordinated in order to provide full-page, four-color print units and 60 seconds for television commercials.

MEDIA PLAN

The media plan shows how the media strategy is to be executed in terms of specific purchases. Since the media strategy sets forth the principles upon which the media plan is based, the media plan itself shows how these principles are brought to bear in individual buying decisions. However, the media plan as it appears in the marketing plan is a summary statement, not a detailed one. Necessary rationale or other background discussion should be relegated to separate, support documents. The following types of statements are characteristic of the media plan:

> The recommended media plan provides for 50 percent sponsorship of *Police Woman*. This show was selected over alternatives because of: (1) overall cost efficiency with adult audiences; (2) concentration of coverage of the target market group; (3) key geographic coverage. An analysis of the *Police Woman* audience is available in a separate media document.

> Six ½ pages are recommended in *Good Housekeeping* magazine because: (1) it provides concentrated coverage of the target market; (2) it has minimal duplication with other media recommended; and (3) it is believed that the *Good Housekeeping Seal of Approval* is a decided asset in this product field.

> The media plan calls for 39 weeks of spot television in 63 key markets. These markets include all U.S. markets of 100 thousand or greater population in which industry per capita consumption exceeded 4.0 units during the past year. The proposed market list is shown in appendix 1. The recommended spot program will provide coverage of 77 percent of all U.S. households and 89 percent of industry sales. Message penetration is estimated to be: (1) 45 percent of total homes, one or more times during each four-week period; and (2) an average frequency of 2.1 times during each four-week period.

SALES-PROMOTION STRATEGY

As pointed out earlier, sales promotion refers to activities that lie outside the areas of media advertising and product publicity. Sales promotion includes such things as point-of-sale material, sampling, couponing, contests, trade incentives, and sales-force incentive programs.

The section on sales promotion should be founded on one or more points in the marketing strategy section; these points should identify the role to be played by consumer or trade promotions. Thus, the marketing strategy establishes the sales-promotion objectives. Typically, the sales promotion strategy will contain the following kinds of statements.

Statements of the promotional techniques that offer the most effective and efficient means of meeting the marketing objectives

> Primary emphasis will be given to consumer-oriented promotions since experience has shown that trade incentives have failed to stimulate dealer cooperation in the past.

> The recommended sales-promotion program will utilize a direct mail coupon to encourage consumer trial following the introduction of the new package in August. Direct mail couponing is recommended in preference to other alternatives because experience has shown that it (1) achieves broad reach in a relatively short period of time, and (2) generates greater retailer display activity than other trial-getting devices.

A statement of how total promotion weight will be allocated by product, by marketing area, by season, and so forth

> All trade support for the product line will be concentrated on the large package size because this package size (1) is most profitable and (2) has the greatest effect on retailer cooperation.

Generally, the selection of a particular sales promotion technique to accomplish a particular marketing objective is based on (1) company experience, (2) traditional practices in a given industry, and (3) the results of specific promotion tests. Chapter 20 discusses sales-promotion techniques and the unique values of each.

SALES-PROMOTION PLAN

The sales-promotion plan explains how the promotion strategy will be executed in terms of specific offers or other activites, geographic areas of application, the key audiences to which the sales promotion will be addressed, and the specific times during the marketing year in which promotions will be used. In addition to outlining the details of the recommended sales-promotion activities, the sales-promotion plan also summarizes the estimated cost of the promotions.

SPECIAL OBJECTIVES, STRATEGIES, AND PLANS

The final section of the marketing plan text is devoted to recommendations in areas such as the product itself, packaging, pricing, research, test marketing, and publicity. Marketing plans for established products will not deal with these areas unless the marketing review section has identified specific problems or opportunities relating to these variables. However, if the marketing review reveals weaknesses in any of these areas, then these weaknesses should be dealt with in some way—by recomminding consumer tests, by initiating developmental work, by revising packages, or by engaging in other appropriate activity.

Often, weaknesses in one or more of the controllable marketing variables will be detected during the course of the marketing year—that is, between plans. Such developments often result from competitive activity such as a product improvement, a redesigned package, or a change in pricing practices. In such cases, the marketer cannot afford to delay action until the next formal planning period. Instead, existing objectives, strategies, and plans must be reexamined immediately, and any necessary adjustments must be made. For this reason, every marketing plan should contain a budget reserve. The budget reserve is a contingency fund that may be used to defray the expenses of unanticipated events so that the planned profit contribution will not be reduced. Even under the best of conditions, the market planner cannot anticipate all of the contingencies that may arise in a competitive marketing situation. It is this factor that surrounds marketing with an aura of uncertainty. But, it is also this factor that makes marketing an exciting, dynamic occupation.

BUDGET SUMMARY

At some point in the marketing plan, all recommended expenditures should be brought together to enable the reader to grasp quickly the full implications of what has been proposed and to show the relationship of the various parts of the marketing plan. This summary usually works best at the end of the plan because the material that precedes it provides its justification. The budget summary should be limited to a single page. Major related expenditures should always be grouped together so that the outline of the spending plan is clear. An example of a budget summary appears in table 3–1. Following the budget summary, it is helpful to provide a calendar of marketing activities in order to give a visual picture of how the various activities fit together. An example of such a calendar is shown in figure 3-2.

PLAN OF PRESENTATION

The marketing plan that has been presented in this chapter will also serve as the outline for the remainder of the text. Each major part of the book will be named after a section of the marketing plan, and the chapters

Table 3–1.   Budget summary

Advertising

1. *Consumer Magazines*
   6 to 9 4-color bleed pages in each of 8 magazines: total circulation of 38.5 million. Net unduplicated coverage of 56% of U.S. households. $940,000
2. *Spot Television*
   60 to 100 Gross Rating Points weekly for 26 weeks in 38 markets.   720,000
3. *Spot Radio*
   15 to 20 sixty-second commercials weekly for 39 weeks on estimated 26 Black stations in 21 major markets.   173,000
4. *Production, Preparation*

Magazines:	$15,000	
Television:	8,000	
Radio:	4,000	27,000
	Total Advertising	$1,860,000

Sales Promotion

1. Major tie-in promotion based on 50¢/case display allowance; national magazine support.   200,000
2. February-March: Repeat fall tie-in promotion: 200,000
3. "Pay Day" Black promotion—SE Region   40,000
4. Promotion materials   30,000

Total Promotion	470,000

Reserves

1. For test marketing 2 new packages   125,000
2. General reserves (5% of budget)   125,000

Total Reserves	250,000
GRAND TOTAL	$2,580,000

in that part of the text will discuss subjects most relevant to that section of the marketing plan.

For example, part three is entitled *The Marketing Review,* and chapters in this section will discuss the situational analysis, consumer behavior, marketing research, forecasting, and the development of the communications budget. Part four is entitled *Strategies for Product, Brand, Packaging, Pricing, and Distribution.* Chapters in this section will deal with product strategy, brand and packaging strategy, and pricing and distribution strategy. Although these subjects are normally dealt with in the "Special Objectives" section of the marketing plan (except in the case of new products), they have been moved forward because of their importance in terms of the total marketing effort. Part five deals with *Advertising Copy—Strategies and Plans.* Chapters in this section deal with identifying copy appeals, the development of copy, and mechanical production. Part six, *Advertising Media—Strategies and Plans,* discusses media strategy, newspapers and magazines, television and radio, and other media. Part seven, *Sales Promotion*

	A	M	J	J	A	S	O	N	D	J	F	M
Consumer Magazines: (Page 4-C Bleed)												
LHJ	x	x	x			x	x	x	x	-x-		x
GH	x	x	x			x	x	x	x		x	x
Redbook	x	x	x			x	x	x	x		x	x
FC	x	x	x			x	x	x	x		x	x
WD	x	x	x			x	x	x	x		x	x
Ebony	x	x				x		x		x		x
TS	x	x				x		x		x		x
MR	x	x				x		x		x		x
Spot Television GRP Weekly	60	60	-	-	-	100	100	60	-	-	100	100
Spot Radio 15-20 Spots—Wk.	x	x				x	x	x	x	x	x	x
Fall Tie-in Promotion						x	x					
Winter Tie-in Promotion											x	x
Black "Pay Day" Promotion (S.E. Region Only)						x	x	x	x	x	x	x

Figure 3-2. Calendar of proposed activities 1963–64

—*Strategies and Plans,* will be devoted to types of sales promotion and their uses. Part eight, *Special Objectives—Strategies and Plans,* will discuss publicity, test marketing, marketing research, and corporate advertising when these subjects are themselves objectives. Finally, part nine, *Measurement and Restrictions,* is devoted to the measurement of advertising effectiveness and some of the legal restrictions that surround the marketing and advertising industry.

I believe that this approach to advertising will place it in the marketing comtext within which it belongs, and point up the way in which effective advertising programs are developed.

SUMMARY

The purpose of this chapter is to identify the role of planning in the marketing program and provide a guide to writing a marketing plan.

The marketing plan is the central document used in organizing, integrating, and developing the advertising and promotion activities of a company. It is, essentially, a mass communications document. It seldom includes a sales plan, which is a major ingredient in the company's marketing effort. Instead, the sales plan is usually a separate document prepared by the sales manager. A major reason for preparing the two documents separately is that many companies market a number of products that are handled by the same sales force. Thus, there will be a number of marketing plans (one for each product), but only one sales plan.

Although it is recognized that a marketing plan may be long range (five years or more) or short range (less than five years), prevailing industry practice is to prepare an annual marketing plan that covers the forthcoming fiscal year.

The functions of the marketing plan are to bring together the key facts and conclusions bearing on marketing decisions, to provide an operating guide for marketing personnel, and to establish benchmarks against which marketing and advertising accomplishments can be judged. In addition, the marketing plan encourages clear and logical thinking, forces the author of the plan to examine the product and its marketing opportunities, and helps identify gaps in information.

There is no universally agreed upon terminology to describe the concepts used in marketing plans. To avoid confusion, the following terms were introduced and used throughout the chapter: *objective*—the end result that is to be achieved; *strategy*—decisions as to how objectives will be accomplished; *plan*—a term used to refer to both the entire document as well as to a detailed presentation of recommended action; *sales promotion*—special incentives for consumers, the trade, or sales force; and *publicity*—nonpaid editorial support by media.

I suggest that you approach the discussion of the marketing plan in the following ways: First, read it all the way through in order to understand how the various sections fit together. Second, study each section in order to understand its purpose and construction.

Third, use it as a guide for preparing a marketing plan of your own. The only way to learn to write a marketing plan is to write one again and again.

Each subsequent section of the book is named for a major part of the marketing plan, and chapters in each section discuss those subjects relevant to that portion of the marketing plan itself.

QUESTIONS

1. Discuss the central idea behind planning and identify the major assumptions on which planning is based.
2. What are the arguments for a three-year versus a one-year marketing plan, and why does it make little practical difference which time frame is used?
3. What are the functions of the marketing plan?
4. Identify the additional values that a marketing plan serves.
5. Distinguish between advertising, sales promotion, and publicity.
6. What are the major areas of interest in the "Marketing Review" section? Why are they important?
7. At a minimum, what should be specified in the "Objectives" section of the marketing plan? What are the three basic criteria that objectives should meet? Explain why these criteria are important.
8. Distinguish between objectives, strategies, and plans. Give an example of each.
9. What does "unnecessary redundancy" have to do with the marketing plan? How can it be avoided?
10. Why is the "Special Objectives, Strategies, and Plans" section of the marketing plan important? What might normally be included in this section in the marketing plan for an established product?

PROBLEM

You are applying for a job as marketing director of a medium size company that has carved out a respectable niche for itself in the condiment market. The company produces a sauce that is used as a flavoring agent in cooking, and there is little direct competition. The company spends over $2 million in advertising and sales promotion, and has sales in excess of $25 million.

The company has never operated under a systematic marketing plan. Each year, the company president approves an advertising and promotion budget based on a sales forecast put together by the sales department. This budget is administered by the advertising manager who, working with the company's advertising agency, decides on a copy approach and a media schedule. Historically, the bulk of the funds are spent in recipe advertising in women's magazines, although recently some of the funds have been shifted to spot TV in a few major markets.

Sales of the company are growing slowly. Mr. Culligan, the company president, is somewhat concerned about the company's future, although it is highly prof-

itable at present. Mr. Culligan has recommended that the company be reorganized, and the board of directors has approved this recommendation. It is the reorganization plan that has created the new position of marketing director.

Your preliminary interview with Mr. Culligan has been quite encouraging. You like and respect the man on the basis of your conversation with him, and you want the job because you believe it represents an excellent opportunity for growth.

Mr. Culligan has expressed an interest in talking about marketing planning and has asked you to put together a short presentation on the values of planning and how a marketing plan can be of value to the company.

Assignment

Prepare such a presentation. The presentation should be about ten or fifteen minutes in length and should contain any charts or visual material that will help make it effective.

The Marketing Review

The marketing review is the starting point of the marketing plan. It is here that the facts and figures are developed that make it possible to set realistic objectives and devise effective strategies and detailed plans. As we pointed out earlier, the value of the marketing review section depends largely on the marketer's ability to—(1) select those facts that are relevant to understanding the current situation; (2) be objective in selecting and reporting these facts; and (3) report facts in a manner that is concise, yet fully intelligible to a reader who is not intimately involved in marketing the product on a day-to-day basis.

The world is full of facts about products and their performances. The marketer must sift through them, selecting some and discarding others, until those that have a direct bearing on the success of the product have been isolated. There are certain procedures and disciplines that help the marketer in this task. The purpose of this section is to examine some of these procedures and disciplines. In chapter 4 we will examine the process of situational analysis, pointing up some of the approaches that are helpful in assessing product performance. Then, in chapter 5, we will briefly examine consumer behavior, the elusive and sometimes mercurial phenomenon that marketing communications seek to influence. Chapter 6 deals with marketing research, an invaluable and irreplaceable tool in the marketing process. Finally, in chapter 7, we will discuss forecasting and the determination of the marketing budget.

Situational Analysis

Purex

Purex markets a line of household cleansers, including Brillo, Old Dutch, Sweetheart, and Fels. It competes with companies such as Procter & Gamble and Lever Brothers. One problem faced by Purex is that it is difficult to match the advertising expenditures of its major competition. Its sales force is severely out numbered by the two thousand or so sales representatives deployed by P&G. A situational analysis of the grocery store business revealed that 17 percent of the stores do 72 percent of the grocery business. This was seen by Purex management as an opportunity to offset some of the disadvantages it faced vis-a-vis its giant competitors.

Purex developed a "national accounts" program, an informational promotion program aimed at the buyers and top executives of the biggest product movers. This program, which includes mail promotions, telephone calls, and face-to-face meetings, keeps buyers and other retail executives informed about new products, retail and consumer sales promotions, and special services offered by Purex. As a consequence of this program, 6 percent of Purex's customers handle two-thirds of the all commodity volume for their product categories, and Purex has a highly successful, minimal cost promotional program.[1]

Frozen Pies

In making a situational analysis, a major marketer of frozen fruit pies found the market share for its brand considerably below the national average in a number of major markets. The first inclination was to increase advertising pressure in these markets in an effort to bolster sales. However, further analysis revealed two separate problems.

In one group of markets brand distribution was good; the brand was distributed in stores selling 80–85 percent of the total grocery volume, but sales per point of distribution were low. For example, on a national basis, the brand was selling approximately one thousand cases per point of retail distribution per month. In the problem markets, however, brand sales were only about six hundred cases per point of retail

1. Purex Borrows from Cosmetics to Market Household Cleaners," *Product Marketing* (February, 1977): 10.

distribution, and there had been some losses in distribution during the past six month period. In the second group of markets, sales per point of retail distribution were equal to or above the national average, but the brand was only distributed in stores doing between 50–60 percent of the grocery volume.

Since the problems in these two groups of markets were distinctly different, they required different solutions. In the first group of markets, where distribution was high, additional consumer advertising and a consumer couponing effort to stimulate consumer purchases was called for. In the second group of markets, however, the problem was one of increasing retail distribution. Advertising is generally an inefficient tool for this purpose. The strategy employed in these markets was (1) to continue the normal advertising effort, (2) to increase sales coverage by the sales force, (3) to offer a stocking allowance of 50¢ per case to encourage retailers to stock the brand, and (4) to use a consumer couponing effort in order to provide initial sales and to persuade retailers that, if the brand were stocked, sales would be forthcoming.

Ohrbach's

Ohrbach's department store was started in 1923, on 14th Street in New York. Later, it moved to 39th Street, and opened branches in suburban New York, Newark, and Los Angeles. It became known as a fashion leader, and the distributor of low-cost copies of Paris originals. Ohrbach's was an anomaly compared to other department stores. It offered no deliveries, no wrapping service, no C.O.D.'s, no mail or phone orders, no alterations. In short, it offered few of the services that department stores customarily use to woo customers. Instead, it offered high fashion, high quality, and low prices.

An analysis of Ohrbach's strengths and weaknesses enabled its advertising agency to develop some of the finest creative advertising in the retail field. One of these ads, "I found out about Joan," developed in 1957, is shown in figure 4–1.[2] Using a skillful blend of artful illustration and cattiness, the following copy from this ad creates a powerful registration of Ohrbach's strengths.

The way she talks, you'd think she was in Who's Who. Well! I found out what's what with *her*. Her husband own a bank? Sweetie, not even a bank *account*. Why that palace of theirs has wall-to-wall *mortgages*. And that car? Darling, that's horsepower, *not* earning power. They won it in a fifty-cent raffle! Can you imag-

ine? And those clothes! Of course she *does* dress divinely. But really . . . a mink stole and Paris suits, and all those dresses . . . on *his* income? Well, darling, I found out about that too. I just happened to be going her way and *I saw Joan come out of Ohrbach's!*

Each of these cases demonstrates the role of analysis in determining strategy. In the case of Purex, an analysis of the retail grocery market led to an innovative sales strategy. In the case of frozen pies, analysis of distribution patterns led to the development of an effective sales promotion strategy and the wise use of advertising funds. For Ohrbach's, a recognition of product strengths resulted in imaginative *and* persuasive advertising. In each case, however, the strategy employed was an outgrowth of careful analysis of the current marketing situation. Analysis, objectives, strategies, plans, and execution is the pattern of successful marketing.

SCOPE OF ANALYSIS

The comprehensiveness possible in the situational analysis depends upon the amount and variety of the factual data available. Some companies will have relatively little marketing data upon which to draw; others will have a great deal. Generally, the amount of data available will depend on the individual company's ability and willingness to invest in research information. Extensive marketing data can be expensive, but it is often worth the cost.

A case in point is the evaporated milk industry in the 1950s. Two major companies, Pet and Carnation, dominated the field. Both companies marketed their products on a nearly national basis prior to World War II. Pet had its greatest strength in the southeast, southwest, midwest, and upper midwest; Carnation's strength was on the eastern seaboard, northeast, mountain, and west coast states. Their total market shares were similar on a national basis, and together they accounted for over two-thirds of all evaporated milk sales. Until 1948, both companies were enjoying sales growth because the total market was growing, and they were maintaining strong share positions. Both companies used industry sales data developed by the Evaporated Milk Association from government statistics on evaporated milk sales categorized by state. This data was useful, but it had limited value because of trans-shipments (that is shipments across state lines after the government data was compiled), and shipments to South America out of southern ports.

After World War II, Carnation shifted its pattern of promotional expenditures, increasing its spending

---

2. Robert Glatzer, *The New Advertising* (New York: The Citadel Press, 1970): 38–45.

The way she talks, you'd think she was in Who's Who. Well! I found out what's what with *her*. Her husband own a bank? Sweetie, not even a bank *account*. Why that palace of theirs has wall-to-wall *mortgages!* And that car? Darling, that's horsepower, *not* earning power. They won it in a fifty-cent raffle! Can you imagine? And those clothes! Of course she *does* dress divinely. But really...a mink stole, and Paris suits, and all those dresses...on *his* income? Well darling, I found out about that too. I just happened to be going her way and *I saw Joan come out of Ohrbach's!*

Ohrbach's

© 1958 by Ohrbach's Inc.

34ᵀᴴ ST. OPP. EMPIRE STATE BLDG. · **NEWARK** MARKET & HALSEY · "A BUSINESS IN MILLIONS, A PROFIT IN PENNIES"®

Figure 4–1. Ohrbach's, Inc.

in the southeastern part of the country and outspending Pet on a per case basis, both in the south and nationally. As a result, the Carnation brand began to make inroads on Pet's share, gaining a competitive edge of four to five share points, nationally. This share advantage translated to about five million standard cases, with a standard case consisting of forty-eight large, or ninety-six small cans of the product.

The reason Carnation shifted its expenditure patterns was that the company started to subscribe to the A.C. Nielsen Food Index. The Nielsen Food Index provides consumer purchase data for grocery store products, measured by store audits conducted in a large, representative sample of food stores throughout the United States. Audits are made on a bimonthly basis (six times a year), and develop information on consumer purchases by region, county size, store size, and chain and independent outlets. It also develops information on prices, in-store promotions, local advertising, shelf stocks, inventories, retailer purchases, and so forth. Special analysis of this data enables users to determine the effectiveness of promotion, the relationship of shelf-facings to sales, as well as other revealing data. Although this data cost Carnation upward to $50 thousand a year, it enabled the company to plan its marketing effort more effectively than in the past, with the result that it gained a profitable marketing advantage over Pet and the remainder of the evaporated milk industry.

Not all industries have data on consumer sales as complete as that offered by retail audit services such as A.C. Nielsen, but most companies have access to a wide variety of data which, when used properly, can provide profound insights into the structure and current conditions in the market place. In chapter 6, sources of data will be described in some detail. The purpose of this chapter is to examine ways in which some of this data may be used in analyzing and making sense out of the wealth of statistics that is often available.

USING MARKETING DATA IN THE SITUATIONAL ANALYSIS

The situational analysis section of the marketing plan proceeds from the general to the specific to enable the analyst to begin with a broad consideration of the market and its potential and progressively narrow the analysis down to specific factors that relate to the marketing problems and opportunities of the individual brand. In this section, we will examine the concepts of market potential, company sales, brand share analysis, distribution analysis, comparative advertis-

ing expenditures, sales promotion expenditures, advertising effectiveness, and special research.

Market Potential

Market potential refers to the *demand for a particular product type at a given time and under defined marketing conditions*. For example, the market potential for automobiles in 1977 was approximately 12 million cars. Under conditions of economic recession, the potential may drop to a little over 9 million cars as it did in 1974 and 1975. During conditions of full employment, consumer optimism, and heavy promotional expenditures by automobile manufacturers, the potential might rise to 13–14 million. Thus, at any given time, the market potential reflects the total size of a particular market in terms of units or dollars.

Some markets are volatile because they are strongly influenced by a variety of economic and personal factors; others are relatively stable. The market forecast (discussed in chapter 7) is highly critical in volatile markets. A forecast that is too low can lead to a severe drop in market position since raw material and production plans must often be formulated months ahead of time. If the market forecast is too high, unsold inventories erode profits and may result in severe losses. Although it is important for planning production and spending levels, the forecast in stable markets is less critical because the possiblity of forecasting error is much smaller. Table 4–1 shows industry sales

Table 4–1

	U.S. Passenger Car Sales—Domestic and Imports				
	1971	1972	1973	1974	1975
Units (in/1000's)	10,900.0	11,200.0	12,000.0	9,400.0	9,100.0
% Change	-	2.7%	7.1%	(21.7%)	(3.2%)
Index (base: 1971)	100	103	110	86	83
	Margarine—U.S. Civilian Consumption				
	1971	1972	1973	1974	1975
Millions of lbs.	2,298.3	2,360.0	2,377.6	2,394.5	2,348.9
% change	-	2.7%	0.7%	0.7%	(1.9%)
Index (base: 1971)	100	103	103	104	102
Per capita (lbs)	11.1	11.3	11.3	11.3	11.0
	Evaporated and Condensed Milk				
	1971	1972	1973	1974	1975
Millions of lbs.	1,408.0	1,336.6	1,262.5	1,186.6	1,025.0
% change	-	(5.1%)	(5.6%)	(6.1%)	(13.7%)
Index (base: 1971)	100	95	90	84	73
Per capita (lbs.)	6.8	6.4	6.0	5.6	4.8

SOURCE: *Brewer's Almanac: 1976*, U.S. Brewers Association, Inc., p. 13.

	Beer—U.S. Consumption				
	1971	1972	1973	1974	1975
Millions of barrels	123,850.0	130,740.00	133,960.0	142,312.0	146,853.0
% change	-	5.6%	2.5%	6.2%	3.2%
Index (base: 1971)	100	103	108	115	119
Per capita (gallons)	18.6	19.5	19.8	20.9	21.4

SOURCE: *Statistical Abstracts: 1975*, U.S. Department of Commerce, p. 95.

for the period 1971 through 1975 for four product categories. Each category presents different problems, and has different implications for the market planner.

The passenger car market is relatively volatile; it is strongly influenced by economic conditions and the level of employment. In such a market, demand may shift dramatically from one year to the next. Note, for example, that demand dropped by 23 percent (almost 3 million units) in 1974. Margarine, on the other hand, was an extremely stable market during the five-year period shown. Per capita consumption was virtually level, and the growth in sales was, essentially, the result of population growth.

Beer represents a relatively dynamic market. A combination of increases in population and per capita consumption led to a 19 percent increase in the five year period shown. Some markets have much stronger growth patterns than beer. For example, one segment of the beer market, lite (low calorie) beers, has grown explosively since 1974, encouraging both new brand entries and investment spending. By contrast, the market for condensed and evaporated milk is sick. Population growth is being offset by decreases in per capita consumption. And, while the market is still large—over a billion pounds annually—it is decreasing each year. Advertising expenditures are down, and price appeals and service advertising characterize the creative approaches in this industry. (Service advertising features recipes, food preparation, etc.)

From the foregoing discussion, you can see that market potential (what is happening in the total market) sets the stage for the marketing plan. Is it a time for optimism or pessimism? A time for investing or retrenching? A time for wooing new customers or holding on to those one has? A time for advertising or a time for price competition?

An analysis of marketing potential can do more than just set the stage for the marketing plan. It can also identify areas of opportunity that will influence the allocation of promotional effort both in space and time. Taking the beer market as an example, table 4–2 shows a regional breakdown for beer consumption, and per capita consumption for each region.

In terms of total consumption, there appears to be little difference between the South Atlantic region (220,514 barrels) and the Mountain region (232,952 barrels). Yet, the Mountain region is a much better beer market because the per capita consumption in this region is 24.76 gallons per person compared to 16.47 gallons per person in the South Atlantic region. This means that each dollar spent on promotion in the Mountain region has an opportunity to generate more sales than a dollar spent in the South Atlantic region. There are many other factors that may influ-

Table 4–2. Regional Consumption of Beer

Region	Population	Sales (Gallons)	Gallons Per Capita
New England	12,150	269,721	22.20
Middle Atlantic	37,276	774,993	20.74
East N. Central	40,862	897,409	21.96
West N. Central	16,682	346,203	20.75
South Atlantic	13,387	220,514	16.47
West S. Central	20,584	459,623	22.33
Mountain	9,411	232,952	24.76
Pacific	27,833	619,488	22.86

SOURCE: USBA Distilled Spirits Institute, Wine Institute, and U.S. Department of Commerce. *Brewer's Almanac*, 1974, p. 57.

ence the allocation of promotional funds: brand position in the market, availability of media, ease of reaching consumers, competitive activity, distribution, transportation costs. Per capita consumption is one of the more important factors. Prudent marketers generally invest funds in areas of high per capita consumption, leaving areas of low per capita consumption to those who are less prudent, and less successful.

Table 4–3 shows the seasonal distribution of beer sales. It is apparent that promotional funds invested in the May through August period will return greater dividends than funds invested in the winter months because 38.7 percent of annual beer consumption occurs in the four months from May through August, while only 28.9 percent of the beer is consumed in the four-month period from November through February. The difference is over 14.2 million barrels. This difference is reflected in the media schedules of brewers who "heavy-up" during the beer drinking season. Further regional analysis might reveal that seasonal variations are not as marked in some regions as in others. For example, the Southeast region with its mild winters has less seasonal variation than the East

Table 4–3. Seasonal Beer Consumption

Month	Thousands of Barrels	% of Total
January	10,967.0	7.5%
February	9,871.1	6.8
March	11,816.2	8.1
April	11,741.2	8.0
May	13,758.1	9.4
June	13,859.4	9.5
July	14,734.3	10.2
August	13,885.9	9.6
September	12,090.4	8.3
October	11,586.1	8.0
November	10,419.2	7.2
December	10,735.0	7.4
Totals	145,363.9	100.0%

SOURCE: *Brewer's Almanac: 1975.*

North Central region with its icy winters. In any case, seasonal analysis provides a basis for the efficient allocation of advertising funds.

Company Sales

If industry sales set the stage for situational analysis, company sales reveal how a particular participant is performing on that stage. Company sales records provide a wealth of information about company performance which, too often, is neglected. E. Jerome McCarthy quotes a top executive of a large consumer products company, which made no attempt to analyze its sales, as saying: "Why should we? We're making money."[3] McCarthy goes on to say:

> But today's profit is no guarantee that you'll make money tomorrow. In fact, ignoring market analysis can lead not only to poor sales forecasting but to poor decisions in general. One manufacturer did extensive national advertising on the premise that the firm was, in fact, selling all over the country. A simple sales analysis, however, revealed that the vast majority of his customers were within a 250-mile radius of the factory. In other words, the firm did not know who and where its customers were and was wasting most of the money it spent in advertising.[4]

The sad fact is that many marketers are incompetent. There are enough incompetents in the field that the road to success is not an impossible one. However, we cannot assume that our competitors are incompetent, even though they may well be. This is, in fact, one of the most dangerous assumptions that can be made because it lulls the marketer into complacency. And there are too many P&G's (whose hallmark is "thoroughness") to pass up any possibility of gaining an understanding of our own market and the performance of our competitors.

There is no best way to analyze sales data. The type of analysis required depends upon the company and the industry involved. Good sales analysis is an innovative and imaginative task; the ultimate goal is to define both problems and opportunities. Sales information can be broken down and compared with past company or industry data in a number of ways. Typical analyses are by geographic region, by product and package size, by size and type of customer, by method of sales, by size of order, by seasonal pattern, by financial arrangement, and so forth.

The Whitman Company, maker of fancy boxed chocolates, analyzed its retail customers in terms of order size. Using data from this analysis, it classified customers in terms of the size of their purchases and developed schedules for calling on customers of different sizes. Whitman stopped calling on thousands of small customers entirely and handled these orders by a postcard system the company developed. This marketing strategy reduced sales costs substantially, enabled the company to increase its coverage of larger customers, and released funds for other, more profitable marketing activities.

The Ralston Purina Company, in the 1950s, concluded on the basis of a situational analysis that they, with their relatively small sales force, could not compete effectively against the Kellog's, the General Mills, and the Quaker's. As a consequence, they disbanded it and developed a system of food brokers, which resulted in better store coverage, increased sales, and additional revenues that could be used for profits or bolstering advertising and other promotional activities. General Electric, a major force in the vacuum cleaner field since 1926, discontinued their product line in the early 1970s. The decision was not made lightly, nor was it made because vacuum cleaners were a declining market. The market had doubled in the past ten years and showed promise of doubling again in the next ten. The problem was that analysis of trends in the market persuaded G.E. that the future of vacuum clearners lay in door-to-door selling, a form of selling in which G.E. had little expertise, and was not structured to pursue. A spokesman for G.E. stated:

> The vacuum cleaner business requires marketing techniques which are somewhat outside the framework of those used in our other product lines. Specialized merchandising and selling at point of sale are necessary for vacuum cleaners to assist the consumer in making a brand selection of a major purchase.[5]

Although many people may disagree with General Electric's decision, it was a decision made on the basis of the company's awareness of its limitations and of the demands on their sales operation.

The analysis of company sales becomes particularly useful when combined with industry data to develop information on brand share.

Brand Share Analysis

Market share measurement is one of the most widely used analytical tools for assessing market perform-

3. E. Jerome McCarthy, *Basic Marketing: A Managerial Approach,* 4th ed. (Homewood, Illinois: Richard D. Irwin, Inc., 1971), p. 123.

4. McCarthy, *Basic Marketing*, p. 123.

5. Milton Moskowitz, "G.E. Leaves a Vacuum in the Cleaner Field," in *Marketing Is Everybody's Business*, Betsy D. Gelb and Ben M. Enis, eds. 2nd. ed. (Santa Monica, California: Goodyear Publishing Company, Inc., 1977), 46–47.

ance. It is widely used because it is a relatively simple device for evaluating the performance of a particular brand in comparison with the total market and with competition. Used properly, market share analysis provides a more critical measure of brand performance than sales alone. This point is demonstrated in table 4-4. During the five year period represented, brand X has shown substantial growth in units, increasing sales by over 10 percent each year. Yet, since the industry grew at an even greater rate, brand X failed to keep pace with the market, was out-stripped by competitors, and its market share declined from 25 percent to 20 percent.

Misleading Market Share Measures.   Market share is sometimes misleading. Most trade associations consider that one of their more important functions is to prepare industry sales estimates compiled from confidential reports from association members or from government statistics. These industry estimates are then distributed to the associations' members so that they can compute their market shares and assess their individual company's performance. Consider table 4-5, which reflects the performance of the Saunders Company when assessed against industry data.

Saunders' sales show a strong growth pattern throughout the year. Market share increases are reflected in every quarter, share position in the final quarter is up over seven points compared to the first quarter, and the company appears to be in a much stronger market position than at the beginning of the year.

In this case, however, market share is a misleading indicator of company performance. The industry in which Saunders competes sells through distributors to retailers who, in turn, sell to the ultimate consumer. In terms of consumer purchases, Saunders' sales have remained relatively stable, with the result that the company has built an excess inventory at the distributor and retail levels of over 15 thousand cases. This is over a two months supply at the current rate of consumer purchases. Until these excess inventories are depleted, distributors and retailers will reduce their purchases, so that Saunders can reasonably expect depressed sales during the next few months. The mechanism of this process is shown in table 4-6.

It is apparent that market share based on sales to channel intermediaries can severely misrepresent the strength of a company's market position. In instances such as that shown in table 4-6, the discrepancy

Table 4-4.   Sales versus Brand Share

	1974	1975	1976	1977	1978
Total market (1000's cases)	33,680.0	38,395.2	46,538.4	54,664.5	65,650.5
Brand X sales (1000's cases)	8,420.2	9,262.0	10,373.4	11,514.5	13,126.5
Brand X % increase	-	10.0%	12.0%	11.0%	14.0%
Brand X market share	25.0%	24.1%	22.3%	21.1%	20.0%

Table 4-5.   Market Share of the Saunders' Company Based on Industry Statistics for 1978

	Quarter 1	Quarter 2	Quarter 3	Quarter 4	Total
	Sales in 1000's of cases				
Industry sales	80,326.6	82,516.3	78,915.7	81,416.5	323,175.1
Saunders' sales	18,957.1	22,609.5	24,069.3	25,239.1	90,875.0
Saunders' share	23.6%	27.4%	30.5%	31.0%	28.1%

Table 4-6.   Inventory Build-up at Trade Level Resulting from Factory Sales in Excess of Consumer Purchases

	Quarter 1	Quarter 2	Quarter 3	Quarter 4
	Sales in 1000's of cases			
Normal inventory	6,300.0	6,300.0	6,300.0	6,300.0
Saunders' factory sales	18,157.1	22,609.5	24,069.3	25,239.1
Consumer purchases of Saunders' product	18,640.0	18,910.1	19,102.0	18,715.0
Excess inventory	317.1	3,699.4	4,967.3	6,524.1
Accumulated excess inventory	317.1	4,016.5	8,983.8	15,507.9

NOTE: Normal inventory is equal to approximately one month's supply at retail level.

between factory sales and consumer purchases has resulted in an inventory situation that may signal the need for a consumer promotion to reduce inventory levels and restore stability to factory shipments. The problem described in table 4–6 is particularly likely to occur in industries with long channels of distribution; that is, where there are several intermediaries (distributors, wholesalers, jobbers, retailers) in the distribution chain.

The possibility of inventory build-ups necessitates a continuing measure of consumer purchases, if it is feasible. In some industries, such as those that sell primarily through drug and food stores, consumer purchases may be measured through services such as A.C. Nielsen. For most manufacturers of consumer goods, similar information can be purchased from MRCA (The Market Research Corporation of America), which operates a nationwide panel of some seventy-five hundred families who maintain a diary of all their purchases. Every week these diaries are sent to MRCA where they are processed by high speed electronic equipment and put into a form for systematic analysis. Some companies, such as major floor covering firms and appliance manufacturers, maintain a sample of major retailers who report on consumer purchases on a daily basis. Such records of consumer purchases are relatively expensive, and many marketers do not have access to such information. However, in many product fields, there are special services that will provide records of warehouse withdrawals by brand at a relatively low cost. Although these figures are less sensitive for measuring consumer purchases than those of the previous services mentioned, they can be reasonably accurate in those product fields in which retail inventories are known to be kept at a minimum, as is the case in grocery stores. The point is that factory sales figures, when not reinforced by consumer purchases, can be misleading and may result in unwise marketing decisions. There are other instances in which market

share data may be misleading, the two most common of which are described below.

Misleading Dollar Share.   Market share can be computed in terms of either units or dollars. When dollars are used as the basis for computing market share a price increase by an individual manufacturer can distort market performance. The price increase may give the appearance of an increased market share when, in terms of units purchased by consumers, sales are actually decreasing. The phenomenon is demonstrated in table 4–7.

Distortions such as this may become calamitous in industries in which retailers normally evaluate the sales of competitive brands in terms of units or cases rather than in terms of gross income or profit, as frequently happens in the grocery field. When unit or case sales for a particular brand drop below a certain point, that brand becomes a candidate for discontinuation, and distribution may be lost.

Misleading Unit Share.   Not only may dollar share be misleading, but also there are instances in which unit share may also be misleading. Consider the manufacturer of both portable and console television sets whose consoles often sell for several hundreds of dollars more than the portable sets and also carry a higher profit margin. A significant increase in the unit sales of the less expensive models may result in both (1) a unit share increase in terms of the total number of units sold and (2) a decrease in both dollar sales and profits. This error in interpretation can usually be avoided by computing unit share for each model so that a decrease in share of the more expensive models is not masked by an increase in share by less expensive sets. This situation makes it particularly important for the marketing analyst to carefully define the particular markets in which the company's products are competing so that appropriate market share calculations can be made.

Table 4–7.   Distortion of Unit Share Caused by Price Increase

	Sales in 1000's units—dollars Quarter 1	Quarter 2	Quarter 3	Quarter 4
Industry sales ($'s)	150,465.0	151,240.3	152,193.8	152,983.5
Brand X sales ($'s)	33,533.7	33,877.8	35,765.5	36,869.0
Brand X shares ($'s)	22.3%	22.4%	23.5%	24.1%
Industry sales (units)	143,300.0	144,038.3	138,358.0	139,075.9
Brand X sales (units)	31,955.9	32,120.5	27,809.9	25,311.8
Brand X share (units)	22.3%	22.4%	20.1%	18.2%

NOTE: During quarters 1 and 2, all brands were priced at $1.05 per unit. Beginning in quarter 3, Brand X increased its price to $1.30 while competitors' prices remained unchanged.

Table 4-8. The effect of Sales-per-Point-of-Distribution on Brand Share

	Quarter 1	Quarter 2	Quarter 3	Quarter 4
Region I				
Industry sales	15,463.5	15,376.2	15,560.3	15,701.0
Brand sales	2,814.4	2,783.1	2,847.5	2,857.6
Brand share	18.2%	18.1%	18.3%	18.2%
Distribution (all commodity basis)	90	90	90	90
Sales per point of distribution	31.27	30.92	31.64	31.75
Region II				
Industry sales	15,000.3	15,216.4	15,110.6	15,198.2
Brand sales	2,640.0	2,723.7	2,629.2	2,659.7
Brand share	17.6%	17.9%	17.4%	17.5%
Distribution (all commodity basis)	68	68	68	68
Sales per point of distribution	38.82	40.05	38.66	39.11

Misuse of Market Share Data. Market share data, even when accurately reflecting consumer purchases, can be misused. Many manufacturers use market share as their primary measure of performance and react vigorously to market share declines. In some instances, though, the cost of maintaining or increasing market share may be excessive and have a deleterious effect on company profits. In some instances, sole reliance on market share performance may inspire marketing decisions that waste company resources and reduce the company's ability to compete effectively in other, more profitable fields. Alfred Oxenfeldt, in a perceptive and thoughtful article on market share analysis, has noted that

> The use of market-share measurement by top management has become almost universal, possibly because of a general unawareness of its flaws as a managerial tool; on the other hand, its widespread use suggests that it has proved useful to some degree. Market-share changes are at best a signal—generally belated and blurred—that difficulties have arisen or have been overcome, but they cannot be interpreted mechanically: market share *may shrink for reasons wholly unrelated to managerial failure and expand in the absence of managerial excellence.* [6]

The Meaning of Brand Share. Brand share is, at best, a descriptive tool. It enables the marketer to assess the performance of a brand vis-a-vis competition. It is not a diagnostic tool since it provides no information as to *why* market share increases or decreases. This requires further analysis. A declining brand share may be the result of inadequate advertising expenditures; it may signal a weak creative effort; it may be the consequence of an improvement in a

competitor's product or the result of a new competitor in the field; it may result from distribution losses. In some instances, a stable brand share at the national level may hide severe problems in specific regions, or in individual markets. In any instance, brand share analysis is only the starting point. But, it is an important starting point, and usually the best the marketer has available. It should be remembered, however, that a change in brand share only indicates that something has happened in the market place. It becomes the task of the marketer to discover what that something is and to devise strategies and plans that will either correct an unfavorable situation, or take further advantage of a favorable one.

Distribution Analysis

Along with market share analysis, distribution analysis is one of the more valuable techniques in the marketer's analytical kit. Variations in brand share among geographic regions for a mass distributed product are more often a function of variations in distribution than any other single factor. This is so because many marketing variables—the product itself, packaging, advertising copy, pricing, and so forth—are similar in all regions. Distribution, however, along with advertising weight and sales promotion activity, often vary from one region to another. In addition, market share analysis can obscure variations in distribution that may be critical to a brand's future health. Consider table 4-8 which illustrates this point graphically by describing two regions which have similar market shares, but distinctly different distribution problems.

The two regions are similar from the standpoint of industry sales and in terms of brand share. However, the distribution patterns within the two regions are quite different. In region I, distribution is excellent: the product is sold in stores doing over 90 percent of

---

6. Alfred R. Oxenfeldt, "How to Use Market-Share Measurement," *Harvard Business Review,* **37,** no. 1 (January-February, 1959), pp. 59–68. Copyright © 1958 by the President and Fellows of Harvard College. All rights reserved.

the volume. Sales per point of distribution, however, are relatively weak, suggesting increased advertising, in-store promotion, or consumer sales promotion as possible strategies for increasing market share. In region II, by contrast, sales per point of distribution are excellent—about 20–25 percent greater than in region I. On the other hand, all-commodity distribution is relatively poor. This suggests that an increased sales force effort and stocking allowances, rather than increased advertising, are more appropriate strategies. This situation is similar to the frozen pie example given at the beginning of the chapter.

All-Commodity versus Store-Count Distribution.
Distribution is often described in two ways: *store-count* distribution and *all commodity* distribution. Store-count distribution refers to the number of stores in which a brand is distributed; it is computed by dividing the number of stores distributing the brand by the total number of stores, and expressing the results as a percent. For example, there were approximately 225 thousand grocery stores in the United States in 1970. If a brand were distributed in 200 thousand of these stores, it would have a store-count distribution of approximately 89 percent (200 thousand divided by 225 thousand). All-commodity distribution, on the other hand, is based on dollar volume. Thus, a product that had 89 percent all-commodity distribution would be distributed in stores doing 89 percent of all the grocery volume. In this instance, the *number* of stores required for 89 percent all commodity distribution would depend upon the *size* of the stores in which the product had distribution. For example, the average chain store had an annual dollar volume of $1,445 thousand in 1970, while the average, small independent store had a dollar volume of only $40 thousand. Obviously, many fewer chain stores than small independents would be required to reach a given level of all commodity distribution.

Figure 4–2 derived from A.C. Nielsen, demonstrates this point graphically. You can see from this figure that it requires 25,143 small, independent food stores (sales under $100 thousand) to generate one point of all commodity distribution, whereas it requires only 844 large independents, and only 362 chain stores. Similarly, in drug stores, it requires 2,298 small independents to provide one point of all commodity drug store distribution, but only 233 chain stores.

Manufacturers of mass-distributed consumer products generally concentrate on the larger volume outlets because they can obtain a given level of all commodity exposure at substantially less sales cost than by calling on the smaller outlets. This was the strategy

of Purex, discussed at the beginning of the chapter. When distribution analysis revealed that 17 percent of the grocery stores accounted for 72 percent of the grocery volume, Purex concentrated its efforts on this 17 percent.

Unfortunately, information on either all-commodity or store-count distribution is relatively expensive and often hard to come by for the marketer of consumer goods. A.C Nielsen provides this information for food and drug stores for its subscribers, and it can be obtained for other retail outlets through specially designed research studies, although the cost of such studies is particularly high. As a consequence, many smaller companies and companies outside the food and drug fields rely on reports from their sales personnel or on distribution studies made by local media in major urban markets.

Selective Distribution.   Many products, particularly in the fashion, appliance, automotive, and fast-food categories, rely on a strategy of selective distribution. That is, instead of seeking distribution in all or most stores selling their product type, they seek distribution in a limited number of independent outlets, in company owned stores, or in franchised stores. The purpose of this strategy is to give the manufacturer greater control over conditions of retail sales. Such a strategy is appropriate when retail sales personnel have a disproportionate role in influencing consumer decisions, such as in furniture, carpeting, or appliance stores, or when a self-sufficient service (fast foods, for example) is being offered. Similarly, in the automotive field, where personalized selling, a wide range of models, consumer credit, post purchase service, and high potential for the product line exist, selective distribution is both desirable and affordable.

Distribution analysis in the case of selective distribution usually involves an examination of the brand's representation in key markets, as well as volume and profit contributions of existing outlets. For example, when General Foods acquired Burger Chef, profit analysis of each outlet in the chain resulted in the closing of some three hundred unprofitable outlets. [7]

In addition to profit analysis, markets can be compared in terms of the share of market being obtained, if data on industry sales are available on a market-by-market basis. Comparisons can also be made in terms of sales per thousand households or in terms of dollar share of certain merchandise categories. For example, *Sales Management's Survey of Buying Power*, the bible of the marketing industry, provides estimates of

---

7. Carol White and Merle Kingman, "Hamburgers? McDonald's Takes It Seriously," *Advertising Age* (May 22, 1972), pp. 3 ff.

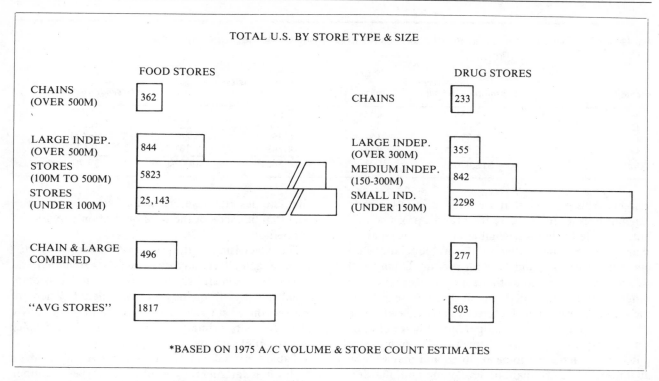

TOTAL U.S. BY STORE TYPE & SIZE

FOOD STORES   DRUG STORES

CHAINS
(OVER 500M)   362   CHAINS   233

LARGE INDEP.
(OVER 500M)   844   LARGE INDEP.
STORES   (OVER 300M)   355
(100M TO 500M)   5823   MEDIUM INDEP.
STORES   (150-300M)   842
(UNDER 100M)   25,143   SMALL IND.
                                        (UNDER 150M)   2298

CHAIN & LARGE
COMBINED   496   277

"AVG STORES"   1817   503

*BASED ON 1975 A/C VOLUME & STORE COUNT ESTIMATES

SOURCE: James O. Peckham, Sr., *The Wheel of Marketing* — (Chicago: A. C. Nielsen Company, 1973), chart 8.

Figure 4–2. The Average Number of Stores Necessary to Obtain One Point of All Commodity Distribution

retail sales by metropolitan county areas for total food stores, supermarkets, eating and drinking places, department stores, apparel stores, furniture and household appliance retailers, automotive outlets, gas stations, lumber and hardware stores, and drug stores. It provides similar information on a county by county basis for the entire U.S. for a somewhat more restricted list of outlet types. Similar information can be obtained from the Census of Business or from industry trade associations, which compile a wide variety of statistics for the use of association members.

In short, distribution analysis, whether for mass or selectively distributed products, is an essential part of the situational analysis. Since a wealth of marketing data is available from company records, government statistics, *Sales Management's Survey of Buying Power*, trade magazines, and industry association, the kinds of analyses that can be made are limited only by the imagination and competence of the analyst.

Comparative Advertising Expenditures.

The share of market should usually equal share of advertising. While all things are never equal among competitive products, this truism emphasizes the importance of weighing competitive advertising expenditures in the marketing review section of the marketing plan. Table 4-9 reflects a hypothetical comparison of these two variables that could easily occur in a particular industry. On the surface, it would appear that brand C is underspending both in total and on a per case basis and that an increase in advertising might reasonably be expected to result in an increase in market share. Such a conclusion is only tentative, however, and could be revised by an examination of competitive pricing, sales promotion, and distribution. However, if we assume that these factors are relatively equal for leading brands in the market, then brand C (possibly because of product quality, package, positioning, media pattern, and/or the effectiveness of its copy appeals) is a reasonable candidate for increased advertising expenditures, at least in a business-building test. The decision to increase advertising on this brand, however, must be weighed against company objectives and the profit contribution of the brand.

In the case of brand A, the relatively unfavorable relationship of advertising and market share *may* result from the brands high share. Products in a dominant market position often find that increased advertising expenditures become marginally less effective as the brand approaches the limit of those consumers to whom its marketing program is appealing. In this

Table 4–9. Comparison of Share of Advertising and Share of Market for a Hypothetical Consumer Product

Brands	Advertising Expenditure in 1000's	share	Sales 1000's cases	share	Expenditure per case
A	$7,388.0	40%	8,971.2	34%	$0.823
B	3,694.0	20	5,804.8	22	0.636
C	2,770.5	15	6,860.3	26	0.404
D	4,617.5	25	4,749.4	18	0.972
Totals	$18,470.0	100%	26,385.7	100%	$0.70

instance, it is possible that a reduction in advertising expenditures would increase the brand's profit contribution while having a negligible effect on its market share position. The relatively unfavorable relationship between advertising and sales for product D may well signal weakness in some other aspect of its marketing program and should alert the marketer to search for the area or areas in which corrective action needs to be taken. The point is that a comparison of share of market against share of advertising raises a number of possibilities that need to be explored and may well be an important determinant in developing both marketing objectives and strategies.

Obviously, a comparison of these two variables requires a relatively accurate measure of both competitive market share and competitive advertising. As pointed out earlier, reasonably accurate measures of market share are obtainable from national store audits such as those provided by A.C. Nielson, from national consumer panes such as that maintained by MRCA, or from services that compile warehouse withdrawal records. Estimates of competitive advertising expenditures are available from a number of industry sources. The better known ones are LNA-PIB and Simmons for magazines; Media Records for newspapers; BAR Network TV, Target Group Index, and Simmons Selected Markets for network TV; BAR Barcume and Rorabaugh for spot TV; BAR Radio and Radio Expenditure Report for network and spot radio; and LNA Outdoor for outdoor advertising. Most of these services are subscribed to by major advertising agencies, and smaller agencies often have access to them through affiliation arrangements with larger agencies.

Sales Promotion

Like advertising, sales promotion activity is an important ingredient in many marketing programs. Because of the wide variety of forms that sales promotion may take, and because there is no published record of such activities, the extent and effectiveness of competitive sales promotion is difficult to assess. The field is not a complete desert, however, and reasonable estimates can often be made of the sales promotion activities of competitors.

The advertising trade press, particularly *Advertising Age*, as well as magazines such as *Promotion* and *Sales Management*, regularly report major promotional activity, frequently in great detail. Then, of course, the company sales force and competitive advertising are primary sources of both the existence and extent of sales promotion programs.

Table 4–10, taken from *Advertising Age*, provides a basis for estimating the cost of various types of coupon offers, a widespread form of sales promotion that involves over 60 billion coupons annually. Current information of this nature is also available from promotional clearing houses such as A.C. Nielsen. Promotional clearing houses are companies that specialize in handling coupon redemptions, a task that few advertisers are staffed to cope with.

Note that table 4–10 indicates wide variations in the effectiveness of the different forms of coupons, with average redemption rates ranging from slightly over two percent for a six-hundred line newspaper ad to over 16 percent for an individual (solo) direct mail coupon. Realistic estimates of the costs for other forms of sales promotion (contests, displays, sweepstakes, and so forth) can be obtained from companies that specialize in these activities.

Advertising Effectiveness

Advertising effectiveness is a major consideration in the market review, since this factor alone can double or halve the value of media expenditures. Many problems are involved in guaging the effectiveness of advertising. (see chapter 22), but some form of advertising evaluation is essential in comparing one's own marketing effort with that of competitors.

At the simplest level, an analysis of competitive advertising in terms of its content will indicate whether competitive claims are unique or stereotyped. Such comparisons with major competitiors should be made routinely. Table 4–11 shows a possible format

Table 4–10. Cost per Coupon Redeemed Based upon Redemption Rates

Circulation method	Cost per M printing/-delivery	Average redemption	Distribution cost (1)	Total number of redemptions (2)	Redemption costs (3)	Total program costs	Cost per coupon redeemed
DIRECT MAIL							
Co-op	$14	11.7%	$ 350,000	2,925,000	$585,000	$ 935,000	31.9ᶜ
Solo	90	16.2 (e)	2,250.000	4,050,000	810,000	3,060,000	75.5ᶜ
MAGAZINE							
Solo	6	3.5	150,000	875,000	175,000	325,000	37ᶜ
Page plus coupon	12	9.1	300,000	2,275,000	455,000	755,000	33.2ᶜ
NEWSPAPER							
600-line r.o.p.	3.75	2.4	93,750	600,000	120,000	213,750	35.6ᶜ
1,000-line r.o.p.	6.25	2.8 (e)	156,250	700,000	140,000	296,250	42.3ᶜ
Co-op r.o.p.							
Coupon only	1	3	25,000	750,000	150,000	175,000	23.3ᶜ
With copy	2	4.5 (e)	50,000	1,125,000	225,000	275,000	24.4ᶜ
Supplements							
Solo	6	3.1	150,000	775,000	155,000	305,000	39.3ᶜ
Free-standing inserts							
Coupon only	2.25	5.4	56,250	1,350,000	270,00	326,250	24.1ᶜ
With copy	3.50	6.4 (e)	87,500	1,600,000	320,000	407,500	25.4ᶜ

(1) Distribution cost based on circulation of 25,000,000; some programs have more, others less distribution.
(2) No allowance made for misredemption, estimated by some industry sources at 20%.
(3) Average cost based on 14ᶜ face value plus 5c handling charge and 1ᶜ internal handling charge.
SOURCE: Redemption rates based on A. C. Nielsen Co. figures where available or industry sources; distribution costs based on published rates and industry estimates.
(e) Estimated.

SOURCE: *Advertising Age* (Oct. 25, 1976), p. 112.

for such an analysis, using two dry dog food brands as an example. The advertisements themselves, taken from the same issue of *Good Housekeeping*, are shown in figures 4–3 and 4–4.

Table 4–11. Comparison of content and format of two dry dog food advertisements

Product: Gravy Train
Headline: Dog's prefer the taste of new improved Gravy Train 3 to 1
Illustration: Side by side illustrations: (1) dog ignoring Gravy Train, (2) three dogs eating new, improved Gravy Train.
Claims: (1) Palatability, (2) natural beef flavor.
Support: (1) Close-up illustration of texture difference between particles of "old" and "new" Gravy Train, (2) reference to tests in which dogs' preferred "new" to "old" Gravy Train 3 to 1.
Package Illustration: Lower, right-hand corner.

Product: Mealtime
Headline: Mealtime. It's just what your dog's been waiting for.
Illustration: Dog on porch, standing over empty food bowl.
Claims: (1) Palatability, (2) meat protein, (3) available in two different sized pellets.
Support: Dog's love meat; "Tail-waggin" taste
Package Illustration: Two packages, lower center—one for large crunchy bite pellets and one for small crunchy bite pellets.

In addition, more sophisticated measures are desirable and often available. Many companies have their own advertisements tested by their own research departments or the research departments of their advertising agencies. There are also a number of independent copy-testing services that are widely used. When independent testing services are used, the service often provides average performance scores for the product type against which the performance of one's own advertisements can be checked.

Special Research

Alert marketers frequently conduct other forms of research which yield valuable information for the marketing review. This research includes such diverse areas as competitive product tests, package tests, price tests, test markets, tests of contemplated promotions, special surveys to gain further information on target markets, business-building tests, and concept tests. This test information should be summarized in the marketing review section of the marketing plan where applicable.

One major marketer of food and drug products takes the point of view that each year the product manager should learn something she did not know

Figure 4-3. (Reproduced with permission of General Foods Corporation.)

before about her product and/or its market. As a consequence, a portion of each budget is earmarked for learning and invested in some form of testing. The outstanding success of this marketer, which has leading products in a number of product categories, is testimony to the effectiveness of this philosophy.

Meaningful approaches to analysis have by no means been exhausted in this chapter. The analyst often must develop her own approaches that are consistent with the data available and that provide insights into the dynamics of the particular marketing situation. This is one of the challenges of marketing analysis, and those who meet this challenge will make valuable contributions to the development of the marketing plan.

SUMMARY

Market planning begins with an analysis of the marketing situation that prevails at the time the plans are being made. A perceptive analysis of the situation develops information which permits the planner to devise effective strategies. Careless or incomplete analysis sows the seeds that blossom into marketing mistakes.

The comprehensiveness of the situational analysis is limited by the amount and variety of factual data that the analyst has available, and the amount and accuracy of this data depends upon the individual company's ability and willingness to invest in marketing research.

Mealtime.® It's just what your dog's been waiting for.

Dogs love the taste of meat. That's why Mealtime gets its flavor from meat protein.

35% of the protein in Mealtime actually comes from meat. So it has the flavor a dog loves. And the protein he needs. Plus all the nutrients required for healthy growth and maintenance.

Mealtime is also the only dry dog food with a choice of either large or small crunchy bites.

Either way, why not get some Kal Kan® Mealtime for your dog?

Here's a coupon for 25¢ to make it easy.

Don't you think he's waited long enough?

Tail-waggin' taste from meat protein.™

©1975 Kal Kan Foods, Inc.

Save 25¢
on any size package of new Kal Kan® Mealtime®

DEALER: Our representative will redeem this coupon for the face value plus 5¢ for handling charges for each coupon redeemed in accordance with the conditions of this offer. Invoices proving purchase of sufficient stock to cover coupons presented for redemption must be made available upon request to Kal Kan or its agents. The customer must pay any sales tax. This coupon void in states where taxed or restricted by law. Cash value 1/20th of a cent. Restricted to one coupon per family. Kal Kan Foods, Inc. P.O. Box 1836, Clinton, Iowa 52734.

LARGE CRUNCHY BITES   SMALL CRUNCHY BITES

STORE COUPON   STORE COUPON

Figure 4–4. (Kal-Kan Foods)

The situational analysis should proceed from the general to the specific. Beginning with the total market and its trends, the analyst progressively narrows the analysis until it focuses upon the specific factors that relate to the marketing problems and opportunities that exist for the particular brand in question.

Market potential—the demand for a particular product type at a given time and under defined marketing conditions—sets the stage for the situational analysis. It also provides a framework for allocating marketing effort, both in terms of geographic regions and in terms of seasonal variations of demand.

The next step is examination of company or product sales as they relate to market potential. This analysis often provides direction for the more effective allocation of company resources. Brand share analysis (often referred to as market share analysis) enables the marketer to evaluate the competitive positions of her products. Although brand share analysis can be misused, it is one of the most valuable analytical devices the marketer has. It should be noted, however, that brand share analysis only reflects changes in marketing position. Further analysis is required to determine why these changes are taking place.

Distribution analysis is a valuable technique in the situational analysis. In distribution analysis, there is a difference between *store-count* distribution (the percent of all stores of a particular type stocking a brand) and *all-commodity* distribution (a distribution measure based on the total dollar volume of a store type rather than on the number of stores). All-commodity distribution is a more accurate reflection of brand availability than is store-count distribution.

It is important to analyze comparative advertising expenditures; an examination of share of advertising as it relates to share of market is sometimes useful. Sales-promotion activity should also be examined in comparison with competition.

Finally, comparative copy effectiveness is an important situational variable. At the very least, an examination of the content and claims of competitive products should be made. Ideally, research information on the effectiveness of one's own and competitive advertising in influencing consumers should be obtained and evaluated.

The basic purpose of this chapter is to point up a few of the more helpful techniques that are often used in making a situational analysis. The actual analytical techniques used in a particular case will depend upon the nature and amount of information available and on the analytical skills and imagination of the analyst.

QUESTIONS

1. Explain how an analysis of market potential can provide guidance for decisions to invest in advertising and promotion and in the geographic and seasonal allocation of funds.
2. What may be the consequences of a market forecast that is too high? too low?
3. Explain why there is not a *best* way to analyze sales, and identify some of the typical bases for sales analysis that are used.
4. What is the primary advantage of using brand-share analysis, and what can be concluded from such an analysis?
5. Explain how brand-share analysis can be misleading.
6. What is the value of distribution analysis? Explain how it is possible to have the same brand share in different regions with different levels of distribution. What are the marketing implications of this situation?
7. Distinguish between store-count and all-commodity distribution. Which is the most useful measure? Why?
8. Explain how Purex uses sales and distribution analysis to increase the efficiency of its marketing effort.
9. What is the assumption underlying a comparison of share of advertising to share of market? Show, by example, how such an analysis might be used.
10. Under what conditions is selective distribution appropriate? How may the effectiveness of selective distribution be evaluated?

PROBLEM

Irvin Richards, a young and relatively inexperienced product manager for Perfect Muffin Mix is in the office of Marge Ratherford, advertising manager of the company.

"Marge," he says, "I want to talk to you about the allocation of our advertising and sales promotion funds for our muffin mix. As you know, our advertising and promotion allowance for next year is $1.30 a case against anticipated sales of 1,671 thousand cases. Company practice has been to allocate 70 percent of this amount for consumer advertising and 30 percent of it for sales promotion. For the past three years the brand manager on the muffin mix has followed this practice in all regions. I just took over as product manager, and I'm not sure that's the best way to do it.

"I've had the research department break down next years estimated sales in terms of our six regions, and also provide me with information on the total number of retail outlets in each region as well as the number of stores stocking our product. Here is the data." (See table 4–12.) "Now that I have it, I'm not sure what it means."

Table 4–12.   Sales and Distribution for Muffin Mix by Sales Region

Regions	1	2	3	4	5	6
Total market (1000's cases)	897.8	1,605.6	676.0	3,242.6	2,640.6	1,499.9
Company sales (1000's cases)	269.3	240.8	135.2	389.1	369.6	267.0
Retail outlets (1000's)	18.7	33.7	14.0	67.6	55.0	31.3
Stores stocking company's muffin mix (1000's)	15.0	28.4	13.3	60.8	33.0	28.2

Marge looked over the data. "Well, Irv, the first thing you have to do is analyze it. After you have done that, allocate the funds the way you think it should be done. Then come back and we'll talk about it. Why don't you come back at 3:00 tomorrow afternoon, and we'll spend some time together to see if we can figure out what you have here."

As he walks out of Marge's office, Irv is thinking, "Well, there goes another evening shot. If I'd paid more attention in my promotion class, I'd have a better idea about how to make sense out of this data.

Assignment

1. Analyze the data and define the problems.
2. Allocate advertising and promotion funds by region, and justify your allocations.

5

Consumer Behavior

El Al Airlines

"On Dec. 23 the Atlantic Ocean became 20% smaller." With this headline, Doyle Dane Bernbach, a leading advertising agency, introduced the jet-age to trans-oceanic travel. (See figure 5–1.)

In 1956 El Al, Israel's airline, put into service the first prop-jet aircraft to be used in the North Atlantic run. Since the new aircraft did not have to refuel at Goose Bay, Labrador, or Gander, Newfoundland, flying time to Europe was reduced by 2½ hours. The business and pleasure traveler was promised a quicker trip and, by implication, less fatigue and hassle. The boring prospect of killing time in another dreary airport while the plane refueled was eliminated. The El Al advertisement was a direct appeal to consumer convenience and comfort.

The Kid in Upper 4

The advertisement in figure 5–2 was run during the early days of World War II by the New Haven Railroad. It is in direct contrast to the El Al advertisement described above. Instead of offering convenience and comfort, it asked for sacrifice and understanding.

(See copy in figure 5–2.) The advertisement appeared at a time when the United States was engaged in a major war. Rationing was a national policy, and everything was in short supply, including railway travel. Airline transportation, an infant industry, was virtually nonexistent. Commercial travel between cities was almost exclusively train or bus. Troop trains criss-crossed the nation, putting a severe strain on the supply of passenger cars and sleepers available for civilian use. It was a time of inconvenience, hardship, frustration, and complaint. The New Haven ad was pure emotional impact at a time when emotions ran deep.

Big Fat Beeyootiful Hair

The Clairol balsam color advertisement is an appeal to beauty, pride, and self-confidence (figure 5–3). Its tone is puckish; the photography excellent; the model superb. The illustration and headline tell the whole story; the copy is almost incidental. What is shown is more persuasive than what is said. The ad is directed to women and addressed to a subject about which

Figure 5–1. (El Al Israel Airlines)

On
Dec. 23
the
Atlantic
Ocean
became
20%
smaller

The first jet-prop
in transatlantic service,
El Al's new Bristol Britannia,
flies you to
London 2¼ hours faster
than ever before.

EL AL
ISRAEL AIRLINES

See your travel agent or El Al Israel Airlines, 610 5th Ave., N. Y. 20, PL 1-3400. Also Philadelphia, Chicago, Los Angeles, Montreal

Figure 5–2.

Figure 5–3. (Clairol, Inc.)

research has shown women to be deadly serious—their hair.[1]

All marketing communications are concerned with consumer behavior, although the appeals that are used to motivate behavior may be vastly different. El Al appealed to convenience and comfort; the New Haven Railroad used an emotion laden appeal to inconvenience and sacrifice; Clairol balsam color appealed to pride and personal attractiveness. Yet, they are all outstanding examples of advertising communications.

How does one appeal to consumers? What are the differences and commonalities of millions of consumers? What are the variables that influence consumers

to behave as they do? These questions are at the heart of marketing communications. And these questions point up the need to examine the entire area of consumer behavior.

AN OVERVIEW OF CONSUMER BEHAVIOR

It is helpful to think of consumers as problem solvers; the problem is defined as *a perceived difference between an existing state of affairs and a desired state of affairs.* Thus, consumers' needs, wants, and desires often present problems that they try to solve through the purchase of goods and services. The housewife who needs a dessert for a dinner party may purchase a cake to solve this problem. A newly married couple needs a place to live; they may solve the problem by

1. G.H. Smith, *Motivation Research in Advertising and Marketing* (New York: McGraw-Hill Book, Co., 1954), p. 229.

buying a house. Or, a young executive who needs some convenient way to carry documents and to establish himself in his new executive role, buys an attaché case. Many of the problems solved by the purchase of goods arise because the consumer's supply of a particular product he or she uses regularly has been exhausted. Other problems arise because of changing needs, improved financial status, or acquisitions which, in turn, create a need for other acquisitions. For example, the purchase of a house gives rise to the need for furniture, carpeting, appliances, and other household objects. But in every case, consumers are solving what appear to them to be problems.

Obviously, where the purchase of goods or services is concerned, problems can be solved in different ways. Consumers are faced with many choices, each of which is urged upon them by manufacturers insisting that their particular product is the best solution. Clairol, Revlon, Max Factor, Elizabeth Arden, Charles of the Ritz, and Helena Rubenstein are but a few of the alternatives available in the cosmetics and personal care field. Ford, Chevrolet, Plymouth, Pontiac, Oldsmobile, Chrysler, Volkswagen, Datsun, and Subaru hardly begin to enumerate the alternatives available among automobiles. Other product fields offer a similar array of choices.

Each manufacturer, through product design, packaging, pricing, advertising, and other communication variables, is attempting to motivate consumers to choose its particular product. Those that are successful in this endeavor succeed and prosper; those that are unsuccessful do not. It is little wonder that motivation is a buzz-word in marketing and that consumer behavior is a subject of intense interest. In this chapter, we will isolate consumer behavior as a subject of study and briefly examine human motivation and the variables that influence it.

CONSUMER MOTIVATION

Few problems in human behavior are more perplexing than the problem of motivation. We even have difficulty in defining the term, even though we know what we mean when we use the term ourselves. This is true because motives cannot be directly observed; they can only be inferred from observations of behavior. We observe someone eating and infer they are hungry; we observe someone drinking and infer they are thirsty; or we observe someone buying airline insurance and infer they are concerned for their safety and for the financial security of loved ones. Yet, these inferences may not be correct. We eat for a variety of reasons other than hunger—to be sociable, because it is time

to eat, or because we are bored. Other activities are also performed for a variety of reasons.

Generically, *motivation may be defined as a theoretical construct involving (1) an energizing force or tensions system that gives impetus to behavior, and (2) a directional component that gives general direction to a variety of responses serving the same general function for the organism.* Although there are many theories of motivation, most of them agree on the major stipulations of this generic definition. Thus, they agree that a motive cannot be directly observed— that it is an abstract concept intended to explain behavior. They agree that motives have an energizing component that gives impetus to behavior and that this energizing force may vary in intensity. Finally, they agree that motives provide a general direction for a variety of behaviors. For example, a safety motive could be used to explain the purchase of flight insurance, the acquisition of steel, radial tires, the installation of a smoke detector, or the purchase of a burglar alarm.

It is beyond the scope of this text to discuss the intricacies of the concept of motivation, but there are three aspects of motivation that have particular relevance to marketing. These are (1) the insatiability of motivation, (2) rational versus nonrational motives, and (3) conscious versus unconscious motives.

The Insatiability of Motivation

Abraham Maslow, a psychologist, has described human beings as "wanting" animals. According to Maslow, human needs are insatiable because as quickly as one set of needs is satisfied another set of needs arise. Maslow postulates that human beings have a hierarchy of needs, and that needs lower in the hierarchy must be satisfied before needs higher in the hierarchy become salient. This hierarchy, arranged from lower to higher order needs, is summarized below.[2]

Physiological needs. If the organism is to survive, physiological needs must be met. They consist, essentially, of biological needs such as hunger, thirst, waste elimination.

Safety needs. Included among safety needs are security, protection, avoidance of pain, order, and structure in the environment.

---

2. Adaptation of "Hierarchy of needs" (pp. 35–46) in *Motivation and Personality*, 2nd ed. by Abraham Maslow Copyright © 1970 by Abraham Maslow. By permission of Harper and Row, Publishers.

Affiliation needs. The human being needs warm and satisfying relationships with other people, affiliation and affection.

Esteem needs. These are needs for recognition, self-respect, and esteem. There are two kinds of esteem needs: (1) needs for acheivement, for adequacy, for confidence, and for independence; and (2) needs for reputation, respect, attention, and appreciation.

Self-actualization needs. The need for self-fulfill-ment, the need to become relatively independent from environmental demands, and to become what one is capable of becoming are included at this level.

Maslow argues that human beings have the capacity for a meaningful, self-fulfilling existence, but they are prevented from achieving this potential because of the conditions of the environment. At a primitive level, where no needs are being met, the physiological ones dominate human behavior. The other needs remain unrecognized until physiological needs are largely met. Once the physiological needs have been satisfied they no longer exert an influence on behavior, and the next higher order needs, those for safety, emerge. At this level of need satisfaction, the safety needs become dominant and remain so until they are largely fulfilled. In order for needs at a higher level to emerge as motivating factors, those on the lower levels must be largely satisfied. When needs at a particular level are frustrated, or only partially satisfied, they persist as a dominating influence in the individual's motivational patterns. Unfortunately, the circumstances of human existence often prevent the satisfaction of all lower-order needs, so that relatively few people ever become self-actualizers, although most of us engage in some self-actualizing behavior.

A key point in Maslow's theory is that our needs are never satisfied. This tends to answer the question of whether marketing creates needs. According to this theory, it does not. Diverse and emerging needs are a unique human experience. Marketing functions as a means to partially meet consumers' needs. Since material products and services only partially satisfy basic human needs, there is a remarkable persistence to human motivational patterns.

A second implication of Maslow's theory is that, in an affluent society such as the United States, lower order physiological and safety needs are largely met. This means that the higher order needs (those for affiliation, esteem, and self-actualization) should be prepotent. An examination of commercials and magazine advertisements quickly shows the importance of these need levels in the appeals that are used. We seldom buy food *just* because we are hungry. Few

of us are starving. We have many choices in what we eat, and advertisers recognize this fact in their advertising copy.

Rational versus Nonrational Motives

A distinction has sometimes been made between *rational* and *nonrational* motives. In this distinction, rational motives—based on biological functions such as hunger or thirst, or on economic considerations—are considered more basic to human behavior than motives that evolve through socio-psychological relationships. In marketing, Copeland siezed upon this distinction to suggest that

1. Rational motives are those motives aroused by appeals to reason. They include such motives as dependability in use, durability, and economy.
2. Emotional buying motives have their origin in human instincts and emotions and represent impulsive or unreasoned promptings to action. They include emulation, satisfaction of the appetite, pride in personal appearance, cleanliness, pleasure in recreation, and so forth. [3]

Although there is a vast amount of motivation research repudiating the importance of this distinction,[4] it is still referred to in marketing and advertising texts. perhaps part of the problem arises from a mistaken attempt to equate *nonrational* with *emotional* when, in truth, they are quite different things. You may be angry (an emotion) but still behave logically (rationally) in dealing with the anger. You may be hungry (a physiological need that in Copeland's terms is unreasoned) but act logically or rationally in satisfying hunger. Beyond this, the usually logical or rational consideration of economy is not always a logical or rational consideration in human behavior. For example, if I were to suffer a burst appendix on a remote trail in the Grand Canyon, it would be neither rational nor logical to refuse to be flown out by heliocopter simply because the pilot charged me more than what I considered to be a fair price.

The point is that consumers have a variety of needs. Some are physiological, some rooted in emotions, some (like economy) learned, and it is pointless to say that some are more rational than others. In fact,

3. Melvin T. Copeland, *Principles of Marketing* (New York: A.W. Shaw Co., 1924), p. 162.
4. Melvin H. Marx and Tom N. Tombaugh, *Motivation* (San Francisco: Chandler Publishing Co., 1967) p. 13; Robert W. White, "Motivation Reconsidered: The Concept of Competence," *Psychological Review*, **66,** no. 5 (1959): 297–333; Richard de Charms, *Personal Causation* (New York: Academic Press, Inc., 1968), p. 97.

needs and motives are *arational*. That is, they are neither rational nor nonrational; they simply exist. Both emotions and logic play a role in influencing our behavior. Either can be appealed to effectively, depending upon the situation. It is pure sophistry to assume that one type of appeal is better than the other in all situations.

Another reason for rejecting the distinction between rational and nonrational or emotional motives is to be found in the motivational theories of David McClelland.[5] In McClelland's system, emotions are not motives, but they are the energizing basis for motives. They provide the force which causes us to act. For example, success in business may be a manifestation of the achievement motive, but the forces which give impetus to the hard work and long hours necessary for business success are pleasure, pride, and self-satisfaction—all emotions that are associated with success. Under this formulation, emotional appeals may be used to arouse motivated behavior, a technique recognized by most competent advertising copywriters. J. Sterling Getchell, one of the great advertising copywriters, insisted that a good advertisement had an emotional "hooker" that attracted our attention as well as a logical justification for the purchase.

It is the position of this text that the distinction between "rational" and "nonrational" motives is a spurious one and that consumers *always act rationally in terms of their understanding of the situation.* If they understood the situation differently, they would act differently.

Conscious versus Unconscious Motives

In the preceding material, we have talked about motives as though they were something that individuals are clearly aware of or could identify if asked to do so. Indeed, many of our motives are conscious; frequently, they are not. Sometimes we don't know why we behave the way we do, and if asked to define our motives, would have a difficult time doing so.

Why do people ride motorcycles? If asked, they might say because it's fun. Usually, when I have asked students in my classes why they ride a motorcycle, they have said the reason is economy. Yet, in view of the danger involved in riding a motorcycle, as measured by the number of injuries and deaths that result from the practice, these reasons seem somewhat shallow. Or, why do people smoke cigarettes? Most of us know that cigarettes are harmful. Medical research indicates that cigarettes are a major contributing factor in heart disease, lung cancer, emphysema, and

other respiratory ailments. Cigarette packages are required by law to warn consumers that smoking may be dangerous to their health, and cigarette advertising is banned from television. So, why do people smoke cigarettes? If asked, they might say that they enjoy it, it is relaxing, or they like the taste. But, in view of the dangers connected with cigarette smoking, these reasons simply are not convincing. Further, the difficulty that people have in trying to stop smoking strongly suggests that there is some underlying factor that is stronger than the reasons given and strong enough to overcome the known dangers associated with the practice.

There is overwhelming evidence, both in experimental and analytical psychology, that unconscious motivational patterns exist and may exert a profound influence on our behavior. Maslow emphasizes this point in his observations about our basic needs.

> These needs are neither necessarily conscious nor unconscious. On the whole, however, in the average person, they are more often unconscious than conscious. It is not necessary at this point to overhaul the tremendous mass of evidence that indicates the crucial importance of unconscious motivation. It would by now be expected, on *a priori* grounds alone, that unconscious motivations would on the whole be rather more important than the conscious motivations.[6]

Since motivation is so important in marketing communications, it follows that writers of these communications should be concerned with unconscious motivations as well as with conscious ones. In the chapter on marketing research, we will refer to certain research techniques that are used to go beyond the surface reasons that consumers give to explain their actions and uncover some of the underlying motivational dynamics of their behavior.

Motivation and Marketing Communications

A survey of motivational theories and research permits us to draw certain generalizations about motivation that are relevant to marketing communications.[7]

1. Consumer behavior is purposeful, goal-directed activity.
2. Consumer needs are diverse. They include biological, safety, social, and individual motivations.
3. Satisfied needs do not motivate behavior.

5. Bernard Weiner, *Theories of Motivation* (Chicago: Markham Publishing Co., 1972), pp. 173–74.

6. Abraham Maslow, *Motivation and Personality*, p. 101.
7. Adapted from Kenneth E. Runyon, *Consumer Behavior and the Practice of Marketing* (Columbus, Ohio: Charles E. Merrill Publishing Co., 1977) pp. 186 and 190.

4. Consumer needs are insatiable. As needs at one level are satisfied, higher-level needs come into play.
5. Needs and motives vary in intensity, with the basic or central needs generally having a greater influence on behavior than instrumental or peripheral needs. Thus, appeals that trigger central motives tend to be more effective.
6. In a relatively affluent society such as the United States, the higher level needs—needs for affiliation, esteem, and self-actualization—tend to have greater centrality and to be prepotent.
7. The goals that consumers seek are related to both conscious and unconscious needs.
8. Since many needs are unconscious and not clearly understood, they are often expressed in the purchase of products and services that are only partially satisfying. As a consequence, unconscious needs are never wholly satisfied and continue to exert an influence on behavior.
9. Feelings (affect) or emotions are intimately involved in the concept of motivation, and emotional appeals often serve as cues for motivational arousal.
10. Finally, consumers often experience motivational conflicts. Sometimes the marketer can, through product development or the creative use of appeals, help consumers resolve such conflicts. In such cases, the marketing program usually meets with a high degree of success.

The identification of relevant motives and the designing of marketing programs that will effectively tap them is not a simple matter. Marketers need research, analysis, sensitivity, creativity, and patience in large measures. However, the results of a well-conceived and carefully implemented marketing program that taps relevant motivational patterns are well worth the effort, both in terms of personal satisfaction and sales results. This subject will be dealt with further in chapter 11 under a section titled Identifying Advertising Appeals.

VARIABLES INFLUENCING BEHAVIOR

In the preceding section, it has been suggested that motives are both diverse and complex. If the author of marketing communications expects to compete successfully, he cannot afford to underestimate the complexity of consumer motivation, nor be unaware of the variables that shape behavior. While a thorough review of these variables is beyond the scope of this book, the remainder of this chapter will identify some

of the major behavioral variables, and briefly characterize their importance.

One thing that must be kept in mind, however, is that the variables that will be identified are not monotonically related to behavior. That is, they are not independent of one another. Most books on consumer behavior attempt to emphasize this point by the use of graphic models to indicate the relationships that are presumed to exist between these variables. Such models are of value to marketing theorists in organizing their thinking and defining the parameters of their theories, but they are of limited value to the marketing practitioner. This is so because we often don't know how these variables are interrelated, nor which variables will be dominant in a given situation. Nonetheless, a knowledge of these variables can often provide insights into behavior that help us to segment markets, or to devise an advertising appeal that will be successful for an established product.

SOCIAL VARIABLES

It has often been said that human beings are social animals, suggesting that the social millieu within which we live exerts a profound effect on our behavior. The very term *human behavior* implies interaction with other people. Studies of feral children (children abandoned in infancy and adopted by infrahuman species) find that such children are virtually devoid of characteristics that we normally think of as human.

Thorstein Veblen, an economist of the early twentieth century, is generally credited as the pioneer of *social determination* in human behavior. Veblen questioned the assumptions of the Victorian economists that behavior was primarily the result of economic forces; he theorized that much behavior is the consequence of social competition and emulation. He coined the term *conspicuous consumption* to describe the behavior of consumers and argued that we purchase products in order to enhance our social prestige. Veblen's influence turned attention to such things as culture, reference groups, and the family as prime determinants of consumption patterns.

Culture

Every society has a cultural heritage that prescribes certain broad patterns of behavior. These patterns extend to such diverse areas as sexual roles, dress, food habits, recreation, patterns of authority, status symbols, artifacts, attitudes, motivation, the use of space, and the meaning of language. We are accustomed to the practices and configurations of our own culture and, when deprived of them, are often unable to deal effectively with our environment. Alvin Toffler refers to the phenomenon of *culture shock* as the psychological effect of suddenly finding ourselves without our accustomed cultural support.

> Culture shock is the effect that immersion in a strange culture has on the unprepared visitor. . . .Culture shock is what happens when a traveler suddenly finds himself in a place where yes may mean no, where a "fixed price" is negotiable, where to be kept waiting in an outer office is no cause for insult, where laughter may signify anger. It is what happens when the familiar psychological cues that help an individual to function in society are suddenly withdrawn and replaced by new ones that are strange or incomprehensible . . . it causes a breakdown in communication, a misreading of reality, an inability to cope.[8]

There is a dominant United States culture, but our society is also highly pluralistic, being composed of a variety of ethnic and religious groups whose values, languages, and mtoivations often differ from those of the dominant culture. Some of these groups, such as blacks, Spanish-Americans, orientals, Jews, and Indians represent significant markets for many products and require special forms of marketing communications. There is always the danger that, unless care is taken to communicate with them in terms of their own values, they will be offended or even alienated.

The problem becomes even more acute when a United States marketer is marketing products in a different country. Jack Stone quotes executives of a United States owned affiliate in Canada as commenting: "Possibly half of the United States prepared advertisements are usable in Canada, but almost never without some change being made in copy or one of the illustrations.[9] And, Edward Hall, in "The Silent language of Overseas Business," details many of the cultural shoals upon which U.S. advertisers run aground when marketing in foreign countries.[10]

The solution is to utilize marketing research in order to gain an understanding of the values, decision-making processes, buying practices, and motivations of the unfamiliar cultural groups to whom the marketing effort is being addressed, and to use "nationals" to help in communications when a foreign culture is involved.

8. Alvin Toffler, *Future Shock* (New York: Random House, 1970) Copyright © 1970, p. 179.
9. J.R. Stone, "American-Canadian Co-Operation: Key to Successful Advertising," in Marketing: Canada, Litvak and Mallen, eds. (Toronto: McGraw-Hill of Canada, Ltd., 1964), p. 262.
10. Edward T. Hall, "The Silent Langue of Overseas Business, *Harvard Business Review*, **38** (May-June, 1960): 87–96.

Social Class

All societies are stratified or structured in terms of social groups. Such stratification arises because, in order for the society to survive, many different societal functions must be performed. Some of these functions are valued more highly than others and, as a consequence, accorded a higher status. Berelson and Steiner observe that

> every known human society, certainly every know society of any size, is stratified. . . . The hierarchical evaluation of people in different social positions is apparently inherent in human social organization. Stratification arises with the most rudimentary division of labor and appears to be socially necessary in order to get people to fill different positions and perform adequately in them.[11]

In a complex society, there may be a number of status hierarchies based on such factors as sex, age, income, occupation, or political position. Social class is one such system of stratification. As the term is used in the United States, it refers to *aggregates of persons or families differing in values and behavior and forming a random order of status levels.* Social class is a useful concept in marketing because members of different social classes have different values, employ different symbols, and spend their resources in different ways. For example, a college professor and a cross-country truck driver will have similar incomes, but their interests and spending patterns may be vastly different. The emphasis placed on education, savings, insurance, housing, and social consumption will vary by social class. The magazines they read will differ. Thus, the *New Yorker*, a sophisticated publication for upper-social-class groups, differs significantly from *True Confessions*, a magazine directed toward lower social groups. The editorial content, the style of writing, the illustrations, the artwork, and even the humor of these two magazines are so different that they have little interest for social class groups outside those for which the magazines are edited. Table 5–1 shows the tables of contents for an issue of each of these publications. It is apparent that these two magazines are addressed to different people.

Social Groups

Groups are the fundamental units of the social system. They are formed to promote survival, carry out

11. G.A. Steiner, *Human Behavior: An Inventory of Scientific Findings* (New York: Harcourt Brace Jovanovich, Inc., 1964), p. 460.

Table 5–1. Comparison of tables of contents of "New Yorker" and "True Confessions"

New Yorker, May 9, 1977
The Talk of the Town
"I Embrace the New Candor"
"Puttermesser: Her Work History, Her Ancestry, Her Afterlife"
"To the Nightingale" (Poem)
Profiles
"The Shore" (Poem)
The Theatre (Off Broadway)
The Race Track
Department of Amplification (India)
A Reporter at Large (Alaska - Part II)
The Current Cinema
"Parent" (Poem)
Musical Events
Letter from Washington
Books

True Confessions, June, 1977
Unforgettable Book-Length:
Am I Having a Mad Love Affair—Or a Nervous Breakdown
Confessions from Life
I Can't Say No to Anybody—Except My Husband
My daughter cried: "My Stepfather Raped Me"
My husband swore: "I'm Innocent." Who can I believe? That Clarence!
I'm Driving My Man to Drink. I Can't Stop Myself!
They Say I Killed a Baby for a Kiss!
Said my 7-year-old: "I Think You and Daddy Should Get a Divorce!"
People Like us—Story 7: Runaway Kidnapper
I Didn't Raise My Little Girl To Be a Cop
Special Extras
True Confessions People
Is Your Personality Ruining Your Love Life?
Your Baby
I Say!
How to Overcome Fear
True Awareness
You and Your Pet
A Wedding Buffet to Remember
Sybil Leek: Star Guide
Martha Matters
My Moment with God
What Your Hair Says About You
Coming Out Even
Ailing Budget?
The Feminine Side of Things
How to Buy a Really Comfortable Bra
Little Brown Bag

work, achieve goals, provide solace and comfort, entertain, and relax their members. We work in groups, learn in groups, play in groups, and much of our consumption occurs in groups. It is little wonder that groups play an important role in influencing the products we use and the brands we purchase.

Although groups may be defined and analyzed in many ways (in terms of size, structure, purpose, decision processes, cohesion, formal and informal, and so

forth) the type of group that holds the greatest interest for marketers is the *reference group*. A reference group may be defined as *a group with which an individual wants to be associated and whose beliefs, attitudes, values, and behaviors the person will seek to emulate.* Sociologists generally speak of reference *groups*, but we may also speak of a reference *person*. A reference person is an individual who serves as an ideal or model and generally embodies the salient group characteristics that are admired.

The influence of reference groups and reference persons on human behavior is confirmed in literature, in common human experience, and in controlled experiments. The role of social imitation or *modeling* as a source of learned behavior is well documented. It is for these reasons that marketing communications frequently employ reference groups or reference individuals in selling products.

Many advertisers portray their products in use in group settings with which consumers can easily identify. In most soft drink advertising, it is difficult to tell whether the advertiser is selling his product or "lovable people having fun." The same thing can be said for chewing gum advertising, beer advertising, and even bank advertising. There seems to be no limit to the ways in which groups are used to persuade consumers.

Along with the use of groups in advertising communications, there is a widespread use of reference individuals. Sports figures, TV stars, and other celebrities grace both the airways and the newstands. In a recent year, no less than sixty-four network television performers were appearing in commercials, either as spokesmen for, or endorsers of a wide variety of products. Financial rewards to members of the Screen Actors Guild approximated $74 million for appearances in commercials, more than guild members earned from television programs and movies combined.[12] Reference figures are not restricted to television stars and celebrities. The IBM advertisement (figure 5–4) features Richard B. Patton, President of Heinz U.S.A., a reference figure that many less successful businessmen would love to emulate.

Some companies, such as General Mills, create their own reference person. Betty Crocker, created in 1921, has reigned for over fifty years as "a sort of 'First Lady of Food,' the most highly esteemed home service authority in the nation and a real friend to millions of women."[13] Ann Pillsbury of Pillsbury Mills

12. James P. Forkan, "From Soap Sellers to Star and Back Again Proves Lucrative Mix for Actors," *Advertising Age* (September 2, 1974), p. 24.
13. Julian L. Watkins, *The 100 Greatest Advertisements* (New York: Dover Publications, Inc., 1959), p. 205.

Heinz U.S.A. President Richard B. Patton

"At Heinz U.S.A., we increased order entry productivity by 75% and saved $200,000 with distributed processing."

"The IBM 3790 distributed processing system has enabled us to integrate our operations throughout the country," says Richard B. Patton, president of Heinz U.S.A., a division of the H.J. Heinz Company. The system links eight customer service centers and five factories with an IBM System/370 Model 125 at the food processor's Pittsburgh headquarters.

"While we wanted to retain centralized management of data processing, we were aware of a growing need for more computing capability in the field," says Mr. Patton. "By giving our production and distribution locations control over order entry and shipments, we achieved immediate gains in operating efficiency of $200,000.

"Among other things, this made it possible for local customer service personnel to determine the exact status of any order, through any of 37 IBM 3277 visual display terminals. Response to the customer is immediate, while duplication of work has been eliminated."

Unified procedures nationwide

In a distributed processing system using the 3790, the workload is shared between the central computer and smaller units, called controllers, which act as small processors. Each controller serves a cluster of terminals at operating departments or remote locations.

At Heinz U.S.A., standardization of procedures throughout the division is a major contribution of the 3790 distributed processing system.

When an order is entered at a terminal, the operator follows step-by-step routines displayed on the screen, eliminating any need for written instructions. Since all procedures originate at the central computer, they are uniform for all locations, facilitating swift data transmission.

Improved customer service

And because the system provides users with automatic accuracy checks, errors are virtually eliminated when data is entered. "The greatest benefit to Heinz of distributed processing is improved customer service," says Mr. Patton. "Moreover, we're communicating better with each other. We've become more of a team than ever before."

Distributed processing systems are one of a number of ways IBM extends the power of the computer to people who need it. For more information, call your IBM Data Processing Division representative. Or write for "Distributed Processing: The Business Benefits" to IBM Corp., Department 83F-3, 1133 Westchester Avenue, White Plains, N.Y. 10604.

IBM
Data Processing Division

In other words, results.

Figure 5–4. (I.B.M.)

and Ann Page for A&P are other examples of corporate personalities created to communicate with consumers. And, although it is extremely expensive to create a corporate personality, the advantage of doing so is that such a personality will never sabotage the communications program through a public indiscretion.

The point is that reference groups and reference individuals (used properly) spell persuasion, a word dear to the heart of the marketing community.

The Family

The family is a unique form of reference group that, perhaps more than any other, shapes the individual and influences his decision patterns and purchase behavior. The family is unique because (1) the relationship between family members is more intimate, the emotional attachments more intense, and the forces holding the group together stronger than those normally found in other groups; and (2) shared consumption and joint decision making are characteristic of family living. It is this latter characteristic that is particularly important to marketing.

Since much family consumption is shared consumption, several family members may participate in the decision to purchase a particular product category or choose a particular brand. Children may have a major voice in purchases of food or child-related products. In some cases, such as dry cereals or snack items, children are the primary users, although parents exercise veto power. In still other situations, such as buying automobiles, the husband and wife share the decision. In any event, knowledge of family decision patterns is necessary both for the selection of media and in the determination of the copy appeals that will be developed.

The family is also worthy of study because of the *family life cycle* phenomenon.[14] A family passes through several stages in its development. At each stage there are different patterns of object accumulation. The newly married couple without children, for example, has vastly different needs and purchase patterns than the older family with several children. Since statistical data on the age, size, income, and so forth of United States families is available from the U.S. Department of Commerce, this information can be used in identifying target markets and in estimating market size.

---

14. William D. Wells and George Gubar, "Life Cycle Concept in Marketing Research, *Journal of Marketing Research,* **3** (November, 1966): 355–63.

Summary of Social Influences

In summary, there are a variety of social variables that must be acknowledged in developing marketing programs. These variables may often be used as a basis for marketing segmentation or in developing advertising appeals within a market segment. Large numbers of products, such as deodorants, mouthwashes, cosmetics are purely social and, since so much of our consumption takes place in social settings, most other products and brands have social implications. Even toilet tissue, a product we might think of as intensely private, is produced in different colors so that we may impress guests with the decor of the family bathroom.

INTRAPERSONAL VARIABLES

Although human beings are inherently social, social variables are inadequate to account for all consumer behavior. Consumers are also individuals who express their individuality within the social context of society in a variety of ways. For an understanding of the intrapersonal variables that influence behavior, we must turn to the field of psychology.

Major areas of psychology include learning, personality, self-concept, attitudes and perception. Each of these areas contain clues that can guide the marketing practitioner in segmenting markets and devising appeals.

Learning

Learning theory is central to understanding behavior, and to devising effective marketing communications. None of us is born with brand names and product attributes engraved in our central nervous systems. Our knowledge of brands and their attributes is learned, and a major function of marketing communications is to facilitate learning. An examination of leading learning theories identifies certain principles that are useful in helping consumers to learn. Four of these principles—repetition, contiguity, reinforcement, and meaning—are described in the following material.

Repetition. The principle of repetition, the repeated exposure of a product message or brand name, is one of the most widely used learning principles in advertising. It is used both in media scheduling and within the copy of advertisements.

It is a point of conventional wisdom in the advertising industry that thirteen insertions a year in a magazine (one every four weeks) represent an optimal media schedule. H.A. Zielske demonstrated experimentally that thirteen exposures, four weeks apart, generated awareness of the advertising among 48 percent of the sample used by the end of the year. A higher awareness of advertising can be obtained by using the same number of exposures over a briefer period of time, although the duration of the effect is sharply reduced. Thus, one advertisement a week for thirteen weeks resulted in 63 percent awareness; however, the advertisement had been forgotten by the end of the year.[15] Figure 5-5 is a graphic expression of Zielske's findings.

The use of repetition to register a product name within a single advertisement is demonstrated in the No Nonsense advertisement (figure 5-6). The name, "No Nonsense," appears nineteen times within the body of the advertisement. Nineteen times! Count them.

Contiguity. Contiguity is most often seen in marketing communications by associating a product with a pleasant situation through spatial or temporal proximity. Beer is shown being enjoyed in a happy social setting; carefully selected models are used in fashion

Figure 5-6. (No Nonsense Fashions, Inc.)

advertising to associate clothing with slim, attractive, and sophisticated people; and dozens of products are associated with sex by placing a beautiful and often scantily clad woman in the advertising, even though her presence may have little or nothing to do with product use. Plate 5-1 is an interesting use of contiguity that associates the Triumph Spitfire with power, speed, and sportiness.

Reinforcement. Reinforcement or reward is the primary learning principle underlying operant conditioning, a leading learning theory. The basic thesis of operant conditioning is that people will tend to engage in activities that are rewarding and avoid situations or activities that are punishing. Reward is usually emphasized through the use of a particular brand. While economic, social, and personal rewards are all widely used, the simple promise of pleasure is the uncomplicated claim in the Michelob advertisement shown in plate 5-2.

Meaning. The concept of *meaning* is a central pillar in cognitive learning theory. Cognitive theory views the individual as a problem solver who seeks the attainment of personal goals. Applied to marketing,

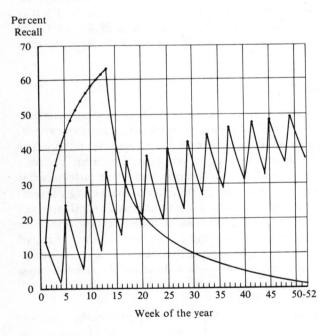

Percent Recall

Week of the year

Figure 5-5. Weekly percentages of housewives who could remember advertisements

15. H.A. Zielske, "The Remembering and Forgetting of Advertising," Reprinted from *Journal of Marketing*, **23** (January, 1959): 239–43. Published by the American Marketing Association.

SAVE AN ENDANGERED SPECIES. BUY ONE.

The convertible, alas, is fast becoming extinct.

Since 1970 alone, 54 foreign and domestic makes have disappeared. Even the Corvette and Eldorado fell victim.

In view of this, we'd like to remind you that you can still invest in the stubborn survivor shown above.

Namely, the racebred Triumph Spitfire 1500.

Being a true open roadster,

the Spitfire lets you feel a wind-in-the-hair freedom almost forgotten in today's boxed-in world.

Being a true sports car, it also offers a high-torque, high-revving 1500cc four cylinder engine. Full instrumentation. Four-speed fully synchronized transmission. Responsive rack-and-pinion steering. Four-wheel independent suspension. And sure-stopping front disc brakes.

Which all helps explain why

the Spitfire is still around while so many convertibles are not.

After all, it's the strongest in any species that survive.

For the name of your nearest Triumph dealer call: 800-447-4700. In Illinois call: 800-322-4400. British Leyland Motors Inc., Leonia, New Jersey 07605.

TRIUMPH

Plate 5-1.

The Triumph ad shows an interesting use of contiguity (British Leyland).

Plate 5-2.

The simple promise of pleasure is the uncomplicated claim in the Michelob ad (Anheuser-Busch, Inc.).

Weekends were made for Michelob.

It's an unexpected pleasure.

MICHELOB BEER

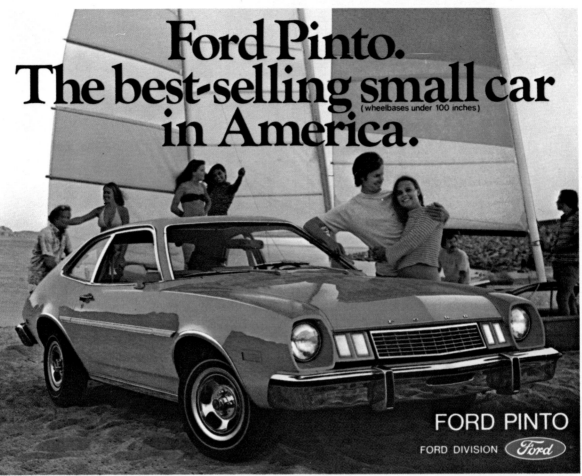

Ford Pinto.
The best-selling small car
in America.

(wheelbases under 100 inches)

FORD PINTO

FORD DIVISION *Ford*

Ford Pinto 3-Door Runabout

Check the facts:

1. Low price plus . . . Pinto starts out with a low price. But that low price includes a powerful cast-iron engine for climbing steep hills, passing quickly, and entering highways confidently. Pinto also has a wide track to help give it a comfortable, stable ride. And every Pinto has a sporty suspension system and rack-and-pinion steering for precise, responsive handling.

2. Excellent mileage.

39 mpg highway	27 mpg city

EPA estimates: With 2.3 liter engine, manual transmission, 2.73 axle without air conditioning, power steering and power brakes. Your actual mileage will vary depending on your car's condition, optional equipment, and how and where you drive. California and high altitude ratings lower.

3-Door Runabout
with new all-glass third door
and flip-up removable roof options.

3. Scheduled maintenance
reduced **$353.**

• Over the past four years, more than 75% of the scheduled maintenance requirements on Pinto's 4-cylinder engine have been reduced or eliminated. That's an estimated reduction in costs of $353.

• So today, the base Pinto's average scheduled service is estimated at only $186 for the first 50,000 miles.

Based on Ford's Service Labor Time Standards Manual, a $13.50 labor rate, and suggested retail parts prices in effect 8/31/76.

4. High resale value.

Pinto consistently has high resale value. Compare Pinto's resale prices to Vega's, for example:

Used Car Retail Prices, January 1977

MODEL YEAR	VEGA	PINTO	Pinto Advantage
1973	$1,264	$1,489	$225
1974	$1,572	$1,861	$289
1975	$1,958	$2,306	$348

Source: National Average N A D A Used Car Guide

It's easy to see why most small cars have a tough time beating Pinto's built-in and lasting value.

And more...

• **Durable and reliable 2.3 liter cast-iron engine.**
• **Roomy, comfortable interior.**
• **Exciting options.**
• **Rugged unit-body construction.**
• **The best rust and corrosion protection system in Pinto's history.**
• **More than 5,500 Ford Dealers.**

FORD When America needs a better idea, Ford puts it on wheels.

Plate 5-3. The Ford Pinto ad is an informational advertisement (Ford Motor Co.).

Marlboro Lights

The spirit of Marlboro in a low tar cigarette.

**Lighter in taste. Lower in tar.
And still offers up the same quality
that has made Marlboro famous.**

13 mg. "tar," 0.8 mg. nicotine av. per cigarette, FTC Report Dec. '76

Plate 5-4. Color is used effectively in this ad for Marlboro Lights (Pall Mall, Inc.).

Vandermint isn't good because it's imported.
It's imported because it's good.

The minted chocolate liqueur from Holland.

Plate 5-5. This ad for Vandermint uses soft focus for the background elements to enhance perception of the central figures (Park Avenue Imports).

cognitive theory emphasizes subjective feelings and perceptions and provides product information that will enable consumers to relate the marketer's product to themselves in a meaningful way. John Deere successfully introduced their lawn and garden tractor by marketing it, not as an oversized lawnmower, but as a "Weekend Freedom Machine," a unique piece of equipment that would enable the purchaser to complete lawn and garden chores quickly, so that the weekend could be enjoyed with family and friends. New Purina Dog Chow was introduced as the dry dog food that "Makes dogs eager eaters," thereby allaying consumers' subjective fears that their pets would refuse to eat the dry dog food they purchased. And the IBM ad mentioned earlier shows managers how they can improve customer service, increase productivity, and save money with IBM equipment.

There are many other direct applications of learning theory to marketing communications. M.S. Hatwick devotes three chapters of his book *How to Use Psychology for Better Advertising* to this topic, [16] and S.H. Britt summarizes twenty applications of learning theory to advertising communications in an article that first appeared in *Printer's Ink*. [17]

Personality

All of us are familiar with the term *personality*. We use it frequently in describing other people; many of us have taken personality tests; and to some of us, personality is synonymous with psychology. Despite our familiarity with the term, few of us normally think of personality as an important marketing variable. Yet, it is a subject of keen interest among marketers. Not all attempts to segment markets on the basis of personality differences have been successful, but there are many instances in which personality differences have been successfully exploited in the development of products and in the devising of appeals.

A classic case of market segmentation that seems to have its roots in personality differences exists in the market for mouthwashes and gargles. Listerine is a straw-colored, astringent, unpleasant tasting mouthwash that is described in its advertising as the "taste you hate two times a day." Scope, by contrast, is deep green in color and pleasant tasting. Both products have the same function, with the only apparent differences being in taste and color. The Listerine user finds it hard to believe that a pleasant tasting mouthwash can be effective. The Scope user cannot understand

why people would subject themselves to the taste of Listerine when better tasting alternatives are available. The differences in preferences seem to lie in the personalities of the users. Similar differences appear to apply to the proprietary medicine field where there are those who behave as though medicines must be ill-tasting and harsh to be effective, while others prefer a gentler approach to medication.

Detergents, cosmetics, cigarettes, beer, alcoholic beverages, automobiles, clothing, and many other products often play on basic differences in the personalities of consumers in achieving acceptance, and a number of advertising agencies use psychologists and psychoanalysts as consultants to help them develop advertising appeals. Earnest Dichter and his Institute for Research on Motivation gained both fame and fortune by identifying unconscious motives which are, by definition, hidden facets of the personality.

Personality has been defined by Allport as "the dynamic organization within the individual of those psychophysical systems that determine his characteristic behavior and thought." [18] Note that there are two aspects to this definition. On the one hand, there is an *internal structure,* referred to as "the dynamic organization within the individual of . . . psychophysical systems." On the other hand, the definition refers to certain behavioral manifestations as "characteristic behavior and thought." These behavioral manifestations are often referred to as *traits.*

The existence of both an internal *structure* and behavioral *traits* make it possible to study personality from either point of view. There are many theories of personality, most of which consider human beings as purposive organisms. Theories differ on a variety of dimensions, such as the weight they give to unconscious factors, reinforcement, structure, heredity, environmental factors, and social influence. One major dichotomy, however, is whether personality is considered primarily in terms of structure or primarily in terms of traits.

Structural Theory. Structural theories emphasize the internal structure of the person as the determinants of behavior. Freud's psychoanalytic theory and its many variants are among the better known theories of this nature. Since structural theories tend to focus on the differences between people rather than on the common traits among them, often emphasize unconscious motivation, and do not lend themselves to quantitative analysis, they have not been subjected to a great deal of empirical research by marketers.

This does not mean that psychoanalytic theory is not used in marketing communications nor that

16. Melvin S. Hatwick, *How to Use Psychology for Better Advertising* (New York: Prentice-Hall, Inc., 1950), chapters 14, 15, and 16.

17. S.H. Britt, "How Advertising Can Use Psychology's Rules of Learning," *Printer's Ink* (September 23, 1955), pp. 77 ff.

18. G.W. Allport, *Pattern and Growth in Personality* (New York: Holt, Rinehart and Winston, Inc., 1967), p. 28.

psychoanalytic themes are not employed in advertising and promotion. Motivation research, which reached its peak in the 1950s and has since become accepted as an established field of marketing research, owes its popularity to the Freudian concept of unconscious motivation. The purpose of motivation research is to get below the surface of conscious rationalizations and to explore the *real* reasons for product preferences and use.

In advertising, the widespread use of sex as a vehicle of interest for a broad spectrum of consumer products is a direct reflection of the Freudian stress on sexuality as a repressed dynamic underlying much of our behavior. Applications of Freudian theory are not restricted to subtle and not so subtle implications of sex, however. Fantasy and wish fulfillment themes are also congenial to Freudian theory. Airlines have offered appealing visions of escape from reality through vacations to exotic places; Schaeffer Beer devotes the better part of one of its commercials to hang-glider flying, capitalizing on the unconscious symbolism of *flying* as a universal escape fantasy; and Honda has used an "escape from convention" theme to sell its motorcycles. In fact, because of the universal nature of psychoanalytic symbolism, it is difficult to find an advertisement or commercial that does not contain some psychoanalytic appeals.

The problem with psychoanalytic theories, as well as other structural theories, is not their lack of use. The problem is that they do not lend themselves to tidy formulations; it is often difficult to make the translation from the theoretical concepts to effective communications.

Trait Theory. Trait theories differ from structural theories in that they stress the response aspect of personality. A trait is a predisposition to respond in a particular way, and personality is described in terms of a particular constellation of traits. There are a number of scales that have been devised to measure the extent to which various traits are present. For example, the *Thurstone Temperament Schedule* is designed to measure the extent to which individuals differ on seven different response characteristics labeled: active, vigorous, impulsive, dominant, stable, sociable, and reflective. Other instruments exist which measure different combinations of traits. Since these scales provide quantitative scores, they lend themselves to marketing analysis and experimentation.

In addition to such standardized scales for measuring traits, tailor-made scales can be devised which measure constellations of traits related to a particular area of activity. For example, I.S. White reports a study in which response traits such as flexible, objective, emancipated, and evaluative were used in relation to household cleaning tasks.[19] The findings were used to segment the detergent market when analysis revealed that housewives could be divided into "modern" and "traditional" groups, which exhibited markedly different preferences for detergent package designs and for advertising appeals. For the most part, tailor-made scales such as that used in the detergent study have been much more productive in adapting personality theory to marketing problems than have standardized scales of traits.[20]

Psychographics. Psychographics, sometimes referred to as *life-style* research, or as *activity and interest* research, is a variation of trait theory that has gained support in the past decade or so. More of a technique than a theory, it attempts to describe the characteristic mode of living of a society, or of a segment of it.[21] The basic procedure for gathering psychographic information is to use an *Activities, Interests, and Opinion* (AIO) questionnaire. The AIO questionnaire is a series of easily administered statements to which subjects respond with an agree-or-disagree answer. Sample statements might be:

I am a swinger.
I am modern.
I like to fish.
I enjoy sports.
I like contemporary music.

The number of statements and the variety of dimensions explored is limited only by the respondent's patience and the researcher's imagination. The same questionnaire may be used to gather demographic information and media preferences. The data are factor analyzed to identify various constellations of answers, and the results are used to segment markets and develop appeals. The assumption underlying the psychographic approach is that people who give similar answers to the questions will be similar in their interests and responsive to similar products and advertising.

Summary of Personality. There is little question that personality plays a significant role in the purchase decisions that consumers make. Some product fields

19. I.S. White, "The Perception of Value in Products," in *On Knowing the Consumer*, J.W. Newman, ed. (New York: John Wiley and Sons, Inc. 1966), pp. 173–86.
20. Runyon, *Consumer Behavior*, pp. 234–40.
21. W.D. Wells, "Psychographics: A Critical Review, *Journal of Marketing Research*, **12** (May, 1975), pp. 196–213.

undoubtedly are more amenable to personality analysis than others, and the particular way in which personality variables can be used in a specific case must be determined by systematic analysis and testing.

Self-Concept

The self-concept or subjective self refers to the way an individual regards himself. Each of us has a self-concept; that is, we have a conscious perception of ourselves as being a certain kind of person, and we reflect the kind of person we perceive ourselves to be by the things we do, the clothes we wear, and the products we buy. Vance Packard, a critic of advertising, makes the following observation in the *Hidden Persuaders:*

> Studies of narcissism indicated that nothing appeals more to people than themselves: so why not help people buy a projection of themselves? That way the images would preselect their audiences, select out of a consuming public people with personalities having an affinity for the image. By building traits known to be widely dispersed among the consuming public, the image builders reasoned that they could spark love affairs by the millions.
>
> The sale of self-images soon was expediting the movement of hundreds of millions of dollars worth of merchandise to consumers, particularly gasoline, cigarettes, and automobiles. And the image builders were offering some surprising evidence of the extent to which American consumers were becoming self-image buyers.[22]

Vance Packard intended his observations as a criticism of advertising and pretended shock at the practice of image building for consumer products, but responsible marketeres have long considered the self-image a legitimate basis for marketing segmentation. Britt, for example, has observed that

> a consumer may buy a product because, among other factors, he feels the product enhances his own self-image. Similarly, a consumer may decide not to buy a product or not to shop at a particular store if he feels that these actions are not consistent with his own perceptions of himself.[23]

All of us are aware that we do use possessions as a way of making statements about ourselves. The teenager who smokes or drinks alcoholic beverages is using these products to say, "I am an adult." The adult who

drives a Cadillac or Lincoln Continental is telling others that he is important. And the host and hostess who serve imported wine are exhibiting their discriminating taste to their guests. In the automotive field, Leon Piconke, Chrysler's director of marketing services in the mid-1970s, made the following observation:

> The automobile is a piece of communication, and the automobile purchase is a very complex expression. When we do attitude studies we ask the question, "Is that your kind of car?" The subject is deciding whether that car fits his image, the kind of personality he wants to project.[24]

This is not to say that all consumption is determined by the self-images consumers hold. However, it should be recognized that self-concepts do exist and may influence many consumer purchases, particularly for those products that have high visibility and are primarily consumed in social settings.

Few, if any, brands can be all things to all people. Those that try to be run the risk of becoming nothing to everyone. As a consequence, the marketer should try to build a strong, unambiguous brand image for the product with which a significant number of consumers can identify. By doing so, marketers can differentiate their products from competition and gain recognition and sales in the market place.

Attitudes

Thus far, we have dealt with a variety of variables that exert an influence on consumer behavior. We have identified social factors such as culture, social class, groups, and the family. We have recognized intrapersonal influences such as learning, personality, and the self-concept. Although all of these variables may exert an influence on behavior, the psychological mechanism through which they operate has not been specified. One useful approach is to consider the concept of attitudes as this mechanism. From this point of view, the net effect of social and intrapersonal variables is to create a structure of attitudes that ultimately govern behavior.

Attitudes may be defined as "predispositions to respond in a particular way toward a specified class of objects" In the context of marketing, the goal of marketing communications is to affect attitudes, thereby creating a predisposition to purchase particu-

22. From the book *The Hidden Persuaders* by Vance Packard. Copyright © 1965 by Vance Packard. Reprinted by permission of the David McKay Company, Inc.
23. S.H. Britt, *Consumer Behavior and the Behavior Sciences: Theories and Applications* (New York: John Wiley and Sons, Inc., 1966), p. 186.
24. Peter Vanderwicken, "What's Really Wrong at Chrysler," *Fortune* (May, 1975), p. 179.
25. C.I. Hovland and M.J. Rosenberg, eds., *Attitude Organization and Change* (New Haven, Connecticutt: Yale University Press, 1960), p.l.

lar brands. For this reason, the measurement of attitudes toward products is a multimillion dollar business, and changing attitudes is a major preoccupation of the advertising industry.

It is generally recognized that attitudes have three components—affective (feeling), cognitive (knowledge), and behavior. That is, our attitudes consist of feelings toward an object, knowledge about the object, and a predisposition to behave in certain ways toward the object. Further, these three components tend to be consistent with one another. For example, if we have a favorable feeling toward a brand, we generally believe favorable things about it and are inclined to buy it.

Since these three components of attitude tend to be consistent, it follows that if we can change one of these components the others will tend to shift in the same direction. Thus, if we can change an individual's emotional response toward a brand from negative or neutral to positive, he may start perceiving the brand differently and be persuaded to purchase it. Or, if we can provide favorable information about a product, thereby changing his knowledge of it, there will be a tendency for his feelings to change, and the probability of purchase will be increased. Finally, if we can change a person's behavior, that is, induce him to use a product he has not previously used, then both the feelings toward the product and the knowledge of it will also tend to change.

These three strategies (changing feelings through emotional appeals; changing knowledge by providing information; and changing behavior by inducing trial) are the primary strategies used by marketers to change attitudes. Generally, the more components of an attitude we can affect, the greater will be the probability of attitude change. For this reason, most advertisers use a combination of strategies.

A diamond is forever, Ford Pinto, and Hamburger Helper are examples of these three approaches. (See plate 5–3 in insert following p. 90; also figures 5–7 and 5–8.) The diamond ad is emotional. It doesn't talk about the product; it talks about love and intimacy. Its purpose is to associate diamonds with our deepest emotional expressions. On the other hand, the Ford Pinto ad is an informational advertisement. It has some emotional appeal, but that is not its central theme. Instead, it provides information on price, construction, mileage, maintenance, resale value, and so forth. Finally, the Hamburger Helper advertisement is a coupon ad. Certainly, it shows the product in appetite appealing photographs (emotional appeal) and provides a recipe for use (information), but the *focus* of the advertisement is on a trial-inducing coupon to get consumers to change their behavior and buy Hamburger Helper if they have not already .

In any case, the purpose of all three ads is to change attitudes. It is only the strategy that differs. For the student interested in marketing communications, a knowledge of attitudes and attitude change is an essential ingredient to success.

Perception

Each of us perceives the world in somewhat different ways. And each of us behaves in terms of what we perceive. Perception starts with the stimulation of the sense receptors (eyes, ears, nose, skin, tongue, and kinesthetic receptors) by a pattern of energy. Each receptor transforms this energy into a neural impulse that is received by the central nervous system. There it is modified and elaborated to create a meaningful experience. It is important to note that incoming stimuli are not passively received by the organism; rather they are organized, interpreted, and given meaning. Thus, perception can be defined as *a process through which incoming stimuli are given meaning,* or *perception is the process through which we make sense of the world.* Within the framework of this definition, there are certain aspects of perception that will be noted in the following material.

Perception Is Subjective. Since perception takes place wholly in the mind of the perceiver, it is a subjective experience. No two people see things in precisely the same way. Two prospective purchasers viewing a new refrigerator may focus on different aspects of the appliance. For one person, design or special features may dominate perception to the detriment of other aspects of the purchase. For another person, price or construction details may be predominant. One ends up buying and the other does not, even though they may have comparable incomes, similar financial obligations, and equivalent requirements for refrigeration.

As consumers, we sometimes block out or ignore things we don't want to recognize, emphasizing only the positive aspects of the product. In other instances, we may focus on product defects, ignoring positive attributes. We tend to see what we want to see, and hear what we want to hear. This is one of the reasons that it is often said we never see things as they really are; instead, we see things as we want them to be, as we expect them to be, or as we need them to be.

Perception Is Selective. During the course of an average day, we are surrounded by thousands of stimuli. At any moment, it is not possible to attend to all

Figure 5-7. (De Beers Consolidated Mines, Inc.)

A diamond isn't the only thing about us that sparkles.

I know love is supposed to be something personal, just between the two of us. But we can't help sharing it with the world. Sometimes we even try to hide our feelings. Especially in a crowd of people. But as soon as our eyes meet, there's a certain way we smile at each other. And anyone can look at us and tell we're head over heels in love. So we really didn't need a diamond to say what's in our future. We wanted one because it says what's in our hearts.

A diamond is forever.

There's a main ingredient for all these oven casseroles.

Sure, Hamburger Helper® from Betty Crocker® added to a pound of hamburger makes delicious skillet dishes. But Hamburger Helper and that same pound of hamburger can make fantastic oven casseroles, too. Easy recipes are on every box. And your kitchen's already full of the handy ingredients the recipes call for.

Hamburger Helper from Betty Crocker. Think of it as a main ingredient.

Lasagne Deep Dish (above right)

1 pound ground beef	⅓ cup grated
1 package Hamburger	Parmesan cheese
Helper® mix for	1 egg, beaten
lasagne	2 tablespoons parsley flakes
2 cups water	¼ teaspoon salt
1½ cups creamed	Dash of pepper
cottage cheese	¼ cup grated
(small curd)	Parmesan cheese

Cook and stir ground beef in 10-inch skillet until light brown; drain. Stir in Sauce Mix and water. Heat to boiling, stirring constantly; reduce heat. Simmer uncovered until slightly thickened. about 10 minutes.

Heat oven to 375.° Cook Macaroni in 6 cups boiling salted water until tender, 10 to 12 minutes; drain

thoroughly. Mix macaroni, cottage cheese, ⅓ cup Parmesan cheese, the egg, parsley, salt and pepper; spread in ungreased oblong baking dish, 10x6x1¾ inches, or square pan, 9x9x2 inches. Spoon beef mixture over macaroni mixture; sprinkle with ¼ cup Parmesan cheese. Bake uncovered until hot and bubbly, 30 to 35 minutes. Let stand about 15 minutes before cutting. 6 servings.

® Reg. T.M. of General Mills, Inc.

It's Hamburger Helper.

Hamburger Helper
EGG NOODLES AND SAUCE MIX
ADD TO 1 LB. HAMBURGER
NOW! Makes exciting new oven casseroles too!

Figure 5–8. (Reprinted with permission of General Mills, Inc.)

of the stimuli that bombard our senses. Thus, we cannot read, carry on a conversation, and watch television at the same time (although we often try). When we try, we find our attention shifting back and forth from one source of stimuli to the other with the result that our comprehension of each of these activities is disjointed and fragmentary. For this reason, we tend to select out of our environment those stimuli that are most important to us, ignoring the rest.

This point is particularly important for marketing. The United States consumer is bombarded with advertising messages from a variety of sources. The marketer's advertising message for a particular product is competing with many others, only a few of which will be consciously seen. Yet, we do see the advertising for those products in which we have a current interest. Were it not for selective perception, it is doubtful that any advertising would be seen by enough people to justify its cost. Thus, all marketing communications are indebted to the phenomenon of selective perception.

Perception and Marketing Communications. The role of marketing communications is to help consumers perceive particular products in desired ways. We do this by surrounding a product or brand with *cues* that help identify it and give it a desired character. Words, colors, shapes, sounds, odors, weight, and other symbols are some of the cues we use. For example, color is used effectively in the advertisement for Marlboro Lights (plate 5–4, insert following p. 90). The idea of masculinity is retained through the action shot of a cowboy, but the advertisement lacks the heavy, dark colors normally associated with regular Marlboro advertising. Instead, the concept of a light cigarette is reinforced through the use of light colors.

Surrogate Indicators. Often, consumers are unable to assess the quality of a brand offered for sale. This frequently occurs with fabrics, furniture, carpeting, electronic equipment, or other products where consumers may not have the technical knowledge to distinguish a superior brand from an inferior one. In such cases, consumers often use *surrogate* or *substitute* indicators. Price, for example, is often used as a surrogate indicator for quality under the assumption that higher priced products tend to be superior. This assumption, of course, may or may not be true. Suds are often used as a surrogate indicator for detergents, which is why detergents frequently contain sudsing agents, even though sudsing has nothing to do with cleaning effectiveness. Blue Cheer is perceived as particularly effective in getting clothes white because *bluing* is associated in consumers' minds with whiteness.

And, the use of the words, "blue magic," in Blue Cheer's advertising supports the consumers' illusion.

There are many other surrogate indicators that consumers use. Bright, garish colors imply cheapness; dark, rich colors imply quality. One of the more important surrogate indicators used by consumers is the brand name. The brand that establishes a reputation for excellence—such as Toro for lawnmowers, Budweiser for beer, Sara Lee for frozen desserts, Titleist for golf balls, or General Electric for major appliances—has a lot going for it in the market place.

A Concluding Note on Perception. There are many ways in which consumers may be helped to perceive products in desired ways so that the image of the brand may be enhanced. There are a number of techniques for emphasizing a product or a product name in advertising. Examples may be found in the ways in which elements are positioned in an illustration, the use of photographic effects, or using musical punctuation in broadcast media. The advertisement for Vandermint (plate 5–5, insert following p. 90) uses soft focus for the background elements to enhance perception of the central figures in the advertisement. It also uses the silhouette of a windmill to reinforce the liqueur's association with Holland.

CONSUMER BEHAVIOR AND COMMUNICATIONS

No one factor that we have discussed holds the key to effective communications. There is no such key. One product may be primarily subject to group influences. Another may be more closely tied to personality or the self-concept. Learning, attitudes, and perception are also important aspects of consumer behavior. Most generally, consumers are acted upon by a number of variables simultaneously, and it is the job of marketing and advertising people to sort out what is most significant.

Human behavior is complex, and consumer behavior is no simpler. There are no easy answers. Knowledge, analysis, sensitivity, intuition, and plain hard work are all ingredients in the creative process, and there are no shortcuts. One of the most important sources of information about consumers and their behavior is marketing research. That is the subject of the next chapter.

SUMMARY

Consumers are problem solvers who perceive their needs, wants, and desires as problems, which they often try to solve through the purchase of goods and services. Marketers compete with one another in trying to influence consumers to use their particular products in order to satisfy their needs. Thus, consumer motivation—the study of human desires and strivings—is a subject of intense interest to advertisers.

Motivation is an abstract concept used to explain why people behave as they do. Most theories of motivation are based on a concept of inherent human needs that give impetus and direction to human behavior. According to Maslow, a leading motivation theorist, these needs include physiological needs, safety needs, esteem needs, affiliation needs, and self-actualization needs, arranged in a hierarchical order. As needs at one level of the hierarchy are satisfied, needs at the next level emerge. As a consequence, human needs are insatiable. Both logical and emotional appeals can be effective in motivating consumers to purchase products; the effectiveness of these different appeals depends upon the situation in which consumers find themselves. The identification of relevant motives in the development of a marketing program is not a simple matter.

The author of marketing communications who expects to be successful in motivating consumers needs to recognize the complexity of the motivational phenomenon and be aware of the variables that shape behavior and give it direction. Although no one of these variables provides a complete explanation of behavior, a knowledge of them often provides insights into behavior that help us in segmenting markets and in defining effective appeals for established products.

A number of variables relate to marketing practices. These variables include social phenomena such as culture, social class, social groups, and the family. They also include psychological or intrapersonal factors such as learning, personality, self-concept, attitudes, and perception. None of these social and psychological variables hold the key to effective marketing. There is no such key. The importance of a particular variable is dependent upon the product, the function it serves, and the target group of consumers involved. Knowledge, analysis, sensitivity, intuition, and plain hard work are necessary in devising product appeals that will be successful in influencing consumers.

QUESTIONS

1. Summarize Maslow's theory of motivation and explain its implications for marketing.
2. Explain the traditional distinction between rational and nonrational motives, and why this is a spurious distinction from the standpoint of marketing.
3. Explain what is meant by a reference group and a reference person. Give some specific examples of how this concept is used in advertising.
4. Identify and explain the four principles of learning derived from learning theory, giving examples of how each is used in advertising.
5. Distinguish between structural theories and trait theories of personality, and explain why most of the research in the field has been done with trait theories.
6. What is meant by *psychographics*? What is the underlying assumption upon which psychographics are based? How is this approach used in marketing?
7. What is meant by the *self concept*? Why is this concept important in marketing?
8. Define the concept of *attitudes*. Identify the basic components of the concept and give examples of how the concept is used in marketing.
9. Define *perception*. How do marketers use this concept in marketing communications?
10. Explain what is meant by *surrogate indicators*. Give examples of such indicators and explain how they are useful in marketing.

PROBLEM

You are a member of a creative team that has been assigned the job of developing a product concept and brand name for a new line of cosmetics that has been developed by one of the agency's major clients.

Consumer research has identified a number of product attributes, all of which received favorable ratings by consumers. Three attributes in particular appear promising. These are (1) a cosmetic line that is easy to apply; (2) a cosmetic line that offers a wide variety of shades, textures, and effects; and (3) a line that contains applicators that permit self-application with results comparable to that obtained by professional beauticians.

The cosmetic line developed by the client organization has all three of these characteristics. And, that's the problem. There is disagreement among the creative group as to which attribute should be emphasized in the product concept. A number of product ideas and possible names have been kicked around. One group member likes the "easy application" approach and has suggested the name "Smooth 'n' Easy." Another wants to emphasize the applicators themselves and has suggested the name "Perfect Face." You prefer the "variety of effects" route and have coined the name "Like Me."

Develop an argument for your approach and name, supporting it with some of the consumer variables discussed in the chapter and your knowledge of competitive products in the market. Magazines such as *Glamour* and *Cosmopolitan* are a good source for competitive product advertising.

In addition, since there is wide latitude in pricing the line, indicate whether it should be priced at the bottom, in the middle, or at the high end of the moderate price range. Explain why your pricing recommendation is consistent with your product concept.

Marketing Research and
The Marketing Information System

Exxon

In the mid-1970s, Standard Oil Company of New Jersey spent an estimated $100 million to change its name to Exxon. The decision to spend $100 million for a name change was not taken lightly, and the name, Exxon, was not selected casually.[1]

The problem was both simple and complex. Jersey Standard could not use its brand name, Esso, in all fifty states because of legal infringement on the rights of other oil companies that included "Standard Oil" (for which Esso is an abbreviation) in their titles. There are seven Standard Oil companies in the United States all resulting from the antitrust suit in 1911 that split the old Standard Oil trust into thirty-four operating companies. As a consequence, Jersey Standard marketed its products under a variety of names, including Esso, Enco, Humble, and Enjay.

The resulting anomalies were both frustrating and expensive; for example, customers in the border areas were understandably unable to grasp the fact that Esso gas, Enco gas and Humble gas were all the same product, and Jersey Standard could not sponsor network television shows without incurring extra costs running into millions of dollars, for making different versions of the same commercial to be shown in different areas.[2]

This was the reason for the change. In 1967, Jersey Standard launched a massive research project to find a name. The directions were simple: find a name that was free of copyright infringements, that conveyed the impression of a large, international enterprise, and that had no negative connotations in any of the countries in which Jersey Standard currently operated, or in which it was likely to make investments.[3] The research task was formidable. The task started with a computer which turned out 10 thousand potential names of four and five letters. Research ultimately

1. J.C. Tanner, "Name Change Brings Excedrin Headache and Costs Approximately $100 Million," *Wall Street Journal,* (January 9, 1973); 32. An excellent write up of Jersey Standard's search for a name has been prepared by B.D. Gelb and B.M. Enis, *Marketing Is Everybody's Business* (Pacific Palisades, California: Goodyear Publishing Company, 1974), pp. 43–44.

2. J. Brooks, "It Will Grow on You," *New Yorker* (March 10, 1973): 106–12.
3. For a detailed list of constraints in selecting a name, see: B.D. Gelb and B.M. Enis, *Marketing Is Everybody's Business,* pp. 43–44.

reduced this list to one name, Exxon. Tests were conducted in 56 languages and 113 local dialects. Enco (one of the company's own copyrighted names) was rejected because phonetically it is part of a phrase that means "stalled car" in Japanese. Other names were rejected for similar reasons.[4] The clear winner was—Exxon—a multimillion dollar nonsense syllable into which Jersey Standard executives could build the meaning and image they wanted for their company.

Seven-Up

The place: Chicago. The time: 1968. The occasion: the annual sales meeting of the Seven-Up company where, among other activities, the company's advertising agencies presented recommendations for the coming year. J. Walter Thompson, the advertising agency for 7-Up, based its presentation on the results of an extensive marketing research study, commissioned by the client to determine how consumers' regarded 7-Up, and to learn why the product was the step-child of the beverage industry. The findings of the research—perplexing and somewhat discouraging—served, nonetheless, as the inspiration for an advertising theme that increased both product sales and company profits.

The research study found that consumers didn't think of 7-Up as a soft drink and, as a consequence, didn't use it for this purpose. Seven-Up was thought of as a mixer for alcoholic beverages, and was spiked with everything from bourbon to vodka; it was thought of as a settler of upset stomachs; and it was thought of as a harmless and soothing drink for children who had colic. But when it came to soft drinks, consumers thought of Coke; 7-Up wasn't even in the running. J. Walter Thompson *made* 7-Up a soft drink by calling it the *Uncola*, and opposing it to Coke as that "other soft drink." Consumer research and a whimsical creative treatment transformed a mixer and medicine into a soda pop.

Bundt Cake Mixes

The introduction of Bundt Cake mixes catapulted the Pillsbury Company from a 14.3 percent dollar share of the cake mix market in 1972 to a 32.1 percent share a year later, adding over $35 million to the company's revenues. But this was only the beginning. For the first six months of 1974, total company sales were

$555,233,000, up 44 percent over the comparable period in 1973, and earnings per share went up 48 percent.[5]

The idea for Bundt cakes came from the Pillsbury Bake-off, an annual consumer promotion conceived by the Leo Burnette Advertising Company, and sponsored by Pillsbury since 1948. The 1968 winner was the Tunnel of Fudge cake which used a round, tubular, fluted pan trademarked *Bundt* by the Northland Aluminum Products Company. This cake became the focus for the Bundt line when marketing research showed that the product concept and the cake mix developed by Pillsbury's research and development department was a hit among consumers.

In each of the three foregoing examples, marketing research played a key role in shaping a company's future. For Standard Oil of New Jersey, it helped find a new name—Exxon. For the Seven-Up Company, it helped find a new advertising concept—the Uncola. And for the Pillsbury Company, it helped find a new product that revitalized the company—Bundt Cake Mixes.

In these three examples, we find the key characteristic of marketing research—*it helps*. Marketing research is not as dramatic as a brilliant marketing success, nor as visible as a highly effective commercial or advertising campaign. But behind the successful marketing plan, and behind the outstandingly successful product, you will usually find a history of marketing research. This is true because few successful companies will risk their reputations and their financial resources on products or advertising messages that have not been submitted to consumers for approval through the unspectacular, but searching inquiry of consumer research.

Marketing research intrudes into every area of company operation—from the product to the sales force to the advertising campaign; from the name to the package; from the manufacturer to the distributor to the consumer herself. If there is one outstanding feature that characterizes the success of the contemporary American marketing enterprise, it is reliance on marketing research. The American Marketing Association, in its 1973 *Survey of Marketing Research*, noted that:

More than half (55%) of all respondent companies answering this question reported that they had a formal marketing research department. Even in the smaller companies with annual sales volume of $5 to $25 mil-

4. D. Duval (Vice-President, Marketing, Exxon, U.S.A.) Address to Houston Chapter, American Marketing Association, November 16, 1972.

5. L. Edwards, "Pillsbury Turnaround: Bundt rises at P&G expense," *Advertising Age* (January 24, 1974): 1 ff.

lion, more than half had either a department or a person assigned to this function.[6]

This same study shows that almost all advertising agencies with billings in excess of $25 million have a formal marketing research department, and over 80 percent of the manufacturers of consumer products with sales of over $50 million have formal departments. In addition, the 815 respondent companies reporting research expenditures in 1973 reported a combined expenditure for marketing research of $233 million, with the mean expenditure for consumer goods manufacturers amounting to $672 thousand. For advertising agencies, the mean expenditure in 1973 was $388 thousand, an increase of 54 percent over a similar survey conducted in 1968, only five years earlier.

Marketing research is pervasive because it is an essential ingredient for successful marketing. To promote a product in a competitive consumer market without the benefits of marketing research is somewhat analogous to trying to play ping-pong blindfolded. For this reason, we need to examine the scope and the uses of marketing research, particularly as it relates to marketing communications.

THE MARKETING INFORMATION SYSTEM

Marketing research is a part of the marketing information system which is designed to gather, process, and disseminate enviornmental information which will be of value to company executives in developing products, in preparing marketing plans, and in assessing the progress of company products. Generally, the marketing information system may be thought of as consisting of three parts: (1) internal records, (2) marketing intelligence, and (3) marketing research.

Internal Records

Internal records provide company executives with a constant flow of information on sales, costs, inventories, cash flow, and so forth. Marketing executives are particularly interested in sales and profits, broken down in terms of individual products, geographic regions, customers, and sales representatives. Most of this information is available from current accounting records, although frequently it must be reorganized and interpreted to be of value to marketing execu-

---

6. D.W. Twedt, ed., *1973 Survey of Marketing Research* (Chicago: American Marketing Association, 1973): 12.

tives. The monthly profit and loss statement, a routine production of the accounting department, is often the central control document employed in assessing the performance of company products.

Marketing Intelligence

Marketing intelligence includes those procedures that a company routinely uses to keep abreast of developments in the external environment and to disseminate knowledge of these developments to the appropriate company executives. Common sources for marketing intelligence are company salesreps who, through their contacts with customers and distributors, are invaluable sources of information on competitive pricing, promotions, and new products. Major consumer goods companies train their field sales staff to be alert to competitive activities, and to be prompt in reporting such activities to their sales manager.

It is generally true that company sales representatives are the prime sources of marketing intelligence, but other sources are exploited as well. Companies and their executives exhibit a great deal of variety in the ways in which they acquire information, and in some instances they use techniques that are reminiscent of the CIA, FBI, and James Bond. Most ethical businesses, however, frown on illegal spying and dubious practices and will cooperate with competitors in order to eliminate them. For example, a few years ago, a young product manager for a large packaged goods company contacted a major competitor, offering to sell the marketing plan for a competitive product being marketed by his company. The competitor immediately contacted the product manager's superiors and cooperated with them and with police officials in apprehending the product manager in the act of selling the plans.

Marketing Research

The third part of the marketing information system is the marketing research department whose specific task it is to gather, evaluate, and report specific information needed by company executives for decision making and problem solving. The marketing research department may be intimately involved in analyzing internal records and other forms of marketing intelligence, but it is uniquely involved in conducting surveys, product and package tests, determining consumer preferences and consumer profiles, evaluating advertising, and so forth. It is these unique activities that most directly concern us because it is these activities that are most closely related to marketing communications.

MARKETING RESEARCH AND THE MARKETING CONCEPT

Rapid acceleration in the growth of marketing information in general, and marketing research in particular, occurred following World War II. This gowth was stimulated by the emergence of the marketing concept as a fundamental philosophy of business. The marketing concept—which recognized that consumer satisfaction was the ultimate key to survival, profits, and growth—placed a premium on marketing information that could guide management in segmenting markets, developing products, preparing market plans, and devising advertising and promotion themes.

The Scope of Marketing Research

Since marketing research is the primary tool used to gather relevant marketing information, we need to examine the scope of the discipline in order to recognize the major areas in which it can be used.

Marketing research has been defined as the *gathering, recording, and analyzing of facts about problems relating to the transfer and sales of goods and services.*[7] Within this definition, it would seem to follow that the activities of a marketing research department are limited only by the information needed, the imagination and ethics of the research personnel involved in devising ways of obtaining needed information, and budget restrictions. And this is essentially true. Because of its versatility, marketing research offers many values for market planning and the determination of communication strategies; as a result, marketing research personnel are often a functional part of the marketing group. There are several reasons why marketing research assumes such importance in marketing communications. Among the more important are the following reasons: (1) consumer behavior is the result of many factors; (2) competitive environments differ; and (3) communications concepts may have unanticipated consequences.

Consumer Behavior Is the Result of Many Factors. A number of social, intrapersonal, and environmental variables interact in producing a particular product preference, or a given pattern of behavior. The fundamental question for marketing strategy is to determine which variables are ascendant in a large enough portion of the population to constitute a viable marketing segment, or a viable appeal. For example, individual motives may be in conflict, as would be the case of the indvidual who was attracted by the social prestige of a luxury car while, at the same time, being morally concerned over the social problems arising from the shortage of oil and financially concerned over the prospects of significant increases in the price of gasoline. Other examples of conflict would be a woman whose frustration and hostility over the tradiional role of women in our society is in conflict with her need for protection or the male whose assertive masculinity is in conflict with an unconscious feeling of inadequacy.

Faced with these conflicting forces, marketing research is needed to determine which forces are predominant, and which are relevant to the product in question in order to formulate hypotheses and develop concepts for testing.

Competitive Environments Differ. No two competitive environments are ever the same. The consumer strategy that would be appropriate for a brand of washing machines may have little relevance for a brand of home permanents. Even in the same product field, products must be differentiated from competition. As pointed out in chapter 1, this may be done through a strategy of market segmentation, or it may be done through a strategy of product differentiation. In either case, the appeals that are effective for one product usually preclude their use for another. Listerine, bad taste and all, is positioned for a particular segment of the mouthwash market. It is doubful that a competitive product with similar positioning could easily dislodge Listerine from its dominant position. In fact, Procter and Gamble struck out when it test marketed Extend in direct competition to Listerine. Extend was withdrawn from the market in 1977. Russell Stover Candy, with its image of candy-store freshness, was successfully expanded through leased departments in department stores. Stephen Whitman Candy, a line developed by the Whitman Company to compete with the Russell Stover line, was notably unsuccessful in its attempt to emulate Russell Stover's distribution strategy. Under diverse competitive conditions, marketing research is a necessary tool for testing alternative strategies in order to find one that is appropriate for the product in question.

Communication Concepts May Have Unanticipated Consequences. Consumers do not always react to

---

7. "Report of the Definitions Committee," *Journal of Marketing,* **7** (October, 1948): 210.

communication concepts in expected ways. The idea that looks great on the drawing board may stimulate adverse reactions that damage rather than help the product to which it is applied. A west coast airline, for example, attempted to allay a fear of flying that keeps many potential customers earthbound. Unfortunately, the campaign instilled fear rather than calming it, and had to be withdrawn. The judicious use of marketing research *before* the advertising ran might have shelved the idea and prevented a public gaffe. In the early 1950s, a major food company developed a promotion built around an identification tag premium. The promotion was designed to tie in with public concern over a nuclear attack and the problems of identifying victims that would result. Research, however, uncovered a vocal minority who violently opposed the idea as an attempt to exploit public fears, and the promotion was discarded thereby avoiding company embarrassment and possible harm to the company's image. G.H. Smith reports an instance in which an advertisement for a hair care product featured identical hairdos for a mother and daughter with the headline "A Double Header Hit with Dad." Marketing research revealed that women have a deep resentment at being compared with their daughters in competition for the husband and father's attention, and the idea was abandoned.[8] In short, marketing research, properly used, can help avoid communication blunders.

BARRIERS TO THE USE OF MARKETING RESEARCH

The rapid growth of marketing research in recent years seems to imply that marketing research has universal acceptance among marketing practitioners and that it is the panacea for marketing woes. Unfortunately, neither of these statements is true. Many marketing executives rely heavily on marketing research in making marketing decisions; others do not. Marketing research can be an invaluable ally of the marketer, but it is no panacea because (1) there are limitations to what marketing research can do, and (2) the world is full of bad research.

Limitations to What Marketing Research Can Do

There are a number of limitations to marketing research. Four such limitations are discussed in the following material.

8. G.H. Smith, *Motivation Research in Advertising and Marketing* (New York: McGraw-Hill, 1954), p. 229

Marketing Research Can Only Measure the Past— Not the Future. Research can only measure what exists—not what may exist tomorrow. All of its predictions are extrapolations of past data. It is not surprising, then, that these extrapolations are sometimes inaccurate because situations change, new variables are introduced into the equation, and people do not always behave tomorrow the way they did yesterday.

Research Can Only Report Findings—It Cannot Make Decisions. Executives sometimes have unrealistic expectations of marketing research. They expect research to make decisions for them, to provide guarantees, and to eliminate complexity. Yet, research may do none of these things. Research provides information on which the marketing executive may base her decision; it doesn't make the decision for her. That is the executive's responsibility and perogative. It is what she is paid for. Research can provide no guarantees or certainties, only probabilities based on past experience. Finally, research may indeed simplify complex situations by eliminating alternatives on some occasions. Yet on other occasions it may make decisions more difficult by uncovering alternatives that heretofore had been unrecognized. Too often, executives fail to realize that research is only a tool to help them make decisions—it is not a decision-making machine.

Research Can Only Deal with the Problem It Is Given—Not with the Problem It Should Have Been Given. Marketing problems are often complex, and it is not uncommon for a marketing executive to define a problem improperly or incompletely. In such instances, research findings are likely to be trivial or useless. Although the possibility of assigning the wrong problem can never be completely eliminated, it can be minimized by having research personnel participate in the problem definition, making them aware of the decision alternatives that management faces.

Research Techniques Are Sometimes Inadequate for Their Tasks. Many research techniques, particularly in the areas of consumer motivation and advertising research, are primitive and provide only gross and tentative measures of consumer motivations or of communications effectiveness. This is unfortunate, but true. A great deal of progress has been made in developing more adequate research techniques for gathering data from consumers, but further development is still needed. In the meantime, motivation and communications research must be supplemented by intuitive feel or creative hunch of competent people. One major packaged goods advertiser, for example, will not run a commerical or print advertisement that has not been subjected to consumer tests. On the other hand, if a particular advertisement or commercial scores poorly in tests but the advertising agency insists it is the right approach and is willing to fight for it, the advertiser follows the agency's recommendation. The advertiser follows this policy because it recognizes the value and legitimacy of creative judgment and because it is aware that its research techniques are fallible.

Taken together, these four factors have limited the acceptance of marketing research among some executives who have been disappointed in their expectations of what marketing research could contribute. A case in point is a feature article by Lois Ernst, an outstandingly effective copy writer and advertising practitioner. The article, titled "703 reasons why creative people don't trust research," details eight grievances against marketing research.[9] Of course, 8 isn't 703, but then Ernst is highly creative. Most of the grievances in this article are trivial and relate to the four factors we have identified as limiting the acceptance of marketing research. Nonetheless, Ernst and other marketing and advertising executives, are sometimes disappointed by the contributions that research has been able to make. Granted that their expectations are often unrealistic or their use of marketing research inappropriate, the fact remains that their disappointment weakens their acceptance of marketing research as an essential element of the marketing process.

The World Is Full of Bad Research

A second barrier to the use of marketing research resides in the field itself and is caused by the fact that the field of marketing research, like every other field of human endeavor, has its share of charlatans, rip-off artists, and incompetents. Much of the marketing research that is done is excellent. A great deal is adequate. Far too much is badly conceived, poorly executed, or misrepresented.

Professionals in the field are conscious of these problems and strive mightily to eliminate them. The American Marketing Association has worked steadily and effectively to establish standards of research and to upgrade the quality of the work that is done. Nonetheless, problems continue. The litany of research abuses range from unnecessary use of research through faulty research design, poor questionnaire development, inadequate sample selection, careless interviewing procedures, superficial data analysis, and blatant misrepresentation of findings. Sometimes

abuses arise out of ignorance and incompetence. Sometimes they occur because inadequate funds are budgeted for the research project and unwise compromises are made. Occasionally, research integrity is deliberately subverted for selfish and irresponsible interests. But that's life, and nobody promised you a rose garden. Nonetheless, the fact that abuses exist have offended many and created distrust of research among executives who could benefit from its use.

MARKETING RESEARCH AND THE CONSUMER

One form of marketing research that is particularly important to marketing is that which deals with consumers. It is sometimes referred to as *consumer* research to distinguish it from sales analysis, forecasting, store audits, and other, more impersonal forms. In the area of consumer research, there are three broad research traditions that differ in terms of their focus or emphasis. These three traditions have been referred to as the *distributive, morphological,* and *analytical* apaproaches.[10]

Distributive Research

Distributive research focuses attention on the outcomes of consumer behavior and is essentially concerned with *who* buys and *what* is bought. The emphasis of distributive research is on demographics—who customers are in terms of geographic and sociological characteristics. It builds profiles of buyers and non-buyers in terms of such factors as age, income, marital status, family size, geographic location. It computes per capita and per family consumption rates for relevant products and brands and defines markets in terms of geographic and sociological descriptions. The distributive approach is both quantitative and descriptive and is the beginning of wisdom.

The Value of Distributive Research. Distributive research is the starting point for all understanding of the consumer; more sophisticated approaches are simply refinements or supplements to the distributive approach. It is relatively simple and straightforward in terms of research techniques employed; as a consequence, it is often less expensive than other forms of consumer research. It has the further advantage that its results can be compared with U.S. census data for purposes of estimating market potentials and pro-

9. L.G. Ernst, "703 Reasons Why Creative People Don't Trust Research," *Advertising Age* (February 10, 1973): 35–36.

10. R.A. Dahl, M. Haire, and P.F. Lazerfeld, *Social Science Research on Business: Product and Potential* (New York: Columbia University Press, 1969), pp. 103–4.

jecting future trends. It is essential for the geographic allocation of advertising dollars, for media selection, and it often provides a rough guide for creative development. This is particularly true when income, family life cycle, or social class are key dimensions influencing product use and/or consumption rates.

Limitations of Distributive Research. Despite its values, distributive research has three major limitations.

It is purely descriptive and fails to deal with the nature of the decision process that underlies the purchase. Often, unless this process is understood, sound marketing strategies cannot be developed. Buying a carpet, for example, involves a completely different decision process than buying a pound of coffee. Since different sources of information, different shopping behaviors, and different influence patterns characterize these two purchases, the marketer of carpeting and the marketer of coffee should allocate their marketing resources differently—each developing a marketing mix that is appropriate for its particular product. While the differences in the decision process for carpets versus coffee may appear obvious, important differences that are not immediately apparent exist for other products as well.

Second, the distributive approach fails to deal with the dynamics of behavior. In order to understand consumers, and communicate effectively with them, the marketer must know something about their motivational patterns, something about the relative importance of various psychological and sociological influences, and something about their media and promotional susceptibilities. In short, she needs to know why consumers behave as they do. Distributive research does not provide this kind of information.

Third, as markets become more competitive, segmentation along demographic lines becomes less adequate for purposes of product positioning. Instead, in order to remain competitive, the marketer must look to psycho-social demensions as possible bases for segmentation.

Morphological Research

The morphological approach starts where distributive research stops. After consumers are identified and described, the morphological approach focuses on the different ways in which different products are bought or the differences in the way the same products are bought by different groups of people (for example, by social class or stages in the family life cycle). Morphological research might be described as *how* research since it concentrates on how decisions are made.

In the carpeting versus coffee example given earlier, the purchaser of carpeting will generally visit a number of outlets in order to see competitive carpeting samples and to gather information. She may consult consumer reports to learn more about fibers, she will undoubtedly talk with friends who have purchased carpeting recently, she will be strongly influenced by retail sales personnel, and share the final decision with her husband. The decision process will tend to be drawn out over a considerable period of time, possibly several weeks. By contrast, the buyer of coffee will probably rely on her own judgment and experience, augmented, perhaps, by advertising and recommendations from friends. Obviously, the marketer of carpets has different points of influence than does the marketer of coffee. Each, however, must know what the points of influence are before company resources can be used well.

Analytical Research

Analytical research, like the morphological approach, starts where distributive research stops. It differs from morphological research in that it involves causal assessment. That is, it asks "why" consumers purchase the products and brands they do. This causal assessment may reveal that the purchase was based on apparent product differences, or it may reveal that it was primarily influenced by psycho-social aspects of the product's image.

Generally, analytical research is the most difficult and is more fraught with ambiguity and error than are the other forms of marketing research. Because of this, a number of indirect techniques have been developed to determine consumer motivations.

It may help to distinguish between morphological and analytical research to turn again to the example of carpets versus coffee. In the case of carpeting, our hypothetical consumer visited carpeting dealers, read consumer reports, talked with friends, and discussed the decision with her husband. This is a morphological description of *how* she went about making the decision, but it doesn't indicate which information source was most influential or why the consumer chose the brand of carpeting she finally bought. Analytical research, on the other hand, might reveal that (1) she purchased a particular type of carpeting because the fiber was resistant to stain and quickly recovered from crushing; (2) she bought the brand she did because of the fashion appeal used in the advertising; (3) she bought from the store she did because it was a high prestige store; and (4) she bought from the salesperson she did because she reassured her in her choice of colors and patterns. By contrast, in the case of coffee, the consumer may have purchased a particular brand because of an endorsement by a celebrity, because of a particular advertising claim such as Folger's "mountain grown" slogan, because of a uniquely appealing package design, because of a price-off coupon offer, or because of a variety of other possible reasons.

The point is that distributive, morphological, and analytical research answer different types of questions. Distributive research asks "who?" Morphological research asks "How?" Analytical research asks "Why?"

All of these questions are important, and the marketing manager should consider all of them when developing a market plan for her product.

One danger that exists is that the novice marketer, intrigued by the "how" and "why" questions and fascinated by esoteric research techniques, will be tempted to by-pass the more mundane province of distributive research and go dashing off into the wild blue yonder of motivation research. Forget it! Successful marketing is systematic and founded on a proper regard for the fundamentals. Distributive research is fundamental; morphological and analytical research, while important, should be added when and where they are applicable. It is true that as markets become more competitive market segmentation and product differentiation depend more on psycho-social distinctions. Under these conditions, the descriptive data of distributive research, while still fundamental, is inadequate to provide marketing direction and must be supplemented by the morphological and analytical approaches.

MAJOR METHODS OF GATHERING DATA

One distinction that is often made in marketing is the distinction between *primary* and *secondary* research. This distinction is not always clear. Primary data is generally considered as data that is originated in view of a specific need; secondary data is that which is already in existence in some organized form, having been searched, organized, and stored by someone else. For example, if *Time* magazine were to undertake a survey of its subscribers in order to define their demographic characteristics, the study would be primary research. This same information provided to advertisers and advertising agencies in published form would be secondary research insofar as the advertisers and advertising agencies were concerned because they did not originate the data. An immense amount of useful secondary data pertaining to industries, markets, products, and consumers is available in the

United States, and those interested in marketing and advertising should know of its existence.

One of the most useful sources of secondary data is Sales Management's *Survey of Buying Power,* an annual publication that provides a plethora of population, household, and income statistics, as well as data on retail sales for several merchandise groups. This data is broken down by geographic regions, states, counties, selected cities, and by one hundred eighty metropolitan county areas. A metropolitan county area consists of a central city of 50 thousand inhabitants or more along with the entire county or counties containing the central city as well as adjacent counties that are essentially metropolitan in character and are socially and economically integrated with the central city. A number of bibliographies of marketing information sources are also available. One of the better general bibliographies is an article in the *Harvard Business Review* authored by Steuart H. Britt and Irwin Shapiro.[11] In addition, the U.S. Bureau of Census publishes data on population, housing, retail and wholesale trade, manufacturers, mineral industries, agriculture, transportation, as well as on other areas. Trade associations, media, and a variety of commercial services also gather and organize marketing data on a number of industry and product groups.

Obtaining secondary information is primarily a matter of digging it out. With perseverance, a great deal of information can be found relevant to almost any marketing problem that can be defined. One problem with secondary data, however, is that it is often not specific enough to the problem at hand and must be supplemented by primary research.

The principal concern of this text, however, is primary research, since we need to examine some of the major methods for gathering data from the consumer. Essentially, there are three ways to collect primary data, although each of these ways may appear in a variety of forms and, in fact, may be combined in order to solve a particular research problem. The three ways are observation, experiments, and surveys. By far, the most frequently used form of primary data collection is the survey, although both observational and experimental techniques have important values and widespread acceptance.

Observational Techniques

Many marketing questions can be answered by simply observing some aspect of the marketing process at work. For example:

11. S.H. Britt and I. Shapiro, "Where to Find Marketing Facts," *Harvard Business Review* **40** (September-October, 1962): 44 ff.

The Pet Milk Company at one point radically changed its evaporated milk label and introduced the new label in the Detroit market. Researchers posted themselves near the evaporated milk section of supermarkets and observed how customers responded to the new label. Since it was apparent from observation that the label was causing a great deal of consumer confusion, and since retail orders were severely depressed, the label was withdrawn from distribution.

A major magazine regularly concealed a television camera in its waiting room in order to observe which magazine articles were read by people who were waiting to see someone in the company. The object was to find out which articles commanded the greatest consumer attention.

Investigators set up a hidden television camera in the ceiling of a supermarket to follow the movements of shoppers through the stores. The object was to develop generalizations on the customer flow pattern that would lead to a more effective arrangement of merchandise and increased customer purchases.

Twenty-four sheet poster companies (billboards) regularly observe traffic flow in various parts of major cities in order to develop statistics on the number of automobiles passing sites at which they have billboards located.

The opportunites for observation are endless: pantry checks, garbage can checks, concealed microphones in order to see how salesreps respond to questions, and a variety of other observational techniques can be employed when they are appropriate, and provide insight into consumer behavior. Observational techniques are most useful when an objective picture of overt behavior will be more useful than subjective responses to questions. One of the major shortcomings of the approach is that it is restricted to overt behavior and provides only inferential material on what the consumer is thinking. It also tends to be expensive and requires careful observation on the part of the investigators. One of the reasons why hidden cameras and hidden microphones are often used is that they provide an accurate, unbiased observation.

One criticism of the observational technique is an ethical one. Normally, consumers are not aware that they are under observation, and, as a consequence, such observation may be considered an invasion of privacy. Not all uses of observational techniques constitute an invasion of privacy, but some do. Since, at this point, the legal guidelines are ambiguous, the researcher must formulate her own standards of conduct.

Experimental Designs

One problem of the observational method is that behavior is usually observed under natural, uncontrolled conditions. As a consequence, it is often difficult to draw meaningful conclusions or to test a marketing hypothesis. In order to test hypotheses about some marketing stimuli or some form of marketing behavior the experimental method is often employed and experimental controls introduced. The experimental method involves a systematic introduction of selected stimuli into a marketing situation and careful measurement of the effects these different stimuli exert on the dependent variable. Extraneous factors that might influence experimental results are controlled by experimental design, by statistical analysis, or both.

A simple example of a marketing experiment would be an in-store test to determine the effectiveness of a product display in generating additional sales. One approach to such an experiment would be to use two groups of stores, a group of *control* stores and a group of *experimental* stores. The control and experimental stores might be given the treatment shown in figure 6-1. Unit sales of the product would be measured during the pretest, the test, and the posttest periods in both control and experimental stores. In the control stores, the conditions would be the same in all three periods. By contrast, in the experimental stores, the display would be erected during the test period. The effectiveness of the display in generating additional sales would be determined by comparing the sales patterns in the control versus the experimental stores and testing the significance of the statistical differences found.

The example just given is a simple experimental design for a controlled experiment in marketing. Other experimental designs could have been used for the same experiment, some of which would be more sophisticated than the design used, and some of which would be less sophisticated. There are a variety of experimental designs that can be employed in testing marketing hypotheses, although a discussion of them is beyond the scope of this text. Some designs are more defensible than others, which means that they use more effective controls. Some designs are highly sophisticated, and some are relatively crude. The highly sophisticated experimental design is not always the best, nor is the relatively crude design necessarily the worst. It always depends on the nature of the problem, the nature of the data, and the nature of the decision to be made. This is why the marketing manager should have at least some experience in experimental design and scientific methodology. With such

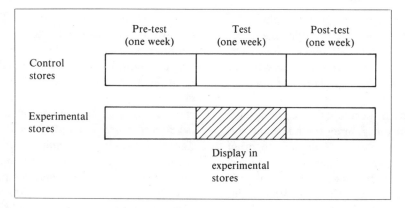

Figure 6-1. A Simple Experimental Design Using Control and Experimental Stores

experience, she will be better able to evaluate the adequacy of a particular experimental design and assess the validity of the results.

Surveys

The third and most common method for developing consumer information is the survey. Compared to direct observation and experimental designs surveys are more versatile, produce a greater wealth of information, and are applicable to a greater variety of research problems. Surveys may be used to develop distributive, morphological, and analytical data and are the work horses of consumer research.

Since surveys are so widespread and their use is so commonplace, it is often assumed that they require no great skill to design and execute. This is not true. The design of a survey, the development of the questionnaire (sometimes referred to as a *schedule*), the identification of the appropriate population, the selection of a sample, the interviewing procedure, and the coding and analysis of data constitute one of the most demanding and technically advanced areas of marketing research. It is true that many surveys are designed and conducted by inexperienced, naïve, and incompetent individuals. It is also true that the validity of the results reflect the level of competence that produced the survey. A number of years ago, a major U.S. company test marketed a new breakfast cereal in the Cincinnati market. The president of the company had many sterling characteristics, but research competence and sophistication was not among them. Against his advertising agency's advice (the company did not have its own research department at the time), the president had the manufacturing department include a post card in each box of cereal. The post card contained a brief message, signed by the company president, thanking consumers for trying the product and asking

them their opinion of the cereal. The results of this "survey" indicated that the product was the greatest innovation since the invention of food and indicated a widespread and enthusiastic acceptance by consumers. Actually, the product was fairly routine, did not sell particularly well (although it is still on the market as one of the minor cereals), and proved to be a major disappointment compared to the survey results. Without making a detailed analysis of the faults of the post-card survey, it should be noted that it violated virtually every rule in the book, provided no useful information for the product group, and there was no way that it could yield a realistic reflection of product acceptance.

Because of the complexity of planning, executing, and analyzing surveys, an extensive literature has developed which details procedures and cautions against common errors. There are innumerable books and articles on questionnaire development, sample design, interviewing procedures, coding, analysis, and presentation of results. One of the better basic references is the *Handbook of Marketing Research,* which devotes some thirteen hundred pages to marketing research, a good portion of which relates to surveys.

Although surveys may employ a variety of specific techniques, there are three basic methods of collecting survey data. These three methods are personal interview, direct mail, and telephone interview. Each of these approaches has certain advantages and disadvantages. The particular method used will depend on the data to be collected, the population to be sampled, and the budget available for the project.

Personal Interviews. Personal interviewing is the most versatile of the three survey methods. It can be used with individuals or with groups; it can accommodate complex interviewing procedures; it can use structured or unstructured questionnaires; it can probe in order to clarify responses; it can employ short or long questionnaires; and it can supplement the subject's responses with personal observations. The flexibility and virtuosity of the personal interview approach are almost unlimited, but it gains these advantages at a relatively high cost.

The financial cost of the personal interview survey is greater than that of the other survey methods, and this fact alone often causes companies to turn to other forms of information gathering. There is another cost associated with personal interviews that is frequently overlooked, however, and that is the possibility of bias arising from the interviewer. As an active participant in the interviewing procedure, the interviewer may insert error into the situation that is specifically attributable to her. She may consciously or unconsciously give the respondent feedback that influences the nature of the response. She may contaminate the interview by using leading probes that introduce her personal point of view into the results. She may serve as a selective filter in hearing or recording the respondents' answers. And, finally, she may deliberately fabricate responses. Careful training, rigorous supervision, comparative tabulation of the responses obtained by different interviewers, spot checking respondents to make sure they were interviewed and that the information they gave was that which was reported are all ways of minimizing interviewer bias. Such procedures are costly and time consuming, and, even when used, do not eliminate all possibility of error.

The shortcomings of the personal interview survey have not been itemized to discredit this form of information gathering. Properly planned and supervised, it is still the most reliable method available. Rather, they have been enumerated to point up the pitfalls of what, on the surface, appears to be a straightforward uncomplicated device for obtaining consumer data. The user of research should be aware of the possible biases that personal interviewing can introduce into the findings and insist that the control procedures employed in a given study be clearly set forth in the written report.

Mail Surveys. Mail surveys are conducted by mailing self-administered questionnaires to selected samples of consumers. The mail survey differs from other survey forms in that there is no interviewer to ask questions and to lead the respondent through the questionnaire. This factor introduces important differences in survey design, questionnaire construction, sample selection, and evaluation of returns. For this reason, it is important to examine the major advantages and disadvantages of mail surveys.

Advantages of the Mail Survey. There are a number of advantages associated with mail surveys that commend their use. First, they permit surveying over a broad geographic area at a minimal cost, and without introducing some of the problems associated with cluster sampling. Second, interview bias is eliminated since no interviewer is present while the questionnaire is being completed. Third, for major surveys, the mail approach usually saves time. Thus, one can complete the interviewing portion of a nationwide survey within about two weeks, a completion time difficult to achieve by personal interviews. Fourth, control can be centralized since the entire operation can be conducted from one office with built-in checks at every relevant point of execution. Fifth, the technique is remarkably versatile, so that a wide variety of information can be obtained through thoughtful question construction. Finally, overall costs are relatively low compared with other survey forms.

Limitations of the Mail Survey. On the negative side, the mail survey has a number of limitations that restrict its use. First, nonresponse is often a severe problem with mail surveys. It is virtually impossible to obtain 100 percent response with any survey method, and even personal interview surveys frequently are able to contact only 80–85 percent of their sample. The problem is even more severe with the mail survey, where nonresponse may be so great as to threaten the integrity of the findings. The Advertising Research Foundation recommends an 80 percent or better response for mail surveys, which bring their returns in line with other survey forms. Through the use of a well-designed survey, a planned program of follow-up reminders (post cards, follow-up letters, follow-up-questionnaires, etc.), and/or established mail panels, it is often possible to meet the foundation's recommended return rate. Many mail surveys, however, achieve a 20 percent return or less and, as a consequence, doubts must be raised about the validity of their findings. Second, population selection and sampling are unique problems for mail surveys. Mailing lists covering a number of general and special populations (teenagers, housewives, pet-owners, home-owners, etc.) may be purchased from any number of sources. However, lists for the desired population are frequently not available, or of doubtful quality. Established mail panels are usually the best sources of quality mailing lists, but even they must develop their lists through quota sampling, a sampling approach that has many technical shortcomings; and, it is not possible to develop a probability sample of survey respondents. Third, mail surveys, obviously, are restricted to those respondents who are able to read and write with sufficient facility to fill out a questionnaire and who are willing to do so. While it might be thought that in an industrial society such as the U.S. literacy could be taken for granted, it cannot be. From a practical point of view, as much as 20–30 percent of the adult population may be functionally illiterate. Of course, it can be argued that the best prospects for consumer goods and those that the marketer is interested in are capable of responding to a mail survey. Generally, this is true, but caution must be observed in many product areas. For example, the primary consumer market for evaporated milk is severely under-represented on mail panels, with the consequence that findings on evaporated milk derived from such panels may be biased and misleading. Similar situations will exist for other products for which markets are concentrated among either the upper or lower socio-economic groups, since these groups are customarily under-represented in mail survey responses. Fourth, mail surveys place limitations on both the length and complexity of the questionnaire that may be used. In general, as the length of the questionnaire increases, response declines. Five- or six-page questionnaires usually present few problems if the questionnaire is well designed, but as the questionnaire exceeds this length, the problem of response rate increases proportionally. Fifth, the subject matter of the research may require the presence of a specially trained interviewer. This is particularly true where the questions are psychological in nature or where it is necessary to probe to clarify or develop answers. In such instances, mail surveys are inadequate. Finally, although mail surveys may save time on major, geographically dispersed studies, they are inappropriate where short deadlines are involved. If the researcher needs an answer in forty-eight hours from a small, localized sample, she will have to rely on either personal or telephone interviews as her source of data.

There are other disadvantages of the mail survey, but they tend to be minor and can often be compensated for through survey design. All in all, the mail survey is an extremely useful device that is used extensively to develop a wide variety of consumer and market information.

Telephone Surveys. The third form of survey is the telephone survey. In many respects, the telephone survey stands midway between the personal interview and the mail survey, neither suffering from the major weaknesses nor having the major strengths of the other two survey approaches. In addition, it has certain unique values of its own.

Advantages of Telephone Surveys. The telephone survey is a fast, convenient, and economical method for obtaining a wide range of consumer information. It is so convenient, in fact, that many market researchers consider it first and only turn to other methods after they have concluded that telephone interviews are inadequate for their problem. Generally, the telephone survey has the following advantages. First, it is fast and efficient. More interviewing can be done by a single interviewer than can be handled through personal interviews. And, for jobs in which there is an extremely short deadline, it may be the only feasible alternative. Second, the telephone directory offers unequalled opportunities to obtain random samples of a number of selected populations. Doctors, lawyers, contractors, automobile dealers, and a variety of other professional and business groups have 100 percent listings in the yellow pages of the directory. Further, the residential pages provide an easy and convenient way of taking a random sample of all listed numbers, although there are a number of sampling errors that need to be avoided.[12] Third, call-backs to reach not-at-homes are easily accomodated by the telephone interview, so that the problem of nonresponse may be less than that for other survey approaches. Fourth, the telephone survey lends itself to different degrees of control more completely than other survey approaches. At one extreme, the interviewer may be permitted to make unsupervised calls from her home; at the other extreme, the interviewer may work from a central office where every word she speaks is monitored. Finally, the telephone survey is economical. It costs substantially less than does the personal interview survey and is often comparable with mail surveys. Before the advent of Wide Area Telephone Service (WATS Line), long distance calls were usually uneconomical for regional and national surveys. With WATS lines, a company can survey by telephone within its WATS area at a cost that is price-competitive with other survey methods.

Disadvantages of Telephone Surveys. Like the other survey methods, telephone interviews have distinct shortcomings. First, the telephone directory represents an incomplete universe of consumers. This is true because not all families have telephones, some telephones are unlisted, and new numbers and number changes cause a turnover of about 20 percent a year, so that the telephone directory is inadequate as a precise sampling instrument. These shortcomings are not critical for many surveys, although they should be evaluated on a survey by survey basis. A classical fail-

12. S. Payne, "Data Collection Methods: Telephone Surveys," in *Handbook of Marketing Research,* R. Ferber, ed., (New York: McGraw-Hill, 1947), pp. 2–105 to 2–123.

ure of telephone sampling occurred in 1936 when the *Literary Digest* published the results of a telephone survey which indicated that Alf Landon, the Republican candidate, would sweep the nation in the coming presidential election. Since lower income voters did not have telephones, this group was seriously underestimated. As a result, contrary to the *Literary Digest's* prediction, Roosevelt won a crushing victory, losing only Maine and Vermont. This forecasting fiasco contributed to the later demise of the *Literary Digest.*

Second, as in the mail survey, there are limits to the length of questionnaire that can be handled by telephone interviews. Although these limits are less restrictive than is often assumed, interviews of over twenty to thirty minutes become awkward and respondents will often discontinue the interview before this limit is reached. Third, the telephone interview does not lend itself to long answers or to complex questionnaires. And, as in the case of personal interviews, interviewer bias may enter into the results, particularly when the interviewer tries to condense a relatively long response to a question.

Summary Comments on Gathering Primary Data

As we have seen, there are a variety of ways of collecting data from consumers. Observational methods, experimental designs, and the various survey techniques all have unique advantages and disadvantages; no single approach is adequate to answer all of the questions that may arise in the marketing of a product or service. The secret of good research is using the proper technique for the proper problem at the proper time.

Good consumer research is rigorously systematic and wholly empirical and may employ a variety of mathematical techniques, but it is as much an art as it is a science, like marketing itself. Identifying appropriate population universes, designing questionnaires, and selecting samples are not absolute procedures. Cost constraints inevitably force compromises; choices have to be made among research techniques, among the problems to be researched, and the precision of the answers that will be acceptable.

There is no universal agreement among research professionals concerning the usefulness of many of the available research techniques or the value of some of the mathematical models that are employed. Creativity and judgment augment technical skill in defining a competent research practitioner. The marketing manager, however, should not be alienated by the lack of agreement in the field. She does need to learn enough about research to understand what the disagreements are about and to recognize situations in which consumer research may be of value.

MAJOR AREAS OF RESEARCH JUDGMENT

Before leaving the general realm of consumer research and turning our attention to specific research techniques, we need to mention three areas that are critical to the research process. These are the areas of research objectives, questionnaire design, and sampling.

Research Objectives

Good research is not done on a haphazard basis. It requires organization, planning, and careful execution. At the heart of the research process are the objectives of the research.

All research should start with a clear statement of the objectives to be achieved. This statement should not only indicate what is to be learned, but it should also indicate how the information is to be used (i.e., the nature of the decision which will be made on the basis of the findings) and the cost constraints surrounding the project. Without this information, it is not possible to select the research techniques to be employed, design an appropriate research instrument, and select an adequate sample.

Most of the disappointments that arise from research findings probably arise because the objectives were not sufficiently clear. When this occurs, the marketing manager has no one to blame but herself. She alone knows the nature of the decisions she has to make; she alone can specify the kinds of information she needs in order to make that decision; and she alone can communicate this information to the market researcher.

Questionnaire Design

Few aspects of surveying are more critical than the design of the survey questionnaire. The art of writing questions may seem simple, but it is full of pitfalls for the naïve and and unwary.

Lorie and Roberts relate a story about measuring readership of *Gone With the Wind.* When respondents were asked "Have you read this book?" more yes replies were received than were known to be possible. When the question was rephrased to "Do you intend to read *Gone With the Wind?*" only those who had read it indicated so, and the affirmative response was much lower.[13]

There are many instances of misleading results arising from poorly worded questions. The type of ques-

13. B. Schoner and K.P. Uhl, *Marketing Research,* 2nd ed. (New York: John Wiley & Sons, Inc., 1975), p. 237.

tions asked,[14] the wording of the questions,[15] and the sequence in which questions are ordered[16] can have a have a profound effect on survey results.

Questions sometimes develop information other than that which is intended. An example used by Boyd and Westfall is a case in point. The simple, apparently straightforward question, "Why do you use Trend detergent?" is actually three different questions because it may give rise to three different types of responses. Consumers responding to this question might give answers such as: (1) to get the clothes clean; (2) it's easier on my hands than others; and (3) my neighbor recommended it. These three answers are actually answers to three different questions. The first answer tells why the consumer used a detergent; the second tells why she likes Trend compared to competitive products; and the third explains how she happened to start using Trend.[17] Questions such as this, that may be answered as several questions, are called *multielement* questions and often lead to ambiguous results.

Guidance in the development of questions is available from a variety of sources, although *The Art of Asking Questions* by Stanley L. Payne is one of the best works on questionnaire construction.[18] Questionnaire development is no job for the amateur, and even the pen of the experienced practitioner slips occasionally. It is for this reason that every questionnaire should be pretested in order to determine how well it works and the kinds of information it develops.

Sampling

Sampling is one area of consumer research that can be pursued with firm guidelines and scientific precision, but frequently it is not because it is felt to be too expensive, unnecessary, and too slow. Before a sample is done, the following things must be determined: the kind of information that is being collected; how it will be used; and how precise the results need to be. If the information being collected is statistical in nature, if it will be used to make forecasts of future events or to draw firm conclusions about the past, if the measuring instrument being used is valid, and if precise

information is needed—then a scientific sample is recommended. If one's purpose is less rigorous and if the measuring instrument itself provides only the grossest of measures, the use of a scientifically drawn sample makes about as much sense as measuring a piece of rusty pipe with a micrometer.

Sampling is an essential part of marketing research. Its theory is well developed; sampling itself is an efficient way of estimating a universe; and it is an accurate and pragmatic way of obtaining empirical data. Suppose that a marketing manager wants to know the proportion of people eighteen years of age and over that drink coffee. If she had the time and money, she might take a census; that is, interview all of them and find out who the coffee drinkers were. Of course, if she used a thousand interviewers, interviewing twelve hours a day, and completing an interview every ten minutes, she could complete the task in about six years. On the other hand, she could obtain an excellent estimate of the number of coffee users from a carefully drawn sample of only a few hundred respondents.

Many people, through lack of experience, are skeptical that one can describe the reactions of several million people by interviewing only a few hundred. Yet, it is done all the time with remarkable precision. A few hundred homes will be monitored to determine the viewing habits of tens of millions of television viewers; two or three hundred people may be used in a comparative taste test of two food products to predict the preferences of the U.S. population; and a carefully drawn sample of 15 hundred voters can predict, quite accurately, how the body politic will vote in a national presidential election.

Not all samples are equally reliable in reflecting the characteristics of the populations from which they are drawn. The size of a sample is a factor in determining its adequacy, but the precision with which the sample is drawn is often a much more critical consideration. Earlier, reference was made to the *Literary Digest* telephone survey that grossly misrepresented the political preferences of the U.S. electorate in 1936. The sample used in that survey was more than large enough; however, it was *not representative* of the voting population it purported to represent because it did not reflect the opinions of millions of voters who were unable to afford a telephone. And this one word, *representativeness,* is the key word in sampling. A sample must be representative of the population from which it is drawn before we can have confidence that it will provide a valid reflection of the relevant characteristics of that population.

A detailed discussion of sampling is far beyond the scope of this text. The American Marketing Associa-

14. B.S. Dohrenwend, "Some Effects of Open and Closed Questions on Respondents' Answers," *Human Organizations* **24** (Summer, 1965): 175–84.

15. D. Rugg, "Experiments in Wording Questions: II," *Public Opinion Quarterly,* **5** (March, 1941): 91–92.

16. E.J. Gross, "The Effect of Question Sequence on Measures of Buying Interest," *Journal of Advertising Research* **4** (September, 1964): 41.

17. H.W. Boyd, Jr. and R. Westfall, *Marketing Research: Text and Cases,* 3rd ed. (Homewood, Illinois: Richard D. Irwin, Inc., 1972), p. 290.

18. S.L. Payne, *The Art of Asking Questions* (Princeton, New Jersey: Princeton University Press, 1951).

tion has published a monograph, *The Use of Sampling in Marketing Research,* that does an excellent job of outlining the issues in sampling theory in clear language and provides a bibliography for the student who wishes to pursue the area further.[19]

There are two aspects of sampling that determine the representativeness of the sample. These are the *type* and *size* of sample that should be employed.

Types of Samples.   Basically, there are two types of samples—*probability* or *random* samples and *non-probability* or *nonrandom* samples. In a probability sample every unit in the universe being sampled has an equal and known probability of being included in the sample. And, although there are a variety of techniques for drawing probability samples, the essential characteristic is that no unit has a greater or lesser chance than any other unit of being included in the sample. Representativeness can be assured with a probability sample and statistical techniques can be used to determine the magnitude of the probable sampling error.

In a nonprobability sample, there is no way of guaranteeing that the sample will be representative of the population being sampled, nor is it possible to determine the magnitude of the sampling error. Generally, there are three kinds of nonprobability samples. In the *convenience* sample respondents are selected on the basis of convenience. An example of a convenience sample would be interviewing passers-by on a street corner or in a shopping center. In the *judgment* or *purposive* sample the researcher chooses respondents believed to be representative of the entire population. An example of a judgment sample would be to select a sample of supermarkets from various sections of town and from various chain and independent organizations in order to measure sales of a food product. The stores selected would not be selected on a random basis but would be chosen because it was thought that their customers would be representative of all supermarket customers. In the *quota* sample the researcher selects sampling units to fill a quota for certain known parameters of the general population. For example, if 20 percent of the population had incomes of over $20 thousand, then 20 percent of the sample would have incomes over $20 thousand. If 10 percent of the heads of households were over sixty years of age, then 10 percent of the sample heads of households would be over sixty years of age. A quota sample is usually much more elaborate than other forms of nonproba-

bility samples, but it resembles them in that factors other than chance determine sample inclusion.

Nonprobability samples are frequently criticized because there is no way of guaranteeing that they will be representative of the population they are intended to represent, and there is no way of calculating the extent of the sampling error. Nonetheless, they are used extensively because: they are less expensive in terms of both time and money than probability samples; and for some research techniques there is no feasible way of drawing a probability sample because of noncooperation among units in the population.

Because of these factors—*cost* and *feasibility*—nonprobability samples are widely used in marketing research. And there is nothing wrong with their use provided: the user of the research is aware of what she is getting, and knows its limitations; and reasonable judgment has been exercised in avoiding gross sampling errors. Nonprobability samples are often used in the early stages of a research project when the market researcher is simply searching for ideas or attempting to develop hypotheses for testing. Nonprobability samples are frequently used in obtaining consumer reaction to advertising and package designs, and they are commonplace among the various motivational techniques that will be discussed in the next section. The use of probability as opposed to nonprobability samples only becomes critical when a high degree of accuracy is required in research data (a situation that does not always prevail).

Sample Size.   A second factor that influences the representativeness of the sample is its size. The size of the sample required to represent a population does not depend on the size of the population itself. Instead, the determining consideration is the complexity of the population. A relatively small sample may be used if the population is known to be homogeneous. If, on the other hand, the population is known to be complex (as is the case of the U.S. population, with its diversity of ethnic, religious, income, and special interest groups) the sample size needs to be relatively large to provide representation of the various population segments.

Generally, an appropriate sample size is somewhere between thirty units and 5 percent of the population. Actual size, however, will depend upon the complexity of the population and the size of sampling error that is acceptable. Specific decisions on the sample's size for a particular survey must be made by the researcher on a project by project basis, with the final decision often being a compromise between the precision desired and the funds available for the project.

19. W.P. Dommeruth, *The Use of Sampling in Marketing Research* (Chicago: The American Marketing Association, 1975).

MOTIVATION RESEARCH

Most marketing research that elicits information directly from consumers is plagued to a greater or lesser extent with response problems. These problems arise because consumers will sometimes mislead survey results by giving false information to avoid embarrassment, to enhance their status, or simply to please the interviewer. These problems become particularly acute when the information sought is of a personal nature, has implications of status, or is causal in nature. Consumers do use products for reasons they are unwilling to admit or for nonconscious reasons. When asked their reason for product use, they will fabricate plausible and sometimes partially true explanations to save themselves from embarrassment and satisfy the requirements of the interview. Motivation research is an attempt to overcome this difficulty.

The term *motivation research* is an umbrella term covering many research techniques, most of which have been borrowed from the behavioral sciences. The field has sometimes been portrayed as an approach for exploring deep, underlying, and unconscious motivational patterns that are normally thought of as the province of the psychiatrist or clinical psychologist. This image is unfortunate because it endows the field with a potency and eroticism that is misleading. The chief value of motivational research is a level of analysis much more superficial and more useful than delving into the depths of the consumer's psyche. Two broad types of motivational research are *projective techniques* and *extended interviews*.

Projective Techniques

Projective techniques, long used by psychologists for clinical diagnosis, have been adapted to a wide variety of marketing problems. The theory behind projective techniques is that when consumers are asked to respond to a relatively unstructured stimulus they will reveal their own need-value systems in their responses. Projective techniques are of particular value in disguising the purpose of an interview and eliciting information that might normally be withheld by consumers or overlooked by more traditional research procedures. Some of the more frequently used projective techniques are briefly described in the following material.

Word Association.   Word association is one of the best known and most widely used forms of the projective techniques. It is relatively easy to apply and can be used effectively to screen brand names for negative connotations or to uncover consumers' feelings about new products, packages, designs, illustrations, or communication themes. Typically, the respondent is asked to give the first word that comes to mind in response to each of a list of unrelated words or to some other stimulus. In most cases, the consumer is asked to respond with a series of words; this modification is referred to as *chain* or successive word association. The name search for Standard Oil of New Jersey used word association to explore the meaning of the name Exxon among consumers.

Sentence Completion.   As its name implies, an incomplete phrase is given to consumers, and they are asked to add words that come to mind in order to complete the sentence. For example, respondents may be asked to complete the thought: "When I have a headache. . . ." A consumer might respond by saying, " . . . I want to be left alone," or " . . . I take Anacin," or " . . . nothing seems to help," or a variety of other responses. An analysis of responses often leads to a product claim or communications theme that can be developed in advertising. For example, a bank used the stimulus: "When I go into a bank . . ." Analysis of the results showed a disproportionate number of responses such as: "I am ignored," "I'm treated like a number," "I feel I'm imposing on them," "I feel all they want is my money." This finding led to the development of a communications theme stressing "personal attention" and "concern for customers." It also led to a training program for tellers and bank officers designed to improve their interpersonal skills in dealing with customers.

Picture and Visual Methods.   In this approach, a cartoon or picture serves as the stimulus object, although there are a number of variations of the technique. For example: (1) the subject may be shown a picture of a marketing situation or of a product in use and asked to tell a story about it; (2) one character in a cartoon may be represented as making a statement or asking a question, and the subject asked to formulate an answer; (3) two cartoon characters may be shown disagreeing on some point, and the subject will be asked to indicate which she agrees with, and why. The picture method is highly flexible because the visual stimulus can be adapted to the marketing question at hand.

One advantage of this approach is that because interviewees seem to enjoy working with pictures it helps build rapport with the interviewer. Since it helps break down barriers between the interviewer and respondent, this factor undoubtedly contributes to the quality of the information that can be gained from the interview.

Situational Methods. Situational methods differ from visual techniques in that a verbal rather than a visual stimulus is used. Typically, in a situational approach respondents will be asked to describe in detail the kind of person who uses a particular product or who shops at a particular store. G.H. Smith cites a study in which young women were asked to write a personality sketch of the type of person who buys "X" brand deodorant and of another who buys "Y" brand. Analysis showed that the "X" brand user was seen as more lax in her standards of cleanliness, less intelligent, and less popular with boys than the user of "Y" brand. These findings led to a recommendation that certain excuses that were given for the "X" brand purchaser (she is thrifty, wants to save time, and wants a less messy deodorant) be exploited in promotion, and the product name be given a positive connotation by linking it more closely with desired features of the product.[20] The situational method, like many other projective techniques, is extremely flexible, easy to work with, and limited only by the imagination of the researcher in terms of the variety of applications that can be devised.

Other Projective Techniques. A number of other projective techniques are used infrequently because they are difficult to use, require highly trained people to gather and/or interpret the data, and do not lend themselves to the collection of data from large samples. One example is *psychodrama*, in which participants are asked to "act out" situations. As the participant becomes involved in the role assigned to her, it is believed that she will express her true feelings and beliefs. Another example is *graphology*, or the analysis of handwriting. These and other projective techniques are cumbersome and, while they may have genuine value in psychological diagnosis, have found little favor with marketers.

Extended Interviews

The term *extended interviews* is used to designate an interviewing approach that can be used with either individuals or groups to obtain qualitative data about consumers' motivations, feelings, and beliefs. Variously referred to as *qualitative, unstructured, depth,* or *focused* interviews, the approach differs from traditional interviewing approaches in the following ways.

---

20. G.H. Smith, *Motivation in Research and Marketing,* p. 102.

The interview is relatively unstructured. Instead of using a formal questionnaire, the interviewer has a list of topic areas that may be introduced in a variety of ways. The interview is more of a discussion than a question and answer encounter, with the interviewer encouraging the respondents to discourse widely over a variety of related and relevant topics. When used with groups, it evolves into a group discussion of relevant topics introduced by the interviewer or brought up by group members. It requires a skillful leader to keep the discussion pertinent and to exhaust one area of discussion before moving to others.

The interview is qualitative. It emphasizes feelings, experiences, and anecdotes rather than tabulatable and quantifiable responses. How something is said (the feeling tone) and what is unsaid (avoided) are often more important than what is said in interpreting the data.

The information elicited tends to be more profound, more detailed, and more comprehensive than that normally garnered from traditional interviewing techniques.

The interview may last for several hours in its efforts to explore all aspects of a given subject.

The interviews are usually recorded, so that a complete transcript is available for analysis.

Since the extended interview approach is relatively expensive, small samples are generally used; and since extended cooperation is required, the sample is generally nonrepresentative. Interpretation is time consuming, difficult, and often highly subjective. Despite these limitations, extended interviews are widely used because they often provide insights into behavior that would otherwise be overlooked. Such interviews are particularly useful in providing hypotheses that can be translated into products or marketing communications that can be tested for appeal or incorporated into more traditional survey techniques for verification or rejection.

SUMMARY

Marketing research is an essential ingredient of marketing. Without sound marketing research data upon which to base a marketing plan one has little guidance in devising marketing strategies and developing effective advertising.

Marketing research is a part of the marketing information system that is designed to gather, process, and disseminate information that will be of value in developing marketing plans and in assessing the progress of company products.

The marketing information system consists of three

parts: (1) internal records, (2) marketing intelligence, and (3) marketing research. Internal records provide data on sales, costs, inventories, cash flow, and so forth. Marketing intelligence consists of those procedures that a company routinely uses to keep abreast of developments in the external environment. Although many sources of information may be used, the company sales force is one of the most important. Marketing research has the task of gathering, evaluating, and reporting specific information needed for company decisions.

Marketing research is important but has its limitations. Because of these limitations, marketing research does not enjoy universal acceptance among marketing and advertising practitioners, although it is widely used by most sophisticated companies.

Distributive research, morphological research, and analytical research are three different marketing research traditions. Distributive research, which is the most basic, is concerned with the questions of "who buys" and "what is bought." Morphological research

is concerned with how decisions are made. Analytical research deals with causal, or "why" type, questions.

Primary research is that research conducted to gather original data to meet a specific need. *Secondary research* refers to information available from published sources. Three basic approaches to gathering primary data are (1) observational techniques, (2) experiments, and (3) surveys.

Surveys are the most widely used method for gathering market data because of their versatility. Basic survey techniques include personal interview, mail surveys, and telephone surveys.

Although marketing research is a systematic and scientific way of gathering information, it still contains a large element of judgment. Three areas of judgment are the determination of research objectives, the construction of the questionnaire, and the sample design.

Motivational research is a form of research developed to overcome some of the response problems associated with traditional research techniques.

QUESTIONS

1. Identify and briefly describe the three major parts of the marketing information system.
2. Explain why marketing research is particularly important for developing effective marketing communications.
3. Identify and discuss the barriers to the use of marketing research mentioned in the chapter.
4. Distinguish between distributive, morphological, and analytical research, pointing up the value of each.
5. Design a simple experiment to measure the effects on sales of a new package design for a food product.
6. What are the primary advantages and disadvantages of personal interview surveys?
7. What are the primary advantages and disadvantages of mail surveys?
8. What are the primary advantages and disadvantages of telephone surveys?
9. Distinguish between probability and nonprobability samples, and indicate the advantages and disadvantages of each.
10. Explain what is meant by *motivational research* and identify the primary reasons for its development.

PROBLEM

Eileen Parsons is the newly appointed marketing research director for the Broadloom Carpet Company. The company is an old-line, moderate-sized company with annual sales of about $80 million, and profits of $4.3 million. The company is successful, highly thought of by both consumers and the trade, and respected by its competitors.

The company owes its success to a succession of managements that had "grown up" in the carpeting business. It had never had a marketing research department, but had operated on management intuition and a sense of the market.

While the firm is financially healthy, there are signs that it has lost touch with the market. Its market share has slipped during the past two or three years, and it has lost several key accounts.

Mr. Foelk, who had been president for over twenty years, recently retired, and the board of directors hired a new president with a background in the home furnishings business and a strong marketing orientation. One of his first acts was to hire Eileen Parsons as marketing research director and give her the job of setting up a small marketing research department.

After Eileen had been on the job for about a week, the president called her to his office for a meeting.

"Eileen," he began, "we know virtually nothing about the carpeting market and, while we are not in trouble yet, we soon will be if we don't start developing some systematic information about the business we are in. I know that we can't do everything at once, so I would like for you to outline a three-year marketing research program which will indicate the kind of information we need to develop, the sequence in which it should be developed, the kind of research approaches—personal interview, mail survey, and so forth—that seem appropriate, and the types of samples we should use at each stage of the research.

"Do you think you could get back to me in a couple of days with your thinking and the rationale behind it. I'm not thinking of specific projects or costs at this point. Just the general approach we should follow."

Assignment:

What should Eileen recommend?

Forecasting and
The Communications Budget

Cold Tablets

A few years ago, a family controlled company held a major share of the cold tablet market. Each year the president of the company asked the marketing department to prepare a forecast of industry and company sales along with an estimated expense budget as a first step in the preparation of advertising and promotion plans. Using a variety of forecasting techniques, the marketing department would prepare their best estimates of sales and expenses and submit the results to the president of the company for preliminary approval. Inevitably, the president sent the forecast back with instructions to "increase the forecest because it did not provide the profit level desired by the family." While some negotiation always took place between family desires and the marketing department's estimates, the forecast that was finally accepted was unrealistically inflated.

By the middle of the cold tablet season, it usually became apparent that sales were falling well short of objectives and company profits were being squeezed. Whereupon, the company president would order an immediate reduction in advertising expenditures in

order to salvage profits. Since cold tablets tend to be highly responsive to advertising, the budget cuts depressed sales even further. The results were predictable. Under this system, it was impossible to carry out a systematic, well-planned advertising program. Over a period of time, market shares decreased, and the brands eventually disappeared from the market.

Beer

A major brewing company traditionally used a two-step approach to forecast sales. The first step involved a forecast of sales by distributor territory which was made by the company's research department. The forecast took into consideration both industry and company share trends. It used population data from the Department of Commerce to estimate the number of eighteen-year-olds coming into the beer market and involved a number of other economic indicators that, historically, had influenced the sales of beer.

The second step was for members of the research department to visit with each distributor so that the distributor could review the forecast for his area in the light of his knowledge of competitive activity and trends in his market. On the basis of these visits, the forecasts were revised in order to provide a realistic reflection of both the research department's estimate and the distributors' local knowledge. The result was a realistic forecast that served as a basis for marketing planning.

Dog Food

Alpo dry dog food was introduced into the Miami and Buffalo markets with promotion expenditures that were estimated at a national rate of $14 million. On the basis of test market results, Allen Products, the manufacturer of Alpo, made a decision concerning the future of its new dry dog food brand. Two factors concerning the test markets are noteworthy: the size of the test market expenditure reflects confidence in the size of the dry dog food market; the use of test markets indicates the importance Allen Products attaches to the need to refine its share estimates prior to committing major resources to the national expansion of the brand.

These three examples point up the role of forecasting in marketing. In the case of cold tablets, the forecast used was arbitrary and capricious; the consequence was a marketing failure. In the beer example, a thoughtful and systematic approach to forecasting provided the company with realistic estimates upon which to base its marketing programs. Finally, the use of test markets by Alpo reflects a common method used by major companies to refine sales forecasts for individual brands and emphasizes the importance attached to accurate forecasts before major commitments of company resources are made.

In this chapter we will examine two critical variables in the marketing plan—*forecasts* and the establishment of *communication budgets*. These two variables are intimately bound together and govern the magnitude of the marketing effort.

FORECASTING

It is hard to overestimate the importance of accurate sales forecasts in the planning of company activities. The company forecast serves as the basis for planning levels of production, the amounts of raw material that will be required, the extent to which capital investments must be made, the salary budgets the company can afford, and the communication expenditures that can be made. If the forecast is too high, unnecessary expenses will be incurred and company resources dissipated. If the forecast is too low, sales and profit opportunities will be irretrievably lost. And, forecast-

ing is not an exact science. Misjudgments are made. Even under the best of conditions, an accurate forecast is often a delicate balance of errors.

Forecasting is a top management responsibility. Although the mechanics of forecasting can be delegated to the marketing or research departments, the ultimate responsibility remains that of management. The final forecast that is used for planning company activities carries the sanction of management to whom has been entrusted the welfare of the company.

A detailed discussion of forecasting and forecasting techniques is beyond the scope of this book. Yet, a general review of the types of forecasts that are often made and the major methods used is desirable because the marketing forecast is an indispensable part of the marketing review section of the marketing plan.

Types of Forecasts

Generally speaking, there are four types of forecasts that may be necessary for individual products, depending upon the nature of the product and the competitive environment within which it is marketed. These are forecasts of general enconomic activity, industry forecasts, product or brand forecasts, and company forecasts.

General Forecasts of Economic Activity. The general level of economic activity in the United States is reflected in the Gross National Product (GNP). The GNP is the value of all goods and services sold in the United States within a given year. Each year, estimates of the GNP are made by the President's Council of Economic Advisors, by a number of leading economists, and by many major companies. There is a reasonably consistent relationship between the GNP and advertising expenditures in the United States, although advertising expenditures as a percent of GNP have decreased somewhat in the past three decades. Immediately prior to World War II, advertising averaged about 3 percent of GNP; today, it averages around 2 percent. One reason for this decrease is that today's GNP has a relatively high quotient of government expenditures and service industries compared to earlier GNPs, neither of which are as advertisable as traditional GNP components. However, predictions of an increase in GNP indicate an increase in general economic activity which, in turn, signals increased sales and optimistic forecasts for individual industries and companies. Some industries, such as the automotive industry, major appliances, and construction are closely related to fluctuations in GNP. For these industries, forecasts of GNP should play a prominant role in making estimates of industry sales. For other industries less closely tied to general economic activity, fluctuations in GNP may not be a major consideration.

Industry Forecasts. Regardless of whether GNP is used to arrive at a forecast for a particular industry, the industry forecast is of critical importance in determining sales of the individual companies making up that industry. Generally, when an industry is depressed the forecasts of the companies composing that industry are also depressed. Conversely, when increased industry sales are anticipated optimistic forecasts and increased promotional activities characterize the behavior of individual producers. A case in point is the market for coffee in 1977–78. High and rising coffee prices resulted in decreased per capita consumption as consumers decreased their coffee purchases and switched to other beverages such as tea. By mid-1977, it was estimated that the market for regular coffee would decrease by 20–25 percent. These estimates led to a sharp reduction in the volume forecasts and promotional activities for traditional brands of coffee and an increase in product development and test marketing of lower priced coffee substitutes such as General Foods' Mellow Roast (half coffee and half natural grains) and Nestle's Sunrise (54 percent coffee and 46 percent chicory).

Occasionally, an individual brand will buck industry trends and plan increased volume despite declining industry sales. In such instances, however, the review section of the marketing plan should contain persuasive reasons to justify optimism, such as: (1) clear-cut product or program superiorities that are expected to lead to substantial brand switching; (2) recent test market evidence that the brand is gaining share at a rate that offsets industry declines; or (3) firm evidence that a number of minor brands will drop out of the market as a result of economic pressures arising from the declining industry, and that the brand in question will be a major beneficiary of their demise.

Product Forecasts. The end result of examining GNP and industry forecasts is to arrive at a realistic forecast for individual products. Industry changes, of course, are not the only factors entering into the brand forecast, although they are major considerations. The performance of a brand in a particular market always relates to the anticipated effectiveness of its marketing effort vis-a-vis competition. Knowledge of unusual developments by competitors as well as the private knowledge that a company has of the effectiveness of its own marketing activities will influence the share of

market it expects to obtain. For example, assuming no significant changes in the magnitude or effectiveness of the marketing programs of a particular brand and its competitors, it is reasonable to assume that the brand will hold approximately the same share of market for future periods as it held in the period just completed. On the other hand, any significant changes in marketing programs may lead to shifts in market share. Normally, one of the primary responsibilities of a marketing group is to strengthen its market and/or profit position through the development and implementation of effective strategies. That's what they are paid for.

Company Forecasts. If a company is a single product company, the company forecast is the same as the brand or product forecast. In multiple product companies, however, the company forecast is the aggregate of its brand forecasts. Frequently, company strategy will require a reduced effort behind a particular brand (a holding action) so that company resources may be placed behind brands that hold greater promise. Each product manager generally finds himself in competition with other product managers for a share of the company resources. It is this competition that recommends the product manager system to many companies. Ultimately, it is the overall welfare of the company, not the individual brand, that is the overriding concern of top management. As a consequence, company strategy may sometimes invoke policy decisions that constrain the activities of individual brands.

METHODS OF FORECASTING

There are a number of methods for forecasting industry sales, none of which is infallible. For this reason, forecasters will often use a number of approaches, hoping for convergence within a narrow range of values. In the last analysis, however, there is a certain subjectivity in the sales forecast, regardless of the sophistication of the forecasting techniques employed. In the following material, a number of common forecasting techniques are briefly described.

Trend Extension. There is a group of forecasting techniques that are frequently used because of their simplicity; these techniques can be classified as *trend extensions*. The trend extension approach may be highly successful for markets that have exhibited a historic pattern of stability, but it is full of pitfalls for volatile markets. Trend extension requires a history of relevant data. For example, if sales data for several years are available, future sales may be forecast by extrapolating the historic sales trend. The assumption underlying trend extension is that the future will be similar to the past and there will be no major changes in the variables that influence sales. There are a number of approaches to trend extension, some more sophisticated than others, but all are subject to the assumption that the future will be similar to the past.

Proportion of GNP. For industries which tend to fluctuate with GNP, the forecaster can attempt to identify the nature of this relationship. For example, automobile sales tend to vary with GNP because auto purchases generally increase as national income rises and decrease as national income declines. However, the relationship is seldom a one-to-one relationship; GNP can provide a rough gauge of automobile sales, but forecasts of the automobile industry must be refined through the use of other factors such as consumer buying intention studies and disposable income.

Simple Regression Analysis. Regression analysis is a statistical technique that is used to extrapolate historical trends. Step-by-step procedures for its calculation can be found in most introductory statistical texts. Through simple regression analysis, one can identify the slope of a line that best describes historical data. Figure 7–1 shows a scatter diagram that reflects time in years on the horizontal axis and case sales for a hypothetical product on the vertical axis. Sales for each year are plotted in this diagram. The line in the diagram represents that line that best describes or "fits" the sales points. One can, of course, prepare a scatter diagram and sketch in a line on the basis of visual inspection. Such a projection

may be fairly accurate, but not as precise as the line derived from regression analysis.

Multiple Regression. A somewhat more sophisticated procedure for forecasting sales uses multiple regression. Whereas the simple regression example shown in figure 7–1 uses only two variables—time and case sales—multiple regression seeks to build a forecasting equation using several variables. For example, a demand equation for evaporated milk might be built by taking into consideration such historical variables as the price of whole milk, the price of evaporated milk, historical sales of evaporated milk, disposable income, sales of other milk substitutes, the number of children under the age of one year (because of the use of evaporated milk for infant feeding), and the sales of prepared infant formulas. The particular variables used are generally selected on the basis of judgment, and various combinations are manipulated mathematically until an acceptable fit is found.

Leading Indicators. The dream of all forecasters is to find one or more leading indicators that can be used for forecasting purposes. A leading indicator is a variable that changes in the same direction, but *ahead* of the sales to be forecast. For example, the number of live births is a leading indicator for a variety of children's products ranging from clothes to baby food to toys. The number of new housing starts is a leading indicator for a variety of appliances and other major household items, and the number of new automobiles sold is a leading indicator for replacement parts. Usually, leading indicators need to be modified by other variables for accurate forecasting purposes, yet they provide a general framework for the forecast.

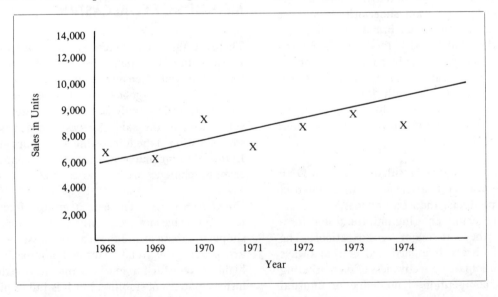

Figure 7–1. Scatter diagram and regression line

Subjective Methods

The trend extension methods referred to above are all based on the extension of past data. There is no assurance that people will behave the same way in the future. As a consequence, a number of forecasting techniques have been devised that attempt to find out, either directly from customers or from other knowledgeable individuals, what the future promises. These methods are often referred to as *subjective methods* because they are based on opinions rather than on hard, objective data. Three frequently used subjective methods are: (1) surveys of buyer intentions, (2) sales force opinion, and (3) expert opinion.

Surveys of Buyer Intentions. Since all forecasting is an attempt to estimate what buyers are likely to do in the future, one approach is to survey all potential buyers for a given product or a representative sample of potential buyers in order to obtain this information from the buyers themselves. The assumption underlying the technique is that people know what they will buy and are willing to share this knowledge. For consumer convenience goods, such as grocery items and personal care products, such surveys often take the form of brand preference surveys in which a sample of consumers are asked to indicate their brand preferences among the available brands. If the survey sample is representative and if the respondents reply honestly, this approach should provide a strong basis for forecasting sales. One limitation, however, is that it fails to take into account future competitive activities and the extent to which this activity will modify existing preferences. Nonetheless, this approach is widely used, and commercial research services (such as *Product Q*) that routinely conduct such surveys have a reasonably good record of forecasting success.

The two areas in which the greatest use of buyer intention surveys has been made are consumer durable goods and industrial products. In terms of consumer durables, several research services regularly produce reports of buying intentions.[1] These reports have proven themselves useful, but not wholly accurate, for short-range consumer durable forecasts. In the field of *industrial buying*, intention surveys for plant, equipment, and materials have been carried out by a number of agencies. Two of the best known capital expenditure surveys are the one conducted by

the U.S. Department of Commerce in collaboration with the Securities and Exchange Commission and one conducted annually by McGraw-Hill, under the auspices of its publication, *Business Week*.

Surveys of buying intentions have been used for a wide variety of products, but they are generally most satisfactory where the number of customers is small, the relationship between buyers and the seller is relatively close, and the costs for obtaining the data is relatively low. For example, a chemical company that has less than a hundred customers for a particular chemical that is purchased in large quantities would generally find intention surveys more useful and economical than a consumer product manufacturer such as Coca-Cola which has millions of potential customers, most of whom buy in relatively small quantities.

Sales Force Opinion. Many companies obtain estimates from their sales forces as a part of their forecasting procedure. The assumption underlying this practice is that sales representatives are more likely to be familiar with customers' reactions and more aware of competitive activity than personnel in the home office. There is a great deal of merit in this assumption since sales reps, in their day-to-day activities, are intimately involved with customers, or with retailers where extended lines of distribution are employed. Sales reps are also more aware of the extent to which point-of-sale material or other forms of local promotion are being used and often have a more current (although unsystematic) picture of sales than do analysts in the home office. On the negative side, sales reps are often "overinfluenced" by purely local activities and usually unaware of larger economic developments and of company plans; further, their perceptions are often distorted by their own proclivities for optimism or pessimism and by their recent experiences in the field.

Few companies use sales personnel's estimates without some modification, and they are most frequently used as checks against home office forecasts. One advantage of involving sales people in the forecasting procedure is that it provides them with a sense of participation; they are often more willing to accept the final forecast and the sales quotas derived from it.

Expert Opinion. Closely related to sales force opinion is the use of opinions from other experts in the product field. These experts may be other company executives who, by virtue of their experience, are able to make valuable contributions to the forecast; they may be company distributors; or they may be members of independent consulting firms. In the brewery

1. Among the better known services are the Survey Research Center at the University of Michigan, Sindlinger and Company, The Conference Board, Inc., and the Commercial Credit Corporation. For a discussion of buyer intention surveys, see: "How Good Are Consumer Pollsters?" *Business Week* (November 9, 1969): 108–10.

example used at the beginning of this chapter opinions of company distributors were sought.

Automobile manufacturers routinely solicit estimates of sales directly from their dealers, and many companies regularly subscribe to forecasts from public and private agencies that sell periodic forecasts of both short-term and long-term business conditions. The advantages of obtaining expert opinions are that: estimates can often be obtained quickly; diverse points of view can be obtained and reconciled to gain a "balanced" forecast; and often, particularly in the case of new products, there is no alternative source of data upon which to base forecasts.

For the most part, subjective methods are used to supplement other sources of data and to serve as a check on estimates derived from trend analysis or from other, more sophisticated techniques. Because forecasting is always an uncertain undertaking, forecasters try to bring as many sources of information as possible to bear on their task.

Market Testing

The use of special tests in selected markets is particularly useful in estimating demand for new products where there is no historic data from which to draw. Test markets are also useful for determining the effects of increased expenditures, sales promotion devices, price changes, or other major changes in existing programs. One problem with market testing is the possibility that the results from a single market will not be characteristic of the response from other markets and in other sections of the country. To compensate for this shortcoming, a number of test markets (usually three or more) are selected from different geographic regions and are carefully monitored through retail audits of purchases and through consumer surveys.

REGIONAL AND SEASONAL FORECASTS

Even after a company has arrived at a forecast of total sales for an industry or a brand, it is usually necessary to break down the forecast by individual regions, or in terms of seasonal factors. This step is necessary to provide guidance in allocating communications expenditures in terms of geographic regions and months of the year. Swimming suits, for example, are sold primarily during the spring and summer months, although they may enjoy a year around market in extreme southern areas blessed by mild winters. Diet foods also have a seasonal pattern that picks up in the spring and summer; hot drinks such as coffee and hot

chocolate enjoy peaks in sales during the winter months. Similarly, gift chocolates and greeting cards may concentrate as much as 80 percent of their annual sales around special seasonal occasions such as Christmas, Valentine's Day, and Mother's Day. This is the reason why greeting card companies such as Hallmark do not employ year around advertising schedules; instead, they concentrate their advertising appropriation in television "specials" immediately preceding peak demand periods. Few products are completely immune to seasonal variations, although these variations are often less extreme than the examples cited above.

Regional variations in sales are also characteristic for most products and brands. Straight whiskeys, for example, have their highest per capita consumption in a band of states extending across the southern part of the country and up the west coast. Blends of straights tend to concentrate in the upper midwest, and Scotch whiskeys have the bulk of their sales in the major metropolitan areas of New York, Washington D.C., Miami, Cleveland, St. Louis, Chicago, Los Angeles, and San Francisco. The per capita consumption of dry dog food is 20–50 percent over the U.S. average in the East Central, North Central, and South Central states, and rice cereals do not sell well in the south.

The regional variations for many products are ideosyncratic and based on obscure or historical developments. Nonetheless, these variations are of the utmost importance to the advertiser whose success depends upon the wise allocation of available funds. Where geographic patterns are unique to an industry, knowledge of regional variations must be derived from industry sources such as trade associations, from a variety of government or private sources, from consumer surveys, or from national retail audits.

In the absence of industry sales by geographic areas, companies often develop *indexes of buying power*. Thus, a marketer might assume that the pattern of sales for his product will follow the distribution of population, retail sales, automotive sales, general merchandise sales, or some other measureable factor. The distribution of the variables listed above can be obtained from *Sales Management's Survey of Buying Power*. For example, a producer of headache remedies might assume that users of this product type are distributed uniformly throughout the population. So, if the state of Virginia accounted for 2.31 percent of the U.S. population, it would account for 2.31 percent of the headache remedy market. Generally, a single factor such as population is an inadequate indicator of sales opportunity. Other variables such as disposable income, population density, retail drug sales, or the number of doctors per thousand families might be important variables in this particular case. This possibility leads to the development of multiple-factor indexes, with each factor being assigned a specific weight in the index.

One of the better known, general-purpose, multiple-factor indexes of area demand is that published in the *Survey of Buying Power*. This index is given by the formula:

$$B_i = .5y_i + .3r_i + .2p_i$$

where:

B_i = percentage of total national buying power found in area i.

y_i = percentage of national disposable personal income originating in area i.

r_i = percentage of national retail sales in area i.

p_i = percentage of national population located in area i.

Sales Management does not contend that his general purpose index will apply to all products; it does contend, however, that this index does reflect the market for many goods that are neither luxury items nor low-priced staples.

Regional market potential estimates reflect the opportunity for an entire industry, not for the individual company. The individual company must estimate its market share based on such factors as distribution, the level of competitive activity, and past performance in the area. In other words, given the market potential in a particular area, companies still must estimate the share of that potential they can acquire. This share represents the company's sales estimate.

DETERMINING THE COMMUNICATIONS BUDGET

The purpose of forecasting is to arrive at a sales projection that will enable a company to compute its income, expenses, communications budget, and profit. Figure 7–2 shows a simplified pro forma budget for a hypothetical company. In figure 7–2, after all expenses *except* advertising and promotion have been subtracted from income, the residual of $9,033,000 is sometimes referred to as "contribution to profit." The contribution figure is what the company has to work with in order to promote the brand *and* to make a profit. Obviously, the more that is spent for marketing, the less the profit will be. In this particular instance, 60 percent of the contribution has been allocated for marketing, leaving a profit before taxes of $3,613,200. The critical role of forecasting can now be seen. Let us assume that actual sales were 10 percent less than forecast, or $48,220,200 instead of $53,578,000. Cost of goods would also be decreased by 10 percent, of course, but gross margin would be decreased by $1,668,600, to $15,017,400. Assuming that no reductions were made in advertising and sales promotion expenditures, profits before taxes would drop from $3,613,200 to $1,944,600—a decrease of approximately 46 percent.

Is $5,419,000 the proper amount to spend for marketing in this case? That all depends. It depends upon the nature of the market and the level of competitive activity. It depends upon how much profit the company needs. It depends on the objectives of the company. It depends upon the effectiveness of the company's programming and the persuasiveness of its creative effort. In short, there is no easy answer. Eldridge has pointed out:

Sales (1000's cases)	6,230,000	
Income ($8.60/case)	$53,578,000	
Minus: cost of goods		
(including packaging)	36,892,000	
Gross Margin		$16,686,000
Expenses		
Sales expense (including		
sales force, freight,		
and warehousing)	3,682,500	
Administrative overhead	2,162,000	
Other fixed and semifixed		
expenses	1,808,500	
Total expense		7,653,000
Contribution to profit		9,033,000
Less: Marketing expense (60%)		5,419,800
Profit before taxes		$3,613,200

Figure 7–2. Pro-forma operating budget

Management is called upon to make no decisions that are more important, or that can more significantly affect the health, growth, and profitability of the business than those involving the marketing budget. In many companies whose success depends upon effective marketing programs, the cost of marketing is the largest controllable expense; in some companies the cost of marketing a product is even greater than the cost of producing it—including raw materials. labor. and packaging costs. [2]

There are a number of methods that are used to establish the communications appropriation, some better than others, but none wholly satisfactory. Each of them, however, speaks to some aspect of the allocation process. Five such methods, along with their advantages and disadvantages are discussed below.

The Affordable Method

One of the least effective methods of determining the advertising and sales promotion budget is to spend what the company can afford. Generally, the determining factor is the level of profit required by the company. In such cases, management earmarks a given amount for profit, and any excess funds in the contribution portion of the budget may be spent for marketing communications. Joel Dean, an economist, has puckishly suggested that everything above a respectable return on capital could be spend for advertising " . . . since excess earnings have low utility to management as such, compared with the *possible* contribution of continuous advertising to the eternal life of the firm."[3] Generally, this approach is most likely to be used in companies where advertising objectives are poorly defined and often serve a general public relations function, as is sometimes the case with public utilities.

The problem with the affordable method, of course, is that it fails to take into consideration the marketing job that has to be done. Consequently, the amount appropriated for advertising and sales promotion may be excessive for the task or sadly inadequate.

At the same time, though, this approach tacitly recognizes the role of budget constraints. Profit *is* a necessary function of a firm. Without an adequate level of profit over the long term, businesses simply do not survive. True, the amount of profit required may vary year by year, and on some occasions a firm may forego profit entirely because of investment requirements or

marketing demands. Nonetheless, the requirement for profit normally places an upper limit on the marketing appropriation.

Percentage of Sales Method

Many companies prefer to set their communications budget as a percentage of sales, or in terms of a fixed amount per case or unit. Automobile manufacturers typically budget a certain amount per car, and oil companies tend to set their communications budget as a fraction of a cent for each gallon of gasoline sold. Similarly, packaged goods manufacturers often appropriate a certain amount per case.

When such appropriations are based on projected or forecast sales, the approach appears to have a certain merit in that the greater the forecast, the greater the expenditure. Conversely, during times of depressed forecasts, communications expenditures are cut accordingly. In addition, when by tacit agreement all factors in the industry utilize a similar percentage advertising wars are averted and a certain stability is incurred by the industry.

Although many companies use this approach, it does have major limitations. First, appropriations are set by anticipated sales or availability of funds rather than in terms of marketing opportunities. Second, the percentage spent, or the amount allocated per unit, is often arbitrary and may bear little relationship to the amount that should be spent in order to develop the total market effectively. Finally, competitive positions tend to become fixed since all competitors are utilizing similar advertising to sales ratios, and real competition is at a minimum.

On the positive side, this approach recognizes the need for a minimum expenditure level to keep abreast of competition. As demand increases, competitive appropriations generally increase, and the firm that fails to keep pace in terms of expenditures may reasonably anticipate a decline in share. Thus, it is reasonable for a firm to establish a standard expenditure rate based on a percentage of sales or a fixed allocation per unit *provided* it is also recognized that marketing opportunities and problems may require a deviation from this standard. One advantage of having a standard is that it enables the firm to evaluate deviations from the standard in terms of the costs involved in pursuing a particular marketing opportunity.

Share of Advertising Method

There is a truism in marketing which states that "all other things being equal, share of market will equal share of advertising." And, while "all other things"

2. Clarence E. Eldridge, *The Marketing Budget and Its Allocation in the Advertising Budget* (New York: Association of National Advertisers, Inc., 1967), p. 25.
3. Joel Dean, *Managerial Economics* (Englewood Cliffs, New Jersey: Prentice-Hall, Inc., 1951), p. 368.

are seldom equal, this concept serves as the basis for the share of advertising method of allocating advertising expenditures. This approach, based on empirical studies in the food and drug fields, was offered by J.O. Peckham, executive vice-president of the A.C. Nielsen Company in the mid-1960s. Peckham observed that, over time, there is a relationship between share of market and share of advertising. If a marketer keeps his product and advertising appeals competitive with the rest of the field, the best insurance for maintaining or increasing market share is to keep share of advertising at a point somewhat ahead of share of sales. For *new* brands being introduced into the market, Peckham found that the initial rate of expenditure should be approximately double the share of sales desired. For example, assume that a new brand is being marketed in a product field in which annual sales are $60 million and annual advertising expenditures are $8 million. Also assume that the market share objective for the new brand is 25 percent. Then

Annual sales goal (25 percent of
$60,000,000)   = $15,000,000
Annual advertising allocation
(50 percent of $8,000,000)   = $ 4,000,000

The *disadvantages* of this approach are that: all other variables are seldom equal; it tends to focus on advertising to the exclusion of other marketing variables; and it does not take profit needs into consideration.

Its *advantages* are that: it emphasizes the need to be aware of competitive activity as one aspect of market performance; it deals with measurable quantities and provides a rough basis for setting the advertising appropriation; and it provides a rough diagnostic tool. For example, if market share consistently lags significantly behind share of advertising, some other aspect of the marketing mix (copy appeals, media selection, product, price, distribution, package, and so forth) is out of kilter and should be re-examined. Or, market share significantly above advertising share may signal an opportunity for improving market position through an increase in advertising expenditures.

Objective and Task Method

In the objective and task method, the firm establishes a sales goal, asks what tasks need to be done to achieve this goal, estimates the cost of each task separately, and then totals these costs to arrive at the marketing allocation required. The objective and task method has a certain logic and appeal that accounts for its growing popularity. Charles A. Mortimer, who

rose through advertising and marketing to the presidency of General Foods, has stated the following:

> The task method is built brick by brick; not pulled out of a hat, or devined with a willow wand. . . . It is based on a concrete estimate of the job to be done. It uses extensively past advertising experience—all that is available—but never accepts any rule of thumb or past statistical relation as a sufficient guide for expenditures without reexamination of the nature of the task and the most promising method of accomplishing it *this* year—not *last* year. It involves constant awareness of what the competitors are doing with respect to advertising themes and expenditures, but it does not blindly follow the competitors program.
>
> The only safe assumption to make in determining advertising expenditures is that each year—or campaign—involves a task that is *new* in some important respect. Old measurements and old answers, accepted uncritically, are not good enough.[4]

On the surface, the task and objective method appears to be the answer to prayer. But its not. Its major strengths are its emphasis on situational analysis, its recognition of the dynamic nature of marketing, and the need to identify the job to be done. It introduces a note of realism into marketing allocations by relating the variety and magnitude of the marketing tasks with the size of the allocation. And this is all to the good.

On the negative side, the objective and task method has two shortcomings: it fails to consider the need for profit and whether a particular objective is worth pursuing in terms of its costs; and it oversimplifies, by implication, the difficulty of determining how much effort will be required to accomplish a given task. Marketing is filled with risks. That is one of its charms. And the best laid schemes do not always accomplish intended goals. That is one of its frustrations.

A Point of View

From a practical point of view, most sophisticated companies use all of these methods in arriving at their marketing allocation.

1. As in the affordable method, the availability of funds and the need for profit *is* a consideration.
2. As in the percent-of-sales method, management does identify a standard or normal rate of expenditure that is based on a percent of sales or a fixed allocation per unit or case.

4. Charles G. Mortimer, Jr., "How Much Should You Spend on Advertising," in *Advertising Handbook*, Rogert Barton, ed. (Englewood Cliffs, New Jersey: Prentice-Hall, Inc.), pp. 113–15.

3. As in the share of advertising method, they do recognize that there is a relationship between share of market and share of advertising, and they often use this rough relationship in defining the level of the marketing appropriation.
4. Finally, all of these approaches are consolidated in the task and objective approach which specifically takes into consideration the variety of tasks that must be done in order to accomplish marketing objectives.

Let's take a look at how this pragmatic approach might be applied by a sophisticated company. To do this, we will introduce three new terms: *return on investment* (ROI), *economic profit,* and *payout plan.*

Return on Investment (ROI).   Return on investment, which will hereafter be referred to as ROI, is a profit criterion frequently used by firms to determine whether they should or should not compete in a particular product field. ROI is a ratio between the capital investment required to enter a business and the annual amount of profit the business will produce. Take the simplified operations statement used in figure 7–2 to demonstrate this concept. The sales income in figure 7–2 is $53,578,000. Let us assume that it cost the company $10,000,000 in capital investment to build the plant and buy the equipment needed to produce this product. Let us also assume that the firm requires an annual ROI of 20 percent before taxes. In order to meet its profit requirements, the $53,578,000 in sales must produce a profit of $2,000,000 ($10,000,000 x .20 = $2,000,000). This $2,000,000 may be considered as a cost of doing business since this level of profit is a policy requirement for making the necessary capital investment.

Economic Profit.   Economic profit refers to that profit that a firm makes over and above its minimal profit requirements. The firm in figure 7–2 made a contribution to profits of $9,033,000. Since the firm only needs $2,000,000 in profits to meet its ROI objectives, it is earning an *economic profit* of $7,033,000 ($9,033,000 − $2,000,000 = $7,033,000) *before* marketing expenses. This $7,033,000, referred to as *available funds,* is the amount the firm has available for economic profit and marketing expenditures.

Now, let us assume that, normally, the firm expects to realize 30 percent of the available funds for economic profit, and to allocate 70 percent of these funds for marketing. Then, normal expenditures for a sales level of $53,588,000 would be $4,923,100. These relationships are shown below:

Sales (1000s cases)	6,230,000
Income from sales	$53,578,000
Contribution to profit	9,033,000
Less: required ROI	2,000,000
Available funds ($1.13/case)	7,033,000
Less: economic profit (30%)	2,109,900
Normal marketing allocation (70%)	4,923,100
Normal marketing allocation as a percent of sales:	9.2%
Normal marketing allocation per case	$0.79

Now, as long as the marketing request for funds falls within the area of $0.79 per case or 9.2 percent of sales, the marketing department and top management will not have any problems; provided, of course, that the marketing forecast appears realistic, the brand is doing reasonable well, the strategies and plans seem to be well conceived, and the creative approach doesn't offend anyone. From management's point of view, the marketing appropriation is in the *normal* range of the cost of doing business, they are getting their profit goodies, and all's well with the world.

But now, let's blow up utopia. Let us suppose that the market is in a real turmoil. A major competitor has just come up with a smashing creative approach; another competitor has launched what appears to be an extremely effective sales promotion program; the company we have been discussing has developed a product improvement that marks a real opportunity for increased sales. In short, the price of doing business has just gone up. And, in the judgement of marketing management, a significant increase in the marketing expenditure is required. This leads us to the concept of payout plans.

Payout Plan

Payout, as it is used here, refers to the length of time it requires a firm to recover an *investment* in marketing. A *payout plan* is a projection into the future that shows funds available, funds spent, and the resulting economic profit. Payout plans may be for any length of time, although they seldom exceed three years because of the difficulty of projecting sales and income with reasonable accuracy beyond this period. Generally, the length of payout plans has been decreasing during the past decade or so because technology and competitive response has tended to shorten the length of time that a product or marketing advantage can be

Table 7-1. Three-year payout

Units and Dollars in Thousands
Except for Cost per Case

	Year 1	Year 2	Year 3
Total market (cases)	31,150.0	32,705.5	34,669.9
Company forecast (cases)	6,230.0	7,552.7	8,667.5
Funds available ($1.13/case)	7,039.9	8,534.6	9,794.3
Expenditures	9,950.0	8,571.5	6,847.3
Economic profit/loss	(2,910.1)	(36.9)	2,947.0
Cumulative economic profit/loss	(2,910.1)	(2,947.0)	-0-
Cost per case	$1.60	$1.13	$0.79
Share of market	20.0%	23.1%	25.0%

maintained. In the 1950s and early 1960s, for example, three year payout plans were common. More recently, one and two year payout plans have become the norm. Table 7-1 illustrates the mechanics of a three year payout plan using the figures we have developed thus far. Note that, in this table, total *available funds* for the entire three-year period are allocated for marketing expenditures; substantial investments in the first two periods cause losses to be incurred. In the third year, marketing expenditures have returned to normal ($0.79 per case), and the investment has been recovered. For the entire period, no economic profit is earned. However, at the end of the three-year period, the firm holds an increased share of an expanded market, and future economic profits will be substantially greater than they have been in the past.

The purpose of the payout plan is to clarify three things for management: (1) the amount of money that will have to be invested to achieve desired results; (2) the length of time during which the investment must be made; and (3) the benefits that will accrue from the investment. With this information, management can make a decision as to whether the risks and potential gain are worth the required investment. The payout approach is commonly used by sophisticated marketers for all new products as well as for other major marketing investments such as business-building tests.

Hedging the Marketing Budget

Both forecasting and budget determination are central considerations in the development of marketing plans. Although sophisticated quantitative models are sometimes used in making these determinations, the dynamics of the marketing situation precludes total reliance on such mechanical approaches. Consequently, the role of experience, judgment, and a sense of marketing opportunity make budget determination as much an art as it is a science.

Since there is always some uncertainty in the marketing forecast, many firms choose to hedge their marketing allocation. A common way of doing this is to hold some amount, say 10 percent, of the budget in reserve, with the stipulation that this reserve will be released for spending *provided* that sales are on forecast after the first six months of the fiscal year. This procedure minimizes the necessity of cutting back the marketing program in order to meet profit objectives if sales lag somewhat behind forecast.

Allocation of the Marketing Budget

Thus far we have talked about determining the total marketing budget. The way in which this total budget will be allocated to particular marketing activities will be dictated by strategic considerations and based on the tasks to be done. For most consumer goods, the bulk of the budget is normally allocated to advertising and sales promotion. Where special objectives and strategies are an important part of the marketing plan, substantial expenditures may be made in research, market tests, or other special activities.

SUMMARY

The company forecast serves as the basis for planning levels of production, the amounts of raw materials that will be needed, the extent to which capital investments must be made, the salary budgets the company can afford, and the communication expenditures that can be made. If the forecast is too high, unnecessary expenses will be incurred and company resources dissipated. If it is too low, sales and profit opportunities may be lost. Because of its crucial nature, forecasting is a top management responsibility.

Four types of forecasts—forecasts of general economic activity (GNP), industry forecasts, product forecasts, and company forecasts—are important to the marketer. Three groups of forecasting methods are: (1) trend extensions, (2) subjective methods, and (3) market tests.

After a forecast of total product sales has been determined, it is usually necessary to decompose, or break down, the forecast in terms of regional areas and seasonal factors in order to provide a basis for the allocation of marketing activity.

Four commonly used methods for determining the communications budget are the affordable method, the percent of sales method, the share of advertising method, and the objective and task method. None of these methods is without flaw. As a consequence, the sophisticated marketer draws lessons from all of them and uses a combination approach to determine the communications budget.

Return on investment (ROI), economic profit, and payout are three concepts often used in the budgeting process. *ROI* is determined by dividing anticipated profit by the capital investment required to produce it. *Economic profit* refers to all profit above that required to meet investment goals. *Payback* is a budgeting procedure that provides for "paying back" a marketing investment within a specified time period .

Including a budget reserve in the communications budget minimizes the impact of forecasting error or unanticipated developments on planned marketing expenditures.

QUESTIONS

1. Explain why the forecast is crucial in the planning of company activities. What are the penalties for a forecast that is too high? For one that is too low?
2. Define what is meant by *GNP*. In what kinds of industries does a forecast of GNP play a role in making industry and company forecasts? Why?
3. Identify some of the conditions that would cause a company to forecast sales increases for a brand in an industry that is stagnant or declining slowly.
4. Explain what is meant by *trend extension* forecasting. What is the primary assumption that underlies its use, and what are its primary limitations?
5. Explain what is meant by a *leading indicator*. Give an example of such an indicator, showing how it might be used.
6. Under what conditions might a survey of buyer intentions be most helpful and least helpful in preparing a forecast for a company brand?
7. Identify the primary advantages and disadvantages of sales-force opinion in preparing forecasts. How are sales-force opinions generally used?
8. What implications do each of the following methods have for setting the communications budget: (a) the affordable method, (b) the percent-of-sales method, (c) the share of advertising method, and (d) the objective and task method?
9. Explain what is meant by the terms: (a) *ROI*, (b) *economic profit*. Relate these concepts to the terms: (a) *profit contribution*, and (b) *available funds*.
10. Explain what is meant by a *payout plan*. Identify how it helps management evaluate a decision to invest additional funds in advertising and promotion.

PROBLEM

Mark Linden, product manager for Cook's Choice instant mix was preparing a marketing plan for the next fiscal year. The pudding market was a relatively stable market, and Cook's Choice held a dominant share. Sales and brand share for the past five years are shown in table 7-2.

Instant pudding mixes, popular both for puddings and pie fillings because of their ease of preparation, were considered by many consumers to be inferior in texture and flavor to regular puddings which took longer to prepare. It was widely felt that these short-

comings of instant pudding mixes had put a ceiling on their market. Cook's Choice's research and development department had been working on an improved formula of the product for several years and, in 1977, had developed an instant pudding product that was comparable to regular puddings in richness, texture, and flavor.

The new mix had been introduced as a "new and improved" product in three test markets in 1978. There were some variations in performance on a market by market basis, but the overall results were highly

Table 7-2. Five-Year Sales and Brand Share Data for Cook's Choice Instant Pudding Mix

	1974	1975	1976	1977	1978
Total mkt. (1000's cs.)	30,550.0	31,466.5	32,095.8	33,219.2	34,547.9
Cook's Choice (1000's cs.)	7,484.7	7,740.8	7,863.5	8,205.1	8,533.3
Market Share	24.5%	24.6%	24.5%	24.7%	24.7%

Table 7-3. Comparison of Cook's Choice test markets with rest of country mix

	Combined Tests Markets		Rest of Country	
	1977	1978	1977	1978
Total market (1000's cs.)	664.4	730.8	32,554.8	33,817.1
Cook's Choice	162.8	208.3	8,042.3	8,325.0
Market share	24.5%	28.5%	24.6%	24.6%

encouraging. The funds available for instant pudding mix were $1.20 per case, of which 65 percent were normally allocated to advertising and sales promotion and 35 percent were retained as profit. In the test markets, however, the company had spent at double the normal rate. A comparison of test market sales compared to the rest of the country is shown in table 7-3.

Mark's question was whether, on the basis of test market results, he should recommend a national program of investment spending to introduce the new product nationally in 1979, and, if so, how long a payout he should recommend.

He knew that competition had been alerted to the product change by the tests markets in 1978, but discussions with R&D personnel had partially assured him that it would take competition at least eighteen to thirty months to duplicate the new product because

the product improvement involved a formula change that would be time consuming to duplicate, a change in the way in which the dry milk ingredient was processed, and a change in cooking temperatures. Even after competition had duplicated the process, it would take them at least six months to acquire the special manufacturing equipment required to manufacture in volume.

Based on the relative consistency of the three test markets, on some consumer tests, and his own evaluation of the new product, Mark felt pretty confident about the test market results.

Assignment

Develop a forecast and spending plan for the national introduction of the new product, recognizing that some kind of a payout plan will be required.

FOUR

Strategies for Product, Brand, Packaging, Pricing, and Distribution

The following three chapters deal with the product, the brand name, packaging, pricing, and distribution. Each of these dimensions of the marketing effort is a channel of communication—a way of expressing the product concept to consumers.

Normally, strategic decisions in all of these areas loom large only for the "new product" and exist as "givens" for an established brand. But, not always. Consumers change. So do markets. A successful product may be driven out of the market if its performance characteristics fail to keep pace with the technological advances of competition. Packaging can become dated and require revision. The brand name itself comes under scrutiny when (1) a product requires repositioning or (2) when new products are developed and the question arises as to whether the new offerings should be sold under the umbrella of an existing brand name (brand extension), or be given brand names of their own. Distribution must continually be examined for its adequacy. Price is a constant problem area, particularly in an economy plagued by inflation and the constant emergence of cheaper substitutes.

Competitive marketing is a dynamic enterprise. The only constants are challenge and change. The marketing review section of the marketing plan must touch every facet of the marketing effort. Wherever a softness or weakness is detected, wherever a new opportunity is perceived, adjustments may have to be made, new strategies may have to be devised, and new plans may have to be developed.

8

Product Strategy

Without a product, there is no marketing. Without a good product, there is little chance of marketing success. The primacy of the product in the marketing enterprise is both an act of faith and a fact of life among successful marketers. Howard M. Morgens, former chairman of the board of Procter and Gamble, the nation's largest advertiser, has observed:

> The only way you can succeed in business is with a good product. You can't do it with advertising. It all gets down to the fact that if you've got a good product, you can be successful with a reasonable marketing expenditure, but if you haven't got the product, the surest way to go broke is to pour your money behind it.[1]

The concept of *product* is not a simple one, however. Witness the following examples.

Sure

Sure is an antiperspirant marketed by Procter and Gamble. It is packaged in an aerosol can. According to its label, the product is aluminum chlorohydrate in

---

an antiperspirant base of propellant 11S, propellant 12, isopropyl myistrate, quaternium-18 hectorite, S.D. alcohol 40, fragrance, citric acid, and water. According to its advertising, the product is confidence. And, according to its use, the product is an antiperspirant, although many consumers think of it as a deodorant. What *is* the product?

Purina Dog Chow

When Purina Dog Chow was introduced in the early 1950s, it was a new form of dry dog food that was more palatable than competitive brands, and contained the sixteen basic nutrients that a dog was known to need. Based on an advertising theme, "New Purina Dog Chow makes dogs eager eaters," it quickly became the nation's number one dry dog food.

During the past twenty-five years, Ralston Purina has made many changes in Purina Dog Chow. Nutritional research at Purina's research farm has led to the discovery of other nutrients, with the result that the number of nutrients has been increased from sixteen to over forty. Manufacturing and ingredient changes have made Purina Dog Chow even more palatable than the initial formulation; ingredients have been added to facilitate the transition from other commer-

1. John S. Wright, Daniel S. Warner, Willis L. Winter, Jr., and and Sherilyn K. Ziegler, *Advertising,* 4th ed. (New York: McGraw-Hill Book Company, 1977), p. 81.

cial dog foods to Purina Dog Chow without untoward effects on the dog's digestive system. This was done because, frequently, dogs experience a period of diarrhea when their diet is changed. As a result of these formula modifications, Purina Dog Chow is now dramatically different from its initial formulation. Its package design has undergone a number of minor changes; different advertising themes have been used during the history of the brand; and even the name has been changed. It used to be *New* Purina Dog Chow. It is still the nation's number one dry dog food. Is Purina Dog Chow the same product it was twenty-five years ago? Many consumers, who have been buying it for years, think that it is.

Automobiles

Consider the following hypothetical—but not impossible—situation. Mr. Ramirez and Ms. Jackson bought the same model of new car on the same day, but from different dealers. The cars were identical in terms of color, trim, upholstery, and accessories. Within a month, both cars developed carboration problems. Both owners took them back to their respective dealers. Ramirez's dealer was friendly, cooperative, and helpful. She fixed the car without charge and gave Ramirez another car to drive while his car was in the shop. Jackson's dealer was uncooperative and suspicious. He fixed the car reluctantly, without charge, but did not give Jackson a car to drive while her car was in the shop. Neither car had recurrent problems with its carboration. During the next five years, both cars had the same mechanical failures—all minor—at about the same time. Ramirez always took his car to the dealer from whom he had bought it and was always satisfied with their work. Jackson did not go back to the dealer from whom she had purchased the car. She took it to another garage, and she was always satisfied with their work. After five years, Ramirez said that the car was the best one he had ever owned and that he was going to buy the same brand again. Jackson said that it was the worst car she had ever owned, and she would never buy that brand again. Were they talking about the same product?

What *is* a product?

DEFINITION OF A PRODUCT

The foregoing examples are designed to point up the complexity of what we mean by the term *product*. A product is not a simple thing. Philip Kotler has sug-

gested that one way to resolve this complexity is to recognize that every product is really *three* products. This is, a product can be defined in three different ways. The three products are the *tangible* product, the *extended* product, and the *generic* product. [2]

The Tangible Product

The *tangible* product is the physical entity or service that is offered to consumers. It is the *object* that is sold. In the case of Sure, the object is an antiperspirant in an aerosol can that is composed of aluminum chlorohydrate in an antiperspirant base of propellant 11S, propellant 12, isopropyl myistrate, quaternium-18 hectorite, S.D. alcohol 40, fragrance, citric acid, and water. In the case of Purina Dog Chow, the tangible product is a dry dog food that has a particular appearance and is composed of a variety of nutrients, cereal grains, meat by-products, preservatives, and so forth. In an automobile, the tangible product is a vehicle composed of wheels, formed metal, circuits, valves, cylinders, a distributor, filters, brakes, upholstery, colors, accessories, and whatever else goes into an automobile. The tangible product, in short, is the physical thing that is manufactured.

The Extended Product

The *extended* product is the tangible product along with the entire galaxy of services, warranties, and psychological overtones that accompany it. Theodore Levitt has suggested that competition

> . . . is not between what companies produce in their factories but between *what they add to their factory output in the form of packaging, services, advertising, customer advice, financing, delivery arrangements, warehousing, and other things that people value.* [3]

According to this definition, Mr. Ramirez and Ms. Jackson in the automobile example given earlier were *not* talking about the same product. The difference was dealer attitude and service. They were indeed talking about the same *tangible* product, but it was the *extended* product (the tangible product plus dealer service) that created the satisfactions and dissatisfactions that resulted in different perceptions of the tangible product itself. Ramirez said it was the best car he had ever owned; Jackson said it was the worst she had ever owned.

2. Philip Kotler, *Marketing Management,* 2nd ed. (Englewood Cliffs, New Jersey: Prentice-Hall, Inc., 1972), p. 424.
3. Theodore Levitt, *The Marketing Mode* (New York: McGraw-Hill Book Company, 1969), p. 2.

The Generic Product

The generic product is the benefit that the buyer expects to derive from her purchase. In the case of Sure, the consumer is buying social confidence. In the case of Purina Dog Chow, the purchaser is buying health and well-being for the family pet. In the case of automobiles, different consumers probably buy different things depending upon their unique needs, although status, style, comfort, dependability, and economy may be among their expectations. The point is that the generic product is hardly a product at all; it is a constellation of benefits that the buyer expects to realize from her purchase.

Obviously, these three definitions are interrelated and exert a mutual influence upon one another. The physical appearance of the product—color, style, shape, weight, texture—often add dimensions that have little to do with product performance per se, and contribute to the extended and generic product definitions. A warranty, clearly a part of the extended product definition, can provide assurance that enhances the tangible product's performance in the mind of the consumer. And the generic product (the consumer's expectations) will clearly influence perception of the tangible product's performance.

It is for these reasons that all aspects of the product need to be coordinated so that they contribute to a unified product image. It is the need for this coordination that makes the marketing plan the central document in the marketing and advertising process.

In the broadest sense, taking all of the foregoing product definitions into consideration, a product might be defined as a *bundle of consumer satisfactions*. Yet, even this definition is awkward because consumer satisfaction is not a simple phenomenon. This is true because the degree of satisfaction may be related to the level of consumer expectation or generic product, rather than to the objective performance of the tangible product. A case in point is the major food processor that developed a superior blueberry-muffin mix. In blind product tests, the new mix was strongly preferred by consumers over competitive offerings. The new brand was priced competitively, convenient to make, and obtained wide distribution in test markets. A strong advertising effort, featuring "fresh-picked Michigan blueberries," performed exceedingly well in copy tests. Initial sales in test markets were excellent, but repeat sales didn't materialize. Consumer research revealed that consumers were disappointed in the brand's performance: "It just didn't taste as good as it looked on TV." This occurred despite the fact that consumers preferred this brand to competition in the blind product tests. Thus, disap-

pointment of expectations, not tangible product quality, led to failure to repurchase.

Theories of Product Performance

A number of theories relating consumer expectancies to product performance have been suggested. Anderson, in a survey of the literature, identifies four such theories: *assimilation, contrast, generalized negativity,* and *assimilation-contrast.* Each of these theories has somewhat different implications for advertising.[4]

Assimilation Theory. Assimilation theory is based on psychological findings that discrepancies between a person's beliefs and experiences result in a psychological tension which the individual unconscously resolves by reconciling beliefs and experiences in some way. As applied to marketing, it assumes that if there is a disparity between product expectations and the objective performance of a product, a psychological tension arises which the consumer tries to resolve by bringing personal experiences with the product more in line with expectations. Under this theory, product advertising should overstate product benefits because high expectancies will result in an upward evaluation of product performance.

Contrast Theory. Contrast theory suggests that when expectations are not matched by product performance, the differences will be exaggerated. Under this theory, a slight understatement of product attributes in advertising should lead to increased customer satisfaction—provided, of course, that product claims are not so understated that the consumer buys a competitive product in the first place.

Generalized Negativity Theory. This theory suggests that any disconfirmed expectancy will lead to a "hedonically negative state," which will generalize to the product, with the result that product performance will be downgraded. The implication of this theory is that advertising should be consistent with product, performance, neither overstating nor understating it.

Assimilation-Contrast Theory. This theory, proposed by Hoveland, Harvey and Sherif,[5] suggests that

4. R.E. Anderson, "Consumer Dissatisfaction: The Effect of Disconfirmed Expectancy on Perceived Product Performance," *Journal of Marketing Research* **10** (February, 1973): 38–44.
5. C.I. Hoveland, O.J. Harvey, and Muzafer Sherif, "Assimilation and Contrast Effects in Reactions to Communication and Attitude Change," *Journal of Abnormal and Social Psychology* **55** (July, 1957): 244–52.

minor discrepancies between expectancies and product performance will be assimilated toward the expectation, whereas large discrepancies will tend to be exaggerated (contrast effect). Under this theory, promotion should create expectancies slightly above product performance but within the consumer's range of acceptance.

While each of these theories may provide insight into consumer behavior under highly specialized circumstances, none of them apply equally well to all product purchase situations, nor are they supported by a substantial body of unequivocal research. The central problem with all of them is that they may oversimplify the complex relationship that exists between product performance and expectation and fail to come to grips with the fact that a "product" may be defined in different ways.

Perhaps a more realistic approach to the concept of consumer satisfaction, and one that lends itself to marketing analysis and action, is the two-factor theory suggested by Swan and Combs.[6] This theory was anticipated by Irving S. White who made a distinction between "expressive products" and "utility products" in 1969.[7]

Two-Factor Theory. Swan and Combs suggest that consumers judge products on a limited set of attributes, some of which (determinant attributes) are relatively important in determining satisfaction. Other factors, not critical to satisfaction, are related to dissatisfaction when performance on them is unsatisfactory. In making this distinction, the authors speak of two aspects of performance:

1. *Instrumental performance* refers to a means to a set of ends. This is essentially the performance of the physical product, per se.
2. *Expressive performance* is the performance the consumer considers an end in itself. It involves psychological attributes such as style and expression of the self-concept.

The determinant attributes in a given purchase may be the *expressive* attributes, while the *instrumental* attributes are relatively unimportant. However, inadequate performance of the physical product (instrumental attributes) may lead to dissatisfaction with the purchase. Thus, Swan and Combs point out

that "a determinant attribute leading to dissatisfaction may not be a determinant attribute leading to satisfaction."[8]

The instrumental performance of Swan and Combs (the performance of the physical product, per se) is thus the performance equivalent of Kotler's *tangible* product. Swan and Combs isolate tangible product performance from the complexities of the *extended* product and the *generic* product, and emphasize the role of the tangible product in consumer satisfaction. Howard Morgens was probably talking about the tangible product with his observation that: "You can only succeed with a good product. You can't do it with advertising."

Retail Stores and Services as Products

Thus far, we have discussed products as though they were tangible objects (such as a car, a refrigerator, a baking mix, or a detergent) that consumers buy, take home, and use. However, a retail store is also a product, as is a service such as that provided by a doctor, a dentist, a television repair person or an insurance policy.

A retail store is a product that sells other products. The store itself has tangible attributes and characteristics about which consumers form preferences. The location, appearance, depth and breadth of merchandise assortments, the name brands carried, courtesy of personnel, credit policies, pricing practices, and so forth are all attributes of a store. We speak of a "store image" in the same sense we speak of a "brand image." Ohrbach's advertisement, used as an example in chapter 4, is an instance of advertising in which a retail store is attempting to create a store image that makes it a desirable place to shop.

Similarly, a service such as that provided by a doctor or a TV repair person is also a product from the standpoint of marketing. The individual who offers a service succeeds or fails in terms of her ability to provide consumer satisfaction.

STRATEGIES FOR NEW PRODUCTS

New products are the future of business. Without a continuous flow of new products, the marketing system, as we know it, would probably atrophy and die. Eberhard Scheuing, in a book titled *New Product Management*, estimates that " . . . eighty percent of today's products will have disappeared from the market ten years from now, while an estimated eighty percent of the products that will be sold in the next decade

6. J.E. Swan and L.J. Combs, "Product Performance and Consumer Satisfaction: A New Concept," *Journal of Marketing* **40** (April, 1976): 25–33.
7. Irving S. White, "New Product Differentiation: Physical and Symbolic Dimensions," in *Marketing in a Changing World,* Bernard A. Morin, ed. (Chicago: American Marketing Association, 1969), pp. 99–103.

8. Swan and Combs, "Product Performance," p. 32.

are as yet unknown."[9] Richard Darby reports a survey of successful firms in which the respondents indicated that three-fourths of the sales growth expected in the next four years would come from products first introduced during that period.[10]

Yet, the failure rate of new products is horrendous. In a study of 366 new product introductions, Booz, Allen and Hamilton (a leading consulting firm) found a 33 percent failure rate.[11] Based on a study of new products by 200 leading packaged goods firms, Ross Federal Research Corporation found the failure rate to be as high as 80 percent.[12] Lippincott and Margulies, a leading package design organization, places the failure rate as high as 89 percent.[13] Different studies of new product introductions yield different failure rates, but it is generally recognized that new product risks are high, and failures all too frequent. It is equally obvious that new product failures are expensive in terms of both time and company resources.

Why do so many new products fail? The most common reason is the lack of a significant difference in the tangible product, as viewed by the consumer, from products already being sold in the market place. Thus, Theodore Angelus, who made a study of 75 new product failures in the food and drug industries, found that the major cause of failure was the lack of a significant product difference, as viewed by consumers.[14] Hugh Davidson supports this conclusion in a study of 100 new products, fifty of which failed and fifty of which succeeded.[15] The results of this study, summarized in table 8-1, clearly show that most of the successful products (74 percent) were *better* than competition, while most of the products which failed were either no different, or worse than competition in terms of tangible product performance.

These findings, which are well supported by the pragmatic experiences of marketing and advertising practitioners, lead to the following broad guidelines for new product strategy.[16]

Table 8-1. Comparison of successful and unsuccessful products

Differences from Competition	% of Successful Products	% of Unsuccessful Products
Better than competition	74%	20%
Same as competition	26%	60%
Worse than competition	-	20%
Total	100%	100%

SOURCE: Adapted from J. Hugh Davidson, "Why Most New Consumer Brands Fail," *Harvard Business Review*, **54** (March-April, 1976), p. 119. Copyright © 1976 by the President and Fellows of Harvard College; all rights reserved.

A new product has the greatest chance of success if it is noticeably better than established products on some dimension that is important to consumers. In introducing food products, for example, the product has the greatest chance for success if it tastes better or is more convenient to use than competitive brands. The whole history of convenience foods supports this observation. The marketer who has such a product can introduce it with a good chance of marketing success.

If the new product is not better, but is distinguishably different from competing brands in some way, it has a reasonable chance for success, but the risk is higher. Golden Fluffo is an excellent case in point. As a shortening, the performance of the tangible product is not superior to leading brands such as Crisco; but it looks different—it is yellow in color. As a result of this difference, the marketer has a unique basis for advertising claims and recommended product uses. For example, it makes fried chicken look "richer," and it gives pie crusts a "golden hue."

If the new product is virtually identical with competitive products, it has little chance of marketing success. In this case, the marketing risk is extremely high, and a disproportionate burden is placed on the packaging, the product name, and the advertising. Further, any brand preference that may be formed through heavy promotion tends to be weak and vulnerable to competitive efforts. There is nothing more discouraging than working with an advertising creative group to find a reason why consumers should use such a product rather than established products already on the market when there *isn't* any reason in the tangible product itself. As a consequence, the best advice for such products is, "Don't introduce them. The probabilities are that they will be nothing but trouble." I know. I've been down that route a dozen times.

If the new product is inferior in its tangible performance characteristics to products on the market, it

9. Eberhard E. Scheuing, *New Product Development* (Hinsdale, Illinois: The Dryden Press, 1974), p. 1.
10. Richard H. Darby, "Market Appraisal Equals Market Insurance," in *Developing a Product Strategy,* Elizabeth Marting, ed. (New York: American Management Association, 1959), p. 143.
11. *Management of New Products,* 4th ed. (New York: Booz, Allen and Hamilton, Inc., 1965), p. 9.
12. John T. O'Meara, Jr., "Selecting Profitable Products," *Harvard Business Review,* (January-February, 1961): 83.
13. Burt Schorr, "Many New Products Fizzle, Despite Careful Planning," *Wall Street Journal* (5 April 1961).
14. Theodore L. Angelus, "Why Do Most New Products Fail?" *Advertising Age* (March 24, 1969): 85–86.
15. J. Hugh Davidson, "Why Most New Consumer Brands Fail," *Harvard Business Review* 54 (March-April, 1976): 119.
16. Kenneth E. Runyon, *Consumer Behavior and the Practice of Marketing* (Columbus, Ohio: Charles E. Merrill Publishing Company, 1977), pp. 213–14.

has virtually no hope of success. The best advice is to forget it.

These guidelines, of course, are not absolute. Exceptions can be found in the market place, but they are relatively rare. And, after all, sound marketing decisions are based on playing the odds. In the case of the third and fourth guidelines, the possibility of success is increased if the product can be sold at a price substantially under competition, so that it still represents a value to consumers. But, even in this case, the product can succeed only so long as a competitor does not undercut its price.

In applying these guidelines, particularly the first, one must be careful to test the product against competition with the appropriate target market in order to avoid what has become known as the *majority fallacy.* Kuehn and Day explain the majority fallacy in the following way:

> If there were five companies marketing a chocolate cake mix and all their products were at the same level of chocolaty-ness, each company might be expected to get 20 percent of the chocolate cake-mix market if all other factors were equal.
>
> Suppose now that a sixth company wants to enter the market. It decides to test two proposed levels of chocolaty-ness against the existing brands. It tests a considerably lighter chocolate cake mix against each of the established brands and finds that 65 percent of consumers prefer the other brand in each test. It tests a considerably darker chocolate against the established brands and again finds that 65 percent of all consumers prefer the brands against which it is tested. Both proposed products have failed the preference tests.
>
> The company then tests a product at the medium level and finds that 50 percent of all consumers prefer it when it is tested against any of the present brands. Now the comparison tests indicate that the new company has a product "just as good" as any of the competing brands. This product will be indistinguishable from the established brands and, if it can overcome the disadvantage of being a latecomer in the market, it might eventually be expected to attain a 17 percent share of the market.
>
> This situation illustrates what is sometimes called the "majority fallacy," i.e., assuming that every product must be acceptable to a majority of all consumers if it is to be successful. A little reflection suggests that a substantial number of consumers might strongly prefer a considerably lighter chocolate cake, and another segment of the market might strongly prefer a much darker chocolate. It is certainly conceivable that each of these groups would amount to a larger segment of the entire market than the one-sixth share that our hypothetical new company might eventually expect to attain with a cake mix just like all the others (if it can

overcome the handicap of being last in entering the market.)[17]

Market Segmentation and Product Differentiation

In chapter 1, market segmentation and product differentiation were identified as alternative marketing strategies. Both, of course, are applicable to new products.

Market Segmentation. Not all forms of market segmentation fall within *product* strategy. Many of the bases for market segmentation do not require a physical modification of the tangible product. Markets may be segmented in terms of distribution channels, geographic areas, income, and so forth without any change in the physical product, although minor product changes are often made to avoid confusion. This is particularly true when consumer income is the basis for segmentation. For example, a major manufacturer of carpet sweepers sold the same sweeper under two different pricing structures in order to appeal to different income segments. In order to avoid consumer confusion and retailer complaints, the higher priced sweeper was decorated with a narrow strip of chrome on the sweeper head and sold through department stores; the lower priced sweeper, sans chrome strip, was sold through discount stores. The basis of segmentation was price. The product difference (the chrome strip) between the two models was a minor, inexpensive concession to provide visual support for the premium price of the more expensive sweeper.

In the discussion of copy strategy in chapter 3, the evaporated milk market was segmented in terms of three types of use: infant feeding, cooking, and coffee creaming. These are three distinct markets, although there is some overlap since some families may use evaporated milk for all three purposes. The tangible product is the same in all three markets, but these three segments require different copy appeals, different directions for use, and different media.

Bases for Segmentation. Table 8–2 shows a list of major variables used in segmenting markets. Obviously, not all of these segmentation variables require physical differences in the tangible product. One way of evaluating whether tangible product changes are requisite for market segmentation has been suggested by Irving S. White:

17. Alfred A. Kuehn and Ralph L. Day, "The Strategy of Product Quality," *Harvard Business Review"* (November-December, 1962): Copyright © 1962 by the President and Fellows of Harvard College; all rights reserved.

Table 8–2. Major Segmentation Variables and Their Typical Breakdowns

Variables	*Typical Breakdown*
Geographic	
Region	New England; Middle Atlantic; South Atlantic; East South Central; East North Central; West South Central; West North Central; Mountain; Pacific.
County size	A; B; C; D.
Climate	Northern; Southern
Demographic	
Age	Under 6; 6-11; 12-17; 18-34; 35-49; 50-65; 65 and over.
Sex	Male; female.
Family size	1–2; 3–4; 5 and over.
Family life cycle	Young, single; young, married—no children, youngest child under 6, youngest child 6 or over; older, married—with children, no children under 18, other.
Income	Under $5,000; $5,000–$7,999; $8,000–$9,999; over $10,000.
Occupation	Professional and technical; managers, officials and proprietors; clerical, sales; craftsmen, supervisors; operatives; farmers; retired; students, housewives; unemployed.
Education	Grade school or less; some high school; high school graduate; some college; college graduate.
Religion	Protestant; Catholic; Jewish; other.
Race	White; Black; Oriental; Spanish-American; American Indian.
Nationality	American; British; French; German; and so forth.
Social class	Lower-lower; upper-lower; lower-middle; upper-middle; lower-upper; upper-upper.
Psychographic	
Personality	(There are any number of social-psychological factors that can be used. Any particu-
Life-style	lar dimension or cluster of dimensions are usually broken down into thirds, or into
Needs/values	upper-half and lower-half.)
Behavioral	
Decision making unit	Father; mother; both; children; other.
Usage rate	Heavy; light; medium.
Readiness stage	Unaware; aware; interested; intends to try; trier; user.
Benefit sought	Variable and product specific.
End use	Varies with product.
Brand loyalty	Strong; medium; light; none.
Marketing-factor sensitivity	Quality; price; advertising; sales promotion.

The consumer market may indeed be organized along the lines of: (a) *physical benefit segmentation*—those to whom specific product advantages represent the critical difference for purchase, and (b) *psychological, or symbolic segmentation*—those to whom a new life style value, usually made explicit in the communications surrounding the physical product, represent the critical difference for purchase.

Examples of the first—physical benefit segmentation— are numerous: the filter tip cigarette which traps more tar, appealing to the tar-conscious consumer, the photocopy machine that turns out copies in three-quarters the time of its closest competitor, appealing to the efficient consumers, the powerful sensory impact of a new toothpaste, appealing to those who want a fresh-feeling mouth. All of these physical dimensions are capable of yielding consumer segments which convert such product differences into purchase acts without their conscious translation into life-style or self-expressive *symbolic* benefits. Examples of the second—*symbolic benefit segmentation*—are also numerous: the youthful energetic spirit of the Continental Airlines image differentiates its passengers sharply from the passengers attracted to the conservative affluent image of TWA. Winston cigarettes differ in their symbolic appeal from Marlboro cigarettes; Time magazine differs from Newsweek. None of the above mentioned products have symbolic benefits which are obvious correlates of actual product-rooted benefits.[18]

Although White's observations are worthy of consideration, as a practical matter, it is probable that a difference in the tangible product that *supports* the symbolic differences in marketing communications will entail less marketing risk, require less marketing expenditure, and provide a sounder basis for segmentation in most instances. In any case, the judgment as to whether market segmentation requires a unique tangible product must be made on a product by product basis in view of company resources, competitive activity, and market characteristics.

18. White, "New Product Differentiation," pp. 99–103. Reprinted from *Marketing in a Changing World* published by the American Marketing Association. See footnote 7, p. 138.

Limits to Segmentation. There are limits to the strategy of segmentation, even when they involve differences in the tangible product. A total market can be segmented into so many subsets that a particular subset is not large enough to support an independent marketing program. Further, some markets do not appear to be susceptible to segmentation, even along traditional lines. For example, many markets are segmented on the basis of sex. Yet, attempts to segment the deodorant market on this basis haven't been all that successful because of the willingness of male family members to use whatever brand is purchased by the housewife. A similar observation may be made about the market for shampoo.

Product Differentiation. As pointed out earlier, product differentiation differs from market segmentation in that marketers utilizing this strategy direct their activities toward the entire market, competing with all other entries, rather than directing their activities to one or more subsets of the total market. Product differentiation is a viable strategy when the market is truly homogeneous or when its size precludes profitable segmentation. As in the case of market segmentation, physical differences in the tangible product may or may not play a role in the strategy of product differentiation. Much product differentiation is simply based on preemptive claims in the sense that the same claim could be made for every competitor in the field; and this approach is sometimes successful. Wonder Bread's "Help's build strong bodies 12 ways" is such a claim.

Product strategy enters into product differentiation when an actual change is made in the tangible product and this difference is used as support for advertising claims. The "secret" ingredient approach is such an example, as are minor, visible product differences. For example, a major manufacturer of lawn and garden fertilizers laced its product with green particles to support its claim of "Green Power;" Oxydol is sprinkled through with green crystals as tangible evidence of its product difference; and the blue color of Blue Cheer supports its claim of "blue magic." As a generalization, product differentiation is simplified and made more believable when there is a *visible* product difference. Many consumers may be gullible, but even the most gullible of consumers are more comfortable when they have something visible to be gullible about.

PRODUCT LIFE CYCLE

Every day, new products are born into the market place. And, every day, old products, no longer in demand in sufficient quantities to justify their continued promotion and distribution, die and disappear from the market place. The period between the birth and death of a product has become known as the *product life cycle.* The concept of the product life cycle is an attempt to recognize that every product has distinct stages in its sales history and that each stage presents unique problems and opportunities for marketing strategy.

Stages in the Product Life Cycle

The product life cycle is generally portrayed as having four stages: introduction, growth, maturity, and decline. The traditional form of the product life cycle is shown in figure 8–1. Note that the product profitability curve does not parallel the life cycle curve but tends to peak earlier. This phenomenon is, essentially, a function of pricing practices and increased competitive activity.

Some authorities portray the life cycle as having five stages rather than four. Chester Wasson inserts a *competitive turbulent* stage between growth and maturity.[19] Booz, Allen and Hamilton insert a *saturation* stage between maturity and decline.[20] Regardless of the number of stages, the general form of the life cycle is essentially the same, although William E. Cox, in a study of 754 drug products, identified six different life cycle curves. The differences resulted from technical developments and promotional activities during the products' lives.[21] The most common variation found by

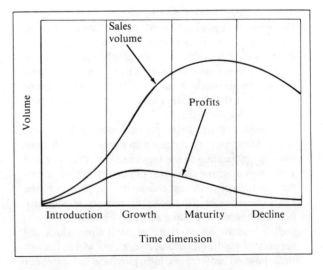

Figure 8–1. Typical four-stage product life cycle and product curve

19. Chester R. Wasson, *Dynamic Competitive Strategy and Product Life Cycles* (St. Louis: Challenge Books, 1974), p. 3.
20. *Management of New Products,* p. 4.
21. W.E. Cox, "Product Life Cycles as Marketing Models," *Journal of Business* (October, 1967): 375–84.

Cox has a second, although smaller rise which results from a final, promotional push during the decline stage. This suggests that marketing activities may modify, or even prolong product life cycles.

The most common reasons for the demise of products are technological obsolescence, psychological obsolescence, and poor product management. In technological obsolescence, a new technology arises that performs the essential function of existing products better or at a lesser cost. The replacement of the horse and buggy by the automobile is an excellent example of technological obsolescence. Fashion is an example of psychological obsolescence since a new fashion—while no better, and certainly no cheaper— may turn last year's wardrobe into a contribution to the Salvation Army overnight. Examples of poor product management are almost too frequent to mention, but once-great names like Pear's Soap, Packard, Uneeda Biscuit, and Twenty Grand have been dead so long that they are no longer mourned.

Some products, such as glass, never seem to die because technology has not produced an economical and superior replacement for mirrors, windows, and dozens of other functional uses. Other products, such as coal (a victim of petroleum, natural gas, and other forms of cheaper, cleaner energy) may have their funerals interrupted by a shortage of their replacement products and be "born again."

Thus, the product life cycle concept is not a good predictive indicator of either product longevity or product vigor. Technological, economic and managerial variables may influence both the cycle's duration and magnitude. Further, the concept of product life cycle does not specify whether the *product* is a product class (vegetables), a product form (canned vegetables), or a product brand (Del Monte). Obviously, different considerations will apply to these three interpretations of *product*. Nonetheless, the product life cycle may have some value in giving us insights into marketing strategy.

For purposes of marketing strategy, let us say that the general form of the product life cycle has four stages. We will characterize the typical marketing situation that prevails during each stage of the life cycle.

The Introductory Stage. The introductory stage of a product life cycle is generally characterized by slow growth, heavy promotional expenditures in relation to sales, relatively high prices, and limited product offerings; that is, limited flavors, styles, forms, and so forth.

Growth is relatively slow during the introductory stage because of: (1) delays in the expansion of productive capacity, (2) technical product problems that have to be worked out, (3) difficulty in gaining widespread distribution, and (4) inertia on the part of consumers in trying the new product.[22] Promotional expenditures are high in relation to sales because of the heavy sales costs involved in obtaining distribution and because of the need for advertising investment in order to create consumer awareness and trial. Prices are relatively high because of the need to recover investment costs in plant and equipment and because the relatively low volume of sales that characterizes the introductory period leads to high production costs. Limited product offerings exist because initial volume is not sufficient to justify a wide variety of flavors, sizes, forms, styles, and so forth.

The Growth Stage. If the introduction is successful, sales start climbing rapidly as distribution increases and as consumers are persuaded to try the product. Promotional expenditures remain high in terms of absolute volume, although their ratio to sales decreases because sales are increasing rapidly. Prices tend to remain high unless they are reduced to stimulate demand or to discourage competition from entering the field. During the growth period, production capacity becomes both more plentiful and more efficient. Competitors enter the field, and major product improvements appear as a response to competition. Product differentiation and market segmentation emerge as marketing strategies; competition for distribution becomes intense; and dealers adopt multiple-line policies (that is, they stock several competitive brands). Sales promotion activities increase, and new forms of the product appear.

The Maturity Stage. Eventually, the rate of growth slows down as the point is reached where most of the potential customers have tried the product. The reduction in growth rate exerts a downward pressure on prices, dealer margins, and profits. Weak competitors and less than adequate brands drop out of the market. Their places are taken by the surviving brands, and sales settle down to the repurchase rate of those consumers who have tried the product and are satisfied with its performance. Any continued growth tends to parallel population growth.

The maturity stage lasts much longer than the preceding stages and, indeed, may continue for many years. Most products on the market are in the maturity stage, which is characterized by well-entrenched brands, consumer loyalty, and relatively stable market shares. Prices are relatively stable because the

---

22. Robert D. Buzzell, "Competitive Behavior and the Product Life Cycle," in *New Ideas for Successful Marketing,* John S. Wright and Jac L. Goldstucker, eds. (Chicago: American Marketing Association, 1966), pp. 46–68.

margin between cost and selling price has dropped to normal levels. Any significant increase in sales for a particular brand must come at the expense of competitive brands, not from growth of the total market.

The manufacturing costs of most competitors are comparable, and promotional expenditures reach a stable ratio to sales. There is little opportunity for price increases because of the existence of established competition. Price decreases offer only a temporary advantage because they will be met by competition with the consequence that profit levels for the entire field will be reduced even further. Deals and price promotions are used on a periodic, short-term basis to clear inventories, to attract customers from other brands, and to increase retail visibility.

The maturity stage is marked by increased efforts to find unique, dramatic, and compelling ways of presenting advertising claims. A larger proportion of the budget is devoted to sales promotional activities. Media analysis, designed to increase the efficiency of the advertising budget, becomes more intense. The maturity stage is often characterized by frenzied efforts to increase usage by current users, to discover new users, new uses for the product, and new channels of distribution.

The Decline Stage. Eventually, most product forms and brands enter a period of declining sales. The decline period may be rapid, particularly in a case where technology devises a new product form that is functionally superior to existing brands. Or, the decline period may continue over a period of years as consumers gradually lose interest and as a variety of substitute forms of the product emerge. The decline stage for most industries and brands is characterized by both dwindling sales and a decrease in competition as more and more competitive companies seek more lucrative uses for their productive capacity and company resources.

MANAGING THE PRODUCT LIFE CYCLE

For the marketing manager, the major question is whether the *brand* life cycle is inevitable, or whether the cycle can be managed in such a way that the vitality of the brand is prolonged. Certainly, many once bright brands have lost their luster. On the other hand, Ivory Soap has been around since 1878, and Kodak cameras have a similar longevity. Kellog cereals, Ford, RCA, Remington typewriters, Chase and Sanborn Coffee, Hires Root Beer, Coca-Cola, Woodbury's Soap, Cadillac, Hershey, and many other brands seem to defy the life cycle concept and retain

their vigor long past the age of reasonable senescence. Some have done so while keeping their original form and formula—Coca-Cola, for example. Others have done so through a variety of brand modifications and marketing strategies. Our focus in this chapter is on *product* strategies that are used to extend the product life cycle and maintain the health of the brand. These strategies focus on the physical form of the tangible product.

STRATEGIES FOR EXTENDING THE PRODUCT LIFE CYCLE

The creation of a successful brand is an expensive undertaking. It represents a major committment of company resources and often takes years of concentrated effort. As a consequence, the demise of a brand represents the loss of an important company asset. There are a number of product strategies that are employed to prolong the life of an established brand. The more common ones—product quality, product differentiation, line extensions, and product obsolescence are briefly discussed in the following material.

Product Quality

Product quality as perceived by the consumer is unquestionably the most fundamental product strategy for maintaining the health of a brand. Reference was made in chapter 1 to a successful laxative which almost disappeared from the market when an "accident of chemistry" made thousands of bottles highly toxic. This, of course, is an extreme example; yet, similar results may accompany nondangerous lapses in product quality. Major companies such as Coca-Cola, Anheuser-Busch, Procter and Gamble, Ralston Purina, Maytag, and many others are sticklers for product quality. These companies maintain extensive systems of quality control, augmented by periodic consumer tests, to make sure that manufacturing standards are being met and that their brands continue to satisfy consumers. Maytag, at one point, closed down the production line of one of its major appliances—at considerable inconvenience and expense—on the basis of three letters of complaint from consumers. All production was halted while plant engineers investigated the complaints to make sure that the problem was a nonrecurrent one and not the fault of material specification, design characteristics, manufacturing procedures, or quality control standards. Production was not resumed until plant engineers were satisfied that the problem was not likely to recur. This same company has used the "high quality" of its products as the theme for an extremely effective advertising campaign—"The Maytag Repairman is the lonliest man in town."

The maintenance of product quality often involves many small product improvements, any one of which is imperceptible to consumers, and none of which are significant enough to mention in advertising. It may involve a better preservative, a manufacturing procedure that provides better quality control, a coating that is more stain resistant or lasts longer. In the aggregate, however, it is often these small improvements that truly maintain quality and keep the brand competitive in the market place. Making continuous, undramatic product improvements that result in only minor changes in the tangible product may, indeed, be one of the most fundamental of product strategies in prolonging the brand life cycle.

Product Differentiation

Companies' employing a strategy of product differentiation often insist that the differentiated claim be based on a perceivable difference in the tangible product and not simply on a preemptive or psychological claim. The "Green Power" example given earlier, in which green crystals were added to a lawn and garden fertilizer, is an example of this approach. Gillette's *promax compact* hair dryer is another. Here, the product difference is one of size, with the *promax compact* being substantially smaller than competitive models.

The product differentiation strategy sometimes involves a systematic program of physical variations, introduced on a periodic basis and designed to create an impression of continuous modification and improvement.

Line Extension

Line extension is a strategy wherein new products are introduced into the line to provide variety, add shelf facings, and increase sales. Line extensions may or may not employ a strategy of market segmentation.

The most common example of line extensions that does *not* involve market segmentation is adding flavors to a food product such as Campbell's soups, Jello, or cake mixes. A classic example of the addition of new flavors in order to increase sales and gain market dominance occurred in the cake mix market in the mid to late 1950s. At that time, prepared cake mixes as a product form were in the late growth stage of their product life cycle. The major brands offered four basic mixes—white, yellow, chocolate, and spice. Analysis of marketing activities at that time suggests

that General Mills launched the following, three-stage strategy of flavor proliferation.

1. First, the company undertook a major research and development effort to create a number of new cake mix flavors.
2. Second, the company cut the price of the basic mixes, virtually eliminating all advertising and promotion funds. Competitive brands quickly followed suit from fear that the price differential would cause them to lose volume and market share.
3. Finally, the Betty Crocker brand started introducing its new flavors on a periodic basis—Peanut Delight, Confetti Angel, Lemon Custard Angel, Black Walnut, Marble Chiffon Cake Mixes, and so forth. Advertising funds were generated from the promotional investments for the new flavors, and copy was designed which introduced the new flavors and supported the entire product line.

Competitors were caught flat footed. By virtue of the price cut, they had no advertising and promotion funds in their pricing structures to fight back. Neither did they have an inventory of new flavors with which to counterattack. If this analysis is correct, it was a highly effective strategy, brilliantly conceived and beautifully executed.

The most common forms of line extension that involve market segmentation are introducing new models or new forms of the product designed to appeal to different consumer groups or different uses. The television manufacturer may extend its product line by adding portable models, thereby appealing to a market segment that is seeking portable entertainment. Or an automobile maker may augment its product line by adding a station wagon, a dune buggy, a truck, and so forth. Or a soap manufacturer may add a liquid or bar or powder form to a brand which initially consisted of soap flakes.

A specific example of a line extension strategy is shown in the Coppertone ad (figure 8–2), which offers three Coppertones—for fair skin, for normal skin, and for dark skin. This is an adaptation of a strategy employed by Breck Shampoo for over twenty-five years in which the company markets different formulas of Breck Shampoo for dry, normal, and oily hair.

Product Obsolescence

Product obsolescence is a marketing strategy that involves the use of features, style, or materials that cause a product to become prematurely obsolete and

Figure 8–2. (Reprinted with permission of Plough, Inc. All rights reserved.)

thereby increases its frequency of purchase. It applies, primarily, to durable and fashion goods which have relatively long use lives, usually several years. Sometimes referred to as *planned obsolescence*, this strategy is highly controversial, and is often unfairly criticized. Basically, there are three forms of product obsolescence: (1) functional obsolescence, (2) style obsolescence, and (3) material obsolescence.

Functional Obsolescence. In functional obsolescence, a new feature or a new function is added that makes the older model less desirable despite its continued use value. Historically, in automobiles the inclusion of electric starters, hydraulic brakes, automatic transmissions, power steering, radios, tape decks, and so forth are examples of functional obsolescence. New refrigerators with freezer compart-

ments, automatic defrosting mechanisms, shelves in the doors, rotatable shelves to provide easy access to refrigerated foods, ice-dispensers, and iced-water spigots may not destroy the functional value of older models which do not have these features, but they certainly make them appear shoddy and old fashioned.

When such improvements are the intermittant result of technological research and are made available as soon as the "bugs" have been worked out of them and manufacturing costs make them affordable, then the strategy of functional obsolescence is both desirable and socially defensible. In following this strategy, manufacturers invest substantial resources in research and development, always with the goal in mind of meeting consumer needs. In the process, they extend the lives of their brands.

On the other hand, if a manufacturer had a number of such improvements on hand at an affordable cost and *deliberately* withheld some of them from the market so that they could be introduced separately in successive model years, a strategy of *planned obsolescence* would be in effect, and the marketer is open to criticism for exploiting consumers. Such a strategy, however, entails substantial risk since there is always the danger that competitors will introduce the improvement first and gain a competitive advantage.

Style Obsolescence. Style obsolescence involves periodic style changes deliberately made to provoke consumer dissatisfaction with last year's purchase. The garment industry was the pioneer in this form of obsolescence, and the automobile industry was quick to follow suit. Yearly model or style changes, with no perceptual product improvements but with design changes that "date" the product at a glance, has a long history in these industries. Whether or not we consider this strategy to be ethically reprehensible depends largely on whether we view cars and fashions as purely functional items or as psychological expressions of their owners. Marketers as well as economists disagree on this point. If, however, we consider the consumer as sovereign, recognizing that the choice to purchase or not to purchase is a personal decision that is made freely, then style obsolescence is a legitimate marketing strategy and the business firm that uses this strategy does so with the risk that consumers may reject its most recent offering. Such was the case of the "midi" in 1970. As Chester Wasson has pointed out:

> Generally, of course, the fashion offerings available in any given season are really quite diverse. In one instance . . . that of the midi introductions of 1970, such was not the case. For once the industry spoke with one strong voice. If customers were manipulatable, the midi should have been a smashing success . . . ; however, it was pure disaster, and one fashion that caught on strong that season was one which both designers and merchants had been rather reluctant to sell—the pants suit.[23]

Material Obsolescence. Material obsolescence means that the manufacturer deliberately chooses materials that are inferior, subject to breakage, corrosion, rot, and wear. Presumably, the purpose in making such a choice is to hasten the return of the purchaser to the market. In a competitive economy, this is *not* a viable marketing strategy. It is a recipe for failure.

The Death and Burial of Sick Products

No brand is ever completely immune to obsolescence or competitive defeat. Even under the best of marketing managements, occasions arise when prudence dictates that a brand should be withdrawn from competition. It is often a painful process because company personnel become personally involved in the products they handle, and "killing" a product seems analogous to drowning a kitten. A great deal has been written about the death and burial of sick products.[24] Marketing and advertising managers should be alert to the possibility that a brand should be eliminated, devise a strategy for brand elimination, act decisively, and then stop worrying about it.

SUMMARY

Every product is really three products. First, there is the *tangible* product, which is the physical entity or service that is offered for sale. Second, there is the *extended* product, which consists of the tangible product along with the entire galaxy of services, warranties, and psychological overtones that accompany it. Finally, there is the *generic* product, which consists of the benefit or benefits that consumers expect to derive from the product's use. These various aspects of the product are interrelated and must be coordinated by the marketing effort in such a way that they contribute to a unified product or brand image.

Consumer satisfaction with purchases is related to their expectancies of product performance. There are a number of theories relating to consumer satisfaction. Consumers are sometimes disappointed with product performance for reasons other than those which accounted for the purchase in the first place. One consequence of this phenomenon is to emphasize the importance of excellence in the tangible product itself.

The concept of *product* applies to retail stores and to services as well as to physical objects. Thus, a retail store is a product that sells other products, and may be marketed as such. The services offered by a doctor, a lawyer, or an appliance repair person are also products in the marketing sense.

In developing new products, those products that are observably superior to, or different from, existing

23. Chester R. Wasson, *Consumer Behavior: A Managerial Viewpoint* (Austin, Texas: Press Educational Division of Lone Star Publishers, Inc., 1975), p. 415.

24. R.S. Alexander, "The Death and Burial of 'Sick' Products," *Journal of Marketing* (April, 1964): 1–7; Walter J. Talley, Jr., "Profiting from a Declining Product," *Business Horizons* 7 (Spring, 1974): 77–84; Philip Kotler, "Phasing out Weak Products," *Harvard Business Review* (March-April, 1965): 107–18; Conrad Berenson, "Pruning the Product Line," *Business Horizons* 6 (Summer, 1963): 63–70.

competition have the greatest chance of success. New products that are similar to existing products involve inordinate risks, and new products that are inferior to competition seldom survive in the market place.

The *majority fallacy* is the fallacy of assuming that the preferences of the majority of consumers represent the preferences of all consumers. It is important to test products with the appropriate target audience.

Market segmentation and product differentiation are product strategies. Both market segmentation and product differentiation may be undertaken with or without a physical difference in the *tangible* product, but an actual physical difference often helps support and give validity to advertising claims.

The product life cycle is made up of: (1) the intro-

ductory stage, (2) the growth stage, (3) the maturity stage, and (4) the decline stage. Although this concept has little predictive value, it is useful in emphasizing that different marketing strategies are appropriate at different stages in a product's history.

Managing the product life cycle in order to extend a particular product's commercial life is a primary concern of marketing managers. There are a number of product strategies for extending the life cycle. One such strategy is the strategy of product obsolescence, sometimes called *planned obsolescence.* Several forms of product obsolescence are functional obsolescence, style obsolescence, and material obsolescence. There is a question of ethics in the strategy of product obsolescence.

QUESTIONS

1. Identify and define the three different definitions of a product discussed in the chapter. Why is it important to recognize these different concepts?
2. What are the advertising implications for the following theories of consumer satisfaction: (a) assimilation theory, (b) contrast theory, (c) generalized negativity theory, and (d) assimilation-contrast theory?
3. Explain the Swan and Combs two-factor theory. What are its implications for marketing?
4. The chapter outlines four guidelines for new product strategy. What are they?
5. When does product strategy enter into the concept of product differentiation? Why may product strategy be an important part of a strategy of product differentiation?
6. Explain the majority fallacy.
7. Distinguish between *physical benefit* segmentation and *symbolic* segmentation. Relate this distinction to the three definitions of *product* given earlier.
8. Briefly describe and evaluate the concept of "product life cycle."
9. Explain what is meant by *managing* the product life cycle. Identify the product strategies that may be used for this purpose.
10. Identify the various forms of product obsolescence. Evaluate them as viable marketing strategies.

PROBLEM

As the new product manager for a major toiletries company, you have been analyzing the market for toilet soaps in an effort to find a market segment that has not been exploited. After several months of research, analysis, and frustration, you finally conclude that there may be an opportunity for a bath soap for children in the two- to five-year-old age group since none of the major companies are advertising a product specifically for use by this segment.

Group interviews have found that mothers of young children complain that giving a small child a bath is a chore, and children in the two to five age

group vigorously resist the process. It has occurred to you that if you can make bathing fun for the child, there may be an opportunity for a successful product in this area. Your major problem is to design a product that meets this requirement.

Assignment

1. Design a soap product that could make bathing fun for children. Define its salient characteristics.
2. Create a name for the product that will position it for this market segment.

Brand and Packaging Strategy

Busch Bavarian Beer

In the mid-1950s, Anheuser Busch marketed Michelob and Budweiser, both premium priced beers. Yet, 80 percent of the beer market was made up of popular priced beers; the premium segment was only 20 percent of the total. In an attempt to crack the popular priced market, Anheuser Busch, working with the D'arcy Advertising Agency, test marketed Busch Lager beer in St. Louis. The new product took off with all the snap and crackle of a wet noodle.

Elmer Marschutz, then chairman of the board of the Gardner Advertising Company in St. Louis, sat next to an executive vice-president of Anheuser-Busch at a civic luncheon. As a conversation starter, Elmer said: "I understand Busch Lager isn't doing very well.

"It could be doing better," the Anheuser Busch executive admitted, grudgingly.

Then Elmer dropped the bomb. "I know why it isn't selling," he said.

"Why?"

"Two reasons," said Elmer. "First, you named it Busch Lager beer. Budweiser is also a lager beer, and no one wants to buy a second-rate Budweiser. Second, your advertising theme, 'the talk of the town,' is dull. It doesn't promise the consumer anything."

"Do you think Gardner could do any better?" asked the Anheuser Busch executive.

"I know we could," said Elmer, modestly.

"Could you develop a campaign for presentation within a month?"

"That's plenty of time," Elmer lied.

Back at the office an hour later, Elmer received a call from the Anheuser Busch executive. "Elmer, you have a two o'clock appointment one month from today to make a presentation to Mr. Busch."

Within half an hour of that call, Elmer Marschutz had a short meeting with the agency's department heads to tell them about the assignment. Pandemonium broke loose. Agency personnel had to become knowledgeable about beer; a product concept had to be defined; product characteristics had to be specified; a brand name had to be selected; packages had to be designed; copy had to be created; point-of-sale material had to be prepared; media had to be identified; and it all had to be assembled into a professional presentation.

The deadline was met, the presentation was made, and Busch Bavarian Beer was born. Busch Bavarian Beer. A new, different kind of beer. Light, refreshing, thirst quenching. A beer like they drink in Bavaria— wherever *that* is.

149

Sego Liquid Diet Food

The Pet Milk Company had made a decision to enter the liquid diet food market, recently popularized by Metrecal, despite the fact that the trade press estimated that over two hundred brands of liquid diet food were being introduced or readied for introduction across the country. A product concept had been prepared, a product developed, distribution strategy determined—but Pet didn't have a brand name for the product. There was no time to develop a brand name, test it, and conduct a "name" search to make sure that no other company had already registered the name selected. The Pet Milk Company owned a few brand names, but most of them (like Brown Cow) were considered completely inappropriate for a diet food. The choice had narrowed down to two names: Pet 900 Liquid Diet Food and Sego Liquid Diet Food.

Both client and agency personnel were concerned about using the name *Pet* for a diet food because that was the name of the company's leading product, Pet Evaporated Milk. Pet Evaporated Milk was advertised for its "richness," and for use in making desserts—foods that were the antithesis of dieting. In fact, the current campaign for Pet Evaporated Milk was using "double the richness of country cream" as its theme.

Sego was the name of an evaporated milk marketed by Pet in Salt Lake City, Utah. The brand had local distribution and was named Sego because the early Mormon settlers of the Salt Lake region survived their first, harsh winter by eating the roots of the Sego lily. So, Sego was rich in tradition and meaning in Utah. But, Utah has a small population, and the name Sego was virtually unknown outside the state. Some quick research in the mid-west indicated that the name *Pet* was associated in the minds of consumers with evaporated milk, infant feeding, chocolate fudge, creamy casseroles, and rich desserts. This same research indicated that the name *Sego* wasn't associated with anything. It drew a blank.

A final meeting was called at the agency to make a decision on the name. We were running out of time. Jo Walsh, a fine copywriter, summed it all up with the following thoughts: "I don't really think we should use the Pet name for a diet food. It has too many associations with high calorie cooking. I'm not really enthusiastic about the Sego name either, but maybe we can give it a diet-food meaning."

Another copywriter said, "Maybe we could say, 'See the pounds go with Sego.'" And everybody laughed because it was such a hokey idea. But we used it. A jingle in the introductory commercials was accompanied by the words, "See the pounds go with Sego." This same line was included in print advertising, and Sego

Liquid Diet food went on to become the best seller in the field, and made Pet several millions of dollars. Moral: hokey ideas sometimes pay off.

Coca-Cola

A brand name is often the most important asset that a company possesses. This observation, exaggerated as it may seem, is amply supported by the following quotation from the legal counsel of Coca-Cola:

> The production plants and inventories of the Coca-Cola Company could go up in flames one night, yet the following morning there is not a bank in Atlanta, New York, or any other place that would not lend this company the funds necessary for rebuilding, accepting as security only the goodwill of its trademark.[1]

These three examples emphasize the role that the brand name plays in the positioning of a product, in communicating salient product characteristics to consumers, and as a valuable resource of an industrial enterprise. In the case of Busch Lager Beer, which failed in test markets, the brand name was a contributing factor in its failure. The Pet Milk Company selected a neutral brand name to which a "diet food meaning" could be attached through advertising and promotion rather than risk using a name associated with rich, fattening foods in consumers' minds; and the quotation by the legal counsel of Coca-Cola reveals the value that a multi-million dollar corporation attaches to the brand name of its major product.

These illustrations point up a fundamental strategy in the selection of brand names:

1. *If at all possible, select a brand name that communicates the essential attributes of the product concept.* Under this strategy, the problems of communicating with consumers will be simplified, and the opportunity for success enhanced. The Carnation company has applied this strategy with great success with such names as *Instant Breakfast, Coffeemate,* and *Slender.* Clairol's *Born Blond,* Bausch & Lomb's *Soflens,* Procter and Gamble's *Pampers,* General Food's *Hamburger Helper* and *Shak'n' Bake* are other outstanding examples of this approach.

2. *If it is not possible to select a name that communicates the essential product concept, select a neutral name into which the desired meaning can be built through advertising and promotion.* Examples of

1. *Trademarks: Orientation for Advertising People* (New York: American Association of Advertising Agencies, Inc., 1971), p. 1.

this strategy are Sego, Ford, Cadillac, Exxon, and Anacin. Initial communication may be more difficult, and promotion costs will be higher, but the task is not an impossible one.

3. *Avoid selecting names that contradict the essential product concept.* Such names erect barriers to communication, and normal competitive activity creates enough barriers to product success without compounding the problem through unwise name selection. I suspect, for example, that it would be a waste of time and money to introduce a diet food called *Fat,* or a brand of tires called *Blowout,* or an automobile called *Lemon.*

LEGAL CONSIDERATIONS IN SELECTING BRAND NAMES

Before we proceed further in the discussion of brand name strategy, perhaps we should define some of the key terms associated with branding, and mention some of the legal requirements that govern the use of brand identification.

Definition of Terms

Confusion often arises in the use of terms such as *trade name, brand name, brand mark,* and *trademark,* although each has a distinctive meaning.

Trade name The name under which a company conducts its business. General Motors, General Mills, Procter and Gamble, Ralston Purina and Anheuser Busch are all well-recognized trade names.

Brand "A name, term, sign, symbol, or design, or a combination of them which is intended to identify the goods or services of one seller or a group of sellers and to differentiate them from those of competitors." [2]

Brand name That part of the *brand* that can be vocalized, such as Instant Breakfast, Sego, Charlie, Winston, Pampers. A brand name may be, but need not be, a trade name. For example, Coca-Cola is a trade name that is also the brand name of the company's leading product. Pampers is a brand name, but the trade name of the company that manufactures Pampers is Procter and Gamble.

Brand mark That part of the *brand* that can be recognized but can not be vocalized, such as a design or symbol, or distinctive coloring or lettering. The Plymouth "ship," the Metro-Goldwyn-Mayer "lion," and the Playboy "bunny" are all brand marks.

Trademark A brand or part of a brand (a brand name or brand mark) that is given legal protection because it is capable of appropriation. A trademark is, essentially, a legal concept which protect's the seller's exclusive rights to use a brand name and or a brand mark. A product may have several trademarks; thus *Coca-Cola* and *Coke* are both trademarks referring to the same product.

Legal Requirements for a Trademark

Trademarks are normally registered with the U.S. Patent Office, although they need not be officially registered in order to be given protection under the Lanham (trademark) Act, passed in 1946. However, the registering of the trademark helps in protecting it by establishing priority of use, which is a major consideration in trademark ownership. A trademark may be registered for a period of twenty years and is repeatably renewable. There are a number of legal restrictions applying to the use of trademarks; the major ones are identified below.

A trademark Must Be Used in Connection with an Actual Product. A design or name that is only used in an advertisement or on a factory does not constitute a trademark within the definition of the law unless it is clearly applied to a particular product, appearing on the product itself or, if that is not possible, on the package or on a dispensing unit such as a gasoline pump.

A Trademark May Not Cause Confusion or Deceive Purchasers As to the Source of the Product. The patent office will not register trademarks that are so similar to existing trademarks that they might cause confusion. The test of confusion is not that the trademarks, when presented side by side, appear similar; but rather that the consumer might be confused when making a purchase. For example, Promise furniture spray was disallowed because it was confused with the Johnson Wax Company's Pledge furniture spray. A list of trademarks that courts have held to be in conflict is shown in table 9-1.

A Trademark May Not Be Deceptive by Implying Benefits That Are Invalid. Names that have been legally barred include "Six Months Floor Wax," which did not last that long: "Lemon" soap that contained no lemon; and "Nylodon" for sleeping bags that did not contain nylon.

There Are Limitations on Names That Are Primarily Surnames, Geographical Names, or Merely Descrip-

2. *Marketing Definitions: A Glossary of Marketing Terms* (Chicago: American Marketing Association, 1960).

Table 9-1. Trademarks in conflict

There is a likelihood of confusion between the following marks when used in connection with the indicated goods, according to various tribunals:

Marks of Successful Party

AFRIN topical nasal decongestant	FA-DRIN chlorphenpyridamine maleate tablets
AFTER TAN lotion for skin grooming	APRES SUN skin lotion
AIR COMMAND air conditioners and parts	CLIMATE COMMAND heating, cooling and air conditioning units
AIREX cellular material of artificial and natural elastomers and plastomers	SEREX plastic forms for use in insulation
AIRVAC dental aspirators and apparatus	VACUUM/AIRE dental equipment and accessories
ARMALON coated fabrics	ARMALONVEST armored vests
AWAKE frozen concentrate for imitation orange juice	ARISE liquid breakfast drink
BALL PARK frankfurters	BALL GAME wieners
BEER NUTS shelled and salted peanuts	BEER POTATO CHIPS potato chips
BIG BOY stick-candy	BIG BOY! powder for soft drinks
BY GEORGE men's toiletries	GEORGE V toilet water
THE CATTLEMAN restaurant and food services	CATTLEMAN canned chopped beef, luncheon meat, etc.
CHICKEN KING drive-in restaurant services	WHERE CHICKEN Is KING restaurant services
COFFEE BREAK non-dairy cream substitutes	COFFEE BREAK non-dairy cream substitutes
COMSAT satellite communications system	COMCET communications computer
CONDITION beauty pack treatment for hair	CURL & CONDITION permanent waving lotion
CORVETTE automobiles	VETTE fiberglass repair panels for automobiles
DISNEY, WALT DISNEY PRESENTS and DISNEY-LAND motion picture films, educational parks and services	DISNEY AREA ACREAGE, INC. real estate
DOT fasteners, connectors and attaching devices of various types used in construction, etc.	RED DOT DOLLY fastening devices used in construction
DURO-LITE incandescent and fluorescent lamps	DURAGLOBE globes for electric lighting fixtures
DUMPMASTER lifting mechanism for true dumping	TRASHMASTER heavy-duty vehicles
EXECUTIVE razors and blades	EXECUTIVE after-shave, pre-shave lotions
FLECTO protective coatings for paint, etc.	FELCO paint
GALLAHER smoking and chewing tobacco, etc.	GALAHAD cigars
GANT SHIRTMAKERS dress and sport shirts	GHENT on Scroll, Design shirts, pajamas, etc.
GP lubricating oil	GP-7 conditioning additives for gasoline, kerosene
HILTON hotels, restaurant and bar services; HILTON HOTELS Scotch whisky, gin, etc. and CONRAD HILTON Scotch whisky and bourbon	HILTON'S gin, vodka, bourbon, etc.
HOLLOWAY HOUSE variety of frozen food products and restaurant services	DOC HOLLIDAYHOUSE pecans
ISI magazine	I.A.I. indexes to books
JVC radio receivers and FM multiplex radio receivers, etc.	IVC magnetic video tape recorders and reproducers
KENTUCKY FRIED CHICKEN CORPORATION restaurants	OLD KENTUCKY HOME FRIED CHICKEN, INC. restaurants
KUD-L-WRAP, KUD-L-DUDS and KUD-L-NAP nightwear for infants and young children	CUDDLER knitted outerwear for infants
LAND YACHT house trailers	SHASTA ROYAL LAND YACHT mobile homes
LAVE soap	LAVANA liquid detergent for fabrics
MAGIC silicone impregnated paper	ITS-MAGIC cleaning pads
MISS MERRY and MY MERRY toy kits	MISS MARY childrens' tea sets
MISTOMETER metered dose dispensers	METER MIST preparation for asthma
NARCO electronic radio and navigational equipment	NACO radios and tape recorders
NOON HOUR pickled and marinated fish, etc.	12 O'CLOCK dietary food in powder form
OCEAN FREEZE frozen seafood	SEA FREEZE and Design frozen seafood
OLD DOUGLAS whiskey	JAMES DOUGLAS blended Scotch whisky
OROGLAS synthetic resinous materials in the form of sheets, rods, etc.	PROGLAS plastics, for snythetic injection molding materials
PENNY WISE and Girl, canned sweet potatoes, hot sauce, etc.	PENNYWISE and Oval Design cookies
PEXENE liquid floor conditioner	TEXENE germicidal cleaner
PLEDGE furniture polish and cleaner	PROMISE dishwashing detergent
PRESCOTT cotton piece goods	PRESSCOTT sweaters, sport and dress shirts, coats, etc.
PRESDFLAKE particle board	CRESFLAKE particle board
Q-TIPS swabs consisting of sanitary absorbent cotton	QUICK TIPS manicure finishing spray
RID-X preparation for liquifying and deodorizing waste materials	RED X insecticides for tobacco crops

Table 9-1. (Continued)

Marks of Successful Party

SAFGUARD mufflers and exhaust systems for automobile engines	SAFEGUARD automotive engine replacement parts
SANSRUN hosiery	SANS topless footwear
SERENE cold wave permanent kit	CERENA products for care of nails
SI-BONNE fabrics	TRES-BONS hosiery
SPECTRUM decorative paper	SPECTRA gift wrap paper
STOP & SHOP grocery store services	STOP 'N SHOP grocery store services
SUDS WITH MUSCLES detergent	MUSCLE detergent
TARACTAN tranquilizer	TARUXAN preparation for treatment of cardiac insufficiencies
THERMIX magnetic stirrer, hot plate for laboratory use	MIX O THERM magnetic stirrer, hot plate for laboratory use
TIC TAC TOE ice cream and sherbert	TIC TAC candy
TITLEIST and FINALIST golf balls	MEDALIST golf balls
TYGON plastic products for surgical use	TYCRON surgical sutures
UNIFLO oils and greases	OMNIFLO motor oil, lubricating greases
UNIVAC tabulating, record handling, computer, etc.	ANAVAC electrically operated entertainment apparatus
VANISH toilet bowl cleaner	BANISH room deodorant
VO 5 and VO 5 CONDITIONER hair conditioner, shampoo, etc.	CONDITIONER #5 pomade for hair
WHOPPER and HOME OF THE WHOPPER burger-type sandwiches and drive-in restaurant services	WHOPPABURGER sandwiches
ZIRCO catalytic agents	COZIRC driers for paints and varnishes

SOURCE: *The United States Trademark Association Year End Report*, 1970, pp. 8-15.

tive Names. There are many surnames applied to products, such as Chrysler, Ford, and Johnson's. Many of these names, however, were in effect before the current trademark laws were enacted. It would be more difficult to get such names approved today. In addition, trademark law does not protect names that are merely descriptive, such as Fresh Bread. Since the word *fresh* is a generic attribute of bread desired by consumers it may not be used as the name for a particular product of a specific manufacturer. As a consequence, the selection of names that impute the essential quality of the product concept may create problems in trademark registration, and need to be checked thoroughly for their acceptability. For example, Sun Oil Company devised a method of blending gasoline at the pump so that the gasoline buyer could regulate the octane rating of the gasoline purchased. Sun Oil referred to this innovation as Custom Blended gasoline, and spent $30 million over a six-year period advertising Custom Blended gasoline as a Sun Oil Company brand. When the company was challenged in the courts, however, the court ruled that *custom blended* was a descriptive term that no company could appropriate for its exclusive use.

BRAND NAME STRATEGIES

The role of the brand name in communicating product attributes is well-recognized in marketing since the brand name not only serves to identify the product, but also to give the product dimension and character. Pierre Martineau has pointed out:

> The Safeway grocery chain conceived these names for its private label brands: Bel Air frozen foods, Sky-lark bread, Old Mill vinegar, Oven Glo crackers, Nob Hill coffee, and canned goods with such names as Honeybird, Lalani, Gardenside, Country Home. There is obviously greater sales appeal in these names than there is in such dry-as-dust labels as "grade A soda crackers." The product in the consumer's mind in some manner becomes different with the mere flick of a name.[3]

The quest for brand names that unerringly project the appropriate product concept is, essentially, a creative act that can and should be confirmed by marketing research, although some marketers have an intuitive knack for sensing the mood of consumers. The late Charles Revson, founder of Revlon, built a $600 million business on his ability to define appealing brand concepts and develop appropriate names for his brands in the promotion-dependent cosmetics industry. His 1952 "Fire and Ice" promotion for a new cosmetics line was a brilliant success. In 1973, he introduced a fragrance called "Charlie" for "the woman who is sort of liberated but who isn't a bra-burner."[4]

---

3. Pierre Martineau, *Motivation in Advertising* (New York: McGraw-Hill Book Company, 1957), p. 109. Reprinted by permission of the publisher.
4. "Merchant of Glamour," *Time* (September 8, 1975): 62.

While competitors smirked at his folly, sales of Charlie exceeded $10 million during its first year, and by 1975 it had become the largest selling American fragrance in U.S. stores. Subsequently, the name was extended to include makeup.

In choosing a brand name for a new product, marketers have a number of broad strategies that may be employed. They may, for example, use one or more of the following four approaches.

Use the Company Name Plus Product Identification. Among companies following this practice are Campbell, General Electric, and Sara Lee. Thus, we have Campbell's Tomato Soup, Campbell's Cream of Chicken Soup, Campbell's Clam Chowder, and so forth. The company name (trade name) acts as a family name or umbrella and is complemented by the brand's generic product name.

Use the Company Name Plus a Brand Name. This practice is characteristic of the automotive and personal-care industries, where we find Ford Pinto, Ford Mustang, Mercury Cougar, Volkswagen Rabbit, Chrysler Cordoba, and so on. The personal-care industry brings us Revlon's Charlie, Revlon's Sun Jewels, Clairol Herbal Essence Shampoo, Clairol Quiet Touch, Clairol Balsam Color, Helena Rubenstein Skin Dew, Helena Rubenstein Strong and Sheer, and many, many others. The intent under this strategy is to offer a familiar family name, while, at the same time, providing each brand an opportunity for differentiated communication through individual brand names.

Use a Brand Name Plus Product Identification. This approach is often found in large companies with several distinct product lines, some of which have been acquired through purchase or merger. It is also characteristic of large retail organizations that have several lines of private labels. Producers following this practice include Betty Crocker baking mixes (General Mills), Duncan Hines Mixes (Procter and Gamble), and Jell-O products (General Foods). Among retailers, examples include the Kenmore and Craftsman lines for Sears, Ann Page and White House for A&P, and Lucerne for Safeway. The logic here is similar to the strategy of using a company name plus product identification. The difference is that companies using a brand name plus a product identification are usually so diverse that the company name may be inappropriate for many of its product lines.

Use a Brand Name Only. Finally, there are those companies that follow a strategy of using only brand names on most of their products. This is common practice in the cigarette field—Camel, Tareyton, Pall Mall, Marlboro, Winston, and so forth; and in the detergent field—Tide, Surf, Fab, Duz, Cheer, All, etc. These manufacturers insist that each brand stand on its own feet with no help from the parent company name. This strategy provides the greatest opportunity for building a distinct and unique brand image for an individual product, unhampered by historic connotations of a company or family name.

The first three strategies described above are referred to as *brand-extension* strategies because an existing brand name is extended to cover other products, often with different product concepts. Although the use of a brand extension strategy inevitably blurs the brand image of the products to which it is applied, at least to some degree, brand extension confers three benefits:

1. It facilitates the introduction of new products by capitalizing on the halo effect of a well-known and reputable brand. That is, the reputation of the existing brand encourages consumers to try a new product carrying the same brand name.
2. It reduces promotion costs since advertising funds spent on any individual product reinforce the entire line through repetition of the family name.
3. In-store impact is increased because the same brand name appears on a number of products.

These are mixed blessings however, and the case against a brand extension strategy rests on two arguments. First, the introduction of a less than adequate product under a family name can have a negative effect (negative halo) on the entire line by causing dissatisfied customers to distrust other products in the line. Second, excessive use of a brand extension strategy can dilute the sharpness of brand images and create confusion among customers. Mennen's brand extension of Protein 21 is a case in point. In 1970, the Mennen Company introduced a shampoo conditioner under the brand name *Protein 21*. The concept was strong, and the name was excellent. Within two years, Mennen gained a 13 percent share of the $300 million shampoo market.

Then Mennen hit the line extension lure. In rapid succession, the company introduced Protein 21 hair spray, Protein 29 hair spray (for men), Protein 21 conditioner (in two formulas), Protein 21 concentrate. To add to the confusion, the original Protein 21 was available in three different formulas (for dry, oily, and regular hair).

Can you imagine how confused the prospect must be trying to figure out what to put on his or her hair? No wonder Protein 21's share of the shampoo market has fallen from 13 percent to 11 percent. And the decline is bound to continue.[5]

There are few hard rules governing whether one should or should not use brand extensions. Their use is always a compromise between dilution of the brand image and possible consumer confusion on the one hand, and advertising efficiency on the other. Generally, brand extensions make a great deal of sense for a line of products that differ primarily in terms of flavor, such as Betty Crocker Cake Mixes. They make some sense for a line of dessert items, such as those marketed by Sara Lee. They make less sense for a diverse line of baking mixes that ranges from everyday, commonplace items such as cornbread and pancake mix to petits fours. And they make no sense at all for many products.

If there is a rule for brand extensions, it is a three-part rule that says:

1. The more similar two product concepts are, the greater the benefits that will accrue from a brand extension strategy.
2. The more different two product concepts are, the greater the risk involved in using such a strategy.
3. Do not automatically use a brand extension strategy just to save money. It may turn out to be the most expensive money you have ever saved.

SELECTING A BRAND NAME

The actual selection of a brand name is often a time-consuming and frustrating assignment. So much so that Fairfax Cone, in a moment of cynicism prompted by his experience with the ill-fated Edsel, complained: "Naming products is a source of constant and usually fruitless mental exercise in advertising agencies (where the client's wife or a guest at a dinner party usually suggests the name that is finally accepted)."[6]

In the case of the Edsel, his cynicism seems justified. Starting with a list of 16 thousand names, judgement and research had reduced the list to four—Corsair, Citation, Pacer, and Ranger. Unfortunately, the Ford board of directors, under a deadline for a name to be used on some vital dies, ignored all recommen-

dations and arbitrarily decided that they would name Ford's new car after the father of the company's president, provided they could obtain the consent of the family. According to Fairfax Cone:

> Consent was forthcoming . . . and so the Edsel was christened in embryo with a name that was at once a surprise and a huge disappointment. As one of our people said, "The name Flab, which had been suggested by a wag in our London office, couldn't have been any less appropriate." Insofar as the public was concerned the name Edsel was devoid of any feeling of action or spirit. It was a proper name, like Elwyn or Ethelbert, and like them, it was faintly effeminate. It had none of the strength of Pontiac or Lincoln, or the spirit of Mercury; nor did it perpetuate a great name in the industry like Chevolet or Chrysler—or Ford itself.[7]

Fortunately, not all names are selected by boards of directors, client's wives or husbands, or dinner guests. And since the selection of a strong brand name is essentially a creative process bolstered by the judicious use of research, there are few hard and fast rules to go by. There are some general guidelines, although most of them have been violated at one time or another by some of America's best-known products.

1. The brand name should *never* contradict the essential attributes of the brand concept. Ideally, the brand name should be supportive of this concept—as is Slender, Coffee-mate, Charlie, and other examples that have been given. But, if that is not possible, at least the brand name should be neutral so that the desired meaning can be created with advertising and promotion.
2. The name should be simple and clear, easy to spell, write, pronounce, and recognize. Names like Purina Dog Chow, Aztec (a suntan lotion), Crest, Ritz, and Hotpoint.
3. The name should be distinctive and not easily confused with other brand names on the market either in terms of sound or appearance. This is important not only because of the danger of trademark infringement, but also to avoid possible consumer confusion.
4. The name should be usable in package and label design, retaining its identity even when it is reduced in size, as often is done on the package or in commercials.
5. The name should avoid unpleasant connotations that may offend customers. Even in marketing, there is no excuse for poor taste. Perhaps I should say, "Particularly in marketing there is no room for

5. J. Trout and A. Ries, "Positioning Cuts through Chaos in Marketplace," pp. 51–53. Reprinted with permission from the May 1, 1972 issue of *Advertising Age*. Copyright 1972 by Crain Communications, Inc.
6. Fairfax Cone, *With All Its Faults* (Boston: Little, Brown and Company, 1969), p. 249.
7. Cone, *With All Its Faults*, p. 250.

poor taste," because, after all, products do not become successful by offending people.

6. Finally, the name should not be too cute, too clever, or too dear. This is difficult. In the search for a distinctive name, there is always the temptation to substitute the clever for the direct, the contrived for the simple, and the phony for the honest.

Despite the difficulty of brand name selection, finding the appropriate brand name is well worth the effort because, everywhere it appears, it communicates some message about the product; and, the stronger and more appropriate the message, the better the communication.

PACKAGING STRATEGIES

Sizzle-Spray

Sizzle-Spray, a pressurized can of barbecue sauce developed by Heublin, Inc., was a marketing disaster in its initial test markets. J.G. Martin, Heublin's chairman at the time, stated:

> We thought we had a good can, but fortunately we first test marketed the product in stores in Texas and California. It appears as soon as the cans got warm they began to explode. Because we hadn't gotten into national distribution, our loss was only $150,000 instead of a couple of million.[8]

Jack Daniel's

Why is Jack Daniel's whiskey sold in a square bottle? The story they tell in Lynchburg (Pop. 361), Tennessee, the home of Jack Daniel's, goes something like this. Many years ago, when Jack Daniel was operating a small Tennessee distillery, a glass salesman approached him with a proposition to supply all of his bottling needs. The glass salesman used the following approach: "Mr. Daniel, before I came to see you, I wanted to find out what kind of a man you were and what you were like to do business with. So, I called on every tavern and business in this part of the country and asked, 'What kind of a man is Jack Daniel?' To a man, they all said, 'You won't find a better, more honest man than Jack Daniel. You can depend on his word. He's a *square* man to do business with.' Mr. Daniel, that gave me an idea. I think you should capi-

talize on your reputation. I think you should put your whiskey in a square bottle and call it 'Square Jack Daniel's'" So the story goes.

L'eggs

The pantyhose boom in supermarkets began in 1969, and was characterized by low prices, poor quality control, and private labels. Hanes Corporation broke the pattern with a relatively high priced product—selling at least 30 percent above competition—consistent quality, a $10 million advertising budget built around the theme, "Our L'eggs fit your Legs," a $5 million sales promotion program, consignment selling, and a unique packaging idea.[9]

Not least in the marketing strategy for L'eggs was an egg-shaped, plastic package that distinguished the product from competition, tied in with the product name, and contributed overtones of brand quality, dependability, and newness in a psychological context that was appealing to women and appropriate to supermarkets.

Each of these examples says something unique about packaging. Its importance from the standpoint of product protection and safety (Sizzle-Spray); what it can say about the manufacturer (Jack Daniel's); and its ability to communicate with consumers (L'eggs).

AN OVERVIEW OF PACKAGING

What is a package? In the automotive, fashion, appliance, home furnishings, fabric, and similar product fields, the product *package* is the styling or design of the product. In the packaged goods field, the package is the container in which the product is sold. In either case, the package is a significant channel of communication with the consumer.

In the fashion field, it is a truism that marketing success is a function of design. In the automotive industry, the strategy of style obsolescence has made Detroit the automotive capital of the world. Since the case for packaging is obvious in those industries in which the product design *is* the package, we will turn our attention to the packaged goods field, where the package is only a container for enclosing and, sometimes, dispensing the product, and where the package is normally discarded after the product has been used.

In the packaged goods field, over $22 billion a year is spent on packaging by United States' industries.

8. "Product Tryouts: Sales Tests in Selected Cities Help Trim Risks of National Marketing," *Wall Street Journal* (10 August 1962), p. 1. Reprinted with permission of the *Wall Street Journal* © 1962, Dow Jones & Company, Inc. All rights reserved.

9. "Our L'eggs Fit Your Legs," *Business Week* (March 25, 1972): 96–98.

About two-thirds of this amount is spent in packaging products for the ultimate consumer.[10] Yet, packaging is one of the most neglected areas of marketing. An examination of marketing texts and journal articles indicates that the subject is either totally ignored or treated in such an off-hand manner that it may as well have been ignored. A stroll through supermarkets, or simple experience as a consumer, indicates that much packaging is badly designed, cheap, and inconvenient. One sometimes gets the impression that for many manufacturers the marketing concept stopped short of packaging. This is unfortunate because packaging is one of the most obvious channels of communication with consumers. Packages are everywhere—on the retail shelf, in displays, in advertising, and, after the product is purchased, in the home. This general neglect of packaging has been noted by others. In a speech prepared for the American Management Association's conference on packaging, one speaker said:

> Packaging is the hottest buy in advertising today—and the least understood. First, packaging is the biggest of the advertising media. The message on the package usually reaches far more people than any type of conventional advertising the product can afford. However, businessmen haven't bothered to measure its coverage. Second, it is the least expensive of ad media. Space which costs millions of dollars elsewhere is free on the package; this space is paid for in manufacturing to contain and protect the product. Additional charges to make the package do a better promotional job are usually infinitesimal in relation to audience size. Third, it is the most potentially effective medium. It is seen by those customers who may buy, at the spot where they buy, and at the moment of the buying decision. Packaging has enormous circulation with virtually no waste. Yet, as a marketing tool, it is poorly understood, generally mismanaged, and barely exploited.[11]

Not all packaging, of course, is poorly done. There are many outstanding packages on the market. The Little Mac (the 60 second burger machine) package, by showing the product in use, dramatizes both its speed and versatility (see figure 9–1). The Pringles package is a packaging idea that earned Procter and Gamble a multimillion dollar share of the potato chip market (see figure 9–2). L'eggs is a superb example of utilizing packaging to express the essential product concept, to facilitate recall of the product name, and to identify the product with the retail outlets through

10. Maurice I. Mandell, *Advertising,* 2nd ed. (Englewood Cliffs, New Jersey: Prentice-Hall, Inc., 1974), p. 168.

11. S.M. Barker, "How to Calculate Package Audience," p. 22. Reprinted by permission of the publisher from *Profitability and Penetration Through Packaging,* an AMA Bulletin No. 65, © 1965 by the American Management Association, Inc.

which it is primarily sold (see figure 9–3). And, the Electrasol package is a clean, straightforward package that communicates the product concept at a glance (see figure 9–4). The Hamburger Helper package, with the ubiquitous Betty Crocker spoon (see figure 9–5), not only dramatizes the product concept with a picture and a few judiciously chosen words, but also seals it with the stamp of approval of "America's first lady of foods."

Figure 9–1.   (Hamilton Beach-Dominion)

Figure 9–2.   (Procter & Gamble)

Each of the above examples appears to be designed with the product concept in mind; each communicates this concept to consumers; each provides visibility on the retail shelf; each tells its story directly and simply;

Figure 9-3. (L'eggs Products, Inc.)

each is adaptable to print and TV advertising; and each protects the product. In short, each of these packages does what a package is supposed to do and thereby makes a tangible contribution to the marketing effort.

The Functions of Packaging

Traditionally, packaging has played a minor role in the marketing mix. More recently, this role has been expanded, although only a few companies have fully realized its potential. Basically, packages have four functions—protection, economy, convenience, and promotion.

Protection. The least the manufacturer seeks in packaging is the protection of the product during its passage from the manufacturer to the warehouse to the retailer and, eventually, to the consumer. To gain this end, double packaging is used—an outer, shipping carton for transportation and delivery to the retailer, and individual packages for shelving and sale to consumers. The minimum requirement for protection is that the package be sufficiently strong to withstand rough handling and sufficiently air tight and leak proof to protect the freshness and integrity of its contents.

Economy. A second function of the package is economy. Unfortunately, many manufacturers regard the package primarily as an expense item, without any redeeming marketing features. This emphasis on cost, more than any other, has retarded the development of the package as a marketing tool and often leads to packaging that is shoddy, unattractive, difficult to shelve, and inconvenient to use. A case in point is the "blister-packs" used for table-ready meats and many other small retail items sold through supermarkets, drug stores, and hardware outlets. The blister-pack, indeed, protects the product and keeps it fresh; it is also economical; but it is an abomination to open.

Convenience. A third function of the package is convenience, both for shipping and shelving and for the consumer. From the standpoint of shipping, warehousing, and shelving, convenience has taken the form of standardization of shipping carton sizes (wherever possible), easy to open shipping cartons,

Figure 9–4. (Economics Laboratory, Inc.)

Figure 9–5. (General Mills, Inc.)

"price spots" for retail pricing, and, more recently, the Universal Product Code and Symbols (UPC), for computerized check-out counters and inventory control. The UPC promises the elimination of price marking (the price is carried in the computer and scanned at the check-out counter), reduction of check-out costs and errors (a major expense item for supermarkets), and improved inventory control (inventory status is automatically monitored by the computer).

Figure 9–6 shows an example of the UPC, as well as a typical sales receipt that is automatically printed for the customer.

For consumers, convenience has also taken a variety of forms—easy to open packages; pour spouts, aerosol cans and other dispensing devices; a wide variety of package sizes for different size families; multiple-packs; heat and serve items; frozen foods packaged in compartmentalized serving trays; shake-and-bake products; boil-in-the-bag foods; dry mixes that the user can mix in the original package; reclosable packages; and so forth. As convenience foods became a big business, the need for convenience packages grew.

Promotion. A fourth function of the package is promotion. Here, the package is recognized for its value in enhancing the brand's appeal through typography, colors, and illustrations; for conveying the desired brand image, describing the product's features, and providing recipes and service suggestions. Often, the package can be designed so that it can be used as an attractive dispenser in the home—on the dining table for food products and in the bedroom or bath for products such as toiletries and facial tissues.

A good package, of course, is one that performs all of these functions in an optimal fashion, always being subject to the mutual constraints of each.

Packaging Strategy

There are a number of ways in which packaging can be used as a strategic tool, in the marketing effort of a product. The strategies employed should enhance or at least be compatible with the product concept. Among the more important packaging strategies are: the small size produced in some fields, such as toiletries, for the convenience of travelers.

Size Strategy. Many markets may be segmented in terms of volume users or the way in which the product is used. Examples of this may be found in the marketing of both "regular" and "family size" packages or the small size produced in some fields for the convenience of travelers.

Size strategy also plays a role in new product introductions, both to encourage retail stocking and consumer trial. In the first instance, shipping cartons of six or twelve individual packages may be used to minimize the retailer's investment and to create the impression of high case movement. The use of this strategy also requires relatively intense sales coverage to avoid out-of-stock conditions. After a new product is well established, the shipping carton can be increased in size—perhaps to twenty-four or forty-eight units to

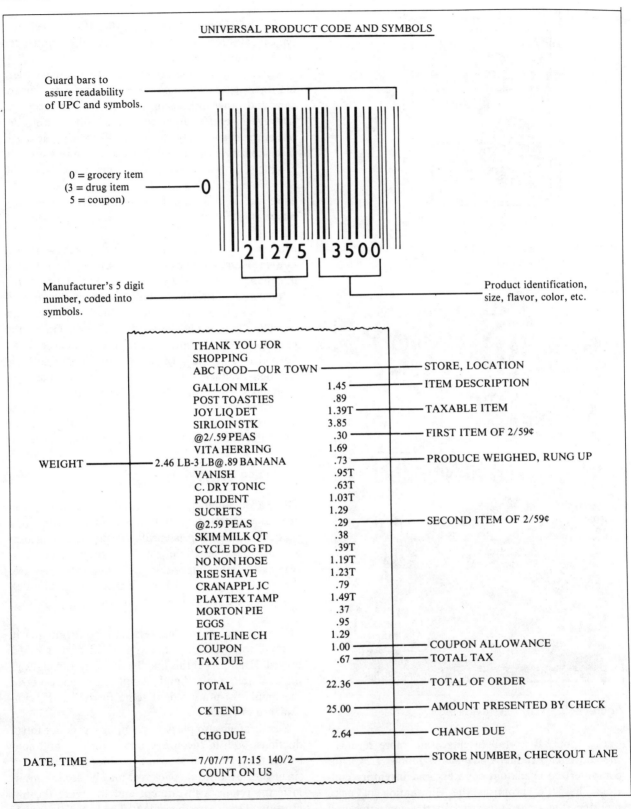

Figure 9-6. Example of the Universal Product Code and Symbols, along with an example of a typical sales receipt. (From GREY MATTER. Grey Advertising, Inc.)

decrease packaging costs. For consumers, a small size package is usually used for introductory purposes to minimize consumer risk; larger sizes are introduced later to meet the requirements of volume users and to provide additional shelf facings and promotional push.

Material Strategy. The material used in a package may play a major role in marketing strategy. For example, packaging materials may be used to impute *quality,* or to insure *safety.* Examples of the first are tasteful display boxes designed for small luxury goods such as jewelry or electric shavers. The second instance is illustrated by nonbreakable shampoo bottles or closures that make it difficult for children to open packages, the contents of which may be dangerous to them.

Shape Strategy. Product shape has long been recognized for its perceptual implications. Smooth, rounded shapes, for example, connote femininity; square, solid shapes imply masculinity. Shapes may also be designed to encourage in-home display on the dining table or in another room of the home where it serves as a visual reminder of the brand. Liquid bath soaps have been packaged in the form of animals, fish, and other objects to provide a pleasant distraction for the child undergoing the unpleasant experience of being bathed. A number of years ago, Log Cabin syrup was packaged in a miniature "log cabin." This practice was abandoned, presumably because of costs and difficulties in shelf stacking.

Design Strategy. Design strategy may, of course, also involve shapes and materials. But here the emphasis is on colors, typography, pictures, and symbols that enhance the product in the consumer's mind. Design strategy is often used to give identity to a line of packages, such as the Betty Crocker "red spoon," or the picture of a quaker on Quaker products. And, of course, packaging a product as a gift is a standard practice in the expensive chocolate and distilled spirits industry.

Convenience Strategy. The world is full of convenience packages designed to make life easier for consumers. A number of such examples have already been given. When convenience is a relevant consideration in terms of the product concept (and it often is) then, it may be possible to use the package to fulfill at least a part of this convenience objective. Sometimes, however, convenience is *not* an attribute that con-

sumers really want. For example, people have complained for years about the difficulty of pouring ketchup out of the traditional long-necked, narrow-opening bottle. Yet, when a ketchup manufacturer introduced a wide-mouthed bottle that made pouring easier, consumers weren't interested.

Promotion Strategies. Packages may be designed or redesigned in such ways as to tie in with major sales promotions. Back or side panels lend themselves to featuring recipes, service suggestions, and special offers. Cents-off and two-for-one offers are often emblazoned on the package face. All of these strategies are possible through packaging. It is for these reasons that packaging is emerging as a major element in the marketing mix, and one that can facilitate or hinder the communication of the product concept.

Designing Packages

A package is not a thing. It is an idea. This thought was aptly expressed by Edward Breck, while president of John H. Breck, Inc., marketer of Breck Shampoo.

> A package is, above all else, an idea. The stronger, the clearer, and the more compelling the idea, the more powerful the package. Many of us in marketing become too absorbed in the details and complexities of package development to realize how important this core idea is to success. Without it the package fails to convey a single impression; its message becomes blurred, and it cannot possibly function with force.[12]

There is no way to tell someone how to design a package. It is a creative, problem solving process. There are, however, certain questions that the package designer should ask. Starting with a clear understanding of the product concept, Walter Margulies, an executive of a leading package design firm, has suggested the following questions.[13]

- How much emphasis should be placed on the brand name? On the product name?
- Toward what segment of the market should be product's basic appeal be aimed?
- In what way will the packaging system best communicate product appeal?

12. E.J. Breck, "Function vs. Aesthetics in Packaging," p. 109. Reprinted by permission of the publisher from *Profitability and Penetration through Packaging,* an AMA Bulletin No. 65 © 1965 by the American Management Association, Inc.
13. From pp. 47–48 in *Packaging Power* by Walter P. Margulies (World). Copyright © 1970 by Walter P. Margulies. By permission of Harper & Row, Publishers, Inc.

- Should the graphics try to convey the size, shape, color, in-use applications? If so, how?

- In dealing with a food product, is it advisable to include recipes on the package? Which ones? Should they be changed in accordance with the seasons?

- Are all package panels being used to their best advantage? Will they effectively sell the product regardless of the way the package is stacked on the supermarket shelf?

- Can the basic design be extended to logically encompass other items in the manufacturer's line? Is it flexible enough to permit the addition of new products at some future date?

- Is there ample space for the inclusion of extra copy to announce special sales offers?

- What about price marking? Has a specific place been set aside where the product can be priced easily by the retailer so as not to mar the total look of the package?

- Is the design flexible enough to permit the addition of new products?

This list is not intended to be exhaustive. But, it is a good starting point.

Testing the Package Design

The finished package should always be tested. Tests of visibility and ease of recognition under different levels of illumination and from different angles are used to check its adequacy for retail display. Shipping tests may be undertaken to ascertain its ruggedness. Accelerated aging tests often need to be made to make sure the package protects product freshness. Consumer tests are employed to determine ease of use and reactions to the overall package design. Sales tests may be undertaken to see how well the package performs under competitive marketing conditions. Only after a package has been subjected to these scrutinies is it truly ready for use.

CHANGING PACKAGES

Normally, it is expected that a particular package design will last for a number of years. Yet, packages do require redesigning from time to time. Reasons for change are manifold: repositioning of the product concept, the availability of new packaging materials or new packaging technology, increased costs of existing materials; competitive innovations; a change in consumer attitudes and values; modernization of the design. All of these factors may raise the question of package change. But, such changes should not be undertaken lightly. A package *is* an important part of the brand's communications with consumers. The

basic question that should always be asked is: "Will this change help or hurt the brand?"

In some fields, package changes are readily accepted by consumers. In others they are not. Several years ago, *Business Week* prepared a presentation for advertising agencies and for distillery managements which demonstrated that, since the turn of the century, no successful, distilled whiskey has made a package design change without suffering a decline in sales. At one point, Camel cigarettes attempted to simplify its package by removing some of the pyramids and palm trees from the package face. Consumer complaints were so vocal that the elements were restored. On the other hand, Ivory Soap has changed the package for its bar soap many times in almost a century of marketing. Many of the changes are almost imperceptible, but in the aggregate, the appearance of the package has undergone a transformation (see figure 9–7).

Stephen Barker, executive of a packaging firm, has offered a checklist of package changes, some of which involve low risk, and some of which involve high risk. This checklist is shown in table 9–2.

How much a package should be changed, and how frequently changes should be made are questions of marketing judgment that must be made on a product by product basis and always in the light of the existing competitive situation.

LEGAL REQUIREMENTS FOR PACKAGING

Within the past few decades, legal restrictions on packaging have grown along with the consumer movement. The Fair Packaging and Labeling Act of 1966 states:

> Informed consumers are essential to the fair and efficient functioning of a free economy. Packages and their labels should enable consumers to obtain accurate information as to the quality of the contents and should facilitate value comparisons. Therefore it is hereby declared to be the policy of the congress to assist consumers and manufacturers in reaching these goals in the marketing of goods.

The Food and Drug Administration (FDA) is responsible for enforcing the law in regard to foods, drugs, cosmetics, and other devices. The Federal Trade Commission (FTC) has jurisdiction over other consumer products.

Since 1970, FDA regulations require manufacturers to submit data on the safety of food, including the packaging materials with which it may come in con-

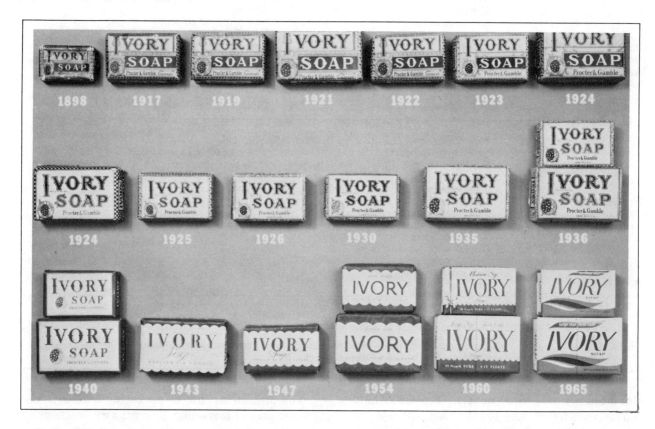

Figure 9–7. Changes in Ivory Soap packages from 1898 to 1965 (Procter & Gamble)

tact. These regulations also specify precise labeling requirements, including descriptive words that may be used, how quantities and volume must be stated, the size and placement of type relating to volume and weight, and background colors. There are also rules governing misrepresentation, slack-fill, health, and a variety of other factors. Obviously, these regulations place restrictions on package design. Some of the restrictions are undoubtedly beneficial; others, merely whimsical. In any case, the package designer under today's legislation should have a good lawyer.

SUMMARY

The brand name plays a major role in communicating salient product characteristics to consumers. As a consequence, great care should go into its choice. Ideally, the brand name should communicate the essential attributes of the product concept. If such a name is not available, then a neutral name should be

chosen; that is, a name into which the desired meaning can be built through advertising and promotion. One should carefully avoid choosing a name that contradicts the essential product concept.

Brand names are covered by a host of legislation. There are certain legal restrictions applying to the use of trademarks.

There are four brand name strategies that may be employed: (1) use of company name plus product identification, as in the case of Campbell's Tomato Soup; (2) company name plus a brand name, such as the Ford Pinto; (3) a brand name plus product identification, such as White House Evaporated Milk, an A&P product; and (4) the use of a brand name only as in the case of Pampers, Duz, or Marlboro. The first three of these strategies are known as *brand extension strategies* because the same name is extended over more than one product. The value of brand extensions lies in the reduction of promotional costs; the disadvantage in the approach lies in the possibility that the use of the same name across several products may

Table 9-2. Packaging threats to a consumer franchise

	Low Risk	*High Risk*
Change in Package Graphics	Directions, cautions* Ingredient line, etc.* Other secondary-panel changes Legal copy requirements Temporary premium offer Temporary deal offer	New name New principal color New illustration, photo New logo New style New design shapes Other new design features on main panel Directions, cautions*
Change in Package Structure	New convenience feature New cap or fitment** New material** Fewer inks** Additional packages† Additional sizes† Temporary premium pack Multipack Sample package Display pack New shipping case New distributor pack New unit load	New type package New shape package Change in only size Obvious but unexplained change in critical material‡

NOTES: *Risk depends on degree of change.
　　　　**If appearance is not dramatically different.
　　　　†Line extension.
　　　　‡As elimination of protective lining.
SOURCE: Stephan M. Barker, "When to change your package—and when not to," p. 49. Reprinted with permission from the May 23, 1977 issue of *Advertising Age*. Copyright 1977 by Crain Communications, Inc.

blur the individual product images. There are no hard and fast rules for selecting brand names, although the name should be simple, easy to pronounce, easily recognizable, and compatible with the product concept.

The promotional use of packaging is often a neglected area in marketing. The primary functions of packaging are product protection, economy, convenience, and promotion.

QUESTIONS

1. Three basic guidelines governing the selection of brand names are given in the chapter. Identify these guidelines and give examples to demonstrate them.
2. Distinguish between the following terms: (a) *trade name*, (b) *brand*, (c) *brand name*, (d) *brand mark*, and (e) *trademark*.
3. Identify the major restrictions applying to trademarks that are given in the chapter.
4. Explain what is meant by *brand extension* strategies. Give examples.
5. What are the advantages and disadvantages of using a brand extension strategy.
6. Identify the guidelines for selecting brand names.
7. What is meant by the statement, "Packaging is the hottest buy in advertising today?" Is packaging really advertising? Why or why not? If it is not advertising, what is it?
8. What are the basic functions of packaging?
9. Identify and give examples of the various packaging strategies listed in the text.
10. Identify some of the package changes that generally involve high risk. What is the key question to ask when considering a package change?

PROBLEM

The nondairy creamer market was established by Carnation with the introduction of Coffee-mate. Coffee-mate was supported by a heavy advertising campaign, and within a year of its introduction had obtained 90 percent all commodity distribution.

King's Dairy, a large, regional dairy products company, felt that the nondairy creamer market offered an opportunity for corporate growth. Research in the company's marketing area—an area that included about 30 percent of U.S. households—indicated that 12 percent of the families had tried Coffee-mate within a year of its introduction. Six months later, another survey revealed that only 13 percent of the families had tried it. While this slow rate of growth was disappointing, King's management was encouraged by the finding that 50 percent of all tryers had repurchased the product. They reasoned that if they should enter the field the combined promotion of the advertising brands could accelerate market growth. They also felt that there was room for two or three competitive products in the market.

King's research and development department was having a great deal of difficulty in developing a product that was preferred over Coffee-mate, however. The basic technology was not too difficult, but certain flavoring agents used in Coffee-mate were difficult to isolate. A series of blind product tests run against Coffee-mate, using successive formulations on samples of one hundred housewives, had yielded the following results.

Formulation:	#25	#26	#27	#28	#29
Preferred Coffee-mate	60%	53%	48%	40%	32%
Preferred King's Product	30%	42%	41%	34%	31%
No preference	10%	5%	9%	26%	37%

Formulation #29 was considered by King's management to be comparable to Coffee-mate, although no better. Nonetheless, because of the comparable preference scores for this formulation, combined with the large percentage of participants who could not distin-guish between the two products, a decision was made to market formulation #29.

Since the King product was no better than Coffee-mate according to the tests they had run, King's management felt they had to differentiate their product in some way. After talking to several packagers, they decided to do so through distinctive packaging. Instead of packaging the product in a standard glass jar, a white, plastic package shaped like a cream pitcher was designed. It was felt that this package had several advantages: (1) the shape of the package suggested cream; (2) it was unique and easily recognizable; (3) the package, because of its attractiveness, could be left on the kitchen table or counter, and would thus serve as a constant reminder of the brand; (4) the shape of the package made it easy to handle; and (5) since it was plastic, it would not break if dropped.

On the negative side, the package had certain disadvantages: (1) it cost 3 cents more per package to produce than a standard glass jar, thus either requiring a slightly higher selling price to retailers or requiring a reduction in company margins; (2) it was somewhat more difficult to stack on retail shelves because of its shape; (3) the plastic was slightly hydrostatic. (That is, it had a tendency to attract dust and soiled easily.) After careful consideration of these factors, King's management decided they were negligible and introduced the product simultaneously throughout its marketing region under the name *King's Instant Creamer.* The product was priced at 25 cents a case higher than Coffee-mate for a case of twelve packages. The introductory advertising featured the "Cream pitcher package with the real cream flavor."

Assignment

1. Evaluate King's strategy.
2. Do you agree or disagree with the company's decision to market the product?
3. Would you have done anything differently?

10

Pricing and Distribution Strategy

Wilkinson Sword, Ltd.

For years, the market for razor blades was uneventful. Innovations were rare, and razor blade manufacturers were complacent and lethargic. Then, Wilkinson Sword, Ltd., a British firm, changed the name of the game. Wilkinson introduced a stainless steel blade into the U.S. market that was clearly superior to American made products. The new blade was heavily supported by advertising and priced at 15.8 cents apiece. The blade was an immediate success.

> Overnight, Wilkinson accumulated a staggering backlog of orders, the sort of thing that usually results in delivery delays and an expensive crash expansion program. Had Wilkinson started at 20¢ a blade . . . it would have been much better able to fortify its position.[1]

Home Permanents

Home permanents were first introduced into the consumer market at a price of twenty-five cents a package. The product was a colossal failure. Women

1. Gilbert Burck, "The Myths and Realities of Corporate Pricing," *Fortune Magazine* (April, 1972), p. 84.

simply were not interested. Then, the same product was repackaged and introduced at $1.25 a package. It was a smashing success. Apparently, women were unwilling to trust their hair to a twenty-five cent product, for fear of hair damage. The higher price increased their confidence in the product's safety, and a new industry was born.

Hickory Hill Bacon

The Independent Packing Company of St. Louis, Missouri, had a problem. It had 11 million pounds of bacon in inventory that the company couldn't sell at prevailing prices. The problem was that, under existing pricing practices, the amount of bacon produced exceeded demand, whereas the other parts of the hog—ham, pork roasts, spare-ribs, and so forth, were disposed of nicely. One approach, of course, would have been the traditional economist's approach to surpluses; reduce prices, let expanded demand dispose of the surplus, and accept the losses in anticipated revenue with good grace. After all, there's a certain amount of risk in all business. But the Gardner Advertising Company had a better idea. Change the product and raise the price.

How do you change bacon? It wasn't hard. Cut it into thick slices, give it a heavier-than-usual smoke, put it into a package designed to simulate a hickory log, and name it Hickory Hill Bacon—"a thick sliced, heavy smoked bacon, with a real country flavor." It worked, and a surplus of hog fat was turned into a surplus of profit.

Each of these examples compounds the complexity of price as a variable in the marketing process. Too low a price for Wilkinson's razor blades produced more consumer demand than the company could handle. Too low a price for home permanents failed to produce any consumer demand at all. In the case of Hickory Hill Bacon, a minor modification of the product, accompanied by a strong selling idea, disposed of an unwanted surplus at a premium price.

Pricing strategy is one of the more complex decisions in marketing. In order to understand its function, we need to turn to some of the basic concepts of economics and trace their evolution into today's marketing practices.

BASIC ECONOMIC CONCEPTS

Historically, economics was founded on the interrelationship of supply and demand, as mediated by the price mechanism. The essentials of this interrelationship are shown in figure 10–1.

Supply and Demand

Figure 10–1a represents a simplified *demand* curve. It slopes downward and to the right; as price decreases, demand increases because more consumers can afford to buy the product. Figure 10–1b represents the *supply* curve. It slopes upward and to the right. As price increases, more suppliers are attracted to the product field because of the increased opportu-

nity for profits. Figure 10–1c represents the *point of equilibrium,* the point where the supply curve and the demand curve intersect and where supply equals demand. A static condition of equilibrium is never achieved because, as prices rise and profit opportunities become more attractive, many suppliers gravitate to the product field and production soon exceeds demand. Then, as prices fall because of excess production, suppliers desert the field in search of more attractive investment opportunities and supply decreases until demand again predominates and prices start to rise. Thus, the equilibrium point is only a balancing mechanism that keeps supply and demand in an ever-changing relationship. All of us have experienced the effects of supply and demand. When cattle production is high, producers lower prices to dispose of their production, the price of beef drops, and we all eat steak. However, as prices decrease, the production of beef becomes less profitable. Production is cut back; marginal producers drop out of the field entirely because they can no longer make a profit; beef becomes scarce. Under the impact of scarcity, demand exceeds supply; prices rise until many consumers can no longer afford to buy beef in the quantities they have in the past and turn to fish, poultry, lamb, pork, cheese, or other substitute products. High beef prices encourage new production, and the cycle begins again.

The foregoing description of the market response to price is based on the assumption that all consumers are aware of price changes and respond to them in the same way. However, from a practical point of view, this assumption is invalid. This gives rise to the concept of price elasticity of demand.

Price Elasticity of Demand

Price elasticity of demand refers to the effect that a change in price has on total income which is computed by multiplying price by demand. For example,

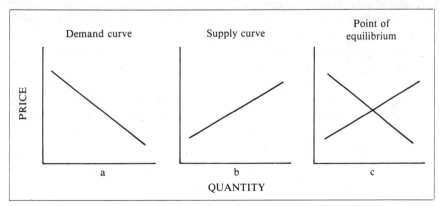

Figure 10–1.   Supply and demand curves

if the price of a product is $1.00, and demand is 100,000 units, then total income is $1.00 x 100,000 = $100,000. There are three forms of price elasticity of demand: *unitary elasticity, price elasticity,* and *price inelasticity.*

Unitary Elasticity. Under conditions of unitary elasticity, a change in price will be compensated for by a change in demand so that total income remains the same.

Price Elasticity. Under conditions of price elasticity, a change in price will yield a disproportionate increase in demand. A price *decrease* will result in an *increase* in total revenue, and a price increase will result in a *decrease* in total revenue.

Price Inelasticity. Under conditions of price inelasticity, a *decrease* in price will result in a *decrease* in total revenue, and an *increase* in price will result in an *increase* in total revenue.

From the standpoint of the individual firm, prices are *too high* if demand is *elastic* because a decrease in price would result in an increase in total revenue. Similarly, if prices are *inelastic,* so that an increase in price would *increase* total income, prices are too low.[2]

TRADITIONAL PRICING

In traditional economic theory, the relationship between supply and demand is wholly a function of price. Practically, it doesn't always work this way—note the examples of home permanents and Hickory Hill bacon. Nonetheless, price considerations continue to dominate most economic thinking. Philip Kotler has pointed out that there are persuasive *historical, technical,* and *social* reasons for economists to emphasize price.[3]

From a *historical* point of view, economics emerged as a discipline at a time when production was characterized by commodities—wheat, cotton, sugar, and other raw materials; even basic foodstuffs and clothing were largely undifferentiated. Branding, packaging, and advertising were virtually unknown. The major factor differentiating one loaf of bread from another, or one bushel of wheat from another, was price.

Further, since most incomes were low, and luxuries were enjoyed only by the wealthy, frugality was a necessary condition for existence.

From a *technical* point of view, price was emphasized because it was easily quantified and unambiguous. Thus, it provided an easy tool for analyzing economic activity. Other considerations such as product quality, brand image, promotion, and customer service were difficult to define and even more difficult to measure since they are essentially psychological in nature.

From a *social* point of view, price offered a defensible rationale for the operation of the marketing system. Price fluctuations served as a mechanism to control surpluses and scarcities. When surpluses existed, there was a tendency to cut prices to get rid of excess production. The lower prices increased demand and discouraged further production. When scarcity prevailed, there was a tendency to raise prices to increase profits. This, in turn, attracted new producers to the field. Supply and demand, aided by the price mechanism, automatically controlled the economy and kept it in balance.

CHANGING POINTS OF VIEW

Over time, two factors emerged in the United States which conspired to change the traditional role of pricing. First, economic growth gave rise to a large body of relatively affluent consumers. Mere subsistence was no longer the rule; discretionary income became commonplace, and millions of consumers discovered that they had a taste for luxuries. Second, dramatic increases in productive capacity, combined with an increased rigidity of costs brought about by the mechanization of production and the emergence of labor unions, generated a perpetual surplus for many products. Manufacturers found themselves faced with the need to increase demand in order to dispose of their production, and they were unable to lower prices sufficiently to do so and still make a profit. As I pointed out in chapter 1, industry responded to this challenge with the *marketing concept* and actively began to seek new ways of attracting consumers. Market segmentation and product differentiation became a way of life, and these strategies gave rise to two new phenomena: *monopolistic competition* and *symbolic pricing.*

Monopolistic Competition

Pure competition exists when there are many suppliers and all products are homogeneous. Thousands

---

2. This statement is contingent on the behavior of costs at various levels of production since an increase in total revenue does not necessarily result in an increase in profits. However, for our purposes, we may consider the suggested relationship to be generally valid.

3. Philip Kotler, *Marketing Management,* 2nd ed. (Englewood Cliffs, New Jersey: Prentice-Hall, Inc., 1972), p. 515.

of wheat farmers offering their harvest for sale represent a condition of pure competition. This is one end of the competitive spectrum. At the other extreme is the concept of *monopoly,* where one supplier controls the entire supply of a product that consumers must buy because there are no substitutes. There is probably no such thing as a true monopoly because there are generally substitutes of one sort or another. Nonetheless, the *concept* of monopoly is still valid. Between these two extremes, there are an infinite number of marketing structures, one of which is *monopolistic competition.*[4]

In monopolistic competition, the product of each competitor differs in *some* way from that of other competitors, so that, in effect, each manufacturer has a monopoly because an exact duplicate of its product cannot be obtained from any other source.[5] True, there are substitute products. For example, one could buy a Ford instead of a Chevrolet and do just as well. But, if the consumer wants a new Chevrolet, the only supplier is the Chevrolet Division of General Motors. Branding, packaging, style, and advertising claims are used by modern marketers to reinforce the concept of a monopoly, and to perpetuate the impression that there is *no real* substitute for the brand being promoted. The major advantage of monopolistic competition for the producer is that it minimizes the need to compete on the basis of price and gives rise to the practice of nonprice competition.

Symbolic Pricing

In monopolistic competition, price is a symbol used by producers to create an *impression* about their products in the minds of consumers. And, as a symbol, price need not function in the traditional manner. For many products, a higher price may lead to an increase in demand rather than a decrease as portrayed by traditional economic theory because, in these instances, price serves as a symbol of quality. Similarly, a low price may discourage demand rather than increasing it because the low price connotes inferiority, as was the case with the home permanents example.

PRICING IN CONTEMPORARY MARKETING

Contemporary marketing does not deny the general validity of traditional economic theory. Generally speaking, a lower prce *does* result in an increase in demand. There are more Chevrolets sold than Rolls-Royces; when the price of steak skyrockets, most of us make do with hamburger, chicken, or fish; and a price reduction on a popular brand can do remarkable things to the sales curve. However, contemporary marketing is no longer a slave to price, having found that product differentiation and consumer psychology can be used to loosen the shackles that traditionally bound supply and demand together in a rigid price relationship. As a consequence, symbolic pricing has *joined* traditional pricing theory as a marketing tool. Together, they make a formidable team.

There are several reasons why symbolic pricing is an effective marketing tool. *First,* most consumers believe that there is a necessary relationship between the price of a brand and its manufacturing cost. This belief is often expressed through the cliché, "You get what you pay for." Studies by Leavitt,[6] as well as Tull, Boring, and Gonsior,[7] and by Gabor and Granger[8] support this observation. Unfortunately, this belief isn't necessarily true. A private-label shaving cream that sells for sixty-nine cents often costs no less for product and package than does the advertised brand selling for double the price. The $2.25 proprietary medicine often costs no more than twenty-five cents for product and package; and the bulk of the cost is in the package. In personal care products, distilled spirits, cosmetics, proprietary medicines, hard goods, home furnishings, art objects, and even in food and clothing, price is often as much of a reflection of product positioning as it is of product costs. Morris and Bronson correlated price with the quality ratings of *Consumer Union* for forty-eight sets of products (mostly, major household appliances) over a period from 1957 to 1968. They concluded that: "Price and quality do correlate, but at so low a level as to lack practical significance." Further, there was no obvious method by which the consumer could identify the set of products for which price-as-an-indicator-of-quality works.[9]

4. Edward H. Chamberlin, *The Theory of Monopolistic Competition* (Cambridge, Massachusetts: Harvard University Press, 1933).
5. Economists generally distinguish between *monopolistic competition* and *differentiated oligopoly.* In monopolistic competition, there are many competitors whose products differ sufficiently to justify branding, advertising, and sales promotion. In a differentiated oligopoly, the same situation prevails in terms of product differences, but there are only a few competitors, rather than many. I have combined monopolistic competition and differentiated oligopoly since my primary focus is on product differences, and not the number of competitors.

6. Harold J. Leavitt, "A Note on Some Experimental Findings about the Meaning of Price," *Journal of Business* (July, 1954): 205–10.
7. D.S. Tull, R.A. Boring, and M.H. Gonsior, "A Note on the Relationship of Price and Imputed Quality," *Journal of Business* (April, 1964): 186–91.
8. Andre Gabor and C.W.J. Granger, "On the Price Consciousness of Consumers," *Applied Statistics* (November, 1961): 170–80.
9. R.T. Morris and C.S. Bronson, "The Chaos of Competition Indicated by Consumer Reports," *Journal of Marketing* (July, 1969): 26–34.

A second reason why symbolic pricing is effective is that, for many products, consumers do not have the expertise required to evaluate product quality. This is particularly true of major appliances, electronic equipment, fabrics, carpeting, furniture, and many other product fields. It is also true for packaged goods, where the goods themselves are concealed by the package and where the list of ingredients on the label would require advanced degrees in chemistry and pharmacology to decipher. In these instances, the consumer is forced to rely on surrogate or substitute indicators such as brand reputation, price, or some other, even more extraneous factor.

A third reason for symbolic pricing is that quality is often in the eye of the beholder; it is a psychological phenomenon that follows the path of the self-fulfilling prophecy. That is, consumers *expect* to be satisfied with their purchases and, barring some blatant product failure, have their expectations fulfilled.

Still a fourth reason for symbolic pricing is the age-old phenomenon of snobbery. Most of us are snobs in one way or another. And, as a consequence, we buy expensive brands to demonstrate our good taste, to impress our friends and relations, and to distinguish ourselves from the crowd.

All of this does not mean that symbolic pricing is completely free from the traditional strictures of the price mechanism or the pressure of competition. In fact, studies have shown that consumers often have a range of prices which they consider appropriate for a particular product type. For example, the Gabor and Granger study referred to earlier found that buyers have two price limits in mind when they consider a purchase: an upper limit above which the product is judged too expensive, and a lower limit below which the quality of the product would be suspect.[10] Similar findings have been reported by Sherif[11] and by Wassen.[12]

Nor can symbolic pricing offset the obvious inferiority of a pair of tennis shoes that fall apart within a few weeks of purchase, nor a television set that spends its life in the repair shop, nor a garment that tears out at the seams after the first washing, nor a thousand other fragilities of the shoddy product. Product performance and price must be generally compatible, and both should project the product concept.

STRUCTURE OF PRICING

Any consideration of pricing strategy must go beyond the price as viewed by the consumer and recognize the pricing practices of the industry in which a particular product is sold. This brings up the problems of manufacturer and channel margins.

Manufacturer Margins

Different manufacturers have different profit requirements and pricing objectives, usually related to traditional practices in the industry, the size of their capital investment, the amount of risk entailed in the product field, the general stability of their respective markets, and the current profit position of the producer.[13] The first requirement of pricing is that it cover manufacturing costs, and provide the margin necessary to meet corporate profit objectives. Only after these minimum requirements are met can symbolic pricing be strategically used.

Distributor Margins

In most distributor and retail fields, there are traditional margins expected for each product class. For example, the traditional margin for cameras in retail department stores is 28 percent; for books, 34 percent; for dresses, 41 percent; for tobacco, 20 percent; and for costume jewelry, 46 percent. It may be possible for the maker of a well-established, high demand brand to "urge" that these margins be shaved somewhat; it is not a prudent practice if channel goodwill is to be maintained. Distributor and retailer margins are sometimes increased to encourage cooperation, but this, too, can lead to problems. For example, the expected cooperation is not forthcoming, but the increased margins are still demanded as a form of legal blackmail. Most frequently, manufacturers only increase distributor and retailer margins on a temporary, promotional basis to increase shelf space, obtain displays, encourage sales support for a special promotion, or to achieve cooperative advertising support.

10. Gabor and Granger, "On the Price Consciousness of Consumers."

11. Carolyn W. Sherif, "Social Categorization as a Function of Latitude of Acceptance and Series Range," *Journal of Abnormal and Social Psychology* **67** (August, 1963): 148–56.

12. Chester Wassen, *Consumer Behavior: A Managerial Viewpoint* (Austin, Texas: Austin Press, 1975), p. 391.

13. For excellent articles on corporate pricing, each taking a somewhat different approach, refer to: Robert L. Lanzillotti, "Pricing Objectives in Large Companies," *American Economic Review* (December, 1958): 921–40; Joel Dean, "Techniques for Pricing New Products and Services," in *Handbook of Modern Marketing*, Victor Buell, ed. (New York: McGraw-Hill Book Company, Inc. 1970), pp. 5:51–5:61; Alfred R. Oxenfeldt, "Multi-Stage Approach to Pricing," *Harvard Business Review* (July–August, 1960): 125–33; Gilbert Burck, "The Myths and Realities of Corporate Pricing," *Fortune Magazine* (April, 1972): 85 ff.; "The Perplexing Problem of Pricing," *Grey Matter*, published by Grey Advertising, Inc., Vol. 37, No. 12 (December, 1966).

PRICING STRATEGIES

The purpose of the foregoing discussion of pricing has been to provide a background for examining pricing strategies. There are a variety of pricing strategies that may be used as a part of the marketing program. The overriding consideration in the use of these strategies is that they support or at least be compatible with the product concept. Some of the most frequently used pricing strategies are briefly described in the following material.

Market Skimming. In market skimming, a new product is introduced at a premium price. Its purpose is to recover investment quickly. Market skimming is a viable strategy when: (1) the new brand has a clear superiority over existing brands; (2) the brand is protected by patents, or the lag time for competitors in developing an equivalent product is relatively long because of technological complexities, or the need to build new plants and equipment; and (3) the market is price *inelastic,* so that a high price will attract enough consumers to be highly profitable. Normally, market skimming is a temporary strategy in the sense that the price will be lowered to a competitive level when other firms enter the field with a comparable product.

Penetration Pricing. Penetration pricing is an introductory pricing strategy in which the new brand is priced relatively low in order to stimulate market growth and capture a large market share. It is a viable approach when the market is highly elastic, or when lag time for competitors is short and management wants to discourage competition by establishing a relatively low profit margin for the product field.

Market Segmentation. Many markets can be segmented on the basis of price; the automobile market is a prime example. Used in this way, pricing strategy is an effective device for appealing to a particular economic segment of the total market.

Prestige and Economy Pricing. As pointed out earlier, consumers in a particular market segment generally have a *range* of prices which they consider appropriate for the product in question. In *prestige* pricing, the brand is priced in the upper region of this range. In *economy* pricing, it is priced in the lower region of this range.

Break-Even Pricing. Break-even pricing is a viable strategy when a product has two or more components, one of which is purchased infrequently, the other fre-

quently. For example, razors are purchased infrequently; razor blades, on the other hand, are purchased much more frequently. One might, in such an instance, price the razor at break-even, or with a slight margin, in order to get the product in use. Blades, then, would be priced with a relatively high margin in order to capitalize on the repurchase pattern of sales. A similar strategy could apply to camera and film, where the manufacturer makes both, or to any other item that requires special refills.

Multiple Pricing. Multiple pricing is, in effect, a quantity discount. A lower price is charged if more than one unit is purchased. This strategy is widely followed by retail stores, particularly grocery and drug outlets, in the form of two-for or three-for combinations. Research has consistently shown that two-for and three-for pricing may double or triple sales over single unit pricing, even though the price savings may be negligible. In many instances, multiple pricing probably steals sales from future periods and does not lead to an absolute increase in usage. In some cases, however, it does increase consumption, particularly for products such as soft drinks and beer, where availability of the product in the home stimulates use. This is the reason why manufacturers of these products use six-packs, or some other multiple unit package.

Line Pricing. Manufacturers who market a line of similar products (such as different flavors of cake mix or soup) or a line of diverse, but related items (such as pet-care products) often find that their manufacturing costs for each item in the line differ. When the differences in costs are substantial, they are usually reflected in the price of the individual items. When the manufacturing costs of the individual items in the line do not vary significantly, a strategy of *average pricing* is often used. Thus, the same price is charged for each item in the line, even though the margins will differ somewhat. On the average, however, the manufacturer achieves the desired margin. The purpose of average pricing is to simplify pricing practices for the consumer and create an impression of comparable quality across the entire line.

Another strategy for price lines is sometimes referred to as *lead* pricing. In this strategy, the high volume items in the line carry relatively low manufacturer margins in order to gain distribution, facilitate consumer purchase, and develop consumer preference. The low volume or specialty items in the line are priced with substantial margins.

Odd Pricing. Odd pricing is most frequently used by retailers, although it may be used by manufacturers when their brands are prepriced (that is, when the price is printed on the package by the manufacturer). Odd pricing is based on the psychological concept that ninety-nine cents is, psychologically, much less than a dollar, or $1.79 is much less than $1.80. One manufacturer of private aircraft consistently suggested odd pricing for its airplanes: $9,990, instead of $10,000; $19,900 instead of $20,000.

Sales Promotion Pricing.　In sales promotion pricing, a price discount is used to deplete inventories, sample consumers, and stimulate sales. This strategy is used by both manufacturers and retailers and involves a variety of price reductions: two-for-the-price-of-one sales, penny sales, various forms of multiple pricing, coupons, and so forth. *Loss leaders* are frequently used by retailers to attract customers. A loss leader is usually a high-volume, frequently purchased item that is price featured in retail advertising near, or below cost. The assumption is that loss leaders will attract customers to the store, and while the customers are there, they will buy other items at the regular price.

Bait Pricing.　Bait pricing is usually used for hard goods and durable items. In this strategy, a stripped-down model is offered at an attractive, low price. When customers inquire about the bargain, salespeople will attempt to trade them up to a higher priced model with more features and a normal margin. Bait pricing is a defensible technique if customers are permitted to purchase the stripped-down model at the advertised price if they wish to. Often, however, unscrupulous retailers have no intention of selling the bargain and offer an excuse that they had only a limited number of the "sale" item and that those have all been sold.

Any or all of the foregoing pricing strategies may be used. It must be recognized, however, that pricing strategy is an integral part of the marketing plan and needs to be coordinated with all other elements of the marketing program through the strictures of the marketing plan.

DISTRIBUTION

Michelob

For many years, Michelob, the premium of premium beers, was sold only in draught form. It was neither bottled nor canned because both required pasteurization or constant refrigeration. Pasteurization caused subtle changes in the flavor of the product, and con-

stant refrigeration was expensive, cumbersome, and difficult to control under conditions of mass distribution. So, Anheuser Busch, the brewer of Michelob, opted for limited distribution in draught outlets. The bars and taverns selected for distribution were carefully chosen and rigorously controlled. Not only were rigid standards imposed concerning the handling of the product (its temperature had to be controlled within specified limits, the dispenser had to be cleaned on a periodic basis, and a keg had to be consumed within a specified time), but also the brewery imposed standards of cleanliness and appearance on dispensing outlets as well as standards for the use of promotional material. In short, retailers of Michelob were selected and policed in such a way as to guarantee the integrity of the product and to enhance the image of the brand.

The strategy of selling Michelob only in draught form was continued until technological developments made it possible to pasteurize the product without injuring the flavor. At that point, distribution strategy was broadened to include a bottled product. Still, control of outlets serving Michelob in draught form remained a strategic concern for Anheuser Busch.

Duncan Hines Cake Mixes

Duncan Hines Cake Mixes were conceived and introduced by Nebraska Consolidated Mills, a small midwestern milling company, several years before the brand was purchased by Procter and Gamble. The initial introductions by Nebraska Consolidated Mills in the midwest were spectacularly successful. Despite heavy advertising and promotion expenditures, the brand "paid out" in well under a year, and achieved 40-50 percent market shares in the backyards of General Mills and Pillsbury which, at that time, dominated the cake mix market.

Dazzled by their success in the midwest, and blinded by dreams of high profits with little effort, the management of Nebraska Consolidated Mills decided to "crash" the California market on a wave of free publicity and with only a token expenditure in advertising and promotion.

General Mills and Pillsbury, belatedly awakened from complacency, countered Duncan Hines' California introduction with every promotional device they had—increased advertising, promotional allowances, massive displays, consumer coupons, the works. As a consequence, Duncan Hines never really got off the ground. In many California markets, it failed to gain a 20 percent share of market, a volume level in the cake mix market necessary, at that time, to maintain widespread distribution and lay a basis for future growth.

Some five years after the California fiasco (after Procter and Gamble had purchased the brand) I had an opportunity to review the national marketing plan for Duncan Hines Cake Mixes. California was characterized as a problem area. The nature of the problem? A weak pattern of distribution and a faltering brand share. Thus, five years later the brand was still suffering from a distribution malaise caused by failure to establish a strong distribution base during its introduction.

Kaiser

Following World War II, Henry J. Kaiser, the industrialist who revitalized the ship building industry and built an industrial empire by mass producing liberty ships, entered the automotive arena with the Kaiser-Fraser Automobile Company. During its relatively brief life, the company manufactured three brands of cars—the Kaiser, the Fraser, and the Henry J. (How do those names grab you?). From the beginning, Kaiser-Fraser was doomed by a weak pattern of distribution, low trade-in values for their products, and a widespread American desire to return to normalcy, a vision which didn't include new brands of automobiles without a tradition of success. In its last throes, Kaiser-Fraser attempted an unsuccessful revolution in automotive retailing. It started distributing the Henry J., a low-priced car, through Sears and Roebuck. In the eyes of consumers, Sears was an appropriate channel of distribution for many items, but not automobiles. They didn't buy, and the Henry J. went down the tubes.

Tractors

One of the principals of a leading management consultant firm relates the following incident:

It was late Friday afternoon in the office of Lester Wadsworth, an elderly Kansas City farm equipment dealer. Larry Richardson, the new regional manager of Benson Tractor Company, had just broken the news that his company was adding a distributor in the Kansas City area. According to his figures, Wadsworth's sales would not suffer. But Wadsworth, who had enjoyed an exclusive franchise for many years, was not taking the decision with good grace.

"Twenty-seven years I've been selling Benson tractors," he was saying. "It's the better part of your lifetime, Larry. Bart Benson and I have come a long way together. We've done a lot of business, and we've shot a lot of duck up at Bart's place in Michigan. I know Bart pretty well, Larry. He doesn't have any use for a sales-

man who isn't out to break every record that's in the book. But Bart's a pretty sound, conservative guy. Sure, he's for growth. But somehow the Benson Tractor Company has stuck with Les Wadsworth for twenty-seven years, while the bright young fellows with the big ideas about expanding distribution have come and gone. It's worth thinking over."

Richardson took a week to think it over and then phoned Wadsworth to tell him that the decision stood. Within a month the new distributorship was a reality, and within a year Benson tractor sales in the Kansas City region rose 40%. Wadsworth's sales had not suffered by the loss, but he was still bitter.[14]

Each of the foregoing examples deals with a somewhat different aspect of distribution. Michelob provides an example of the use of *selective* distribution in order to protect the product and enhance its brand image. Duncan Hines represents a failure to obtain *intensive* (widespread) distribution in a field where intensive distribution is essential to product success. Kaiser emphasizes the role that *tradition* plays in distribution and points up the fact that consumers sometimes have expectations concerning appropriate channels of distribution that restrict manufacturers' freedom in establishing distribution channels. Finally, Benson Tractors is an example of *channel conflict*, which may result in bitterness. And, while Benson's sales were not harmed in this instance, such a happy outcome is not always the case. Together, these examples demonstrate that distribution is not a cut and dried, mechanical process of marketing logistics, but a complex marketing activity that involves strategy, tradition, and emotional involvements.

Most marketing texts deal with distribution from two points of view—from the point of view of *distribution strategy,* which focuses on the selection of appropriate distribution channels; and from the point of view of *logistics* and the costs involved in transporting, warehousing, and controlling the physical flow of goods. Our focus will be on *distribution strategy.* This does not mean that logistics are unimportant. On the contrary, the cost of logistics or physical distribution is a major area of marketing expense and represents one of the greatest opportunities for cost reduction through innovations in materials handling and through the computorization of sales records and inventories. Yet, it is the *strategy* of distribution that reinforces or fails to reinforce the product concept, that facilitates consumer purchase, and that occupies a critical role in market planning.

14. A.L. McDonald, Jr. "Do Your Distribution Channels Need Reshaping," *Business Horizons* (Summer, 1964): 29–38. Copyright, 1964, by the Foundation for the School of Business at Indiana University. Reprinted by permission.

SYSTEMS OF DISTRIBUTION

There are a number of alternatives for making products available to consumers. These alternatives range from direct mail and catalogue sales to complex distribution systems that involve a hierarchy of intermediaries such as agents, wholesalers, jobbers, and retailers. Table 10–1 lists some of the most common intermediaries which, in a variety of combinations, constitute the distribution channels used by manufacturers.

Figure 10–2 shows some of the possible distribution systems that are commonly used for industrial and consumer products.

Table 10–1. Definitions of various marketing intermediaries

Agent. A business unit which negotiates purchases or sales or both but does not take title to the goods in which it deals. The agent usually performs fewer marketing functions than does the merchant. He commonly receives his remuneration in the form of a commission or fee. He usually does not represent both buyer and seller in the same transaction. Examples are: broker, commission merchant, manufacturers agent, selling agent, and resident buyer.

Branch house (manufacturer's). An establishment maintained by a manufacturer, detached from the headquarters establishment and used primarily for the purpose of stocking, selling, delivering, and servicing his product. A branch office is similar, although it is limited to the last two functions.

Branch store. A subsidiary retailing business owned and operated at a separate location by an established store.

Broker. An agent who does not have direct physical control of the goods in which he deals but represents either buyer or seller in negotiating purchases or sales for his principal. The broker's powers as to prices and terms of sale are usually limited by his principal.

Commission house (sometimes called *Commission merchant*). An agent who usually exercises physical control over and negotiates the sale of the goods he handles. The commission house usually enjoys broader powers as to prices, methods, and terms of sale than does the broker, although it must obey instructions issued by the principal. It generally arranges delivery, extends necessary credit, collects, deducts its fees, and remits the balance to the principal.

Consumers' cooperative. A retail business owned and operated by ultimate consumers to purchase and distribute goods and services primarily to the membership; sometimes called *purchasing cooperatives*.

Dealer. A firm that buys and resells merchandise at either retail or wholesale.

Discount house. A retailing business unit featuring consumer durable items, competing on a basis of price appeal, and operating on a relatively low markup and with a minimum of customer service.

Distributor. In its general usage this term is synonymous with *wholesaler*.

Facilitating agencies in marketing. Those agencies which perform or assist in the performance of one or a number of the marketing functions, but which neither take title to goods nor negotiate purchases or sales. Common types are banks, railroads, storage warehouses, commodity exchanges, stock yards, insurance companies, graders and inspectors, advertising agencies, firms engaged in marketing research, cattle loan companies, furniture marts, and packers and shippers.

Industrial store. A retail store owned and operated by a company or governmental unit to sell primarily to its employees. Nongovernmental establishments of this type are often referred to as *company stores* or *commissary stores*. In certain trades the term *company store* is applied to a store through which a firm sells its own products, often together with those of other manufacturers, to the consumer market.

Jobber. This term is widely used as a synonym of *wholesaler* or *distributor*. The term is sometimes used in certain trades and localities to designate special types of wholesalers.

Mail-order house (retail). A retailing business that receives its orders primarily by mail or telephone, and generally offers its goods and services for sale from a catalog or other printed material.

Manufacturer's agent. An agent who generally operates on an extended contractual basis; often sells within an exclusive territory; handles noncompeting but related lines of goods; and possesses limited authority with regard to prices and terms of sale. He may be authorized to sell a definite portion of his principal's output.

Merchant. A business unit that buys, takes title to, and resells merchandise. The distinctive feature of this middleman lies in the fact that he takes title to the goods he handles. Wholesalers and retailers are the chief types of merchants.

Middleman. A business concern that specializes in performing operations or rendering services directly involved in the purchase and/or sale of goods in the process of their flow from producer to consumer. Middlemen are of the two types, merchants and agents. The essence of the middleman's operation lies in the fact that he plays an active and prominent part in the negotiations leading up to transactions of purchase and sale. This is what distinguishes him from a marketing facilitating agent who, while he performs certain marketing functions, participates only incidentally in negotiations of purchase and sale.

Rack jobber. A wholesaling business unit that markets specialized lines of merchandise to certain types of retail stores and also provides the special services of selective brand and item merchandising and arrangement, maintenance, and stocking of display racks. The rack jobber usually, but not always, puts his merchandise in the store of the retailer on consignment. Rack jobbers are most prevalent in the food business.

Resident buyer. An agent who specializes in buying on a fee or commission basis, chiefly for retailers.

Retailer. A merchant, or occasionally an agent, whose main business is selling directly to the ultimate consumer.

Selling agent. An agent who operates on an extended contractual basis, sells all of a specified line of merchandise or the entire output of his principal, and usually has full authority with regard to prices, terms, and other conditions of sale. He occasionally renders financial aid to his principal. This functionary is often called a *sales agent*.

Voluntary group. A group of retailers, each of whom owns and operates his own store and is associated with a wholesale organization or manufacturer to carry on joint merchandising activities, and who are characterized by some degree of group identity and uniformity of operation. Such joint activities have been largely of two kinds: cooperative advertising and group control of store operation.

Wholesaler. A business unit which buys and resells merchandise to retailers and other merchants and/or to industrial, institutional, and commercial users, but which does not sell in significant amounts to ultimate consumers. In the basic materials, semifinished-goods, and tool and machinery trades merchants of this type are commonly known as *distributors* or *supply houses*. Generally these merchants render a wide variety of services to their customers. Those who render all the services normally expected in the wholesale trade are known as *service wholesalers*; those who render only a few of the wholesale services are known as *limited-function wholesalers*. The latter group is composed mainly of cash-and-carry wholesalers who do not render the credit or delivery service; drop-shipment wholesalers, who sell for delivery by the producer direct to the buyer; truck wholesalers, who combine selling, delivery, and collection in one operation; and mail-order wholesalers, who perform the selling service entirely by mail.

SOURCE: Reprinted from *Marketing Definitions: A Glossary of Marketing Terms*, compiled by the Committee on Definitions of the American Marketing Association, Ralph S. Alexander, Chairman, published by the American Marketing Association.

The *length* of a particular distribution system is measured in terms of the number of *stages* or intermediaries that exist between the producer and the ultimate consumer. In figure 10–2, examples I–1 and C–1 represent *zero* stages because the producer sells directly to the consumer without the use of intermediaries. Direct mail and catalogue selling are the most common forms of zero stage distribution systems among consumer products. In the case of industrial sales, zero stage systems are most frequently represented by firms whose sales representatives call on their customers. In contrast, C–4 is a *long* distribution chain since there are four stages or intermediaries between the producer and consumer. Many firms use a combination of distribution chains to reach their ultimate customers.

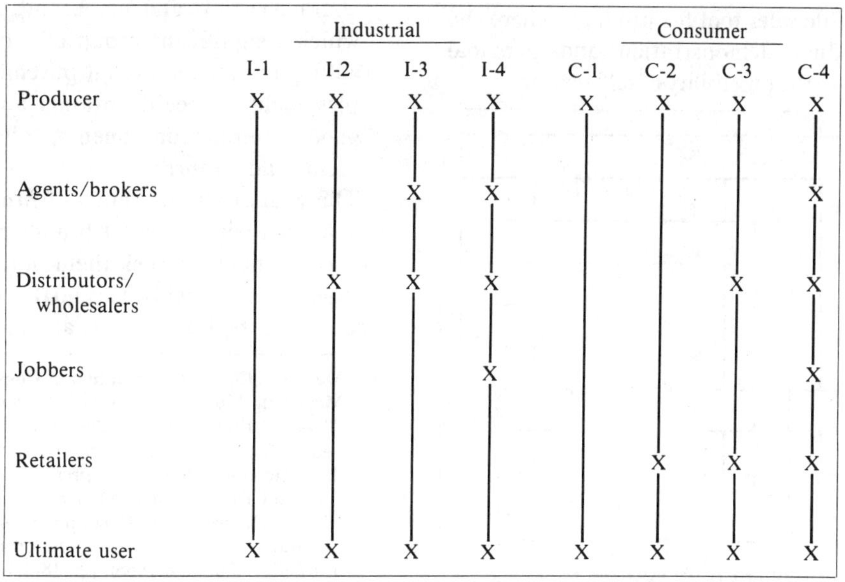

		Industrial				Consumer		
	I-1	I-2	I-3	I-4	C-1	C-2	C-3	C-4
Producer	X	X	X	X	X	X	X	X
Agents/brokers				X	X			X
Distributors/wholesalers		X	X	X			X	X
Jobbers				X				X
Retailers						X	X	X
Ultimate user	X	X	X	X	X	X	X	X

Figure 10–2. Selected examples of channels of distribution for industrial and consumer products.

Figure 10–3 shows a typical channel system for a manufacturer of grocery products that has its own sales force. In this instance, a variety of channels are employed because of the number and size of grocery outlets that must be used in order to make the product available to consumers. Sales to large corporate chains (such as Safeway, A&P, Kroger) are usually direct; whereas sales to independently owned grocery stores require the services of wholesalers and jobbers to provide adequate coverage. If the manufacturer of grocery products reflected in figure 10–3 also sold to other outlets (such as drug stores, plant cafeterias, and restaurants) still other distribution channels would have to be set up to serve these customers.

One problem with *long* channels of distribution is that the producer tends to lose control over the conditions under which its products are sold. Thus, control is lost over the price charged the ultimate consumer, the way in which the brand is displayed, the size of inventories maintained, retail advertising, and the freshness of the product, when this is a relevant factor.

FUNCTIONS OF DISTRIBUTION

Often, when we speak of distribution, we think only in terms of product availability. However, availability is only one dimension of distribution. Practically, distribution serves four distinct functions in marketing.

1. It is a mechanism for making a product available to those consumers for whom it is intended.
2. It is a symbolic communication of product worth.
3. It is a guarantor of consumer satisfaction and customer service.
4. It is an invaluable sales tool for products where the need for product demonstration and personal selling repudiate the possibility of self-service.

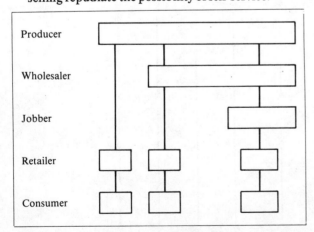

Figure 10–3. Typical channel system for a manufacturer of grocery products that has its own sales force.

Only one of these functions (the first) deals solely with product availability. The other three are concerned with the *type* of retail outlets employed.

The type of distribution used is more important for some products than for others. This is true because the amount of retail service and support required varies by product type. For example, the first function of distribution listed above, product availability, is often the only essential requirement for low-priced, mass-distributed, packaged goods such as cigarettes and soft drinks. By contrast, all four functions of distribution are important for a variety of high-priced, luxury goods, ranging from automobiles to carpeting.

For this reason any consideration of distribution strategy must recognize that consumer goods may be divided into a number of classifications based on the shopping habits of consumers. There are a number of systems for classifying consumer goods; one of the most widely used systems is that developed by Copeland.[15] Copeland classified consumer goods as convenience goods, shopping goods, and speciality goods.[16]

Convenience goods Those consumer goods which the consumer purchases frequently, immediately, and with a minimum of effort in comparison and buying. Examples include cigarettes, soap, many food products, newspapers, and so forth.

Shopping goods Those consumer goods which the customer, in the process of selection and purchase, characteristically compares on such bases as suitability, quantity, price, and style. Examples include furniture, clothing, used automobiles, and appliances.

Speciality goods Those consumer goods with unique characteristics and/or brand identification for which a significant group of buyers are habitually willing to make a special purchasing effort. Examples include specific brands and types of luxury goods, stereo components, photographic equipment, and so forth.

The goal of all marketers of *branded* merchandise is to make their particular brands a speciality good so that consumers will seek them out, accepting no substitutes. In most fields, this goal is only partially realized since substitute brands are usually available and

15. Melvin T. Copeland, "Relation of Consumer Buying Habits to Marketing Methods," *Harvard Business Review* (April, 1923): 282–89. Other systems of classification have been devised by: Leo V. Aspinwall, "The Characteristics of Goods Theory," in *Managerial Marketing: Perspectives and Viewpoints,* rev. ed., William Lazer and Eugene E. Kelley, eds. (Homewood, Illinois: Richard D. Irwin, Inc., 1962), pp. 633–43; Gordon E. Miracle, "Product Characteristics and Marketing Strategy," *Journal of Marketing* (January, 1965), pp. 18–24.
16. *Marketing Definitions: A Glossary of Marketing Terms,* compiled by the Committee on Definitions of the American Marketing Association and Ralph S. Alexander, 1963.

acceptable to consumers if their preferred brands are difficult to obtain.

Having identified the functions of distribution, and having recognized that different types of products are purchased in different ways by consumers, we are now ready to examine distribution strategy as a part of the marketing plan.

DISTRIBUTION STRATEGY

The particular distribution system used by a firm depends on the nature of the markets being served, the types of products involved, and the resources of the producer. Generally, there are three distribution strategies available in the consumer field: *intensive* distribution, *selective* distribution, and *independent* distribution.

Intensive Distribution

In intensive distribution, the marketer seeks widespread availability of the brand, often using multiple channels for this purpose. Intensive distribution is generally appropriate for *convenience* goods. Cigarettes, candy, and soft drinks are commonplace examples of an intensive distribution strategy; these products are found in grocery stores, drug stores, eating and drinking establishments, and in vending machines—a modern American art form that graces most public and many private establishments.

Many, if not most, of the products sold through food and drug outlets fall within the convenience goods classification. For these brands, type of distribution is relatively less important than widespread availability. Even in these instances, however, there are cases in which intensity is sacrificed for other considerations. For example, a product which has a relatively short shelf life may be distributed only in outlets that have high volume turnover in order to protect product freshness. Or, consider proprietary cold tablets that are commonly sold in both food and drug stores. A particular brand in this category that is attempting to project a "clinical" or "prescription" image may adopt a strategy of restricting distribution to drug stores and use this strategy as a device for enlisting the support of registered pharmacists and medical doctors in recommending the brand to consumers. This strategy, in fact, was followed by Coricidin for years. It was also the initial distribution strategy of Contac.

Multiple channels of distribution are often necessary to reach different segments of the same market. Fancy chocolates are a case in point. Fancy chocolates are generally sold through three types of retail outlets:

specialty candy shops, department stores, and drug stores. However, many consumers reject "drug store" candy as inferior or stale and insist on buying in one of the other outlet types. So, for market coverage, drug stores need to be supplemented with other forms of distribution. Interestingly enough, attempts to sell fancy chocolates in food stores have been unsuccessful, even though many food store customers are also buyers of fancy chocolates. Apparently, food stores symbolize "window box" or inexpensive candies and are an inappropriate source for expensive chocolates in the minds of consumers.

Selective Distribution

In a selective distribution strategy, the producer does not seek intensive distribution but elects instead to distribute through a limited number of outlets that complement the brand image and/or provide the level of personal selling and customer service that is required. This distribution strategy is often critical for *shopping* and *speciality* goods where the images of the retail outlets themselves may have a profound effect on the consumer's perception of the brand. For example, a television set that has a marketing emphasis on stylish design, quality performance, and prompt customer service will probably not be sold in an automobile accessories store, even though such a store may be appropriate for more utilitarian television sets. Why? Consumers do not shop for stylish furniture in automobile accessories stores.

Similarly, makers of clothing and other household furnishings that rely on high style, expensiveness, and snob appeal as selling points cannot afford to have their products distributed by retail outlets that do not reflect these same dimensions. The consumer does not expect to find a flawless diamond at K-Mart or Yellow Front and is likely to be suspicious if these outlets purport to carry such items. On the other hand, one does not go to Tiffany's in search of cheap costume jewelry.

Independent Distribution

Independent distribution is a form of selective distribution in which producers bypass existing distribution channels and set up a private distribution system that meets their particular needs. Independent distribution systems take a number of forms.

Direct-mail and catalogue selling are particularly appropriate for speciality items that are infrequently purchased and/or for which buyers are widely, but thinly dispersed throughout the general population. A great deal of hobby equipment and supplies is sold in this way, although this approach has also been used by clothing manufacturers, producers of gift cheeses, and book publishers in order to avoid both the cost and difficulty of obtaining distribution through conventional channels. A relatively recent development in catalogue sales is the offering of a wide variety of nationally advertised brands of durable and semidurable goods at substantial price reductions.

Direct sales agents are used by a number of firms to sell directly to consumers on a door-to-door basis. Avon has successfully used this approach for cosmetics; the Fuller Brush Company was a pioneer in this field; Tupperware has developed in-home selling into an art; and carpet sweepers appear to be moving in this direction.

Company owned stores often sell a particular manufacturer's brands exclusively, although they may also distribute noncompetitive items for other manufacturers. The Delmar Corporation, the retail division of International Shoe, uses this strategy, as do the tire industry and major oil companies.

Franchise distribution uses independent entrepreneurs to make its products or services available to consumers. Under the franchise system, the parent company executes an exclusive agreement with independent business people. The parent company generally provides a protected geographic area, technical service, and managerial help in return for compliance with company standards and capital to establish the local outlet. This strategy has long been used by automobile manufacturers and, in recent years, has found favor in the tourism industry (Holiday Inns, Travelodge, Motel-6), in food service (Kentucky Fried Chicken, McDonald's, Baskin-Robbins, Burger Chef), as well as in a number of other industries.

The primary advantage of an independent distribution strategy is that it guarantees maximum control by the manufacturer at the sacrifice of either immediate service (direct mail and catalogue sales) or widespread product availability.

OBTAINING DISTRIBUTION

Obtaining and keeping distribution is a major problem for most marketers selling through established channels. This is true because the decision as to whether a particular brand will be stocked is made, not by the brand's producer, but by retail management. Further, shelf space is limited, and retail management is often reluctant to take on new products because it increases its inventory and complicates its billing. In the grocery field, for example, a major supermarket may carry over 14 thousand different items. Each week, store management will be offered

as many as 100 new items—5 thousand a year. Since shelf space is not elastic, the addition of a new item requires some adjustment in existing stocks. Either the number of shelf facings on existing products must be decreased, or an item must be discontinued. Reduction in the number of shelf facings is often uneconomical from the retailer's point of view because it increases stocking costs and the danger of out-of-stock. Consequently, when a new brand is added, an existing brand must be dropped from inventory. A similar situation exists in other retail fields such as drug stores, hardware stores, department stores, and clothing stores. It is this difficulty of obtaining distribution that often causes producers to opt for an independent distribution system, by-passing conventional channels. For most marketers of consumer products, however, manufacturer-controlled outlets are not feasible because the costs are high and the distribution they afford is too limited. As a consequence, it is the retail outlet that ultimately determines what brands are and are not made available to consumers.

The primary responsibility for obtaining and servicing distribution lies with the sales force. As a consequence, good trade relations are a priceless ingredient in sales effectiveness. In addition, sales presentations are designed to magnify the profit potential to the retailer for stocking the brand, and advertising schedules are carefully explained (merchandised) to buyers. For maximum effectiveness, these activities are also supplemented by other marketing activities such as trade magazine advertising, stocking allowances (price discounts for all initial purchases), display allowances, and advertising allowances. Heavy consumer advertising, consumer coupons, and other consumer promotions are often scheduled to bring pressure against retailers to stock a particular brand. A classic use of consumer pressure was related to me several years ago by a buyer for a major grocery chain in Chicago. According to this buyer:

One day this nondescript little guy came in and wanted me to stock a new liquid cleaner called Lestoil. I hadn't heard of the brand nor the company, and wasn't very interested because we had shelves full of cleaning products of every size, shape, and description. When he finished his sales call, he left me his calling card which I casually tossed in my desk drawer only because I didn't want to hurt his feelings by throwing it in the waste basket.

About three weeks later, Lestoil hit Chicago. And I do mean *hit*. It was a blitz! I think they used every newspaper, TV and radio station in the market, with heavy schedules. My telephone went wild with calls from our store managers saying that consumers were demanding the stuff. I tore my desk apart trying to find that damn calling card.

Although massive efforts like that of Lestoil are common in the food and drug trade, more modest efforts may also be successful. Pet-Ritz, for example, was having trouble getting distribution of its frozen pies in A&P stores in a number of key markets in which A&P was an important outlet. A marketing strategy was designed to bring selective pressure against A&P. Pet-Ritz advertising was scheduled in *Woman's Day,* a women's service magazine sold only through A&P stores. Consumer coupons were mailed to selected residential areas surrounding A&P outlets. This activity was merchandized or "sold" by Pet-Ritz food brokers in their calls on A&P regional buying offices. The program accomplished its purpose in a number of key markets. The point is that distribution strategy and activities must be coordinated with other marketing considerations—with advertising, with sales promotion, and with the sales force—in order to be effective. And, the marketing plan is the instrument of this coordination.

DISTRIBUTION CONFLICTS

Many books on marketing treat the relationship between the producers of branded products and the intermediaries who distribute these brands as though they were joined together in a harmonious partnership through bonds of affection and mutual interest. In truth, both have a stake in pleasing the consumer, but their mutuality of interests stops at that point. The cooperation that exists between the producer and the retailer is a forced cooperation based on mutual interdependence. Producers need retailers to distribute their brands to consumers, and retailers need the producers' brands to attract consumers to their stores. Each would be delighted to do without the other, if it were possible. The extent of their differences can be seen in the following comparisons shown in table 10-2.

Since it is the retailer who selects the brands that will be sold at the retail level, it is the producer who suffers from the inevitable conflicts caused by these differences in interest. Whether or not a retailer will continue to carry a particular brand will depend on whether or not it is profitable to do so. When demand drops, causing brands to become unprofitable, loss of retail distribution is a foregone conclusion. Thus, the producer is always under pressure to develop brands and marketing programs that provide profit not only for herself, but also for retailers.

Another form of distribution conflict arises when producers use multiple channels of distribution. Although multiple channels are commonplace for many product categories, they are often difficult to initiate in product fields where they have not been traditionally used. Adding new channels of distribution without alienating established channels is often a test of both distribution strategy and selling skill.

SUMMARY

Pricing is one of the more complex decisions in marketing. In order to understand its function, we need to turn to some of the basic concepts in economics.

Historically, price is the central mechanism that mediates the relationship between supply and demand. Economists have traditionally emphasized price, almost to the exclusion of other marketing activities, because of historical, technical, and social reasons.

The rise of consumer affluence and increased production capacity has given rise to monopolistic competition and symbolic pricing in the marketing equation. In monopolistic competition, the product of each competitor differs in some way from that of other competitors; thus, each competitor has a monopoly because an exact duplicate of its product is not available from any other source. Symbolic pricing refers to the use of price as a symbol of quality because of a widespread belief among consumers that there is a necessary relationship between price and quality, although this belief is not supported by fact. The consequences of monopolistic competition and symbolic pricing have been to loosen the ties that traditionally bound supply and demand together in a rigid price

Table 10-2.

Producers Are Interested in	Retailers Are Interested in
Multiple distribution.	Exclusive distribution.
Sales of their brands.	Sales of their stores.
Producers' profits.	Retail profits.
Consumer loyalty to brands.	Consumer loyalty to stores.
Display of their brands.	Display of the most profitable items.

relationship and turned pricing into a formidable marketing tool.

Pricing is structured in terms of manufacturer and distributor margins, and several pricing strategies are commonly employed.

There are two aspects to distribution—distribution strategy and logistics. Distribution agencies come in several forms.

Four functions of distribution are (1) product availability, (2) symbolic communication of product worth,

(3) guarantor of product satisfaction and customer service, and (4) personal selling.

Consumer products are classified as convenience, shopping, and specialty products, and each classification has its own channels of distribution.

There are several common distribution strategies, each with its own advantages and disadvantages. Often, multiple channels are used for a single product. Distribution conflicts can cause difficult problems for the producer.

QUESTIONS

1. Explain the interrelationship of supply, demand, suppliers, and price.
2. Explain the relationship between total income and price changes under the following conditions of elasticity: (a) unitary elasticity, (b) price elasticity, and (c) price inelasticity.
3. What are the historical, technical, and social reasons underlying the traditional emphasis on price?
4. Explain what is meant by *monopolistic competition* and why it is important in marketing.
5. Explain why symbolic pricing is an effective marketing tool.
6. Explain the strategies of price skimming and penetration pricing. Identify the conditions under which each is appropriate.
7. Explain what is meant by channel length; explain the basic problem to which long channels of distribution give rise.
8. What are the functions of distribution?
9. Explain what is meant by *intensive, selective*, and *independent* distribution, and the conditions under which each is appropriate.
10. Identify the sources of conflict between manufacturers and producers.

PROBLEM

A key consideration in pricing a new product is often the volume that must be sold in order to break even. The *break-even point* in units can be determined by dividing the gross margin per unit into the fixed costs. Gross margin is the difference between the selling price and the cost of manufacturing the product. Thus, if the selling price is $1.00, and manufacturing costs are $0.40 per unit, the gross margin is $1.00 − $0.40 = $0.60.

The *fixed costs* are the costs for plant and equipment to manufacture the product. They are fixed because they represent costs that must be met whether or not any product is being manufactured. Now, let us take an example to demonstrate the computation of the break-even point. Assume fixed costs (the cost of plant and equipment) to be $50,000. Assume the gross margin to be $0.60 per unit. Break-even in terms of units would be:

$$\frac{\text{fixed costs}}{\text{gross margin}} = \frac{\$50,000}{\$0.60} = 83,333 \text{ units.}$$

After break-even has been achieved, and fixed costs met, the entire gross margin is a contribution to profit and other expenses, such as selling expense and advertising expense.

You are the product manager of a camping products company that has developed a new type of lightweight, collapsible drinking cup for backpackers. You are considering two alternative prices for the product—$2.50 and $2.00. Research has estimated that at the $2.50 price the first year market will be 200 thousand units, plus or minus 20 percent. At the $2.00 price the first year market is estimated at 600 thousand units, plus or minus 30 percent. In either case, manufacturing costs will be $1.80 per unit, and fixed costs will be $50 thousand. Since the product will simply be added to the company's line, other expenses, such as selling costs and advertising costs, will be minimal. You estimate $15 thousand at either volume level.

You are trying to decide whether to use a price skimming strategy ($2.50 a unit) or a penetration pricing strategy ($2.00 a unit). Because you have heard that a major competitor is working on a similar unit, you are afraid that you will have very little lead time—a month or two at the most. You have filed for a patent on the product but are not sure that it is patentable. At the same time, you have to introduce the product immediately to be in the market in time for the back-packing season.

Assignment

1. What decision do you make?
2. What are the considerations that led you to this decision?

FIVE

Advertising Copy—
Strategies and Plans

Thus far, attention has been devoted to those sections of the marketing plan that deal with marketing analysis, marketing objectives and strategy, and strategies for the product, brand name, packaging, pricing, and distribution. All of these, of course, are basic, and all must be carefully coordinated if the marketing effort is to be effective. Now, however, we come to that section of the marketing plan that carries the main burden of marketing communication—the advertising itself. For many, this is the most exciting part of marketing. Certainly, it is the most visible.

There is probably more controversy about what constitutes good advertising than there is in any other area of marketing. It is a highly volatile area in which different theories, personal opinions, likes and dislikes rule the day. Yet, effective advertising does not occur by chance. Advertising creativity is a "disciplined" creativity. It is firmly rooted in the marketing plan and directed by the logic of the product concept.

Normally, the advertising section of the marketing plan is divided into three parts, which are outlined below:

1. **Advertising Objectives and Strategy**
   a. **Advertising objectives** specify the target group or groups to be reached, as well as specific, measurable, and realistic communication goals.
   b. **Advertising Strategy** (optional) is only included in the plan when additional specifications for the advertising are required, such as the timing of the schedule, how advertising weight will be distributed within a line of products, and how advertising will be used to support other marketing activities.

2. **Copy Strategy and Plan**
   a. **Copy Strategy** reflects basic decisions that will direct and shape the content and form of the advertising copy.
   b. **Copy plan** details how the copy strategy will be executed in a specific advertisement or advertising campaign.

3. **Media Strategy and Plan**
   a. **Media strategy** indicates how media will be se lected and used in accomplishing mar-marketing objectives.

b. The **Media plan** details the specific media to be used.

Since chapter 3 details the salient features of the advertising objectives and strategy portion of the marketing plan, the two following sections of the book will deal with the general area of copy and its development and with media.

The material dealing with the broad area of copy will be divided into five chapters. Chapter 11 is an overview of creativity and the role of advertising in the marketing mix. Chapter 12 discusses how to approach the task of writing advertisements. Chapter 13 is devoted to print advertising and deals with headlines, illustrations, and body copy. Chapter 14 discusses print production, and chapter 15 is concerned with broadcast advertising and its production.

Advertising is an art, not a science. There are no hard and fast rules for designing advertisements or for writing copy. Yet, it is through the creativity of advertising copy that the product concept takes wing and systematic strategy statements are transformed into persuasive communications. In a sense, advertising creativity is the soul of marketing. Without it, mass marketing is not possible.

Advertising Creativity— an Overview

The Rabbit and the Tortoise

In Aesop's fable, the tortoise beat the rabbit. But, maybe rabbits are getting smarter, because in 1977 the rabbit beat the tortoise. The rabbit in this modern fable is the Volkswagen Rabbit, VW's leading entry in the economy car market. The tortoise is General Motors, one of the slower, more reluctant participants in the economy car race.

The Buick Division of General Motors tested five economy cars, including Volkswagen's Rabbit and its own Opel. The exhaustive comparisons measured such features as interior space, trunk capacity, acceleration, steering quickness, and maintenance schedules. To its credit, Opel used the test results in its advertising, candidly admitting that the Rabbit outscored the Opel by 50 points to 47.

Unable to pass up this unexpected windfall, Volkswagen prepared its own advertising, using the Opel advertisement for its illustration. The headline read, "General Motors Names Rabbit Best of Five Economy Cars." (See figure 11–1.) In its body copy, the Rabbit ad states: "We are grateful to General Motors for providing what we suspected all along." The ad, prepared by Doyle Dane Bernbach, goes on to say: "It

takes a very big company to admit that our car is better than their car. And we want to take this opportunity to thank them publically for saying so."

Curiously, General Motors may be the beneficiary of its candor. Mail generated by the Opel ads is running four to one in favor of the approach, with the bulk of the positive response coming from young people.[1] Whether or not this "positive response" will show up in the sales figures for the Opel or the Rabbit is an open question.

Creative Talent

William Tyler, a long-time contributor to *Advertising Age*, laments the lack of foresight by advertising agencies in the following comment.

> It looked a little too good to be true. And sure enough, it was. I'm talking about the way agencies have been getting along the last few years with only half as many people per dollar billed. They claimed they did it without reducing the quality of their services. Short

---

1. John J. O'Connor, "VW Rabbit latches onto GM findings for latest ads," *Advertising Age* (August 8, 1977): lff.

185

Figure 11–1.   (©Volkswagen of America)

In a major hospital study, Excedrin relieved pain better than regular aspirin. Here's why that could be important when you have a headache.

Doctors know headache pain is not readily measured. So they used hospitalized patients suffering a different kind of pain to compare regular aspirin and Excedrin.

In this study, doctors found that Excedrin worked significantly better. And this evidence indicates how well Excedrin could work for you.

So the next time you have a headache, get Excedrin, the extra-strength pain reliever. See if it doesn't work better for you.

The extra-strength pain reliever.

Plate 11–1.   In this Excedrin ad, the words ''major hospital study'' in the headline and the picture of a woman in a hospital setting lend legitimacy to the product claims (Bristol-Myers Co.).

Jack and Avocado get together for a dip.©

Tired of the same old chip dip? Here's an idea guaranteed to wow you. Brightly seasoned avocado dip scooped up on tasty morsels of Monterey Jack cheese. It's a natural. The mellow flavor of Jack and the nutlike taste of avocados were made for each other. So whip up the recipe and invite some friends over for a dip. They'll flip.

Guacamole (Classic Avocado Dip)
4 California avocados, mashed & pureed, 1 teaspoon seasoned salt, 2 tablespoons lemon or lime juice, 1/2 teaspoon Worcestershire, 1/8 teaspoon Tabasco, 1 medium tomato, chopped fine. Combine and chill all ingredients. Serve with cubed Monterey Jack cheese speared on picks.

CALIFORNIA MONTEREY JACK CHEESE
Manufacturing Milk Producers of California
LOVE FOOD FROM CALIFORNIA
©1973, California Avocado Advisory Board

Plate 11-2. In this ad, the headline is meaningless without the illustration (California Avocado Advisory Board).

term, they were probably right. But now it's long-term time—time to take another look.

On the alter of profits, we've sacrificed the development of new creative talent to take the place of the old ones now gone. And now we're paying the price: a critical shortage of mature creative people.

What's the answer? Agency training programs? Okay, but necessarily superficial. Frantic raiding and trading? I'm afraid so, until we go back to the time-honored apprentice system, by hiring promising youngsters and bringing them along the slow and costly way by putting them under experienced hands (where they will learn more from their own errors than their successes, that being the nature of our business.)

We're facing an era of wildly escalating creative salaries to make up for the ones we didn't pay the last few years. We dealt the golden goose an almost mortal blow. And she'll be in intensive care for quite a while yet.[2]

Creative Philosophy

The Ted Bates Advertising Agency believes in U.S.P.—the Unique Selling Proposition—as the keystone for successful advertising (the U.S.P. is a unique difference in a product or in the use of a product that distinguishes it from competition).[3] Ogilvy, Benson, and Mather tout "image advertising," as exemplified by the "Man in the Hathaway Shirt" (see figure 11–2).[4] Norman B. Norman of Norman, Craig, and Kummel believes that conscious suggestion is a waste of the advertiser's money, and that effective advertising taps the unconscious, resulting in *empathy* (the personal identification of the reader with the product being advertised).[5] Doyle Dane Bernbach depends on *execution*, insists that "execution becomes content," and argues that a good ad is different.[6] McCann-Erickson's orientation is toward *motivational* advertising " . . . built on the 'real reason' why people use this kind of product."[7] And, an executive of Batten, Barton, Dursten, and Osborn summed up his agency's position with the humerous observation: "You can always tell an Ogilvy ad or a Bates ad, but you can't spot a BBDO ad because we'll steal from everybody."[8]

Competition! Lack of creative talent! Controversy! These are the messages of the foregoing examples. And these are the dimensions of advertising copy.

What is good advertising? There is little agreement among advertising professionals about the philosophy underlying effective advertising, and even less agreement about how advertising effectiveness should be measured. Yet, hard-headed, cost-conscious business executives, who wouldn't approve a $10 thousand expenditure for a new piece of equipment without a complete study of its proposed value, replete with cost and performance documentation, will blithely approve $10 million for an advertising campaign based on a slick presentation and confidence in the presenter. Rosser Reeves quotes a company president as saying:

Advertising, to me, is really one of the mysteries of American business. I can inventory my stock. I can calculate the cost of my factories. I can figure my taxes, estimate my depreciation, determine my sales cost, derive my return per share. Yet, there are times when I spend as much as $18,000,000 a year on advertising—and have no idea what I am really getting for my money.[9]

Yet, despite disagreement and despite ambiguity, good advertising does exist. Perhaps one reason why there is so much disagreement about the philosophy that should underly effective advertising is that great copywriters have their own systems of beliefs to which they adhere. As one admirer of David Ogilvy said: "Let's face it. David's a snob. He patronizes waiters. Everybody does best what he really believes in, so David gives his products snob appeal."[10]

SOME BASIC IDEAS

In the remainder of this chapter, we will briefly examine a number of basic ideas about advertising. Some of the ideas are controversial, but they are still important to the understanding of advertising.

We will examine the state of theory in advertising and suggest a point of view that may be helpful in reconciling some of the disparate views that exist about what constitutes good advertising.

We will turn to the question of identifying relevant advertising appeals. This moves us a step beyond general advertising theory and emphasizes the importance of having some convictions and beliefs about what is important to consumers.

We will recognize the problem that advertising writers and marketers have in "keeping in touch"

2. William D. Tyler, "Agencies return to time-honored apprenticeship for young creatives," *Advertising Age* (August 15, 1977): 50.
3. Rosser Reeves, *Reality in Advertising* (New York: Alfred A. Knopf, 1961).
4. David Ogilvy, *Confessions of an Advertising Man* (New York: Atheneum, 1964), p. 100.
5. Martin Mayer, *Madison Avenue U.S.A.* (New York: Harper Brothers, Publishers, 1958), p. 59.
6. Robert Glatzer, *The New Advertising* (New York: The Citadel Press, 1970), p. 18.
7. Mayer, *Madison Avenue,* p. 69.
8. *Ibid.,* p. 70.
9. Reeves, *Reality in Advertising,* p. 11.
10. Mayer, *Madison Avenue,* p. 57.

The man in the Hathaway shirt

AMERICAN MEN are beginning to realize that it is ridiculous to buy good suits and then spoil the effect by wearing an ordinary, mass-produced shirt. Hence the growing popularity of HATHAWAY shirts, which are in a class by themselves.

HATHAWAY shirts *wear* infinitely longer—a matter of years. They make you look younger and more distinguished, because of the subtle way HATHAWAY cut collars. The whole shirt is tailored more *generously*, and is therefore more *comfortable*. The tails are longer, and stay in your

trousers. The buttons are mother-of-pearl. Even the stitching has an ante-bellum elegance about it.

Above all, HATHAWAY make their shirts of remarkable *fabrics*, collected from the four corners of the earth—Viyella® and Aertex® from England, woolen taffeta from Scotland, Sea Island cotton from the West Indies, hand-woven madras from India, broadcloth from Manchester, linen batiste from Paris, hand-blocked silks from England, exclusive cottons from the best weavers in America. You will get a

great deal of quiet satisfaction out of wearing shirts which are in such impeccable taste.

HATHAWAY shirts are made by a small company of dedicated craftsmen in the little town of Waterville, Maine. They have been at it, man and boy, for one hundred and twenty years.

At better stores everywhere, or write C. F. HATHAWAY, Waterville, Maine, for the name of your nearest store. In New York, telephone OX 7-5566. Prices from $5.95 to $20.00.

with consumers. This is a perennial problem since consumers change, as do advertising writers.

We will review the problem of verbal and nonverbal communications. It is one thing to have a theory of advertising and understand consumers. It is another to communicate with consumers in terms that they understand and respond to. Here, we will focus on the problem of *meaning* and its importance in advertising communications.

We will identify certain other dimensions of advertising that are widely discussed, but about which little agreement exists. These dimensions include the question of *believability* in advertising, the role of *liking and disliking* of advertising in terms of its influence on advertising effectiveness, and the perennial problem of *tasteless* advertising.

We will consider what advertising does and the effects it has on consumers in persuading them to purchase particular products or services.

Finally, we will recognize that advertising may take different forms and describe the major forms of advertising which exist. Not all advertising is intended to do the same thing and, unless the objectives of an advertisement or campaign are clearly identified, there is little opportunity that effective advertising will result.

THEORY IN ADVERTISING

Generally, advertising is short on theory, and long on execution. Because most economists are primarily concerned with supply and demand, they have either tended to sweep advertising under the rug because it interferes with the "rational" relationship between demand and price, or they have treated it as a cost of bringing the seller and the buyer together. Most practitioners of advertising are too busy creating advertising to worry about what they are creating. And most other people don't think about it very much. Perhaps that is one of the reasons why there is so much disagreement about what constitutes a good ad. Ben Gedalecia, while research director of BBDO, lamented that there is no general theory of advertising that gives coherence to advertising practice.[11]

There is general agreement, of course, that one of the functions of advertising is to provide information. But this doesn't explain why some advertising is effective and some is not. Further, an advertisement that

contains a great deal of information may be a real dog. Consider the following hypothetical ad copy.

The Galaxy 8 is a car. It has four wheels, brakes, and lights. It has an engine that runs on gasoline, a carburetor, a crankshaft, springs, a universal joint, a distributor, an electrical system, cylinders, sparkplugs, doors, and a place to sit. It comes in a variety of colors.

Now that's a lot of information. But who cares? It doesn't do anything for anybody. Clearly, effective advertising does something other than provide information.

The Value-Added Theory

Martin Mayer had suggested that people inside and outside of the advertising industry could think more clearly about the subject if they would recognize that advertising, in addition to its informative function, also *adds a new value to the existing value of the product.* He refers to this concept as the *value-added theory* of advertising,[12] and suggests that this added value is relatively slight since advertising is highly effective in good times, and relatively ineffective when the financial squeeze is on. Thus, when money is plentiful, a slightly more attractive product may seem worth the extra cost, but:

. . . when money is precious for the security that it alone can offer, the incremental value of advertising will seem slight indeed if a similar, less advertised or even unadvertised product can be bought for less . . . (p. 312).

As a matter of strict logic, advertising *must* somehow change the product to which it is applied. In recent years, some advertising research psychologists have gingerly approached this question, via Burleigh Gardner's concept of the "brand image." But the psychologist's habits of work lead him to assume that the image is something present in the consumer's mind, rather than something pervasive in the product itself. It is remarkable how many people who readily see that a new package or a new brand name will change a product fail to see that advertising inevitably has a very similar effect (p. 313).[13]

The theory that advertising *changes* the product in some way is a challenging concept. If we further

---

11. *Ibid.,* p. 310.

Figure 11–2.   (C.F. Hathaway Co.)

12. *Ibid.*
13. *Ibid.,* p. 312. For another excellent discussion of the value-added theory, see: Vincent Norris, "Advertising and Value Added," in *The Role of Advertising,* C.H. Sandage and Vernon Fryburger, eds. (Homewood, Illinois: Richard D. Irwin, Inc., 1960), pp. 145–56.

postulate that advertising changes a product by *endowing it with a consumer benefit that relates to conscious or unconscious human needs,* we have the basis for a theory that might reconcile much of the controversy that surrounds the field.

The Consistency of the Value-Added Theory with Other Theories

U.S.P. The Unique Selling Proposition of Ted Bates becomes an effective device for advertising provided the U.S.P. is a comsumer benefit. A U.S.P. that has no *benefit-relevance* for the consumer would be ineffective. True, it would provide information, but it would add no appreciable value to the product. Rosser Reeves emphasizes this point in his three-part definition of the U.S.P.

1. Each advertisement must make a proposition to the consumer. Not just words, not just product puffery, not just show-window advertising. Each advertisement must say to each reader: "Buy this product, and you will get this specific benefit."
2. The proposition must be one that the competition either cannot, or does not, offer. It must be unique—either a uniqueness of the brand or a claim not otherwise made in that particular field of advertising.
3. The proposition must be so strong that it can move the mass millions, i.e., pull over new customers to your product.[14]

Reeves' definition is consistent with the observation made in chapter 8 that *a new product has the greatest chance of success if it is noticeably better than established products on some dimension that is important to the consumer.*

Image advertising. The concept that advertising adds value to a product by translating the product concept into a consumer benefit is also consistent with the *image* advertising of Ogilvy wherein advertising endows the product with a meaningful, intangible value such as status, excellence, confidence, or potentiality—*provided* the product's performance is consistent with the advertising promise. The importance of an advertising promise is emphasized in the following quotation from Ogilvy:

> Two hundred years ago, Dr. Johnson said: "Promise, large promise, is the soul of an advertisement." When he auctioned off the contents of the Anchor Brewery, he made the following promise: "We are not here to sell boilers and vats, but the potentiality of growing rich beyond the dreams of avarice."[15]

14. Reeves, *Reality in Advertising*, pp. 47–48.
15. Ogilvy, *Confessions*, p. 93.

Earlier (chapter 8), it was pointed out that products are often bought for their *expressive* value, that is, psychological attributes (image) such as style and expression of the self-concept. Certainly, if there is a perceivable difference in the product, the believability of an image claim is enhanced by this tangible difference. This observation is consistent with the second guideline for new products stated in chapter 8: *If the new product is not better, but is distinguishably different from competing brands in some way, it has a reasonable chance of success, but the risk is higher.*

Empathy Advertising. The value-added concept of advertising is consistent with Norman, Craig, and Kummel's emphasis on *empathy* (which deals with *expressive* values); with Doyle Dane Bernbach's preoccupation with "execution and uniqueness" (where uniqueness is translated into a consumer benefit); and McCann-Erickson's motivational advertising, built on the "real reason" why (a consumer benefit) people use this kind of product.

The Role of Advertising. Finally, and more importantly for the exposition of this text, the value-added concept is totally consistent with the role of advertising in the marketing process and its relationship to the product concept. In this context, advertising, in addition to providing information, *translates the product concept into a consumer benefit that can be understood and appreciated by consumers.* The highly successful advertisements translate the product concept into a strong consumer benefit; unsuccessful advertising fails to do so, either through poor communication or because the product concept is not based on considerations relevant to consumer needs. *If* the product concept represents a viable position in the product space, and *if* advertising does its job properly, there is every reason to believe that the product will be a success.

IDENTIFYING ADVERTISING APPEALS

Thus far, I have defined the role of advertising as that of providing information and translating the product concept into a consumer benefit that can be understood and appreciated by consumers. This raises the question, "What is a consumer benefit?" Within the framework of motivation theory (discussed in chapter 5) a consumer benefit is anything that will help consumers solve problems or achieve goals. For example, if a dry skin condition causes consumer concern for appearance, then Oil of Olay or any number of other moisterizers will solve, or help solve, this problem. The following copy was taken from the Oil of Olay package.

Discover the secret of Oil of Olay . . . shared by women around the world. This mysterious beauty fluid works with your skin's own natural moisture to quickly ease away dryness, leaving your skin feeling soft and smooth. An abundance of pure moisture, tropical oil and emollients impart a renewed radiance and glow to your skin. Oil of Olay is remarkably fast penetrating, with no greasy after-feel. Gentle it on every morning and night to help your skin live in its own moist climate. And it's marvelous under makeup, too.

Does it work? I don't know; it sounds good. Apparently my wife as well as millions of other women believe that it does work and that it solves their problem within the framework of their expectations. The product promises and delivers a consumer benefit.

Of course, dry skin is only an apparent problem. The real problem—or goal—is probably a desire for beauty or confidence in one's appearance,; the elimination of dry skin is an instrumental way of achieving this goal.

The bases for all advertising promises or claims lie within the motivational structure of the individual consumer. Some of these needs or motivations may be universal; some may be highly idiosyncratic. It is for this reason that a knowledge of consumer motivation is an integral part of marketing. It is also the reason that psychologists and advertising practitioners alike have sought to identify a list of basic motivations or needs that will enable them to understand the apparent vaguaries of consumer behavior.

Many attempts, none wholly satisfactory, have been made to draw up a list of basic needs that would provide guidance to understanding and influencing behavior. Melvin S. Hattwick, a psychologist, spent a number of years in the advertising field with such outstanding advertising agencies as BBDO and Needham, Louis and Brorby, Inc. In 1950, Hattwick wrote a book titled *How to Use Psychology for Better Advertising*. In this text, he listed eight basic "wants" that characterize consumer behavior. These "wants" are: (1) food and drink, (2) comfort, (3) freedom from fear and danger, (4) to be superior, (5) companionship of the opposite sex, (6) welfare of loved ones, (7) social approval, (8) to live longer.[16] In addition to these basic appeals, Hattwick also indentified a number of secondary appeals (appeals that are learned or acquired, and not as powerful as the basic appeals). These secondary appeals included such things as: bargains, information and education, cleanliness, efficiency, convenience, dependability and quality, style and beauty, economy and profit, and curiosity.

Victor Schwab, in his book *How to Write a Good Advertisement*, offers a somewhat longer list which is divided into four major divisions.

People want to *gain* . . .
(1) Health, (2) Time, (3) Money, (4) Popularity, (5) Improved appearance, (6) Security in old age, (7) Praise from others, (8) Comfort, (9) Liesure, (10) Self-confidence, (11) Personal prestige.
They want to *be* . . .
(1) Good parents, (2) Sociable, hospitable, (3) Up-to-date, (4) Creative, (5) Proud of their possessions, (6) Influential over others, (7) Gregarious, (8) Efficient, (9) "First" in things, (10) Recognized as authorities.
They want to *do* . . .
(1) Express their personalities, (2) Resist domination by others, (3) Satisfy their curiosity, (4) Emulate the admirable, (5) Appreciate beauty, (6) Acquire or collect things, (7) Win others' affection, (8) Improve themselves generally.
They want to *save* . . .
(1) Time, (2) Money, (3) Work, (4) Discomfort, (5) Worry, (6) Doubts, (7) Risks, (8) Personal embarrassment.[17]

While he was executive vice-president of a major advertising agency, Charles F. Adams drew up a much shorter list of advertising appeals. His list and his comments about the importance of having convictions concerning consumer motivation are shown below.

1. *First, the Promise of Economy and Greater Financial Ease.* This does not necessarily imply cheapness, but rather a sound purchase and excellent value received for the money spent. And, of course, it embraces freedom from service and maintenance. The dependability of the product is also of great importance.
2. *Second, the Promise of Self-improvement.* Everyone wants to be liked, if not admired. Anything you can tell the prospect about what your product will do to enhance his image in his own eyes or in the eyes of others and add to his community standing and prestige should have a telling effect.
3. *Third, the Promise of Self-gratification.* This concerns the creature comforts of life, health, the satisfaction of hunger, bodily comfort, relief from physical labor and effort. Obviously any appeal to these needs will be soundly based.
4. *Fourth, the Promise of Increased Family Happiness.* Anything that will add new zest to living, a spirit of togetherness for the people the prospect loves and needs, will put your presentation on solid ground.

16. Melvin S. Hattwick, *How to Use Psychology for Better Advertising* (New York: Prentice-Hall, Inc., 1950), p. 89.

17. Specified excerpt from p. 47 in *How to Write a Good Advertisement* by Victor O. Schwab. Reprinted by permission of Harper & Row, Publishers, Inc.

My own list of appeals has stood me in good stead over the years, but whatever list the admaker prefers, he should at least *have* one. If he does not, he should then either create one of his own or borrow someone else's. For if his advertisements or commercials do not appeal in some way to at least one of these mainsprings of human action, then they will probably not sell anything. And it is also true that no amount of semantic dexterity or graphics ingenuity can take the place of such an appeal.

I have gone through this brief explanation for a very definite purpose. For it is my belief that modern admakers are coming more and more to rely on their mechanical and technical skills, and less and less on their understanding of what sells things.[18]

Other successful admakers will have other lists; some items will be the same, some different. There is no magic in any particular list of consumer motivations. The magic lies in what the lists imply—that the admakers have some understanding, and some convictions about consumer motivations. Without this understanding and conviction, there is little chance that effective advertising will be written. The successful admaker never loses sight of the consumer—never loses touch with what people worry, think, and dream about—because that's the stuff of effective advertising.

KEEPING IN TOUCH WITH CONSUMERS

In chapter 5, reference was made to Abraham Maslow and his contention that human needs are insatiable, that, as fast as one set of needs is satisfied, another set of needs arises. Changing economic conditions and changing values in a society may give certain needs greater prepotence at one time and give another constellation of needs greater prepotence at another period. For example, needs of security and economy may become more important in times of social and economic stress. Similarly, the women's movement may change many of the consumer benefits that women will respond to. As more women work, as opportunities for broader participation in society increase, and as sexual freedom becomes more explicit, traditional appeals to women consumers may have to be modified if advertising effectiveness is to be maintained.

This puts the admaker in a paradoxical position. Most admakers are successful because they intuitively understand the people to whom they are writing. Earlier, I quoted an admirer of David Ogilvy as saying, in effect, that "David is good at writing snob copy be-

cause he is a snob." Most successful copywriters are good at writing for particular kinds of people because that's the kind of people they are. But, as copywriters become more successful, they change. This change process is called *psychological mobility*. Higher income, a different standard of living, an emerging life style start to insulate them from the consumers for whom they are writing. It is difficult to write about a bargain basement with understanding if you buy all of your clothes at Brooks Brothers or Saks Fifth Avenue. And you quickly lose empathy for lunch-pail dining when you become accustomed to martini lunches at "21" or the Four Seasons. It's a different world.

An admaker can try to keep pace with target groups of consumers by digesting the results of consumer research findings. But it's not the same thing. The facts and figures in a research report fail to capture the experience. As a consequence, most successful advertising writers seek other methods of keeping in touch with the pulse of the market. One excellent creative supervisor I knew religiously read the "advice" columns in the daily newspapers—Ann Landers, Abigail Van Buren, and others. Another devoted some of his leisure time working at a check-out counter in a supermarket. A third participated as a personal interviewer in gathering research data on the products to which he was assigned. It is commonplace for advertising writers to attend group interviewing sessions conducted by the agency research department in order to get the first-hand experience of listening to consumers express their likes and dislikes, their feelings and frustrations, their expectations and their disappointments.

The point is that consumer motivation is the fuel that fires successful advertising and the search for viable product concepts, and advertising appeals is an endless preoccupation of successful advertising practitioners.

VERBAL AND NONVERBAL COMMUNICATIONS

Advertising is based on ideas, but it communicates these ideas through signs—words, phrases, pictures, and actions—that give rise to meaning. A *sign*, as it is used in communications, is merely a stimulus that represents an object or an idea. The sign *apple* for example, means a certain kind of fruit with which we are familiar. The sign *run* means a certain kind of action. Thus, a sign is a label that is associated with the object or idea it represents. Signs gain their meanings through learning, and insofar as two people have the same learning experience they use the same signs

18. Charles F. Adams, *Common Sense in Advertising* (New York: McGraw-Hill Book Company, 1965), pp. 70–72.

to represent the same things. Without common signs there can be no communication; anyone who has traveled in a foreign country without knowing the local language knows how awkward communications can become.

People reared within the same culture have certain common experiences (in the home, in school, and in society at large) that facilitate their communication. But because no two people ever have an *identical* history of experience, even common signs may become distorted. For example, the sign, *mother* has a core meaning in our culture that is shared by most people. Yet, even this sign will have a somewhat different meaning to two people if the mother of one was loving and concerned and the mother of the other was harsh and critical. To the first person, the sign, *mother*, will give rise to feelings of affection; to the other, it will trigger feelings of hostility and resentment. Since even common signs can have somewhat different meanings, communications are seldom perfect. The problems that arise in communications are represented in figure 11–3.

The sender of a message can communicate with the receiver of the message to the extent that their fields of experience overlap. Signs that fall outside the area of shared experiences will either not be understood, or will be misinterpreted. Since signs may have different meanings to different people, we need to more closely examine the concept of *meaning*. Generally, signs have four kinds of meanings: (1) *denotative* meaning, (2) *connotative* meaning, (3) *structural* meaning, and (4) *contextual* meaning.

Denotative Meaning

Through learning we associate signs with objects, actions, and ideas. The sign *chair* denotes a particular class of objects with certain characteristics which,

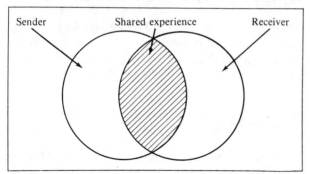

Figure 11–3. Fields of experience of the "sender" and "receiver" of a message. Only signs that fall within the region of shared experience will be understood.

by common agreement, is called *chair*. Denotative meaning involves a relatively simple sign-object relationship. Words high in denotative meaning most often refer to concrete objects. The dictionary definition of a word refers, essentially, to its denotative meaning.

Connotative Meaning

Many objects and ideas are much more complex than that represented by a simple sign-object relationship. The idea or object becomes surrounded by a complex constellation of meanings so that the meaning of the sign varies somewhat among different people. *Communism, socialism,* and *capitalism* all have a denotative meaning as a form of economic organization. At the same time, these words have rich connotative meanings which differ among different people and are often associated with strong feelings. Many people, for example, respond to *communism* as *bad, threatening, oppressive,* and *undesirable.* Others, by contrast, respond to it as *good* and *desirable,* and perceive it as a reasonable attempt to introduce rationality, equity, and justice into economic relationships. Sometimes, words that have the same denotative meaning may have somewhat different connotative meanings. For example *naked* and *nude* denotatively mean "to be without clothing." Yet, connotatively, *naked* is a masculine word and *nude* is a feminine word. When great precision in communication is desired, one should try to use words that are high in denotative meaning and low in connotative meaning. Conversely, when *persuasion* is the object of communications, words high in connotative meaning become more important.

Since the object of advertising communications is persuasion, words high in connotative meaning are its basic tools. Herein lies a danger in the communications process. Words should be chosen carefully so that they complement each other. When words with noncomplementary connotative meanings are used together, confusion and ambiguity mar attempts at communication. There is generally a "right" word to express every thought, and the careless use of a single word can destroy a carefully constructed argument.

Advertising writers must be adept with words, sensitive to their nuances, and conscious of their power.

Structural Meaning

Single words are insufficient for most communications. Normally, we need to use combinations of words to express our meanings. Syntax and grammar provide the rules for stringing words together in a meaningful relationship. These rules permit us to express complex ideas through sentences and paragraphs. The receivers of messages respond to sentences in the same way they respond to individual words. A sentence has a coherent unity if it is properly constructed. Again, advertising writers need an understanding of syntax and grammar.

Writers of advertising sometimes deliberately violate the rules of syntax and grammar in order to gain impact and euphony. "Winston tastes good like a cigarette should" is grammatically incorrect. It should read "Winston tastes good as a cigarette should." Yet, this grammatical violation adds force to the slogan, even though it may offend some grammarians. Violations of syntax and grammar need to be used jusiciously, if at all. When syntax and grammar are used either carelessly or ignorantly, the intended meaning may be lost or the reader may be confused.

Contextual Meaning

Signs often derive their meanings from the context in which they occur—that is, from the signs that surround them. Consider the following sentences:

We crossed the river on the *bridge* north of town.

I have never played worse *bridge* in my life.

It was a difficult billiard shot. Even with the *bridge,* I could hardly reach the cue ball.

Did the dentist have to install a *bridge?*

I'm having trouble building a *bridge* between the key ideas of the presentation.

In each case, the word *bridge* has a different meaning, depending upon the context within which it appears.

Context is extremely important for advertising. The meaning of a sign is often clarified and sometimes enhanced by the context within which it occurs. The context may be other words, a picture, an object, or an action. Consider the Excedrin ad (plate 11–1, insert following p. 186). The signs, "major hospital study," in the headline and the picture of a woman in a "hospital setting," lend legitimacy to the product claims. Or, in the California Avocado Advisory Board ad (plate 11–2), the headline is meaningless without the illustration. The refrigerator that carries the sign, "General Electric," is a very different refrigerator from the one that carries the sign, "Hickory Hollow Manufacturing Company."

Thus far, we have dealt with words and pictures as signs. Colors and shapes are signs also. The Eagle Printing Company printed the following suggestions for enhancing the appetite appeal of food illustrations as a guide to advertisers.

Orange is one of the dominant hues of high appetite appeal. The color is rich and luminous. Avoid yellow-orange. Clear yellow, however, slightly warm in tone, is savory. But again avoid the goldenrod cast (which appears rancid) and the greenish cast (which appears raw).

Among the reds, use bright vermillion, suggestive of porterhouse steaks and ripe apples. Purplish reds seem "tough" and unfit for human consumption.

As to greens, select clean ones, crisp and clean in quality. Avoid yellowish greens which are bilious, and bluish greens which seem poisonous.

Your other colors will then consist of warm browns and tans, remindful of well-cooked meats and breads. For a definitely "sweet" color choose pink. For wines and liquors choose transparent purples. This is the appetite palette. Blues may be used to set them off, for while blue is not a good food color it does seem to suggest cleanliness and freshness.

However, purples, grays, magentas, chartreuse greens, and the like are to be avoided. We would not care to "eat" them—so why should they feature any products meant for our tables.[19]

The goal of advertising writers and artists is to use signs to persuade consumers. Advertising is successful only to the extent that it conveys the intended meaning to consumers. This thought is summed up in a sign that Bill Spencer, former creative director of the Gardner Advertising Company, displayed on the wall of his office. It read, as I recall:

Advertising can survive many imperfections as long as it says what it has to say clearly and distinctly, always keeping in mind the audience to whom it is directed.

OTHER DIMENSIONS OF ADVERTISING

There are other important dimensions of advertising; each relates to effectiveness. Three that will be touched on in the following material are: (1) the *believability* of advertising, (2) whether the advertising itself is *liked* or *disliked,* and (3) *tastelessness* in advertising.

Believability

It seems reasonable to assume that believable advertising should be more effective than nonbelievable advertising. It was pointed out earlier that the believability of

---

19. Eagle Printing Company, "What Colors Look Good Enough to Eat," No. 5, *Facts from the Research Department of the Eagle Printing Ink Company,* 100 Sixth Ave., New York.

an advertising claim is enhanced by an observable product difference that can be used to support the claim. Believability, however, is a complex idea.

For example, John Maloney makes a sharp distinction between two types of *nonbelief,* which he refers to as *disbelief* (or outright rejection) and *curiosity.* The statement of a consumer that an advertising claim is "hard to believe" may mean two different things. It might mean, "I do not believe that, and I won't try the brand" (disbelief), or it might mean, "That's hard to believe, but I think I'll try the brand to see if it is true" (curiosity). Maloney found that housewives he surveyed who found an advertising claim "hard to believe" were just as willing to try a brand as those who found the claim "easy to believe." Consequently, Maloney concluded that absolute believability is not an essential ingredient of effective advertising.[20]

This conclusion is consistent with the use of fantasy in advertising. No one, for example, believes that a white knight, charging around on a white horse and pointing a white lance at a bunch of dirty kids, will make them sparkling white. Yet, the "white knight" advertising of Ajax was extremely successful. The use of fantasy as a device for overstating claims is a legitimate tool. Even the courts have conceded that fantasy that exceeds the bounds of credibility does not constitute false and misleading advertising.

Liking versus Disliking

A frequently raised question in advertising is whether advertising itself must be liked in order to be effective. Few advertising writers deliberately attempt to write advertising that consumers dislike, but they sometimes use strident claims, or poor taste, or a technique that offends some group of consumers.

The problem of "liking" is a difficult one because the people who are most vocal in their dislike of a particular advertisement are often not the people for whom the advertisement was written. For example, I have found that many male college students are vociferously critical of detergent advertising, perceiving it as dull, far-fetched, and trivial. Practically, though, detergent advertising isn't written for male college students, but for housewives who are inundated with dirty children, dirty husbands, dirty clothes, dirty linens, and dirty dishes. Further, the "slice of life" technique that is often used in such advertising is not taken from the lives of college students, but from the lives of housewives. As another example, advertisements directed to women are often criticized because of the stereotyped roles in which women are cast. Such

criticisms are generally valid. However, many women are not offended by these stereotypes, but respond positively to them.

There are many opinions on whether ads that are liked are more effective than those that are disliked, but there is little hard data. One of the reasons, of course, is that there is little agreement on how one measures the effectiveness of advertising. However, Maurice Kelly, while vice-president of marketing and planning for Eastern Airlines, stated the following opinion.

> Noisy promotions alienate the consumer. . . . The public today wants to be persuaded softly, not rudely; to be coaxed, not commanded. They're tired of shouting.[21]

On the other hand, Draper Daniels, basing his opinion on thirty years in the advertising business, states:

1. The consumer tends to prefer advertising that does *not* make her remember the name of the product or make her want to buy it.
2. If there is any correlation between how consumers feel about advertising and sales power of advertising, it would appear to indicate that advertising about which consumers most often complain is the advertising most likely to sell them.
3. While highly offensive advertising is frequently highly effective, it is also largely responsible for the rise of Consumerism and the trend toward more stringent government regulation of advertising.[22]

One research study, reported by Treasure and Joyce, used the percentage shift in brand preference before and after exposure to commercials as a measure of effectiveness. The study found that:

1. Specific commercials that are especially well liked or especially disliked are not substantially different in effectiveness.
2. Adjective choices used to describe commercials with high liking scores clustered around entertainment values. Adjectives used to describe highly effective commercials focused more on creative and communication values. This suggests that liking and effectiveness are *not* the same thing.[23]

Perhaps the most balanced view is that suggested by David Ogilvy. "A good advertisement," he says, "is

20. John C. Maloney, "Curiosity versus Disbelief in Advertising," *Journal of Advertising Research* (June, 1962): 2–8.

21. "They're tired of shouting," *Advertising Age* (April 13, 1970): 3.
22. Draper Daniels, *Giants, Pigmies and Other Advertising People* (Chicago: Crain Communications, Inc., 1974), pp. 252–53.
23. John Treasure and Timothy Joyce, "As Others See Us," *Occasional Paper 17,* Institute of Practitioners in *Advertising,* London, 1967.

one which sells the product *without drawing attention to* itself. It should rivet the reader's attention on the product. Instead of saying, 'What a clever advertisement,' the reader says, 'I never knew *that* before. I must try this product.'"[24] According to this point of view, the advertisement that is doing its job properly stays in the background, neither pleasing nor offending.

Tasteless Advertising

Young writers will always face the temptation to shock people in order to gain their attention. Further, it is probably impossible to write anything that will not be offensive to someone, somewhere. Nonetheless, the temptation to shock or offend in order to gain attention should probably be avoided. After all, advertising exists and will continue to exist at the sufferance of the public. And the use of tactics that violate good taste is an open invitation to further government regulation. Fairfax Cone, a widely admired and highly respected advertising practioner, deplores "tastelessness in advertising," and suggests that there *must* be a better way to present the product.[25] And, *Advertising Age,* in the following editorial, echoes this point of view.

Shock: A Creative Short-cut

The double entendre is a perennial industry problem, one that will from time to time belch forth its bad taste and blanket the industry. We see evidence of this each week as readers send us what are called "Ads we can do without," usually ads that play off anatomical features or sexual activities.

We recall the commotion that greeted National Airlines' "Fly me!" campaign a few years ago, and the eyebrow-lifting that occurred when the "My men wear English Leather or they wear nothing at all" campaign broke. More recently, we've had the "Flick your Bic" campaign. Such efforts, obviously in questionable taste, nevertheless managed to link product or service to a fresh slogan and thereby earned grudging recognition in some quarters as hard-working creative solutions to marketing problems.

How, then, does one justify the tv commercial for Speidel's new digital watches? Speidel has a prospective groom telling his bride-to-be, "Honey, this is the day. Today, I'm going all the way." The future bride registers shock, unaware that he's only talking about the Speidel watch and watchstrap he has bought. The theme then becomes, "Speidel goes all the way," thus linking Speidel to a phrase that already draws snickers from every boastful adolescent. By attaching its brand

name to that expression, Speidel hopes to gain instant recognition and identification for the new entry. Where the budget is weak, the competition strong, and time short, the temptation is to treat the creative short-cut as a creative solution; too bad creative people can't make their talents transcend such temptation.[26]

THE EFFECTS OF ADVERTISING

Since the role of advertising is to provide information and to translate the product concept into a consumer benefit that can be understood and appreciated by consumers, it follows that advertising, to be successful, must *communicate* with consumers. In order to ascertain how well advertising is accomplishing its communication task, we need some way of measuring or monitoring its accomplishments.

One approach that has been given wide currency since the early 1960s is the "hierarchy of effects" concept. This concept describes advertising communications as a series of steps ranging from simple *awareness* of a brand or service to the actual *purchase* of it. There are a number of hierarchy of effects models, five of which are summarized in table 11–1.

The similarity between these various models is apparent. They differ only in the number of steps involved and in the particular words used to describe the steps. The Association of National Advertisers commissioned R.H. Colley to develop the DAGMAR model (an acronym for Defining Advertising Goals for Measuring Advertising Results) in an effort to devise a method of measuring advertising effectiveness.[27] The Lavidge and Steiner model conceives of advertising as a force that moves people up through a series of steps in which "the actual purchase is but the final threshold."[28] The AIDA model has traditionally been used by salespeople to visualize the process of moving a prospect along a series of mental steps to the final sale.[29] The Adoption Process model has been borrowed from sociology and is primarily associated with the introduction of new products. Finally, the National Industrial Conference Board developed its model as an aid in visualizing the sales process. The presentation of this model noted: (1) the influence of

24. Ogilvy, *Confessions* p. 90.
25. Fairfax Cone, *With All Its Faults* (Boston: Little Brown and Company, 1969), p. 304.
26. "Shock: A creative short-cut." Reprinted with permission from the November 28, 1977 issue of *Advertising Age.* Copyright 1977 by Crain Communications, Inc., p. 10.
27. R.H. Colley, *Defining Advertising Goals for Measured Advertising Results,* 1961.
28. R.L. Lavidge and G.A. Steiner, "A Model for Predictive Measurements of Advertising Effectiveness," *Journal of Marketing* **25** (October, 1961): 59–62.
29. K.K. Cox and B.M. Enis, *The Marketing Research Process* (Pacific Palisades, California: Goodyear Publishing Company, Inc., 1972), p. 41.

Table 11-1. Hierarchy of Effects Models

Dagmar	*Lavidge-Steiner*	*AIDA*	*Adoption Process*	*Industrial Conference Board*
Action	Purchase	Action	Adoption	Provoking sale
Conviction	Conviction	Desire	Trial	Intention
Comprehension	Preference	Interest	Evaluation	Preference
Awareness	Liking	Attention	Interest	Acceptance
	Knowledge		Awareness	Awareness
	Awareness			

advertising at each stage depends on the industry, the product, and the type of advertising as well as factors peculiar to the company, its selling methods, and its previous marketing position; (2) the influence of advertising tends to diminish at each successive stage, playing a smaller role in "provoking the sale" than in "awareness;" and finally, (3) much advertising is only intended to achieve some intermediate objective such as increasing awareness or arousing a desire to buy.[30]

In order to examine the hierarchy of effects concept more closely, let us take one of the models and consider it in detail. Although any of the models could be used equally well, let us use the Industrial Conference Board model since: (1) its terms are relatively unambiguous; (2) it has an intermediate number of steps that, in my experience, seem to parallel the stages that consumers often go through; and (3) it explicitly recognizes that the importance of advertising may diminish as consumers move up the scale in terms of their familiarity with the brand and their propensity to purchase it.

This scale, like the others, assumes that the progress from awareness to purchase is a laborious one that takes place over a period of time, that the consumer moves only one step at a time, and that each step upward increases the probability of purchase. Although these assumptions may hold true in many cases (many of us can recall personal experiences that required repeated exposures before we finally made a decision to purchase a brand), the rule is not inviolate. If the consumer benefit is strong and relevant to needs that are prepotent, one may traverse the ladder from awareness to purchase in a single leap. Kristian Palda has also questioned the assumption that each step up the ladder leads to an increased probability of purchase.[31] Certainly, one can imagine situations in which Palda's criticism is valid. For example, I have clearly progressed from "awareness of" to a "prefer-

ence for" a Rolls-Royce with no increase in the probability that I will ever buy one. Not only do I not have the money, but the thought of spending over $40 thousand for an automobile (even though I think the car is probably worth the price) violates my sense of propriety. This simply means that advertising often has effects on individuals who lie outside the target market for which the advertising was intended.

Aside from these exceptions, the hierarchy of effects model seems reasonably descriptive and offers a way to monitor the extent to which advertising is progressing beyond the role of providing information toward achieving its goal of translating the product concept into an appealing consumer benefit. So, let us appraise each of the steps in the Industrial Conference Board model to see how it works in practice.

Awareness

As a first step in the purchase process, broad awareness among relevant consumer groups is critical. Few brands are positioned to appeal to an entire market; each, on some basis, identifies a target segment to which it is directed. The extent to which brand awareness is achieved can be measured fairly simply through market surveys of the appropriate user groups.

Yet, awareness is often difficult to attain because it means breaking through the fog of lethargy, apathy, and distraction that surrounds consumers. In order to create awareness, the advertisement or commercial must first attract attention, and this usually requires a dramatic device of some sort. In magazine advertising, the advertiser has only a fraction of a second to arrest the attention of the reader before he flips the page. Dramatic headlines, provocative illustrations, and the ostentatious use of color are all used for the purpose of attracting attention. This is undoubtedly one of the reasons for the excessive use of scantily clad or provocative women in advertising illustrations, even though it is not always clear what they have to do with the product or its use. After all, there is nothing like sex to attract attention in a society where sexual hang-ups are the national neurosis.

30. H.D. Wolfe, J.K. Brown, and G.C. Thompson, *Measuring Advertising Results,* Studies in Business Policy, No. 2, The National Industrial Conference Board (1962), p. 7.

31. K.S. Palda, "The Hypothesis of Hierarch of Effects: A Partial Evaluation," *Journal of Marketing Research* **13** (February, 1966): pp. 13–24.

In broadcast advertising, it is generally believed that the first five seconds of the commercial must capture the active attention of viewers. Otherwise, their minds will wander; they will flip to another channel; or they will engage in some other activity. All of this places a premium on developing attention-getting devices that tests the ingenuity of advertising writers and illustrators.

Sometimes, preoccupation with gaining attention becomes so single minded that inadequate thought is given to other tasks that the advertisement should perform. Thus, there are brands whose advertisements have achieved wide awareness, but have done little to move the consumer to the next step in the hierarchy, acceptance.

Acceptance

When a product has gained acceptance, it is seen as an alternative brand, a brand that might be bought if the preferred brand is not available. In some product fields where leading brands are seen as similar, gaining acceptance may be about as much as advertising alone can accomplish. In the gasoline industry, for example, it is generally recognized that brands with which consumers are familiar fall into two groups. The *golden circle* group includes brands that are considered acceptable and interchangeable. An individual will use any brand in his golden circle without concern and with equal confidence. The *off-brands* group includes those brands about which the consumer is a little suspicious and will avoid using if possible.

The level of acceptance requires a greater familiarity with, and more information about, the brand than the level of awareness. Familiarity and information is often achieved through *reason why* copy, or by showing the brand in appropriate use situations. Sometimes, sheer repetition of the brand name may move it to the level of acceptance. This expensive way to gain acceptance is used because the consumer's logic seems to be: "I've seen that brand name so often, it must be all right. If it weren't, the manufacturer couldn't sell enough to justify its continued advertising."

Reason why copy may take many forms. It may take the form of a "secret ingredient"—"The mysterious beauty fluid" in Oil of Olay that "works with your skin's own natural moisture to quickly ease away dryness, leaving your skin feeling soft and smooth." It may take the form of a product endorsement by a celebrity; thus, Everynight Astringent Shampoo by Helene Curtis has Chris Evert, the tennis star, saying: "It super cleans oily hair without drying it out." It may take the form of demonstrations, or simple reas-

surances. Whatever form it takes, it enables the consumer to make the subjective decision that: "This brand is all right. I won't go too far wrong if I use it."

Preference

The goal of most advertising is to gain preference for brands; to bring consumers to the point where they prefer a particular brand over all others. From the standpoint of advertising's capabilities, preference is always tentative; product purchase may result in disappointment, with the consequence that the product will fall back to the bottom rung of the ladder and not be repurchased. Also, when the preference stage is reached, it is quite possible that other factors are entering into the process of product evaluation—factors such as word-of-mouth advertising, exposure to the product through friends or other social occasions, the experience of users, and so forth. It is at this point that the contribution of advertising may become severely contaminated by personal experience, the experience of others, or by other marketing activities.

The advertising techniques used to create preference are the same ones that are used to promote acceptance, since it must be recognized that an argument or appeal that is sufficient to generate preference on the part of one consumer may only generate acceptance by another and leave still a third consumer untouched.

The extent of preference can be measured by marketing research—both in terms of the proportion of the target market preferring the brand and in terms of preference strength (how strongly the brand is preferred over competitive brands). If consumer research finds that relatively few consumers prefer a particular brand compared to competition, the problem may lie in many areas. It may be the product itself, the brand name, packaging, pricing, service, and so forth. Only when these other areas have been ruled out, may it be assumed that a new advertising approach needs to be developed. Far too often, advertising is blamed for a lack of consumer interest when the real problem lies elsewhere.

On the other hand, if a brands "share of preference" is greater than its "share of sales," then the evidence is fairly clear that advertising is doing its job, and some other part of the marketing effort needs strengthening. A case in point is that of a major household appliance. Consumer surveys consistently revealed that 40–45 percent of the potential customers preferred the brand *before* they began shopping for actual purchase. Yet, the brand obtained less than 30 percent of sales. Investigation in this instance indicated that lack of sales support at the retail level was the culprit. The company had neglected retail sales people in their marketing program, and it was these sales people who were switching customers to other brands. Or, take the case of Alka-Seltzer in the late 1960s. Frequent shifts in advertising direction did little to revitalize a sales curve that had leveled off at about 21 percent of the market. The real problem is not clear, but the brand probably had exhausted that segment of the market that was interested in an Alka-Seltzer type product. Further expansion in the upset-stomach–analgesic field could only be obtained through a different product formulation aimed at a different market segment.

Intention to Buy

This stage refers to the psychological committment to purchase a particular brand. For many low-priced, packaged goods, preference and intention are virtually synonymous. For more expensive items, where price is a limiting factor, intention becomes a critical stage in the buying process. To refer to an earlier example, I prefer a Rolls-Royce to all other cars I have seen. The thought of owning a Rolls-Royce really excites me. But I have no intention of buying one.

For relatively expensive products or brands, the advertising of warranties for extended periods, such as "Five years or 50,000 miles" for an automobile, may move a consumer from the preference state to a psychological intention to buy. Or, advertising the lifetime guarantee of the J.C. Penney sealed battery may be sufficient assurance. Similarly, the safety emphasis in the advertising for radial steel belted tires may overcome the price differential and transport the consumer from a state of preference to the committed customer state. In most instances, where intention to buy is a distinct step from preference, the advertising needs to be substantive to cause that step to be taken.

Provoking the Sale

Again, the role of advertising in provoking the final sale will differ widely, depending upon the product class. For relatively inexpensive, frequently purchased items, the development of brand preference is usually sufficient to cause trial. However, for products requiring demonstration and/or personal selling (automobiles, insurance, clothing, furniture, carpeting, and so forth) the contribution of advertising in closing the sale is usually minimal. Advertising may make the consumer receptive to a particular brand, but other marketing activities usually occupy the dominant role in closing the sale.

However, the one form of advertising that may be the

determining factor in this final stage is *promotional* advertising that features a major price reduction. If the consumer has already formed a brand preference and made the psychological committment to purchase sometime in the future, promotional advertising may precipitate immediate action.

Summary Observation on "Hierarchy of Effects" Models

It is doubtful that the "hierarchy of effects" concept provides a pure, unadulterated description of advertising's contribution to marketing; too many other marketing activities also enter into the process. The hierarchy of effects concept is useful, however, because it suggests that advertising should be evaluated on the basis of that which it does best: namely, creating awareness, acceptance, and preference for a brand.

However, it is difficult to determine just how much advertising is required to achieve a given level of awareness, acceptance, or preference. The amount required depends on the nature of competition, the strength of the product concept, and the effectiveness of the advertising itself.

KINDS OF ADVERTISING

Throughout the discussion of advertising, our focus had been on *product* advertising. That is, advertising designed to provide consumers with information about the product and to translate the product concept into a consumer benefit. Such advertising is sometimes referred to as *display* advertising since it displays the product for everyone to see. There are other kinds of advertising with somewhat different objectives. Four of the major kinds of advertising are described in the following material.

Sales Promotion Advertising

Whereas display advertising is generally designed to affect consumer beliefs about a product over a period of time and through repeated exposures, *sales promotion* advertising is intended to create immediate action. Thus, it generally carries an urgent message, such as an announcement of a sale, a contest, a coupon, or some other offer. Major sales promotional activities (which will be discussed in chapter 20) are frequently supported by advertising, and the specific objectives of the advertising are determined by the nature of the promotion being used. Advertising in support of a consumer contest or sweepstakes, for example, is designed to describe the *prize structure*, the rules of the contest, and what consumers must do to enter. The Homecare Sweepstakes advertisement (plate 11–3, insert following p. 218) is an excellent example of a sales promotional ad. Note that the entire advertisement is devoted to the sweepstakes, and in this particular example, the only way Homecare products get in the ad is by being a part of the prize structure.

Trade Advertising

Trade advertising for a consumer product is generally directed to members of the retail trade and designed either to help gain distribution or to enlist retail cooperation in a product promotion. In the first instance, such advertising usually emphasizes the profit that the retailer can realize by stocking the brand and often offers a *stocking allowance* for all initial purchases. In the second instance, announcing a promotion, the trade advertising usually describes the promotion, specifies its dates, indicates the extent of consumer advertising support, and often offers a *promotion allowance* for in-store displays during the promotion period. Both of these goals—gaining distribution and announcing promotions—are supported by the activities of the sales force. The advertising is used to provide broad coverage of the retail trade, and to pave the way for personal sales presentation. Figures 11–4 and 11–5 are examples of trade advertising. The Vlasic example is directed toward gaining distribution. The Sylvania example announces a promotion.

Corporate Advertising

A third form of advertising, *corporate advertising*, may have a variety of objectives and be directed toward any number of audiences. Some corporate advertisements are directed to consumers, with the intent of conveying a particular corporate image that will serve as a backdrop or umbrella for product advertising. Other corporate advertising may be directed toward members of the financial community (investors, investment analysts, brokers, etc.) in order to inform them about the company's financial performance and/or other qualities that might help increase the attractiveness of company stock as an investment. Sometimes companies use corporate advertising to promote a social philosophy which management believes to be in the company's best interest. The advertisement by Eaton Truck Components (figure 11–6) is an interesting use of corporate advertising. Ostensibly, the advertising is addressed to the general

public and protests possible misuse of highway funds by Congress for nonhighway-related items such as mass transportation. At the same time, it is indirectly addressed to the trucking industry, and says, in effect: "Hey, fellows! We're on your side." Crafty.

In any event, corporate advertising may be used to accomplish any number of corporate communications objectives. The structure and content of a particular advertisement or campaign will depend on the nature of its objectives, and the audience for which it is relevant.

Retail Advertising

Retail advertising generally takes one of two forms. Either it is *display* advertising designed to create a store image and communicate the store's unique benefits to consumers, or it is *sales promotion* advertising, the purpose of which is to increase store traffic or clear inventories. The Orhbach's advertisement shown in chapter 4 is an outstanding example of retail advertising to communicate a store image. It offers no particular product for sale. It represents Orhbach's as a source of stylish, inexpensive clothes.

Retail *sales promotion* advertising features products, bargains, and sales. The January "white sale," with its discounts on linens and flat pieces and the "back to school" sale of children's clothes are examples of traditional sales promotions by department stores. Similarly, the advertising of weekly food features is a traditional food store sales promotion activity, as is Rexall's annual "penny" sale—"Buy one item at the regular price, and get a second one for a penny."

All in all, advertising may serve many objectives. It is essential, however, that the objectives to be served are clearly specified *before* the advertising is developed. Otherwise one is liable to end up with creative garbage. In addition, after the advertising has been developed (and before it is approved for use) an enormous amount of time and company resources could be saved by asking the following three questions:

Does the Advertisement Execute the Creative Strategy? If it does not, it is inappropriate and should be rejected without wasting any more time on it. No one needs a great campaign that doesn't do what it is supposed to do.

Figure 11–4. (Vlasic Foods, Inc.)

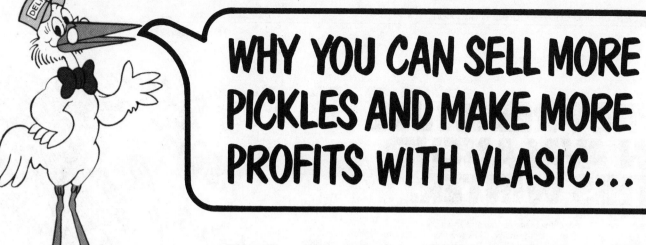

WHY YOU CAN SELL MORE PICKLES AND MAKE MORE PROFITS WITH VLASIC...

In the pickle business, sales and profits are the name of the game. Here's how vlasic helps you increase both.

ADVERTISING/MERCHANDISING SUPPORT—Vlasic wrote the book on advertising and merchandising support in the pickle business. Only Vlasic advertises on prime time network TV throughout the year. Our highly recognizable spokesman presents one of the most effective advertising messages in any food category. And no one's better at stimulating promotional sales than Vlasic.

CONSUMER PREFERRED—Vlasic's superior quality products are guaranteed to the consumer and to you. Consumer tests prove Vlasic products are preferred for taste, flavor and quality over all national and regional brands. Our high standards in each step of processing assure your customers always receive the very best pickle money can buy.

REGIONAL RESPONSIVENESS—Our six pickle-packing plants are strategically located across the U.S. for two important benefits: One, we can serve you most efficiently. Two, we can serve up superior product which is actually taste-tailored to local consumer preferences.

COMPLETE VARIETY—Vlasic's line of over 96 pickle, relish, pepper and specialty items offers you variety unequalled by any competitor. We help you please all your customers all the time with processed, refrigerated and fresh pack; sweet, dill or candied . . . giving them the selection they expect and the satisfaction they demand.

SHELF MANAGEMENT—Vlasic's unique shelf management program is designed to build total pickle sales and profits. We can provide this kind of support because, as America's #1 pickle, we have the experience and resources to make it possible. Our specialists are ready to help you with item selection and shelf layout, based on local sales data, as well as proven shelving and merchandising ideas.

AWARD-WINNING PACKAGING—Vlasic is the best at capturing impulse sales by giving shelves a bright, compelling look. Our color-keyed labels have won a national design award, and the jars come from our own custom molds. Even the lids are specially designed. All of this results in more sales and increased turns.

vlasic outsells the number 2,3,4 and 5 pickle brands combined!

Vlasic Foods, Inc., 33200 W. 14 Mile Road, W. Bloomfield, MI 48033. Sales data available upon request.

WE'RE PREDICTING AN AVALANCHE THIS WINTER.

Conditions are perfect for it.
When you take America's biggest selling brand of flash and give it one of the
biggest promotions the industry has ever seen, the dollars
are bound to fall fast and heavy. Right into your cash
register.

OUR BIGGEST NETWORK TV PROMOTION EVER.

Starting November 14th, we'll be running Sylvania
Blue Dot™ Flash commercials night after night on prime-
time TV all through the key Thanksgiving/Christmas selling season. Nearly 700 million advertising messages!
Add to that, full-page ads in *Family Circle, People, Ladies' Home Journal*
and *Redbook* (total circulation 21 million). All with store coupons offering 20¢ off
on any Sylvania Blue Dot Flash product: Flip Flash, Magicube, Flashcube,
Flash Bar, Hi-Power Flashcube, and Flashbulbs.

COLORFUL DISPLAYS WITH REFUND COUPONS WORTH UP TO $1.25.

We'll also have sen-
sational in-store displays
featuring an offer no
picture-taker can pass up:
a consumer refund worth
50¢ on one package of
Sylvania Blue Dot Flash,
and $1.25 on two packages.
No doubt about it.
With promotional dyna-
mite like this, there's going
to be a sales avalanche of
major proportions.

OVER 21 MILLION MAGAZINE COUPONS.

So ask your Sylvania Blue Dot sales representative about our special "Save the Holidays"
promotion. And make sure you lay in an emergency
supply of Sylvania Blue Dot Flash products.
This way, when the avalanche hits, you know
you'll be well covered.

GTE SYLVANIA

Sylvania Lighting Center, Danvers, Mass. 019

Figure 11–5. (General Telephone and Electronics)

Is the Advertisement Clear and Understandable? If
it is not, it should be rewritten. Draper Daniels,
advertising writer, creative director, and agency principal, has suggested:

A big reason why so much advertising doesn't work is
because it is the product of writers who have a far
greater love for and understanding of words than most
people do, and of artists who understand and love art
far more than the average housewife does. The resulting
advertising is frequently highly pleasing to other artists
and writers and either incomprehensible or without
interest to prospects of the product.[32]

*Will the Advertisement Arouse Interest, Gain Read-
ership, and Have an Effect on the Consumers to
Whom It Is Directed?* And, here's the rub. It is not
difficult to determine whether an advertisement executes strategy. Neither is it too difficult to tell whether
the ad is clear and understandable. But, when it
comes to the question of interest and effect, we are in
the realm of creative judgment where rules go out the
window, and marketing research sometimes hinders
as much as it helps.

---

32. Daniels, *Giants*, p. 253.

Figure 11–6. (Eaton Corporation)

The $8.9 billion misunderstanding

Your highway taxes should not be detoured while roads and bridges remain inadequate or incomplete.

In 1976, the Highway Trust Fund had a balance of $8.9 billion, all of it paid by the people who use the nation's roads. $38 from each typical motorist and $1,335 from each large truck annually, derived from taxes on gas, oil and tires and several other taxes on heavy trucks and buses.

The $8.9 billion is supposed to pay for highway construction and rebuilding—nothing else. That's why Congress created the Highway Trust Fund. Yet today, Congress is under pressure to detour part of the Fund for projects not related to highways.

Herein lies the big misunderstanding.
The Highway Trust Fund balance is needed for federal highway projects already committed. In 1976, federal highway project authorizations exceeded $22 billion. The trucking industry strongly opposes funding non-highway projects, however worthy, with highway tax dollars. Efficient trucking operations depend on good roads for trucks to deliver most of the food and other consumer goods on which we all depend. The Highway Trust Fund should be spent only on highways and bridges because many of them are in desperate need of rebuilding or replacement. If you drive, we think you'll agree.

This message is brought to you by Eaton Corporation, makers of truck components for the American Trucking Industry.

SUMMARY

The chapter is devoted to a number of general considerations, each of which is important to an understanding of advertising and the ways in which it works.

Little attention has been given to theory in advertising despite the fact that theory is needed to give coherence to the field and to reconcile some of the disagreements that exist as to what constitutes good advertising. The value-added theory of advertising suggests that advertising adds value to a product or service by endowing it with a consumer benefit that relates to conscious or unconscious human needs. This theory is then used to reconcile some of the disparate views that are rampant in the field.

The next general consideration is the developing of basic appeals that can be used to persuade consumers. Since consumer motivation is complex, there is no universal agreement among advertising writers on a single list of consumer motivations. Aspiring advertising writers need to develop a list of motivations that represent their convictions about what is important to consumers.

Even with an understanding of consumer motivation, there is still the problem of translating this understanding into persuasive communications. In this regard, the role of verbal and nonverbal communications and the concept of *meaning* must be understood to avoid some of the problems of effective communications.

Three controversial areas of advertising are: (1) believability in advertising, (2) the role of liking and disliking advertising in advertising effectiveness, and (3) the problem of tastelessness in advertising.

The question of how advertising affects consumers is crucial, and the effects of advertising are essentially communication effects. There are several *hierarchy of effects* models that begin to describe contributions that advertising makes to the marketing effort.

The major kinds of advertising are: product, display, sales promotion, trade, corporate, and retail. It is important to clearly define advertising tasks before individual ads or campaigns are developed.

QUESTIONS

1. Explain the value-added theory of advertising and relate it to (a) the U.S.P. (unique selling proposition) concept, and (b) image advertising.
2. Discuss the problem of keeping in touch with consumers, both in terms of the consumers themselves and in terms of the advertising writer.
3. Explain the following concepts of meaning: (a) denotative meaning, (b) connotative meaning, (c) structural meaning, and (d) contextural meaning.
4. Discuss the concept of *believability* in advertising.
5. Relate the concept of liking and disliking of advertising to advertising effectiveness.
6. Select one of the hierarchy of effects models and describe it. In these models, what is the primary function of advertising?
7. Identify the different kinds of advertising described in the text. What is the primary purpose of each?
8. What are the three basic questions that should be asked in reviewing a proposed advertisement? Which is the most difficult to answer? Why is it most difficult?

PROBLEM

Since the advent of margarine, which sells for about half the price of butter, the sales of butter have declined significantly. In 1950, per capita consumption of butter was 10.7 pounds; by 1975, per capita consumption of butter had dropped to about 4.0 pounds. By contrast, during the same period, the per capita consumption of margarine increased from 6.1 pounds to almost 12.0 pounds. In addition to the price differential, the flavor of margarine has been improved during this period, and the development of "soft" margarines has increased the versatility and appeal of this product type. Beyond this, the concern of the medical profession over the high cholesterol content of dairy products has caused many older consumers to severely limit dairy products in their diets.

As the advertising manager of a major producer of dairy products, you are a member of the advisory council of a national dairy association. It has been suggested that members of the association be assessed in order to generate $5 million for an advertising campaign to increase butter consumption. In considering whether or not you should support this proposal, you are wondering: (1) how effective such a program might be, (2) what kinds of consumer appeals might be used, (3) what the basic purpose of the campaign should be (awareness, interest, desire, action), and (4) what the target audience should be.

Assignment

1. Evaluate each of these four considerations.
2. Relate this problem to the value-added theory of advertising.
3. Do you support the proposal?

12

Advertising Creativity—
the Preparation

Contac

Contac was introduced into the market in September, 1961, at the beginning of the cold season. In three months, it was being distributed in 90 percent of all U.S. drug stores. The product concept behind Contac was a "tiny time pill" concept of medication—hundreds of tiny pills that were designed to dissolve at different rates, providing continuous medication. The name, *Contac*, a contraction of "continuous action," was selected to reinforce the product concept. Initial distribution was restricted to drug stores to gain druggist's support, since discount houses and food stores were pirating sales from drug stores by selling competitive products at discount prices. The advertising was clear, straight-forward, and concise; it consisted of a dominant headline and short body copy (see figure 12-1).

Note the body copy references to "600 tiny time pills," "relief up to 12 hours," and "get Contac at your pharmacy." The package is the only illustration in the advertisement. It, too, reinforces the product concept by prominantly featuring a close up of a capsule with hundreds of tiny time pills.

Pampers

The Pampers advertisement (plate 12-1, insert following p. 218) is very different in format from the Contac advertisement. Pampers uses a dominant illustration that "selects" the audience, a headline that is conversational and "confidential," a picture of the product in use, and a package that graphically indicates a product for babies. It is advertising that clearly translates the product concept into a consumer benefit.

Lysol Spray Disinfectant

Consider the Lysol Spray Disinfectant ad (plate 12-2, insert facing p. 219). The headline, the illustrations, and the body copy tell the same story. The headline announces "Six reasons why even the cleanest homes need Lysol Spray." These six reasons are then illustrated by product-in-use pictures that are clearly numbered. The body copy clarifies each of the illustrations and signs off with the consumer benefit: "Lysol Spray kills household germs, including germs that cause odors." It is a hard-working advertisement. It features the product, shows how

Figure 12-1. (Menley & James Laboratories)

Here comes Daddy with a cold for everybody.

A few sneezes here and there and suddenly your whole family could be sharing Daddy's cold. Which is good reason for keeping Contac® on hand. Because a single Contac capsule works fast to help check your sneezes, stop your sniffles, and clear your stuffy nose. And the 600 tiny "time pills" inside keep on working up to 12 hours.

You get gentle relief all day or all night from the good medicine in just one Contac capsule. And when you're not sneezing and sniffling and blowing, you're not spreading as many cold germs. And you'll be a family hero for that. Get Contac at your pharmacy.

shows how easy it is to use, and it deals with a common household problem.

Each of these advertisements does its job in a different way. They use different headline approaches, different illustrations, different layouts. Yet, each clearly and simply translates the product concept into a consumer benefit that can be understood and appreciated by the audiences to which each is addressed.

STRATEGY AND STYLE

Every advertisement starts with an idea. But, ideas can be executed in a variety of ways. Ten different creative groups, given the Contac, the Pampers, or the Lysol Disinfectant assignment, would probably produce ten different executions of the basic idea. Some might be more effective than others in communicating with consumers, yet all the ads would be written within the framework of the copy strategy. The Ted Bates agency, for example, once tested four of its own commercials for the same brand of cigarettes. All of the commercials used the same U.S.P. (unique selling proposition), expressed in the same words. But, the advertisements were written differently. The copy tests indicated that the commercials varied widely in terms of their ability to register their message with consumers. The best commercial was fifteen times more effective than the worst.[1] Thus, creative execution can make a substantial difference in carrying out a copy strategy. Because of this, we need to take a closer look at the questions of strategy and style.

Copy Strategy

In chapter 3, it was pointed out that the copy strategy contains four elements. All of these elements may not appear in every copy strategy, but they should appear because they provide basic guidance for the execution of copy. These four elements are:

1. A statement of the *principal benefit* offered by the product.
2. A statement of the *principal characteristics* of the product—the "reason why" the benefits exist.
3. A statement of the *character or personality* of the product which will be reflected in the *mood, tone, and overall atmosphere* of the advertising.
4. A statement of *what the product is,* and *what the product is used for.*

---

1. Rosser Reeves, *Reality in Advertising* (New York: Alfred A. Knopf, 1961), p. 92.

Precisely *how* these four dimensions of strategy are reflected in a particular advertisement or campaign is a question of execution and style. Sometimes the principal benefit is explicitly stated in words; sometimes it is illustrated; sometimes it is strongly implied. But, in a good ad, it is always there. Let's see how these strategy elements were executed in the Lysol advertisement.

What Is the Principle Benefit? It cleans, disinfects, and removes unpleasant odors from homes. These benefits are stated or implied in several ways: in the headline in the name, Lysol, which is an established disinfectant; in the body copy which specifies six areas of effectiveness; and in the graphics on the package.

What Is the Principal Product Characteristic That Provides this Benefit? It kills household germs that cause odors. This assertion appears in the body copy and in the secondary headline at the bottom of the page. The advertisement could have specified the particular ingredients that cause Lysol Spray to kill germs, but the writer chose not to. Instead, a direct assertion was made. Generally, consumers aren't all that interested in the anatomy of products. They are more concerned with *what* the product does.

What Is the Mood, Tone, or Overall Atmosphere of the Advertising? It is straightforward, businesslike, yet informal. It uses models and a home with which consumers can easily identify. It could have been funny, or sexy, or chic, or sophisticated, or clinical, or threatening, or moody, or exuberant, or fun. But it isn't. And, it is doubtful whether any of these moods would have been appropriate for this product.

What Is the Product, and What Is It Used for? It is a spray disinfectant, a germ killer, and it is used for cleaning and eliminating odors. This is stated in a number of ways in the advertisement. Further, its ease of use and versatility are reflected in the illustrations and body copy.

Examine the Pampers and Contac advertisements in terms of these same dimensions, and you will see how each of these elements of copy strategy is executed. All good ads will have these elements—either explicitly stated or clearly implied. The use of a written copy strategy simply guarantees that *what* is stated or implied will always be the same. If you were to obtain different advertisements written from this strategy, you would immediately recognize their similarity, even though they might use different headlines, different illustrations, and different body copy. The same ideas, even if expressed in a different writing or artistic *style*, will still give rise to the same overall impression of the product, if the same copy strategy is followed.

Style

Style refers to the unique way in which a particular writer or artist expresses herself. Most good writers and artists have a style of their own. It is not a formula for writing or drawing; rather, it is a characteristic mode of expression. Edward Buxton quotes Paula Green, a partner in the Green Dolmatch advertising agency in New York, on the question of style:

> *Interviewer:* How did you—or how do you—think creative people develop a style of their own?
> *Green:* (Before answering she picks up a doll from a nearby table. It is a sad-sweet, old-fashioned doll called Holly Hobby. Paula is currently preparing an advertising campaign to launch the doll). Maybe this is part of the answer. It is a curious thing—the creator of this doll, a young woman, looks exactly like her doll. She recreated herself—or a fantasy of herself. Creative people are like that. I used to see it during my years at Doyle Dane. Art directors always drew themselves in their layouts. There is always something of the creator in all creative work.[2]

George Gribbin, a copywriter who later became chairman of Young and Rubicam, a large and extremely successful advertising agency, recalls that when he first joined the agency he was assigned to the Packard account and was told to write the way his predecessor, Jack Rosebrook, had been writing. Gribbin says:

> I got lost in the minutiae of it, imitating Rosebrook. In six weeks they took me off the Packard ads. I said to myself. "Well, maybe I can't write the Packard account. I don't know. But what I do know is that I can't write like Rosebrook. I've got to write like Gribbin." Over the years, I've learned that if we have a writer and we tell him, "Do it in this particular style," we'll get less good advertising.[3]

Most of us express ourselves best when we express ourselves naturally. When we try to use someone else's words, or style, or format, we become awkward, stilted, and unconvincing. And, when an advertise-

ment becomes stilted and unconvincing, that is the death of effective communications.

DEVELOPING ADVERTISING

Earlier, it was pointed out that most major advertising agencies work through creative groups, with each group consisting of writers, artists, and producers. Copywriters generally do the writing; artists generally conceive the illustration; and producers generally produce the final advertisement or commercial. But there is no rigid division of labor when trying to come up with an idea for an advertisement or campaign. All members of the group work together, contributing their ideas and talents to a common venture. The importance of coordinating these talents from the outset is dramatized by the following quotation:

> It is possible to leave a piece of copy on an art director's table, go away, and hope that something good will come of it. Sometimes it does; more often it doesn't.
> It is possible for a copywriter to sketch an ad *exactly* the way she wants it to appear. With the copy attached to the sketch, the copywriter hands it to the art director with the instruction, "Just clean this up a little for me, will you?" Something good may come of this. Usually it doesn't.
> Of all the important moments in the birth of an ad, the one we arrive at now can be the *most* important: the moment when art director and copywriter sit down together to discuss what the ad is going to look like.
> This is important for you to understand. Because if it does not happen, your chances of getting an attractive, hard-selling ad are going to be greatly reduced. The fact is that often this meeting of the minds does *not* take place. As we mentioned earlier, many of the smaller agencies in your city do not have art directors. By choice they rely on an art service to make their layouts for them. The busy copywriter may find it inconvenient to drive across town to the studio, or he or she may feel that some scribbled instructions on the copy sheet are enough. Often it is not.
> When you have something to say about your company's advertising, you will be doing everyone a favor if you insist that the art director and the copywriter get together—even if you have to take them to lunch.[4]

Because of this need for coordination, I will not talk about copywriters or art directors in the following discussion on the developing of advertising. Instead, I will talk about admakers—be they copywriters, art directors, or creative groups.

2. Edward Buxton, *Creative People At Work* (New York: Executive Communications, Inc., 1975), p. 155.
3. Judith Dolgins, "Because he loves the feel of words," in *Advertising: an Omnibus of Advertising* prepared by Printers' Ink (New York: McGraw-Hill Book Company, Inc., 1963), p. 118.
4. James S. Norris, *Advertising* (Reston, Virginia: Reston Publishing Company, Inc., 1977), p. 158.

William Bernbach has said, "Properly practiced creativity can make one ad do the work of ten."[5] Properly practiced creativity doesn't come easily, however. Good advertisements don't just happen. They take work. John Crawford, author of a text on advertising, says that the admaker's job consists of two parts:

1. *A never-ending search for ideas*—the "what to say" in an advertisement that provides the brilliant answer to an advertising problem, and
2. *The never-ending search for new and different ways to express those ideas*—the "how to say it" and "how to show it" techniques of preparing an advertisement that provides the brilliant execution of the ideas the copywriter wants to convey.[6]

Not all advertising is brilliant, of course. Some of it is downright dull. But no admaker ever starts out with the intention of writing a dull ad. When advertisements fail to live up to their expectations, it is often because the admaker has failed to expend the effort that effective advertising demands, or has lost patience with the time it requires. In discussing the development of advertising, let us look at two separate but interrelated activities—the search for facts and the creative process.

THE SEARCH FOR FACTS

Good advertising begins with facts. All the facts that one can gather. Some will be trivial and of little value, but at the outset it isn't possible to know what is dross and what is gold. "Lynchburgh (Pop. 367), Tennessee" is a fact about Jack Daniel's whiskey. It's the location of the distillery. As a fact, it is completely trivial. Yet, it has been made important in Jack Daniel's advertising as a symbol of the tradition and care that go into the making of the product. And this points up a curious characteristic of facts in advertising. No fact is important until someone makes it so. That's why it is necessary to begin with facts. Advertising practitioner Charles Adams emphasizes this point with the observation: "Before you pick up the pencil, pick up the facts. Detachment is fine, but ignorance is inexcusable."[7]

Fact gathering can be quite complex, depending on the nature and variety of sources used by the admaker. A primary source of facts is the client organization itself. One admaker has said that, before he started work on a new project, he had over a hundred questions that he submitted to the client.[8] Beyond this, there are relevant research studies conducted by the agency, the client, and by media. Often there is a substantial amount of secondary or published research available through the government or trade associations. Facts can be obtained from the account group, as well as from contact with consumers and the wholesale and retail trade. Appendix 2, at the end of the text, lists 279 questions that might be asked. Not all of these questions are equally important, or even relevant for all writing assignments, but they do serve as a comprehensive reference list. At the very least, the admaker should become a repository of information about the product itself, about the people who use it, about the marketing practices in the product field, and about the advertising of the product and its competitors.

The Product

The starting point for any advertising campaign is the product itself. Some of the more important questions about the product are identified below.

What Is the Product? This may sound like an obvious question, but the answer is sometimes complex. Before it became a brand of coffee, Brim was the brand name of a powder that made a delicious drink when mixed with milk. Since four servings of Brim met all of the daily nutritional requirements and contained approximately 900 calories, the product could be several things. It could be a liquid diet food; it could be a dietary supplement; it could be a beverage to drink with meals; it could be a between-meal snack. Since the makers of Brim were unable to decide what the product was, its advertising reflected this confusion, and it failed in test markets. Carnation developed a similar product, called it Instant Breakfast, advertised it for people who did not have time for a regular breakfast, and built a multimillion dollar market.

When dealing with a complex product, such as McDonalds, it may be difficult to define precisely what the product is. Is it a hamburger? A fast-food concept? Or what? When Gainsburgers was first introduced into test markets, the product performed

5. William Bernbach, "Advertising's Greatest Tool," in *Speaking of Advertising*, John S. Wright and Daniel S. Warner, eds. (New York: McGraw-Hill Book Company, Inc., 1963), p. 313.
6. John W. Crawford, *Advertising*, 2nd ed. (Boston: Allyn and Bacon, 1965), p. 173.
7. Charles Adams, *Common Sense in Advertising* (New York: McGraw-Hill Book Company, Inc., 1965), p. 20.

8. *Ibid*, p. 15.

poorly because pet owners weren't sure whether the product was a "snack" or a "complete nutrition" dinner. The advertising wasn't clear on this point, and neither were consumers. The product did not succeed until it was clearly positioned as a "complete nutrition" dinner.

Claude Robinson, one of the founders of the Gallup-Robinson copy testing service, remarked one time that advertisers frequently overlook the obvious, and, by doing so, make grievous mistakes. Never make the mistake of assuming *what* the product is. Ask what it is. Sometimes you get strange answers. And, that's the beginning of product knowledge.

What Does the Product Do? Most products have more than one function or use: the makeup that is also a skin moisterizer, the shampoo that is also a conditioner, the all-weather topcoat that keeps us warm while also protecting us from rain, the fabric softener that is also a "freshener," the detergent that both bleaches and cleans. All of these examples are of products that have more than one *instrumental* function. Products also have *expressive* functions. That is, they permit us to make a statement about ourselves. Thus, a sportscar is *more* than transportation; a fashion by Dior is *more* than a dress; Chateau Haute Brion is not just another dinner wine; and Marlboro country is as much an image of masculinity as it is a cigarette.

The admaker must determine what the essential product benefit is—whether it is instrumental or expressive—and not let it become lost in a swarm of secondary and tertiary claims.

What Is It Made of? The ingredients of a product may offer the key to its advertising. Crest, with flouristan, prevents tooth decay; Coors beer is made with clear mountain water; Dial soap contains At–7, which attacks skin bacteria that causes body odor; for years, Shell gasoline got better mileage because of TCP; and don't forget Contac's "tiny time pills."

Although consumers generally don't get too excited about the anatomy of products, there are occasions when an ingredient provides a justification for the primary product benefit which, without a justification, would be a hollow claim. Thus, in addition to the above examples: Purina Puppy Chow contains *extra* protein to help puppies grow stronger; Alpo canned dog food is *all* meat; and the flavor of Tareyton Lights is improved by *charcoal*, if you happen to like charcoal.

Services also have ingredients—raw materials, courtesy, and special features. Burger King makes your hamburger the way *you* like it; American Airlines offers fine dining; and Avis Car rental tries harder. In any case, the admaker should know what the ingredients in the product are and what they do. After all, it was steel-belted radial tires that revolutionized the tire industry.

How Is It Made? The process by which a product is made may, like its ingredients, inspire an advertising approach, or at least provide support for a product claim. Budweiser floats beechwood chips through its brewing vats, and Jack Daniel's whiskey is "charcoal mellowed drop by drop." In fact, much of Jack Daniel's tremendously successful advertising is based on the process by which the product is made. A process, incidentally, that not only gave distinction to the brand, but resulted in a whole new classification of whiskeys (charcoal mellowed whiskies) as competitors attempted to capitalize on Jack Daniel's success.

One of the classic advertising campaigns for beer was developed by Claude Hopkins, a genius at writing copy. It was based on a process that was only marginally related to the product. While touring the Schlitz brewery, Hopkins was unimpressed by the Brewing process itself, but when he saw the empty bottles being sterilized by live steam he came alive. His campaign theme, "Our Bottles Are Washed with Live Steam," was a blockbuster. Of course, for a process or an ingredient to have advertising impact, it must be relevant to a consumer benefit. When Hopkins wrote his "live steam" campaign, consumers were deeply concerned about just how sanitary all of those returnable bottles were. Sanitation was a relevant benefit. Today, the same campaign would probably have all of the impact of a stifled yawn.

How Does It Compare With Competition? Advertising does not take place in a vacuum, but in a competitive environment. Few branded products are identical. Similar, yes. Identical, no. This is what is meant by monopolistic competition. The admaker should know the strengths and weaknesses of the product upon which she is working, and those of competition. One cold tablet may have a more effective analgesic for easing aches and pains; another, a more effective antirhenetic for reducing fever; still another, a more effective antihistamine for relieving nasal congestion. One may work more quickly than another, or work longer, as in the case of Contac. One detergent may be more effective for getting out stains, while another is safer for delicate fabrics. One brand of paper towels may be more absorbent, while another is stronger.

Are there differences in the appearance of the ad-maker's product, or in the way in which it is used? Can these differences or methods of use be made relevant in terms of a consumer benefit? A careful comparison of the physical and performance characteristics of highly similar brands often reveals a minute difference that can be magnified. However, these differences must be such that their emphasis is relevant to consumers and to the consumer benefit the brand offers.

Some brands may be so similar to competition that differences are virtually nonexistent. In this instance, the job of the admaker becomes infinitely more complex. In some cases, the admaker may not find a difference in the brand itself, but in consumers' perceptions of the brand. Bayer aspirin is perceived by millions of consumers as being more reliable and efficacious than other brands of aspirin, although from the standpoint of analgesic qualities, aspirin is aspirin. Yet, Bayer aspirin continues to dominate the aspirin market because of its "quality" story. If there are no differences between brands *and consumers perceive different brands as the same*, the admaker is dealing with a commodity; and, writing advertising for a commodity is a thankless task. Perhaps through a dramatic technique or through sheer advertising weight, one commodity may be made better known than another. But this is seldom a profitable undertaking. It is at this point that advertising has reached the limits of its persuasion, and other marketing activities (pricing, reciprocity, trade deals, and so forth) become the most effective mode for generating sales. But it is also at this point that the admaker must have the courage to say, "This brand has nothing to sell." Then attention can be turned to the really pressing question: "How can this brand be changed in such a way that it becomes advertisable?" Few brands are completely hopeless. Only people are hopeless, and the most hopeless are those without the imagination and the will to improve a brand that has sunk into the quagmire of commodities.

How Can It Be Identified? Most product advertising is concerned with the stimulation of *selective* demand (demand for a particular brand) rather than *primary* demand (demand for a product type). In some instances, when a particular brand dominates a market, greater attention will be given to the stimulation of primary demand under the assumption that if the entire market grows the dominant brand will be the principal beneficiary. However, even in this case selective demand is seldom totally neglected. Sometimes, trade associations such as the Dairy Institute or an association of citrus growers will assess its members for funds to develop an industry-wide promotion to increase the use of dairy products or orange juice. But most product advertising is concerned with the selective demand for individually branded items.

Because of this, one of the jobs of the admaker is to determine how the brand can best be identified at the point of sale. Usually, this is done through a prominant display of the package or trademark in the advertisement. Sometimes, it is done through a unique color. For example, the John Deere tractor is a particular shade of green with the John Deere name emblazoned on a yellow swatch. In any case, the copy writer must ask: "What is there about this brand that will make it easy to identify?" The Betty Crocker "spoon," the Duncan Hines "old English" sign, or the Quaker Oaks "Quaker" are identifying symbols that work both on the package and in advertising.

What Does It Cost? Price often serves two functions (chapter 10). On the one hand, it is a basis for market segmentation; on the other, it is used symbolically to position a product vis-a-vis competition within a particular market segment. The role of price in *display* advertising depends largely on the importance of price as a relevant strategic consideration. When price is a critical factor in product positioning, some reference to price should appear in the advertising. The Chrysler Le Baron, for example (figure 12–2), featured price in its introductory advertising even though one could hardly describe the Le Baron as an economy car.

However, for most competitively priced packaged goods, price is ignored in advertising because it isn't a relevant consideration. Nonetheless, the admaker should be familiar with the price of the product she is writing about, as well as that of competition. Sometimes, this knowledge will serve as a basis for an "economy " or "snob" appeal.

Usually, it isn't possible to quote a specific price in display advertising. This is true because prices will vary somewhat by geographic region because of freight rates or between retailers within a particular region. This difficulty can often be overcome by using a "list" price as is done in the Le Baron ad, or by indicating a "suggested" retail price, or by the general acknowledgement that the brand is "less than" or "more than" competitive products, or by using a price range.

In *sales promotion* advertising, particularly for a retail store, a knowledge of price is critical since much of this advertising depends on bargains for its appeal. Obviously, the admaker must be familiar with the regular price of an item being promoted in order to communicate the magnitude of the savings.

Figure 12-2. (Chrysler Corporation)

INTRODUCING CHRYSLER LEBARON.

A PERSONAL CAR. A ROAD CAR. A NEW SIZE CHRYSLER.
$5,667. AS SHOWN.

Never before has one automobile combined such desirable features with such an attractive price. This unique combination makes Chrysler LeBaron the beginning of a totally new class of automobiles.

The two-door LeBaron shown above has the performance of a road car, powered by Chrysler's computer-controlled Lean Burn Engine. LeBaron is a lighter, leaner Chrysler. A personal car. The two-door LeBaron has such personal features as overhead lighting, individually directed for driver and passenger. A complete list of options, including genuine leather seating, rivals that of any luxury car.

The standard LeBaron features listed below will show you how much car it really is.

The total will show you how little it's priced. The Chrysler LeBaron two-door and four-door are now offered for sale or lease at your Chrysler dealer.

Two-Door LeBaron Medallion
Base Sticker Price	$5,436
318 cu. in. V-8	Std.
Power Steering	Std.
Power Front Disc Brakes	Std.
Automatic Transmission	Std.
Landau Vinyl Roof	$132
Wire Wheel Covers	$35
Whitewall Tires	$43
Bumper Guards, Front	$21
TOTAL	$5,667*

*Sticker price, including options as shown. Taxes and destination charges extra.

CHRYSLER

A PRODUCT OF
CHRYSLER
CORPORATION

Optional leather seat $208 extra. LeBaron Medallion only.

CHRYSLER LEBARON. THE BEGINNING OF
A TOTALLY NEW CLASS OF AUTOMOBILES.

The Consumer

A second group of facts needed by the admaker concerns the consumer. There is almost an endless array of questions that can be asked about consumers; five key question areas are recognized in the following material.

Who Uses It?   Here, the admaker must identify the target market. Is the product used by men? Women? Children? Families? Who are the primary users? Both men and women use diet foods, for example, but women account for 80 percent of the market. Special K is an adult cereal. Life cereal is for young adults, and Coco Puffs is for children. Peanut butter is a child product; toothpaste is for the entire family; and shaving cream is used by men. Beer is drunk by both males and females, but no brewery has ever succeeded by advertising beer primarily to women. Why? Men are the heavy beer drinkers, and the male ego apparently shrinks at the thought of drinking a "woman's" beer. Not too long ago, cigarettes were advertised primarily to men; today, there is a significant market for cigarettes among women.

Age groups are also important. Most beer is consumed by young adults. Scotch, by older people. Teenagers are heavy buyers of records; it is estimated that they account for 90 percent of the single record sales, and 50 percent of the albums—except for classical music. Most products have a target age range, and the family life cycle (referred to in chapter 5) is often used as a guide to the patterns of object accumulation that exist. Thus, the newly formed family is a primary market for refrigerators, ranges, and for inexpensive, durable furniture. The families with young children are heavy buyers of washing machines, dryers, baby furniture, baby foods, and so forth. The older family—with the children grown—is an excellent market for tasteful furniture, travel, recreation, self-education, and hobbies.

Other socio-economic considerations are also important. Income is a major factor for many products, and social class is often a segmentation variable. The point is that the admaker needs to know precisely whom the product is intended for so that the appropriate appeals and "signs" may be used in advertising communications.

Who Influences Brand Choice?   The user of a product or brand may not be the one who makes the purchase or specifies the brand. About 80 percent of all United States' dwelling units are occupied by families. Individual family members purchase products for their personal use as well as for other family members. Sometimes the pattern of brand influence is simple. In other cases, it is quite complex. The question, "Who uses the product?" generally has to be supplemented by two other questions: (1) Who specifies the brand? and (2) who actually makes the purchase? These questions are necessary because brand influence can occur at any stage of the decision process.

Both men and women use shampoo. Yet in most families, the housewife selects the brand. Many children's products must be approved by parents, usually the mother. As a consequence, many children's products require a dual appeal—a direct appeal to children and a secondary appeal to the mother to enable her to rationalize the purchase. Often, this dual requirement demands two different advertising campaigns.

Table 12–1 shows the results of a buying influence study for a selected group of products. This study, jointly supported by five magazines, was made available to client organizations and advertising agencies. That this particular study does not deal with child influence is one of its shortcomings. It does indicate, however, that both husbands and wives exert an influence on both the types of products used and on the particular brands purchased. It also shows that there are wide variations in the extent of husband-wife influence.

How Is the Product Used?   This question really involves two questions: how? and where? Some products are used in social situations; some, in private. Some products are highly visible (cars, clothing, cosmetics, home furnishings, and so forth) some are seldom seen by others (deodorants, shaving cream, shampoo, underclothing, etc.). The advertisement by Soflens (figure 12–3) is an interesting approach because it shows a close-up of an invisible product—a product that is worn in public, but is not meant to be seen.

Highly visible products are used by consumers not only for their instrumental functions but also for their expressive functions. That is, they are used to make a public statement about the user. Whether we are talking about the blue jeans of a college student, or the Lincoln Continental of a surgeon, each is making a public statement about himself or herself. The admaker needs to understand the importance of that public statement in order to surround the brand with the proper symbols.

If a product is a highly social one, like beer, it is usually desirable to show it in a social setting. If the product is an intimate one, it should convey intimacy. An outdoor product belongs outdoors; an indoor pro-

Table 12-1. Who Makes the Buying Decisions?
Relative purchase influence: Husbands and wives (% influence)

	Purchased by:		Direct Influence Product		Brand		Indirect Influence Product		Brand	
	W	H	W	H	W	H	W	H	W	H
Cereals:										
Cold (Unsweetened)	84	16	74	26	71	29	65	35	67	33
Hot	84	16	67	33	67	33	63	37	59	41
Packaged lunch meat	73	27	60	40	64	36	56	44	57	43
Peanut butter	81	19	70	30	74	26	65	35	68	32
Scotch whisky	35	65	18	82	18	82	22	78	23	77
Bar soap	85	15	65	35	64	36	60	40	61	39
Headache remedies	67	33	67	33	67	33	64	36	65	35
Cat food (dry)	66	34	75	25	81	19	80	20	80	20
Dog food (dry)	76	24	60	40	59	41	60	40	61	39
Fast-food chain hamburgers	68	32	55	45	55	45	53	47	52	48
Catsup	75	25	68	32	68	32	60	40	62	38
Coffee:										
Freeze-dried	68	32	57	43	62	38	56	44	59	41
Regular ground	74	26	65	35	65	35	58	42	60	40
Mouthwash	72	28	56	44	56	44	52	48	53	47

Share of influence

	Purchase Decision Influence Product		Brand		Initiation Product		Brand		Product		Brand	
	W	H	W	H	W	H	W	H	W	H	W	H
Vacuum cleaner	60	40	60	40	80	20	69	31	66	34	65	35
Electric blender	59	41	53	47	67	33	50	50	53	47	52	48
Broadloom carpet	60	40	59	41	82	18	74	26	72	28	69	31
Automobiles	38	62	33	67	22	78	21	79	18	82	18	82

Source of Data: "Purchase Influence Measures of Husband/Wife Influence on Buying Decisions." Haley, Overholser & Associates Inc., New Canaan, Conn., January, 1975. Percentages reflect relative purchase activity, direct and indirect influence of husbands and wives in the sample. For durables and services, percentages reflect relative activity in purchase decision, initiation of idea to purchase, and the gathering of information.
Source: "Buying Study Called Good Support Data," p. 52. Reprinted with permission from the March 17, 1975 issue of *Advertising Age.* © 1975 by Crain Communications, Inc.

duct belongs in the house; and most food products belong on the table or in the kitchen. Effective advertising seldom blazes new trails in the realm of social mores. It bows to the prevailing values and conventions of society. For attention value, products are sometimes shown in bizarre settings. Sometimes it works. But, when it does, the bizarre setting usually has some relevance to dominant product attributes.

How Is the Product Purchased? Different products are purchased in different ways. Frequently purchased packaged goods are generally bought without too much thought or conflict. Carpeting and expensive furniture, on the other hand, involve considerable information gathering, shopping, comparison, and uncertainty. Advertising should be adapted to the role it occupies in the consumer decision process. Perhaps advertising for expensive furniture should display its elegance in a handsome setting, surrounding it with symbols of quality and discriminating taste. The facts of construction, durability, fabric, and price may be better left to retail sales personnel or point-of-purchase

brochures. For Hamburger Helper, on the other hand, a simplified "how to prepare it" approach may be more meaningful. If the admaker doesn't know how a product is purchased, it is unlikely that the advertising will be used in the most effective way.

Why Is the Product Purchased? There is a great deal of disagreement about this question, and there is probably no universal answer. Some successful advertising practitioners, such as Rosser Reeves, prefer direct, straightforward, conscious reasons, firmly embedded in tangible product characteristics. Others, like David Ogilvy, insist that " . . . it is almost always the total *personality* of a brand rather than *trivial product differences* which decide its ultimate position in the market." [9] Norman B. Norman goes even further by saying that conscious suggestions are usually a waste of the advertiser's time and money; what is meaningful is the unconsious suggestion. This latter

---

9. Martin Mayer, *Madision Avenue, U.S.A.* (New York: Harper Brothers, Publishers, 1958), p. 58.

Figure 12-3. (Bauch & Lomb, Inc.)

point of view is purely psychoanalytic and suggests that sex, aggression, power, fantasy, security, etc. underly all consumer behavior.

Each of these practitioners probably has a vision of the truth, but none of them see it in its entirety. Consumer motivation is complex and poorly understood. Some of the reasons for buying a particular product or brand are undoubtedly conscious; others are merely conscious rationalizations of obscure motivational dynamics. J. Sterling Getchell, a much admired copywriter of the past, said: "People buy for emotional reasons, and then justify their purchases with rational reasons why." The purchase of a Lincoln Continental may be clearly understood by the buyer as an expres-

sion of prestige and power. On the other hand, it may be a compensation for unconscious feelings of personal inadequacy. A motorcycle may be bought for its convenience and economy; or it may be an expression of an unconscious wish for self-destruction—the Freudian death instinct. The conscious rationalizations of those who hang-glide might be interesting.

Since there may be many motivational bases for the purchase of a particular product, the admaker should know as much about them as possible. Whether the admaker ultimately chooses the route of conscious motivativation, unconscious motivation, or a combination of the two is a matter of choice. But, in order to make a choice, one must be aware of alternatives.

The Marketing Situation

A final group of facts that are relevant to the admaker concerns the marketing situation. By *marketing situation*, I mean such things as: (1) What is the brand's marketing position? (2) How is it distributed? and (3) What is the advertising history of the brand and its competitors?

What Is the Brand's Marketing Position?   Whether a brand is the leader in its market, a major contender, or a poor performer may, in itself, be a source of advertising inspiration. The self-confidence of Budweiser's dominant position in the beer market is reflected in the jingle that accompanies the use in television advertising of a beer wagon drawn by the company's Clydesdales. The opening words of the jingle are: "Here comes the King! Here comes the King! Here comes the big number one." It is a deliberate use of a market leadership that is summed up in the slogan, "Budweiser, the king of beer."

Only one brand can occupy the dominant position in a market. Avis, in 1962, lagged far behind Hertz in the car rental field. The company was also losing money, and had been for a number of years. A new president of Avis was given the task of turning the company around and, as an effort in this direction, he hired Doyle Dane Bernbach to develop an advertising approach. The advertisement shown in figure 12–4 is the beginning of the "We try harder" campaign that took its cue from Avis' market position and the new management's dedication to upgrading the entire operation.

The new management and its advertising were successful. In 1962 Avis' revenues were $34 million, with a loss of $3,200,000. In 1964, revenues were $44 million, with a profit of $3 million. Anyone who didn't have a "We try harder" button wasn't really in style.

How Is It Distributed?   Contac, used as an example at the beginning of the chapter, is an example of a brand in which method of distribution played an inte-

When you're only No. 2, you try harder. Or else.

Avis can't afford to relax.

Little fish have to keep moving all of the time. The big ones never stop picking on them.

Avis knows all about the problems of little fish.

We're only No. 2 in rent a cars. We'd be swallowed up if we didn't try harder.

There's no rest for us.

We're always emptying ashtrays. Making sure gas tanks are full before we rent our cars. Seeing that the batteries are full of life. Checking our windshield wipers.

And the cars we rent out can't be anything less than spanking new Plymouths.

And since we're not the big fish, you won't feel like a sardine when you come to our counter.

We're not jammed with customers.

© AVIS RENT A CAR SYSTEM, INC.

Figure 12–4.   (© 1964, Avis, Inc.)

gral role in its advertising. In this instance, reference to getting Contac at your pharmacy was used to give an ethical connotation to the brand, to enlist the support of pharmacists, and to direct consumers to the place of purchase. For many products with selective distribution, telling consumers where the brand can be found is an important function of copy. While everyone may know that Plymouths are sold by Plymouth dealers, many people may not know that Opels are sold by Buick dealers, Fiestas by Ford dealers, Johnny Miller menswear at Sears, or that Elancyl (a shampoo massage) is available at Saks Fifth Avenue. Some advertisers with limited distribution, such as De Weese Designs (swim and sun fashions) or Pantene (a specialty shampoo), list a toll-free number in their advertising so that consumers may call to find the location of the nearest outlet. Since cosmetics, as well as many other products, can be purchased in drug stores or department stores or variety stores or supermarkets or some combination of these outlets, the least the admaker can do is to direct consumers to the appropriate places of purchase.

What Is the Advertising History of the Brand and Its Competitors? The admaker should be thoroughly steeped in the advertising approaches that have been used in the past by the brand and its competitors. She should also be aware of the strengths and weaknesses of these approaches, as measured by research or sales results. There is little virtue in creating an advertising appeal that has been preempted by competitive brands through prior use, or in repeating a campaign that has not distinguished itself in the past.

On the other hand, there is little profit in replacing an advertising campaign that is still highly effective, simply for the sake of doing something new and different. Advertising campaigns do wear out through use, but not as quickly as most advertisers think they do. It is not unusual for an admaker or an advertiser, because of constant contact with a campaign idea from its inception, to become bored with it by the time it makes its first appearance in consumer media.

Frequently, however, a product that starts out with a unique consumer benefit finds itself inundated by competition with similar products and look-alike advertising. Initially, the brand may benefit from the competitive advertising, particularly if it has advertised heavily enough to have preempted the product benefit in the eyes of consumers. Eventually, though, its primary association with the benefit may be eroded through the activity of competition. At this point, either the product concept needs to be modified (often the best solution), or a fresh and distinctive advertising campaign should be developed. In any event, the

admaker should keep an active file of past and current advertising so that she will be constantly aware of competitive activity and of changes that are occuring in the field.

The search for facts is an important part of the admaker's job, but it is not an end in itself. It is only the starting point. No fact is important until it has been made important by translating it into a consumer benefit that will attract attention and persuade consumers to try the product. This point is well demonstrated by the following anecdote related by Charles E. Scripps, when he was board chairman of the Scripps-Howard newspaper chain:

"Gentlemen," said the sales manager, "I want to show you the very latest thing out of our laboratories." At this point he paused and took from his pocket a small twist drill, the kind everyone uses to drill holes in wood or metal. "I want you to know all about this," the sales manager continued enthusiastically. "This is a 5/8" drill. It's exactly 6 3/4" long. It's made of a new secret alloy that will outlast anything on the market." He went on and on, describing how their research department had determined just the right degree of twist, the angle at the point, the strength and hardness. Then he said, "Gentlemen, there are 3.5 million 5/8" drills sold in the U.S. every year. Every garage mechanic, carpenter, machinist, plumber, electrician, home mechanic—everyone who works with tools—has to have one. But, gentlemen, let's just keep one thing in mind: *Not a single one of those people want a drill. What they want is holes.*" [10]

This, then, is the job of the creative admaker. To translate drills into holes. To persuade consumers that one particular drill will make holes better than competitive brands. It is not an easy task. The facts that are relevant to this translation are not always apparent.

THE CREATIVE PROCESS

The development of advertising is a creative process. But it is a process that takes place within the constraints of the problem to be solved and usually under the pressure of time. Unfortunately, not all creative ideas solve the problem at hand, and good ideas cannot be programmed to arrive precisely when they are needed. As a consequence, effective creativity demands discipline—a discipline that some consider foreign to the creative act itself. It also requires a systematic procedure, although many sophisticated

10. Charles E. Scripps, "Money, Media and Minutes," An address before the Advertiser's Club of Cincinnati, January 7, 1959.

Plate 11-3.

This Homecare Sweepstakes
ad is an excellent example
of a sales promotional ad
(Riegel Textile Corp.).

"I wouldn't use anything but Pampers. I've been through this before."

"My first baby taught me all about
how great Pampers are.
"The reason I love them is simple.
They help keep my baby dry after he
wets.
"Pampers have this Stay-Dry lining.
After he wets, the lining helps keep
the moisture in the wet padding away
from his tender skin.
"There's nothing like
experience to show you
what really works."

Ask any mother about Pampers dryness.

©1976. The Procter & Gamble Company

Plate 12-1.

This Pampers ad clearly translates the
product concept into a consumer benefit
(Procter & Gamble).

Six reasons why even the cleanest homes need Lysol® Spray.

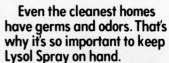

Even the cleanest homes have germs and odors. That's why it's so important to keep Lysol Spray on hand.

Lysol Spray kills household germs, including germs that cause odors. Make Lysol Spray the important final step in cleaning—every day.

1. Get rid of smoke and stale odors trapped in fabrics.
2. Clean the air of cooking and other odors.
3. Kill the germs that cause odors in garbage cans.
4. Eliminate pet odors.
5. Kill athlete's foot fungus on shower floors.
6. Kill mold and mildew and their odors on the shower curtain.

Lysol® Spray kills household germs, including germs that cause odors.

Plate 12-2.   This Lysol ad features the product, shows how easy it is to use, and deals with a common household problem (Lehn & Fink Products Co.).

advertising people resent step-by-step procedures. Many good admakers have developed a systematic procedure of their own that is so thoroughly integrated into their normal work habits that they don't think of it as systematic, even though it is.

Traditionally, the creative process has been divided into the three steps beautifully described by Charles Adams:

> First, there should be a period of *ingestion*. Drink in all the facts and information you can about the subject. Acquaint yourself with the purposes and objectives of the campaign. Familiarize yourself with competitive efforts. Look at the history and the track records of previous efforts for this advertiser. Familiarize yourself with the product. Make yourself as informed as possible. Generally immerse yourself in the advertising challenge.

> The second stage I call *incubation*. This is the period during which you put the problem aside. Or, metaphorically, you let it simmer on the back burner. You don't ask for a solution or even for an intelligent analysis. You let it stew, or as has been said, you "just walk around it" for a while. But you will be surprised and delighted to find it coming to the surface every now and again, almost involuntarily. And when it does surface, it will probably be showing some new side or sparkling in some new way in the light of your current thoughts and experiences.

> The final stage might be termed *inspiration*. Here you try in earnest to come up with a solution. You force yourself into action, lay the problem out in the open, search avidly and determinedly for the answer. And, usually, if you give it enough time and effort, it comes—that moment of insight, that triumph over ignorance that makes the total effort worthwhile. It may be something as simple as a phrase—something as complicated as a new photographic process. But whatever it is, you will know it when you find it. And then you will shelter it, nourish it, elaborate on it, change it, and polish it until it reaches that point where it is presentable, salable, and workable.

> This, in endless variation, is the creative process. It is essentially a lonely task, a private agony. And it is best not hurried.[11]

Walter Joyce, while not rejecting the three stages of the creative process summarized by Adams, is more specific in suggesting ways to put the creative process to work. Joyce identifies eleven steps that are helpful in stimulating ideas and gaining new insights into the problem. These eleven steps are identified below.[12]

1. *Define the problem.* Since creativity in advertis-

ing is a problem-solving activity, the first step is to identify the problem. Sometimes, this is the most difficult part of the job, and, obviously, it is the most critical. If the problem is improperly defined, there is little chance that an acceptable solution will be found. Is the problem one of identifying the primary consumer benefit of the product or service? Or, is it one of dramatizing this benefit? Is the problem one of gaining name registration? Or, is it one of demonstrating a unique brand feature? Is the problem one of developing a rationale to support the central claim? Or, is it one of overcoming consumer apathy? What is the problem?

2. *Consciously question every accepted assumption of the problem.* Most of us enter a new situation with a mass of preconceptions. Our heads are filled with beliefs, some of which are true, some of which are partially true, and some of which are patently false. The admaker is also exposed to members of the client organization and other people who have had experience with the product. They, too, have questionable preconceptions that they are willing to share as the literal truth. Because of this, the admaker needs to adopt an honest skepticism, a willingness to question her own beliefs, as well as those of others.

3. *Get involved with the problem.* Creating good advertising is an engrossing proposition. The admaker can't be a dilettante. She must make each assignment the most important thing there is to be done. Sometimes it may be difficult to get totally involved with a cake mix, or a jar of peanut butter, or a box of soap. Surely, there are more important issues in the world. Of course there are. But not from the standpoint of creating advertising. The talent or skill (whichever it is) of total involvement is a necessary ingredient in the creative process.

4. *Begin to ask questions.* Asking questions at this point is the road to new insights. Question! Question! Question! It's the way we learn. Some of the answers we get may be trivial, but many will not be. It is through questions that new information is developed and new perspectives gained. Sometimes, the right question opens up a totally new line of inquiry. For example, when Ralston Purina was trying to find a way to get a profitable share of the growing dry dog food market, the planning group kept wrestling with the question, "How can we gain a major share of the dry dog food market?" And, they were geting nowhere.

11. Adams, *Common Sense*, pp. 142–44.
12. Walter Joyce, "Care and Feeding of the Idea," in *Advertising*, an omnibus of advertising prepared by Printers' Ink, p. 113.

One day, in a particularly unproductive meeting, a member of the planning group said: "I think I know what the problem is. We've been asking the wrong question. Instead of asking, 'How can we get a major share of the market,' we should be asking, 'What does the consumer want in a dry dog food?'" This broke the logjam.

5. *Consciously begin to adopt new assumptions, or try to renovate old ones.* This is a major step in breaking out of our preconceptions. Here, we deliberately try out new beliefs and new ways of thinking. In short, we start playing the game of "What if . . . ?" Then, we begin to question our new assumptions.

6. *Consciously let the inductive process start to work.* In this step, we start to look for new relationships that have not been articulated before. Let imagination flow freely; speculate; go beyond the facts.

7. *Begin to form a judgment.* Ultimately, a creative idea is a judgment. It is a personal conclusion about what is important, drawn from one's own experience and exploration. Sometimes it is called, a *hunch;* sometimes an *intuition.* Whatever it is called, it is something unique that the individual brings to the situation.

8. *Try to make a prediction.* At this point, Joyce says, " . . . try to see if there is a new unity in the world that surrounds your problem." Perhaps another way of expressing this thought is to ask, "Do I still see the problem the same way as when I started, or do I see it in a new light?" Then ask, "Do my ideas make sense? Do they have a natural coherence, a logic of their own? Are they too complex or involved?" Good ideas do have a logic and coherence of their own, and the test of their usefulness is often their simplicity.

9. *Now take action.* Once an idea that makes sense starts to take shape, try it out. It may have to be tried a dozen ways before it comes out right. But, ultimately, it has to be committed to paper. If it has any value, it will survive this test. However, this is often a traumatic experience for admakers because it means they have to venture outside their private world and expose their fledgling ideas to the harsh realities of criticism. Unfortunately, while few people can create a good ad, critics are legion. When it come to criticism,

everyone is an expert. And this leads to Joyce's tenth point.

10. *Develop the drive, the competence, to demonstrate the validity of the new theory.* In other words, develop the guts to survive criticism; to fight for an idea you believe is right; and not to be demoralized because others carp or disagree. And, finally,

11. *Be ready, however, to question the new hypothesis—and to start all over again if it doesn't solve the problem.* There is a difference between defending an idea and being blind to its faults. Criticism is often justified; it points up flaws and shortcomings. Sometimes these weaknesses are not serious, and honest criticism gives rise to modifications that strengthen the concept. Sometimes, however, the flaws are fatal. At this point, the difference between the amateur and the professional comes to light. The amateur self-righteously continues to defend a lost cause; the professional literally goes back to the drawing board.

No one can tell anyone else how to be creative. Creativity is highly idiosyncratic. The foregoing guidelines only represent an approach to problems that recognizes that creativity requires data to work with, fluidity of thought processes, and an ability to change perspectives. Gathering data, asking questions, deliberately taking another point of view, and engaging in imaginative speculation are only techniques that are helpful. Most people who make their livings by exploring new ideas bring an innate curiosity to the process. They are curious about everything. Having an assignment and a deadline only gives the admaker an opportunity to be curious in a defined area.

PITFALLS OF ADVERTISING CREATIVITY

Although advertising thrives on new ideas, it is often inhospitable to them. New ideas are not really popular in business, and there are good reasons for this to be so. Most businesspeople are fairly conservative. A business enterprise requires major investments in plant and equipment, people, organization, and training. It functions best in a somewhat stable environment where forecasts can be made with reasonable confidence, where plans can be laid and carried out with a minimum of revisions, and where risk is reduced to an acceptable level. A stable world is one in which decisions can be programmed, in which rules and formulas can be devised and followed, and where sensible caution will avoid catastrophe.

New ideas always involve risk, and there is constant temptation to avoid the new for the sake of the safe. Edward Weiss, chairman of Edward H. Weiss & Company, has summed up this thought with the observation that: "The greatest danger in modern technology isn't that machines will begin to think like men, but that men will begin to think like machines."[13] This, then, is the first pitfall for the admaker, that under the influence of caution, she will fall victim to formula-advertising that is defensible because it has worked in the past.

The second pitfall is that of substituting techniques for ideas. Such substitutions may take the form of a dramatic photographic treatment, a bizarre illustration, humour, sex, exaggerated claims, news, rhetoric, or a dozen other attention-getting devices. There is nothing wrong with any of these devices, *provided they are subordinated to, and enhance the consumer benefit.* When they take precedence over the consumer benefit or ignore it, mediocrity is the inevitable consequence.

A third pitfall is tastelessness—the use of vulgarity for its shock value in order to gain attention. Granted, values change, and the age of Victoria has been supplanted by a certain degree of enlightenment and sophistication, but the world is still full of those who are uncomfortable with many of these value changes. And, for mass consumer goods, these people are your customers.

Fourth, never fall into the trap of assuming that consumers are witless pawns, to be manipulated and beguiled. Consumers may have many faults, and they often act unwisely, but they are not stupid.

Finally, beware of losing touch with the consumer for whom you are writing. It's easy to do. Advertising people talk to advertising people, and the advertising business tends to develop its own idiom. But, outside the advertising business, there are millions of people who have problems and concerns and who don't talk the way advertising people do. They are called *customers.*

SUMMARY

The chapter is introduced by three examples of advertisements, each of which does its job in a different way. Effective advertising comes in different forms— different headlines, illustrations, body copy, and formats. These differences trace to differences in strategy and style.

Strategy provides basic guidelines for the execution of copy and generally contains four elements: (1) a statement of the principal benefit offered by the product, (2) a statement of product attributes or characteristics of the product that provide a basis for the principal benefit, (3) a statement of the character or personality of the product, which is manifested in the advertisement as a mood or tone, and (4) a statement of what the product is and what it is used for.

Style refers to the unique way in which individual writers express themselves; most successful advertising writers have a characteristic style through which they can express ideas easily and naturally.

Coordinating writing, illustrations, and production in the development of advertising is important. Unless this coordination is consciously undertaken at the outset, the possibility of developing an effective advertisement is appreciably diminished.

The development of advertising is a never-ending search for ideas and for new and different ways of expressing these ideas. Fundamental to this search are: (1) the search for facts upon which to base ideas, and (2) the creative process itself.

The first step in developing advertising is to search out the facts—all of the facts that one can find. Major areas in which facts are needed include: (1) the product itself, (2) the consumer, and (3) the marketing situation.

The creative process itself is divided into three stages. First, *ingestion*, in which the admaker absorbs facts and information about her subject. The second is *incubation*, a period during which the information that has been gathered is unconsciously assimilated. The third stage is *inspiration*. In this stage, the admaker consciously tries to arrive at a creative solution to the problem at hand. The chapter also outlines eleven steps that are often helpful in stimulating ideas and facilitating the creative process.

There are five common creative pitfalls. One is the temptation to avoid risks and "play it safe." A second is to substitute techniques for ideas. A third is to succumb to the temptation to use devices that are in poor taste in order to gain attention. A fourth is to assume that consumers are naïve and gullible. And the fifth is the danger of losing touch with consumers. These temptations are ever present, and they are all destructive to the creation of effective advertising.

13. *Ibid.*, p. 105.

QUESTIONS

1. What are the four elements that should be included in the statement of copy strategy?
2. Analyze the Contac advertisement at the beginning of the chapter in terms of these four strategy elements.
3. Distinguish between strategy and style. What is the key to an effective style?
4. What determines whether a fact is important or trivial in developing advertising?
5. Demonstrate by an example other than those offered in the text why the question, "What is the product?" is not an obvious question.
6. Discuss the role of ingredients and manufacturing processes in developing advertising.
7. What is meant by the statement: "Writing advertising for a commodity is a thankless task"? Demonstrate with an example how this problem might be overcome.
8. Identify and describe the three stages in the creative process.
9. Identify the five major pitfalls that the admaker needs to avoid.

PROBLEM

Select a magazine advertisement for a consumer product with which you are familiar. Make sure that the ad contains body copy which talks about the product and its benefits.

Analyze the advertisement in terms of the four basic elements of copy strategy that are discussed in the chapter, and write a copy strategy for the advertisement.

Now, on the basis of the information contained in the advertisement, write a *different* copy strategy for the product. In what ways do you think *your* strategy is stronger or weaker than the one that has been used?

13

Print Advertising

Figures 13–1, 13–2, and 13–3 are print advertisements. Each communicates an idea clearly and forcefully. Yet, they are dramatically different.

Volkswagen

The Volkswagen advertisement is nothing but a headline with white space where one would normally expect to find an illustration or body copy. Yet, the white space tells the headline story more clearly than any illustration or any amount of body copy could. The advertisement takes a single feature of the product—the fact that the engine is air cooled—and turns it into a consumer benefit that supports the basic idea behind the Volkswagen; namely, the concept of a car that is economical, dependable, and trouble free. This advertisement is effective *because* the basic concept of the Volkswagen had already been established through previous advertising. Standing alone, without this background, much of the impact of the advertisement would have been lost.

Vanity Fair

In contrast to the Volkswagen example, the Vanity Fair advertisement depends wholly on the illustration. It has no intelligible headline, and the small amount of body copy used is telegraphic jargon. The ostensible purpose of the advertisement is to display the style, quality, and sophistication of the product through a direct visual experience. The original ad ran in color which, combined with "high style" photography, communicated the essence of the product.

Zareh

The third advertisement has neither headline nor illustration. It is all body copy, tightly set. In form, it is a newspaper column. Yet, the success of this advertisement is vindicated by the following quotation from a *Fortune Magazine* profile on Zareh Garabed Thomajan, the proprietor of Zareh. Thomajan referred to himself as "The Thief of State Street."

Zareh's column is probably the most widely read advertising copy in Boston and environs. At State Street he receives a steady stream of visitors who, if they do not come to buy, come to seek his advice in advertising their own products. A few of his fan letters are "scurrilous" like the one he got recently that began, "Zareh, you cur." Magazines and trade journals have run articles on his copy. The *New Yorker* reprinted one of his ads featuring a "positively insulting" scarlet corduroy loafer coat. Little, Brown & Co., publishers, asked him to write a book, and finally, he has been propelled into after-dinner speaking. He must have been the only haberdasher ever to address a group of 1,000 genuine Boston notables.[1]

1. "Zareh Garabed Thomajan," *Fortune* (November, 1947): 148.

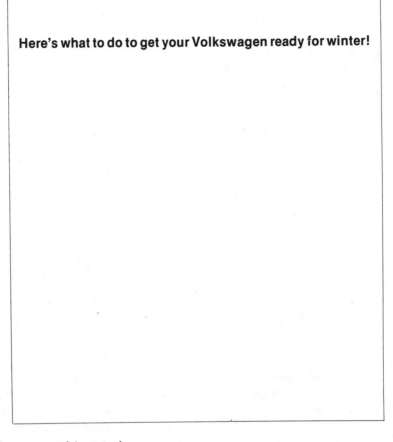

Here's what to do to get your Volkswagen ready for winter!

Figure 13-1. (Volkswagen of America)

Admittedly, these three advertisements represent extreme cases. Few advertisements are all headline, all illustration, or all body copy. That, however, is precisely the reason for citing them. Taken together, they emphasize the point that advertising need not be forced into a mold, or written by formula, in order to be effective. The ultimate test of a good advertisement is whether it communicates the idea it is intended to communicate in such a way that it reaches and influences its target audience. There are many literary and visual devices that can be used to convey an idea. The job of the admaker is to discover and use those devices that convey the particular idea that he or she is seeking to communicate.

EXECUTING THE IDEA BEHIND THE ADVERTISEMENT

All advertising starts with an idea, and finding the right idea is often a frustrating task. However, James Webb Young, in a treatise titled, *A Technique for Producing Ideas,* suggests that the execution of an idea, the final step in the creative process, may be the most difficult one. Specifically, he says:

In this stage you have to take your little newborn idea out into the world of reality. And when you do, you usually find that it is not quite the marvelous child it seemed when you first gave birth to it.

It requires a deal of patient working over to make most ideas fit the exact conditions, or the practical exigencies, under which they must work. And here is where many good ideas are lost. The idea man, like the inventor, is often not patient enough or practical enough to go through with this adapting part of the process. But, it has to be done if you are to put ideas to work in a work-a-day world.[2]

In addition to starting with an idea, a good advertisement is a *gestalt*. That is, it gives a single, unified impression. This demand for a single unified impression places two restrictions on the creation of ads. First, it is unwise to try to put too many things into an advertisement. Too many ideas start to get in the way of each other so that none of them comes through clearly. A central idea, adequately buttressed with

2. James Webb Young, *A Technique for Producing Ideas,* 4th printing (Chicago: Crain Communications, Inc., 1970).

Figure 13-2. (Vanity Fair Corp.)

NEAL BARR

Our Luxurious Gleam-Liners. Spring's most romantic departure, pairing a soft satin shine with the new shimmer-shade: Seaspray. Softcup bra, 32 to 38 B, 32 to 40 C, about $8.50. 32 to 40 D, about $9.50. No Ride-Up pettiskirt, S, M, L, short, average, long, about $5.50. Both in Satin Glisanda® of anti-cling Antron® III nylon. Also in Powder Puff, Honey Beige, Star White, Midnight Black. Vanity Fair Mills, Inc., 640 Fifth Avenue, New York, N.Y.

VANITY FAIR   A company of *vf* corporation

I'll never forget the first time he came into our shop about a year ago. He was a little man in a green elevator operator's uniform, oldish and very shy. We were quite busy that day, but he awaited his turn patiently and then asked to see some "fine sweaters." Now "fine sweaters" in this shop means twenty or thirty dollars, so I showed him some for ten, thinking that by so doing I could save him some embarrassment and still meet his requirements. He said they were "nice," but would I please show him our "best" ones. So I did, some Scotch cashmeres, in the meantime making a mental note never again to judge a man by his jacket. He selected one at $27.50 and then asked if I would "lay it aside" and accept "$2 weekly" until it was paid for. I said I would and he came in every Saturday for a month and lived up to his agreement. On his fourth payment he asked to see some more "fine sweaters," selected one at $25, and then asked if I'd lay this aside, too. He wanted still to pay $2 a week (not $4) and pick up both sweaters when the whole amount, $52.50, had been paid. I consented only after I had tried to dissuade him from spending so much money. I didn't know what his income was, but I suspected $52.50 was most of two weeks' wages. Believe it or not, after about six more payments he propositioned me again. It seems we had *four* English alpaca

sweaters in our State Street window and would I please lay these aside, too! Well, this was obviously ridiculous. While we had nothing to lose (*all* his selections would remain in our hands until *all* were paid for, and this by his request), I felt I had to do something if my unusual client wasn't to go into hock for life. But it wasn't easy. This gentleman was obviously the sensitive type. I told him, and as gently as I could, that our arrangement was a bit top heavy, that there was no need to buy so many sweaters because the foreign markets were opening up again, that even prices might soon come down, and finally, I suggested something that was really none of my business—that he was spending too great a part of his income for things he could do without. He was very courteous. He listened intently to everything I said but could he still have the sweaters? He said he didn't drink or smoke, that $2 a week was no hardship, and that if I was worried he could pay $2.75 or $3 weekly! I got nowhere. I asked him then if he would at least take out a couple of sweaters and enjoy wearing them while he was paying me. He said, "No, thanks," that he expected to pay his total bill by the following August, at which time he'd take them out in time for his two-weeks' vacation in Nova Scotia, his childhood home. Right after he left, Tim came up and informed me that, contrary to my belief, Mr. "C" now had *thirteen* sweaters in the "hold" department instead of the seven I had believed. It seems our little friend had bought half a dozen more in the weeks past while making his Saturday payments to other clerks!

So I called my boys together.

What to do without offending our passionate friend. It was finally agreed I should go to his place of employment, and, as gently as possible, call the deal off and refund his payments or, if that proved too difficult, settle for the first three sweaters that were now paid for in full. Well, partly because I was very busy, but chiefly because I dreaded the job, I did nothing for a few weeks more. Finally, one Saturday afternoon, I asked my bookkeeper to give me Mr. "C's" account. It was—13 sweaters totalling $284, 39 payments totalling $78. Roxy also told me something that wouldn't be significant ordinarily but which was in this instance—no payments had been made these past four weeks. I walked up to the building where our friend worked, and, not seeing him about, asked the starter where I could find him. Possibly you have guessed the rest. Mr. "C" had died suddenly just four weeks before and was there anything he could do? No, there wasn't. I trudged back to the store and told the boys. Everybody felt low. About the only consolation we could find in the whole affair was my failure to deliver the ultimatum we had planned.

I shall be grateful for that failure as long as I live.

P. S.—What happened to the $78? Mr. "C's heirs have been reimbursed in full.

Figure 13-3.   (Zareh Men's Clothing Inc.)

validation, is about all that a single advertisement can handle.

Consider the advertisement for Everynight Astringent Shampoo and Everynight Moisturizing Shampoo by Helene Curtis. (See figure 13-4.) The central idea is embodied in the headline: "'I've never met anyone who doesn't have a problem with her hair,' says tennis star Chris Evert." The rest of the ad is addressed to this point.

The second demand that a single, unified impression places on an advertisement is that all elements of the ad should fit together as the pieces of a jig-saw puzzle do. This often requires an endless process of shifting and modifying elements until they do, indeed, fit together comfortably.

Again, taking the Helene Curtis ad as an example, note that the major illustration uses a close-up of Chris Evert, easily identified as an active sports figure for whom frequent hair washing is a problem. The headline reinforces the identification of Chris Evert. The first paragraph of the body copy is a personalized message from Chris Evert. Two hair problems are prominently identified in the body copy, along with the solution to these problems—Everynight Astringent Shampoo and Everynight Moisturizing Shampoo. Finally, the two shampoos featured in the ad are shown, one on each side of the body copy. This is a complex advertisement because it features two pro-

Figure 13-4.   (Helene Curtis Industries, Inc.)

"I've never met anyone who doesn't have a problem with her hair," says tennis star Chris Evert.

"Everybody I know has a problem with her hair. Even me. I use problem-solving Everynight® Astringent Shampoo for oily hair. Now my hair is no problem. Why don't you use *the problem-solving shampoo* for your hair problem?"

THE PROBLEM:
Oily, greasy hair.

THE SOLVER:
Everynight Astringent Shampoo

Works on oily hair the way astringents work on oily skin. Has lots of oil removers that actually blot up excess oil without drying out your hair. Leaves hair soft and shiny, full of body and highlights. Your hair actually feels cleaner, longer.

THE PROBLEM:
Dry, heat-styled hair.

THE SOLVER:
Everynight Moisturizing Shampoo

Softens and conditions hair that gets dry during styling. Works on dry hair the same way moisturizers soften and condition dry skin. Makes normally dry hair feel soft and full ...don't just shampoo, moisturize too.

HELENE CURTIS

ducts. Yet, it give a unified impression, using the concept of "hair problems" as the unifying theme.

Most advertisements are like this Chris Evert ad in that they have four elements: (1) a headline and, possibly, subheads, (2) an illustration, (3) body copy, and (4) a logo or brand identification. Some advertisements do not use all four of these elements, as was demonstrated by the Volkswagen, Vanity Fair, and Zareh examples. If all four elements are used, they are not always given the same weight or importance. Nonetheless, each of these elements makes a specific contribution to an advertisement, and together they provide a logical sequence or progression of the idea being communicated. The admaker should thoroughly understand the functions of each of these elements because only then is it possible to make a judicious decision as to which element or elements should be emphasized in a particular case or whether one or more of the elements may be eliminated entirely. If one is eliminated, its function must be assumed by the remaining elements of the ad. The primary functions of the four key elements of a print advertisement are discussed in the following material.

The Headline

The headline generally has three functions. First, it is an *attention getting* device that arrests the attention of the reader as he leafs through a magazine or newspaper. Because of its importance in gaining attention, writers often try to capture the essential idea of the advertisement in the headline. For example:

Wella Balsam Shampoo not only conditions your hair, it even repairs split ends.
or
The April Honda: lowest priced car in America.

Second, the headline is often used to select the target audience by appealing to a particular group of people, as the following examples do:

More and More small shippers are discovering we're the Cargo Coddlers.
or
As the head of a business, I read Barron's to keep ahead.

The first headline identifies "small shippers" as the target audience. The second singles out "heads of businesses."

Third, The headline, often assisted by a subhead, is used to entice the reader into the text or body copy of the advertisement. Both of the following headlines are deliberately designed to lead the readers into the body copy of the ad.

8 great ways a Playboy Club Key turns the finer things your way.
or
A Significant Breakthrough in the Fight Against the Effects of Aging.

The headline assumes added importance when it is recognized that, for most ads, 80–90 percent of the audience never read more than the headline. David Ogilvy, for example, states:

The headline is the most important element in most advertisements. It is the telegram which decides the reader whether to read the copy.

On the average, five times as many people read the headline as read the body copy. When you have written your headline, you have spent eighty cents out of your dollar.

If you haven't done some selling in your headline, you have wasted 80% of your client's money. The wickedest of all sins is to run an advertisement *without* a headline. Such headless wonders are still to be found; I don't envy the copywriter who submits one to me.[3]

Illustrations

In addition to headlines, most advertisements contain illustrations. Like headlines, one of the functions of the illustration is to attract attention. As an attention attracting device, however, the illustration should be relevant to the idea upon which the ad is based and not simply a source of borrowed interest. (*Borrowed interest* is the use of irrelevant illustrations of high interest value.) Properly used, illustrations not only attract attention but also reinforce the headline, demonstrate the product, convey abstract ideas that are hard to express in words, and set the tone or mood for the entire advertisement.

Body Copy

Copy is a somewhat ambiguous term that often applies to all of the words appearing in an advertisement, including the headline and subheads. When the term, "copy," is modified by the word, "body," it refers to the text of the ad, excluding headlines, subheads, illustration, and logotype. The function of body copy is to provide information about the product, to develop support for the headline, and to persuade readers to use the product being advertised. Body copy is sometimes referred to as the "reason why" of an advertisement because it permits the

3. David Ogilvy, *Confessions of an Advertising Man* (New York: Athenum, 1964), p. 104.

writer to develop reasons why the product should be used, rather than competitive products.

Logotypes and Brand Identification

Logotypes (logos), or signature cuts, are special designs of the advertiser or its products which are used to facilitate identification. The logo in a particular ad may be a name, a trademark, a package, or some combination of these elements. There is no rule as to where a logo should be placed; it is often placed in the lower, right-hand corner of the advertisement, although it may appear elsewhere in the ad as well. The logo is the only element that always appears in an advertisement. Headlines, illustrations, or body copy may sometimes be dispensed with, but the logo always appears somewhere to identify the advertiser.

WRITING HEADLINES

Not all advertising practioners are as adamant about headlines as is David Ogilvy, who was quoted earlier. Most, however, will agree that the headline is a major element in the advertisement. All advertisers will deplore the *empty,* or *hollow,* headline—a headline that is a weak or meaningless statement. Yet, many headlines convey no information and have about as much inherent interest as the sex life of a head of cabbage. Consider, for example, the following headlines:

Power Pal (a hairdryer)

So French you can feel it (a cosmetic)

Don't Interrupt Life's Great Performances (a cassette deck)

How very you (luggage)

It tastes like today (a soft drink)

Strip to our bare essentials (shoes)

Unsurpassed (a cleaner)

Sometimes, these headlines were rescued by an arresting illustration; in most cases they were not. When we consider that 80–90 percent of magazine readers only see the headline, we must question how much selling was done by these examples, how effective they would be in drawing readers into the body copy, and what they contribute to registering the name of the product being advertised. By way of contrast, consider the following headlines:

World's only dog food that makes its own gravy (Gravy Train)

How to *fix* any part of *any* car (Motor Book)

Charlie, I just love what your makeup does for my skin. Even after I take it off. (Charlie)

Why is any size headache The Excedrin Headache? (Excedrin)

This remarkable makeup gives you a fresh look that stays fresh all day. (Maybelline)

Now, these headlines will not be of interest to everyone. They aren't meant to be; the products they advertise aren't for everyone. But, they do say something to those consumers who have an interest in the product fields they represent.

If there are any rules, perhaps the first rule of headline writing is that the headline should *do* something. It should state a benefit, create interest, identify the brand, give information, select the audience, or *something.* It shouldn't just lie there like a lump of mud. One obvious difference between the headline examples that said something, and those that did not, is that the former were longer than the latter. And this brings up the question of headline length.

Headline Length

How long should a headline be? There is no mechanical answer to this question other than that it should be long enough to say something. Generally, you can say more in five words than you can in one word. And, you can say more in ten words than you can in five. At some point, however, the point of diminishing returns is reached where the cost of reading the headlines exceeds the value of what it has to say. Consumers glance at an ad. The headline should be short enough to be read in this glance. It is for this reason that most writers strive for relatively short headlines. This is sound practice *provided* that the headline doesn't become so short that it becomes meaningless. Sometimes, a short headline may have enough intrigue or be so well integrated with the illustration that it retains its power. Generally speaking, however, more sins are committed with short headlines than with long ones. One agency writer, Whit Hobbs, wrote this seventy-word headline:

I seem to spend my whole day picking up; pickup the laundry and the groceries and the mail; picking up Jim at the station and the children at school—and picking up after them all! Sometimes I feel like a squirrel in a cage . . . running in circles all day and never getting a chance to collect my thoughts and take a look at what's going on in the world.

Why seventy words? Mr. Hobbs' answer was, "Because it took 70 words to say what I wanted to say." [4]

4. S.W. Dunn and A.M. Barban, *Advertising,* 3rd ed. (Hinsdale, Illinois: The Dryden Press, 1974), p. 327.

By contrast, one of the most effective advertisements ever run by an advertising agency has a single word headline (see figure 13–5). In this instance, much of the power of the headline derives from the illustration. Raymond Rubicam acknowledges this point in the following quotation:

> Vaughn Flannery, then our art director, Anton and Martin Bruehl, photographers, and I, worked long and hard to make that ad register as well as say *"Impact"* in every detail. Oddly, the very first picture idea that we rejected was a picture of two prize fighters, one getting a good sock in the jaw. Before we came back to it we tried at least 20 other ideas, none of them with sufficient *"Impact."* It was only when Bruehl posed two negro fighters instead of two white fighters that the picture took on the fresh and dramatic character we wanted.
>
> I had the same kind of trouble, but perhaps not so much of it, with the text. It had to be short, it had to be emphatic, it had to be conclusive. So I adopted the device of two definitions of the word *"Impact,"* and stopped there.[5]

Subheadlines.   Sometimes the problem of long headlines can be solved by the use of subheadlines (subheads), which may explain the headline, qualify it, amplify it, or develop it in some way. A subhead is subordinated to the main headline but distinguished from body copy by being separated from it physically, and shown in larger type. For example:

Headline: More Than Gentle!
Subhead: Earth Born Baby Shampoo combines a fresh honeysuckle fragrance with a low pH, non-alkaline formula!
or
Headline: Flatter your Filet!
Dramatize your dessert!
Glorify your goulash!
Subhead: Introducing Pyrex Fireside.
or
Headline: The beauty secret that keeps Royal Velvet Towels young.
Subhead: Our secret is invisible. It's locked in the weave.

A Summary Position on Headline Length.   There are many examples of short headlines that have worked and of long headlines that have worked. On balance, though, about six to twelve words is the optimum length for a headline. Less than six words runs the danger of becoming telegraphic jargon. On the other

hand, if more than twelve words is required, the idea may be too complex to be expressed in a headline. Perhaps the real question is not, "How long is the headline?," but "What does the headline say?" Margot Sherman, who gained recognition throughout the advertising industry as a copywriter at McCann-Erickson, touches on the real basis for judging the length of headlines with the following questions about advertising in general:

> Ask yourself, If I were a flesh and blood human being instead of an advertising thinker, would there be any reason in God's earth for reading or listening to this message? Is there really something here for me?[6]

Direct and Indirect Headlines

Headlines may be classified in many ways. For example, some headlines are direct in that they identify the principal message of the ad. Others are indirect in that they are designed to arouse curiosity and lead the reader into the body copy. Two examples of direct headlines are given below. Both headlines are relatively long—seventeen to eighteen words. Although the body copy amplifies the headline in each instance, the basic message is delivered by the headline itself.

Max Factor creates
Mistake-proof nail enamal.
Pre-measured for perfect application.
In the plastic shatter-proof bottle.

The headline not only identifies the consumer benefit, "mistake-proof," but also provides reasons for this benefit—"pre-measured" and "shatter-proof" bottle. In addition, it identifies the manufacturer, Max Factor. Such headlines are often referred to as *hard-working* headlines because of the amount of information they convey relatively quickly.

The following headline from a Pioneer advertisement is also direct in that the primary sales point is summed up in the headline.

MOST $600 RECEIVERS SOUND AS GOOD AS THIS ONE.
UNFORTUNATELY FOR THEM THIS ONE SELLS FOR UNDER $300.

The following headline from a General Electric corporate advertisement is *indirect*, almost to the point of misdirection. (See figure 13–6.)

What was Thomas Edison's biggest blunder?

---

5. Julian Lewis Watkins, *The 100 Greatest Advertisements* (New York: Dover Publications, Inc., 1959), p. 97.

6. *Advertising,* An omnibus of advertising prepared by Printers' Ink in its 75th year of publication. (New York: McGraw-Hill Book Company, Inc., 1963), p. 316.

Figure 13–5. (Young & Rubicam, Inc.)

IMPACT

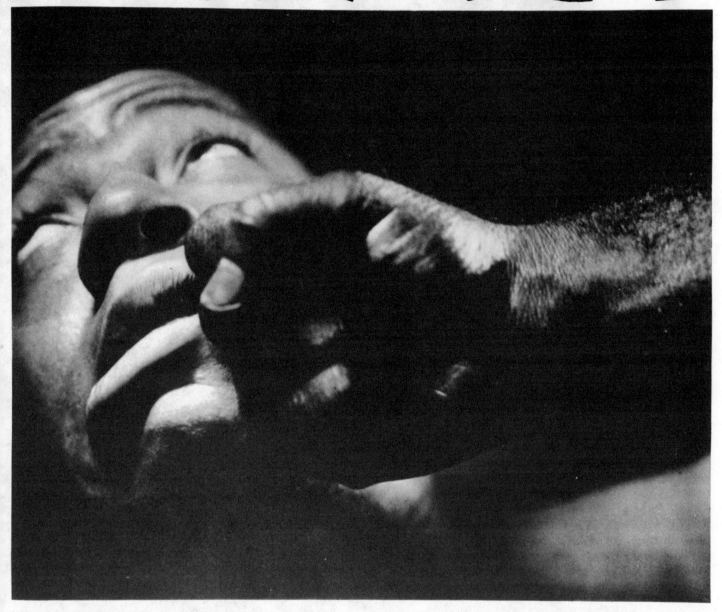

ACCORDING TO WEBSTER: The single instantaneous striking of a body in motion against another body.

ACCORDING TO YOUNG & RUBICAM: That quality in an advertisement which strikes suddenly against the reader's indifference and enlivens his mind to receive a sales message.

YOUNG & RUBICAM, INCORPORATED · ADVERTISING

NEW YORK · CHICAGO · DETROIT · HOLLYWOOD · MONTREAL · TORONTO

Figure 13-6. (Courtesy of General Electric Company)

What was Thomas Edison's biggest blunder?

Here's what we think Edison himself would have said:

"Some people give me credit for being the man who put electricity to work in America. Not completely true.

A lot of people had a hand in it. Thomson. Tesla. Steinmetz.

Charley Steinmetz.

Queer-looking duck. Not even five feet tall. With an enormous head.

Inside that head, there was an enormous brain.

Shortly after he arrived in this country, Steinmetz came to work for General Electric.

Those were exciting times at GE. It was the beginning of the whole age of electricity. Some of the top scientists and engineers in the country were there. Ideas were bouncing around like marbles.

Steinmetz started working with alternating current. The kind of electricity we all use today.

I thought it was a fool idea.

I favored direct current. Of course, it couldn't be transmitted more than two miles. But I didn't see that as any real problem.

That was the biggest blunder of my life.

If people had listened to me then, we'd have power plants all over the country. Every two miles.

Well, Charley kept on working at it. Kept on calculating.

The big test came at Niagara Falls in 1894. GE built a transformer and strung a line to Buffalo. 26 miles away.

The switch was thrown at Niagara and the lights came on in Buffalo.

Steinmetz once told me he was almost refused admission at Ellis Island as an unfit immigrant. It's funny. One of the men most responsible for the electrification of America was almost turned away at its gate."

Edison may not have been wrong after all. New solid-state equipment and technology developed by General Electric make it possible to send direct current efficiently over great distances. It will soon be transmitted 450 miles from North Dakota to Duluth, Minn., over a line being built. In some cases, direct current may become the most economical way to transmit electricity.

Progress for People
GENERAL ⓖ ELECTRIC

The foregoing examples suggest that the type of headline used depends largely on the purpose of the advertisement and the nature of the message to be communicated. If the primary purpose of the advertisement is to register the brand name or if the consumer benefit can be expressed easily in a few words, then a direct headline is preferable. If, on the other hand, the message is too lengthy or complex to be expressed in the headline, then the headline must be written in such a way that it will attract readers to the body copy. In this instance an indirect headline may be required.

Often a direct headline may be provocative by the simple addition of a word. For example, consider the following headline for BMW (Bavarian Motor Works).

PEOPLE WHO DRIVE A BMW ENJOY DRIVING MORE THAN YOU DO.

Now, that's nice; but who really cares? The headline is direct because it communicates the product name and makes a statement about people who drive a BMW. As it stands, it might draw some people into the body copy, but it has all of the characteristics of a "brag and boast" headline; all air and little content. Now examine this headline, as it actually ran, with one word added.

WHY PEOPLE WHO DRIVE A BMW ENJOY DRIVING MORE THAN YOU DO.

When the word *why* is introduced into the headline, it takes on substance, suggests that there are valid reasons for the claim, and suggests that these reasons will be explained in the body copy of the ad.

But when a headline lures readers into the body copy, the body copy had better be worth reading. It should say something worthwhile about the product to compensate readers for their time and effort. Otherwise, the entire ad may be rejected as being irrelevant, and the product, without even having put up a fight, will have lost a chance to create a customer.

Other Types of Headlines

In addition to being classified as direct or indirect, headlines may also be classified in other ways. For example, they can be classified in term of content—the type of appeal or consumer benefit that is offered. They may be classified in terms of grammatical form—questions, statements, exclamations, or conversations. The Pampers advertisement shown in chapter 12 is a conversational statement:

"I wouldn't use anything but Pampers. I've been through this before."

There is little evidence that one form of headline is more effective than another. It all depends on the ad and what the headline is supposed to do. Some practitioners argue that (in product advertising at least) the brand name should *always* appear in the headline. "After all," they say, "most people only read the headline." Others disagree.

Many writers insist that one should avoid clichés in the headline. Others disagree. Ogilvy, for example, says:

> The two most powerful words you can use in a headline are FREE and NEW. You can seldom use FREE, but you can almost always use NEW—if you try hard enough. . . . Other words and phrases which work wonders are HOW TO, SUDDENLY, NOW, ANNOUNCING, INTRODUCING, IT'S HERE, JUST ARRIVED, IMPORTANT DEVELOPMENT, IMPROVEMENT, AMAZING, SENSATIONAL, REMARKABLE, REVOLUTIONARY, STARTLING, MIRACLE, MAGIC, OFFER, QUICK, EASY, WANTED, CHALLENGE, ADVICE TO, THE TRUTH ABOUT, COMPARE, BARGAIN, HURRY LAST CHANCE.
>
> Don't turn up your nose at these cliches. They may be shopworn, but they work. That is why you see them turn up so often in the headlines of mail-order advertisers and others who can measure the results of their advertising.[7]

Some of the more frequently used forms of headlines are described in the following material.

News Headlines. Most consumers are interested in news about products: new developments, new styles, new ways of doing things. The news headline takes advantage of this interest. Facts about a product are news as long as a large number of potential consumers are unaware of them, but the news headline always implies that these facts are of recent origin. Sometimes, the news headline contains the word *new*, but there are many ways of saying *new* without using the word. For example:

NOW.
VACATIONS AND AIR TRAVEL FOR
1-A-DAY (Braniff)
or

Datsun introduces the family cars with a 240-Z engine. (Datsun)
or

---

7. Ogilvy, *Confessions*, pp. 105–6.

The new Volaré T-Bar Roof: our answer to the vanishing convertable (Volaré)

or

FINALLY
VANTAGE
LONGS

The first long cigarette to bring good taste to low-tar smoking. (Vantage)

or

A significant Breakthrough in the Fight Against the Effects of Aging. (Ribomins)

or

Now you can keep your lips in the shape you've always wanted. (Sally Hansen "Perfect Lips")

or

NEW IMPROVED (Triumph)

or

New! The sexy Seamless Instead Bra. (Instead)

All nine of these headlines are news headlines, even though only three of them use the word, *new*.

Question Headlines. Psychologically, a question demands an answer. A provocative question generates a psychological tension that is only removed by finding the answer. Many headlines attempt to take advantage of this phenomenon by raising questions that are then answered in the body copy. Some examples:

"What am I afraid of?" (Psychology Today)

or

ARE YOU BLAMING YOUR TAPE RE-CORDER FOR PROBLEMS CAUSED BY YOUR TAPES? (Maxell Tapes)

or

"Dear General Foods,
If your products are so good, why are you making them 'New' and 'Improved' all the time? (General Foods)

Sometimes the answer is given in the body copy. Sometimes it is given in the headline itself, or in a subhead. For example:
Headline: When is a haircolor not a haircolor?
Subhead: When it's Happiness . . . The Beauty
Treatment for your hair.

Obviously, the more provocative the question, the greater the interest in the answer.

Command Headlines. A command headline tells consumers to do something, often to try or buy a brand. Properly used, they can be effective. Two interesting examples of command headlines are shown below.

Remember this before you rent a tuxedo for your wedding day. The tuxedo is returnable. The day is not. (gingiss formal wear centers)

or

Drive a car that impresses people who aren't easily impressed. (Volvo)

More often, though, a command headline gains in effectiveness when it is stated in some other way. After all, most of us don't need any more people telling us what to do. Consider the following way in which a command headline can be modified so that it gains in effectiveness.

Meet your copier-duplicator needs.

As a command headline, it is weak and offers little of interest to the reader. Interest can be enhanced by making it into a "how to" headline through the addition of three words:

6 ways to meet your copier-duplicator needs

The headline becomes even more provocative as it actually appeared in an advertisement.

Kodak Offers
6 ways to meet your
copie-duplicator needs.

The point is, of course, that headlines often require work and rework before they say precisely what we want them to say in precisely the way we want them to say it.

Testimonial Headlines. Testimonial headlines provide personal testimony about a product or service. Experts are often used to lend credence to advertising claims for products ranging from automobiles to zircons. Sometimes celebrities are used to give prestige to a brand, even though they have no expertise in the particular product field. Plain, ordinary people are often used simply to give assurance of product satisfaction. For example, a businessman, a sports figure, and a consumer are used in the following three headlines:

"As the head of a business, I read Barron's, To *keep* ahead." (Alfred Fromm, Chairman of the Board of Fromm & Sichel, San Francisco, California)

"Short & Sassy is just perfect for my hair" (Dorothy Hamill, figure skating champion)

"My hands became so rough and raw . . . I was about to call a doctor . . . " (Unsolicited testimonial for Neutrogena hand cream from a Massachusetts housewife.)

There are other ways to classify headlines: *benefit* headlines identify a consumer benefit; *comparison* headlines draw a comparison between the brand being advertised and competition; *how to* headlines tell consumers how to do something (how to fix a car, how to lose weight, how to retire at 50).

However, the various forms of headlines are only *techniques*, and a technique is only useful insofar as it has relevance in a particular situation. Far too frequently, young copywriters try to be "cute," or "funny," or "creative" purely for the sake of being cute, funny, or creative. When this happens, technique usually gets in the way of the idea, and mediocrity is the result.

Guidelines for Effective Headlines

Earlier, it was emphasized that there are no hard rules governing the writing of headlines. This is so because each advertisement is different and the requirements of the headline varies with the situation. The following guidelines should be thought of as a check list of elements to consider.

1. The headline should have *content*. It should say something relevant to the consumer benefit inherent in the brand being advertised. Avoid generalizations that could apply to any brand.
2. The headline should employ words that will help select the target market.
3. Brevity is desirable, but it should not be used to the sacrifice of saying something meaningful.
4. The headline should be provocative and draw the reader into the body copy.
5. It should be written in the language of the consumer for whom it is intended. Avoid advertise-ese.
6. Finally, the headline should be coordinated with the other elements of the advertisement.

ILLUSTRATIONS

In some advertisements, the illustration, not the headline, is the most important feature of the ad. The Vanity Fair advertisement used at the beginning of the chapter is a case in point. More often, the illustration amplifies the headline.

Effect of Illustrations

Normally, the illustration contributes to the overall effect of print advertising in one or more of the following ways: (1) it attracts attention of the target audience; (2) it communicates relevant product ideas or benefits; (3) it stimulates interest in the headline and body copy; and (4) it expresses ideas and feelings that are difficult to express in words. In a well-conceived advertisement, the illustration often accomplishes all four of these functions.

Selecting the Target Audience. There are many ways of attracting attention with an illustration: run it upside down or sideways; use bizarre settings; shoot through filters; use dramatic subjects; use action shots; resort to pornography. But, simply attracting attention is not the purpose of an illustration. A good illustration is one that attracts the attention of the *relevant* target audience in a *relevant* way. There is a cliché in advertising that if you want to attract the attention of women, use the picture of a baby. If you want to attract the attention of men, use a picture of a puppy. And, if you want to attract the attention of everyone, use both a baby and a puppy. Sometimes babies and puppies are appropriate, as in the Gaines Puppy Choice advertisement (figure 13–7); but for most products, they are not.

Examine a copy of *Fortune* magazine. Many of the advertisements use illustrations that may seem to be devoid of interest. Now, assume that you are a business person faced with a variety of operational problems—production, marketing, transportation, packaging, insurance, data processing, finance. Reexamine the illustrations from this point of view to see if they do not assume added relevance.

Communicating Relevant Product Benefits. The illustration can often be used to communicate a product benefit. A high-gloss table shows the benefits of a furniture wax (see plate 13–1 in insert following page 250); an appetite appeal photograph can enhance the attractiveness of a food product (see plate 13–2); a before and after picture photograph may be used to show the results of a diet plan; a simplified one-two-three demonstration of product use may be used to dramatize product convenience; a fashion shot can reveal the beauty and style of apparel; tastefully decorated rooms enable the reader to visualize how carpeting, floor tile, draperies, or furniture will look in an actual setting. And, the Lysol Spray Disinfectant advertisement (plate 12–2) demonstrates both variety and ease of product use.

The end benefits of some products (fashions, home furnishings, cosmetics, and so forth) are easier to illustrate than others. Once a principal benefit has been defined, however, finding ways of visualizing it is sometimes the admaker's most challenging job. Volkswagen used a series of illustrations of the bug being driven through snow, over rocky terrain, through

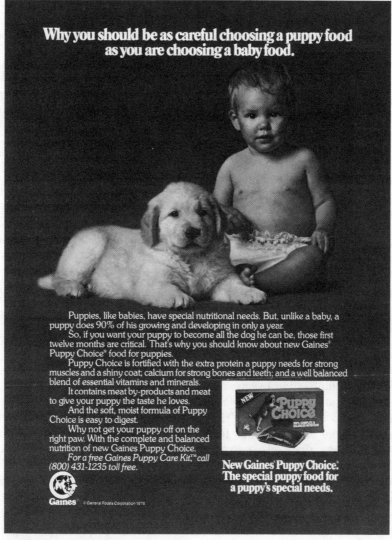

© General Foods Corporation 1977.
Reproduced with permission of General
Foods Corporation.

Figure 13-7. (General Foods Corp.)

mud, and through water, summing up with the caption: "Few things in life work as well as a Volkswagen." Volvo demonstrated the strength of its roof
construction by showing seven Volvos stacked on top
of one another, and Sound Guard, a dry lubricant for
protecting phonographic records, used a magnified
illustration of stylus damage to show the difference in
wear for an unprotected record versus one protected by
Sound Guard.

Generating Interest in Headline and Body Copy. In
addition to attracting attention of the target audience,
the illustration should intrigue the readers so that they
want to know more about the product. Usually, the

illustration and headline work together in this respect:
the headline makes a statement or asks a question.
Together, they dramatize a product benefit and create
curiosity about the product on the part of the reader.
A well-conceived illustration will cause the reader to
ask: "Why is this so?" or "What is going on here?" or
"Will this work for me?"

Contrary to general opinion, women are interested
in photographs of women in the advertising they read,
and men are interested in photographs of men. The
reason is that people in general are interested in themselves and those with whom they can identify.
Research conducted by George Gallup for the movie
industry has demonstrated that moviegoers are more

interested in actors of their own sex than in actors of the opposite sex, and analysis of dreams has shown that male characters outnumber female characters in men's dreams by a ratio of two to one. [8]

Expressing Ideas and Feelings. Feeling and mood can often be expressed more dramatically and communicated more quickly in an illustration than in words. Happiness, serenity, confidence, concern, as well as other emotions, can be expressed in words, of course. Poets and novelists do it all the time. Yet, it often takes several paragraphs or pages to do so. Print advertising, with its requirement for instant communication to capture reader interest, doesn't have the luxury of using several paragraphs to establish a feeling. Instead, it relies on the illustration for this purpose. An action photograph, a quizzical look, an intimate scene, fresh complexion, a sad face, or a happy gathering can be grasped instantly by the reader and create empathy and curiosity about the advertising message.

Illustration Techniques

The admaker has a variety of illustration techniques with which to work (photographs, original artwork, cartoons, line drawings, and so forth). Although the subject of the illustration is more important than the technique, experience indicates that, in general, photographs are far more effective than other illustration forms in attracting reader attention and involvement. Ogilvy, for example, states:

> Over and over again research has shown that *photographs* sell more than *drawings*. They attract more readers. They deliver more appetite appeal. They are better remembered. They pull more coupons. And they sell more merchandise. Photographs represent reality, whereas drawings represent fantasy, which is less believable. [9]

The findings of Gallup-Robinson, a firm that has specialized in copy research, support Ogilvy's endorsement of photographs as more effective than other illustration techniques. But, perhaps the most convincing evidence is what the advertising industry does. With all of its faults, the advertising industry utilizes those techniques that tend to work best. Pick up any magazine, and compare the proportion of photographs to other forms of illustration. Photographs win, hands down. There are a number of reasons why photographs are more effective than other art forms.

1. *Realism:* People like to see the "real thing" in their ads. Good color photography does wonders for all kinds of products, from gleaming motor cars to steaming bowls of soup. Just look at the food photography in any homemaker's magazine!
2. *The feeling of "it's happening now:"* Photographs—particularly news type photographs—put you right on the spot when it is happening. You are standing on the goal line when the touchdown is scored. You get involved. Remember, one of our big objectives in advertising is to put the reader "in the driver's seat" . . . to make him relate and see himself in that same situation.
3. *Making the "cartoon effect" come alive:* Photographers have done some wonderful things in taking "cartoon situations" and giving them the added dimension of realism. A drawing of the eye-patched Hathaway man, for instance, simply wouldn't come off.
4. *The beauty and sensitivity of film:* Photographers are sometimes able to achieve a high artistic level with their pictures. A photograph can carry a tremendous emotional wallop.
5. *Photographs make excellent "convincers:"* What better proof do you need than the unretouched photo of the weight reducer, before and after? [10]

All of the foregoing advantages are consumer oriented, and they should be. In addition, some practical advantages that photography has for the admaker, are *speed, flexibility,* and *economy.* A drawing or painting takes longer to complete than a photograph. Further, a variety of shots can be taken in the same session and, if desirable, stock photos can be purchased inexpensively.

This does not mean that other illustration techniques should never be used. For example, photographs often do not reproduce well on the coarse paper stock used by newspapers. Here, original artwork and stylized drawings may be much more effective. Note, the extent to which department stores use original artwork and line drawings in depicting clothing, furniture, and other products in their newspaper ads. Even in magazines, where high gloss paper stock lends itself to photographic reproduction, original artwork may be used effectively. For example, the Container Corporation ran a highly effective corporate campaign using nonrepresentative illustrations by artist Walter Paepcke; Massachusetts Mutual Insurance Company successfully used a series of Norman Rockwell paintings to convey a feeling of warmth and friendliness and to imply that the company was concerned with simple, homey virtues. Similarly, graphs and charts

---

8. *Ibid.,* p. 119.
9. *Ibid.,* p. 18.

10. Stephen Baker, *Advertising Layout and Art Direction* (New York: McGraw-Hill Book Company, 1959).

may sometimes be used effectively in illustrations to convey important information quickly and dramatically. The point is not that nonphotographic illustrations should never be used. Certainly, if photographic reproduction is a problem because of paper stock, some other illustration technique will be more effective. However, where reproduction fidelity is not a problem, nonphotographic illustrations should be used cautiously because research has indicated that photographs are far more effective than other illustration techniques in attracting reader attention and gaining consumer involvement.

Size of Illustration

Marplan, a totally owned subsidiary of the Interpublic group of advertising agencies, analyzed over 250 thousand advertisements, using the *Starch "noted" score* as the critierion for attention value. It found that single, large, well-structured illustrations, with a single focal point, were more effective than other illustrations in attracting attention. The Leo Burnette advertising agency confirmed this finding in a review of recent studies of advertising.[11] The use of the Starch "noted" score as the measure of attention may be a relatively superficial measure of readership. However, Gallup-Robinson, used the more rigorous "recall' readership measure and made similar findings.

One limitation of all of these studies is that they only measured general recognition or recall, not the recognition of the specific target group to which the ads were directed. Nonetheless, the findings are probably valid for the target groups as well since the basic question is how much work does the reader have to do in order to understand the advertising message. A complex illustration, or several illustrations in the same advertisement, signal work; work involves time. In the busy world of most consumers, an advertisement that demands a great deal of time will tend to be ignored. Instead, consumers will note and read those ads in which the main elements of the message can be grasped quickly. Robert Plisken, while vice-president in charge of art for Benton and Bowles, looked into the future of advertising illustrations and predicted:

> Eventually, of course, print ads will be all picture, like TV, the bigger and brighter the better. And, maybe at the bottom somewhere, there will be a small line of type . . . [12]

The Use of Color

The first *full* color advertisement appeared in 1937. Since then, the use of color has grown steadily until, today, a majority of full page advertisements are printed in color, as well as many fractional page units. There are a number of reasons for using color in print advertising:[13]

1. Attracting attention to an advertisement.
2. Representing objects, scenes, and people with complete fidelity.
3. Emphasizing some special part of the message of the product.
4. Suggesting abstract qualities appropriate to the selling appeal.
5. Creating a pleasant first impression for the advertisement.
6. Creating prestige for the product, service, or advertiser.
7. Fastening visual impressions in memory (partly because of the performance of the other functions listed above, and partly because of inherent power to stimulate interest).

These are all persuasive reasons, but they do not mean that color should automatically be used. Color costs more than black and white, commanding a premium of up to 30 percent. Color is not equally important for all products. Consider the following three ads (see plates 13–3 and 13–4 insert following p. 250, and figure 13–8, p. 240). Both the Aynsley and the Frost and Tip ads require full color. Much of the impact of these two advertisements would be lost without it. By contrast, color is not an essential ingredient of the Smith-Corona ad. Color might detract from the ad.

When considering the use of color, the creative group can use a four-color process that will provide a complete range of color reproduction, or a more limited, and less expensive range of color such as: black and one color; two colors; black and two colors. When only one or two colors are used, they are generally used to attract attention or to highlight a part of an otherwise black and white ad. Such limited use of color often defeats its own purpose. Gallup and Robinson have found that when color is used *functionally* (such as showing green grass in what is basically a black and white ad for lawn seed) it may increase readership. However, when color is used nonfunctionally (a color headline or a splash of color for attention value only) it tends to reduce readership.

In 1967, Daniel Starch reported a study of 25,081 advertisements in seven product categories in national

11. Donald Wayne Hendon, "How Mechanical Factors Affect Ad Perception," *Journal of Advertising Research*, (August, 1973), pp. 39–43.
12. Robert Pliskin, "Some of the most carefully chosen words are pictures," in *Advertising*. An omnibus of advertising prepared by Printers' Ink, p. 133–46.
13. Thomas B. Stanley, *The Technique of Advertising Production*, 2nd ed. (New York: Prentice-Hall, Inc., 1954), p. 59.

WHY SMITH-CORONA IS AMERICA'S BEST SELLING PORTABLE.

There are 15 brands of portable typewriters on the market.

But this year, like the last 10 years, more people will buy a Smith-Corona than any other brand.

Here are just five among many important reasons why:

THE TYPEWRITER WITH A HOLE

When we designed our cartridge, we re-designed our typewriters.

In place of spool cups, posts, reversing levers, ribbon guides and messy ribbons, there's a hole.

The hole is for our cartridges.

Next to the hole is a lever. Depress the lever and the cartridge pops out.

In three seconds, just by inserting a new cartridge, you can change a ribbon without getting your fingers dirty.

mistakr
mistak
mistake

CORRECTS MISTAKES IN 10 SECONDS

The hole also accommodates a correcting cartridge.

So when you make a mistake, you can snap out the typing cartridge, snap in the correcting cartridge, type over the mistake, snap the typing cartridge back in and type the correct character—all in ten seconds or less.

FIVE COLORS

Cartridges come in black, red, blue, green, and brown.

If you're typing along in black, but you want to type a line in red for emphasis, snap out the black cartridge and snap in the red cartridge. In just three seconds you can see red!

NYLON
FILM

EXECUTIVE LOOKING CORRESPONDENCE

The Smith-Corona electric portable with a film ribbon will give you the sharpest typing image of any portable.

When you want to type a letter that looks like an executive's, snap in the black film cartridge

and type with real authority.

The black nylon is not quite so authoritative but is more economical. One cartridge lets you type about 325,000 characters.

FOUR YEARS OF COLLEGE AND BEYOND

We could make some remarkable statements about how we test out typewriters. But that's not necessary.

Most typewriter retailers have typewriters on display. Type a few sentences on a Smith-Corona. Snap a cartridge in and out. Smith-Corona looks and feels sturdy because it is sturdy.

So, for your high school graduate, we suggest you follow this simple formula:

Buy a doctor a Smith-Corona when he or she graduates from high school.

Buy a lawyer a Smith-Corona when he or she graduates from high school.

Buy a successful businessperson a Smith-Corona when he or she graduates from high school.

SCM® SMITH-CORONA
SCM CORPORATION

magazines. A comparison, based on the Starch "noted" score, of the various uses of color is summarized below.[14] This table should be read in the following way. First, each column should be read separately. In the first column (half page ads), the table shows that: if the average number of readers noting a black and white, half page ad is indexed at 100, then the average number of readers noting a two-color, half page ad will be 2 percent greater (index 102), and the average number of readers noting a four-color, half page ad will be 87 percent greater (index 187). Note that, for full page ads, the average number of readers noting a two-color ad is 8 percent *less* (index 92) than the average number of readers noting a black and white ad, while the average number of readers noting a four-color ad is 52 percent greater than those noting a black and white ad.

	Half page	Full page	Two page
Black and white	100	100	100
Two color	102	92	100
Four color	187	152	149

In the final analysis, the decision to use or not to use color in advertisements is a creative decision. For example, when Jack Daniel's began advertising in the 1960s, virtually all distilled spirits advertising was full page, four color. Against this competitive background, the Jack Daniel's creative group deliberately decided to use black and white, fractional pages. This decision was made for three reasons: (1) to set Jack Daniel's advertising apart from competition, (2) to communicate the simple, rustic setting in which the product was made, and (3) to broaden coverage with a limited advertising budget. This same Jack Daniel's campaign is still running and has been highly successful for almost twenty years (see figure 13–9).

Nonetheless, the communication power of color is widely recognized. Blues and greens are cool and relaxing; red is exciting; pastels are feminine; dark browns are masculine; white is pure; black is the color of mourning; golds and purples are rich and expensive. Colors have many connotations and can be used to express a variety of feelings and moods. However, they need to be used thoughtfully, and some colors are hard to control. The Pet Milk Company, for example, devised a campaign for evaporated milk built around the headline, "Start cooking with a golden spoon. Start cooking with Pet." Research indicated that the symbolism of a "golden spoon" was highly effective and that it reinforced the inherent richness of evapor-

14. S.W. Dunn and A.M. Barban, *Advertising,* p.375.

Figure 13–8   (SCM Corporation)

IF YOU'RE EVER in need of an experienced photographer, Mr. Joe Clark is your man.

Mr. Clark was born and reared right over in Cumberland Gap, a Tennessee town that's even smaller than ours is. And, since about 1954, he's been taking just about all the pictures that appear in our ads. Over the years, Joe's good snapshots have told you a lot about Jack Daniel's Whiskey. But, as even he would admit, one sip will tell you a whole lot more.

CHARCOAL MELLOWED

◊

DROP

◊

BY DROP

Tennessee Whiskey • 90 Proof • Distilled and Bottled by Jack Daniel Distillery
Lem Motlow, Prop., Inc., Lynchburg (Pop. 361), Tennessee 37352
Placed in the National Register of Historic Places by the United States Government

Figure 13–9.   (Jack Daniel Distillery)

ated milk. Advertising illustrations featured a golden spoon, as well as appetizing food photography. Unfortunately, gold is a somewhat ambiguous color which ranges from a light yellow to a burnished bronze, and it is difficult to control in terms of color fidelity. The same advertisement, appearing in different magazines, reproduced a wide range of gold colors—some were absolutely unattractive. Pet's advertising agency dispatched an art director to the printing plants of all of the magazines on the media schedule to work with printers in selecting the right combination of inks to produce a uniform gold color. After a year of frustration, Pet's advertising manager insisted that the campaign be discontinued, despite its strengths, because of the inability to reproduce a consistent gold color.

Types of Illustrations

Illustrations may also be classified in terms of their subject matter. A typical classification along these lines is shown below:

1. The product itself.
2. The product package.
3. The product in use.
4. The benefit derived from using the product.
5. The consequences of not using the product.
6. Comparisons—"before and after" comparisons, as well as comparisons with competitive products.
7. Testimonials about the product.
8. Dramatizations of a situation.
9. Illustrations that create a feeling or mood.

Obviously, the list is not complete. The types of illustrations that may be used are limited only by the imagination of the admaker. Equally apparent, many illustrations can be classified in more than one way. Further, multiple illustrations can be used (and often are) to show different product attributes and/or benefits. The point is *not* that there are various ways of classifying illustrations, since there is little firm evidence that one type of illustration is better than another. The point *is* that many types of illustrations may be used, depending upon the key idea or benefit that is depicted in the advertisement.

For certain products where fashion or design is particularly important, the illustration usually features the product in some way. Clothing, automobiles, furniture, carpeting, floor tile, draperies, and so forth fall in this category. The Solarian ad by Armstrong (plate 13–5, insert following p. 250), for example features a tile pattern in an in-use setting. The major purpose of this advertisement is to demonstrate the beauty of the tile. The Flexalum ad (plate 13–6, insert following p. 250) also shows the product in use. Here however, in addition to showing the beauty of the product in an appropriate setting, a major purpose is to demonstrate its functional value.

It is usually desirable to illustrate the major product benefit, but the visualization of this benefit is often difficult. Robert Pliskin comments on the difficulty encountered in developing a campaign for the Glass Container Manufacturers Institute:

> The objective of the advertising: Demonstrate the superiority of glass over other packaging materials. Most glass, of course, is transparent, almost invisible.

Glass also adds beauty and dimension to anything it contains. How do you make an invisible product highly visible on a printed page?

Peaches. Peaches are packed in glass. Photograph a jar of beautiful, halved peaches—you will discover that the peaches simply take over the ad. Women will look at the pretty peaches, drool a little, and pass on to the next page. Worse yet, the peach packers may do the same thing. We want them to drool over the glass. How do you flag the inattentive reader? How do you tell him the ad is for glass containers and not peaches?

Here are some thumbnails we tried.

Why not do the obvious? Simply say GLASS loud and clear. Give the ad a logo, make the logo as big and important as possible. Not bad. But can we say it with imagination, a new way? Try setting the word "glass" and putting it inside a glass jar, to make the distortion created by the glass enhance the meaning of the word. We run smack-dab into a problem here. We did not want to distort to that degree that would suggest a flaw in the material, but when we distorted the word only a little, we lost the effect we were after.

But the word "glass" alone is dull. We thought of glass letters, or of making the letters look like glass. Tallyho. The idea.

Use the word "glass" very large like a masthead, subdue the values so that it does not detract from the picture values, keep the copy to an absolute minimum.[15]

Figure 13–10 shows what happened.

A key point that emerges from the above quotation is that headline, copy, and illustration cannot be developed independently. They must all work together to create a single, overall impression.

Characteristics of Effective Illustrations

While, as in the case of headlines, there are no inviolate rules about how a product or service should be illustrated, effective illustrations often have the following characteristics:

1. The illustration visualizes the central idea or benefit underlying the advertisement.
2. It should work with, and reinforce the headline; not compete with it.
3. Large illustrations are generally more effective in attracting attention than small ones.
4. Illustrations with a single focal point are preferable over illustrations with multiple focal points.
5. When multiple illustrations are used, they should be used purposefully, and in an orderly fashion.

15. Robert Pliskin, "Some of the most carefully chosen words are pictures," p. 134.

Figure 13–10. (Glass Packaging Institute)

Glass goes to parties best.

GLASS

Nothing comes between you and the flavor

see "Glass" through Jar show distortion

Packers who are proud of their produce pack them in GLASS

PROBLEM
SOLUTION

Thumbnails like these save time, require no refinement or execution. When the marriage of art and copy is consummated, these little layouts are born. They grow up to be larger roughs, then comps, eventually are rendered and some become magazine ads

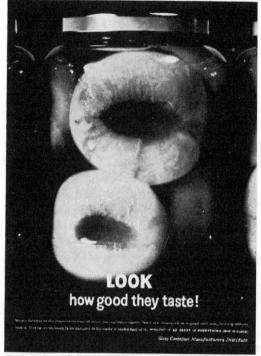

LOOK
how good they taste!

Glass Container Manufacturers Institute

Comprehensives above and below show some of development of campaign beyond "roughs" and before the finished ads are finally produced

GLASS

Best thing next to peaches

You can't taste glass. Clean, clear glass never intrudes, never changes flavor. Luscious fruit tastes as good as it looks in glass. **Wouldn't it be great if all fruit came in glass?**

Glass Container Manufacturers Institute, 99 Park Avenue, New York 16

(You see more than you think when you buy soft drinks in returnable bottles.)

Glass Container Manufacturers Institute

NOTHING COMES BETWEEN YOU AND THE FLAVOR WHEN ITS BOTTLED IN GLASS

How do you say "fresh," "clarity" and "never changes flavor" in one picture? Above finished ad solution, with photo by Ben Rose, does, as do the two below. Left photo is by Stone-Langley, right by Irving Penn

GLASS

GLASS

Nothing comes between you and the flavor when it's bottled in glass

6. Color is effective in generating readership when it is used functionally.
7. Photographs are generally more effective in attracting consumer interest and readership than other illustrative techniques.

BODY COPY

Whereas a primary purpose of the headline and illustration is to attract attention and to arouse interest, the primary purposes of the body copy are to satisfy the curiosity of the reader, answer relevant questions about the brand, and persuade the reader to try the product. Littlefield and Kirkpatrick have suggested that good copy follows the pattern of a well-planned presentation and develops along a sequence of organized steps:

1. Recognize a buyer problem or a buyer desire. This recognition is usually made in the headline so as to get maximum attention of prospects. The problem or desire should be true to life and present the prospect's own experience.
2. Recommend the product being advertised as the best solution or best answer to the problem or desire. The emphasis here is on the product as a solution—not on the product itself. The problem or desire is still the major consideration.
3. Promise benefits and advantages. Spell out in adequate detail and in attractive terms the satisfaction to be had.
4. Personalize these benefits and advantages if possible. Reassure the reader that the satisfactions to be had are available to *him,* that he will benefit *personally,* that the satisfactions are designed for *his* situation and for *his* circumstances. Specific information is especially helpful here.
5. Offer proof of the advantages claimed, the benefits claimed, and the benefits promised.
6. Ask for action. Be absolutely and completely clear to the reader about what he is to do. Tell him *where* the product can be found and its *price* if those bits of information are appropriate. If there is a particular reason why the reader should act now, include it.[16]

Not all copy performs all of these steps in the same way. Nonetheless, good copy carries out the spirit of these suggestions. To a large extent, the content of the copy is determined by the headline which, in turn, flows from the central idea upon which the advertisement is based. Consider the following Purex copy.

16. James E. Littlefield and C.A. Kirkpatrick, *Advertising, Mass Communication in Marketing* (Boston: Houghton Mifflin Company, 1970), p. 178.

The headline makes a statement about the product benefit. The body copy amplifies this statement in clear, understandable terms.

Headline: (interest)	Even in cold water there's one sure way to whiten and disinfect.
Body copy:	Use Purex Bleach. Because hot water or cold, hard-working Purex Bleach does so many things that need to be done.
(benefits (personalize)	It whitens. It helps keep clothes from getting dingy. It helps you handle really tough laundry stains. It deodorizes everything in the wash. And it disinfects. Even in cold water, Purex Bleach kills germs and bacteria.
(proof)	Our Purex symbol promises you good, honest value—and that is what Purex Bleach delivers, in the laundry and all around the house. Try it.
(ask for action)	And get things Purex clean.

Note that in this instance the "proof" is simply the reputation of the company—"Our Purex symbol promises you good, honest value."

The Minolta XG–7 (figure 13–11) is somewhat different from the Purex ad. The headline arouses interest by suggesting that "easy to use" competitive cameras aren't all that easy to use. The body copy then identifies eleven reasons why the Minolta XG–7 *is* easy to use. Proof consists of explanatory copy elaborating each of these reasons. Personalization is woven throughout the body copy. The ad concludes with an invitation to "Try the Minolta XG–7," and encourages readers to see a Minolta at the nearest photo dealer or to write to the company.

There is no magic formula for writing body copy, just as there is no magic formula for writing headlines or preparing illustrations. The body copy must always be tailored to the demands of the idea that lies behind the advertisement and must be coordinated with the headline and illustration.

Classifications of Body Copy

As in the case of illustrations, body copy can be classified in a variety of ways such as *reason-why copy,*

Figure 13–11. Minolta

SOME OF THE NEW COMPACT, AUTOMATIC CAMERAS SEEM VERY EASY TO USE. UNTIL YOU START USING THEM.

There's more to an easy-to-use camera than automatic exposure. Yet that's what most of the new 35mm reflex cameras are: automatic, but hard to use.

Here's why the Minolta XG-7 makes fine photography both automatic *and* easy.

It's easy to take perfectly exposed pictures. Just point, focus and shoot. The electronic shutter in the XG-7 sets itself automatically up to 1/1000th of a second.

But it's hard to take an over-exposed picture. On automatic operation, the shutter locks to prevent over-exposures. It also locks when your batteries are too weak.

Easy focusing. The XG-7's viewfinder is big and bright, even in the corners. Your subject snaps into critical sharpness.

It's easy to be creative. You can make the automatic exposure setting brighter or darker for creative effects.

An easy-to-understand electronic viewfinder. Light emitting diodes tell how the XG-7 is setting itself and warn against under- or over-exposure.

An easy-to-see electronic self-timer. The self-timer lets you get into your own pictures. It's a large flashing light mounted on the front of the camera. The flashing speeds up to let you know when the picture is about to be taken.

An easier-to-use auto winder. It automatically advances film, as fast as two pictures a second. You attach the optional Auto Winder G without having to remove (or lose) any caps from the XG-7.

The easier-to-be-creative flash. The optional Minolta Auto Electroflash 200X synchronizes continuously with the winder. This feature allows you to take a sequence of up to 36 flash pictures in about 18 seconds.

The important "little" extras. The XG-7 has a window that shows when film is advancing properly. A memo holder holds the end of a film box as a reminder. There's even an optional remote control cord.

Fast, easy handling. The way a camera feels has a lot to do with how easy it is to use. Is it comfortable or awkward? Are the controls placed where your fingers naturally fall, or are they cramped together? The Minolta XG-7 is human engineered for comfort and smooth handling. It's quiet, with a solid feeling you find only in much more expensive equipment.

Easy-to-change lenses. Remove or attach lenses with less than a quarter turn. And a system of almost 40 different lenses, from fisheye to super-telephoto, makes the XG-7 a key to virtually unlimited creativity.

Try the Minolta XG-7. See it for yourself at your nearest photo dealer, or write for literature to Minolta Corporation, 101 Williams Drive, Ramsey, N.J. 07446. In Canada: Minolta Camera (Canada) Inc., Ontario.

EASY DOES IT.
MINOLTA XG7

human-interest copy, humerous copy, and so forth. However, the copywriter doesn't normally set out to write a particular kind of copy. Instead, he sets out with a clear understanding of the purpose of the advertisement, with a massive array of facts and information about this product and its uses, and with the basic questions: "How can I make this copy interesting?" "How can I make this copy persuasive?" "How can I make this copy believable?" When the job is done, then the copy can be classified as reason why, human interest, humerous, and so forth. Even copywriters are sometimes surprised with what they end up with. And, if they are satisfied with what they have done, the only things they know for sure is that it "feels right" and it does what it was supposed to do.

Reason-Why Copy. This is a broad classification of body copy that starts off with a consumer benefit or statement about the brand being advertised and explains why the statement or benefit is true. The Purex copy shown earlier fits easily into this classification. Sometimes, we think of reason-why copy as being a straightforward, unemotional recitation of facts about the product. But, it needn't be. The following example is reason-why copy, but it is other things as well. It is human interest; it is narrative; it is emotional; it is conversational; and it has quiet bits of humor tucked in here and there. It is an outstanding advertisement used by the Traveler's Insurance Company.

The Greatest Reason in the World

"Why did you buy life insurance?" I asked him.

"Well," he said, "it was because once I met a young person coming up the stairs of an apartment house with her arms full of packages, one of them dangling from a slender string. I didn't think she'd mind, so I offered to help her. At the door of her apartment, I saw that she was quite pretty. She still is.

"Because late one night, while she and I were waiting at a dimly lighted railway station for the Owl to take me home, I said, 'We could live on the money I'm spending for railroad fares! What do you say we try it?' We did, and it worked.

"Because one day I was offered a job by another company, and when I told my boss, he promised me ten dollars more a week if I'd stay. When I told *her* of the boss's generosity, she said, 'What do you mean, generous? If he knew you were worth that much to him, he should have paid it to you before he had to.' So I quit and took the new job.

"Because one night she woke me up and said, 'I think I'd better go.' We went, and the last I saw of her that night, she was being trundled down a long corridor in a wheelchair, in spite of her protests that she could walk. When I saw her the next morning, she was lying

very still and white with the sweetish smell of ether on her breath. A nurse came in and asked, 'Wouldn't you like to see him?' But I wasn't interested in babies just then—not even our own.

"Because one autumn evening, while we were driving leisurely along a country road, we came upon a small white cottage, its windows ablaze with the light of the setting sun. She said, 'What a place this would be for us!' Yes, what a place it has been for us!

"It's because of these memories, and many others that I wouldn't tell you and that wouldn't interest you even if I did, that I bought life insurance.

"And if the premiums could be paid in blood, instead of money, pernicious anemia would be a pleasure."

Moral: Insure in the Travelers. All forms of insurance. The Travelers Insurance Company, The Travelers Indemnity Company, The Travelers Fire Insurance Company, Hartford, Connecticut.

Copy like this is hard to write. That's one reason not much of it is seen. The copywriter has to be a bit of a playwrite. The copy is also long, but it enjoyed high readership.

Humorous Copy. Humorous copy is also difficult to do well, but there appears to be a trend toward the use of wry humor in advertising. Donald Herold, in a book called *Humor in Advertising,* defends the use of humor in the following way:

By humor in advertising I don't mean jokes.
I don't mean gags.
I don't mean gimmicks.
Maybe I don't even mean humor . . .
By humor in advertising, I mean a quiet and sensible and legitimate use of amusing copy and/or cartoons, or perhaps amusing illustrations or photographs, to do a job of merchandising—first by attracting attention in a relevant way, then by imparting pleasant information and making a soft sell, all in a mixed atmosphere of relaxation and integrity.[17]

Agency head Draper Daniels identifies four "rules" for using humor in advertising but suggests that these rules are only guides until the copywriter acquires the experience and judgment that makes them unnecessary.

1. In most cases humor is better for selling a low-priced product than it is for selling a high-priced one.
2. Humor is an effective way to put new life and memorability into an old story.
3. Humor is effective in telling a simple story in a memorable manner.

17. Donald Herold, *Humor in Advertising* (New York: McGraw-Hill Book Company, Inc., 1963), p. 1.

4. Humor is effective in driving home the ridiculousness of an outmoded practice which militates against the use of a new product or method. [18]

The Volkswagen bug made a good use of humor in its attacks on both the size and yearly model changes of American cars. Maytag uses humor effectively in its story of the Maytag repairman—"The loneliest man in town." And the Leo Burnette Agency developed the following copy for Del Maiz Niblets Corn:

1. A very wealthy man had once forgotten everything about his early life except the name of the town he came from.
2. He had not given a thought to his dear mother for twenty years, being too busy stacking up the shekels.
3. One night his cook sprang a new one on him. It looked like a dishful of gold. It had a big glob of butter melting on it. He took a helping and tasted—lo! it was "Corn-on-the-cob-without-the-cob." It was Del Maiz Niblets Corn.
4. That big-kerneled, tender corn made scenes of his boyhood flash before his eyes. The old home. His mother standing over the washtub. The red-checkered table cloth. The big platter of sweet, golden ears of corn he used to love.
5. The man ate and reminisced—and vice versa. He was a boy again. So the very next morning he dropped his mother a postcard with a picture of Radio City on it.

Humor is not applicable to all products, and may be offensive in some instances. Serious problems, illness, misfortune, and death are obviously inappropriate for humorous treatment. At one point, I was involved in a test of humorous copy for a diet food product. The copy bombed out, dismally. We quickly learned that dieting is not funny to people who are overweight.

Testimonial Copy.   Body copy written in the form of a personal testimony can often provoke interest and be highly persuasive, provided the reader can identify with the individual giving the testimony. Professional athletes in a variety of fields are often used to give expert testimony in support of a brand. Often, celebrities with no particular expertise are used to attract attention and gain brand acceptance. Indiscriminate use of celebrities, however, may give rise to incredulity on the part of readers. It is difficult to believe that a leading actress keeps her hands soft and smooth by washing dishes with a particular brand of soap. As a consequence, testimonials should be given by someone who is relevant, and with whom readers can easily associate the brand being advertised.

The following body copy from an Avon advertisement demonstrates this point. The purpose of the advertisement is to recruit Avon representatives. The spokeswoman is Cynthy Gravitt, a housewife in Tustin, California.

"I'm not the aggressive type, and I'm shy about meeting new people. But selling Avon cosmetics really is a friendly business. My customers are happy to see me and make me feel welcome. It's amazing how much confidence I've built up since I became an Avon Representative.

And running my own business gives me so much freedom. I'm able to work Avon around my family life. If my son Chad gets a cold, I can be with him as long as he needs me. That's the beauty of being your own boss.

All in all, Avon has made a beautiful difference in my life. It keeps me fresh and young. I'm more conscious of the way I look. And I've made a lot of new friends. Best of all, Avon has taught me I can just be myself, and everything else falls right into place."

If Cynthy Gravitt's story interested you, why not find out how *you* can become an Avon Representative. Simply call 800–325–6400 (toll free) and someone from Avon will be in touch with you as soon as possible to answer all your questions. Of course, there is no obligation.

There are, of course, other forms that body copy can take: conversational, descriptive, question and answer, and so forth. The form is not as important as the content. If there is nothing worthwhile to say in the body copy, then the advertisement is better off without it.

Length of Copy

Generally speaking, short copy will attract more readers than long copy. This is true because long copy spells work insofar as the reader is concerned. But, if readers are interested in a product, they will often read long copy avidly in search of more information. One of the greatest mistakes the copywriter can make is to leave out relevant information purely for the sake of avoiding long copy.

Sometimes, illustrations and headlines make long copy unnecessary. Marlborough advertising is a case in point. The picture *is* the idea behind Marlborough. Body copy is not necessary because there is nothing more to say. On the other hand, long copy is sometimes necessary to develop key selling points, to tell the product story, or to establish a mood. The only sound advice on length of copy can be summed up in

18. Draper Daniels, "Humor in Advertising," in *The Copywriter's Guide,* Elbrum Rochford French, ed. (New York: Harper & Row, Publishers, 1959).

two admonitions: (1) try to keep it brief, but don't sacrifice relevant content for the sake of brevity; (2) say what you have to say, then shut up.

Guidelines for Writing Body Copy

There are no hard and fast rules for writing body copy, but there are some guidelines that may be useful to the novice copywriter.

Make the First Paragraph of the Body Copy Short and Interesting. The first paragraph, after all, is the reader's introduction to the body copy. Unless this introduction is worthwhile and provocative there is little incentive to procede further. Consider these examples:

> Now you can make Chinese-style fried rice in less time than it takes to cook ordinary rice. (Minute Rice)

> Puppies, like babies, have special nutritional needs. But, unlike a baby, a puppy does 90% of his growing and developing in only one year. (Gaines Puppy Choice)

> Sears Superplush towels are Sears' thickest towels. As thick as towels that usually cost much more. (Sears)

> Let's say you are looking for a new car. And, just for the sake of argument, let's also suppose that, like many people, you're in the market for a mid-size. (Buick Regal)

Each of these examples invites the reader to continue reading because each provides some information and implies that more is forthcoming.

If the Copy Is Long, Open It Up with Captions or White Space between Paragraphs. Closely set, densely packed copy can be foreboding. The use of captions to separate copy blocks helps make long copy less formidable. The Glenfiddich advertisement in figure 13–12 is an example of this technique.

Keep the Copy Simple. Although copy may be written at different levels of sophistication for different audiences (the vocabulary used for an advertisement in *Junior Scholastic* will differ from the vocabulary used in an advertisement for the *New Yorker*), the presentation of ideas should be clear and easily understood. Most ideas can be presented simply with a little effort. Jargon and telegraphese should be avoided. Ideally, copy should flow smoothly, containing no words that interrupt the reader's train of thought. Few consumers have advanced degrees in

English literature, and it is unreasonable to expect the remainder to keep a dictionary at hand while reading advertising.

Keep the Copy Concise. Every word in an advertisement should work. Excessive verbiage adds nothing to the persuasiveness of copy. The writer should get to his points quickly, without beating about the bush. However, conciseness should not be confused with brevity. *Brevity* refers to the length of the copy; if there are a number of points to be made, there is no way to make them with short copy. *Conciseness* refers to how directly each point is made. Consider the following copy for Christian Brothers' Sherry. It is spare, lean copy that makes its points simply and directly.

> There is a wine to enjoy after the dinner is over.
> Creamy. Smooth. Rich. This is a wine to serve with fruit and cheese, desserts, or to offer with coffee.
> Of course, many people enjoy its delicious flavor on other occasions as well. Whenever you serve it, you will always find the quality and care that is there in each bottle from the Christian Brothers Cellars.

Make the Copy Specific. Consumers are not interested in generalities. They read body copy to find out specifically what the product advertised will do for them. If an automobile battery is guaranteed to give forty-eight months service, say so. Don't say "It's long lasting." Contac's statement that its "600 tiny time pills give relief up to twelve hours" is a specific statement about product performance. Avoid empty superlatives, generalities, and platitudes. Be factual. It is all too easy to leap into the wild blue yonder of the meaningless statement. For example, a gasoline extolls the "joy of driving;" a beer promises, "know the joy of good living;" a whiskey informs us it's a "gift in good taste;" a tire is a "marvel of engineering;" and a liqueur is "splendor in a glass." An effective advertisement is one that says to the reader, "Buy this product and you will get these specific benefits."

Search for the Right Words. In chapter 11, reference was made to the connotative meanings of words. A word may produce a positive or negative effect quite different from its literal meaning. "Half empty" and "half full" have the same literal meaning, but the first phrase reflects concern; the second phrase does not. *Inexpensive* and *cheap* have quite different connotations. Few people object to belonging to a large organ-

Figure 13–12. William Grant & Sons, Ltd.

"Glenfiddich may have an acceptance not dissimilar from Rolls-Royce. Americans have the unique ability to identify the best in the world and acquire it, irrespective of price."

—from an interview with David Grant, Director, Wm. Grant & Sons, Ltd. Banffshire, Scotland—Distillers of world famous Glenfiddich Unblended Scotch

(You already may be enjoying the seductive hint of Glenfiddich® in your favorite blended Scotch!)

Good news for old friends

I have taken this advertisement to advise our many American friends of some good news.

Now, many of your better spirit shops have available, in limited supply, original Glenfiddich Unblended Single Malt Scotch Whisky.

Invitation to new friends

I wish also to invite those who have not yet tasted Glenfiddich while traveling abroad, to take advantage of this new opportunity. (You've probably enjoyed a hint of its dry fragrance in your favorite blended Scotch.)

How Glenfiddich became the world's most preferred unblended Scotch

Glenfiddich is sought by connoisseurs in over 150 countries because of its flavor and elegance. This single malt, unblended Scotch tastes superb 'neat' and retains its undiluted flavor over ice or with water, as well. This rare 10-year-old unblended single malt Scotch is still being created in the same distillery built by my great-grandfather in 1886 on the site of the Robbie Dubh Spring—well known then as now for the quality of its water.

The cognac of Scotch Whiskies? Yes.

Because of its pleasing dry fragrance, Glenfiddich is often served in a brandy inhaler after dinner. Perhaps of equal significance is its purchase in substantial amounts by some of Scotland's foremost distilleries to add its special fragrance to their famous Scotch blends. (So now you can enjoy *more* than the seductive hint of Glenfiddich you've probably found in your favorite blended Scotch.)

The only 'Distillery Bottled' Scotch in the Highlands

We have also continued another family tradition. As with the Continent's most cherished wines where perfection is maintained by close personal supervision at the chateaux where they are bottled, Glenfiddich is the *only* Highland distillery in *all* of the Highlands of Scotland that bottles its creation on the premises to ensure perfection in every drop.

Remarkably, the best-selling despite its price

As a source of undiminished pride, Glenfiddich has become the most preferred, best-selling unblended single malt Scotch in the world. This achievement came despite its costly process to create, which has made it one of the most expensive Scotches available. (Since we make only very small batches under constant personal supervision, this virtual hand craftsmanship has truly earned Glenfiddich the right of comparison with the famous Rolls-Royce* motor car.)

R.S.V.P.

I wish to extend my personal invitation to try Glenfiddich Single Malt Scotch Whisky. If your favorite spirit shop does not have Glenfiddich, please write directly to me for the addresses of those shops most convenient to you.

If you already appreciate the unique taste of Glenfiddich, I extend my personal invitation to apply for a complimentary membership in **The Academy of Malt Scotch Whisky.** By sending you a personalized, hand-inscribed scroll, the Academy bestows recognition that you are one of those knowledgeable individuals whose discriminating tastes demand the finest.

Simply write directly to me for your membership application to my American offices, c/o The Academy of Malt Scotch Whisky, 1271 Avenue of the Americas, Suite 3572F, N.Y., N.Y. 10020.

David E. Grant, Director
William Grant & Sons, Ltd.
The Glenfiddich Distillery,
Dufftown, Banffshire
Scotland

ization, but most people do object to being part of a bureaucracy. Usually, there is a right word to express a particular thought. Be dilligent in searching for that word.

Be Truthful. With all of their faults, consumers are not stupid. They are quick to spot the spurious, the frivolous claim. Say what you have to say honestly, and stick to the facts.

Make Every Advertisement a Complete Sales Pitch for the Product. It is unreasonable to expect consumers to read a series of advertisements to find out about a product. Their time is precious to them, and they have little interest in serialized copy.

LOGOS AND BRAND IDENTIFICATION

The final element of most print advertising is the logotype (logo), which identifies the brand and/or the advertiser. The logo may be a name, a trademark, a package, or some combination of these elements. Generally, the logo appears in the lower, right-hand corner of the page, although there is nothing inviolate about this position. Often, when the logo is a package, it may appear elsewhere in the advertisement as well. The point is that the logo should be sufficiently prominent so as to be easily seen, and should always be used so as to identify the advertiser and to facilitate recognition at point of sale.

SUMMARY

The chapter is devoted to the development of print advertising. There are no hard and fast rules about how an advertisement should be written. The major elements of a print advertisement are the headline, the illustration, the body copy, and the logo.

The headline is often considered the most important part of the advertisement because it is the most frequently read part of the ad. Optimal headline length is about six to twelve words. Several types of headlines are direct, indirect, news, question, and testimonial.

When using illustrations, the advertiser must consider functions, techniques, size, use of color, and types of illustrations frequently used. A checklist of the characteristics of effective illustrations may be helpful.

The purposes of body copy are to satisfy the curiosity of the reader, answer relevant questions about the brand, and persuade the reader to try the product. The particular type of body copy used will depend upon the purpose of the advertisement. Although brevity in body copy is desirable, relevant content should not be sacrificed in order to be brief. Finally, general guidelines for writing body copy are outlined.

Each ad has a logo or signature. The logo should always be used to identify the advertiser and to facilitate recognition at the point of sale when this latter point is a relevant consideration.

QUESTIONS

1. Identify the four major elements of a print advertisement, and indicate the purpose of each.
2. Distinguish between *direct* and *indirect* headlines. Find an example of each in current advertising.
3. Select a headline from a current advertisement, and express it in the following forms: (1) news; (2) question; (3) command; (4) testimonial; (5) benefit; and (6) comparison.
4. Select a headline from a current advertisement, and evaluate it in terms of the guidelines for an effective headline.
5. What are the primary functions of the illustration?
6. Select an illustration from a current advertisement, and evaluate it in terms of the primary functions of an illustration.
7. What do research findings indicate in terms of the size of the illustration?
8. Evaluate the use of color in print advertisements.
9. Summarize the functions of body copy.
10. Select a current advertisement, and analyze the body copy in terms of the functions it should perform.

LET'S FACE IT.
PLEDGE® MAKES
A BEAUTIFUL DIFFERENCE.

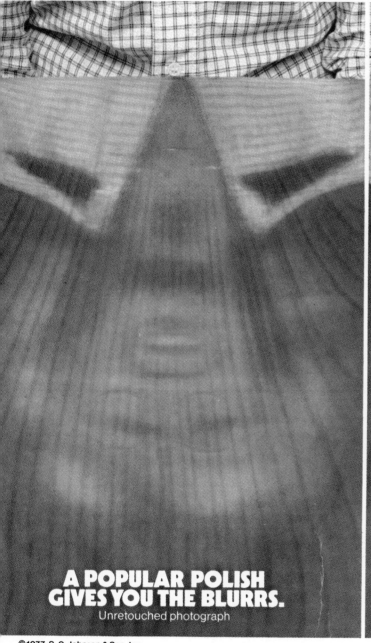

A POPULAR POLISH GIVES YOU THE BLURRS.
Unretouched photograph

PLEDGE® GIVES YOU THE BEAUTY.
Unretouched photograph

You're looking at unretouched proof that Pledge does more for the beauty of your furniture than any other polish. Because Pledge shines better.

See, the popular polish on the left gives you the Blurrs. It hides the natural beauty of the wood, because it doesn't have enough shine.

But, look on the right. When you dust with Pledge, you get a clearly more beautiful shine. So you get the beauty of the wood. Not the Blurrs.

Change to Pledge. It's for the better.

Lemon   **Natural Wood Scent**   **Regular**

GET THE BEAUTY. NOT THE BLURRS. EVERYTIME YOU DUST.

Plate 13-1. In this ad, the high-gloss table shows the benefits of a furniture wax (S. C. Johnson & Sons, Inc.).

"See how Shake'n Bake keeps chicken more moist and tender."

COATING MIX

Photograph is approx. 2 times actual size.

Fried chicken can be dry.
Baked chicken can be dry.
But chicken made with Shake'n Bake®
coating mix comes out more moist
and tender—because the crispy
coating seals in the juices.

"With Shake'n Bake® coating mix
you get crispy chicken at its tender best."

© General foods corporation 1977. Reproduced
with permission of General Foods Corporation.

Plate 13–2.

In this ad for Shake'n Bake, the photograph enhances the attractiveness of the food product (General Foods Corp.).

WHEN THE QUEEN OF ENGLAND
WANTED BONE CHINA FOR HER WEDDING,
SHE CHOSE AYNSLEY.

A timely investment
in a timeless art.
Free booklets.
Aynsley English Bone China,
225 Fifth Avenue,
New York 10010
The English member of
the Waterford Crystal family.
By hand. With heart.

Plate 13–3.

This Aynsley ad requires full color for best effect (Aynsley Bone China).

© 1976 Clairol Inc.

"Mother Nature gave me plain hair. I gave it pizazz."

Don't give up on plain hair. Give it a Frost & Tip® look. The kind of excitement you can't get with brush-on lighteners. Anything from a single streak to a full head of frosting. It's easy. And remember, you won't be changing your whole haircolor.

With Clairol's Frost & Tip, you can do terrific things for your hair. And you. And that's why it's the number one frosting kit.

Frost & Tip.
It's more than a look. It's a feeling.

Plate 13-4.   This Frost and Tip ad requires full color for best effect (Clairol, Inc.).

Armstrong Designer Solarian® with the richness of Inlaid Color.
As different from other no-wax floors as an oil painting is from a print.

No matter how fine a print is, it's still just a print—a reproduction of the original. An oil painting is built up layer on layer, shade on shade, creating depth and realism.

Armstrong's exclusive Inlaid-Color process gives Designer Solarian the same richness, depth of color, and realism of design as a painting . . . that quality of "an original" that no print can hope to achieve.

And because of its Mirabond® wear surface, Solarian keeps its sunny shine without waxing or buffing far longer than ordinary vinyl floors. The cleaner you keep it, the brighter it shines. Just sponge-mop with detergent, and rinse

thoroughly. If heavy-traffic areas eventually show some reduction in gloss, your retailer can supply a special Solarian Floor Finish which can be applied occasionally as needed to help maintain the shine.

For free color brochure and names of retailers, write Armstrong, 7705 Tock Street, Lancaster, Pa. 17604.

Armstrong

CREATORS OF ☐ THE INDOOR WORLD®

Plate 13–5.

The major purpose of this Solarian ad is to demonstrate the beauty of the tile (Armstrong Cork Co.).

Most blinds are made for windows...
Décor blinds are made for rooms.

Ask any good decorator.

No other window covering combines all the benefits of a one inch blind.

Open—they become virtually invisible.

Closed—they allow you complete privacy.

And inbetween, you're able to select any degree of softly-diffused sunlight.

But we think a window covering should do more than cover the glass. That's why we make Flexalum Décor Blinds—not just with your windows in mind—but with your walls, and floors, and furniture, and carpeting and everything else that makes your home your personal creation.

Décor Blinds come in 50 of the most popular colors. According to House & Garden, many of these colors are the ones you'll be decorating with this year.

And Flexalum Décor Blinds are the only blinds with a one inch headrail—leaving you more room for curtains and drapes.

Just check the Yellow Pages for your local representative of the slimmest blinds in the world.

Or ask us for a copy of Window Moods. (Please enclose 50¢ to cover postage and handling.) It's a complete guide on decorating with one inch blinds. From the people who introduced the first aluminum blind. Mail to: Hunter Douglas Inc. 20 Campus Rd., Totowa, N.J. 07512.

Flexalum
Décor Blinds

Plate 13–6.

This Flexalum ad not only shows the product in use, but demonstrates its functional value (Hunter Douglas, Inc.).

PROBLEM

R.D. Cline, Inc., a manufacturer of toiletries, has developed a competively priced men's hair grooming product to be advertised to the under twenty-five-year age group. The product is a clear, nongreasy, colorless, nonsticky grooming agent that is invisible on the hair. It provides excellent hair control while permitting the hair to appear natural to both look and touch. The product is a clear gel that is packaged in a tube. It differs from similar products in that it contains a harmless ingredient, Protex 5, that gives it superior hair control. The name selected for the product is Diablo. The copy strategy and copy plan are shown below.

Copy Strategy

1. Diablo men's hair dressing will be sold to men under the age of twenty-five on the basis of its superiority over competitive products in providing hair control while retaining the natural look.
2. This benefit is possible because of a harmless, invisible ingredient, Protex 5.
3. The overall mood of the advertising will be dashing romantic, and dynamic in order to attract the interest of, and appeal to, the target audience.
4. The product itself is a crystal clear, odorless gel that will be packaged in a plastic tube. Used sparingly (one or two dabs), it will provide hair control that improves the appearance of a man's hair. It washes out easily with a shampoo.

Copy Plan for Print Advertising

1. All magazine advertising will be built around an individual who will always be positioned as a highly masculine, sophisticated, romantic man who is successful in all of his activities . . . both business and personal.
2. The Diablo character, will have a scar on his right cheek, and he will always be shown in situations where he is totally in command.
3. He will always be shown involved in an activity of some type (business, racing, playing tennis, etc.), and he will be shown associated with beautiful women.
4. A large illustration will be used depicting Diablo and his activity.
5. The headline will emphasize the chief product benefit.
6. Body copy will develop key copy points and provide justification for product claims.
7. The product logo will always appear in the lower, right-hand corner of the ad.

You have just joined the agency creative group. Your group supervisor has given you the foregoing material and asked you to develop a magazine advertisement.

Assignment

1. Describe the illustration.
2. Write a headline.
3. Write body copy.

14

Design, Layout, and Mechanical Production

Design in print advertising refers to the way in which the elements of an advertisement are arranged in the space available. And, as often is the case in advertising, there is disagreement as to what constitutes the most effective design. Consider the following issues:

Picture-Headline Format

One point of view in advertising argues that the most effective design for an advertisement uses an "editorial" format, such as that usually employed by magazines, with a dominant illustration at the top of the page, followed by a headline, body copy, and logo. The Miss Clairol ad (plate 14–1 in insert following page 282) uses this design. Marplan, following an analysis of the Starch "noting" scores of 250,000 advertisements, supports this point of view.[1] Similar findings have been reported by other advertising research organizations.

Yet, an examination of advertisements in any current magazine will reveal that many ads violate this rule. Art directors often insist that the editorial

format places too many restrictions on the design of advertisements, that it hinders the creative expression of ideas, and that if all advertising followed this practice, it would result in a monotony of design that would make all advertising look alike—a consequence that is considered anathema in the advertising industry. Rudy Czufin, former art director of the Gardner Advertising Company, expressed his contempt for the editorial format by charging: "If that's good advertising design, you don't need an art director. All you need is a straightedge and a photograph."

Over-printing and Reverse Type

Two controversial practices that are widely used in contemporary advertising involve over-printing and reverse type. In *overprinting,* the headline and/or body copy is printed on the illustration instead of being segregated from it. True, this practice economizes on space and permits the use of a larger illustration. It also gives greater flexibility in arranging elements in an ad. It may even help draw attention to the headline, and some headlines need all of the help they can get. Nonetheless, on the basis of its research, Gallup-Robinson cautions against this practice, and

---

1. Donald Wayne Hendon, "How Mechanical Factors Affect Ad Perception," *Journal of Advertising Research* (August, 1973): 39–43.

Ogilvy states that it reduces the attention value of advertisements by an average of 19 percent.[2]

A probable reason for these research results is that over-printing tends to clutter up the illustration, reducing its clarity and communication value. As a result, the headline and illustration compete for attention. Opponents of over-printing argue that, in a well-constructed advertisement, the illustration and headline should never compete; instead they should complement each other. Critics of over-printing have suggested that admakers should take their cue from editors of newspapers and magazines. Editors seldom hide their illustrations behind their headlines, and it is the practices of magazine and newspaper editors that shape the reading habits of consumers.

The second controversial practice, that of using *reverse type,* is particularly prevalent in contemporary advertising. Reverse type is printing the headline and/or body copy in white against a dark background instead of following conventional practices and using black type on a white background. A probable reason for the widespread use of reverse type is the growing tendency to use larger illustrations. If the illustration fills the entire advertising space available (as it often does) over-printing must be used. And, if the illustration uses dark colors, the advertising designer has little choice but to use reverse type in order for the headline and copy to be read.

Again, critics of this practice deplore it, often pointing to research findings to support their criticism. They also argue that consumers are unaccustomed to reading reverse type since books, magazines, and newspapers do not use it. They further contend that the effect of using reverse type is "arty," and signals to the reader that the communication is just another ad. In a book titled *How to Advertise,* Kenneth Roman and Jane Maas point out that although reverse type may look attractive, it reduces readership. As an example, they refer to the Save the Children Foundation, which used a reverse plate (white type on a black background) in soliciting funds. When the organization tested black type on a white background (the conventional way of printing) contributions increased 65 percent.[3]

Coupons

Traditionally, advertisements that include a consumer coupon place the coupon in the lower-right-hand cor-

ner of the ad. In their admonitions to admakers, Roman and Maas suggest that the advertiser who is planning a coupon ad should request a right-hand-page position and place the coupon in the lower-right-hand corner where it can easily be torn out. Ogilvy, on the other hand, says: "When your advertisement is to contain a coupon, and you want maximum returns, put it at the top, bang in the middle. This position pulls 80 percent more coupons than the traditional outside-bottom of the page."[4]

With such conflicting advice it is little wonder that the designers of ads often find themselves in a quandary and usually throw counsel to the winds by doing what seems right to them. There are a number of reasons why conflicting practices in advertising are rampant. First, the basic strength of a good advertisement lies in the idea behind it. If the idea is strong, this strength can overcome many of the limitations of a weak presentation. But if the idea behind the ad is weak, there is not much that good advertising design can do except reveal the idea's weakness by drawing attention to it. Second, different ideas may well require different treatments. The design that works well for one idea may be poorly adapted for another. Third, even poor designs sometimes have redeeming features. A powerful headline or compelling illustration may overcome the inadequacies of an awkward design. Fourth, most research studies that draw generalizations about advertising design are based on large numbers of ads—some of which are well read, some poorly read, and some indifferent. These studies do not conclude that a particular design should *never* be used. They only conclude that, on the average, certain design features *tend* to be more effective than others. Fifth, most research studies of advertising design are based on *general* readership rather than on readership by target audiences. An ad that is poorly read by the general public may still have high readership by those consumers who represent key prospects.

It is this ambiguity that makes advertising design a complex undertaking, and leads to the conclusion that effective advertising is more of an art than a science.

DESIGN CONSIDERATIONS

Three terms that are sometimes used ambiguously in advertising design are *visualize, layout,* and *design.* To visualize refers to the mental picture that a copywriter or art director has of an advertisement before

2. David Ogilvy, *Confessions of an Advertising Man* (New York: Atheneum, 1964), p. 125.
3. Kenneth Roman and Jane Maas, *How to Advertise* (New York: St. Martin's Press, 1976), p. 36.

4. Ogilvy, *Confessions,* p. 125.

anything is put on paper. In the process of developing an idea, and as the idea starts to take shape, its originator begins to imagine or visualize how the advertisement will look in its final form. Sometimes this visualization is quite specific; other times it is fairly general because there are many details that have to be worked out. It is this "picture in the mind" that is the starting point for getting something down on paper.

The term *layout* is an advertising colloquialism both as a verb and a noun. As a verb, it refers to the actual process or steps that are involved in translating the admaker's idea into a finished product. As a noun, it is the result of this process. Thus, an art director may say, "I have to layout an ad," referring to work to be done. Or, she might say, "This is a layout of the idea we discussed," referring to the result of work that has been done. The term itself is a contraction of the phrase, "laying out the elements of an advertisement." (*Layout* will be discussed later in the chapter.) In the layout process, the art director starts arranging and rearranging the elements of the advertisement on paper until a satisfactory *design* is obtained.

The *design* of an advertisement is the final result of visualization as developed and modified through a number of layouts.

Space Units

There are certain pragmatic considerations that, ultimately, influence the final design of the advertisement. One of these, the space unit available, is often influenced by budget considerations. If the advertisement can afford a two-page spread, the art director has more flexibility than if she is forced to work within the constraints of a single page, a half page, or even a single column. Further, some page and multiple page advertisements are *bleed* ads, which means that the illustration extends beyond the normal margins to the edge, or *trim line,* of the page. In a two-page spread, the advertisement may bleed across the gutter; that is, the illustration and/or type may run across the center binding (gutter) of the magazine. Still other advertising units are gatefolds—double and triple pages that fold out to reveal one advertisement; or dutch doors, pages that partially cover each other to lend interest, or to create a particular effect.

The following three plates in the insert following p. 282 demonstrate some of the most frequently used page and multiple page units. Plate 14–2, for Smirnoff, is a conventional page unit in which the illustration and print areas are surrounded by white, "trim" space. The Charlie ad (plate 14–3) is a double-page, bleed ad that bleeds across the gutter. The Le Car ad (plate 14–4) is a single-page, bleed ad.

Since nonconventional page units generally carry a premium price, their use frequently stumbles against the harsh reality of the advertising budget. A single-page, bleed ad, for example, usually costs 15–20 percent more than a standard page.

Major consumer magazines usually offer a variety of page units. They may range from gatefolds and dutch doors to both vertical and horizontal fractional pages, as well as other unusual units. The point is that the art director must always work within the confines of the space units available and affordable, regardless of what she would like to do.

TYPES OF DESIGNS

There are any number of ways in which the elements of an advertisement may be laid out in a major space unit of one page or more. Leon Quera has identified four basic designs which he has titled: *picture and words, open contrast, vertical sequence,* and *multiple block.*[5] These formats differ in (1) the size and number of illustrations used, (2) the extent to which white space is incorporated in the ad to provide contrast for the printed material, (3) whether multiple illustrations are arranged in a vertical, horizontal, or block sequence, (4) and the particular way that headlines, illustrations, body copy, and logo are arranged in the space. The particular design used, however, is important only insofar as it dramatizes or fails to dramatize the main idea on which the advertisement is based. In some instances, a single, dominant illustration is desirable; in other instances, a sequence of illustrations may be employed to tell a picture story of how the product is used, or of its benefits. The main point that the ad designer should keep in mind, however, is that the design should *always* be subordinated to the idea being communicated. After all, the purpose of design is to focus attention on the idea, not dominate it. Most advertising practitioners are highly critical of advertising designed as art without consideration of its business function, and Rosser Reeves suggests that we should always be suspicious of such advertising because it usually obscures the product message.[6]

CHARACTERISTICS OF EFFECTIVE DESIGN

Although there are many ways in which a print advertisement may be designed, good designs have several

5. Leon Quera, *Advertising Campaigns: Formulation and Tactics* (Columbus, Ohio: Grid, Inc., 1973), pp. 164–67.
6. Rosser Reeves, *Reality in Advertising* (New York: Alfred A. Knopf, 1961), pp. 122–23.

things in common. Some of the more important characteristics of effective design are identified below.

Focal Point

A well-designed ad has a single focal point that attracts the consumer's attention. The focal point is generally the headline or illustration. It draws the reader into the ad and provides a logical place to start. A cluttered design with several focal points often appears confusing, spells work to the reader, and reduces reader interest.

Movement

Movement refers to the way in which the attention of the reader flows from one element of the advertisement to another. An effective design generally has a dominant or logical starting point (the focal point), and is so constructed that the reader's gaze is drawn successively through the major elements of the ad. A number of devices may be used to obtain this effect.

A Logical Sequence of Elements. Most readers of advertising have, through constant exposure to magazine and newspaper editorial material, become accustomed to proceeding from the top down and from left to right. Because of our experience, this method of presentation seems logical. Thus, advertisements laid out along these lines are easy to read and (according to readership studies) tend to enjoy higher than average readership. The Shake 'n Bake ad (plate 13–2 in insert following page 234) follows this design. The dominant appetite appeal photograph is the focal point, or starting place for the ad. The reader's gaze flows easily through the headline, package, body copy, to the slogan at the bottom of the page.

Pointing Devices. Hands, arrows, lines, blocks of type, numbers, and so forth can also be used to lead the attention of readers from one part of the advertisement to another in a sequential fashion. In the Shake 'n' Bake advertisement, for example, the chef is pointing to the package. The Eastman Adhesive advertisement (figure 14–1) uses numbers to direct eye-flow. And, while this advertisement contains many elements, the numbering device helps the reader to sort out, and dwell on each of them.

Gaze motion. Research studies, as well as our everyday experience, show that eyes direct other eyes. Gaze motion involves placing persons or animals in such a way that they are looking toward an important element of the advertisement. Although this device is not widely used, the KitchenAid advertisement (plate

14–10, insert following p. 282) uses this approach to (1) focus attention on the product being advertised, and (2) draw attention downward into the ad and toward the body copy.

Clarity of Presentation

It is the responsibility of the art director to see that the elements of the advertisement work together to give a single, unified impression. This becomes particularly important when the advertisement contains a number of design elements, such as several illustrations. Although the Ivory Liquid ad (figure 14–2), contains several illustrations, it does not violate this principle.

Simplicity

Simplicity in design sounds easy, but it is often difficult to accomplish. It is usually violated by trying to include too many elements or ideas in a single communication. Often, the use of a variety of type faces to attract attention or highlight copy points or printing headlines and body copy in different colors creates unnecessary complexity. The ad designer should always remember that reading advertisements is not a major preoccupation in the lives of consumers. Few consumers will waste time on an ad that appears unduly complex.

Arrangement of Headlines

Headlines, particularly long headlines, often need to be arranged to facilitate reading. This can often be done by grouping words in meaningful sequences, on different lines. Take the following heading from a Pledge ad, for example:

LET'S FACE IT. PLEDGE MAKES A BEAUTIFUL DIFFERENCE

Although the headline is not particularly long (only eight words) its readability is enhanced by breaking it up into three lines, as it actually appeared:

LET'S FACE IT.
PLEDGE MAKES
A BEAUTIFUL DIFFERENCE

Or, the following, longer headline for Maybelline:

This remarkable makeup gives you a fresh look that *stays* fresh all day.

Written in this form, it is fairly formidable, and difficult to grasp. However, as it actually appeared, it was broken up into three distinct, easily graspable thoughts:

Here's the adhesive you can count on.

1 One drop of Eastman 910® adhesive can hold up to 2½ tons.

2 And it forms strong bonds in just seconds to minutes.

3 With a variety of materials like rubber, metal, glass, most plastics, ceramic and hardwood.

4 Or combinations of these to one another.

GLASS RUBBER RUBBER
GLASS RUBBER
METAL PLASTIC

5 The least Eastman 910 adhesive that will cover the area to be bonded works best—one drop per square inch is usually about right.

6 And there's seldom any need for clamps or holding devices other than simple fingertip pressure.

7 This remarkable adhesive has been proven in industrial use for nearly 20 years.

8 Eastman 910® adhesive, the tool in a tube, is available in stores nationwide.

910 One drop is stronger than you are.

Eastman Chemical Products, Inc. Plastics Products Division
Kingsport, Tennessee 37662

Kodak

Figure 14-2.   (Procter & Gamble)

This remarkable makeup
gives you a fresh look
that *stays* fresh all day.

TYPES OF LAYOUTS

As pointed out earlier, the term *layout* is a contraction of the phrase, "laying out the elements of ad advertisement." Thus, it is both an object in itself, as well as the process for developing the final design of the advertisement.

As an object, the layout begins as a rough, preliminary sketch of how the admaker visualizes the ad. As a process, it often moves through a number of successive stages, with elements of the ad being modified and shifted around until a satisfactory design is obtained. Before starting a layout, the artist usually has a tentative headline, a good idea of how much space will be required for body copy, and general agreement on the subject matter of the illustration. There are several stages in the layout process, some of which may be omitted in the development of a particular ad. The major layout stages are: *thumbnail sketches, rough layout, finished layout, comprehensive,* and *working layout.*

Thumbnail Sketches

Frequently, the artist begins with a number of small, rough sketches of possible layouts. These sketches are usually about one-eighth to one quarter the size of the finished ad, and provide a quick and convenient way of getting different design ideas down on paper. The

Figure 14-1.   (Eastman Chemical Products, Inc.)

headline and illustrations are roughed in, and the location of the logo and body copy are indicated. The artist may prepare two, three, or several thumbnail sketches before arriving at one that holds promise for further development. Plate 14–5 (insert following p. 282) shows six thumbnail sketches for a magazine advertisement for Kellogg Company.

Rough Layout

In the second step of the layout process, the thumbnail sketch or sketches selected for further development are roughed out in the actual size in which they will appear. For example, if the advertisement is to appear in *Woman's Day, Time,* or a similar sized magazine, the rough layout will measure 7 1/16 inches wide and 10 inches deep. Some artists prefer to start with a rough layout, bypassing the thumbnail sketch stage. Whether or not you begin with thumbnail sketches or a rough layout largely depends on personal preference, and how clearly the advertisement is visualized prior to the layout stage. One or several rough layouts may be prepared. Rough layouts are crude. Illustrations are hastily sketched; headlines are roughed in; body copy is indicated by wavy lines. But these crude layouts help the experienced eye to evaluate the appearance of the final ad. A rough layout, developed from one of the thumbnail sketches for Kellogg Company is shown in plate 14–6 (insert following p. 282).

Finished Layout

The next stage is the preparation of a finished layout. The finished layout is much more detailed and carefully drawn than the rough layout. The style of the illustration is indicated; headlines are carefully lettered as they will appear in the final advertisement; the logotype is carefully executed; and body copy is neatly ruled in lines and blocks of copy of varying lengths to indicate indentation and paragraphs. The finished layout is virtually a facsimile of the finished ad. It is this layout that is generally shown to the client for approval. A finished layout of the Kellogg Company's ad is shown in plate 14–7 (insert following p. 282).

Finished layouts are usually mounted on cardboard and covered with cellophane when being presented for approval. This is a common practice, but it is probably a bad one. A layout should be designed for the publication or publications in which the advertisement will appear. Its design should be compatible with the graphic appearance of these publications. As a consequence, a layout can best be evaluated when it is pasted in the publication. That's the way consumers see it—not as a piece of art, mounted for hanging in a private gallery. And, that's the way it should be seen prior to its final approval.

Working Layouts

Working layouts, sometimes referred to as *mechanicals, keylines,* or *paste-ups,* are not actually layouts. Instead, they are "blueprints" for production. The working layout indicates the exact placement of all of the elements in the ad, specifies type face and size, and includes relevant instructions for the typographer and engraver. The final advertisement is prepared from the working layout. The finished ad for the Kellogg Company example is shown in plate 14–8 (insert following p. 282).

PRINT PRODUCTION

The production of print advertising is handled by specialists in the advertising agency, and by outside suppliers. Nonetheless, anyone who works closely with advertising—agency account executives and supervisors, client product managers and advertising personnel, sales promotion managers, and so forth—should have at least a rudimentary knowledge of advertising production.

The job of the print production department in an advertising agency is to work with the creative groups in translating the working layout into the finished advertisement. In carrying out this function, the production department selects suppliers, instructs them, and reviews their work to make sure that it meets agency standards. Type specification is often handled by the production department in consultation with the art director, or it may be handled by a type specialist (typecaster) who is a member of the art department.

THE PRODUCTION PROCESS

After an advertisement has been approved, a series of production operations still have to be performed. The design and size of type are specified, and a typographer sets the type to fit the working layout. "Type proofs" are returned to the agency for correction and/ or approval. Art work or photographic material for the illustration and other graphic elements of the advertisement are sent to the engraver, along with instructions on size, screen, the type of engravings to be made, and other specifications. The job of the engraver is to reproduce as faithfully as possible the photographs or art work. Some colors are difficult to reproduce with modern inks and high-speed presses, and some black and white photographs lack enough contrast for good reproduction. As a consequence, it is usually desirable to discuss any potential problems with the engraver and make needed modifications *proofs* are approved, they are sent along with the engravings to the typographer. The typographer assembles them in a form with the type, following the specifications on the working layout. Proofs of the completed advertisement are then made for final approval and correction, and *printing plates* or *mats* (matrices) are made for shipment to the media.

This procedure describes the basic steps in the production of advertisements printed by the *letterpress* process, a process which will be described later in the chapter. Many publications, however, use *offset lithography* or *gravure* processes instead of letterpress. For these processes, the medium is supplied with a paste-up, or *camera ready* copy instead of printing plates. Line artwork and proofs of type are cemented into the exact positions in which they are to appear in the final ad. They are then photographed and *line negatives* are obtained. Photographs and other continuous-tone art are usually submitted separately. This material is photographed through a screen and stripped into position with the line negatives. The stripped-in negatives are used by the publications to make offset and gravure printing plates. In all printing processes, however, each step needs to be carefully proofed and corrected in order to assure accuracy and quality reproduction.

PRODUCTION SCHEDULING

Advertising is a business of deadlines. The *closing date* (the date by which print advertising material must be received by the publication) ranges from a few days before publication date for newspapers to two or three months for consumer magazines. This means that creative work must often start several months before the publication date of the magazine in which the advertisement is to appear. The following production schedule is typical for a four-color advertisement appearing in a monthly, consumer magazine:

Date of issue	September
On sale date	August 15
Closing date	July 10
Plates must be shipped by	July 5
Engravings go to electrotyper	July 1
Engraver should deliver final proof	June 26
Engraver should have first proof	June 21
Material should go to engraver	June 4
Art and mechanical layout should be ready by	May 28
Type and mechanical layout should be ordered by	May 22
Finished artwork should be delivered by	May 21
Finished artwork should be ordered by	May 1
Creative work should be approved by	April 31
Creative work should start by	April 10

In this example, over four months elapse between the time the creative work starts and the time the magazine carrying the ad appears on the newsstand. This schedule assumes that there are no delays and that everything happens on schedule, which it seldom does. Few ads proceed from conception to appearance without at least one emergency. If the advertisement is running behind schedule and the closing date can't be met, the order can usually be cancelled anytime before the closing date. In the case of back cover positions and unusual space units, however, the cancellation date may be as much as three months prior to the closing date. Cancellations resulting from failure to meet production schedules do little to build client confidence in its agency. As a consequence, they are considered a major tragedy (on about the scale of World War II) by agencies. If the agency is running only a few days behind schedule, extensions of the closing date can usually be obtained by calling the production manager of the publication for which the advertisement is intended.

Since advertising is often prepared on tight schedules, a production order is issued to keep it on track. A sample production order (often referred to as a *requisition*) is shown in figure 14–3. Armed with the production order, the traffic department of the agency shepherds the advertisement through its various stages.

TYPOGRAPHY

Typography refers to both the selection and arrangement of type. There are many varieties of type, differing both in style (type face) and size, which can be used to create different effects. Some type faces are delicate and feminine; others are bold and masculine. Some are modern; some old fashioned. Some are easy to read; some difficult. Since readability is a prerequisite for advertising, difficult-to-read type faces are used sparingly, usually to create a special effect. Generally speaking, *lower case* type (small letters) is easier to read than *upper case* type (capital letters).

Type Groups

There are over a thousand different type faces, with new faces being created all of the time. Many of these

LEO BURNETT U.S.A.
A DIVISION OF LEO BURNETT COMPANY, INC.

PRINT REQUISITION   JOB NO. M- 53883

AD NO. __M-3483B__   ESTIMATE NO. _____

COMPANY 10	CLIENT Kellogg Company	MEDIA PMG					EST JOB $
PRODUCT(S) Various	PROD CODE 999	YEAR F'77	JOB START DATE 1/25/77	EST COMPL DATE 12/31/77			SHIPPING

DESCRIPTION (AD SIZE, COLOR, TITLE, PUBLICATIONS)	HOLD	OPEN	TYPE	KIND OF BILLING	TAXES (OOP-BL)
Thought Leader Series	☐ YES ☒ NO	☒ YES ☐ NO	☒ BL ☐ UB ☐ UD	☒ A (AS INC) ☐ C (COMPL JOB) ☐ Q (QUOTE)	EST COST (OOP-UB) 100
"A good breakfast..."					
	CLIENT I.D.			MONTH OF APPL	EST COMM (FEE) 20

BY PS MGR Bob Kubis	DATE 1/25/77	COMM %	BILL ADD 010	A/S 02	JOB GROUP 740680	EST TOTAL

COPY REQUEST

Per _____   Memo dated _____

Copy Due _____

LAYOUT REQUEST   ☐ NSP   ☐ MAG   ☐ OTHER _____

☐ Rough
☐ Comprehensive

Layout Due _____

FINISHED ART

☐ Complete assembly
☐ Illustration
  ☐ B/W   ☐ Color
☐ Photography
  ☐ Retouching
  ☐ Line drawing
  ☐ Halftone drawing
☐ Prints
☐ Lettering
☐ Color swatches
☐ Record stat by Studio
☐ Slides

Art Due _____

PRODUCTION

☐ Composition
☐ LP Engraving(s)   ☐ Cronars
☐ Repro material _____
☐ Offset material
☐ Gravure material
☐ _____ Client reprints
☐ Electros
☐ Quantity proofs _____
☐ Cromalin
☐ Press proofs

NEWSWEEK
Eastern Region   5/2
Chicago   5/9
Los Angeles   5/9
San Francisco   5/9
Atlanta-Dallas   5/23

TIME
Chicago   5/9
Atlanta   5/9
Dallas   5/9
Los Angeles   5/9
San Francisco   5/9

TIME (cont)
Eastern Region 5/30

US NEWS & WORLD REPORT
Eastern Region 5/16
Chicago   5/23
Los Angeles   5/23
San Francisco   5/23
Atlanta   5/30
Dallas   5/30

BUSINESS WEEK
Northeastern
Region 5/2

NATIONAL GEOGRAPHIC
Eastern Region 5/1

NUTRITION TODAY
May/June

Production Due _____

Form No. 9-54   5 76

— TERMINAL/BUDGET CONTROL —

Figure 14-3. Production Order

type faces are similar enough in appearance to be regarded as a group. Although there is no agreement as to how many groups there are, the following broad classifications are widely used: *roman, block, cursive* or *script,* and *ornamental.* These groups are often divided into subgroups, but for our purposes, consideration of these major groups is sufficient.

Roman. The most popular type group is roman. This group probably contains a larger number of designs than any of the other three groups. The two most distinguishing features of roman type are: (1) the small lines, or *serifs,* that cross the ends of the main strokes, and (2) variations in the thickness of the strokes themselves.

This line is set in roman.

Roman type, of course, varies in size and contains a number of subclassifications that vary in terms of: (1) the thickness of the strokes, (2) the amount of variation in the thickness of the strokes, and (3) the size and regularity of the serifs.

Block. The block-letter type is sometimes referred to as *gothic, sans serif, contemporary,* or *uniform strokes.* It also has two distinguishing characteristics: (1) the lines forming the strokes are of uniform thickness, and (2) it lacks serifs (hence the name, sans serif).

This line is set in block.

There is a form of type called *square serif* that is generally classified as a block type, although it is a combination of block and roman. Like block type, the lines forming the strokes are of uniform thickness. However, like roman, it has serifs, although the serifs have the same thickness and weight of the main strokes. Block type is somewhat less readable than roman because of the uniform width of the strokes in the type face, and because of the general lack of serifs. Nonetheless, the simple, clean lines of block type give it a modern appearance that is often desirable in advertising. For this reason, it is widely used.

Cursive or Script. The cursive, or script, group includes a number of type faces that resemble handwriting. Although script is attractive, it is somewhat difficult to read.

This line is set in script.

In some varieties of this group, the letters appear to be joined together; in others, they are discrete. Script conveys a feeling of formality and femininity but, be-

cause it is less readable than roman or block, it is generally used sparingly in advertising. Its use is generally restricted to emphasizing names and short phrases.

Ornamental. The final major group of type faces includes a large number of designs that do not fit into any of the foregoing classifications. Although these type designs differ widely in appearance, they are all ornamental or decorative in nature.

This line is set in ornamental.

Some of these designs are extremely difficult to read and, when used, are selected to create an atmosphere—a feeling of antiquity, mystery, another culture, or a different era.

Type Families

There are type families within each of the major type groups. A type family consists of a related group of designs identified by such names as Bodoni, Caslon, Futura, and so forth. The basic design remains the same within the family of type, but it will vary in terms of weight, width, and the angle of the characters. These differences provide for contrast and emphasis within the same basic type design. The most common variations include bold, extra bold, condensed, extended, and italic, although all of these variations may not be available in a particular type family. Figure 14–4 shows a number of variations in the Helvetica family.

Note that while each variation is set in the same size in terms of height (it is all set in 30 point type), the number of letters that can be printed in a given space varies because the characters vary in width. This brings up the question of type measurement.

Type Measurement

Since even a brief discussion of type measurement may be helped by some familiarity with basic type terminology, figure 14–5 shows a *slug* of type, with its anatomy labeled. Type measurement is a language in itself. Some of the key terms are defined below.

The Point. The size of type (height) is measured in points. There are 72 points to an inch, so that a point is 1/72 of an inch. The most common type sizes used in advertising are 6, 8, 10, 12, 14, 18, 24, 36, 42, 48, 60, 72, 84, 96, and 120 points. The smaller sizes—6 to 14 points—are generally used for body copy; the larger sizes are reserved for headlines and subheads. Figure 14–6 shows a variety of type sizes for comparative purposes.

Helvetica Light

The Helvetica family of type

Helvetica Light Italic

The Helvetica family of type

Helvetica Regular

The Helvetica family of type

Helvetica Regular Italic

The Helvetica family of type

Helvetica Medium

The Helvetica family of type

Helvetica Medium Italic

The Helvetica family of type

Helvetica Bold

The Helvetica family of type

Helvetica Bold Italic

The Helvetica family of type

Figure 14-4   Variations in the Helvetica type family

The Pica.   The pica is the unit of measure used for designating the width of lines. A pica is 12 points wide, so that there are six picas to an inch.

The Agate Line.   The agate line is a vertical measure of space in which type may be set; it is generally used in referring to fractional space in newspapers and magazines. The agate line is one column wide; there are 14 agate lines to an inch. Thus a newspaper or magazine advertisement that is two columns wide and three inches deep would contain 84 agate lines

(2 x 3 x 14 = 84). Since the agate line is a measure of space only, regardless of the type size used, the foregoing example would still be 84 agate lines, whether it were blank, contained only one line of type, or contained several lines of type.

Making Type Readable

Not only are some type faces more readable than others, but readability can be improved by the way in which type is set. There is a small amount of space

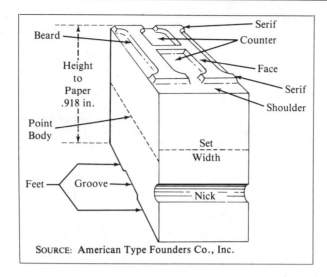

SOURCE: American Type Founders Co., Inc.

Figure 14–5 Slug of type with anatomy labeled

between lines of type because the type character is slightly smaller than the metal block on which it is cast. This difference between the size of the character and the metal block is called the *shoulder* (see figure 14–5). When lines of type are set without any additional space between them, they are said to be set *solid*. Often, to increase readability or to adapt the body of type to the space allotted to it, additional space between lines is desirable. This may be accomplished in two ways: (1) the compositor may cast the characters on a larger block of metal, thus increasing the shoulder and the space between lines; or (2) thin metal strips called *leads* (pronounced "leds") are inserted between the lines. Leading is specified by adding its value in points to the size of type. For example, 12 point type set with two points of space between lines would be specified as "12 on 14," or as "12/14."

Specifying Type

There are a number of considerations when specifying type for an advertisement. Of course, one of the primary ones is *readability*. An advertisement that is hard to read, or looks hard to read, will attract few consumers. A second consideration is *appropriateness*. Since type may be selected that creates impressions of masculinity, femininity, modernity, tradition, exoticness, and so forth, the typographer needs to select type that is appropriate to the overall impression which the advertisement is intended to create. A third consideration is *harmony*. It is generally unwise to use too many type styles in an advertisement, since a number of styles gives the appearance of clutter and

suggests difficulty in reading. As a consequence, one or two styles is usually enough. Contrast can be achieved by using heavier weights for the headline, subheads, and captions than is used in body copy. Key words and slogans can be emphasized by using italics from the same type family as is used for other copy.

When specifying type, the typographer needs to provide the following information: (1) type size and leading, (2) type face, by name, and (3) type width in picas. There are also a number of guidelines that facilitate readability, when specifying type.

1. Solid lines of capital letters or italics are difficult to read. Both, however, can be used effectively to emphasize individual words, names, or slogans.
2. Leading between lines helps increase readability.
3. Sizes below eight point are usually difficult to read. Don't forget that many consumers either wear reading glasses or should wear them.
4. Readability is improved and the body copy is "opened up" by allowing more white space between paragraphs than between lines in the same paragraph.
5. Short paragraphs and lines are easier to read than long ones. This is the reason why copy is often set in columns with thirty or forty characters to the line.
6. Spacing between words should be watched carefully. If characters are jammed together, they are difficult to read. Similarly, if characters are too far apart, words tend to lose their integrity, and it is difficult to tell where one ends and another begins.

SIZE of type	8 POINT	
SIZE of type	10 POINT	
SIZE of type	12 POINT	*text type*
SIZE of type	14 POINT	
SIZE of type	18 POINT	
SIZE of type	24 POINT	
SIZE of type	30 POINT	*display type*
SIZE of type	36 POINT	
SIZE of type	42 POINT	
SIZE of type	48 POINT	

Figure 14–6. Sample variations in type size

Typesetting

There are a number of methods for setting type; that is, for arranging letters to form words, sentences, and paragraphs. Each has certain advantages and disadvantages, and all can be broadly classified as *hand setting* or *machine setting*.

Hand Setting. Hand setting is the oldest form of setting type. In this process, the compositor selects letters individually from a type *font* or *case,* where each letter of the alphabet is assigned to a separate compartment. The letters are placed in a three-sided, metal box referred to as a *composing stick.* After it has been set, the type is transferred to a metal form and locked together. After it has been used, the form is unlocked, and the letters are returned to the appropriate compartments in the type case.

Although hand setting is slow and expensive, it provides wide latitude in spacing and design and is easy to correct since individual characters can be replaced with minimum effort. Because of its expense, however, handsetting has generally been replaced by various forms of machine setting, although hand setting is sometimes used for handbills and small jobs.

Machine Setting. There are a number of forms of machine setting that are widely used in commercial printing because of their speed, economy, and/or versatility. Each of the major methods is briefly described in the following material.

1. Monotype. Monotype is a mechanical method of casting letters or characters one at a time. A monotype system consists of two machines. The first utilizes a typewriter-like keyboard, which produces perforations on a ribbon. The ribbon is then fed into a type-caster which casts and assembles the letters one at a time. Since the letters are cast and assembled individually, it is easy to correct by replacing a single letter. All types of faces may be used, and spacing between words is easy to adjust. Because of these advantages, monotype is frequently used for tables and charts and certain kinds of fine book work.

2. Linotype. Linotype is a machine setting process which casts type a line at a time. The linotype operator types out the material on a keyboard that resembles that of a typewriter. When a line has been typed, it is cast into a metal slug, with the complete line of type on its printing edge. When the slugs have been used, they are returned to the melting pot of the machine where they are melted for reuse.

Linotype is faster than hand setting or monotype. However, it is more difficult to correct because the entire line in which the correction occurs must be recast. Also, irregularly shaped type areas may be difficult to set by linotype. Thus, while linotype is quicker and less expensive than monotype for routine work, monotype may be less expensive for complicated jobs or tabular composition.

3. Ludlow. This method is really a combination of hand setting and machine casting. The type matrices (brass molds for each character) are set by hand and locked in a frame. The entire line is then molded by machine. The Ludlow process insures clean, sharp reproduction because it provides new type for each job, as does monotype and linotype. Since it is essentially a hand setting process, it tends to be slow and relatively expensive. It can be used for setting small type, but its primary use is in casting headlines for newspapers and magazines.

4. Photocomposition. Photocomposition, also called *cold type,* is increasing in use because of its sharpness, clarity, greater choice of type sizes and faces, faster reproduction, and lower costs. The basic process involves a letter keyboard that operates an electric camera and a film printing device which makes a photographic negative, or a *reproduction* proof. Photocomposition is primarily used for offset and gravure printing, but it can also be adapted for publications that print by the letterpress method. These different methods of printing will be described in the next section of this chapter.

Cold type composition can also be produced by equipment such as the IBM Executive typewriter, the Varityper, and the Justowriter. These machines, which offer a variety of type faces and spacing variations, produce a printed image from which plates can be made. All three of these machines offer greater speed and economy than conventional typesetting processes. They are often used for catalogues, direct advertising material, and house organs.

METHODS OF PRINTING

There are four basic printing methods used in advertising. Three of these methods—*letterpress, gravure,* and *lithography*—are widely used for magazine and newspaper reproduction. The fourth form, *silk screen,* is a relatively simple process used primarily for limited quantity production runs, such as for posters and point-of-sale material. Letterpress, gravure, and lithography are generally printed from special plates made by a photoengraving process. Letterpress can print directly from set type, but in high-speed printing (such as that required for metropolitan newspapers and magazines) and for printing illustrations, a special plate is required. There are a number of methods of photoengraving, which will be described later in the chapter. The basic process involves photographing completed artwork (including type) and transferring the negative to sensitized metal plates, usually of zinc or copper.

The basic principle underlying all four of the major printing processes is essentially the same; namely, the transfer of an inked image from one surface to another. The methods by which this transfer takes place differ dramatically, however.

Letterpress

In letterpress, the ink is transferred from a raised surface to the paper. The process is similar to the use of a rubber stamp with which most of us are familiar. The letters or image to be transferred are in relief and backward. The stamp is pressed on an inked pad and then pressed on a piece of paper or other surface to transfer the image.

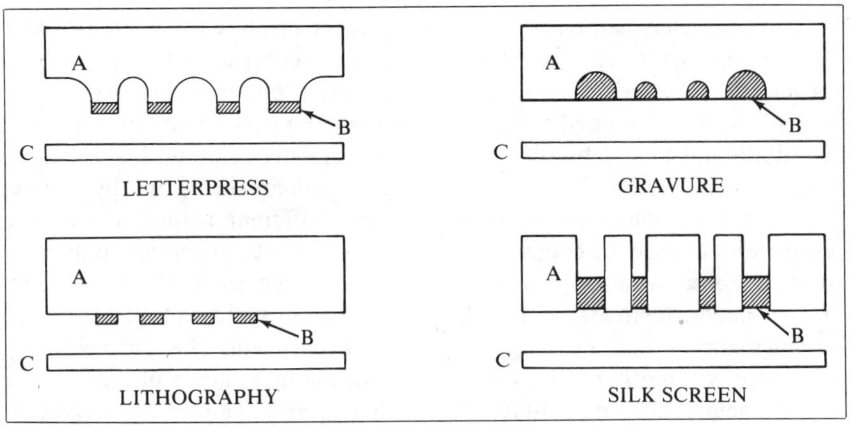

Figure 14-7. Basic printing processes. These diagrams illustrate the basic principles of the major printing processes. "A" represents the printing plate or screen; "B" is the printing ink; and "C" is the surface on which the design is to be printed.

When letterpress is printed from plates rather than from type, the raised printing surface is obtained by etching a metal plate with acid. The parts of the plate to be printed are protected by an acid resistant coating, so that they are not affected. The acid eats away the nonprotected part, leaving the areas to be printed on a raised surface. Figure 14-7 diagrams the principle of the letterpress process.

There are three types of modern letterpress equipment: *platen, cylinder,* and *rotary* presses. The *platen* press transfers the impression by bringing two flat surfaces together. The *cylinder* or *flatbed press* rolls a cylinder of paper across a flat surface or *bed* which contains the printing plates. The *rotary* press, which is particularly suited for large quantity, high-speed work, uses a curved printing plate which is wrapped around a rotating cylinder. Another revolving cylinder carries the paper. Printing is transferred by rotating the cylinders against one another.

Letterpress is used by most newspapers, as well as for many magazines and books. It produces a sharper, cleaner image than the other methods and is an excellent process for halftone and color printing. It is relatively expensive, but it is ecnomical in large quantities.

Gravure or Intaglio

In contrast to letterpress, which prints from a raised surface, the gravure process prints from a depressed surface (see figure 14-7). The design is etched into a metal plate, leaving depressions. The surface of the plate is inked and then wiped clean with a metal blade, leaving ink in the depressions. When printing takes place, the depressions give up their ink, transfering the design from the plate to the paper.

The primary value of gravure is its excellent reproduction of color illustrations and tonal effects, even on soft, inexpensive papers. This is why it is generally used by newspaperes for special sections and color printing. Compared to letterpress, however, its reproduction of type is a little fuzzy. Since the process is relatively expensive, it is used primarily for long production runs.

Lithography

Lithography, as opposed to letterpress and gravure, prints from a smooth surface (see figure 14-7). The principle underlying lithography is the incompatibility of oil and water, and the fact that ink (which is oily) will not adhere to a wet surface. The design is deposited on a plate, either by hand or photographically, with a greasy crayon or ink. The nonimage areas of the plate are treated with a stain that retains water. A water roller is then applied to the surface. Since grease and water are incompatible, the design area rejects the water while the nondesign areas are dampened. An ink roller is then passed over the surface. Since the ink is oily, the design area accepts it. Because the nondesign area is dampened, it will not accept the ink.

There are two forms of lithography: *direct* and *offset.* In *direct* lithography, the printing plate prints directly on the paper. In *offset* lithography, the plate transfers the image to an intermediate rubber surface called a *blanket.* The blanket then transfers the image to the paper. Offset lithography provides a richer effect than does direct lithography and is frequently used for long production runs. In contrast to letterpress and gravure, lithography is relatively inexpensive, although obtaining the proper balance of ink and water is sometimes tedious. In addition, however, offset lithography will print on almost any surface. It is especially suitable for printing on metal; for this reason, many packages, such as soft drink and beer cans, are printed by the lithographic process.

Silk Screen or Seriography

Silk screen is one of the oldest and simplest methods of reproducing printed materials. The process operates on the stencil principle and requires no printing plates. Instead, a special screen (originally of silk) is stretched tightly on a frame over the surface on which the message or image is to be printed. A stencil (prepared by hand or photographic process) is used to block out areas that are not to be printed, and a rubber roller is used to force ink through those portions of the screen not blocked out by the stencil (see figure 14–7). Today, printing screens are usually made of nylon or stainless steel mesh rather than silk, from which the process derived its name. With photographically produced stencils, tonal qualities similar to those obtained from lithography are possible.

Originally, silk screening was a *hand process,* but today fully automated presses are available. Since silk screening does not require printing plates as the other major printing processes do, silk screen is economical for small quantity production. In addition, it can be used to print on virtually any surface, from bottles to barrels to sweatshirts. It is particularly useful when short production runs are required, when there are

severe time and cost limitations, or when an unusual printing surface makes other processes impractical.

Choosing a Printing Process

When preparing advertising material for commercial media such as magazines or newspapers, advertisers have no choice. They must prepare the material for the process by which the particular magazine or newspaper is printed. When preparing brochures, catalogues, inserts, point-of-sale, and other promotional material, however, the choice of printing process will depend on such things as cost and time restrictions, the quantity to be produced, the quality of reproduction desired, and the material on which the message is to be printed. Table 14–1 summarizes some of the major characteristics of each method.

PHOTOENGRAVING

In modern, high-speed printing, photoengraving is used for both type and illustrations. Technically, photoengraving is the process for making plates for letterpress printing. The following description of the process is based on this use, although, with minor variations, the same process is used for the other printing methods as well.

Photoengraving involves a photochemical process in which a camera is used to make a negative. The nega-

Table 14–1. Summary of comparative printing methods

	Cost	Appearance	Paper stock	Quantity
Letterpress	Relative high cost of plates, but less waste than lithography. No delays in obtaining proper water/ink balance.	High quality color reproduction. More body and brilliance than other methods. Inks glossier, and less problems with metallic inks.	Works particularly well with high quality paper and special stock.	Almost no limits on quantity; but small sample runs are more expensive than offset.
Gravure	Relatively expensive plates. Economical only on runs of 100,000 or more.	Rich color effects, particularly on cellophane, acetate, and metallic foils.	Can use softer paper than letterpress, but fails to reproduce in as sharp detail.	Ideal for long production runs for periodicals, catalogues, or package wraps.
Offset Lithography	Lowest plate cost, but complete new plates required for changes or corrections.	High quality even on rough surfaces.	Sensitive to moisture changes. Problems of paper curl and dimensional stabilities.	Good for both long and short runs, and is often used for books and folders. Widely used for promotion materials and direct mail.
Silk screen	Low cost since there are no plates involved.	Good quality, but not as good as can be obtained by other processes.	Extremely versatile. Can be printed on all sorts of material, and on any thickness.	Best for small quantity runs. Recently, high speed machinery has made it feasible for some long run work.

tive is then transferred to a sensitized metal plate of zinc or copper, and etched to create the printing surface. The photoengraving process may be used to obtain either *line* or *halftone* engravings.

Line engravings are the simplest, since line plates produce only solid tones. They do not produce shades, or gradations of color. If continuous tones (say from solid black through various shades of grey) are desired, the halftone engraving process must be used. Intermediate shades of a color are produced by breaking up solid lines and areas in the artwork into minute dots of different sizes. Each dot becomes a printing surface for carrying ink. Thus, whereas line cuts print from solid lines or areas, halftone engravings print from dots.

The same basic photochemical process is used in the production of both line and halftone engravings. However, in making halftone engravings, the original artwork is photographed through a halftone screen, which generally consists of a sheet of glass (although plastic film is also used) on which fine black lines have been drawn at right angles to one another so that they form little boxes of clear glass. The number of lines to the inch in the screen will vary with the degree of fineness of the printing to be done. Course paper, such as that used in newspapers, requires a course line screen, usually 65 lines to the inch. On high quality

paper such as that used in "slick" magazines, a finer screen may be used. The finer the screen, the better and more detailed the reproduction. The most frequently used line screens are 55, 65, and 85 for newspapers and 110, 120, or 133 for magazines. Extremely smooth paper can accept up to 150 to 200 line screens without blurring.

The halftone screen is placed between the lense of the camera and the artwork to be photographed. Light from the artwork passes through the screen and spreads on its way to the film negative. The dot pattern on the negative is determined by the amount of light reflected from various areas of the artwork. Dark, solid areas reflect little light, and show up on the negative as large dots; bright areas or highlights reflect a greater amount of light, and show up as widely scattered, small dots. Whereas the *number* of dots will depend on the fineness of the screen, the *size* of the dots will depend on the amount of light reflected by the artwork being photographed. Figure 14–8 shows a greatly enlarged halftone showing the effect of screening.

Occasionally, it is desirable to combine the clarity of line engravings with the tonal qualities of halftones in a single plate. This can be done by using a combination of line and halftone negatives that are stripped together to make a composite or combined unit.

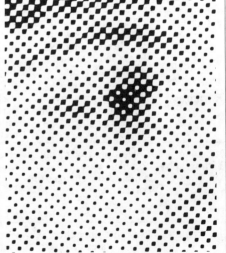

Figure 14–8. Enlarged halftone showing the effects of screening

PRINTING COLOR

The most common process for producing full-color advertisements with tonal values, such as those seen in most magazines, is the four-color process. All colors can be reduced or decomposed to the three primary colors—red, yellow, and blue. When black is added to these three colors, detail strength and neutral shades of grey are obtainable. Color artwork is photographed through filters—a green filter for red, a violet filter for yellow, orange for blue, and a special filter for black. This decomposes the artwork into four separate negatives referred to as *color separations.* After the color separations have been corrected (that is, improved for color accuracy), the separations are photographed through a halftone screen to make four halftone plates, one for each color. In photographing the color separations, the halftone screen is rotated to a different angle for each separation. As a consequence, when the four plates are printed—superimposing them over one another—the resultant dots do not completely overlap, so that they reproduce a faithful rendition of the original colors. The most commonly used screen sizes for magazines are 133 lines for yellow, and 120 line screens for the other color plates. The color plates are printed separately—usually in the sequence of yellow, red, blue, and black—using transparent inks. The transparent inks "mix" the primary pigments and result in a color blended illustration. The illustrations in plate 14–9 (insert following p. 282) show *progressive proofs* of a four-color, halftone advertisement.

SUMMARY

There is widespread disagreement about what constitutes effective design in advertising. Four issues that are at the heart of much of the controversy are the use of a picture-headline format, the use of overprinting, the use of reverse type, and the placement of the coupon in coupon ads.

In any discussion of design, there are three terms—*visualize, layout,* and *design*—that need to be clarified. To *visualize* refers to the mental picture that a copywriter or art director has of an advertisement before anything is put on paper. The term *layout* is used in two ways. As a verb, it is the actual process of translating the admaker's idea into a finished product. As a noun, it is the result of this process. The *design* is the final format of the ad—the final result of visualization as developed and modified through a number of layouts.

One of the major variables influencing advertising design is the space unit available. The larger the space unit, the greater the freedom to manipulate design elements.

Although there are a number of ways in which design elements can be arranged, an effective design has the following characteristics: a single focal point, a logical progression of eye movement, clarity of impression, and simplicity.

Advertising layouts progress through a series of steps. The major layout stages are: thumbnail sketches, rough layout, finished layout, comprehensive, and working layout.

The actual production of print advertising is handled by specialists in the advertising agency and by outside suppliers. After an advertisement has been approved, a series of production operations still have to be performed. The design and size of type have to be specified, type proofs have to be made and approved, artwork must be engraved, all elements of the advertisement must be assembled, and printing plates must be made for shipment to media. Because of the complexity of the production process, a system of production scheduling must be devised to coordinate the various activities so that time schedules can be met.

Typography refers to both the selection and arrangement of type. There are over a thousand different type faces to select from. Many of these different type faces are similar enough in appearance to be classified as a type group. Four broad type groups that encompass most type faces are *roman, block, cursive or script,* and *ornamental.* Within each major type group, there are type families. A type family is a related group of designs identified by names such as Bodoni, Caslon, and Futura. Because of the many type faces available, it is possible to select type to convey impressions of modernity, old-fashionedness, formality, futurity, mystery, and so forth.

Terms used in measuring type and the space it occupies are the *point* (1/72 of an inch), and the *agate line.* An agate line is one column wide and 1/14 of an inch high.

Type may be set either by hand or by machine. The particular typesetting method used will depend upon the particular job since each has advantages and disadvantages for various forms of work.

There are four basic methods of printing: *letterpress, gravure, lithography,* and *silk screen.* The particular printing method used depends on such factors as the surface being printed, cost and speed considerations, and the fidelity required in the finished work.

Modern, high-speed printing uses photoengravings. *Photoengraving* is a photochemical process in which a camera is used to make a negative of the material to be printed. The negative is then transferred to a sensitized metal plate and etched to create the printing surface. The photoengraving process is used for both *line* engravings (solid lines) or *halftone* engravings (used to produce gradations of tones).

The most common process for producing full-color printing is the four-color process. Color artwork is photographed through filters, and a separate engraving is made for each of the basic colors in the process—red, yellow, blue, and black. There four engravings are printed separately. They are superimposed over one another using transparent inks, which yield a color-blended result.

QUESTIONS

1. What are the reasons given in the text for conflicting practices in designing advertisements?
2. Distinguish between the terms (a) *visualize*, (b) *layout*, and (c) *design*.
3. Identify the characteristics of an effective design.
4. Analyze a current magazine advertisement in terms of the characteristics of effective design given in the text.
5. Define the following terms: (a) *typography*, (b) *lower case*, (c) *upper case*, (d) the *point*, (e) the *pica*, and (f) the *agate line*.
6. Identify and indicate the major characteristics of the four major type groups mentioned in the text.
7. Briefly describe the following methods of setting type: (a) *handsetting*, (b) *monotype*, (c) *linotype*, (d) *Ludlow*, and (e) *photocomposition*.
8. Distinguish between the printing processes for: (a) letterpress, (b) gravure, (c) lithography, and (d) silk screen.
9. Distinguish between the methods of printing for the following processes: (a) platen, (b) cylinder, and (c) rotary.
10. Briefly describe how color photographs are printed.

PROBLEM

As art director of a copy group, you have been working on an ad for the Buick Regal that will appear in *Psychology Today*. You have agreed that five illustrations will be used: one exterior shot of the automobile and four interior shots of different seats (bucket seats, bench seats) in different fabrics or materials.

The following headline and body copy have been written, but not layed out.

Headline: Regal. The Buick you buy by the seat of your pants.

Body copy:

The reasons for buying a mid-sized car are pretty well established, wouldn't you say? Small. Light. Maneuverable.

Mid-sized cars make a lot of sense, in other words.

Well, Buick's new mid-sized Regal Coupe is trying to do more than just make sense.

And we maintain that once you sit in one, you're going to have more than practical arguments for acquiring one.

You settle into cushiony notchback seating, covered this year with either fabric or soft vinyl. On your right, a big, soft, fold-down armrest makes things a tad more comfortable.

But that's just the standard seating. There are a number of available choices in a Regal Coupe. All of them are luxurious. All of them worthy of a Buick.

Facing you is the instrumentation. Rich and readable. An available Delco stereo sound system provides atmosphere.

You turn the key, and the Regal Coupe's V–6 engine comes to life.

You drop the shift lever into drive, and the Regal Coupe's available Buick-smooth automatic transmission takes it from there. Those power, front-disc brakes are standard. So is the power steering.

The car is tight, the interior surprisingly quiet.

No, Buick's Regal Coupe isn't the sort of mid-sized car you buy just with your head.

Don't be surprised if you end up buying it by the seat of your pants.

Assignment

1. It has been agreed that the ad will be a single-page bleed, but no agreement has been reached as to whether it will be in color. You have to make a recommendation on this score.
2. Lay out the ad, showing how the illustrations, headline, and body copy will appear. If you decide to use color, indicate where it will be used (background, illustrations, type, headline, etc.). Also indicate what colors you will use.
3. In addition to the illustrations, headline, and copy you have been given, you will have to include two other things in the ad somewhere: the GM logo and the Regal logo. The GM logo consists of the letters *GM* in a rectangular box. (You will probably want to look up a GM ad to see what it looks like.) The Regal logo consists of the word *Regal* with an eagle alighting on it.
4. Decide whether the illustrations should be drawings, photographs, or a combination of the two. Write a brief set of instructions for the photographer or artist explaining the effect you hope to create with the illustrations.
5. Consult the Consumer Magazine Standard Rate and Data Catalogue for production specifications for *Psychology Today*. Production specifications include (a) mechanical measurements for the ad, (b) method of printing, (c) what materials will be required for the magazine, and (d) closing date.

15

Broadcast Advertising

As in print advertising, there are few hard and fast rules for writing broadcast commercials. Charles Wainwright, when vice-president of the Tatham-Laird and Kudner advertising agency, said: "Selling commercials come in all sizes and shapes. It's impossible to categorize them except to say that a *selling commercial convinces the consumer to buy the product.*"[1] The following three examples of award winning commercials demonstrate this point (see figures 15–1, 15–2, and 15–3).

Alka Seltzer

The Alka Seltzer commercial, "Small Things" (see figure 15–1), relies wholly on a voice-over technique. Conversational voices present a series of tension producing situations. After each situation, a hand is shown dropping an Alka Seltzer tablet into a glass of water. The video portion of the commercial alternates a blank screen with pictures of the product—no people, no drama, no action, no excitement. Yet, the commercial is highly effective in demonstrating the product's

copy strategy—that Alka Seltzer is effective in relieving headaches caused by tension.

Cracker Jack

The Cracker Jack "Train" commercial (see figure 15–2) is quite different from the Alka Seltzer commercial. Throughout the commercial, not a word is spoken. The entire commercial is in pantomime, and relies wholly on the video. The story is simple: the hero—played by comedian Jack Gilford—is returning from the washroom to his berth in a Pullman car. Two other passengers, who have retired to their berths and drawn the curtains, are passing a large box of Cracker Jacks back and forth across the aisle. Gilford stops, intercepts the package, and shares in the late snack until he is "discovered." The payoff line is a *super* in the last frame of the commercial that reads: "The Big Pass Around Pack. Cracker Jack."

World Book Encyclopedia

The "Eggs" commercial for World Book Encyclopedia (figure 15–3) is an entirely different creative problem. In the words of Paul Blustain of the Post-Keyes-Gardner advertising agency:

---

1. From *The Television Copywriter* by Charles A. Wainwright. © Copyright 1966, permission by Hastings House, Publishers, p. 90.

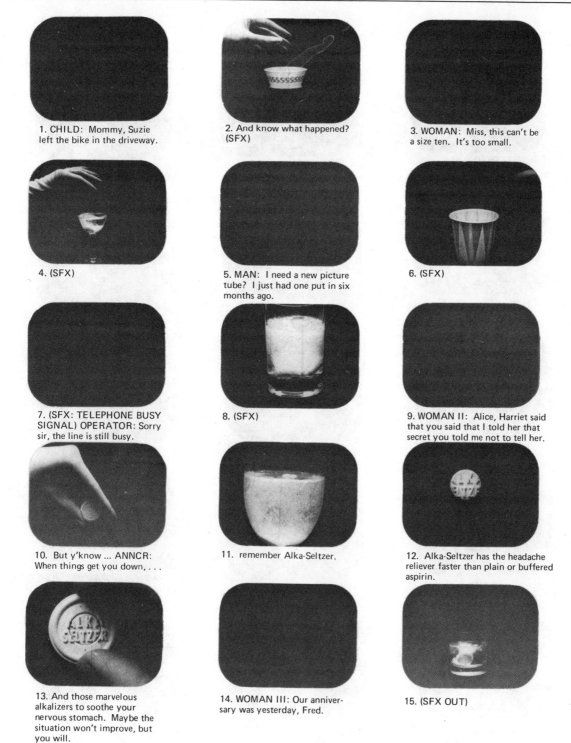

1. CHILD: Mommy, Suzie left the bike in the driveway.

2. And know what happened? (SFX)

3. WOMAN: Miss, this can't be a size ten. It's too small.

4. (SFX)

5. MAN: I need a new picture tube? I just had one put in six months ago.

6. (SFX)

7. (SFX: TELEPHONE BUSY SIGNAL) OPERATOR: Sorry sir, the line is still busy.

8. (SFX)

9. WOMAN II: Alice, Harriet said that you said that I told her that secret you told me not to tell her.

10. But y'know ... ANNCR: When things get you down, . . .

11. remember Alka-Seltzer.

12. Alka-Seltzer has the headache reliever faster than plain or buffered aspirin.

13. And those marvelous alkalizers to soothe your nervous stomach. Maybe the situation won't improve, but you will.

14. WOMAN III: Our anniversary was yesterday, Fred.

15. (SFX OUT)

Figure 15–1. (Copyright 1965 by Miles Laboratories, Inc.)

In the beginning there was no egg commercial. There was simply this strategy:

1. To make an interesting and entertaining commercial that would create high awareness for World Book Encyclopedia.

2. To define World Book not just as reference material but as books children enjoy reading.

3. To appeal to the parents of young students.

4. To produce the commercial with a "reasonable" budget.

1. (SFX: TRAIN)   2. (SFX: TRAIN)   3. (SFX: TRAIN)

4. (SFX: TRAIN)   5. (SFX: TRAIN)   6. (SFX: TRAIN)

7. (SFX: TRAIN)   8. (SFX: TRAIN)   9. (SFX: TRAIN)

10. (SFX: TRAIN)   11. (SFX: TRAIN)   12. (SFX: TRAIN)

13. (SFX: TRAIN)   14. (SFX: TRAIN)   15. (SFX: TRAIN OUT)

Figure 15-2. (Cracker Jack Co.)

With these objectives in mind, our conversation centered on the famous people in World Book. The commercial itself grew out of a casual remark that intellectuals have been referred to (by anti-intellectuals) as *eggheads.*

We decided to paint eggs with the faces of famous people. We wanted them to be as real as possible, not cartoons or caricatures.[2]

2. CLIO Awards Teacher's Guide, CLIO Enterprises, Inc., 30 East 60th Street, New York, N.Y. 10022, p. 31.

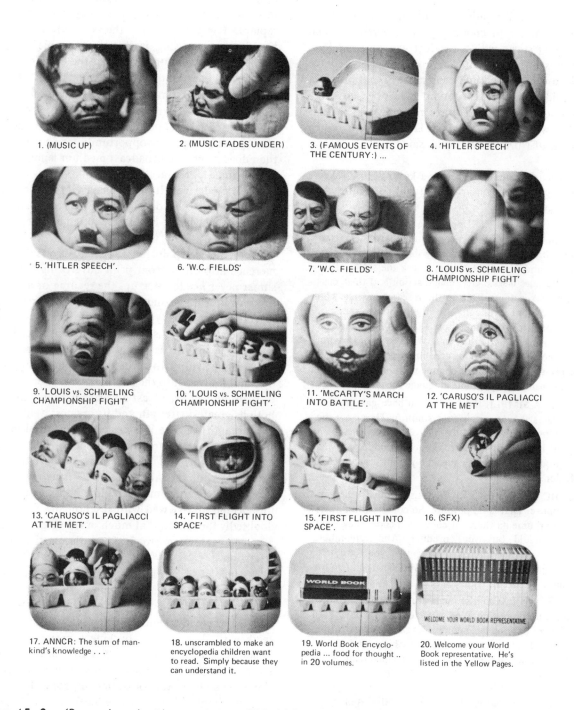

1. (MUSIC UP)

2. (MUSIC FADES UNDER)

3. (FAMOUS EVENTS OF THE CENTURY:) ...

4. 'HITLER SPEECH'

5. 'HITLER SPEECH'.

6. 'W.C. FIELDS'

7. 'W.C. FIELDS'.

8. 'LOUIS vs. SCHMELING CHAMPIONSHIP FIGHT'

9. 'LOUIS vs. SCHMELING CHAMPIONSHIP FIGHT'

10. 'LOUIS vs. SCHMELING CHAMPIONSHIP FIGHT'.

11. 'McCARTY'S MARCH INTO BATTLE'.

12. 'CARUSO'S IL PAGLIACCI AT THE MET'

13. 'CARUSO'S IL PAGLIACCI AT THE MET'.

14. 'FIRST FLIGHT INTO SPACE'

15. 'FIRST FLIGHT INTO SPACE'.

16. (SFX)

17. ANNCR: The sum of mankind's knowledge . . .

18. unscrambled to make an encyclopedia children want to read. Simply because they can understand it.

19. World Book Encyclopedia ... food for thought .. in 20 volumes.

20. Welcome your World Book representative. He's listed in the Yellow Pages.

Figure 15–3.   (Reproduced with permission of World Book—Childcraft International, Inc.)

The result is a 120-second commercial. The sound effects (SFX) behind each character reinforced its identification. For example, the introduction to Beethoven's Fifth Symphony was played behind Beethoven, the first character; for Hitler, part of a tape of one of his speeches was played; behind W.C. Fields, a recording of Field's voice telling a humorous story about Philadelphia was used; and so forth. The result was a highly dramatic and unusual commercial that executed the creative strategy superbly.

SPECIAL CHARACTERISTICS OF BROADCAST MEDIA

In many respects, creating commercials for broadcast media is similar to creating print advertising. The commercial starts with a product concept—an idea that needs to be translated into a consumer benefit. This idea is expressed in a copy strategy that provides basic guidance for its execution. Like print advertising, broadcast writing requires research and a thorough knowledge of the product. Don Natheson, when president of North Advertising, said:

> When a young man or woman asks me what it takes to be a good television writer, I usually pass out these four suggestions:
>
> 1. BE A DIGGER! Don't live in an "isolation booth." Get out among people and talk to them, find out what they want, what they like about your product—and what they dislike. Check the stores. Talk to the sales clerks. Get their reaction and their customers' reactions. Talk to the research people who created your product. Use the product yourself. Compare it with competitors. Talk to the men who sell your product to dealers. What are they saying and not saying? Read the consumer research reports, especially the un-aided comments. Learn to talk to the consumer in the same language she talks to you.
>
> 2. BE A SIMPLIFIER! After you have gathered all the facts about your product, simplify. Throw out the unimportant ideas and the bad ones. Keep the good ones. Remember—it only takes one good idea to sell a product. Too much mumbo-jumbo creates confusion. Simplify!
>
> 3. BE A CONVINCER! Advertising must sell merchandise. That is its purpose. So convert those facts into arguments that will convince people they need and should buy your product. And remember, people are not interested in you or your product. They just want to know what your product can do for them.
>
> 4. BE AN EXCITER! Facts aren't enough! They're dull, uninteresting. You must embellish facts with bizazz. Use music, humor, novelty, pace, lighting, atmosphere, camera tricks—anything and everything to attract attention to your convincing arguments.[3]

On the other hand, broadcast media has certain unique characteristics that are not present in print advertising. Whereas print advertising deals with space, broadcast media—whether radio or TV—deals with time. The consumer can study a print advertisement, if he is so inclined, spending as much time as he wishes in looking at the illustration, reading the body copy, relating the product and its benefits to his situation. But broadcast media is different. It's there for a moment, and then it's gone; there are no instant replays. For this reason, the key admonition for broadcast advertising is "Keep it simple." Writer Hanley Norins has suggested that the broadcast message should be so simple that you should " . . . be able to sum it up in your mind in one sentence—just as you would with a billboard."[4]

At the same time, however, broadcast commercials often provide a greater opportunity for showmanship than does print; the broadcast medium lends itself to jingles, music, dramatic effects, and a variety of attention getting devices. It also lends itself to "personality selling" better than does print. Broadcast personalities, particularly in radio, are often powerful persuaders.

From the viewpoint of audience, broadcast commercials also differ from print advertising. The consumer never *has* to interrupt the reading of an article or story in a magazine to look at an advertisement. Advertising can easily be ignored. In broadcast, however, the advertising is intrusive; the consumer has no choice. Viewing or listening to editorial matter, music, or drama stops when the commercial comes on. It does not resume until the commercial is over. It is this intrusiveness of broadcast advertising that constitutes both its greatest strength and its greatest weakness. It is a strength because it is easier to get initial interest for a broadcast commercial, although the consumer can always "turn off" his attention, or leave the room when the commercial comes on. Intrusiveness is a weakness because commercial interruptions are often unwelcome and viewed with resentment. This is undoubtedly the reason that much of the criticism of advertising centers on broadcast media, particularly on television.

Because of its aural character, slogans, key words and phrases, and rhymes are more effective in broadcast media than in print. A classic of radio—"you'll wonder where the yellow went when you brush your teeth with Pepsodent"—became a national byword. When Busch Bavarian Beer was first introduced, its theme song (replete with yodeling) earned it recognition by over 95 percent of adult consumers. The Salem cigarette jingle, "You can take Salem out of the country, but . . . (musical ping)," made it almost impossible for the listener not to complete the phrase.

Rhyme can be used effectively in broadcast, but it can also be overdone. At one point, I conducted some

---

3. Wainwright, *Television Copywriter,* p. 5.

4. Hanley Norins, *The Compleat Copywriter* (New York: McGraw-Hill, Inc., 1966), p. 153.

research on rhymed versus prose commercials for one of our food clients. Our research indicated three things.

1. Rhymed commercials were more effective than prose commercials in capturing attention, and creating interest.
2. Sales points in rhymed commercials tended to get "lost" and did not register as well as in the prose version.
3. Listeners became satiated with rhymed commercials more quickly than with prose commercials.

A major conclusion of the study was that rhyme, to be effective, should be used sparingly. A key sales point or slogan stood out and was better remembered if it was couched in rhyme in a commercial that was primarily prose. However, if the entire commercial was in rhyme, sales point recall was reduced.

Radio and TV are both broadcast media, but they are quite different in character. For this reason, they need to be discussed separately. Radio will be taken first because, in many respects, it is the simpler of the two media.

RADIO COMMERCIALS

In the 1930s and 1940s radio occupied a role similar to that of television today. It was truly a mass media, reaching audiences of millions, providing a leading form of home entertainment. With the advent of television, the decline of radio as a major advertising medium was precipitous. Today, radio is widely used for local and regional advertising, but for national advertising, radio is often considered as a supplemental medium.

Radio presents two major challenges for the copywriter: (1) it is completely an aural medium, and everything has to be accomplished with sound effects; (2) the radio listener is usually doing something else at the same time—washing, cooking, cleaning, reading, driving a car, or some other activity. This places a major burden on the radio writer to capture and hold attention. Generally, the commercial must capture the listener's attention in the first eight seconds, or lose him altogether. Thereafter, the structure and content of the commercial needs to be sufficiently striking to hold interest.

Types of Radio Commercials

There are many forms that radio commercials may take. Kevin Sweeney, while president of the Radio Advertising Bureau, identified four basic forms or "schools of thought" about radio commercials: (1) the jingle approach, (2) narrative commercials, (3) straight delivery, and (4) personality commercials. [5]

The Jingle approach. In this form, the commercial uses a jingle or rhyme, often accompanied by a catchy tune to carry the content of the commercial. Such an approach can be effective for short phrases or ideas, but the excessive use of rhyme can lead to reduced recall for salient product attributes.

The following radio commercial, prepared for LIFE SAVERS®, uses the jingle approach. Written for young people, it is set to rock music. Five different musical arrangements were made to avoid wear-out and to sustain listenership.

Life Savers
The flavor goes on and on
When everything but the hole is gone.
The flavor goes on and on, so long.
So strong,
That you can't go wrong with
Life Savers . . .
A part of livin'
Life Savers . . .
A part of livin'.
'Cause their great taste has been around for
Years and years
And folks have found there's nothing
Quite like . . . nothing quite like
Life Savers . . .
A part of livin'.
The flavor goes on and on.
Life Savers.

Narrative commercials. Narrative commercials tell a story, often in dialogue, and frequently with humor. Since most commercials are limited to 60 seconds at most, it takes careful writing to set up the plot, make the sales point or points, and deliver a punch line.

The following example for Renault's Le Car demonstrates the structure of a narrative commercial. In this particular instance, celebrities Mike Nichols and Elaine May are used to lend emphasis and impact.

MIKE: Mrs. van Rennep, Mr. van Rennep has asked me to discuss the divorce settlement with you.
ELAINE: Yes, Mr. Hagger.
MIKE: He wants it to be a happy divorce. He suggests that you have the house in town, the house in Cortina d'Impezzo.

5. S.W.D. Dunn and A.M. Barban, *Advertising* (Hinsdale, Illinois: The Dryden Press, 1974), p. 406.

ELAINE: Don't want it.

MIKE: The house in Tierra del Freigo.

ELAINE: Don't want it.

MIKE: The Rolls Royces, both children, the dog. . . .
He would like to keep the two cats and Le Car.

ELAINE: Yes. I don't want the children; I do want Le
Car. I only want one Rolls and I'll take the house in
town.

MIKE: Mrs. van Rennep, the children, of course, can
be discussed, but I am afraid Le Car is out of the
question. I know that Mr. van Rennep was very firm
about that. He said it was the only quality and fun
left in his life.

ELAINE: Ah . . . Mr. Hagger. The Rolls is boring, the
house in town is unspeakably dull, I am 28 years old,
I have given him the best year of my life.

MIKE: Ah . . . Mrs. van Rennep. Would you consider
letting Mr. van Rennep keep Le Car if he throws in
Hawaii?

ANNCR: That was Mike Nichols and Elaine May for
Le Car by Renault.

Straight Delivery. In this form of commercial, an announcer presents a straightforward message about the
product, emphasizing its salient features, and usually
ending with a request to "try it." A straight delivery
commercial may or may not be accompanied with appropriate sound effects (SFX). The following Spalding
Australian Tennis Ball commercial uses the sound effects of a tennis ball being hit to emphasize and reinforce the product message.

(SFX: BALLS BEING HIT—VERY RESOUNDING)

ANNCR: The crucial part of your tennis game is that
fleeting moment when racket contacts ball—your
only chance for control. Control isn't a new idea to
tennis. (STOP SFX.)

But did anyone every think a tennis *ball* is important to control? Spalding did.

(SFX: BALL CAN BEING OPENED. "WHOOSH"
OF PRESSURE RELEASED. SLOWLY WIND
DOWN INTO STRETCHED POINT OF CON-
TACT.)

The new Spalding WCT Australian . . . an amazing
new championship ball. It stretches the fleeting moment of contact . . . exclusive fabric and com-
pound flatten with the force of your swing . . . ball
and racket become one. By now, other balls would
have left your racket . . . left your control.

(SFX OF OTHER BALLS LEAVING RACKET
UNDER MAIN SOUND.)

But the Spalding WCT Australian is *still there.* It stays
on your racket longer than any other ball, to give you
more time for control.

(SFX AS BALL FINALLY LEAVES RACKET.)

The new Spalding WCT Australia . . . distinctive

Championship Tennis. Look for it at fine tennis
stores.

(MUSIC FADES OUT)

Personality Commercials. This approach gains its
strength from the presenter—an Ed McMahan, a
Johnny Carson, or a local radio personality. In some
instances, the personality is given a script to read. In
other instances, he or she is simply given a product
fact sheet and asked to ad lib the commercial. Both
approaches have advantages and disadvantages. The
first controls what is said, but often loses the impact of
the personality. The second capitalizes on the presenter's natural style, but often loses control over content. Thus, a number of years ago, Arthur Godfrey,
using a fact sheet for a peanut butter commercial,
started off with: "Ugh! I hate peanut butter. But, if
you like peanut butter, Skippy is the best you can buy."
Then he went ahead and covered the salient product
characteristics.

Ross and Landers drew on the Radio Advertising
Bureau's library of over 10,000 commercials to devise
a classification system that contains seventeen different categories. Their list is shown below.[6]

1. *Product Demo*—Communicating how a product is
   used, or what purposes a product serves.

2. *Voice Power*—Use of a unique voice adding special
   qualities to the copy. May blend in other sounds or
   music, but the power of the commercial is essentially in casting the voice.

3. *Electronic Sound*—Through synthetic sound-mak-
   in machines or through devices that alter sound,
   commercial attempts to establish original product-
   sound associations.

4. *Customer Interview*—A spokesman for the product
   plus a customer, discussing the merits and advantages of the product or service. Often the most rewarding interviews are those done spontaneously.

5. *Humorous Fake Interview*—Variation of the customer interview in humorous fashion. Has the advantages of preplanning plus the interest the interview generates.

6. *Hyperbole or Exaggerated Statement*—Use of exaggeration, extreme understatement or overstate-
   ment to arouse interest in legitimate, often basic
   product claims that might otherwise pass unno-
   ticed. Can often be a spoof.

7. *Sixth Dimension*—Compression of time, history,
   happenings into a brief spot. Can often be a sequential narrative ultimately involving listener in
   future projections.

6. Wallace A. Ross and Bob Landers, "Commercial Categories,"
in *Radio Plays the Plaza* (New York: Radio Advertising Bureau, 1969), p. 29.

8. *Hot Property*—Commercial that latches on to a current sensation. Can be a hit show, a performer, or a song. Hit is adapted for product.

9. *Comedian Power*—Established comedians do commercials in their own unique style. Has advantages of humor and inferred celebrity endorsement.

10. *Historical Fantasy*—Situations or historical characters are revived to convey product message.

11. *Sound Picture*—Sound used to help put the listener into a situation by stimulating his imagination. Sounds are usually easily recognizable to facilitate listener involvement.

12. *Demographics*—Commercial appeals particularly to one segment of the population (an age group, interest group, etc.) through use of music, references.

13. *Imagery Transfer*—Spots reinforce effects of other media through use of musical logos, or other sound associations identifiable with a particular campaign for a particular product.

14. *Celebrity Interview*—Famous person provides celebrity endorsement of the product in informal manner.

15. *Product Song*—Music and words combine to create a musical logo as well as to sell product. In style of popular music with orchestration.

16. *Editing Genius*—Many different situations, voices, types of music, sounds combined in a series of quick cuts to produce one spot. Every cut contributes in some way to strength of message.

17. *Improvisation*—Copywriter conceives situations that might be good backdrop for a product and then allows performers to work out the dialogue extemporaneously. Requires postediting of tapes to make spot cohesive.

Obviously, no classification system can do justice to the variety of effects that can be created with sound. The purpose of identifying these various approaches is simply to emphasize the versatility of radio. The particular approach or combination of approaches used, however, must always be selected in terms of the product dimensions to be featured and the impression that is to be created. A number of years ago, for example, the Chrysler Motor Company used a series of humorous commercials in support of the Dodge automobile. The entire approach was inappropriate to the basic image of the car, and the net result was to create confusion about how the product was positioned and to cheapen the product.

The Length of Commercials

Since time is the controlling factor in terms of how much can be said in a commercial, commercial length is a critical consideration. Normally, radio commercials run for 10, 20, 30, or 60 seconds, although longer time segments can be purchased. For example, a few years ago, a con artist used a fifteen minute radio commercial to advertise the "Rose of Shangri-la" to aspiring horticulturists. The commercial wove a romantic legend of how explorers, lost in the remote reaches of Tibet, wandered into a hidden valley where they discovered an exotic rose which, at great expense, they imported to the United States, and which could be used to turn a routine garden into a place of wonder and beauty. Listeners were urged to create their Shangri-la by sending their order, accompanied by their personal check, to a post office box number. Those who responded received a species of multi-flora rose, a thorny, sprawling shrub (*Rosa multiflora*) having clusters of small fragrant flowers, that is widely used as a windbreak in agricultural areas of the midwest. It was a real rip-off.

Normally, however, radio commercials run for 10, 20, 30, or 60 seconds. If the commercial contains a musical introduction and close, or introduces special sound effects, the length of the product message is correspondingly reduced. Thus, the number of words that may be spoken in a commercial will vary with the length of the commercial and its structure. The average word count for radio commercials is:

10 seconds	25 words
20 seconds	45 words
30 seconds	65 words
60 seconds	125 words

Since 60-second commercials often include a musical introduction and close as well as identification of local dealers and their addresses, the actual amount of message time is often only 35 or 40 seconds.

Guidelines for Writing Radio Commercials

Although there are no hard and fast rules for writing radio commercials, the following guidelines can be helpful for the beginning writer.

Keep it simple. Complex verbal messages are hard to comprehend. The listener must grasp the important sales points at the time of presentation. There are no instant replays.

Use a dramatic device or provocative statement early in the commercial. If interest is not flagged in the first 8 or 10 seconds, the message will probably be lost.

Speak to people in their own language.   Monologues and conversations should sound natural (unless, of course, satire is being used), not stilted or contrived. Use familiar words, simple sentences, and easily understood references.

Repeat the product name.   Use the product name several times in the commercial and, if the name is confusing, spell it, more than once if possible.

Be specific.   Have something specific to say about product features or consumer benefits. Avoid generalities; they are meaningless.

Choose words carefully.   Radio commercials should be sparse and lean. Eliminate unnecessary words; use action words, not passive ones; personalize the message.

Repeat basic ideas.   If a sales point is important, repeat it. If it's not important, leave it out. The same point can often be made in different ways to avoid the sound of redundancy.

Identify the package.   Help the consumer visualize the package. If it is red, say "look for the red label." Or, if it has some other identifying characteristic—a picture, a special shape, or special material—use this feature to help identification.

Read the commercial aloud.   After it has been written, read it aloud to make sure it has no tongue trippers, that it flows smoothly, and that it is the proper length.

The Form of Radio Commercials

Radio commercials are usually prepared in the form of a script, much like the script for a play, that identifies the speakers and the sound effects to be used. Figure 15–4 shows a typical radio script for a 60-second commercial. If a script is not used because a personality is employed to deliver the commercial, the personality is simply given a fact sheet from which he or she can ad lib.

RADIO PRODUCTION

There are two basic ways of delivering a radio commercial: live and prerecorded. Sometimes both methods are combined in a single commercial.

Live Commercials.   A live commercial is one delivered on the air by an announcer or a station personality. The advantages of live commercials are that they are inexpensive and that local announcers may have popular followings that have confidence in what they say. The disadvantages, of course, are that the announcer may not stick to the script or may "flub" the delivery. When strict control of the presentation is desired, advertisers prefer to use prerecorded commercials.

Prerecorded Commercials.   Prerecorded commercials may be simple (using an announcer to deliver a straightforward message) or highly complex (using a number of voices, music, and sound effects that may require split-second timing). Prerecorded commercials are generally more expensive than live commercials—often considerably more. But they combine the advantages of control and the opportunity to use special effects to increase the impact and effectiveness of the commercial delivery.

When prerecorded commercials are used, they are assigned to a radio producer whose job is to set up a budget, select a recording studio, cast the voices, arrange for music and special effects, edit the results, and follow the commercial through to its completion. Music, sound effects, and the spoken message are often recorded separately and then combined on a *master tape* by the recording studio. Duplicates (*dupes*) of the master tape are made for distribution to local radio stations, or to the radio network. When local dealer identifications are *tagged* at the end of the commercial, these are generally dubbed in by a local announcer.

TELEVISION COMMERCIALS

Television commercials are immensely more complex and more costly than radio commercials. They also reach larger audiences and, generally, are more effective. A fairly complex prerecorded radio commercial may cost $4 thousand. A fairly simple television commercial of comparable quality may cost $20 to $25 thousand. A recent commercial package for Levi's— two 30-second and one 60-second commercial—cost $250 thousand.[7] The advertiser can get almost anything he wants in television, provided he is willing to pay the costs.

---

7. "Abel's technique lights the way for advertising," *Advertising Age* (August 22, 1977): 3

```
LEO BURNETT U.S.A.                          PRUDENTIAL PLAZA • CHICAGO, ILLINOIS 60601
                                                      312-565-5959


KELLOGG COMPANY                             As Recorded:
60-Second Live Radio Announcement           Typed:  6/20/78  lkh
("Personality"—Announcer)
"VITAMIN FORTIFIED"
CORPORATE


L-640-CORP-60

1                                           (TO BE USED WITH RECORDED "VITAMIN FORTIFIED"
                                            RADIO DONUT #0683-CORP-60)

2                                           (MUSIC UNDER :11)

3   ANNCR: (LIVE WITH MUSIC UNDER)          You might be doing something very smart every morning,

4                                           and not even know it.

5   SINGERS: (MUSIC TRK.)                   YOU OFTEN START YOUR DAY

6                                           SOME TASTY KELLOGG'S WAY

7                                           THAT'S SMART, THAT'S VERY SMART.

8                                           (MUSIC UNDER :21)

9   ANNCR: (LIVE WITH MUSIC UNDER)          If you had a Kellogg's fortified cereal with milk as part

10                                          of your breakfast this morning, you were smart. Because

11                                          a typical serving of a Kellogg's fortified cereal with milk

12                                          contains twenty-five percent of your daily allowance

13                                          for eight vitamins, plus ten percent of the iron. So

14                                          if you had a nutritious Kellogg's cereal this morning,

15                                          congratulations. You're smart.

16  SINGERS: (MUSIC TRK.)                   GIVE YOURSELF A BRAVO

17                                          A GREAT BIG HIP HURRAH

18                                          KELLOGG'S IN THE MORNING

19                                          IS A VERY SMART START FOR THE DAY.

20                                          KELLOGG'S

21                                          A VERY SMART, VERY SMART . . . START.
```

Figure 15–4. A radio script for a 60-second commercial

In the early days of television, the emphasis was on the product story; *double-spotting* (running two commercials back-to-back) was the measure of the industry's greed; and the novelty of the medium guaranteed viewer attention. Since then, the cost of television has skyrocketed. Three, four, five, six, seven, or more commercials are often run in succession, and commercial clutter has turned the medium into an endless succession of commercials. Joseph Ostrow, a senior vice-president and director of communications at Young and Rubicam, has charged that "The television industry, and most particularly the networks, seem unable to control their lust for greater and greater profitability." [8] There is a growing concern in

8. "Agency exec blasts tv pricing; CBS blames sudden demand," *Advertising Age* (August 22, 1977): 1.

the advertising industry that television is pricing itself out of the market.[9]

Rising costs and increased competition on television have had two consequences that affect TV commercials: (1) 60 second commercials are becoming a rarity, with most commercials being written for 30-seconds or less; (2) there has been an increased emphasis on technique (presentation), often at the expense of the product idea. Hank Seiden has addressed himself to this second point with the following classification of commercials.

> All commercials fall into one of four categories:
> Commercials with bad concepts and bad execution.
>   They're the worst.
> Commercials with bad concepts and good execution.
>   They're almost as bad.
> Commercials with good concepts and bad execution.
>   They're inexcusable.
> Commercials with good concepts and good execution.
>   That's advertising.[10]

Despite all of its problems, television is an exciting advertising medium. It is a slice-of-life, a view of the world in action, color, and sound, intruding itself into the viewer's living room. And, because of its versatility, it is exciting to write for.

The same creative process enters into the development of television commercials that underlies the other media. The commercial starts with an idea, and the stronger the idea, the stronger the commercial. The commercial is written within the framework of a copy strategy, but the opportunity for demonstrating the product is infinitely greater than in single dimension media such as magazines, newspapers, and radio.

As in all advertising, one of the major problems the writer faces is separating the essential facts, condensing and simplifying the basic idea behind the product. One highly successful television writer has described his approach to developing television commercials in the following way:

> Intelligent advertising should begin with the ability to condense a complicated sales message down to its basic form: a headline and a picture. The further we get away from these two elements, the poorer our communication becomes. So, far from being ends in themselves, TV techniques should operate only to make the headline and picture more interesting, more exciting, and more convincing as clearly, quickly, and simply as possible.

With that in mind, I ask you to consider my plan: Every creative team, before starting a TV campaign or commercial, should first rough out a print ad communicating the same message to be communicated in the TV commercial. Needless to say, the team should execute this print ad, consisting of headline, rough visual, and copy points, just for themselves. No one else should see it. To be on the safe side, they should also consider several approaches before deciding on the best way to go. In the end, it's not only conceivable but entirely probable that they'll spend more time on the ad than on the actual television storyboard, because the storyboard will come easily after this basic conceptual groundwork has been laid.

If nothing else, this technique is bound to sharpen creative thinking by forcing a team to determine, first, the single most important point to be made, and, second, how best to make it.

As for the rest, it's easy. The print ad should be used as a blueprint for the TV storyboard and the final execution. All along the way, the storyboard should be judged against this ad to see that the idea hasn't been lost, obscured, or slowed down in translation from print to TV. And it would be a good idea if, in the final production of the commercial, the print ad were prominently displayed so that every time a production technique begins to crush the basic idea, it can be stopped then and there.

As a guide for the final editing, nothing could beat the print ad. It should also be compared to the finished commercial, just to see how closely the technique of one medium has approximated the other.

The print ad, you might say, is ideally suited to serve as the conscience of our industry. If we paid more attention to our consciences, as theologians and thinkers have advised for solid centuries, we would see better and more effective TV commercials in the future.[11]

The forms that TV commercials can take are endless—stand-up presentations, dramatization, song and dance numbers, testimonials, dialogues, cartoons, fantasy, and so forth. But the real key to the effective use of television is *demonstration*. Television was made for demonstration. It is its ultimate weapon. The fact that so many commercials fail to use it suggests that they have nothing to sell, or that the medium is being misused. I suggest that any product that has an excuse for existing has something to demonstrate. Finding that *something* is the job of the copy group. It's what they are paid for.

Not all demonstrations are equally effective, of course. The demonstration of a weak idea is the sign of a weak product or a lazy copy group. A demonstration that is in poor taste is inexcusable. And the substitution of technique for content is the bane of much television advertising. Although advertising is

9. "Advertisers restless, but stay with tv," *Advertising Age* (September 26, 1977): 1.
10. Hank Seiden, *Advertising Pure and Simple* (New York: AMACOM, a division of the American Management Associations, 1976), p. 35.

11. *Ibid,* pp. 93–94.

"If it doesn't look natural, it's not for me."

As kids, we grew up with "Does she...or doesn't she?"® So when I made that important decision to use haircoloring, I picked Miss Clairol.® Now I know why it's famous. The color has a soft, lively look to it that does a lot for me. My hair has a healthy sheen, nice highlights, and I like the way it feels. But it's really the color! It looks totally natural <u>every</u> time. And that's what I care about most...if it doesn't look natural, it's not for me.

<u>Miss Clairol</u>®...first for natural looking hair color.

Plate 14-1. This ad uses an <u>editorial</u> format: dominant illustration followed by headline, body copy, and logo (Clairol, Inc.).

The Smokey Mary

We never dreamed when we first launched the Smirnoff Bloody Mary it would become a global classic.

That doesn't mean, however, that most folks know how to make a really good one, or even care to bother.

One fellow we know "cops out," as he says, with the Smokey Mary. "To put the bite in, I just add red barbecue sauce." A capital idea, for those who hate to fuss.

If you should become a Smokey Mary

enthusiast, do pace your drinks. Try to remember that where there's smoke, there's fire.

To make a Smokey Mary pour 1½ ounces of Smirnoff into a glass with ice and fill with tomato juice. Add about a tablespoon of barbecue sauce to taste, a squeeze of lemon, and stir.

leaves you breathless.

Plate 14-4. ▶

This Le Car ad is a single page bleed ad (Renault U.S.A., Inc.).

Plate 14-2.

This Smirnoff ad is a conventional page unit in which the illustration and print areas are surrounded by white trim space (Heublin, Inc.).

Plate 14-3.

This ad is double page; it bleeds on all sides and across the gutter (Courtesy of Revlon, Inc.)

Charlie, I just love what your makeup does for my skin.

Even after I take it off.

Do you ever feel like you're still wearing makeup even after you take it off? Your skin kind of dull and cloudy? Well, Charlie Makeup (Fresh New Makeup and Real Live Blush) will eliminate that feeling.

Charlie Makeup has a gel formula. A gel formula eliminates the necessity for a lot of complicated ingredients. That keeps Charlie Makeup very simple, indeed.

Just fresh pure makeup that looks and feels fresh, pure, and touchingly moist on your skin. And when you take it off? You'll have skin that looks and feels fresh, pure, and touchingly moist.

Is it any wonder Charlie Makeup is so lovable?

© 1976 Revlon, Inc.

Introducing Le Car

In Europe, where driving is a passion, where people demand economy, performance and a car that's fun to drive, over one million people have bought Le Car. Now, a proven success, Le Car comes to America.

Les Features

Le Car is a sports car with a back seat. With front wheel drive, rack and pinion steering and Michelin steel-belted radials standard, it offers fantastic handling, cornering and traction.

Le Performance

Le Car will not bore you. During 1976, it took first in its class in 12 out of 16 races, beating Hondas, Datsuns, Pintos, Vegas, Toyotas, and Fiats. Le Car combines great performance with 41 MPG highway, 25 MPG city.* *Remember:* These mileage figures are *estimates*. The actual mileage *you* get will vary depending on the type of driving you do, your driving habits, your car's condition and optional equipment. *California excluded

Le Fantastic Ride

Unlike other little cars, Le Car rides so smoothly, even on rough roads, it'll amaze you.

Le City Car

Le Car maneuvers in and out of, around and through traffic. And it fits in a smaller parking space than the Honda, Chevette or Rabbit.

Le Price

Le Car prices start at only $3345.†
Call 800-631-1616 for nearest dealer. In N.J. call collect 201-461-6000.

†P.O.E. East Coast: Price excludes transportation, dealer preparation and taxes. Stripe, Mag wheels, Sun roof and Rear wiper/washer optional at extra cost. Prices slightly higher in the West.
Renault U.S.A., Inc. ©1977

Le Car by Renault ◆

Plate 14-5.

Thumbnail sketches for a proposed ad (Courtesy of Kellogg Company and Leo Burnett U.S.A. Agency).

It's no accident our cereals are an excellent nutritional complement to milk.

Kellogg's

"A very smart start"

Plate 14-6.

Rough layout (Courtesy of Kellogg Company and Leo Burnett U.S.A.).

It's no accident our cereals are an excellent nutritional complement to milk.

Kellogg's
"A very smart start"

It's no accident our cereals are an excellent nutritional complement to milk.

97% of all ready-to-eat cereals get teamed up with milk. And nutritionally, they make great partners.

Take a look at the chart below. You will see that, in a typical serving of Kellogg's Corn Flakes® cereal and milk, it's the milk that supplies the most calcium, phosphorus and magnesium. But it's the cereal that provides virtually all the iron, and most of the vitamins, while they both contribute protein.

That two foods should complement each other so well is no accident. We fortify our cereals with essential nutrients milk alone does not supply.

Kellogg's cereal and milk. Great partners in nutrition. A very smart start.

Relative contribution of the nutrients in a serving of 1 oz. Kellogg's Corn Flakes® cereal and 4 oz. Vitamin D Fortified Whole Milk

Nutrient	% U.S. RDA	% Contributed by One-Ounce Kellogg's Corn Flakes	■ % From Cereal □ % From Milk	% Contributed by ½ Cup Vitamin D Fortified Whole Milk
Iron	10	100		trace
Folic Acid	25	100		trace
Niacin	25	100		trace
Vitamin B₆	25	100		trace
Vitamin C	25	100		trace
Thiamin	25	100		trace
Vitamin A	30	93		17
Riboflavin	35	71		29
Calories	*	61		39
Vitamin D	25	40		60
Protein	15	27		73
Magnesium	4	trace		100
Phosphorus	10	trace		100
Calcium	15	trace		100

*US RDA for Calories not established.

Kellogg's®
A very smart start.

®Kellogg Company ©1978 Kellogg Company

Plate 14-9.

Progressive proofs are proofs of all color
plates used separately for one operation
and of the combinations. They indicate color
quality. The proofs shown here are seen in
the following order:
(a) yellow
(b) red
(c) yellow and red
(d) blue
(e) blue, yellow, and red
(f) black
(g) final combination of four colors (Aynsley Bone China)

a

b

c

d

WHEN THE QUEEN OF ENGLAND
WANTED BONE CHINA FOR HER WEDDING,
SHE CHOSE AYNSLEY.

A timely investment
in a timeless art.
Free booklets.
Aynsley English Bone China.
225 Fifth Avenue.
New York 10010
The English member of
the Waterford Crystal family.
By hand. With heart.

e

f

WHEN THE QUEEN OF ENGLAND
WANTED BONE CHINA FOR HER WEDDING,
SHE CHOSE AYNSLEY.

A timely investment
in a timeless art.
Free booklets.
Aynsley English Bone China.
225 Fifth Avenue.
New York 10010
The English member of
the Waterford Crystal family.
By hand. With heart.

g

With KitchenAid, the dishes come out clean no matter who loads them.

The KitchenAid® Load-As-You-Like Dishwasher.

Loading a KitchenAid dishwasher is so easy anyone can do it.

 That's because there are wash arms above and below both racks. Which means you can put pots and pans in either rack and know they'll come out thoroughly clean because of the up and down, all-around scrubbing action.

The top rack on the KitchenAid Superba adjusts to 16 different positions so there's plenty of room for big things above and below.

A built-in Soft Waste Disposer means you don't have to pre-rinse.

And the KitchenAid Superba has a Soak 'n Scrub™ pot cleaning cycle that gets dirty pans and casseroles really clean.

With all this, the KitchenAid dishwasher is the most energy efficient we've ever built.

People who own dishwashers  say KitchenAid is the best. So, for quiet, dependable dishwashers, see your KitchenAid dealer. He's listed in the Yellow Pages under "Dishwashing Machines."

KitchenAid®
People say it's the best.

Plate 14-10.   In this KitchenAid ad, <u>gaze motion</u> is used to focus attention on the important ad elements.

indispensable to modern marketing, it is not marketing. Marketing begins with a consumer benefit and a product concept that provides that benefit. It is the job of advertising to present the concept clearly, interestingly, and dramatically.

Development of TV Commercials

Like a radio commercial, a TV commercial first appears as a script. However, a TV script differs from a radio script in that it is usually written in double columns, with the audio on one side and the video on the other (see figure 15–5). For presentation purposes, the script is rendered in the form of a storyboard which visualizes the action, scene by scene, as it occurs. Fig-

ure 15–6 shows how the script in figure 15–5 was transformed into a storyboard.

Like a magazine layout, the storyboard may be presented in rough, finished, or comprehensive form. The purpose of the storyboard is to permit the client to visualize the commercial, to facilitate communication between the writer and producer, and, sometimes, for estimating costs.

In describing the action and sounds in a TV script or storyboard, the industry has developed its own jargon. Some of the most commonly used symbols and expressions are identified in table 15–1.

Although these terms are often used in a TV script or storyboard to help explain what is happening, their actual use in production of a commercial is usually at

LEO BURNETT U.S.A.
A DIVISION OF LEO BURNETT COMPANY, INC.
ADVERTISING

PRUDENTIAL PLAZA • CHICAGO, ILLINOIS
312-236-5959

KELLOGG COMPANY
30-Second Film
"BUILDING BREAKFAST"
CORPORATE
KLKL6280

Approved for Bidding: 8/17/77

VIDEO		*AUDIO*
OPEN ON KID HOLDING BLOCK WAVING ARM.	KID:	Hey, give us a hand. We're building a better breakfast.
	KID:	What's that?
SHOW KIDS AND BLOCKS IN 4 FOOD GROUPS.	KID:	That's a breakfast with foods from at least three of the four basic food groups.
CU OF KID AND ORANGE JUICE BLOCK.	KID:	I've got orange juice from the fruit and vegetable group.
CU OF KID AND MILK BLOCK.	KID:	Here comes milk from the milk group.
CU OF KID AND CORN FLAKES BLOCK.	KID:	Make room for corn flakes and toast from the cereal and bread group.
KIDS PILING BLOCKS TOGETHER.	KID:	Now that's a well built breakfast.
KIDS ADMIRING BLOCK BREAKFAST.	KID:	Yep! It's got the energy you need for an active day.
	KID:	Build a better breakfast tomorrow.
SHOW 4 BREAKFASTS. SUPER: "KELLOGG'S".	ANNCR:	(VO) This better breakfast message is from Kellogg's.

Figure 15–5. TV script

1. OPEN ON KID HOLDING BLOCK WAVING ARM.
   KID: Hey, give us a hand.

2. SHOW KIDS AND BLOCKS IN 4 FOOD GROUPS.
   KID: We're building a better breakfast.
   KID: What's that?
   KID: That's a breakfast with foods from at least three of the
   four basic food groups.

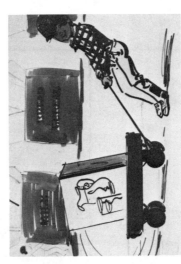

3. CU OF KID AND ORANGE JUICE BLOCK.
   KID: I got orange juice from the fruit and vegetable group.

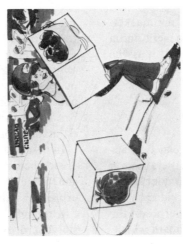

4. CU OF KID AND MILK BLOCK.
   KID: Here comes the milk from the milk group.

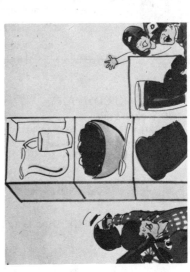

5. CU OF KID AND CORN FLAKES.
   KID: Make room for corn flakes from the bread
   and cereal group.

6. KIDS PILING BLOCKS TOGETHER.
   KID: Now that's a well-built breakfast.

7. KIDS ADMIRING BLOCK BREAKFAST.
   KID: Yep! It's got the energy you need for an active
   day.
   KID: Build a better breakfast tomorrow.

8. SHOW 4 BREAKFASTS. SUPER: "KELLOGG'S."
   ANNCR: (VO) this better breakfast message is from
   Kellogg's.

Table 15-1. Terms Commonly used in TV Scripts

Term	Definition
SFX	Sound effects
VO	Voice over
ANN	Announcer
Music up and out	A final blare of music
Music under	Background music that is under the dialogue
Music down and out	The music fades out
CU	Close-up shot
ECU	Extremely close up
Pan	To sweep the camera across the scene
LS	Long shot
MS	A medium distance shot
Dolly	To move the camera in and out of a scene
Cut	To move abruptly from one scene to another
Dissolve	To fade out one scene while fading in another
Optical	Any special visual effect such as dissolving a scene with a diamond effect, stopping motion in midflight, dividing the screen into quarters, and so forth.
Super	To superimpose something— usually a word, phrase, or product name—over the picture

the discretion of the producer. As one television writer has pointed out:

> For years advertising copywriters and TV producers have been playing a little straight-faced game in which the copywriter . . . lards his script with all kinds of cuts, dissolves, fades, ECU's and dollies. The producer gravely accepts this script, reads it over, and then goes ahead and shoots the thing as he pleases—which is probably just as well.[12]

The guidelines for writing an effective TV commercial are not much different from those for writing an effective radio commercial. The most important admonition is still "keep it simple." There are, however, certain considerations that are unique to television.

Use the video. That's what it is for. Don't waste time talking about something that can be more easily shown in a picture. Further, the video should carry the burden of the commercial. The audio serves to interpret and enhance the action.

Coordinate the audio and video. Make the audio and video work together. Few things are more confusing in this world than audio and video tracks that don't relate to one another.

Use action where possible. Ideas can be comprehended quickly in visual form. So, action should be used to maintain attention and keep the commercial moving forward. Agnew and O'Brien, in describing television advertising, have suggested: "A picture should be simple enough to grasp in five seconds; so, as a rule of thumb, a picture should not be kept static any longer than that."[13]

Don't let the desire to entertain get in the way of the message. This is the greatest danger in television writing. TV is such an outstanding entertainment medium that there is always the temptation to entertain rather than to persuade. Entertainment is fine as long as it is not done for its own sake, but used in *support* of the advertising message.

TELEVISION PRODUCTION

Television production begins with the approval of the storyboard and the budget by the client. In the process of production, a TV commercial will change more than any other form of advertising. This is true because the TV script and storyboard are essentially static, whereas the finished commercial is enhanced by casting, action, sets, optical devices, music, voices, and other sound effects. Although the script and storyboard provide direction and a constraint on what will be produced, an experienced, sensitive director can often strengthen a commercial immeasurably. As a consequence, on-the-spot modifications and changes are commonplace, and often necessary. This is why many major advertising agencies often insist that the TV writer be present on location during production to make sure that such changes add too, and do not detract from, the original concept of the commercial.

Methods of Television Production

TV commercials may be delivered as live presentations, or produced on film or video tape. The choice of production techniques depends largely on the nature of the commercial, the budget available for production, the effects to be obtained, and the preferences of the producer.

Live Commercials. Live commercials are usually delivered on camera by a station announcer or by a program personality. While live commercials were used extensively in the early days of TV, they are rarely

---

12. James S. Norris, *Advertising* (Reston, Virginia: Reston Publishing Co., Inc., 1977), p. 209.

13. Clark M. Agnew and Niel O'Brien, *Television Advertising* (New York: McGraw-Hill, Inc., 1958), p. 98.

Figure 15-6. TV storyboard

used today except on local news shows, some talk shows such as the Tonight Show, and audience participation shows where members of the studio audience compete for prizes or cash awards.

The advantages of live commercials are their spontaneity, the opportunity to capitalize on a program personality, and the ability to relate the product to topical subjects. Their disadvantages, however, are immense. There can be no retakes, no editing, no corrections, and few special effects. Other reasons for the decrease in the use of live commercials are that some stations will not accept them because they do not have adequate production facilities, and the widespread use of *spot television* announcements in local markets make them unfeasible.

Filmed Commercials. About 80 percent of the commercial production of national advertisers is made on 35-millimeter film, similar to that used in commercial motion pictures, although there is a growing use of 16-millimeter film for this purpose.[14] Film is the most versatile and flexible production medium, although it is also the most expensive and time consuming. It lends itself to complicated visual effects and trick photography—such as the "invisible man" sequence used by Haynes underwear, or the miniature chuck wagon used in Purina's Chuck Wagon Dog Food commercials. It is easy to edit, so that scenes can be shot at different locations and assembled for the final commercial.

Videotape. Both the video and sound portions of commercials can be recorded by videotape cameras on magnetic tape similar to that used on home tape recorders. Initially, it was thought that videotape would replace film as the primary production medium for TV commercials because of its cost advantages over film, its high quality of reproduction, and its speed. Videotape, like the instant replays of professional football broadcasts, can be broadcast almost immediately after filming. However, this has not been the case for practical reasons. Film has continued to flourish because of its greater versatility in editing and in creating special visual effects. The development of new videotape equipment and production techniques is beginning to overcome these limitations of tape production, and a recent survey by Eastman Kodak indicates a substantial increase in videotape production, particularly among local and regional advertisers who do not have easy access to film production facilities.[15]

Further, more and more advertising agencies are shooting on film and then transferring to videotape. This is being done for a variety of reasons.

1. Higher fidelity sound can be obtained, since the original sound track is cut on magnetic tape and its transfer to film causes a slight loss in clarity.
2. It is possible to take a badly timed piece of film and electronically color-correct it on videotape in a matter of minutes; whereas the same color correction on film would take several days at an optical house.
3. When a network is supplied with film, it transfers it to videotape before it is broadcast, so there is no reason the network should not be provided with videotape in the first place.[16]

Preparing for Production

Regardless of the production method, thorough preplanning prior to the actual shooting of a commercial is essential. Production studios and shooting crews are paid according to the time they spend on the set or on location. A cost of $10 thousand for a day's shooting is not unusual. As a consequence, the details of production should be worked out before the actual shooting begins to avoid costly delays. Live commercials also require careful preplanning because there is only one chance to do the commercial right.

Selection of a Production Studio. Although many local and regional advertisers use television stations for their commercial production, national advertisers generally use production studios that specialize in commercial production. The particular studio used should be selected early in the prepreparation stage because studio personnel play an important role in preproduction planning. There are two primary considerations in the selection of a production studio: *capability* and *cost.* Studios differ in their capabilities. Some specialize in film, and some in videotape. Some are uniquely equipped for shooting on location; others have elaborate studio facilities. Some specialize in animation; others specialize in live action. It is particularly important to select a production house that is adept in the techniques required for the commercial in question.

Since television production is expensive, a number of qualified production studios are usually asked to bid competitively. Bids are based on discussisons of the storyboard, as well as other specifications provided by the advertiser or its advertising agency. These discussions not only provide comparative cost esti-

14. Arthur Bellaire, "Nat Eisenberg tells agencies: Videotape commercials merit more consideration," *Advertising Age* (May 5, 1975).
15. Hooper White, "Is videotape an art form or hardware convention?" *Advertising Age* (August 22, 1977): 44–45.
16. *Ibid,* p. 44.

mates, but they often uncover opportunities for cost reductions or indicate that a particular studio is better qualified than others for achieving the desired end result.

The selection of a recording studio for sound tracks follows the same procedures as those used in choosing a production studio. Since sound studios are less specialized than film or tape houses, the selection process is less complex.

Preproduction Meetings. After a production house has been selected, one or more preproduction meetings are scheduled to plan the actual shooting or recording sessions. Normally, these meetings include the agency producer, the production house producer, the director, and often the commercial writer or art director. Sometimes the advertising manager of an agency account executive may attend, but this is not normal procedure.

The purposes of the preproduction meetings are to explain the concept behind the commercial, to anticipate any special problems that may arise during the shooting sessions, and to reach agreement as to how each scene is to be handled. These meetings also assign responsibility for obtaining props, wardrobes, actors and actresses, selecting locations for scenes that cannot be shot in the studio, and making whatever arrangements are necessary. Assembling props is a tedious chore, and a talent for detail is a prerequisite for those assigned this responsibility.

Casting. Casting for commercials is often critical since the people used must be selected so as to project the personality attributes envisioned in the commercial. In many cases, professional models are used; in other instances, professional actors or actresses are required because some models can't act. In still other instances, nonprofessionals may be employed, particularly if the commercial requires testimonials from consumers. Usually the agency producer serves as casting director, although he is often assisted by the production studio. Since professional models and actors belong to unions, most payments are standardized; however, when well-known actors or actresses are employed, a special fee is often negotiated.

Sound Tracks. Sound tracks are often shot separately and then synchronized with the video portion of the commercial. When background music is required, a special score has to be prepared. This score is recorded separately and then synchronized with the action in the editing process. It is not uncommon to shoot the video portion in one section of the country and record the sound track in another, especially if a particular musical group or announcer is desired.

Shooting the Commercial

When shooting with actors, each sequence is shot separately and assembled during editing. Frequently, scenes are not shot sequentially in order to minimize set changes and actors' time. Individual scenes are rehearsed and shot several times from different camera angles and under different direction, so that a good take is assured.

In the case of animation, the sound track is prepared first, and then the action is designed around it. Next, artwork is prepared and transferred to clear plastic sheets called *cells* for photographing. Finally, the video and audio portions are assembled and synchronized.

When actors have speaking parts in the commercial, the sound is often recorded "on camera" at the same time the picture is shot in order to insure that the audio and video portions are synchronized. In the case of *voiceover,* where the announcer is heard but not seen, and in animated commercials, the sound track is recorded separately and joined with the video during editing.

Editing

Editing is the process of selecting, splicing, and synchronizing the video and audio portions of the commercial. In this process, several thousands of feet of film may be viewed in selecting the scenes that will be used in the final commercial. There are a number of sequential steps taken in the editing process. After the commercial has been shot, the film is sent to a laboratory for processing or developing (in the case of videotape, this step is unnecessary). The unedited film, called *rushes,* is viewed to make sure that the material on hand is adequate and that no further shooting or retakes are necessary. The next step is to select scenes from the rushes, assemble them in sequential form, and synchronize them with a separate soundtrack. This process yields a *rough-cut* or *interlock* which is usually viewed by the agency account executive and the client. After the interlock has been approved, the film is sent to an optical house so that special visual effects, such as *wipes, dissolves, fades,* and *supers* can be added. Finally, the audio and video portions are assembled on a single film or tape referred to as an *answer print.* The answer print is corrected for color, quality, density, and synchronization of sound. The corrected answer print becomes the *master print* from which duplicates are made for distribution to the stations carrying the commercial.

The production of a television commercial is a complex operation, requiring the talents of many specialists and using highly sophisticated equipment.

Normal production time runs from six weeks to two months from the approval of the storyboard until prints are shipped to television stations for use.

SUMMARY

A major difference that distinguishes broadcast media from print advertising is that broadcast deals with time, whereas print advertising deals with space. Since the consumer has no opportunity to study and reflect on a commercial, the central idea must be presented simply, clearly, and memorably. At the same time, however, broadcast advertising lends itself to a variety of special effects and attention getting devices that are not available to the print writer.

Radio commercials can be classified in many ways, such as humorous, jingle, narrative, dialogue, and straight delivery. There is no classification system that can do justice to the variety of effects that can be created with sound, however. The primary reason for recognizing the various classifications of commercials is to emphasize the versatility of the medium.

Since time is the controlling factor in terms of what can be said in a commercial, commercial length is a critical consideration. Normally, radio commercials run for 10, 20, 30, or 60 seconds.

Although there are no hard and fast rules for writing radio commercials, there are guidelines that can be helpful to the beginning writer. These guidelines include admonitions such as: keep it simple; be specific; repeat basic ideas.

Radio commercials are usually prepared in the form of a script, although fact sheets rather than scripts are often used when well-known personalities are employed to deliver commercials. Radio commercials may be delivered live or prerecorded; each approach has its own strengths and limitations.

Television commercials are much more complex than radio commercials because they involve both sight and sound. The key to effective television commercials is *demonstration,* and the greatest danger in developing TV commercials is to let the technique of presentation get in the way of the product story.

One useful approach to developing a TV commercial is first to develop a print ad that condenses the selling message into its basic form: a picture and a headline. This print ad should then be used as the guide for the commercial.

Television has its own jargon, which is used in scripts and storyboards to describe how the commercial will be filmed. However, regardless of the instructions written on the script or storyboard, final decisions on filming are the responsibility of the producer.

As in the case of radio, there are certain guidelines that can be helpful to the novice television writer. Basically, these guidelines emphasize the use of video, the need for coordination between video and audio, and the use of action.

Television production is much more complex than radio production. Because of its complexity, preproduction meetings are essential when preparing to shoot a television commercial. The method of production (film versus video tape), the selection of a production house, decisions on casting and sets, and the determination of how various scenes will be shot must be made ahead of time in order to conserve both time and money. Television production proceeds through several well-defined stages: the actual shooting of the film, the assembling of the commercial, the coordination of sight and sound, editing, color corrections, and the production of a master print.

QUESTIONS

1. Identify and explain the four suggestions at the beginning of the chapter for being a good television writer.
2. Identify the major ways that broadcast writing differs from print writing.
3. Evaluate the use of rhyme in broadcast writing. What are its advantages and disadvantages?
4. Identify the guidelines for effective radio commercials. Why are they only guidelines rather than rules?
5. Distinguish between *live* and *prerecorded* radio commercials. What are the advantages and disadvantages of each?
6. Translate a print ad for a current product into a radio commercial.
7. Develop a TV script and/or storyboard from a current magazine print ad.
8. Identify and explain the guidelines for an effective TV commercial.
9. Distinguish between and evaluate the following forms of TV production: (a) live, (b) filmed, and (c) videotape.
10. Outline and explain the major steps in TV production.

PROBLEM

Select a consumer magazine ad for a product that can be advertised on TV.
1. Write a 30-second TV script from it.

2. Write a 60-second TV script from it.
(Bring the ad to class so that it can be compared with your TV scripts.)

Advertising Media—
Strategies and Plans

As pointed out at the beginning of part 5, the advertising portion of the marketing plan consists of two areas—copy and media. These two aspects of advertising are inseparable because copy, no matter how well conceived and executed, has no business value until it is exposed to a target group of consumers; and media, without advertising copy, is simply a public service. In fact, one of the specters that haunts most advertising agencies is that they will fail to meet a magazine closing date. I doubt that a day passes without someone in some advertising agency making the wry comment: "Well, we can always run a blank page and say, 'This blank page is brought to you through the courtesy of our client.' "

In this part of the book, we will deal with media strategy and the major and minor media that are used to carry advertising messages to consumers. Chapter 16 deals with media strategy, and some of the considerations that enter into media selection. Chapter 17 will discuss the characteristics of major print media—newspapers and magazines. Chapter 18

will address itself to broadcast media—television and radio. And chapter 19 will discuss some of the minor media—outdoor advertising, transit advertising, program media, and so forth.

Media strategy, selection, scheduling, and coordination is a highly complex task that must consider both the quantitative and qualitative aspects of media. Major quantitative consideration are:

1. "reach"—the number of consumers exposed to at least one advertising message
2. "frequency"—the number of times that the average, target consumer is exposed to an advertising message during a particular period of time, usually a four week period
3. "budget constraints"—all media programs are limited by the available budget, and compromises between what one would like to do and what one can afford to do are the realities of media planning.

Qualitative aspects of media include such things as the editorial climate—its appropriateness and its mood.

Media planners in major advertising agencies are highly skilled professionals. Their jobs, like most jobs in advertising, are filled with deadlines, compromises, and frustrations. But, those jobs can also be exciting and rewarding, both personally and financially.

16

Media Strategy

Panasonic

Panasonic spends approximately $17 million annually in the United States and includes consumer magazines, television, newspapers, and business magazines in its media schedules. *Media Decisions* (MD) magazine explored Panasonic's media philosophy with Russ Johnson, who is responsible for advertising and public relations policy in the United States for Matsushita Corporation of America, the manufacturers of Panasonic. Excerpts from this interview are shown below:

MD: Does the creative and product decision affect the media you will use?

Johnson: It should and does.

MD: When are media decisions made?

Johnson: The media plan is never set until after the creative plan is finalized. The number of ads, the individual creative strategies of each ad, the particular people we are trying to reach, the editorial environment of individual magazines, all play an important part in our media selection. We have certain strategy guidelines that affect both creative and media. One we call the "environment" situation where we put the product in a situation that emphasizes the use or uniqueness of the item. But it must be a natural en-

vironment, not a forced one. For instance, we do not use people as props. They must enforce the creative strategy, not obscure it. Then we look for magazines or TV programs with an "editorial" or "story" environment to complement the environment of our ad.

This sounds very basic, but most basic principles are forgotten. . . .

MD: Does such a matter as good times/bad times also affect what media you use?

Johnson: Yes, it does. During that period of economic recession, we shifted a good deal of our TV investment from network to spot. Based upon the simple fact that it takes heavy-up, creative pressure to separate a man and his money during bad times. The consumer is worrying about paying his mortgage, his overhead, and building up his savings account for tomorrow. So it takes a lot of pressure to convince him to buy, not on price but on value.

During the recession we put our weight in the major markets where income is more plentiful, where there was at least some economic chance to move the consumer.

MD: With such a varied line of merchandise, you must have a lot of different target audiences. How do you decide your targets?

Johnson: We decide on the basis of the product itself. We watch warranty card returns. We listen to our sales personnel. Our dealers. We sent project teams out into the big markets, small markets, urban markets, rural markets. But in most cases, our products are male-oriented. And we decided a long time ago to target in at the male 18 to 34 group. We wanted to zero in and not zero out. We felt this group was an active group, more easily persuaded to change on the basis of sensible, creative arguments. . . .[1]

Furniture

Another article in *Media Decisions* discusses general strategic considerations for advertising furniture, with particular emphasis on the strategy of Thomasville.

The furniture business is what you call a slow sell.

No impulse buying here. The choice of furniture is a carefully considered decision involving life style, aesthetic taste, budget, and future plans.

The nature of that market is reflected in the media most often selected to reach the prospective furniture buyer. Save for occasional adventurous excursions into television, furniture advertising has been at home in magazines.

The target audience for furniture is vast. Nearly all Americans at one time or another buy and own furniture. So it's often not a question of who buys furniture, but who buys it when, and in what price range.

Furniture is one of the more lightly advertised product categories in the home furnishings field. Leading National Advertisers shows $27,935,100 spent on the product category in 1976. And $5.5 million of that was for mattresses. . . .

A view of that market and Thomasville's approach is provided by William E. Beste, a vice president at BBDO, acct. sup. of the Thomasville account.

Thomasville is in the upper bracket of the price range, specializing in dining room and bedroom suites. The art and copy approach is sumptuous. Their advertisements don't just entertain your eyes with elegant furniture, but with complete living environments. If they've sold you the mood of their artwork, they've probably gone a long way toward selling you their furniture.

Thomasville had a brief flirtation with television in the late 1960s, but found the impression left with viewers was all too fleeting, the wastage in audience extreme, and the cost of reaching the target audience selectively, too high. . . .

And furniture, being a product the buyer wants to see, if not feel, requires a visual color medium.

Beste explains the media requirements for Thomasville this way: "First off, we're talking about an upper-medium to upper price range. Now our principally advertised products are dining room and bedroom suites. So we are looking for selectivity, not general exposure. And you can do that better in magazines than any other medium.

"Another factor is that furniture falls into a big ticket considered purchase category. Our research shows that people take between a year and a year and a half to make a purchase decision.

"Before making that purchase, the consumer wants to accumulate a number of options. Ads from magazines can be clipped and saved. The television image goes by too quickly, although home TV cassette recording could change that.

"The aesthetic details of the art work are another factor in media selection," Beste says. "With print we can concentrate on the aesthetic angles most pertinent to the impression we want to make."

To determine what magazines to use, BBDO and Thomasville researched the target audience and who is influential in the purchase decision.

They discovered that furniture purchase comes at measurable points in the family life cycle. Newlyweds make furniture purchases, but not often in the up-scale Thomasville range. The arrival of children is another trigger for furniture purchase, as are changes in economic status that provide greater disposable income, family moves, the acquisition of a second home, the departure of children for college or marriage, and retirement.

When those times arrive, Thomasville is after the up-scale family with an eye to greater elegance in bedroom and dining room furnishings.[2]

Campbell's Soup

Campbell soup faced an entirely different strategy problem from that of Panasonic and Thomasville. Unlike electronic equipment and furniture, soup is a convenience food. Further, Campbell is the unchallenged leader in the field. The soup section of any supermarket is dominated by Campbell soups, and, on any given day, the pantry shelf of the average consumer will contain several cans and a variety of flavors carrying the red and white Campbell label. The Campbell marketing effort is a well-organized and smoothly functioning operation. Campbell advertising is well-conceived, and the "soup for lunch" slogan and the "Campbell Kids" are a part of Americana.

The question: "How can media strategy be used to increase the effectiveness of Campbell's marketing program? Herb Maneloveg, while media director of the BBDO advertising agency, found a way. Campbell's media strategies were reexamined, and a substantial sum of money was transferred to prelunchtime radio. The result was a substantial increase in sales volume, attributed to more frequent use of soup for lunches.[3]

1. "We Pick the Media to Match the Message," *Media Decisions* (September, 1977): 125.

2. "Why Furniture Favors Magazines, Long Term," *Media Decisions* (September, 1977): 72 ff.
3. Arnold M. Barban, Stephen M. Cristol, and Frank J. Kopec, *Essentials of Media Planning* (Chicago: Crain Books, A Division of Crain Communications, Inc., 1976), p. 1.

All three of these examples are concerned with media strategy. The Panasonic example emphasizes the importance of coordinating media strategy with creative strategy, with the editorial environment of the media used, and with the economic climate that dominates the product decision. Thomasville points up the importance of selectivity in media, and the need to recognize consumer buying practices in media selection. Campbell soup demonstrates how media strategy can be used to increase the effectiveness of an already effective program by the use of "reminder" advertising immediately prior to lunch—a time of major soup consumption.

THEORIES OF MEDIA USE

It is doubtful that any aspect of the advertising industry is free from disagreement and controversy. Media is no exception. Each medium has its advocates and detractors; there is disagreement among professionals about how media can be used most effectively; and there is little hard evidence that there is one best approach. Yesterday's gamble is today's practice, and today's practice is tomorrow's anachronism.

There are a number of theories of media use, each of which seeks some compromise between the multiple demands of *reach, frequency,* and *continuity,* all three of which few advertisers can afford.

Reach is defined as the unduplicated proportion of a defined audience that is exposed to an advertising message within a particular period of time, usually four weeks. Why four weeks? Arbitrary. But that is the traditional time horizon on which most media data is based.

Frequency refers to the number of times within a given four-week period that a particular audience or a portion of that audience is exposed to the message. Frequency can be expressed in two ways: (1) in terms of *average frequency,* or (2) in terms of the *frequency distribution.* If frequency is stated as an average of 4.0, this means that the average member of the target market is exposed to the advertising message 4.0 times during the four-week period. Not all members of the target market will be exposed precisely this number of times, of course. Some will have more, and some will have fewer exposures. For example, the *frequency distribution* might look something like this:

0 - 1 exposures	10%
2 - 3 exposures	20%
4 exposures	40%
5 - 6 exposures	20%
6 + exposures	10%

Average frequency is generally used for media planning purposes, and the frequency distribution is often used to measure the amount of variability around this average that is actually attained. Both average frequency and frequency distributions are based on extremely gross estimates that imply a precision much greater than that which actually exists. Nonetheless, the concepts of average frequency and frequency distribution give a *rough* gauge for planning and evaluation purposes.

Continuity, as it is used in reference to media, refers to the *continuous* use of advertising over a specified period of time, usually for the duration of the marketing plan, which is one year. Thus, an advertiser whose advertising appeared every week for fifty-two weeks would be employing high continuity. Often, however, advertising will not be used throughout the year, but, instead, will be concentrated during peak buying seasons. For example, the advertiser of suntan lotion usually concentrates advertising during the summer months when the product is in greatest demand. Thus, *continuity* is sacrificed in order to gain *reach* and *frequency* during the peak buying period.

Most media plans end up as a compromise between reach, frequency, and continuity, with the nature of the compromise being determined by the judgment of the media planner and based on her understanding of the competitive situation and the product's advertising needs. Broadly speaking, there are four theories or approaches that may be used in seeking a viable compromise between these variables: *wave* theory, *media dominance* theory, *media concentration* theory, and *reach* theory.[4]

Wave Theory

Wave theory sacrifices continuity in order to achieve reach and frequency goals. In this approach, the advertiser purchases time and/or space in various media for a relatively short period of time (four weeks, for example), and moves in and out of these media in "waves." The assumption is that the effects of the advertising will carry over from periods of heavy concentration to those in which no advertising appears.

Media Dominance Theory

In media dominance theory, the advertiser buys an unusually large amount of time or space in one medium. After building dominance in that medium, funds are shifted to another medium for a short period of time. Through this process, the advertiser

4. Lyndon O. Brown, Richard S. Lessler, and William M. Weilbacher, *Advertising Media* (New York: The Ronald Press, 1957), p. 122.

achieves frequency in a variety of media for a short period of time, achieves reach through the use of several different media, and gains continuity of advertising through the use of successive media, although the continuity in any one medium is relatively low.

Media Concentration Theory

Through media concentration, reach is sacrificed in order to gain frequency and continuity by concentrating all funds in a single medium during the marketing period. For example, an advertiser might buy 12, two-page spreads (one each month) in *Reader's Digest,* or a similar schedule in two or three smaller circulation magazines, or a 30-second spot per week in a popular TV detective series or some other television vehicle.

Reach Theory

Reach theory maximizes reach at the sacrifice of both continuity and frequency. In this approach, a variety of media is used to attain maximum reach, with little consideration given to either frequency or continuity. For example, an advertiser might buy a package of 30-second TV spots appearing in a wide variety of television shows. An advertiser might schedule a single insertion in a wide list of magazines or use a combination of print and broadcast media, each on a limited basis.

Since these four approaches represent different ways of using media, an advertiser may also use some combination of them. For example, one might schedule a major space unit in each issue of a magazine (media concentration theory) and then supplement this schedule with four-week flights of radio spots run every three months (wave theory). Again, it must be emphasized that the particular pattern of media used will depend upon the competitive situation and the needs of the product in question.

Each of the foregoing approaches (or any combination of them) is a compromise between reach, frequency, and continuity. Such compromises must be made because few advertisers have sufficient funds to maximize each of these variables. As a consequence, the media planner seeks an optimal solution—that is, the best solution possible within the limits of the funds available. This, then, introduces the role of media strategy.

THE ROLE OF MEDIA STRATEGY

In chapter 3, it was pointed out that media strategy is subordinate to both the marketing and advertising strategies. These strategies establish general media constraints such as: (1) the amount of money available, (2) the definition of the target group or groups of consumers, (3) the relative emphasis to be given to each target group when more than one exists, and (4) when, during the year, advertising support is to be delivered. The basic function of media strategy is to show how media will be selected and used to meet these general objectives.

Generally, media strategy statements cover the following decision areas:

1. *Decisions concerning the general kinds of media to be used, along with a rationale for these decisions.*
   a. The use of local versus regional versus national media.
   b. The use of print versus broadcast media.
   c. The ways in which two or more media will be combined to meet specific marketing and advertising objectives.

2. *Decisions concerning types of media within broad media classifications, and the rationale for these decisions.*
   a. Types of programming within broadcast media—sports, drama, situation comedies, adventure, game shows, and so forth.
   b. Types of magazines, such as women's, men's, special interest or general interest magazines.

3. *Decisions concerning space and time units, and the reason for these decisions.*
   a. The particular time or space units that will be used.
   b. The way each medium selected will be used to meet the requirements of reach, frequency, cost efficiency, and other factors concerning media scheduling.
   c. The ways in which specific broadcast time periods or space positions will be used to achieve advertising objectives. For example, "drive time," "women's sections," "home furnishings sections."

4. *Decisions concerning the ways in which other marketing factors will influence media timing.*
   a. Seasonality of sales.
   b. The timing of media supported promotions.
   c. The availability of copy.

Within the framework of such strategy statements, specific media may be selected and justified, schedules may be assembled, and costs estimated.

Obviously, there are a number of factors that affect the development of a particular media strategy and the preparation of specific media plans. Some of these factors are discussed in the next section.

FACTORS INFLUENCING MEDIA STRATEGY

Different media have inherent characteristics which recommend their use. Magazines, for example, provide high quality color reproduction and varied editorial climates. They permit leisurely perusal of the advertising message and can be used selectively to reach highly specialized audiences such as brides, sports car buffs, hunting enthusiasts, bridge players, new mothers, and an incredible array of other specialized consumer groups. Newspapers, which are generally thought of as a mass medium, can also be used selectively through position requests in the sports section, the financial section, or the women's pages. However, the outstanding strength of newspapers lies in their ability to localize advertising, to provide intensive coverage of a particular city, or even of specific suburbs within a major metropolitan complex through the use of suburban editions and community newspapers, and to impart a sense of immediacy to the advertising. Television, while also providing some measure of selectivity through types of programming (sports, soap-operas, game shows, family programs, children's programs, and so forth) derives its greatest strength from its unique combination of sight and sound and its ability to demonstrate product use. Radio, because of its ubiquitous nature (there are over 400 million radios in homes, cars, and public places in the United States), not only provides audience selectivity through programming, but is also unique in terms of its flexibility in time of broadcast and its local nature. Other media such as outdoor posters and transit advertising also have characteristic strengths.

The task of media strategy and selection is to match the characteristics of individual media with market requirements of the product being advertised. This task is not always an easy one because there are many marketing considerations that influence media strategy and the selection of particular media. In the following material, eleven such considerations are identified and discussed briefly. These are:

The target market
Product characteristics
Distribution channels
Pricing policy and strategy
Sales promotion activity
Stages in the product life cycle
Flexibility
Size of advertising appropriation
Media availability
Media discounts
Editorial climate

This list is not exhaustive. It does, however, include the major factors that are frequently considered.

The Target Market

Few products are used by all people. Market segmentation is a fact of life. Even products that enjoy universal use (clothing and furniture, for example) are segmented in terms of style and price. An effective media program is one that concentrates on the target market with little waste circulation.

Table 8–2 in chapter 8 identifies a variety of geographic, demographic, psychographic and behavioral variables that may be used in identifying markets. Media can often be found that will match many of these markets to an amazing degree. Sources of media data, such as the Target Group Index (TRI) and Simmons (which will be discussed later in this chapter), provide product usage data and media habits for a wide range of demographic characteristics. Through the use of such information, media can be selected to reach target markets with a minimum of waste circulation. Media efficiency in reaching target markets is not the only consideration in selecting media, however. Often, efficiency will be sacrificed for impact or for the opportunity to demonstrate the product. This thought leads to a consideration of product characteristics.

Product Characteristics

Some media are better suited than others to expressing the unique attributes of particular products. The Thomasville example given at the beginning of this chapter is a case in point. Here, the nature of the product—elegant furniture—and the way the consumer buying decision is made require the use of magazines. In this particular instance, the desire for media efficiency does not have to be compromised in order to display the product properly because audience selectivity is a characteristic of magazines. In other instances, however, compromises have to be made. Automobiles are a case in point. Media efficiency in reaching the target markets for most new automobiles can best be served by using magazines, and magazines are widely used for this purpose. Although it involves substantial waste circulation, television is also widely used because it is an ideal medium for showing the performance characteristics of cars. Similarly, women's magazines are highly efficient in reaching the target market for dog food. But because they neither provide the breadth of coverage that is desired nor offer the opportunity to show the dog's enthusiasm over mealtime, as does television, compromises have to be made. Morris the cat has become well known as the television "spokesman" for 9-Lives cat food, although there is a great deal of waste circulation since not all television-viewing families have cats—in fact, some hate them.

Distribution Channels

The location, structure, and sales coverage of distribution channels may also influence media strategy to a major extent as noted in the following examples.

Location.   While many brands have national distribution, others are regional or even local in their sales. Still other brands may have spotty distribution. That is, while they are sold from coast to coast, and from the Canadian to the Mexican border, distribution may be nonexistent or extremely thin in some major metropolitan areas. In all of these instances, the efficient use of media requires that advertising pressure be deployed only in those areas in which the brand is available.

Still other brands that have truly national distribution may vary substantially in market share from one region of the country to another, or among major metropolitan areas. In still other cases, market potential for the product type will show marked regional differences. In such cases, a national advertising program in network television and/or magazines may be used to provide umbrella coverage for the total U.S., with local media being employed to heavy up the schedule in selected metropolitan markets, or even regions, where market share and/or market potential is substantially above average.

Distributor and retailer reactions to media.   Distributors and retailers often have personal preferences that influence media schedules. Some distributors and retailers are vocal in their insistence on local media which they believe (rightly or wrongly) to be more effective than national vehicles. Others may prefer national media because they are believed to lend prestige to the brand. It is often necessary to take these distributor and retailer viewpoints into consideration in formulating media plans. This is particularly true for products such as beer, in which the success of the brand is heavily dependent on the quality and cooperation of local distributors.

Equalizing sales force coverage.   In some instances, there are disparities in sales force coverage in various regions of the country. Such disparities may arise for a variety of reasons, ranging from a rapid expansion of sales that taxes the company's ability to provide the needed sales support to regional differences in product potential that makes it uneconomical to provide comparable sales coverage in all areas. In such instances, media weight is often expected to compensate for these differences by providing dealer and distribu-

tor contacts through regional trade publications in those areas in which sales coverage is the weakest.

Distribution Policies.   In the discussion of distribution (chapter 10), it was pointed out that some companies follow a policy of *intensive* distribution, while others follow a policy of *selective* distribution. Selective distribution is common in fields such as clothing, shoes, furniture, and some major appliances. Intensive distribution, on the other hand, is characteristic of most grocery products, proprietary drug products, and competitively priced personal care items. Under a policy of selective distribution, dealer support through retail advertising and dealer promotions often carries much of the manufacturer's communication burden. In the case of intensive distribution, however, dealer support is minimal to nonexistent, and the manufacturer's advertising program must bear the responsibility of reaching and influencing consumers. Obviously, media strategy will be influenced by the distribution policies employed by the manufacturer.

Pricing Policy and Strategy

Pricing policy and strategy influence media strategy in a number of ways. First, pricing strategy is often a key consideration in product positioning. A brand that is premium priced, either for market segmentation purposes or to impute quality to the brand within a given market segment, may require "prestige" media to support the basic product concept. Second, an economy or competitively priced brand may have limited contribution margins which, of course, reduce the funds available for advertising. Third, margins offered to distributors and dealers will often affect the amount of channel support that is given a brand. Where channel margins are high, the resulting advertising and promotional support from distributors and dealers may influence both the size of the manufacturer's media expenditures and the type of media that are used. Thus, if distributors and dealers provide extensive local support, the manufacturer's expenditures may be confined to national media.

Sales Promotion Activity

For many product groups, sales promotion plays a major role in the marketing plan. Sales promotion includes such activities as coupons, contests, sweepstakes, cents-off deals, self-liquidating premiums, display allowances, and trade deals. (See chapter 3.) The effectivenesss of a particular sales promotion often depends upon the amount of advertising support it receives as well as the particular type of media used. For example, a coupon promotion requires some method for distributing the coupons. Magazines, newspapers, and direct mail are often used for this purpose. A trade deal, while supported by sales force activity, also usually requires the use of trade publications for adequate trade coverage. Contests and sweepstakes often require magazine advertising to spell out the prize structure and rules. Thus, media expenditures must be diverted from product advertising to provide adequate support for sales promotion activity, and the nature of the sales promotion being employed will directly affect the type of media used.

Stages in the Product Life Cycle

The stage of a brand's life cycle will also exert an influence on the size of the media expenditure and the particular media used. During the introductory stage, for example, broad coverage—using newspapers, magazines, television, and outdoor advertising—may be required in order to gain quick and widespread brand recognition. From an efficiency standpoint, such a widespread use of media is wasteful. Nonetheless, this kind of media coverage is often necessary if the brand is to gain distribution and obtain the initial trial that is necessary to launch it successfully.

In the maturity stage of the brand's life cycle, a different media strategy may be required. Audience selectivity becomes more important; media efficiency takes precedence; frequency of message may become more important than reach; and, in the case of food products, "service" advertising (which features recipes showing how to use the product in new and interesting ways) may demand primary reliance on magazines.

Flexibility

Media differ in the length of the commitments that they require and in the closing dates by which advertising materials must be submitted. For example, the purchase of a television program on a weekly basis—affordable only by major advertisers—requires a year's commitment of funds. The purchase of a spot in the Super Bowl must be concluded many months before "Super Sunday," and the scheduling of a TV special just prior to Christmas may require a commitment in the preceding January or February. Similarly, the closing dates for magazines, particularly for unusual space units or cover positions, may require a commitment several months before the magazine appears on the newsstand.

In a volatile market, an advertiser may need greater flexibility in scheduling than these commitments permit. In such instances, marketing strategy will call for flexibility in the commitment of funds, and media strategy must reflect this marketing requirement by specifying the use of media that have short closing dates and which accept cancellations with minimum notice.

Size of the Advertising Appropriation

The size of the advertising appropriation will, of course, affect media strategy. Some advertisers cannot afford network TV, and despite attempts to reduce the cost of network television through the use of *scatterplans* (buying infrequent participating spots in a variety of TV programs) it is, essentially, a medium that requires a substantial investment in advertising dollars. An adequate schedule in national magazines may also be beyond an advertiser's means and, while spot TV can be purchased in individual markets for a relatively small outlay, the aggregation of markets necessary to provide adequate national coverage may be completely beyond reason. The point is, of course, that the size of the advertising budget does impose constraints on media strategy.

Media Availability

The desired media is not always available when and where it is needed. Although this is normally not a problem with magazine and newspaper advertising, unless position requests are a key part of media strategy, it is often a major factor in network TV and in both radio and TV spot announcements in key markets. If a particular time slot has been sold, there is nothing the radio or TV station can do to create more time, and premium time slots are often not available in all markets in which the advertiser would like to have her advertising appear.

Media Discounts

Media discounts are often a major factor in planning media strategy. Discounts, based on the size of the expenditure and/or the frequency of use, exist for virtually all media. These discounts are often complex and take one or more of the following forms:

1. Published, formal discounts based on volume, frequency, continuity, or some combination of these considerations.
2. Distressed media pricing in which the cost of a

given media exposure is reduced because it remains unsold. This occurs primarily in broadcast media.

3. Special media "plans" where a combination of media exposures will be priced at a cost below the total cost of the individual exposures, priced separately. This occurs, primarily, in broadcast media, print, and newspapers. In broadcast media, there is an infinite number of such plans.

4. Negotiated prices for media exposures. This situation is characteristic of network TV and exists, in the form of nonstandard space units, in the print media field.

In computing media discounts, the time and/or space used by different brands of the same manufacturer is accumulated to qualify for discounts. Table 16–1 shows the average maximum discounts available to national advertisers, based on published rates.[5]

Table 16–1. Discounts for selected media

	Average & maximum discount	Range of maximum discounts
Network TV	10%	5 - 15%
Newspapers	18%	0 - 31%
Spot TV	20%	0 - 50%
Consumer Magazines	32%	27 - 41%
Spot Radio	36%	0 - 59%
Network Radio	36%	23 - 53%

SOURCE: Gardner Advertising Company.

It is apparent that, for a major advertiser, the discounts that can be earned are significant. For a company such as Procter and Gamble, which spends over $400 million a year in advertising, the judicious use of media as well as coordination of media among its various brands can result in substantial savings. These savings can be used to extend media coverage, to increase profits, or both. For this reason, large companies that use a number of advertising agencies for their different brands often appoint one or more of their agencies as *coordinating agencies* to keep track of possible opportunities for media discounts through the coordination of media schedules. Obviously, the magnitude of the savings available through media discounts may exert a profound effect on media planning.

5. The study upon which these discounts are based was made by the Gardner Advertising Company (St. Louis, Missouri) in 1967. Although minor changes may have occurred since the study was made, the general structure will still hold true.

Editorial Climate

Editorial climate, although an intangible or qualitative factor, may play a major role in influencing media selection. Even among media that reach similar audiences, editorial climate may vary significantly. Some media are considered more reliable than others; some, more fun. Some are educational in nature; some, prestigious. Shelter books such as *Better Homes and Gardens* catch readers who are thinking about home improvements as opposed to the news weeklies, which catch readers who are thinking about national or world events.

Media planners attempt to place their advertising in an editorial setting in which the readers or viewers will be particularly receptive to their advertising messages. And media, particularly magazines, often provide a great deal of audience research data which attempt to define the orientation of their readers.

SOURCES OF MEDIA DATA

Media analysis and planning require a great deal of information on markets, media rates, advertising materials required by media, closing dates, circulation, audience duplication, competitive expenditures, and so forth. And such information is available from a number of sources ranging from the media themselves to a variety of subscription services that audit media claims and monitor advertising activity. Some of the most widely used sources of media and market information are identified below.

Reports by Media

The media themselves are a source of considerable information. They publish rate cards which provide information on rates, available advertising units, closing dates, mechanical requirements, circulation figures, nonacceptable advertising, and so forth. Media also undertake special research studies on the demographic characteristics of their audiences, their penetration of markets, product usage and brand preferences among members of their audiences, and other market related data. Although this information is often useful, it must be interpreted cautiously—not because the studies themselves are dishonest, but because media search out and present data that tends to put them in a favorable light.

Reports by Media Associations

All of the major media have national media associations which publish material concerning the nature and merits of advertising in the media they represent. Leading associations include the *Bureau of Advertising of the American Newspaper Publishers Association, The Magazine Publishers Association,* the *Radio Advertising Bureau,* the *Television Bureau of Advertising, Outdoor Advertising, Inc.,* and the *Advertising Specialty Association.*

Standard Rate and Data Service (SRDS)

SRDS is the most widely used service by national advertisers for information on rates, circulation, mechanical requirements, issuance and closing dates, and other basic information on media. Published monthly, it is compiled from the rate cards of the various media and eliminates the need for advertising agencies to maintain a file of rate cards on each medium. SRDS issues separate volumes for magazines, newspapers, television, radio, and so forth.

Audit Bureaus

There are a number of organizations that impartially audit the claims of media. The Audit Bureau of Circulation (ABC) and the Traffic Audit Bureau (TAB) check and verify the circulations of many newspapers, magazines, business publications, and outdoor advertising. In order to be audited, media have to comply with certain standard reporting practices, and all advertising agencies of any stature subscribe to the audited reports.

Independent Research Services

There are a number of independent research organizations that provide viewer data on broadcast media and readership information for print vehicles. Some of these services also contain marketing data on product use for a wide range of products. Still others monitor advertising and publish data on competitive advertising expenditures. Table 16–2 lists the major services, along with a brief description of the data provided by each and the method of pricing the information that each supplies.

Thus, there is a great deal of information available to the media planner. The biggest problem is to make sense out of it. This can be done, but it isn't easy.

COMPARING MEDIA

After media strategy has been defined, the major task of the media planner becomes one of matching media selection with strategic considerations. Since there are many possible media vehicles, the job is a monumental one which is compounded by conflicting claims, and often by ambiguous research information. For example, in 1975, Time, Inc., brought suit against W.R. Simmons and Associates for allegedly underrepresenting *Time* magazine's total audience in their audience survey. Since Simmon's data is widely used by advertising agencies in making their media selections, Time, Inc., contended that such misrepresentation would severely depress its advertising revenues. At first, this controversy seemed to threaten the future of syndicated services such as Simmons, and the advertising trade press was in an uproar. However, the advertising industry's dependence on such data is so great that much of the industry rallied around efforts to devise validity studies for gathering audience data, and Time's lawsuit was dropped.[6]

Again, in 1977, serious questions were raised by wide discrepancies between the total audience figures for consumer magazines developed by Simmons and Target Group Index (TGI). Table 16–3 shows comparisons between these two services for a list of 36 magazines. Examination of this table reveals that: (1) the audience sizes reflected by the two services differ, sometimes substantially; and (2) Simmons indicates a general picture of readership decreases from the previous year, while TGI reflects a general picture of readership increases.

These differences arise, not because of chicanery or malfeasance, but simply because the task of developing valid data on magazine readership and program viewing for over 200 million U.S. consumers is an exceedingly difficult and costly one. Different sampling techniques, different interviewing procedures, different ways of asking questions, and different ways of validating media exposure inevitably lead to discrepancies in the final results. Further, the harsh reality of the cost involved in gathering such data results in pragmatic compromises being made in sampling procedures and in the collection and processing of the findings. These compromises, while both justifiable and necessary to keep survey costs within affordable limits, nonetheless increase the probability of error.

Probably there is no solution to this problem as long as the advertising community insists on playing a "numbers game." Regardless of the care taken by audience measurement services, their best efforts will never achieve perfection. *Advertising Age* has addressed itself to this problem through the following editorial.

---

6. "ARF kills proposal for magazine study, but wants new plan," *Advertising Age* (January 19, 1976), p. 1.

Table 16-2. Thirty-six syndicated media research services available to agencies in 1977

Services and Description	Method of Pricing
Arbitron TV Market Report. Estimates audience among households and sex/age categories by time period, station and program; three to eight times a year for 210 markets.	According to agency billings.
Arbitron Day-Part Summary. Estimates market-by-market audiences by station within day-parts; 210 markets; three times yearly.	Either part of TV package or bought separately
Arbitron TV Markets & Rankings Guide. Annually offers TV market definitions and rankings by size, audience, station revenue, plus consumer expenditures.	Either as part of TV package or bought separately.
Arbitron TV Ethnic Reports. Estimates audience among Black or Spanish Metro households exclusively; four to 15 markets; two or three times a year.	Priced separately
Arbitron Radio Market Reports. Surveys 160 markets; 60 two times a year; 90 markets one time a year, two markets three times a year, eight markets four times. Day parts and demographics in all markets covered.	Based on agency billing.
Arbitron Nationwide Radio Audience Estimates. Uses 880,000 diaries once a year to compile a national network report for both line and nonline networks; estimate by station or network.	Part of radio package.*
Nielsen TV Index Basic Service. Reports bi-weekly on household rating nationally; options offered for fast weekly household report, including SIA dailies.	Based on agency billings.
NTI Analysis Service. NTI ratings with persons data, including NTI/NAC (audience demographics) and market section audience (MSA); also 11 optional reports, supplements about persons, costs, household and persons rankings, brand cumes, cpms, cume audiences, etc.	Part of NTI package.
Nielsen Station Index. Offers a four-week viewers-in-profile report, with options for daily and weekly reports in New York, Chicago, L.A.; two-week reports in four to 10 markets, network programs by Dominant Market Area (DMA), syndicated programs, DMA trends by season, DMA-CATV audience distribution.	Based on agency billings.
Pulse Radio Service. Measures local radio audiences in 150 markets.	Based on agency radio billings.
Pulse Local Qualitative Radio Service. Measures income, educational levels, family size in approximately 50 markets.	Flat rate.
Pulse Special Radio Service. Measures approximately 100 smaller markets.	Depends on the market size of desired report.
Pulse Ethnic Radio Service. Measures Black and Spanish audiences.	Included in radio package or sold on special order.
Pulse Syndicated Newspaper Service. Measures about 150 markets in alternate years.	Based on market size.
BAR Network TV and Radio Service. Monitors three networks full time. Reports activity/estimated expenditures by brand, parent company, product class. Publishes weekly, with monthly, quarterly cumulative summaries.	Scaled to agency total broadcast billings.
BAR National Spot TV Service. Monitors N.Y., L.A. full time, 73 other top markets one week per month. Reports activity, estimated expenditures by brand, market, parent company, product class. Publishes monthly market reports, with monthly, quarterly cumulative summaries.	Scaled to agency total TV billings.
LNA Magazine Analysis Service. Monthly analysis of PIB member publications; pages, dollar revenue; includes product category.	Scaled to agency domestic billings.
LNA Regional Advertising Service. Monthly analysis of regional advertising activity and dollars in selected PIB publications.	Scaled to domestic billings.
LNA Multi-Media Reports Service. Three types: quarterly revenue reports; magazines, newspaper supps, network TV, spot TV, network radio, outdoor. (BAR furnishes broadcast data.)	Scaled to agency domestic billings.
LNA Outdoor Advertising Expenditures. Expenditures of national outdoor advertisers in markets of over 100,000 population; quarterly.	Scaled to agency domestic billings.
W. R. Simmons Study of Selective Markets. Measures 1976-77 magazine reading, radio listening, TV viewing, newspaper and supplement reading audiences; household and/or product consumption rates, brand usage of over 500 categories of package goods, durable goods and services and basic demographic characteristics.	Scaled to agency domestic billings.

Table 16-2. (continued)

Services and Description	Method of pricing
W. R. Simmons Local Multi-Media/Marketing Studies. Sample of 5,000 adults, 1000 clusters; first personal interview: yesterday's newspaper reading, magazine reading, radio listening, shopping/marketing behavior, with week's personal diary left behind. Second interview TV diary retrieved, other media observations. All projected to total ADI. Field work: January-March 1977.	Scaled to agency domestic billings.
Media Records Blue Book. Contains general and automotive linage and dollar expenditures taken from newspaper reports of over 200 daily and Sunday newspapers in 70 cities.	By subscription fee annually, $1500; special sections at own fees.
Media Records Green Book. Offers much the same format as Blue Book; national investments in 61 Media Records measured cities covering 191 daily and Sunday publications; shows expenditures only in dollars.**	Also by annual subscription; 10% discount to buyers of both services.
Media Records Local All-Media Syndication Studies. Figures on getting into the local measurement field in spring of 1977 with O'Brien and Sherwood doing the field research. Aiming at Detroit, Philadelphia, Chicago, St. Louis.	Not determined.
Starch Inra Hooper Ad Readership Service. Measures performance of about 1000 issues of 90 consumer, general, business, trade newspaper publications. Also offers Profiles of Magazines Subscribers at $2,000 minimum; standardized surveys by mail of magazine subscribers.	$140 per report.
Trendex TV/Radio Coincidentals. Measures viewing or listening activity at time of phone call; minimum sample size per day, 1000 calls.	Depends on number of calls.
Media Statistics. Measures 280 small radio markets. Although basically for station groups, reports are available to agencies. Same owner, Jim Seiler, provides alternate service to Arbitron in big markets. Measures every two weeks and delivers on third week. Expanding from top 10 markets in 1977.	$5 per station report.
Sigma 3 Local Multi-Media/Marketing Studies. A Bill Simmons operation, which started off with a study of the New York market. Charter supporters: New York *Post, Newsday,* Bergen *Record* and 13 radio and TV stations. Aiming at Philadelphia market next.	Flat rate per report to agencies.
Scarborough Report (Scarborough Research Corp.). Initial local multi-media/marketing study: Washington market. Based on random sample of 3,000 adult respondents. Besides media/product usage, measures frequency of shopping and where. Charter subscriber: Washington *Post.*	Available on subscription basis to agencies.
The Source Reports (Dimensions Unlimited, Inc.). Surveys twice a year in L.A., San Francisco, Chicago markets re. consumer radio and newspaper usage and marketing habits (food stores, department stores, fast food patronage, movies, airlines). Original supporter: L.A. *Times.* Will measure New York market this spring. Places weekly diary after prequestioning of respondent.	$25 per market report for agencies.
St. Louis Shoppers Quarterly Survey. Lee Creative Marketing conducts annual survey among 1000 randomly selected housewives in St. Louis metro area, newspaper readership by day of week, radio, TV habits by day, hour, grocery, drugstore, hardward store shopping habits, plus awareness of selected TV commercials and demographic information.	Priced on annual or quarterly basis, or info. desired.
Target Group Index National All-Media Study. On-going media/marketing survey of over 30,000 adults each year.	Sliding scale based on billings.
TGI Target Teen Index (TTI). Measures media and consumer habits of 8,000 teenagers between 12–19.	Scaled to billings.
TGI Major Market Index (MMI). Surveys each of the top 20 ADI markets. Emphasis on local media plus product usage. Spinoff of TGI's national all-media study.	Scaled to national revenue. Local agencies may buy just local books.

*NOTE: Radio package also includes overview of all markets surveyed in either spring or fall sweep; small market reports; trading area reports; regional, state, sport network reports, ADI information; 15 Black and two Spanish market diary surveys issued in fall.

**NOTES: Gray Book contains summary data report from Green Book with 125 classifications and subclassifications; top 100 newspaper advertisers.

NOTES: *Erdos & Morgan's EM/CPM* surveys are not included in the above since they are custom-originated (they are underwritten in individually by 19 magazines) and the reports are free to the top 100 agencies ($25 to others). However, the 19 magazines agreed to standardized questions for the basic demographics.

Belden Market Studies are not included since they are not a syndicated service.

SOURCE: *Media Decisions*, February, 1977.

Table 16-3. Comparison of Simmons' and Target Group Index data

Magazine	Simmons' Totals	Simmons' % change	Target Group Index Totals	Target Group Index % change
ACTION				
Field & Stream	8,472,000	− 16%	7,998,000	+ 15%
Golf	1,235,000	− 23%	2,081,000	+ 16%
Golf Digest	1,793,000	− 13%	2,437,000	+ 3%
Ziff-Davis Network	10,503,000	− 9%	9.737.000	+ 9%
BUSINESS				
Barron's	811,000	− 23%	1,223,000	+ 30%
Business Week	3,452,000	− 10%	3,627,000	+ 1%
Forbes	1,825,000	+ 3%	1,994,000	+ 25%
Fortune	1,874,000	+ 13%	1,469,000	—
Scientific American	1,804,000	− 9%	1,866,000	+ 5%
MENS				
Esquire	3,694,000	− 20%	3,727,000	− 5%
Oui	3,705,000	− 10%	3,640,000	− 4%
Penthouse	8,981,000	− 9%	10,921,000	+ 15%
Playboy	14,019,000	− 12%	17,844,000	—
NEWSWEEKLIES				
Newsweek	17,762,000	—	14,934,000	− 2%
Sports Illustrated	12,282,000	− 3%	9,863,000	− 2%
Time	21,236,000	+ 3%	17,280,000	+ 2%
U.S. News	8,255,000	− 2%	7,749,000	+ 2%
SHELTER				
Better Homes	22,117,000	− 11%	24,546,000	+ 7%
House & Garden	6,509,000	− 21%	11,513,000	+ 4%
House Beautiful	5,064,000	− 16%	7,681,000	+ 9%
WOMENS				
Cosmopolitan	9,816,000	+ 3%	8,813,000	+ 14%
Family Circle	19,661,000	− 6%	21,165,000	+ 9%
Glamour	6,497,000	− 10%	5,903,000	+ 8%
Good Housekeeping	17,689,000	− 14%	21,669,000	+ 6%
Ladies' Home Journal	15,063,000	− 9%	17,403,000	+ 8%
Mademoiselle	2,844,000	—	3,214,000	+ 2%
McCall's	19,051,000	− 8%	20,024,000	+ 8%
Ms.	1,868,000	− 4%	1,609,000	+ 9%
Redbook	10,988,000	− 14%	12,672,000	+ 3%
Vogue	4,550,000	+ 6%	4,256,000	+ 14%
Women's Day	18,421,000	− 1%	20,839,000	+ 4%
GENERAL INTEREST				
National Geographic	21,442,000	− 4%	20,634,000	+ 10%
The New Yorker	3,022,000	− 5%	1,791,000	− 17%
People	13,966,000	+ 21%	11,542,000	+ 20%
Psychology Today	4,223,000	− 4%	4,320,000	+ 19%
Reader's Digest	40,900,000	− 4%	41,827,000	+ 3%

SOURCE: "Poles Apart," *Media Decisions* (November, 1977): 74–75. Sources of original data: W.R. Simmons & Associates and Target Group Index.

The numbing numbers game

Once again the magazine industry is wallowing through a research crisis, although the hue and cry so far is muted compared to the anguish of the 1974–75 controversy over syndicated total audience surveys. Perhaps the latest flap is less dramatic because publishers, agencies and advertisers have a more mature understanding of syndicated survey limitations. But it is more likely that the 1976-1977 ad boom, which isn't seriously threatened by puzzling survey results, has taken the edge off controversy so far.

Now W.R. Simmons & Associates, the leading audience estimator, has accorded readership declines to fully 70% of the 70 titles it measures. The data look "funny" compared to widespread increases claimed by the Target Group Index survey whose findings are more in line with publishing's current self-congratulatory outlook.

Sparing a review of the accusations and technical detail, we would stress a more fundamental point. The ad and media industries apparently haven't developed a mature enough approach to syndication data. Publishers still play audience numbers games to sell their space, in part because agencies and advertisers find numbers the easy way of justifying magazine choices. Publishers generally are neither seriously encouraged nor inspired by their own lights to advance research into sophisticated analyses of exactly how and why consumers read magazines. Yet they force syndicated researchers to pump ever greater complexities into the surveys, then disingenuously complain of "overloaded" survey mechanisms.

All of this has been said before, many times over. But we feel it warrants saying again and again, until the industry finally understands the sensitivity and limitations of the survey numbers game.[7]

In 1978, Simmons and Target Group Index merged. Although this merger may or may not improve the quality of the media data produced, it will eliminate some of the uneasiness that existed in the past when these two services issued conflicting reports.

Given the data available—whatever its limitations may be—the media planner still has the task of using this information to compare and evaluate alternative combinations of media in order to arrive at a reasonably efficient media buy.

Media Efficiency

Efficiency in media is generally measured in terms of the cost-per-thousand exposures among members of a target audience.[8] Cost-per-thousand (CPM) is computed by multiplying the *rate* (cost of an advertising message) by 1,000, and dividing by the number of people exposed to the message.

$$\frac{\text{rate} \times 1000}{\text{number exposed}} = \text{CPM}$$

A media program that costs $11.55 for a thousand exposures is obviously much more expensive than one that costs only $9.50 for a thousand exposures. To demonstrate this difference, let us take an example. Let us assume that the target market for these two media programs consists of women between the ages of 35 and 49, of which there are approximately 18 mil-

lion in the United States. Let us also assume that media strategy requires an average of 3.0 exposures against members of this audience during a four-week period, for fifty-two weeks. The total number of exposures required is shown below:

Target audience		3.0 exposures each four weeks		13, 4-week periods		Total exposures
18,000,000	×	3.0	×	13	=	702,000,000

At a cost of $11.55 per thousand, the total cost of the media buy would be $11.55 x 702,000 = $8,108,100. At a cost of $9.50 per thousand, the total cost would be $9.50 x 702,000 = $6,669,000. This represents a difference of $1,439,100, a substantial savings for the lower cost-per-thousand campaign.

Comparing Efficiency in Multimedia Programs

In a complex media schedule, where a number of media combinations are being considered, thousands of comparisons must be made in arriving at the most efficent combination of media for the schedule in question. Joseph St. Georges points up the magnitude of this problem with the following commentary:

As an example of the potential complexity of the media decision . . . in the simplest circumstances, a media buyer selecting 3 media from a group of 6 has 20 potential different choices. The same media buyer selecting 10 media from a group of 100, has 17,310,000, 000,000 different alternatives available to him. If he could analyze 1 alternative per second, 24 hours a day, 7 days a week, he could cover all of his choices (in) one-half million years.[9]

Obviously, such comparisons are impossible to do by hand. It takes a computer.

COMPUTER MODELS IN MEDIA SELECTION

Computer technology came to the rescue of the media planner in the early 1960s. *Advertising Age,* on October 1, 1962, announced: "Y&R, BBD&O unleash media computerization." Subsequently, BBD&O ran full-page newspaper and magazine advertisements claiming that their computerization system showed one BBD&O client how to get $1.67 worth of effective advertising for every dollar in his budget. Other major advertising agencies accepted the challenge and began to investigate a variety of ways for using computers in

7. "The numbing numbers game," p. 16. Reprinted with permission from the November 7, 1977 issue of *Advertising Age.* Copyright 1977 by Crain Communications, Inc.

8. Although cost-per-thousand is a standard measure of cost in the advertising industry and is used by magazines and broadcast media, other media may use a variation of this measure. For example, newspapers commonly use the *milline* rate, which is the cost per agate line for each million readers. Outdoor advertising uses sometimes *showings* for comparing costs. A 100 showing in a particular market, for example, is considered sufficient to expose virtually every mobile person in the market to the message in a 30-day period.

9. Joseph St. Georges, "How Practical is the Media Mode," *Journal of Marketing* (July, 1963): 31–32.

media selection. Often, their investigations led them to dead ends. William Moran of Y&R said that his agency had spent two years trying a linear programming approach, finally abandoning it in favor of another alternative.[10]

Since computers burst into the media scene, a number of computer models have been developed as aids in the selection of media. Some of the better known models are briefly discussed in the following material.

Linear Programming

A linear programming model for selecting media is an *optimizing* model. That is, from a number of alternatives, it attempts to select the one best alternative within the framework of strategic considerations such as the size of the advertising budget, the minimum and maximum usage of specific media vehicles and media classifications, and the minimum exposure frequencies for target buyers. These constraints—along with information on media rates, audience size, audience characteristics, target market data, and the relative value of exposures in each medium versus the value of exposures in other media—are fed into the computer. Push a button and presto! Out comes a recommendation indicating what specific media and what size units will give maximum exposure. But it's not that easy.

Linear programming has a number of severe limitations. First, it assumes that repeat exposures have the same effect as the initial exposure, which may or may not be true. Second, it cannot handle the problem of media discounts. Third, it cannot handle the problem of audience duplication between media. Fourth, it does not indicate *when* advertising should be scheduled. Fifth, it requires highly suspect or nonexistent quantitative data.

High Assay Models

The high assay model, developed by Y&R, avoids many of the problems of linear programming by choosing media on a sequential basis rather than a simultaneous one. Using data similar to that used in linear programming, it starts off by considering all of the media available during the first week of the schedule and selects the single best buy. Then a second selection is made for the same week if the *achieved* rate of exposure is below the *desired* rate. When optimal exposure for the first week is achieved, the program proceeds to the second week and so on until the entire

schedule is developed. The advantages of the high assay model are that: (1) it develops a schedule simultaneously with the selection of media; (2) it handles the problem of audience duplication; (3) it deals with media discounts; and (4) it can incorporate theoretically important variables such as brand-switching rates and multiple-exposure coefficients.[11] Its major limitation? As in the case of most media models, some of the data required is either suspect or nonexistent.

Simulation

Unlike linear programming and high assay models, simulation models don't attempt to find the "best" media plan. Instead, they estimate the exposure value of any given media plan submitted for analysis.[12] In simulation exercises, hypothetical buyers—along with their demographic characteristics, media habits, and program use patterns—are stored in the computer. Then, alternative media plans are fed into the computer, which develops an estimate of the exposures provided by each plan. The media planner then examines the results and determines how well each of these alternatives meets the advertising needs of the product. Simulation has been criticized for three reasons. First, it does not include an overall "effectiveness" measure for each alternative. Rather, it yields a multidimensional picture of reach and frequency for each plan. Second, it lacks a procedure for finding better media combinations. Third, the representativeness of the hypothetical population is suspect.

MEDIAC

One of the newer generation media models for computers is MEDIAC (Media Evaluation Using Dynamic and Interactive Applications of Computers).[13] Designed as a sophisticated mathematical model, this program incorporates a number of important marketing considerations such as market segments, sales potentials, exposure probabilities, diminishing marginal response rates, forgetting, seasonality, and cost estimates. Obviously, hard data on many of these variables is simply not available. And, while this model overcomes many of the deficiencies of the earlier linear programming models, it still assumes a linear cost structure for media. This assumption is not consistent

10. William T. Moran, "Practical Media Decisions and the Computer," *Journal of Marketing* (July, 1963): 26–30.

11. Philip Kotler, *Marketing Management,* 2nd ed. (Englewood Cliffs, New Jersey: Prentice-Hall, 1967), p. 689.
12. *Simulmatics Media-Mix: Technical Description* (New York: The Simulmatics Corporation, October, 1962).
13. Philip Kotler, *Marketing Decision Making: A Model Building Approach* (New York: Holt, Rinehart and Winston, 1971), pp. 460–64.

with the complex discount practices that exist in the field.[14]

Other computer models have been developed by other advertising agencies and concerned organizations. Some are better than others. None are wholly satisfactory. All must rely on ambiguous and inadequate quantitative data, as do media planners. The difference is that professional media planners have good sense. Computers don't. Once this data is pumped into a computer's memory bank, there is a tendency to forget its inadequacies and to become enamored with the volume of pristine numbers that flash on the display screen or pour forth from the printer.

Properly used (and most sophisticated advertising agencies do use them properly) computer models are a major asset in the selection of media. They do not and cannot replace the role of judgment and imagination in media planning, but they can process an unbelievable amount of data in a remarkably short period of time. They summarize it and organize it into a usable form for the media professionals who must, in the final analysis, make judgmental decisions on media selection and scheduling.

MEDIA COSTS

Costs vary substantially between media and within the same medium for various target groups. For example, the average cost per thousand for reaching men with a

60-second commercial on radio (during drive time) was $2.45 in 1971. The average cost per thousand for reaching these same men with a prime-time, 60-second TV commercial was $7.15—almost three times as much. Within the same medium, the average cost per thousand for reaching a women with a 60 second, prime-time TV commercial was $5.75, whereas the average cost per thousand for married women, 18–24 years of age was $52.25, and for single women in the same age group, $115.00. Tables 16–4 and 16–5 show a cost-per-thousand comparison for selected media and for various target groups. It should be born in mind that these are *average* costs for the media in question, based on 1971 media rates. The cost per thousand for *selected* vehicles within these media types would be somewhat lower provided the media vehicles were selected for their cost efficiency in reaching particular target groups.

MEDIA USE AND PRICE TRENDS

Advertising expenditures by media vary significantly. Table 16–6 shows a comparison of advertising expenditures by selected media for 1967 compared with 1976 as well as the split between national and local advertising. From this table, it can be seen that: (1) newspapers account for the largest expenditure ($9,910 million), followed by direct mail ($4,754 million); (2) the greatest percentage growth in the ten year

Table 16–4. Cost per thousand comparison for selected target groups in selected media—men

	% Pop.	Television Day Net. (60'')	Early Eve.* (60'')	Prime Net. (60'')	Late Eve.* (60'')	Radio Drive-Time* (60'')	Maga-zines P4/C
Total Men	100	$8.95	$5.70	$7.15	$5.15	$2.45	$3.35
By Demographics:							
$15,000+	23	111.85	56.50	55.00	35.70	13.30	16.90
$10,000+	50	45.90	21.30	21.65	12.85	5.20	6.90
A County, $10,000+	22	119.30	41.85	43.35	24.40	9.20	12.90
Prof.-Mgr., $10,000+	16	149.20	56.50	55.00	29.40	12.55	15.30
Under $5,000	18	21.35	18.25	27.50	21.75	12.20	24.35
White Collar	30	47.10	22.60	24.65	14.70	6.30	7.90
18–24 Single	11	105.30	66.45	75.30	50.00	17.60	22.35
18–34	36	36.50	20.15	21.65	13.85	5.50	7.45
18–34 $10,000+	15	89.50	70.60	65.00	41.65	13.80	16.65
35–49	28	40.65	22.60	25.55	15.60	7.10	11.05
35–49 $10,000+	14	162.75	59.50	65.00	31.25	14.70	18.80
Blue Collar	36	23.55	14.10	17.00	12.65	5.25	9.05
Blue Collar $5–10,000	21	59.70	31.40	34.90	25.65	10.75	16.35
50+	36	16.55	11.80	17.85	15.15	8.05	19.80
65+	13	28.90	28.25	47.70	41.65	27.50	50.45

*Spot in top 100 Markets.
NOTE: All incomes referred to are on a household basis.
SOURCE: BBS BBDO Audience coverage and Cost Guide, 1971, BBDO media department.

14. Dorothy Cohen, *Advertising* (New York: John Wiley & Sons, Inc., 1972), p. 501.

Table 16-5. Cost per thousand comparison for selected target groups in selected media—women

	% Pop.	Television Day Net. (60'')	Television Early Eve.* (60'')	Television Prime Net. (60'')	Television Late Eve.* (60'')	Radio 10 A.M.– 3 P.M.* (60'')	Maga- zines P4/C
Total Women	100	$2.15	$4.35	$5.75	$4.00	$1.70	$3.45
By Demographics:							
$15,000+	19	30.70	47.75	52.25	35.45	14.95	18.65
$10,000+	43	8.95	17.20	18.55	11.15	5.70	7.05
A County, $10,000+	20	17.20	29.65	35.95	20.00	10.90	13.80
Under $5,000	24	6.50	13.05	19.80	15.60	7.70	15.00
18–24 Single	7	53.75	107.50	115.00	78.00	31.90	43.10
18–24 Married	10	13.45	35.85	52.25	35.45	15.90	25.55
Mothers, Children under 2	11	14.35	40.95	52.25	32.50	15.05	24.60
Working:							
Prof.-Mgrs.	8	86.00	66.15	82.15	48.75	33.65	25.55
Cler.-Sales	16	48.85	43.00	39.65	24.35	14.85	15.70
Full Time Homemaker	55	3.15	7.45	10.05	6.80	3.05	5.40
18–34	35	5.80	15.40	17.40	11.15	4.95	7.75
18–34, $10,000+	13	21.50	53.75	52.25	30.00	14.75	19.30
35–49	27	9.35	17.90	19.80	13.00	6.35	9.20
35–49, $10,000+	13	23.90	39.10	44.20	24.35	13.85	17.40
50+	38	5.50	8.95	15.15	11.15	5.70	9.15
65+	16	10.25	20.45	38.35	35.45	13.25	26.15

*Spot in top 100 Markets.
NOTE: All incomes referred to are on a household basis.
SOURCE: BBDO Audience Coverage and Cost Guide, 1971, BBDO Media Department.

Table 16-6. Comparisons of expenditures in selected media, 1967–1976 (expenditures in millions)

Media	Expenditures 1967	Expenditures 1976	Percent increase	% of total expenditures by media, 1976
Newspapers	4,910	9,910	101.8%	29.6%
Magazines	1,245	1,789	43.7	5.4
Farm Pub.	68	86	26.5	0.3
Network TV	1,455	2,857	96.3	8.5
Spot TV	1,454	3,765	158.9	11.3
Network Radio	64	104	62.5	0.3
Spot Radio	984	2,173	120.8	6.5
Direct Mail	2,488	4,754	91.0	14.2
Business papers	707	1,035	46.4	3.1
Outdoor	191	383	100.5	1.1
Misc.	3,304	6,604	99.9	19.7
Totals	16,870	33,460	98.3%	100.0%
Total national	10,210	18,450	80.7	55.2
Total local	6,660	15,010	125.3	44.8

SOURCE: Adapted from Robert J. Coen, "No let up in boom: '77 ad spending rates momentum," pp. 30–31. Reprinted with permission from the July 18, 1977 issue of *Advertising Age.* Copyright 1977 by Crain Communications, Inc.

period occurred in spot TV (158.9 percent) followed by spot radio (120.8 percent); and (3) approximately 55 percent of all advertising in 1976 was national advertising, while approximately 45 percent of all advertising was local.

Media prices also increased during this period. Some of the price increases were accompanied by increases in audience size. Some were not. The failure of audience growth to keep pace with price hikes is re-

flected in table 16–7, which shows the percent increase in cost-per-thousand exposures for selected media, using 1967 as the base year. It is apparent from this table that the cost of advertising is increasing in all media and increasing at an alarming rate in some. For example, the estimated 1978 cost-per-thousand exposures in network TV was 105 percent (index 205) greater than in 1967, and the estimated 1978 cost-per-thousand exposures in newspapers was

Table 16-7. Media price trends; 1967 = 100

Media	1967	1970	1973	1976	1977*	1978*
Magazines	100	106	109	125	132	143
Newspapers	100	115	126	169	183	199
Network TV	100	108	114	149	174	205
Spot TV	100	99	109	147	156	167
Network Radio	100	96	95	111	122	135
Spot Radio	100	102	106	122	129	138
Outdoor	100	101	136	161	173	187

*Estimated.
SOURCE: Adapted from Robert J. Coen; Herbert Zeltner; *Advertising Age* estimates. Reprinted with permission from p. 60 of the September 26, 1977 issue of *Advertising Age*. Copyright 1977 by Crain Communications, Inc.

up 99 percent (index 199) over 1967. Of course, these trends are a source of deep concern for advertisers because it means that the cost of doing business is rising rapidly.

SUMMARY

Four theories or approaches to media use are *wave* theory, *media dominance* theory, *media concentration* theory, and *reach* theory. They all represent a compromise between three basic media variables, namely, *reach, frequency,* and *continuity.*

The basic decision areas covered by media strategy are (1) decisions concerning the general kinds of media to be used; (2) decisions concerning specific types of media within broad media classifications; (3) decisions concerning space and time units; and (4) decisions concerning the way other marketing factors will influence media timing.

A number of factors influence media strategy. The task of the media planner is to select media that meet the requirements of these variables.

Media analysis and planning require a great deal of information on markets, media rates, circulation, audience duplication, competitive patterns, and so forth.

The media themselves as well as a number of independent research organizations are the sources of much of this data.

Using this data, the media planner is faced with the problem of comparing media, a comparison which often tends to overemphasize the quantitative aspects of media.

Cost per thousand is a basic media concept used for determining media efficiency.

Because of the large number of different media available, the job of evaluating alternative media combinations is a herculean one that can only be handled through the use of computers. A number of computer models are commonly employed. While these computer models, properly used, are an unquestioned boon to the problem of media selection, the validity of the quantitative data upon which they are based is often suspect or nonexistent.

Although the cost per thousand for reaching various target groups varies widely, media costs have risen rapidly in the past decade. The rapid escalation of media costs is a matter of deep concern to advertisers and agencies because it increases the cost of advertising substantially and often forces undesirable constraints on media planning.

QUESTIONS

1. Distinguish between *reach, frequency,* and *continuity.*
2. Explain how wave theory, media dominance theory, media concentration theory, and reach theory offer a compromise between the three variables of reach, frequency, and continuity.
3. Identify the major decision areas that are normally dealt with in the media strategy statement.
4. How can media be used to equalize sales force coverage for a consumer product sold through retail outlets? What kinds of media would most likely be employed?
5. Why is it suggested that research reports by media should be interpreted cautiously?
6. What does SRDS stand for? What kinds of information does it provide, and why is it used?
7. Explain what *Advertising Age* means by the "numbing numbers game." Why does it exist, and what does *Ad Age* suggest is the solution?

8. Explain what is meant by *media efficiency*. Given a media expenditure of $60 thousand and an audience exposure of 12 million, what is the CPM?
9. Assume a target audience of 24 million consumers, to be reached an average of 2.5 times each four-week period for 52 weeks. What would the total cost of a media program be that met the above requirements if its CPM were $4.50?
10. What are the primary advantages and shortcomings of computer models in the selection of media?

PROBLEM

Circus Time protein spread is a soy-protein based spread that is manufactured in three flavors—chocolate, grape, and blackberry. With its protein base and enriched with vitamins, it is a highly nutritious children's snack food that is spread on bread or crackers.

Company sales of the product during the past year were $28.5 million, and the bulk of the advertising and sales promotion expenditure of $2.28 million had been directed toward the 6–12 age group via weekend children's TV.

Joan Weston, product manager for Circus Time protein spread, and Frank Claxton, advertising director for the company, were discussing the advertising and promotion plan for the forthcoming year.

"Joan," Frank said, "it seems to me that we should devote a significant part of our advertising budget to mothers this next year. The recent survey conducted by the research department indicates that they have doubts about the nutritional value of Circus Time. We know that our kid TV advertising is doing a good job in getting the kids to ask for the product, but mothers still have veto power, and their lack of acceptance is hurting our sales."

"I don't disagree with you," Joan said, "but I'm not sure we can afford to do everything that needs to be done. Our forecast next year is for $29 million, with an advertising and promotion budget of $2.3 million. The sales department wants $500 thousand of that for a consumer coupon, which I also think we need."

"Is that forecast with or without the couponing effort?" Frank asked.

"Without," Joan answered.

"Based on our past couponing experience, plus an effort against both mothers and children, I suspect we could justify increasing the forecast by another million dollars," Frank suggested.

Joan thought for a minute, then said, "I think you're probably right; at least I'd be willing to recommend it. Frank, making the assumption that we can get the forecast revised, could you have someone rough some costs together to see what the program would look like? Let's plan on $500 thousand for couponing, and split the rest between women in the 25 to 49 age group who are full-time homemakers, and kids 6 to 11, with a heavier emphasis on kids than on mothers. I don't know the best split; it depends on how much reach and frequency we can get with each group."

After Joan left, Frank pulled out some of his media references and started putting some numbers together.

There are approximately 25 million children between 6–12 years of age, and the cost per thousand for reaching them on weekend TV is $2.70. Thus, ignoring duplication, it would cost $67,500 (25,000 x $2.70) to reach all of them once. Frank knew he couldn't afford to reach all of this age group with adequate frequency, but he could probably get adequate frequency on a part of this group, particularly if he used a wave approach.

Full-time homemakers between 25 and 49 were a different problem. He could use daytime radio, daytime TV, or women's magazines. There are about 30 million women in this group. Cost-per-thousand for daytime TV is about $7.60. For magazines, the cost-per-thousand is about $8.50 for a full page ad. Radio has a cost-per-thousand for this group of about $5.80.

Frank estimated that TV production would cost about $40 thousand, and print production, about $25 thousand. If he used radio, production costs would run about $5 thousand.

Assignment

1. Prepare a recommendation for advertising Circus Time.
2. Show how available advertising funds will be split between children and mothers, and recommend the size audiences that will be reached and the average frequency that will be attained. Ignore the question of audience duplication.

Newspapers and Magazines

The Philadelphia Story

On December 5, 1977, a new newspaper hit the streets of Philadelphia. The *Philadelphia Journal* was launched with high ambitions and a $300 thousand promotional expenditure by a Canadian company, the Montreal-based Quebecor, Inc. Pierre Peladeau, publisher of the new tabloid-sized newspaper, announced: "We will publish the facts, no biases, no editorials, only letters from readers and opinion columns. . . ."[1] This is a far cry from the original "Philadelphia Story," which was a broadway play about a courageous newspaper editor's battle against corruption, although one can argue that it takes a certain amount of courage to launch a new newspaper in these uncertain times.

The target circulation for the new newspaper was 200 thousand. Initial advertising linage was light, although the first edition carried ads for Gimbel's, Wanamaker's, and Strawbridge and Clothier, three of the areas largest department stores. Department store advertising is the bread-and-butter of metropolitan newspapers.

Between 1970 and 1975, the number of daily newspapers (including morning and evening editions) increased by 13, from 1,776 to 1,789.[2] Whether or not the *Philadelphia Journal* will survive to become a permanent member of this group will depend on the outcome of the Philadelphia story.

American Home

Following the February 1978 issue, Charter Company folded *American Home* into *Redbook*. *American Home* had 368 advertising pages and $4,847,522 in advertising revenue for the first eight months of 1977. Nonetheless, the publisher lost $4 milliion trying to make the magazine solvent by converting it from a home service to a women's magazine. Charter will continue to publish five *American Home* special interest magazines, covering such areas as foods, crafts, furniture, and the home.[3]

---

1. "'Phila. Journal' hits the streets," *Advertising Age* (December 12, 1977): 8.

2. *Editor and Publisher's Yearbook,* 1975.
3. "Charter folds 'American Home' into 'Redbook,'" *Advertising Age,* (December 5, 1977): 8.

The demise of *American Home* as an independent publication is simply another casualty in the competitive magazine field, which has grown by almost $1 billion in advertising revenues in the past 10 years—from $1,245 billion in 1967 to $2,145 billion in 1976.[4]

The ABCs of Publishing

For years, the Audit Bureau of Circulation (ABC) has represented stability in the publishing industry. The Audit Bureau has kept the publishing field honest through semiannual audits of publishers's statements, validating circulation data by type of circulation (that is, subscription versus newsstand), by area of circulation (county, state, and region), and by issue. Also, for years, election to the bureau's board of directors was a "rubber stamp" affair, with little evidence of dissent or displeasure on the part of the members of the bureau.

In 1977, however, a group of small publishers challenged the incumbent board, charging that the board has long been dominated by the giants in the publication field even though the majority of the members of the ABC are small circulation publications. As a consequence of this dominance by large publications, it was alleged that the interests of the small publishers are often ignored.[5] The revolt of 1977 failed but it is reasonable to expect that continued pressure by small publishers will eventually bring about some basic changes in ABC.

These three news items, all of which appeared in 1977, help to characterize the turbulence of the print publication field. Other 1977 news items were the refurbishing of *Esquire* to position it as the leading men's magazine; the rebirth of the Brooklyn Eagle, once Brooklyn's largest newspaper; the organization of a group of "senior citizen" publications into a sales group; the controversy which arose over discrepancies in Simmons and TGI audience figures; the almost monthly appearance of a new magazine; the anticipated shift of television dollars into women's magazines as television costs go higher, and its audience shrinks. These events, normally, don't make headlines in the consumer press. But, despite the lack of widespread publicity, the print field is alive and healthy. Beneath what appears to be a placid surface, there is a great deal of activity and fierce competition for advertising revenues.

Since newspapers and magazines differ significantly in their strengths and weaknesses and the ways in which they are used, they need to be discussed separately.

NEWSPAPER ADVERTISING

In terms of total advertising revenue, newspapers have the lion's share by far. Estimated advertising revenues for newspapers in 1976 were almost $10 billion. The bulk of this revenue, however, came from local advertisers who accounted for $8,408 million, or 84.8 percent of the total. National advertising in newspapers was only $1,502 million, 15.2 percent of the total.[6] Nonetheless, $1.5 billion is a substantial amount, and newspapers are a formidable national advertising medium.

Overview of Newspapers

Daily and Sunday newspapers have a combined circulation of approximately 113 million, broken down in table 17–1.[7]

The total circulation figures shown in table 17–1 are for editions, not separate newspapers, since almost 200 of these newspapers have both morning and evening editions. Although these daily and Sunday newspapers account for the bulk of newspaper advertising, in addition there are almost 10 thousand semiweekly, weekly, biweekly, monthly, and bimonthly newspapers serving suburban communities, small towns, and rural areas. In addition to these general circulation newspapers, there is a multiplicity of small newspapers serving various special groups, including a variety of foreign language newspapers, ethnic and religious newspapers, labor and professional groups, high school and university students, and so forth. Thus, newspapers may not only be used as a mass medium, but also to reach highly specific target markets.

A number of newspapers also distribute Sunday supplements, often referred to as *Sunday magazines*. Some of the major newspapers publish their own localized Sunday supplements; there are other supplements that are nationally syndicated. *Family Weekly*, for example, is distributed by 307 newspapers with a combined circulation of 10,700,000, and *Parade* is distributed by 111 newspapers with a combined circulation of 19,033,000.

4. "Estimated annual U.S. ad expenditures: 1958–1976," *Advertising Age* (July 18, 1977): 31.
5. "Audit Bureau Uprising falls short," *Advertising Age* (November 14, 1977): 2 ff.

6. "Estimated annual U.S. ad expenditures: 1958–1976," *Advertising Age*.
7. *Editor and Publisher's Yearbook*, 1975.

Table 17–1. Breakdown of circulation of daily and Sunday newspapers.

Edition	Number of papers	Circulation in 1000's
Morning	340	26,145.0
Evening	1,449	35,732.0
Sunday	641	51,569.0
Total		113,556.0

KINDS OF NEWSPAPER ADVERTISING

Newspaper advertising may be classified in a number of ways. One widely-used classification system and one on which rates are often based is: classified advertising, retail advertising, national advertising, and reading notices.

Classified Advertising. While classified advertising may be used either by national or local advertisers, the bulk of the classified section of newspapers (often referred to as *want ads*) are local in nature, being placed either by local firms or individuals. These ads are arranged by subject matter for the convenience of readers, and generally do not include headlines or illustrations. There is a form of classified advertising known as *classified display,* which uses different type sizes, white space to attract attention, and simple illustrations.

Retail Advertising. As the name implies, retail advertising is that advertising placed by retail merchants and other local businesses. Normally, it takes two forms: *sales promotion* advertising, which is based on price-features, sales, or specials of some kind, and *image* advertising, designed to position a retail store or business to appeal to a particular group of consumers. Retail advertising may be paid for entirely by the retailer, or its cost may be shared by a manufacturer. This latter form of advertising is referred to as *cooperative* advertising; it is run under the name of a local retailer in order to encourage retailer support and in order to take advantage of local rates, which are usually lower than national advertising rates.

National Advertising. National advertising refers to that advertising used by manufacturers and producers in support of their products. Such advertising is part of the manufacturer's national advertising plan and is used to intensify coverage in a local area. National newspaper advertising is often used in the introduc-

tion of new products, particularly in test markets, to assure widespread consumer recognition and to aid in gaining retail distribution.

Reading Notices. Some newspapers accept reading notices, which are advertisements made up to resemble editorial material. Reading notices are charged at a higher rate than retail advertising. In order to prevent reading notices from being confused with news stories or editorial material, the word *advertisement* must appear at the top of the notice.

NEWSPAPER RATE STRUCTURE

The physical dimensions of newspaper pages vary in size, generally ranging from five to nine columns in width and from 300 to 315 lines in depth. The *standard* newspaper is eight columns wide and 300 lines deep, allowing 2400 lines to be printed on a page. Since the line measure in newspapers refers to *agate lines* and there are 14 agate lines to an inch, the standard newspaper is about 22 inches in depth. A *tabloid* newspaper, which generally appears only in major metropolitan areas, is five columns wide and 200 lines deep. This size is more convenient for users of mass transportation who read the newspaper while commuting. The country's largest circulation newspaper, the *New York Daily News,* is a tabloid.

The Rate Card

Rates for newspaper advertising vary in accordance with the kind of advertising used—classified, retail, national, and reading notices—and, in many instances, in terms of the volume of advertising used. Newspaper rates are relatively stable and are made known through published rate cards. Further, the circulations upon which the rates are based for all major newspapers are audited by the Audit Bureau of Circulation.

The published rate card contains all of the information that an advertiser needs to contract for space in the newspaper including information on rates as well as copy and mechanical requirements. Figure 17–1 shows the anatomy of a rate card as recommended by the American Association of Advertising Agencies, Inc. (the 4 A s). A major feature of this card is that all information is given standardized numbers and listed in a standardized sequence. If a newspaper has no information for a particular category of data, it simply skips the number, but does not alter the numbering of the rest of the card.

Published Morning, Evening, Sunday
Publication Address
Telephone Number

NAME OF NEWSPAPER

Rate Card Number
Issue Date
Effective Date

1—PERSONNEL

a. Name of publisher.
b. Names of advertising executives
c. Name of production supervisor.

2—REPRESENTATIVES

a. Names, addresses, and telephone numbers of advertising representatives.

3—COMMISSION AND CASH DISCOUNT

a. Agency commission.
b. Cash discount.
c. Discount date.

4—GENERAL

a. Policy on rate protection and rate revision notice.
b. Regulations covering acceptance of advertising.
c. Policy regarding advertising which simulates editorial content.

5—GENERAL ADVERTISING RATES

a. Black and white rates for standard space units. Bulk and/or frequency discounts.
b. Starting date if sold in combination.

6—COLOR—ROP

a. Color availability—days of week and number of colors available.
b. Minimum size for ROP Color advertisements.
c. Rates for standard units—1 page, 1500 lines, 1000 lines—with black and white costs as base for comparison.
d. Rates for non-standard units—black and white line rate plus applicable flat or % premium.
e. Closing dates for reservations and printing material.
f. Cancellation dates.
g. Leeway on insertion dates, if required.

h. Number of progressive proofs required.
i. Registration marks on plates and mats.
j. Full page size for direct casting, in inches.
k. Number of mats required for direct casting.
l. Running head and date line for direct casting, if required.
m. Bulk or frequency discounts on color.

7—MAGAZINE SECTIONS
(Name of Sections and when issued)

a. Rates for letterpress—black and white, color.
b. Rates for rotogravure—monotone, color.
c. Minimum depth and mechanical requirements.
d. Closing and cancellation dates.

Figure 17-1. Anatomy of the rate card recommended by the American Association of Advertising Agencies.

Not all newspapers follow the numbering sequence recommended by the 4 As. For example, the *Standard Rate and Data Service* listing for the *St. Louis Post Dispatch* (See figure 17-2) departs from the sequence recommended, although all of the relevant information is still presented.

Newspaper Rates

There are a number of terms used in referring to newspaper rates. The major ones employed are listed below.

8—COMIC SECTIONS (When issued)

a. Rates for color units.
b. Minimum depth and mechanical requirements.
c. Closing and cancellation dates.

9—CLASSIFICATIONS

a. Rates for special classifications (amusements, financial, political, etc., and special pages.)

10—SPLIT RUN

a. Availabilities and rates.

11—POSITION CHARGES

a. Availabilities and rates.

12—DAILY COMIC PAGES

a. Rates.
b. Minimum requirements.
c. Regulations covering acceptance of advertising.
d. Closing and cancellation dates.

13—CLASSIFIED

a. Rate per word, line or inch; number of words per line.
b. Minimum requirements.

14—READING NOTICES

a. Available pages.
b. Rates and requirements.

15—CONTRACT AND COPY REGULATIONS

a. Regulations not stated elsewhere in rate card.

16—CLOSING AND CANCELLATION DATES (Black and White)

17—MINIMUM DEPTH ROP

18—MECHANICAL MEASUREMENTS

a. Type page size before processing— inches wide by inches deep.
b. Depth of column in lines.
c. Number of columns to page.
d. Number of lines charged to column and to page.
e. Number of lines charged to double-truck and size in inches.
f. Requirements as to mats, originals and electros.

g. Screen required.
h. Address for printing material.
i. Other mechanical information.

19—CIRCULATION INFORMATION

a. Circulation verification (details in Publisher's Statement and Audit Report).
b. If unaudited, basis for circulation claim.
c. Milline rates, if desired. Daily ...., Sunday ....

20—MISCELLANEOUS

a. Year established.
b. Subscription price; single copy price.
c. News services, e.g. AP, UP.
d. Other information not listed elsewhere.

(Standard Form Rate Card recommended by the American Association of Advertising Agencies, Inc.).

Figure 17-1. (continued)

Flat Rate. When the line rate is fixed, regardless of the volume of advertising, it is designated as a *flat rate.*

Open Rate. If a newspaper offers discounts, the *open rate* is the rate charged advertisers who do not use a sufficient volume to qualify for a discount.

Discounts. Many newspapers have established discount levels for advertisers using an unusual amount of advertising space. These discounts, while initially arrived at through negotiation, become established, are published, and apply to any future advertisers offering a similar volume of linage. Discount practices vary significantly among newspapers. For example,

MISSOURI

POST-DISPATCH

900 N. 12th Blvd., St. Louis, Mo. 63101.
Phone 314-621-1111; 910-761-0479.

 (ABC) ads C

Media Code I 126 8200 0.00
EVENING AND SUNDAY
(Evening edition not published on Jan. 1, Memorial Day, July 4, Labor Day, Thanksgiving or Christmas. If holiday falls on Sunday, no publication on Monday.)
Member: INAE; Newspaper Advertising Bureau, Inc.

1. PERSONNEL
Publisher—Joseph Pulitzer, Jr.
Advertising Director—James D. Cherry.
Advertising Manager—Clyde Pinson.
General Adv. Manager—Lowell C. Iler.
Retail Adv. Mgr.—William L. Glenn.

2. REPRESENTATIVES and/or BRANCH OFFICES
Million Market Newspapers, Inc.
Florida and Caribbean—The Leonard Co.
Hawaii—Lenha Hawaii, Inc.
Mexico—Al Nadal representing The Leonard Company.

3. COMMISSION AND CASH DISCOUNT
15% to agencies 15th of month following previous month's advertising; 2% cash discount—15th following month.

4. POLICY—ALL CLASSIFICATIONS
30-day notice of any rate revision given to contract holders.
Alcoholic beverage advertising accepted.
R.O.P. linage does not apply toward completing feature section contract.

ADVERTISING RATES
Effective November 13, 1977.
Received November 14, 1977.

5. BLACK/WHITE RATES

	Daily	Sunday
Open, per line	1.97	2.60
Within 1 year:		
1,000 lines	1.91	2.54
2,500 lines	1.89	2.52
5,000 lines	1.85	2.46
10,000 lines	1.79	2.40
25,000 lines	1.76	2.36
50,000 lines	1.73	2.33
100,000 lines	1.71	2.30

FULL PAGE CONTRACT RATES

	Daily Per page	Sunday Per page
Open	5,496.30	7,254.00
1 page	5,273.10	7,030.80
5 pages	4,966.20	6,640.20
10 pages	4,822.50	6,556.50
20 pages	4,687.20	6,333.30
25 pages	4,547.70	6,110.10

APPLICATION OF DISCOUNTS
When both less-than page units and full page units are used during contract period, full page linage may be combined with less than page linage to earn lowest contract rate. If bulk contract rate is greater than page contract rate, the former applies to full pages. If page rate is greater, bulk contract rate will apply on less-than-page units.
Rotogravure, Comic and TV Magazine linage can be combined with b/w linage to determine earned contract rate.

5a. ZONE EDITIONS
Individual Neighborhood Sections:
South/West Zone and North/West Zone published Thursday. Minimum 42 lines.

Zone Flat Rates:	Per line
South/West	.80
North/West	.60
Zone Pick-Up Rates:	
South/West	.70
North/West	.50

Average net paid circulation for 6 months ending March 31, 1978: North/West 74,950; South/West 166,100.
Advertising must be picked up from full run to one zone only within 8 days at pick-up rate. Advertising may be picked up in either zone one time only within 8 days at pick-up rate. Copy changes on pick-up ads limited to dealer names and addresses. Pick-up must be ordered with initial insertion to qualify for pick-up rate. No ad may be scheduled for both zones same day.

7. COLOR RATES AND DATA
Availability b/w 1c daily and Sunday; b/w 2 c and 3c daily (except Saturday) and Sunday. No leeway required. Minimum b/w 1 c. 2c or 3c 1,000 lines.
Use b/w line rate plus the following applicable flat costs:

	b/w 1 c	b/w 2 c	b/w 3 c
Daily, extra	815.00	1,000.00	1,210.00
Sunday, extra	1,000.00	1,210.00	1,470.00

Standard red, yellow, blue and black colors used. Special inks at advertiser's expense. Require: repro proofs. 3 progressive proofs, 4 registration marks and b/w repro proofs on each color. Running head and dateline not required.
Closing Dates: B/w 1c reservations and printing material 3 days before publication; b/w 2 c or 3 c reservations and printing material 7 days before publication date.
Cancellation 1 week before closing date.

8. SPECIAL ROP UNITS
SPACE SPOTS
Minimum 50 lines, maximum 250 lines per spot. 13 consecutive weeks, minimum 6 spots per week, no maximum (short rate to volume discount earned, if curtailed). Insertion at publisher's option. 33-1/3% discount from open rate. Linage not applicable to other contract.

9. SPLIT-RUN
Accepted on alternate press run basis at .10 per agate line extra; minimum charge 75.00; minimum size 200 lines.

11. SPECIAL DAYS/PAGES/FEATURES
Best Food Day: Wednesday.

12. ROP DEPTH REQUIREMENTS
As many inches deep as columns wide. Minimum depth for Travel, Resorts, Hotels and Steamships on Sunday Travel Page, 7 lines. Regular minimums apply to daily and Sunday R.O.P. Ads ordered for 290 lines or more deep, on any page, charged full column—310 lines.

13. CONTRACT AND COPY REGULATIONS
See Contents page for location of regulations—items 1, 2, 4, 6, 10, 11, 12, 13, 14, 18, 19, 20, 22, 24, 25, 26, 30, 31, 32, 33, 34, 35, 39, 45.

14. CLOSING TIME
Deadline daily: 7:00 p.m. 2 days before publication; Sunday, noon Friday. No copy, corrections, or cancellations accepted after deadlines.

15. MECH. MEASUREMENTS (Offset)
For complete, detailed production information, see SRDS Print Media Production Data.
9/9/3—9 cols/ea 9 picas/3 pts betw col.
Lines to: col. 310; page 2790; dbl. truck 5735.

16. SPECIAL CLASSIFICATION/RATES
POLITICAL
Full run, flat, per line daily 1.79; Sunday 2.40.
RESORT AND TRAVEL
Rates apply to Resorts, Hotels, Tourism, Tour Agencies and Transportation in Sunday Resort and Travel pages and/or sections. General contract rates apply to daily and Sunday R.O.P.

YEARLY CONTRACT RATES

Open rate, per line	2.60
6 insertions, per line	2.33
13 insertions, per line	2.30
26 insertions, per line	2.26
52 insertions, per line	2.21

POSITION CHARGES
Next to reading 30%, full position, 42-line minimum, publisher's option, 50%. News illustration is equivalent to reading matter.
Specified Page Positions:
Page 2 or 3 (publisher's choice)—guaranteed—100%
Sports, and Women's pages, guaranteed............ 50%
Full position guaranteed on any of these pages for an added 50% of basic rate. Ads accepted with guarantee of any of these pages will be inserted as ordered or omitted at publisher's option. Except for above pages publisher does not guarantee to place advertising on any named page nor in a specified location.
DAILY COMIC PAGE
Inside back cover: 30 lines x 4 columns or 60 lines x 4 columns.
Accepted at R.O.P. rate. Minimum 13 times in 13 weeks. Closing time 3 days prior to publication; cancellation 1 week prior to closing.

17. CLASSIFIED RATES
For complete data refer to classified rate section.

18. CIRCULATION
Established: daily 1878, per copy .15; Sunday 1887, per copy .60.

Figure 17-2.

while discounts on retail advertising to large users are commonplace, a number of newspapers offer no quantity discounts to national advertisers. In addition, a study of the discount structure for national advertisers in the top fifty United States markets revealed the pattern shown in table 17-2[8].

The most blatant discrimination in media discounts occurs between types of advertisers. For example, as a generalization, large local advertisers such as major

Table 17-2. Maximum newspaper discounts—top fifty markets

Percent maximum discount	Number of papers offering
0%	18
1 – 15%	14
16 – 20%	11
21 – 25%	7
26 – 30%	9
31 – 36%	4
No. of papers represented	63

department stores may often earn rates 50 percent below national advertisers.

Historically, federal regulatory agencies have tended to ignore media discounts. However, this practice may be coming to an end. In August, 1977. the Federal Trade Commission filed suit against the *Lost Angeles Times,* charging that the *Times'* discount structure provides large retail advertisers unfair competitive advantages.[9] At this point, the FTC case is restricted to the retail discount structure and does not include the widespread discrepancies which exist between retail and national advertisers. However, an FTC spokesman said that this facet of price discrimination could be developed later in the case.

Short Rate. When newspapers offer volume discounts, the advertiser estimates the amount of space that will be used during the next 12 month period, and contracts for that amount at the discount earned, subject to year-end adjustments. Let us assume that a newspaper has the following rate structure:

8. *Current Practices in Media Pricing and Discounts,* Gardner Advertising Company, St. Louis, Missouri, 1967.

9. "FTC hits L.A. Times' discounts for ad volume," *Advertising Age* (August 22, 1977): 1 ff.

Open rate	$0.60 per line
5,000 lines	0.55 per line
10,000 lines	0.50 per line
15,000 lines	0.40 per line

An advertiser estimates (not guarantees) to run 10 thousand lines and contracts for this amount at $0.50 per line. During the year, each advertisement is billed at the $0.50 rate. However, the advertiser runs only 6 thousand lines during the contract period, thereby actually qualifying only for the 5 thousand line rate of $0.55. At the end of the year, the following adjustment is made:

Charged:	6,000 lines @ $0.55	$3,300.00
Paid:	6,000 lines @ $0.50	3,000.00
	Short Rate due:	$ 300.00

Had the advertiser run 15 thousand lines instead of the 10 thousand contracted for, he would have qualified for the $0.40 rate and would received a *rebate* at the end of the year.

Combination Rate. Combination rates are discounts for advertising appearing in the morning and evening editions of the same newspaper, for combining a weekday insertion with a Saturday or Sunday insertion or for advertising in more than one newspaper in a newspaper group. At one point, some combination rates were forced, that is, advertisers were required to use the combination of insertions or newspapers. However, courts have ruled against this practice, and such combinations are now optional.

Position Charges. An advertiser may place his advertisements R.O.P. (run of paper). This means that the newspaper editor can place the advertisement anyplace in the paper; the advertiser has no control over where the advertisement will appear. Or the advertiser may specify a particular position on the page or a position within a particular section of the paper. Higher rates are generally charged for these *preferred* positions. Such charges vary, depending upon the particular newspaper involved, and the nature of the preferred position.

Color Charges. Normally, newspaper advertising appears in black and white. Color advertising is available in many papers on an R.O.P. basis, and can be used in any paper through the use of preprinted inserts. R.O.P. color does not provide dependable quality because of highspeed presses, porous paper stock, and problems of *off-register* reproduction. *Off register* is a term used to described a situation in which colors overlap and demarkations between colors are not clear. For this reason, R.O.P. is used sparingly and chiefly for making ads distinctive with bold backgrounds, designs, color headlines, and so forth. When R.O.P. color is used, there is an extra charge, and newspapers usually have a minimum space requirement for color ads.

One use of four-color in newspapers that has gained widespread popularity is knows as *HiFi* color or *SpectaColor* pages. The advertiser preprints the advertisement on a better quality paper than is normally used by newspapers. The advertisement is printed on one side of huge rolls of paper, and consists of a continuous, repetitive illustration or design, so that no matter where the paper is cut to form a newspaper page, the complete ad will appear on each page. The rolls are supplied to the newspaper, which prints its own material on the blank side. Generally, the advertiser pays for the color preprints plus the black and white page rate. Still another form of color that appears in newspapers consists of multipage, preprinted inserts, often of tabloid size. The advertiser prints the entire insert and sends it to the newspaper where it is inserted after the newspaper has been printed. The charge for such inserts is negotiated, but once a newspaper has established a price for such an insert, this same price applies to other advertisers with similar requests.

Split Runs. Many newspapers offer *split runs* at a slight extra charge. The simplest form of split run is one in which an advertiser prepares two ads of the same size, differing in some respect—headline, illustration, coupon value, or even product. The plate for one ad is printed on press A, and the plate for the other ad is printed on press B. Both presses feed alternately into a common stacking of newspapers, so that the two ads appear in alternate copies of the paper which are distributed throughout the newspapers distribution area. In more complex forms of split runs, some papers can take up to three different ads which can be distributed to discrete areas. For example, one ad to the central city, another to one group of suburbs, and the third to another group of suburbs.

Advertisers use split runs for a variety of testing and advertising purposes. For example, an advertiser might prepare two different ads of the same size, each offering a free sample of the product in the body copy, in order to see which ad would produce the largest consumer response. The responses to each ad could be identified by having consumers enclose a copy of the ad with their responses or write to a different department of the company (Dept. A for one ad and Dept. B for the other). Different headlines could be tested in the same way. Or the relative effectiveness of two coupons of different face values could be ascertained through the use of a split run.

NEWSPAPER CIRCULATION

As pointed out earlier, newspaper circulation is audited by the Audit Bureau of Circulation, an organization established in 1914 to provide an independent audit and verification of newspaper circulation claims. These circulation figures appear on newspaper rate cards, and in the Standard Rate and Data Service (SRDS) newspaper catalogue. Newspaper circulation is generally divided into three categories: *city zone, retail trading zone,* and *all other.* The all other category includes all qualified circulation not included in the city zone or retail trading zone. Sometimes circulation is shown only for the primary market (city zone and retail trading zone) and *outside* circulation. See the *St. Louis Post Dispatch* listing (figure 17–2) for an example of this practice.

Newspapers differ in the extent to which they provide coverage in these three areas. Some newspapers in a multiple-newspaper metropolitan area provide better coverage of the city zone that they do of the retail trading zone; others will provide better coverage of the retail trading zone. Still other newspapers may have unusual strength in the *all other* category, which generally consists of small towns and rural areas. For example, the *Phoenix Republic* provides fairly good coverage of Flagstaff, Arizona, a town of 30 thousand population 140 miles north of Phoenix. The *Des Moines Register* offers coverage of small towns throughout Iowa, and the *Kansas City Star* has substantial out-of-state coverage in Kansas and Missouri. These circulation patterns are taken into consideration in selecting newspapers by national as well as local advertisers.

In selecting newspapers, the advertiser is concerned with both circulation and costs. Since newspapers differ on both of these dimensions, a standardized basis for comparison is needed. The basis used is the *milline rate.* Technically, the milline rate is the cost for reaching a million people with an agate line and is computed on the following basis.

$$\frac{1,000,000 \times \text{agate line rate}}{\text{circulation}} = \text{milline rate}$$

Thus, if the agate line rate for a particular newspaper is $0.90, and the circulation of the newspaper if 520 thousand the milline rate is:

$$\frac{1,000,000 \times \$0.90}{520,000} = \$1.73$$

Why multiply by 1 million? Convenience. If you didn't, the line rate divided by the circulation for the above example would be .00000173, and that is too many decimals.

Standard Rate and Data Service also provides computations of the *maximil* and *minimil* rates for newspapers that offer volume discounts. The *maximil rate* is the milline rate computed on the basis of the *open rate.* The *minimil* rate is a milline rate computed on the basis of the lowest rate available, that is, the one qualifying for the greatest discount offered by the paper.

HOW NEWSPAPERS ARE SOLD

Newspapers have local sales people who take orders for classified advertising and local representatives who call on retail advertisers. Often these representatives help small retailers and classified advertisers in preparing their advertising and make them aware of any special marketing services or information that the newspaper has to offer.

National advertising is generally handled by newspaper representatives' (reps) organizations which have offices in major advertising agency centers such as New York, Chicago, St. Louis, and Los Angeles. These *rep organizations* represent a number of independent newspapers and newspaper chains and are paid commissions by the individual newspapers on the advertising space they sell. Since newspaper rates are relatively firm and not subject to negotiation, the job of the newspaper rep is threefold: (1) to make sure that advertisers and advertising agencies are familiar with the strengths of the newspapers and the markets they represent; (2) to keep them informed about any merchandising or marketing services offered by the newspapers; and (3) to perform a general public relations function.

MERCHANDISING AND MARKETING SERVICES

Newspapers provide a variety of merchandising and marketing services for advertisers and potential advertisers. Merchandising aids to the smaller advertisers include the creation of promotional pieces, the planning and budgeting of advertising, and the actual creation of copy and rough layouts for the advertising.

For national advertisers, newspapers may conduct trade surveys, provide route lists for retail sales people, which enable them to use their time efficiently, give presentations to trade groups, and send promotional pieces to major retailers. Some of the larger newspapers conduct annual consumer surveys to determine brand preferences and/or purchases for a wide list of consumer products. The *Chicago Tribune* became renowned for a permanent consumer panel that it maintained to measure consumer purchases.

STRENGTHS AND WEAKNESSES OF NEWSPAPERS

Like all media, newspapers have certain strengths that commend their use, and certain weaknesses that limit their value. In order to evaluate the medium properly, one should be aware of these plus and minus characteristics.

Strengths of Newspapers

The Bureau of Advertising of the American Newspaper Publishers Association promotes the use of newspaper advertising by disseminating marketing information concerning its use. Among the strengths of newspapers identified by the Bureau are the following.

Broad coverage. Newspapers are truly a mass medium. Seventy-eight percent of adults twenty-one and over read newspapers on an average weekday. Over a five weekday period, newspapers will reach a cumulative audience of 94 percent of all adults, eighteen and over; and, on the average, 82 percent of all newspaper readers will be exposed to the page carrying the advertiser's message.

High reader interest. Interest in advertising is as high among newspaper readers as is interest in the editorial material. Because of the preponderance of retail advertising, newspaper advertisements are the most popular part of the paper for women, and second only to sports for men. Further, readership is constant throughout the year, and the news value of newspapers adds immediacy to the advertising.

Flexibility. Newspapers are flexible in a number of ways: (1) space units ranging from one inch to multiple pages can be used; (2) advertising can be scheduled any day of the week; (3) closing dates are late, so that ads may be prepared on extremely short notice; and (4) since newspapers are essentially a local medium, they provide a great deal of geographic flexibility, allowing the advertiser to pinpoint his advertising pressure in terms of his advertising needs.

Low Cost Per Exposure. On a cost-per-thousand basis, newspapers are relatively inexpensive compared to other media.

Cooperative Advertising. Newspapers are excellent vehicles for cooperative advertising and for dealer-tie-ins.

Weaknesses of Newspapers

As one would expect, newspapers' greatest strengths are also their greatest weaknesses. The major shortcomings of newspapers include the following.

High Waste Circulation. Because of their mass coverage, newspapers do not provide audience selectivity except on a geographic basis. It is true that there are special interest newspapers, but these are generally small circulation publications and useful, at best, on a supplementary basis.

High Cost for National Coverage. While newspapers offer a relatively low cost-per-thousand for intensive coverage of a particular market, their high waste circulation makes them an expensive vehicle to use on a national basis. For example, the cost of a 1000 line ad in newspapers necessary to provide 60 percent metropolitan area coverage in the top 50 markets is in excess of $145 thousand.

Shortness of Message Life. There is nothing older than yesterday's news. Newspapers are read hurriedly, and the life of a newspaper advertisement is short. Unlike magazines, newspapers are unlikely to be put aside and read later.

Poor Color Reproduction. One of the greatest limitations of newspaper advertising is the general poor quality of its color reproduction and the lack of opportunity to use fine artwork. A great deal of progress has been made in this area, but there is still a long way to go.

Competition from Retail Advertising. The volume of retail advertising in newspapers detracts from the readership of national ads. Further, poor position often reduces readership even more.

These are the major pro's and con's of newspapers. Used properly, the newspaper is a powerful medium. Used improperly, it is a waste of company resources.

MAGAZINES

Magazines, like newspapers, are a major print medium. However, whereas newspapers are primarily local in nature, magazines are, essentially, national. Whereas newspapers excel in mass coverage, magazines are recognized for their audience selectivity. Thus, in a real sense, these two print media complement one another.

In 1977, Standard Rate and Data Service listed about 3600 business and professional publications, and some 1200 consumer and farm magazines, about two-thirds of which are classified as *consumer.* The SRDS listing does not contain hundreds of small publications that are not audited, and that lead a marginal existence. In addition, new magazines are founded every month, and, every month, some of them go out of business. *Media Decisions* reported that 200 new consumer magazines were started in 1976, but by December, 1977, only 18 were still in business. Undoubtedly, some of these survivors will cease publication by the end of 1978.

Most of the existing magazines lie outside the mainstream of advertising. For example, in 1977, Target Group Index, a major magazine readership service, reported on only 119 consumer magazines. These 119 magazines, however, had an audience of 145,434,000 readers. Consumer magazine advertising revenues for 1978 were estimated at $2,145 million, a 20 percent increase over 1977. And there is widespread speculation within the advertising industry that disillusionment with network television and skyrocketing television costs will see an even greater swing to magazines in the future.

TYPES OF MAGAZINES

Magazines may be classified in a number of ways. Geographically, some magazines are classified as "national," although their circulation patterns tend to parallel retail sales distribution rather than population. Others, such as *Sunset Magazine,* are regional in nature. *Sunset,* one of the most successful magazines in the industry, is edited primarily for residents of the Pacific states, including Alaska and Hawaii. Little more than 10 percent of its circulation of over one and a quarter million is delivered outside of these states. Sunday supplements, such as *Family Weekly* and *Pa-rade,* are often considered as magazines because their size, format, and color reproduction characteristics are more similar to magazines than to newspapers.

Magazines may also be classified in terms of size—pocket size, such as *Readers' Digest* or *TV Guide* (about 4 3/4" x 6 1/2"); standard size, such as *Time* or *Newsweek* (about 8" x 11"); or large size, such as *Better Homes & Gardens* (about 9" x 12"); and there are a variety of miscellaneous sizes. Or, they can be classified by frequency of publication—weeklies, biweeklies, monthlies, quarterlies, and annuals.

By far, the most frequent way of classifying magazines is by editorial content and audience appeal. Business and professional magazines are classified by *Standard Rate and Data Service* into 176 different classifications, ranging from "advertising" to "woodworking." Farm publications are classified by SRDS according to subject matter: dairy and dairy breeds, diversified farming and farm home, farm education and vocations, field crops and soil management, livestock and breed, poultry, and so forth. Consumer magazines are classified into 58 subclassifications by SRDS, ranging from "airline inflight" at one end of the alphabet, to "youth" magazines at the other end. Magazines such as *Time* and *Newsweek* are classified as "newsweeklies," and magazines such as *Readers' Digest* and *TV Guide* are considered "general editorial" magazines.

Even these classifications do not do justice to the variety of magazines that exist. For example, *The Atlantic Monthly, The New Yorker,* and *Grit* are all classified as "general editorial" magazines, yet their editorial orientations are quite different. *Atlantic Monthly* is an intellectual magazine; *The New Yorker* has a sophisticated, urbane appeal; and *Grit* is clearly edited for the small town market. The point is that magazines are edited for a variety of audiences. One can buy magazines edited to appeal to prurient interests and voyeurism, or magazines that appeal to philanthropy, aesthetic tastes, and intellectual discourse. There is virtually no end to the variety of markets represented by magazines.

KINDS OF MAGAZINE ADVERTISING

Generally, magazines are characterized by three kinds of advertising: *display, display classified,* and *classified* advertising. Different rates and minimum size requirements apply to these three kinds of advertising in the published rate schedules.

Display advertising, sometimes referred to as *product* or *general* advertising accounts for the bulk of magazines' advertising revenues. This advertising is characterized by the use of attention-getting devices such as illustrations, typographical variations, and the use of white space, thereby standing in contrast to the closely set and uniform type size that is associated with classified advertising. The primary purposes of display advertising are to project a brand concept and to influence consumer attitudes.

Display classified advertising, as in the case of newspapers, appears in the classified section of the publication but uses simple illustrations, different type sizes, and limited white space for attention value. Much of the display classified advertising appearing in magazines is *direct mail* advertising since the products and services being offered are not available through retail outlets. Some magazines run the display classified and classified advertising in the same section; others do not. For example, *Popular Mechanics* has a special section for display classified advertising called "The Bargain Hunter."

Classified advertising, sometimes referred to as *nondisplay advertising,* is usually segregated in the back pages of the publication and is available both to individuals and companies. Usually, different rates and minimum requirements apply to commercial products as opposed to individuals who have personal items to buy or sell. For example, in *Psychology Today* the rate for "commercial products" is $4.90 per word with a 15 word minimum; the rate for a personal classified ad is $2.90 per word, with no minimum.[10]

MAGAZINE RATE STRUCTURE

Like newspapers, magazine advertising rates are well structured and, normally, not subject to negotiation. The published rate card and discount conditions are, by and large, inviolate. Unusual space units are subject to negotiation, but once a price has been set for a particular unit, this price applies to other advertisers with similar requests. Price concessions do occur occasionally in the rate charged for cover positions. The magazine must have a cover, and if no advertiser can be found that is willing to pay the normal premium, these will sometimes go at the published rate for standard pages.

The Rate Card

Magazines, like newspapers, are audited by the Audit Bureau of Circulation, and audited circulation statements appear on the rate card. The structure of the

magazine rate card is similar to that of newspapers and contains all of the information that the advertiser needs to schedule and prepare an advertisement. A sample *Standard Rate and Data Service* listing for *Cosmopolitan* is shown in figure 17–3.

Magazine Rates

Magazine rates are quoted in terms of pages, fractional pages, column inches, agate lines, and special units. Since discounts and premium charges are common in magazines, these pricing practices are examined in the following material.

Discounts. Some magazines operate under a *flat rate* policy—where all advertising is charged at the same rate. Most magazines offer a variety of discounts. The most common discounts are *volume* and *freqency* discounts, although *combination* discounts exist for some magazine groups. *Frequency* discounts are based on the number of insertions used during a contract period, with the size of the discount depending on the number of insertions (note section 5 of the *Cosmopolitan* listing in figure 17–3). In addition, some publications offer discounts for the renewal of a schedule beyond one year. *Volume* discounts are offered according to the total space used during a contract period and are offered in addition to frequency discounts. As in the case of newspapers, the advertiser contracts for space based on an estimate (not a guarantee) of the amount and frequency of the planned advertising. Should he use less space than anticipated, he is subject to the *short rate*. Should the advertiser use more space than contracted for and fall into a higher discount bracket, a *rebate* will be given by the magazine at the end of the year.

Combination rates are offered by publications that are under the same corporate ownership or sold as a group to reach a particular market. For example, Condé Nast Publications publishes *Mademoiselle, Vogue, Glamour,* and *House and Garden.* Special discounts are offered for running the same advertising in various combinations of these magazines.

Maximum discounts in magazines may run as high as 35–40 percent. Because of differences in the size of circulations and the page rates charged, the amount of money which must be spent in order to earn the maximum discount in different magazines may range from less than $200 thousand to several million dollars.

Position Charges. With the exception of *cover* positions, magazines do not normally charge a premium for preferred positions since advertising throughout

10. Rates based on the December, 1977, issue of *Psychology Today.*

Figure 17–3.

the magazines receives about the same consumer exposure. There are *preferred* positions which the advertiser may request and, while some magazines will try to grant these requests, they do not guarantee to do so. For example, an advertiser running a horizontal half-page may prefer a top-of-page position; or an advertiser may prefer to be in the first third of the book. In the case of a departmentalized magazine such as *Better Homes and Gardens,* a food advertiser may prefer to appear in the "food" section, and a furniture advertiser may prefer to be in the "home decoration" section.

In the case of *cover* positions, there is often a premium charged for the *2nd cover* (the back of the front

cover), and the 4th cover (the back of the magazine). The premium for 2nd covers, when charged, is generally about 10 percent more than the 4-color page rate, and the 4th cover premium generally ranges from 15 to 25 percent above the four-color page rate. In addition, many publications do not offer discounts on any of the cover positions.

Color. Color reproduction is available in almost all of the leading magazines, including business and farm publications. There is a wide variation in the premium charged for color, however. The premium for two-color pages may range from as low as 5 to 6 percent over the black and white page rate to 20 or 25 percent. Four-color may carry a premium over black and white pages ranging from 20 percent for the larger circulation magazines to as high as 70 percent for some of the smaller circulation publications. The average premium for four-color advertising is probably about 30 percent.

Bleed Pages. A bleed page is one in which printing runs to the edge, or "bleeds" off the page. The premium for bleed ads generally ranges from 10 to 30 percent, depending upon the publication.

Splits, Halves, and Sectional Editions. Some magazines offer split runs for a slight premium. In addition, some of the larger publications offer partial runs and special editions. *Playboy,* for example, will run an advertisement in every other issue at a premium of about 20 percent over its normal cost-per-thousand rate. That is, a 4-color page will cost about 20 percent more than half the cost of the same unit in the full edition. It also offers five regional editions—Eastern, Central, Western, Southeast, and Southwest—for which it charges premium rates. Some magazines, such as *Time,* even offer metropolitan editions for a limited number of major metropolitan areas.

Having reviewed some of the major rate practices of magazines, you should now examine the *Cosmopolitan* listing (figure 17–3) more closely. Note, in particular, the types of discounts allowed, the treatment of "position" requests, how covers are charged in comparison to four-color rates, special rates, and regional editions.

MAGAZINE CIRCULATION

In preparing a media plan, magazines are evaluated on a variety of bases: circulation, the demographic characteristics of their audiences, cost, editorial content, and general tone. Since magazines differ in size of circulations and page rates, the standardized basis for comparing costs is the cost-per-thousand (CPM) discussed in chapter 16.

The page rate used in the numerator in the cost-per-thousand computation may be the cost of a black and white page or some other space unit, depending on the nature of the schedule and the preferences of the media analyst. Cost-per-thousand computations are usually designated as B/W cost-per-thousand, four-color cost-per-thousand, and so forth to indicate which base has been used.

The denominator of the cost-per-thousand equation may be based on the *average issue circulation* (delivered circulation), *guaranteed circulation, reader exposure,* or *target audience exposure.* Any of these may be used

as long as the analyst indicates which he is using. Each of these terms, however, requires some explanation.

Average Issue Circulation

Circulation for magazines will vary from issue to issue, depending on the number of copies sold on the newsstand and the number of subscriptions that are in effect for a particular issue. *Average issue circulation* is determined by dividing the total number of copies distributed during the past January through December period by the number of issues published. These are the circulation figures audited by the Audit Bureau of Circulation.

Guaranteed Circulation

Magazine advertising rates are based on a *guaranteed* circulation that, generally, is somewhat less than the average issue circulation figure. If the magazine fails to meet its guaranteed circulation, the publisher gives a pro rata rebate to the advertiser. Thus, if the delivered circulation of a magazine fell 5 percent below the guaranteed circulation for the issues in which a particular advertiser contracted, the publisher would rebate 5 percent of the cost of the advertising space at the end of the year.

Reader Exposure

Magazines are generally read by more than one person. Sometimes, two or more people in a magazine household will read the magazine. The magazine may be given to a friend or relative after the immediate family has seen it. And, all of us have had the experience of passing time in a doctor's or dentist's waiting room, or in a barber shop or beauty parlor, reading magazines that are kept there to keep us from getting bored. Readership in the subscribing household is referred to as *primary* readership. Readership by someone outside the subscribing household is referred to as *secondary* or *pass-along* readership. The *total exposure* of a magazine includes both its primary and secondary readers and is substantially greater than its delivered circulation. Total exposure is measured by audience measurement services such as Simmons and Target Group Index.

Table 17–3 shows the delivered circulation, the guaranteed circulation, and the total exposure for *Newsweek* and for *National Geographic.* Several points should be noted in this comparison. First, for 1978, *National Geographic* is guaranteeing a substantially larger circulation than it delivered in 1977, suggesting that it has completed a successful circulation drive. Second, the *secondary* readership of *Newsweek*

Table 17-3. Comparison of delivered circulation, guaranteed circulation, and total exposure for "Newsweek" and "National Geographic"

Magazine	Ave. issue circulation (1977)	guaranteed circulation (1978)	Total exposure		
			Men	Women	Total
Newsweek	2,900,000	2,789,785	8,473,000	6,461,000	14,934,000
National Geographic	8,650,000	9,601,727	10,539,000	10,105,000	20,643,000

SOURCE OF DATA: Guaranteed and average issue figures obtained from Publisher Information Statements, dated December 27, 1977; total exposure obtained from Spring, 1977, report of Target Group Index.

is proportionally larger than the secondary readership of *National Geographic*. This is revealed by the fact that *Newsweek's* total exposure is 5.15 times as large as its delivered circulation, whereas *National Geographic's* total exposure is only 2.39 times as large as its delivered circulation. This is a normal pattern since newsweeklies tend to enjoy a large secondary readership while *National Geographic* is a magazine which subscribers tend to save. Third, while male readership is greater than female readership for both publications, female readership's proportion of total exposure tends to be greater for *National Geographic* than for *Newsweek*.

Target Audience Readership

Target audience redership or *exposure* refers to the number of people in the target audience that are exposed to the advertising. In dealing with magazine readership figures, target audiences are defined in terms of demographic variables such as age, education, marital status, product usage, and so forth. Because target audience data is provided by services such as Simmons and Target Group Index, the advertising industry gets upset when the accuracy of these services is questioned.

MARKETING AND MERCHANDISING SERVICES

Magazines, like newspapers, provide a variety of marketing and merchandising services for advertisers and advertising agencies. They often undertake readership and product usage studies of their audiences, and they sometimes prepare basic marketing studies in fields of interest to advertisers or potential advertisers. The research departments of major magazines are often repositories of a great deal of marketing information in a variety of product fields, which they supply to advertisers and advertising agencies upon request.

Magazines do not supply creative help in preparing advertising, as do newspapers, but most magazines have departments that will prepare or assist in the

preparation of counter cards, folders, special letters to distributors and retailers, and similar merchandising aids. Few magazines offer these services without charge or without a major purchase of advertising space. Some of the major magazines will have merchandising specialists in areas such as fashion, cosmetics, department store selling, and so forth. These specialists are available to help present advertising plans to client sales meetings and to meetings of distributor organizations.

STRENGTHS AND WEAKNESSES OF MAGAZINES

Magazines have a number of advantages as an advertising medium. Full realization of these advantages by advertisers is dependent upon a number of variables such as: type of product, the nature of the product's distribution, the effectiveness of advertising copy, competitive activity and so forth.

Advantages of Magazines

Some of the major advantages of magazines are listed below.

High Audience Selectivity. With the exception of direct mail, magazines are the most selective of media for reaching target audiences, except in those cases where the target audience is restricted to local, geographic areas. There are a vast number of special interest magazines available for use, and magazines can even be selected to appeal to a variety of temperaments.

High Quality Reproduction. The paper on which most magazines are printed is excellent for detailed, four-color reproduction. It enables food advertisers to capture "appetite appeal," and permits fashion advertisers to portray "style" in an arresting manner. Further, through the use of unusual space units, interesting effects and high impact can be achieved.

Long Life and Reader Interest. The exposure life of magazines is longer than that of most other media. Magazine advertising can be perused and studied at leisure and, after the primary reader is through with the magazine, its life is extended through pass-along readership. Some magazines, particularly in the home service and fashion fields, are purchased as much for their advertising as for their editorial content.

Audience Characteristics. Magazine readers tend to be above the national average in terms of income and education. And, since magazine circulation tends to follow retail sales rather than population, it parallels the nation's purchasing power.

High Prestige. Magazines lend prestige to products that appear within their covers. Although there is a certain amount of prestige attached to all national media, magazines are particularly strong in this respect—a fact that derives from the education and relative affluence of magazine readers.

Weaknesses of Magazines

Against these strengths, magazines have the following limitations.

Lack of Penetration. Magazines are essentially a national medium and cannot be used to dominate local markets. Sunday supplements can be used for this purpose, but the selectivity of the medium is lost in the process.

Inflexibility. Magazines are relatively inflexible in two respects: (1) although regional and metropolitan editions are available in some magazines, it is generally difficult to vary pressure geographically with magazines; (2) magazine closing dates are often two or three months prior to the date of issue. This precludes moving quickly to take advantage of marketing opportunities.

Lack of Message Immediacy. There is no immediacy to magazine advertising as there is in newspapers and broadcast media. It is basically an *image* medium, designed to sell over the long term.

High Costs. Production costs for magazines are relatively high, particularly for four-color advertising. In addition, even though the cost-per-thousand may be relatively low for a high circulation magazine, the page cost may be well beyond the reach of many small advertisers.

SUMMARY

This chapter is devoted to describing the salient characteristics of the major print media—newspapers and magazines.

In terms of advertising revenues, newspapers are by far the largest advertising medium, although local advertisers account for over 80 percent of newspaper advertising revenue. Although there are only about 15 hundred daily newspapers (with a combined circulation of over 113 million), there are almost 10 thousand semi-weekly, bi-weekly, monthly, and bi-monthly newspapers serving suburban communities, small towns, and rural areas. In addition, there are a variety of newspapers serving ethnic and special interest groups.

Newspapers are characterized by several kinds of advertising: *classified* advertising, used primarily by local advertisers; *retail* advertising, placed by retail merchants and other local businesses; *national* advertising, placed by manufacturers in support of their products; and *reading notices,* advertisements made up to resemble editorial material. Different rates are charged for these different kinds of advertising, but the rates are relatively stable and made known through published rate cards. Most newspapers offer volume discounts. The size of the discount depends upon the amount of space used, and local advertisers are given more favorable rates than national advertisers.

Newspaper circulation is audited by the Audit Bureau of Circulation, and circulation figures are shown on the newspaper rate card. Since newspapers differ both in line rate and size of circulation, the basic device for comparing newspaper costs is the *milline rate.* The milline rate is the cost of reaching one million people with an agate line of newspaper space.

Newspaper space is sold to local advertisers through local salespeople. National advertising is generally sold through newspaper representative organizations that have offices in major advertising centers. These organizations represent a number of independent newspapers and newspaper chains.

Although newspapers have a number of advertising values, their primary values are their ability to provide broad coverage and high readership. The primary weakness of newspapers is their high waste circulation.

Magazines, like newspapers, are a major print medium but, whereas newspapers are recognized for their mass coverage, magazines are known for their audience selectivity.

Standard Rate and Data Service lists about 3600

business and professional publications, about 800 consumer magazines, and about 400 farm journals. Magazines may be classified in many ways, but the most frequent way of classifying them is in terms of editorial content and audience appeal. SRDS classifies magazines into 176 different groups, some of which appeal to highly specialized interests. These categories only partly describe the diversity that is available through magazines.

Magazines generally carry three kinds of advertising: *display* advertising (from which they derive the bulk of their revenues), *display classified,* and *classified* advertising. These forms of advertising have different rate structures and different minimum size requirements.

Like newspapers, magazine rate structures are relatively stable and made available through published rate cards. Magazines offer a variety of discounts based on the volume of space used and the frequency of insertions. They also have premium charges for such things as cover position, color, bleed, and regional editions.

Cost per thousand (CPM) is the basic device for comparing the costs of magazines. Cost per thousand comparisons may be made on the basis of *guaranteed* circulation, *average issue* circulation, or *total readership.* Target audience exposure refers to the number of people in the product's target audience that are exposed to its advertising. Target audiences are defined in terms of demographic variables and based on data published by readership services such as Simmons and Target Group Index.

Magazines, like newspapers, provide a variety of marketing and merchandising services to advertisers and advertising agencies. Further, the research departments of magazines are often repositories for a great deal of marketing information which is supplied to advertisers and agencies upon request.

The primary strengths of magazines lie in their audience selectivity, their high quality of reproduction, long life, quality audiences, and high prestige. Their primary weaknesses are their lack of penetration of markets, their relative inflexibility, their lack of immediacy, and their relatively high cost.

QUESTIONS

1. What are the fundamental differences between newspapers and magazines from the standpoint of the advertiser?
2. Assume that a newspaper has the following rate structure:

Open rate	$0.90 per line
5,000 lines	0.85 per line
10,000 lines	0.80 per line
15,000 lines	0.70 per line

   An advertiser contracts for 10 thousand lines and is billed at this rate. During the contract year, however, 15 thousand lines are used. Show the computations for the year-end adjustment.
3. Advocates of Sunday supplements claim that they offer the advertiser the best of both magazines and newspapers. How would you defend this point of view?
4. Explain what is meant by a *splitrun* and indicate why it might be used by an advertiser.
5. Explain, without formulas, what the milline rate reveals and how it differs from the magazine cost-per-thousand. Why don't newspapers, like magazines, use a cost-per-thousand measure?
6. Identify the major strengths and weaknesses of newspapers.
7. Using the *Cosmopolitan* SRDS listing (figure 17–3), identify: (a) the maximum discount shown, (b) the difference in cost between black and white and color pages, (c) the premiums for bleed pages, (d) the policy on pricing covers, (e) method of printing, and (f) closing dates.
8. Explain what is meant by volume, frequency, and combination discounts.
9. Distinguish between *average issue circulation, guaranteed circulation,* and *reader exposure.* If you were recommending a schedule in a magazine, which of these bases would you use to compute cost-per-thousand? Why?
10. What are the major strengths and weaknesses of magazines?

PROBLEM

You are a space buyer in an advertising agency. One of your clients sells a nutritional cattle feed supplement to dairy farmers and has been using six pages in *Hoard's Dairyman* as his primary medium. Analysis of his sales indicates there is a need to increase coverage in four regions: (1) West North Central, (2) South Atlantic, (3) East South Central, and (4) West South Central.

The budget for next year's effort is approximately $30 thousand for space costs. This is to include six black and white pages in *Hoard's Dairyman,* with the balance placed in dairy magazines that will strengthen coverage in the desired areas. You prefer to use magazines that are audited, although you recognize that it may be necessary to use unaudited magazines to obtain the desired coverage.

Using your SRDS, you turn to the section on "Dairy and Dairy Breed."

Assignment

1. Schedule *Hoard's Dairyman* for six B/W pages.
2. Select one or more additional media to supplement coverage in the desired areas.
3. Prepare a recommendation showing:
   a. The media you have selected, and the number of B/W pages you will use.
   b. The percent of total circulation by geographic regions that you achieve.
   c. Your dollar allocation for space by geographic region.

18

Television and Radio

The Year That Rain Fell Up

All fall, broadcast and ad executives nervously peeked at the figures on their desks, then shut their eyes and turned the tallies face down, as if they had hoped the whole thing would go away. Like scientists who had discovered that rain also falls up, they could not believe what they were seeing. Last week, however, the two rating services, Nielsen and Arbitron, confirmed their fears: in 1977, for the first time in history, television viewing declined.

For daytime audiences, the numbers were startling. From November, 1976, to November, 1977, Nielsen put the drop-off at 6.4%—roughly equivalent to the combined population of Detroit and San Francisco. The Arbitron figures were even more dramatic. From 9 A.M. to noon, they said, viewing was down 11%—or goodbye Chicago. The arithmetic for the prime-time evening hours was less dramatic, but significant nonetheless. Nielsen said the nighttime decline was 3.1%; Arbitron said it was 5%.

On Madison Avenue, where the ad agencies are spending an estimated $7.65 billion of their client's money on TV this year, the news was dismaying. "Nobody *ever* assumed that viewership would go down," observes Bill Tenebruso of Wells, Rich, Green. "I think it's a little premature to start saying that something devastating happened to TV in 1977," says Wal-

ter Reichel of the Ted Bates agency. "But something is going on."[1]

Listen Before You Shop

Except for the major department stores, shopping mall stores have traditionally had limited advertising budgets. Most of the advertising has been done in mall bulletins and some local newspapers. However, competition is increasing, not only between individual stores in each mall, but also between malls. And it has become more and more difficult for the junior specialty stores to maintain their share of the consumers' dollar.

Competition breeds invention. In 1977, Paul Harris (a 100 unit chain of specialty stores) started experimenting with radio by running a three-week flight of spots in September which reached 63 percent of its target audience. Casual Corner, with 250 stores in shopping malls across the country, experimented with a four-week spot television campaign in October. The future of radio and television advertising for mall

---

1. "The Year That Rain Fell Up," *Time* (January 9, 1978): 69. Reprinted by permission from *Time, The Weekly News Magazine*; Copyright Time, Inc., 1978.

shoppers is uncertain; it depends on how well these experiments work. If they are successful, other specialty chains will follow suit because nothing succeeds in advertising like success. [2]

Who Listens in Drive Time?

"Drive time" in radio parlance means that time during which job holders drive to and from work. Normally, it is considered to be from 6:00 A.M. to 10:00 A.M., and from 3:00 P.M. to 7:00 P.M. Traditionally, drive time has been considered the best time to reach men with radio advertising. The assumption has been that car radios are the only thing that stand between the driver and madness. At the same time, it was widely believed that the best time to reach women was between 10:00 A.M. and 3:00 P.M., a time period referred to as "housewife time."

Research by RADAR market surveys is beginning to explode these beliefs. Surveys in the fall of 1976 and the spring of 1977 indicated that: (1) there are nearly as many people listening to car radios during housewife time as during drive time; and (2) more women listen to radio (at home and while driving) during drive time than during housewife time.

Harper Carrine, director of research at CBS radio, says "Agencies and clients are beginning to see that these myths about more men listening in drive time, or women in housewife time, are cockeyed."[3]

Such is the face of broadcast media: surprise, experimentation, and exploded beliefs.

The decline of network television viewing should not be unexpected. After all, there are limits to growth. Yet, the decline came as a surprise to network executives whose first response was to attack the bearers of ill news and to reject their findings.

There are many reasons why TV viewing should decline, and may decline even more. For example, an increasing number of women are joining the work force; in-home computer games that are played on the TV set have undoubtedly eroded, and will continue to erode, TV viewing. And then there is programming. Network programmers have, more and more, programmed for the 18 to 29 age group, thereby alienating older viewers. During 1976–77, there was a trend to convert half-hour soap operas to hour-long programs, a move that many believe has had a deleterious effect on daytime viewing. Beyond this, there has been a shift from game shows, preferred by older women, to soap operas, which are preferred by younger women.

Stunting (shifting prime-time programs around so much that no one knows when his or her favorite show will be broadcast) has not helped the situation. And then there are the unimaginative, routine formula shows in prime-time hours and "look alike" situation comedies (sitcoms) with built-in laugh tracks to compensate for their lack of humor. All of these factors are bound to have an impact on TV viewing.

The possibility of a significant decline in TV viewing is particularly threatening to the industry when one also recognizes that the cost of network TV has risen spectacularly in recent years. An average minute of prime-time television cost $100 thousand in 1977, up more than 50 percent since 1975. A minute spot in the Johnny Carson show cost $120 thousand in 1977, and a thirty-second spot on the Super Bowl cost about the same. Daytime price increases have been almost as steep, from $11,600 in 1975 to $17,000 in 1977, an increase of 47 percent. National magazines and network radio are delighted with the turn of events. It can only mean increased advertising revenues for their coffers.

Radio is still alive and reasonably healthy. It is a $2.25 billion industry. And, as advertisers grow increasingly concerned over TV costs and ratings, radio promises to become even healthier.

AN OVERVIEW OF BROADCAST MEDIA

Broadcast media differ from print in a number of significant respects. They differ both in terms of the characteristics of the media themselves and in terms of the structure of the industry. Let's look at some of these differences.

Differences in the Characteristics of the Media

In one sense, broadcast and print media are different worlds. A magazine buyer in an advertising agency, for example, can move fairly easily to newspapers. But, without special training in broadcast, she is not prepared to deal with broadcast problems, and vice versa. Some of the major differences between the two media are identified in the following material.

Broadcast Is a "Time" Medium whereas Print Is a "Space" Medium. Consumers have no opportunity to study broadcast commercials as they can study print ads. The commercial is there for a few seconds or a minute, and then it is gone.

Broadcast Is Basically an Entertainment Medium. People turn on their television and radio sets to seek

2. "Mall stores experiment with radio and tv use," *Advertising Age* (November 28, 1977): 20.
3. "Who's Listening in Drive Time," *Media Decisions* (November, 1977,): 70 ff.

entertainment programs, or to catch up on the news. They do not tune in to listen to or view commercials. Advertising, in fact, is often viewed as an unwelcome interruption—something consumers would prefer to do without. How different this is from a magazine, which is often bought because of its advertising.

Since people differ in their interests and tastes, broadcasters attempt to appeal to different groups through their programming. In radio, for example, there may be several stations in a market. Each is beamed at different target audiences through "country and western" music, through "rock," through "sweet" or "classical" music. The problem of appealing to different audiences is more difficult in TV because there is a limited number of channels. As a consequence, most TV stations are directed toward a general audience, and different programs on each channel are used to appeal to different audience segments via children's programming, soap operas, game shows, sports, adventure, situation comedies, and so forth.

Further, unlike print, which is the private property of individual publishers, the airwaves are public domain, so that the Federal Communications Commission, which licenses radio and TV stations, exerts some control over program content and over advertising.

Broadcast Is a Glutton for Entertainment and Editorial Material. In radio, this problem is met by programming an abundant supply of music (it's not always good, but it is abundant). But in television, the problem is more pressing. Material has to be written and produced in an unending stream. Magazines, which are printed once a week or month, don't have this problem in the same degree. And although newspapers are printed daily, because they have a world of happenings to draw from, there is always more news than editors care to print.

The never-ending demand for new material is one of the major reasons why much of television's programming is mediocre. There simply are not enough creative people to meet TV's voracious appetite for good material, and TV production is expensive.

Broadcast Time Is Perishable. Each day there is a certain amount of commercial time. If the time is not sold, it is irrecoverable. Demands are less pressing in print. The amount of editorial material appearing in a publication is adjusted in accordance with advertising revenues. This difference between print and broadcast media leads to different pricing and selling practices (these differences will be discussed later in this chapter). Further, unlike magazines, where advertising readership is relatively uniform throughout the publi-

cation, broadcast has prime listening times during which the audience is greatest. For radio, it is the daytime hours; for television, it is during the evening.

There Is a Difference between Print Circulation and Broadcast Coverage. Print *circulation* is the number of copies of a publication that are distributed to consumers. In broadcast, *coverage* refers to the potential audience of a station or network, and circulation is equated to exposure (that is, the average number of listeners or viewers during a given time period).

There are other differences between print and broadcast, of course. The foregoing ones are simply some of the more significant.

THE STRUCTURE OF BROADCASTING

The basic unit of broadcasting is the local station, which is privately owned but licensed by the Federal Communications Commission (FCC). Some stations are affiliated with networks; some are not. A local station that has a network affiliation is referred to as an *affiliate.* One that does not is referred to as an *independent.*

A station gains network affiliation by signing a contract with one of the national networks. Under the terms of this contract, the local station agrees to sell the network a certain amount of programming time for about 30% of the station's normal time charges. The local station, particularly in television, benefits from this arrangement in two ways: (1) it receives professional programming that it could not afford to develop itself, and which attracts large audiences; and (2) because of these large audiences, the local station is able to sell time between network programs at a premium price. Figure 18–1 shows the basic structure of the broadcast industry.

Since television and radio are significantly different as advertising media, each will be discussed separately in the following material.

TELEVISION

There are approximately 69 million television homes in the United States. This represents 97 percent of all homes. Of these 69 million television homes, approximately 71 percent (48,990,000) have color TV, 45 percent (31,050,000) have more than one television set, and about 12 percent (8,280,000) are served by CATV systems. CATV stands for "community antenna television" and is popularly referred to as *cable TV.* Initially, cable TV was established to provide TV cover-

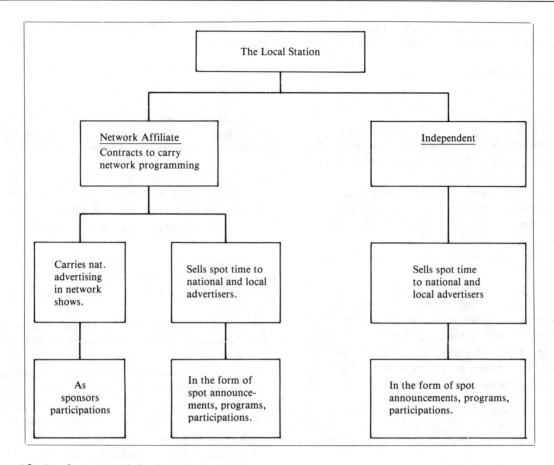

Figure 18-1. Structure of the broadcast industry

age in remote areas or in areas where surroundings interfered with television reception. Subsequently, the concept of cable TV has been expanded beyond the provision of better reception in remote areas to that of providing a diversity of programming, even in relatively populous regions.

The 69 million television homes in the United States are served by over one thousand local television stations, three national television networks—The American Broadcasting Company (ABC), the Columbia Broadcasting System (CBS), and the National Broadcasting Company (NBC)—and approximately 3200 CATV systems. Networks, local stations, and the CATV systems are all licensed by the FCC and must meet certain minimum operating and programming requirements in order to obtain and keep their licensed authority.

Basic Television Terms

There are a number of terms that are used in connection with television planning and audience measurement. These terms are: *penetration, coverage, sets-in-use, share of audience,* and *rating.* Perhaps the eas-

iest way to explain them is to borrow an example from Paul Roth's book, *How to Plan Media.* [4]

Penetration   Start with a theoretical "universe" of 100 households. Ninety-seven of these 100 households own TV sets. TV *penetration* or *set ownership* is 97/100 = 97%.

Coverage Area   The TV signal of a theoretical network covers 80 TV households. The *coverage area,* therefore, is defined as: 80 out of 97 TV households in the universe = 80/97 = 82% *coverage.*

Sets-in-use   At 9–10 P.M., 60 TV households are watching TV. Thus, *sets-in-use* = 60 out of 97 households = 60/97 = 62% *sets-in-use.*

Rating   During the 9–10 P.M. period, 20 TV households are watching a particular program. The *rating* of this program is 20/97 = 21. A rating point therefore, is one percent of all the households having a TV set.

Share-of-audience   During this 9–10 P.M. period, 20 households are watching a particular program. How-

---

4. Paul Roth, *How to Plan Media* (Skokie, Illinois: Standard Rate and Data Service, Inc., 1969).

ever, 60 households are watching TV. Therefore, that particular program's *share-of-audience* is 20/60 = 33.

Evaluating a Television Commercial

Television commercials are evaluated in terms of *reach, frequency,* and *weight.*

Reach The reach of a commercial refers to the number of people or households exposed to it, generally in a four-week period.

Frequency The *frequency* of the commercial refers to the number of times the average member of its audience (or the average household) is exposed to it within a four-week period.

Weight The *weight* of a television schedule is measured in terms of *gross rating points.* Gross rating points are computed by multiplying the *rating* of the commercial by the number of times it is run. For example, suppose that a commercial appeared in a program with an average rating of 10. Further, suppose that this commercial appeared in this program four times in a four-week period. The gross rating points earned would be: 4 x 10 = 40.

Now, let's take a simplified example (using households) to see how a particular TV schedule can be evaluated in terms of weight, reach, and frequency.

Example of a TV Audience

Since there are 69 million television homes in the United States, a weekly program with an average rating of 10 would reach 10 percent of the homes. This would be equal to 6,900,000 homes. In a four-week period, it would accumulate (cume) *40 gross rating points* (4 x 10 = 40), and, theoretically, reach 27,600,000 homes (4 x 6,900,000 = 27,600,000). Thus, 40 gross rating points in a four-week period would generate 27,600,000 exposures for a commercial that appeared in the program once a week for four weeks.

However, not all of these exposures are *new* exposures. Some households will watch the program every week and thereby have an opportunity to be exposed to the commercial four times. Some will only watch three weeks out of four; some two weeks out of four; and some will see the program only once. Thus, 40 gross rating points represents a certain amount of duplication in the 27,600,000 exposures it provides.

Now, let's make some more assumptions about our theoretical commercial and the program in which it appeared. Let us assume the pattern of exposures given in table 18–1.

Now, we can describe our theoretical commercial in terms of its *weight,* its *reach,* and its *frequency.* In this

Table 18–1.

No. of households	× No. of exposures	= Total exposures
2,760,000	× 4	= 11,040,000
2,760,000	× 3	= 8,280,000
2,760,000	× 2	= 5,520,000
2,760,000	× 1	= 2,760,000
11,040,000	10	27,600,000

particular example, a weight of *40 gross rating points* provides a *net* or *unduplicated reach* of 11,040,000 households, with an *average frequency* of 2.5

$$(27,600,000 \div 11,040,000 = 2.5).$$

A commercial with a similar weight (that is, 40 gross rating points) but more or less duplication would deliver a different net reach and a different average frequency.

This is a simplified example because we have dealt with households and have not taken into consideration the composition of the audience *within* households. In order to do this, we need audience composition figures such as those provided by the audience measuring services. With audience composition information, we could provide comparable weight, reach, and frequency information for men, women, children, and even for particular age groups. The essence of media planning is to develop an optimal balance between reach and frequency against some defined target audience, such as women between the ages of 18 and 39, or men between the ages of 29 and 49, or some other specified group.

TELEVISION COMMERCIAL TIME

Classifications of Television Time

Commercial rates for television time vary by time of day, with those time periods attracting the largest audiences commanding a higher price. The period of highest television viewing is referred to as *prime time.* On the east and west coasts, prime time is between 7:30 and 11:00 P.M. In the Midwest and Mountain states, it is 6:30 to 10:00 P.M. On network affiliated stations, the FCC permits 2½ hours of prime time to be programmed by the networks, and local stations are permitted to sell commercial time between programs. The hour or so adjacent to prime time is called *fringe time. Early fringe* precedes prime time; *late fringe* follows prime time. Fringe time ranks next to prime time in terms of costliness.

Local television stations often set up a variety of rate classifications defined in terms of the time of day in which the broadcast occurs. For a small station, the time classifications may be as simple as:

Class A—7:30 P.M. to 11:00 P.M.
Class B—All other times

On the other hand, a key station in a major market may have an extremely complex rate structure. For example, KMOX-TV in St. Louis, Missouri, has 33 rate classifications ranging from 8A to Z. In this particular instance, Z rates for a 60-second commercial cost only 2 percent as much as *8A* rates. But, of course, only the worst of insomniacs are liable to be awake during the Z time period.

Availability of Commercial Time

The actual amount of television time available for advertising is sharply limited by the Television Code of the National Association of Broadcasters, to which most stations subscribe. A portion of the Television Code relating to nonprogram (commercial) material is reproduced below.

In order that the time for non-program material and its placement shall best serve the viewer, the following standards are set forth in accordance with sound advertising practice.

1. Non-Program Material Definition: Non-program material, in both prime time and all other time, includes billboards, commercials, promotional announcements and all credits in excess of 30 seconds per program, except in feature films. In no event should credits exceed 40 seconds per program. The 40-second limitation on credits shall not apply, however, in any situation governed by a contract entered into before October 1, 1971. Public service announcements and promotional announcements for the same program are excluded from this definition.
2. Allowable Time for Non-Program Material
   a. In prime time on network affiliated stations, non-program material shall not exceed nine minutes in any 60-minute period.
   b. In prime time on independent stations, non-program material shall not exceed 12 minutes in any 60-minute period. In the event that news programming is included within the three and one-half hour prime time period, not more than one 30-minute segment of news programming may be governed by time standards applicable to all other time.
      Prime time is a continuous period of not less than three and one-half consecutive hours per broadcast day as designated by the station between the hours of 6:00 PM and midnight.

   c. In all other time, non-program material shall not exceed 16 minutes in any 60-minute period.
   d. Children's Weekend Programming Time—Defined as that contiguous period of time between the hours of 7:00 AM and 2:00 PM on Saturday and Sunday. In programming designed primarily for children within this time period, non-program material shall not exceed 12 minutes in any 60-minute period.
3. Program Interruptions.
   a. Definition: A program interruption is any occurrence of non-programmed material within the main body of the program.
   b. In prime time, the number of program interruptions shall not exceed two within any 30 minute program, or four within any 60-minute program. Programs longer than 60 minutes shall be prorated at two interruptions per half-hour.
      The number of interruptions in 60-minute variety shows shall not exceed five.
   c. In all other time, the number of interruptions shall not exceed four within any 30-minute program period.
   d. In children's weekend time, as above defined in 2c, the number of program interruptions shall not exceed two within any 30-minute program or four within any 60-minute program.
   e. In both prime time and all other time, the following interruption standard shall apply within programs of 15 minutes or less in length:

      5-minute program—1 interruption;
      10-minute program—2 interruptions;
      15-minute program—2 interruptions.

   f. News, weather, sports and special events programs are exempt from the interruption standard because of the nature of such programs.
4. No more than four non-program material announcements shall be scheduled consecutively within programs, and no more than three non-program material announcements shall be scheduled consecutively during station breaks. The consecutive non-program material limitation shall not apply to a single sponsor who wishes to further reduce the number of interruptions in the program.[5]

Unfortunately, not all subscribers to the code are as conscientious in their adherence to code stipulations as reasonable integrity would dictate. For example, during the late movie on a major Phoenix, Arizona, television station, I counted eleven consecutive commercials between 11:30 and 11:35 P.M.; twelve minutes later, I counted six more consecutive commercials. I don't know how many more commercials were run before midnight because I turned off

5. *The Television Code,* 17th ed., April 1973 (Washington: Code Authority, National Association of Broadcasters, 1973), pp. 14–17.

the set in disgust. It is practices such as this that undermine the entire televison industry and help discredit it as an advertising medium.

OPTIONS IN TV ADVERTISING

The television advertiser has a number of options available in terms of the geographic areas covered by her advertising schedule. These options may be broadly described as network versus local scheduling.

Network Scheduling

Network scheduling may be either national or regional in nature. Normally, the major networks—ABC, CBS, and NBC—require that the advertiser contract for a minimum number of their affiliated stations. These stations provide what is, essentially, national coverage, although there will be some remote or isolated areas that will not be reached by the network stations. Under certain conditions, an advertiser can purchase only a portion of the network, referred to as a *network leg*. One network leg may cover the Mountain and Pacific states; another the Southeast region; still a third the Eastern Seaboard; and so forth. NFL football, for example, is often broadcast on a regional basis with various sections of the country receiving the games of those teams based in their region. NCAA basketball and other sports are often broadcast in a similar fashion.

In addition, there are regional networks that cover certain portions of the country, such as the Northeast and Southeast. Finally, there are *tailor-made* or *ad hoc* networks in which a group of stations join together for a special program. As soon as the program has been broadcast, the network passes out of existence. The stations carrying the David Frost interviews with former President Nixon are an example of such a network.

Advertisers sometimes put their own regional network together in order to obtain the type of programming they want. Thus, in the 1960s, the Pet Milk Company produced a country music television program and then negotiated an arrangement with a line-up of television stations in the Southeastern region to carry the program in exchange for commercial time within the program itself. This commercial time was then sold by the participating stations to local advertisers. The project was eventually abandoned by Pet because production costs for the program made it economically unfeasible.

Local Scheduling

Local scheduling refers to those programs or commercials that originate with local television stations. An advertiser can, of course, build up regional or even national coverage through the use of local stations. Building national coverage in this way is usually undesirable. (1) Buying is more complex since each local station must be contacted individually, whereas a network purchase requires a single contract. (2) High rated, local time is often unavailable when and where it is needed. This means that the advertiser must run more commercials in order to achieve equivalent gross rating points, and reach and frequency estimates are both more difficult to prepare and less accurate than those based on network programming. (3) Commercials purchased on a local basis often lose their effectiveness because of commercial clutter. They may be surrounded by other commercials, some for competing products. (4) A separate film or videotape must be sent to each participating station. As a result, the flexibility that is offered by building national coverage through local purchases is often offset by higher costs. (5) The problem of control—confirming the fact that the commercial ran when and where it was supposed to—is much more difficult through local stations than through the network.

As a consequence of these factors, most national advertisers that invest heavily in television use network schedules to provide basic national coverage. Then, they supplement their network schedule with local spot purchases in those markets where additional coverage is needed.

Methods of Buying Time

A television advertiser has several alternative methods for buying time. These are: *sponsorship, participation,* and *spot announcements.* Sponsorship and participation are available on both a network and local market basis. Spot announcements are available only from local stations.

Sponsorship. When an advertiser sponsors a program, she assumes total financial responsibility for the production of the program as well as for the advertising appearing within it. The advertiser may or may not control the content of the program. In the mid-1970s, the question of program control became a major issue in the advertising industry.[6] It became

---

6. "Protests mount against more advertiser control of tv content," *Advertising Age* (November 14, 1977): 1 ff.

an issue because television networks, in their frenzied race for ratings, were resorting to excessive use of violence, sex, and night-club humor—practices that many viewers found offensive. Since viewers tend to blame the advertiser whose products appear on the offending programs rather than the networks, advertisers live in constant fear of consumer boycotts. For example, a major package goods company cancelled the Smothers Brothers from their schedule during the Vietnam war because their protests against the war offended many viewers who wrote irate letters to the advertiser. General Motors withdrew its sponsorship of "Jesus of Nazareth" because of a storm raised by some fundamentalist religious groups. In the later instance, General Motors lost some six million dollars that it had invested in producing the program, and Procter and Gamble, which picked up the broadcast after GM's cancellation, ended up with one of the best buys in television history.

Nonetheless, despite these contretemps, program sponsorship offers worthwhile values. First, the advertiser does have control over the type of program in which her commercials appear—sports, drama, adventure, situation comedies, variety, and so forth. Second, sponsorship offers the opportunity for extensive merchandising and collateral advertising, often taking advantage of the star of the program as a product spokesperson. Third, sponsorship offers the opportunity to run two and three minute commercials in order to develop the product's story fully. Unfortunately, the cost of television is such that few advertisers can afford the luxury of sponsorship, particularly in prime time. One alternative is multiple sponsorship, in which two or more advertisers will underwrite the costs of production and share the commercial time. This approach is frequently used for sports events such as the World Series and the World Series of Golf and for prestigious, prime-time programs.

Participation. About 90 percent of network commercial time is sold on a participating basis. Each of a number of advertisers pays for 30 seconds or 60 seconds of commercial time in one or more programs. An advertiser may participate in a particular program one time only or have multiple participations on a regular or irregular basis. In contrast to sponsorship, the participating advertiser does not assume financial responsibility for the production of the program. The network or the individual station underwrites programming costs and then prices commercial time within the program at a rate that will recover costs and provide a profit.

There are a number of advantages to using participations rather than outright sponsorship. First, since the advertiser may use any number of participating spots, the size of the television expenditure can be adjusted to the available budget. Second, the use of participating spots on a number of programs enables the advertiser to achieve greater reach while reducing frequency within the same number of gross rating points. Third, the advertiser's cost-per-thousand may be substantially reduced over the cost-per-thousand for sponsorship.

There are two disadvantages of participations. First, since there are a number of advertisers on each program, the individual advertiser loses "program identity" and the merchandising opportunities that exist for program sponsors. Second, advertisers normally lose some control over the programs in which their commercials appear. But, then, all media planning and buying is a trade-off. One balances reach against frequency, weight against budget, impact against continuity, and control against flexibility.

Spot Announcements. Spot announcements are bought from local TV stations and appear between programs rather than within them. There is little opportunity for an advertiser to identify a product with a show since the announcements are isolated from the shows themselves. Another disadvantage of spot announcements is that the break between programs is often filled with competing commercials, station identification, and promotional spots for coming programs. Since viewers expect several minutes of solid advertising, they often use the time in other ways. A number of studies have shown that the volume of sewage increases substantially between programs, suggesting that many viewers are doing something other than watching commercials.

BUYING TELEVISION TIME

Network time is sold by network representatives who negotiate directly with advertisers and advertising agencies. Local stations use local sales people to contact local advertisers, and national "rep" organizations, which operate on a commission basis, represent a number of stations throughout the country, although one organization will normally represent no more than one station in a particular market. Since network and local selling practices differ in some respects, each needs to be discussed separately.

Network Selling Practices

Network selling can be divided into four periods, each with different pricing practices. These periods are: (1) early preseason, (2) late preseason, (3) beginning of the season, and (4) seasonal selling.

Early preseason. Historically, the network season starts in September. Early in the preseason (six to eight months before the season starts) prices are established by the seller. Presumably, these prices are related to the seller's costs and projected profit needs. At this point, prices are relatively inflexible.

Despite the relative firmness of price at this point, negotiation still enters in as a major factor because of the diversity of the buying needs that the seller faces. For example:

1. Some buyers have options on, or control, programs and are seeking desirable time segments.
2. Some buyers have options on time segments and are seeking desirable programs.
3. Some buyers (having neither program nor time options) are seeking a limited number of programs and time slots designed to reach well-defined audiences that will provide an appropriate commercial environment for their products.
4. Other buyers are seeking a large number of programs and time segments and are in a position to participate in a wide variety of programs with quite different audience characteristics.

Late preseason. This period (one to six months prior to the TV season) is the time during which the buyers' influence becomes apparent. Unit prices fluctuate widely because the seller is constantly aware of her unsold position versus the availability of buyers. Unit prices begin to give way to *packages,* wherein the cost of each element in the package is not defined. A number of time units, usually scattered among many shows, are offered at an arbitrary price.

Beginning of the Season. At the beginning of the actual TV season, pricing of unsold inventories is a reflection of the individual network's profit position, the size of its unsold inventory, and the availability of buyers. Packages of commercial time may be available for purchase at half the price at which they were offered six months earlier. On the other hand, the buyer is at this point often in the position of evaluating for purchase a limited number of opportunities consisting of shows with little prospects for large audiences.

Seasonal Buying. After the season in under way, the size of the unsold inventory and the availability of buyers continue to be the prime determinants of pricing. The performance of each unsold show or segment of a show in terms of audience ratings becomes a major factor in focusing buyer interest and results in further volatility in the market.

As a result of the buying and selling climate described above, the role of published discounts is minimized. This is particularly true since published discounts in network TV apply only to time charges and are not applicable to program costs. Considering the importance of negotiation and renegotiation (regardless of when network purchases are consummated), it is all but impossible to determine whether two advertisers in the same network program at the same time are paying the same price, even though they both may be earning the same published discount. The variable is not the discount, but the sum of the base prices upon which discounts are taken. As a result, in evaluating network value one needs to look at the cost-per-thousand-viewers paid, not the discount earned.

The following example illustrates the variations in pricing that often occur in network television. For an expenditure of $4,160,000:

. . . Company A buys (preseason) one minute a week for 52 weeks at $80,000 per minute.

. . . Company B buys opportunistically (after the season is under way) two minutes a week for 45 weeks at $46,000 per minute.

. . . Company C spends $1,000,000 and purchases 24 minutes in a four-week period at $42,000 per minute.

This is not to say that the average audience (as reflected by ratings) per minute purchased by Company C will be of similar size to those purchased by Company A. But it is quite possible that some of the twenty-four minutes purchased by Company C were offered months earlier to Company A at double the price paid by Company C. As a consequence of the foregoing considerations, published discounts for network television aren't all that important.

Generally, network TV is a national medium, oriented to the national advertiser whose product has broad, national distribution and sales. In some instances, network TV can be purchased on a regional basis through the use of network legs. The premium for such purchases is generally about 30 percent over national rates for the same coverage area.

Local (Spot) Selling Practices. The pricing policies and published discounts applying to advertising placed with local television stations vary widely, depending on the station involved, its competitive position in the market, the size of the market, and the number of competitive stations.

Some of the factors present in network television buying and selling are present in spot television. However, the large inventories of available time on network-affiliated stations are found outside of network time. The supply of local time on these stations during and immediately adjacent to prime time is quite limited. It is in this prime evening time that the largest television audiences are available. Therefore, it is common practice to price these time segments at premium, nondiscountable rates. During the remainder of the broadcast day, the supply of local commercial time is greatest, and audience are usually much smaller. These time segments are discounted to a substantial degree.

Stations without network affiliations have a sizable supply of commercial time, regardless of the time of day. The pricing policies of these stations are generally characterized by liberal discounts, flexible pricing, and negotiation.

The demand for spot television fluctuates widely from market to market and by time of the year. In periods of low demand, negotiation by buyer and seller may result in concessions in terms of the requirements for discounts and, in some cases, price-cutting. As in the case of newspapers, the rates charged national advertisers are generally higher than the rates charged local purchasers.

The volume of *weekly activity* is the common determinant of discount levels in spot television. A company spending a million dollars to run twelve announcements per week for four weeks may earn a 50 percent greater discount than another company spending five million dollars to run six announce-

ments for thirty-seven weeks. Additional discounts may be earned by accepting preemptable schedules (schedules in which the station has the right to preempt any particular spot at its discretion). Table 18–2 shows the number of stations in the top fifty markets offering maximum discounts at various levels. These discounts include both dollar volume and "preemptability" discounts.

STRENGTHS AND WEAKNESSES OF TELEVISION

Television is generally considered the most powerful of advertising media. It is so considered because of its unique combination of sight and sound, its ability to deliver large audiences, and the flexibility it offers for varying coverage on a market-by-market basis.

Product demonstration. To a much greater extent than other commercial media, television provides an opportunity for product demonstration.

Captive audience. Unlike print media where advertising can be easily ignored, one has to make a special effort to avoid being exposed to commercials in a television program that one is viewing.

Wide coverage. Because 97 percent of U.S. households have TV sets, television provides penetration of 69 million homes. In the average week, TV will be viewed by 70 percent of all adults and teenagers, and 80 percent of all children between the ages of two and twelve.[7] A popular program can easily reach 13 million households, and a major event like the super bowl will reach almost 30 million homes.

Flexibility. Television is highly flexible in terms of both time of day and in terms of geographic coverage. Advertisers may use as many commercials as they can afford within a single year and may buy a single market, national coverage, or anything in between. In addition, advertising weight can be adjusted by market in terms of the advertiser's needs.

On the negative side, television has two major limitations.

Expense. Television is expensive, both from the standpoint of commercial production and the cost of

Table 18–2. TV discount ranges in top fifty markets

Discount range	Number of stations
0 – 9%	3
10 – 19%	34
20 – 29%	34
30 – 39%	59
40 – 49%	33
50 –	25
Total stations	188

SOURCE: Gardner Advertising Company

7. BBDO Audience Coverage and Cost Guide, 15th ed., (Batton, Barten, Durstine, & Osborn, Inc., 1976), p. 7.

television time. The cost for a 30-second commercial in a popular prime time, network show may exceed $70 thousand. A 30-second spot in a major market such as Chicago may exceed $2 thousand. Many advertisers cannot afford a significant television effort throughout their areas of distribution.

Lack of selectivity. Although some selectivity is available in television, it is not really a selective medium. For example, although the average soap opera is thought of as a "woman's" program, it will reach an audience that consists of about 58 percent adult women over 18 and 42 percent men, teenagers, and children.[8]

RADIO

Radio is the most ubiquitous of media. There are some 400 million radio sets in use in the United States—over five sets per household. This figure includes some 85 to 90 million car radios, as well as stationary and portable radios of every size, shape, and description. The radio audience is served by approximately 4300 AM stations, approximately 2200 FM stations, and four national networks—the *American Broadcasting Company,*[9] The *Columbia Broadcasting System,* the *Mutual Broadcasting System,* and the *National Broadcasting Company.* In addition, there are a number of regional networks. Some of them are highly specialized, such as the Country Music Network, Farm Directors Network, National Spanish Language Network, and the Ivy Network Corporation (college radio).

Prior to the advent of television, radio occupied a position similar to that of television today. Network programming was a major form of family entertainment, and programs such as *The Fitch Bandwagon, Fibber McGee and Molly, Burns and Allen, Jack Benny, Bob Hope, The Big Story, The FBI, Gangbusters, Gunsmoke,* and numerous others were major, national advertising vehicles.

With the appearance of television, many people forecast the death of network radio. Radio was in critical trouble for some time, but it has survived and grown stronger since about 1961. The character of radio has changed substantially, however. Table 18-3 compares advertising expenditures in radio for 1948 and 1976. It is apparent from this table that radio has become, primarily, a local and spot medium.

RADIO COVERAGE

Radio coverage varies from station to station depending on the station's power, its antenna system, soil conductivity, and the *Heaviside layer.* The Heaviside layer is an atmospheric condition consisting of a ceiling of electrical particles that bounces radio signals back to earth, particularly at night. Because of this phenomena, night coverage for a radio station is generally greater than day coverage. In order to minimize interference between stations, the FTC may require a station to operate under a lower power output at night. The FCC also assigns station licenses on the basis of four classes of channels:

Class 1. Clear channel stations are assigned 50,000 watts, receive almost exclusive use of a particular frequency, and serve a wide area free from interference.

Class 2. Class 2 stations are clear channel dur-

Table 18-3. Comparison of advertising expenditures in radio: 1948–1976.

| | Expenditures in millions of dollars: | | % of total expenditures in: | |
	1948	1976	1948	1976
Network radio	211	104	37.5%	4.6%
Spot*	121	493	21.5	21.7
Local*	230	1,680	40.9	73.7
Totals	562	2,277	100.0%	100.0%

* The term *spot* refers to advertising bought from a local station by a national advertiser; the term *local* refers to advertising bought from a local station by a local advertiser.

SOURCE: Robert J. Coen, "No let up in boom: '77 ad spending retains momentum," p. 3ff. Reprinted with permission from the July 18, 1977 issue of *Advertising Age.* Copyright 1977 by Crain Communications, Inc.

8. *Ibid.,* p. 14.
9. The American Broadcasting Company is segmented into four operating divisions: American Contemporary Network; American Entertainment Network; American FM Network; and American Information Radio Network. Each appeals to the particular programming formats of their affiliated stations.

ing the day only and must go off the air at sunset (because of the Heaviside effect) so that they will not interfere with class 1 stations.

Class 3. Regional stations have a power range up to 5000 watts and may cover several markets. The actual coverage of a regional station will be limited by other, distant stations that share the same frequency.

Class 4. Local stations, designed to serve a single community fall in this class. Generally, they operate on 250 watts or less and have a receiving range of about 25 miles.

The actual coverage of a station is measured in terms of its *field intensity*. Using portable measuring equipment mounted in a car, signal strength is measured at various distances and in different directions. On the basis of these measurements, coverage maps are drawn showing primary and secondary coverage areas. A primary coverage area includes those areas in which the signal is consistently strong. The secondary coverage area is that area in which the signal is strong most of the time.

BUYING RADIO TIME

Radio is sold in the same way television is; like television, radio may be bought on a network, spot, or local basis. However, network pricing practices differ in some respects from local and spot practices.

Network Radio Selling Practices

Pricing in network radio (as in the case of network television) is influenced by the same conditions attendant to a perishable, volatile commodity. However, compared to network television, the total amount of time available for sale on network radio is relatively small, being restricted for the most part to network news shows and a few other news or sports features. Further, production and programming costs are quite low compared to television, so that the financial risks are substantially less in radio, and the networks have a much lower break-even point.

In periods when the market is "soft," and especially when a large advertiser withdraws from the medium, network radio selling practices become fiercely competitive. Concessions in base price, as well as in conditions required to earn discounts, are common incentives for prospective advertisers. Because the medium does not have a programming season like network television, these concessions are not seasonally predictable. Instead, they are triggered by the individual network's profit position at any time. Since network radio is nationally oriented, the advertiser who desires to use it regionally generally pays a premium for this privilege. The size of the premium, however, is determined by negotiation and is heavily influenced by the network's inventory position.

Because of the importance of negotiation and wide variations in base prices, the actual price of a network radio buy may have little relation to published discounts, which range as high as 53 percent for some of the national networks.

Local and Spot Radio

The pricing policies and practices in local and spot radio are more liberal than those generally found in spot television. This results from two factors. First, on the average, there are four to five times as many radio stations per market than there are televison stations. Thus, selling competition is more intense. Second, the amount of commercial time for sale on network affiliated radio stations is about twice as great as that available on network affiliated TV stations because there is substantially less network programming in radio.

As in the case of television, local radio stations establish several classifications of time based upon audience size, and they price these time segments accordingly. Figure 18–2 is an example of a radio listing for station WQQW in Waterbury, Connecticut. Note (item 6, spot announcements) the rate differences between time classifications and the discounts based on the number of spots per week.

There are wide differences in the pricing practices of different radio stations in the same market for the following reason: generally, three or four stations will attract 60 to 70 percent of the listeners in a major market. These stations adhere fairly rigidly to published prices and discounts. The other stations in the market compete for the scraps with liberal pricing and discount policies, with an emphasis on negotiation, and with frequent price concessions.

Like spot television, weekly rather than annual volume is the most significant factor in earning discounts on spot and local radio. An examination of the 500-odd radio stations in the top fifty markets indicates that maximum discounts range from zero to 60 percent.

STRENGTHS AND WEAKNESSES OF RADIO

Radio is an interesting medium and, since it is overshadowed in the broadcast field by television, its unique virtues are sometimes overlooked.

Low cost. Radio costs are relatively low both in terms of time and production, radio advertising is

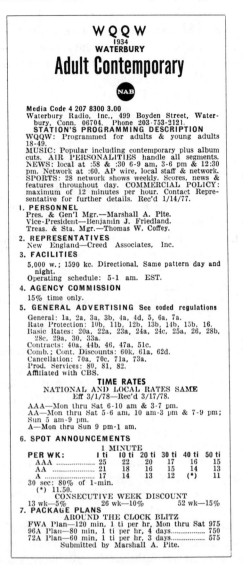

WQQW
1934
WATERBURY
Adult Contemporary
NAB

Media Code 4 207 8300 3.00
Waterbury Radio, Inc., 499 Boyden Street, Waterbury, Conn. 06704. Phone 203-753-2121.
STATION'S PROGRAMMING DESCRIPTION
WQQW: Programmed for adults & young adults 18-49.
MUSIC: Popular including contemporary plus album cuts. AIR PERSONALITIES handle all segments. NEWS: local at :58 & :30 6-9 am, 3-6 pm & 12:30 pm. Network at :60. AP wire, local staff & network. SPORTS: 28 network shows weekly. Scores, news & features throughout day. COMMERCIAL POLICY: maximum of 12 minutes per hour. Contact Representative for further details. Rec'd 1/14/77.

1. PERSONNEL
Pres. & Gen'l Mgr.—Marshall A. Pite.
Vice-President—Benjamin J. Friedland.
Treas. & Sta. Mgr.—Thomas W. Coffey.

2. REPRESENTATIVES
New England—Creed Associates, Inc.

3. FACILITIES
5,000 w.; 1590 kc. Directional. Same pattern day and night.
Operating schedule: 5-1 am. EST.

4. AGENCY COMMISSION
15% time only.

5. GENERAL ADVERTISING See coded regulations
General: 1a, 2a, 3a, 3b, 4a, 4d, 5, 6a, 7a.
Rate Protection: 10b, 11b, 12b, 13b, 14b, 15b, 16.
Basic Rates: 20a, 22a, 23a, 24a, 24c, 25a, 26, 28b, 28c, 29a, 30, 33a.
Contracts: 40a, 44b, 46, 47a, 51c.
Comb.; Cont. Discounts: 60k, 61a, 62d.
Cancellation: 70a, 70c, 71a, 73a.
Prod. Services: 80, 81, 82.
Affiliated with CBS.

TIME RATES
NATIONAL AND LOCAL RATES SAME
Eff 3/1/78—Rec'd 3/17/78.

AAA—Mon thru Sat 6-10 am & 3-7 pm.
AA—Mon thru Sat 5-6 am, 10 am-3 pm & 7-9 pm; Sun 5 am-9 pm.
A—Mon thru Sun 9 pm-1 am.

6. SPOT ANNOUNCEMENTS
1 MINUTE

PER WK:	1 ti	10 ti	20 ti	30 ti	40 ti	50 ti
AAA	25	22	20	17	16	15
AA	21	18	16	15	14	13
A	17	14	13	12	(*)	11

30 sec: 80% of 1-min.
(*) 11.50.
CONSECUTIVE WEEK DISCOUNT
13 wk—5%   26 wk—10%   52 wk—15%

7. PACKAGE PLANS
AROUND THE CLOCK BLITZ
FWA Plan—120 min, 1 ti per hr, Mon thru Sat 975
96A Plan—80 min, 1 ti per hr, 4 days.................. 750
72A Plan—60 min, 1 ti per hr, 3 days.................. 575
Submitted by Marshall A. Pite.

Figure 18-2.

within the reach of most national or local advertisers. On a cost-per-thousand basis, radio is the most economical of the major commercial media for reaching consumers.

Selectivity. Radio can be highly selective in reaching certain target markets. Farm radio, for example, with its reports on the weather, livestock, and grain markets zeros-in on the farmer. Teenagers can be reached efficiently with "rock" music. And there are dozens of stations that broadcast partly or entirely in a variety of foreign languages for various ethnic groups.

Flexibility. Radio is highly flexible, both geograph-

ically and in terms of time segments of the day. On the average day radio will reach 75 percent of U.S. adults.

Useful supplementary medium. Radio is an excellent supplementary medium that can be used to intensify coverage for relatively short periods of time at a minimum cost. Many advertisers use it only as a supplementary medium, but it can be used as a primary medium through intensive schedules.

Local personalities. Some local radio personalities have loyal followers and are extremely effective in selling products.

Weaknesses. On the negative side, the reach of individual programs is relatively small. Ratings of two and three are not uncommon. As a consequence, intensive programming is necessary to build reach. Also, radio is wholly an aural medium; it is relatively easy to "tune out" a radio commercial and, once broadcast, the commercial is gone.

SUMMARY

Broadcast media differ from print media both in terms of the characteristics of the media themselves and in terms of the structures of the industries. TV and radio differ in terms of their characteristics, the ways in which they are used, and in the selling practices that characterize their industries.

In discussing television, it is important to understand the relationships between weight, gross rating points, unduplicated reach, and frequency.

Television time can be bought on either a network or local basis, and there are advantages and disadvantages of each method of buying. In addition to these geographic options, advertisers may buy television in terms of program sponsorship, participations, or spot announcements. Each of these approaches has strengths and weaknesses.

At one time, radio occupied the role that television does today. With the rapid growth of television, radio has become primarily a local and spot medium.

Like television, the basic unit of the radio industry is the individual station. Unlike television, however, local radio stations vary in terms of their power output. Four classes of stations are licensed by the Federal Communications Commission.

QUESTIONS

1. Identify the major differences between print and broadcast media.
2. Describe the structure of the broadcast industry.
3. Explain the following terms: (a) *penetration*, (b) *coverage area*, (c) *sets-in-use*, (d) *rating*, and (e) *share-of-audience*.
4. Explain what is meant by the *weight* of a television schedule. How is weight related to reach and frequency?
5. Explain the major geographic options that an advertiser has in buying television time.
6. Distinguish between sponsorship, participations, and spots as ways of buying TV advertising. Given no budget constraints, which would you prefer to use and why?
7. Briefly characterize the selling practices in network TV in the: (a) early preseason, (b) late preseason, (c) beginning of the season, and (d) during the season.
8. Identify and distinguish between the four classes of radio stations licensed by the FCC.
9. How does the selling of time in spot radio differ from the selling of spot TV? Why do these differences exist?
10. Why is it suggested that radio is an excellent supplementary medium rather than a basic medium for national advertisers?

PROBLEM

As advertising manager for a major food marketer, you are negotiating with the networks for a one-third sponsorship of a prime-time, variety show. You are considering two offerings, both popular shows with an established history of success.

Your costs for show A, which is expected to achieve an average rating of 20, is $3,659,760 for a one-minute commercial per week for 52 weeks. Based on last year's experience, you expect the following exposure pattern:

40% of the exposures will be one time in a 4-week period.
25% will be two times in a 4-week period.
20% will be three times in a 4-week period.
15% will be four times in a 4-week period.

Show B is expected to achieve an average rating of 23, and will cost $3,994,120 for one commercial a week for 52 weeks. You estimate the following exposure pattern for a four-week cume.

30% of the exposures will be one time.
25% will be two times.
25% will be three times.
20% will be four times.

You want to achieve a net unduplicated reach over a four-week period of approximately 34 to 35 million households. Also, in selecting a television vehicle, you are interested in one that has the greatest unduplicated reach as long as the cost-per-thousand for unduplicated reach is not out of line.

Assignment

Knowing that there are approximately 69 million television households in the United States, analyze the audiences of the two shows in terms of:
1. Four-week cume.
2. Net unduplicated reach in a four-week period.
3. Cost-per-thousand unduplicated reach.
Then, recommend one of the two programs, based on the criteria you have set.

Other Media

Burma Shave

Superhighways are not an unmitigated blessing. These four-lane symbols of speed and efficiency, isolated by billboard restrictions, have all but destroyed a bit of Americana that will be remembered with nostalgia by almost everyone over 30.

At one point, Burma Shave dominated the country's byways with advertising signs. These signs, six to a set and spaced in groups about 100 feet apart along the country's main highways, relieved driving tedium, moralized, helped teach children to read, and made Burma Shave one of the best known brands of shaving cream in the United States.

Beginning in 1926, Burma Shave installed over 7 thousand sets of these roadside posters, with heaven knows how many different verses. For years, it was the company's primary advertising medium.

Some examples:

> Use our cream
> And we betcha
> Girls won't wait
> They'll come
> And getcha
> Burma Shave

> Don't take
> A curve
> At 60 per
> We hate to lose
> A customer
> Burma Shave

Screenvision

Commercials in movie theaters predate home television by many years. Often refered to as "trailers" or "minute movies," this medium has been used by local and national advertisers alike. But now it is running into trouble. The trouble began with an expansion of this medium in recent years. Screenvision, a company founded to exploit cinema advertising, developed distribution in some three thousand movie theaters. It numbers among its clients such products as Chanel No. 19 fragrance, Chrysler, and Seiko Time. Cinemavision, a Nashville based company, has been testing movie commercials in more than a dozen markets in anticipation of entering the field.

In the current age of protest and individual rights, movie goers are objecting to theater commercials when given an opportunity to express their opinions. Even the FTC is getting into the act. The head of FTC's Seattle office has notified two theaters in Seattle that it was "unfair and misleading" to run ads in theaters without first telling customers that it was doing so.[1]

Best Kept Secret in Town

Industry groups at the twenty-third annual meeting of the Exhibit Designers and Producers Association have decided to undertake an industry-wide effort to promote trade show exhibits as a major marketing medium and to elevate this medium from the "best kept secret in town" to the "talk of the market place."[2] The nucleus of the industry effort is the creation of a national Trade Show Board (TSB), supported by nine trade show organizations. The immediate goal is a first year budget of $100 thousand to launch the new organization.

According to an industry spokesman, trade show producers have spent $2.3 billion for capital improvements on 10 million square feet of new exhibition facilities in the past ten years. Annually, more than 50 thousand exhibitors use over 4 thousand trade shows in over 100 cities to promote their products. Obviously, it is a big business.

Highway posters, in-theater commercials, and trade show exhibits are but three examples from a group of media that are sometimes called *minor* media, *secondary* media, *supplementary* media, and *unmeasured* media. All of these terms are, to some extent, misnomers when one considers the diversity of the media involved and the scope of their activities. Direct mail, for example, is generally considered a *minor* medium, even though it is estimated to account for almost five billion advertising dollars a year. And, while $5 billion is probably an understatement (no one knows how much is spent on direct mail) it is still substantially larger than the expenditures in magazines, in radio, or in business papers.

Outdoor advertising, which is generally thought of as a supplementary medium, has, nonetheless, been used as the primary advertising effort by some national brands, as the Burma Shave example makes clear. Outdoor advertising is, technically, a *measured* medium, but there is more uncertainty and dissatisfaction over its measurement than there is for broadcast or print media, even though audience measure-

ment in these two areas comes in for more than its share of criticism. For example, the editor-in-chief of *Advertising Age* told the 1977 convention of the Outdoor Advertising Association that "advertisers' biggest concern about outdoor advertising seems to be in the area of audience research."[3]

The purpose of this chapter is to briefly examine some of the more widely recognized miscellaneous media, pointing up their salient characteristics, their strengths and weaknesses. All of them, under appropriate conditions, may have value for a particular advertiser. None of them however, have the stature and prestige of print and broadcast. The advertising media covered in the following material are: (1) outdoor, (2) transit, (3) directories, (4) direct, (5) program, (6) films, (7) exhibits, (8) specialty, and (9) point-of-purchase.

OUTDOOR ADVERTISING

Outdoor advertising is generally considered the dominant "out of home" medium. Not all advertising that appears outdoors is considered outdoor advertising, however. Over a period of time, and under the auspices of the Outdoor Advertising Association of America (OAAA), only those signs or billboards that meet certain standards established by the OAAA, and which are placed by recognized *plant operators* are so considered. Under OAAA definitions, most of the signs and posters seen along roads on buildings, restaurants, bars, and so forth are not considered *outdoor* advertising in the technical sense. In fact, it has been estimated that only about 5 percent of all outdoor signs are accounted for by the organized outdoor advertising industry.[4] The organized industry, however, accounts for an estimated $409 million, about two-thirds of which is placed by national advertisers.[5] Since there is no dependable data on outdoor signs not placed by the organized industry, and since national advertisers generally contract only with recognized outdoor plants, it is this segment of outdoor advertising that will be treated in the following material.

Organization of the Industry

Outdoor advertising is a local medium, and the basic unit of the industry is the local plant operator. There

1. "Patrons vote no on theater ads; FTC office orders a warning," *Advertising Age,* (November 21, 1977): 1.
2. "Trade show groups unfold one umbrella," *Advertising Age,* (December 5, 1977): 1.
3. "Marketers want more outdoor data, Crain says," *Advertising Age* (November 7, 1977): 78.
4. Report, *This Outdoor Advertising,* Institute of Outdoor Advertising, 1971.
5. *Advertising Age,* (July 17, 1977): 31.

are over 1,000 recognized plant operators in the United States, covering 11,000 markets. Plant operators are independent business firms which own or lease sites for outdoor displays, erect the structures for the signs, and sell space to advertisers for a period of time ranging from one month to five years. Plant operators are also responsible for physically placing the advertising on the sign structure and for its maintenance. In major markets, there may be several plant operators competing for sites which have high traffic counts— that is, streets or intersections which carry heavy traffic.

The Outdoor Advertising Association of America (OAAA) is the trade association for the industry. A division of the OAAA, the Institute for Outdoor Advertising (IOA), serves as a marketing and promotional arm for the industry. Its activities include the publication of *The Buyers' Guide to Outdoor Advertising,* a quarterly publication containing the rates and number of panels (billboards) per showing in all markets represented by association members.

Until 1977, the National Outdoor Advertising Bureau (NOAB), a service organization owned by a group of advertising agencies, performed a contracting function for major outdoor advertisers for a commission of 3.66 percent. In addition to contracting for space, the NOAB also handled billing and paying, sent instructions to plant operators, and carried out field inspections to guarantee that instructions were being followed and that outdoor posters were being properly maintained. As more and more advertising agencies began assuming these services themselves (generally to save money) NOAB became unprofitable and closed shop.

Forms of Outdoor Advertising

The major types of outdoor advertising used by national advertisers are *posters, painted bulletins,* and *spectaculars.* Posters are the most commonly used of these three forms and are the mainstay of the industry. Painted bulletins are more costly and usually placed in better locations. Spectaculars are the largest, most expensive, and most dramatic of the outdoor forms. They may have moving parts, belch smoke, or employ other attention-getting devices. Spectaculars are usually reserved for locations where the traffic count warrants their cost.

Posters. Poster sizes are referred to in terms of *sheets.* The term orginated when it took twenty-four of the largest sheets of paper that printing presses could hold to cover a sign 12 by 25 feet. Even though the size of presses has changed, the term *24-sheet* is

customarily used to refer to a standard sized poster. Today, posters are still mounted on 12 by 25 foot signs, but three sizes of posters are generally used.

1. *24-sheet posters* (104" x 234"). The rest of the board area is a margin of blank paper.
2. *30-sheet posters* (115" x 259"). Twenty-five percent more advertising space than 24-sheet, surrounded by a blank margin.
3. *Bleed posters.* Extends artwork to the edge of the frame. Bleed posters average 40 percent larger than 24-sheet.

In addition to these large-sized posters, there are also 6-sheet and 3-sheet posters, which are generally found in suburban shopping areas and on a neighborhood store walls.

The most commonly used poster size is 30-sheet. This size is available in all major markets in the continental United States, except Alaska. Posters may be illuminated or regular (nonilluminated) and, in markets of over 100 thousand population, about two-thirds of the posters are of the illuminated type. The percentage of illuminated posters drops to about 5 percent in markets under 10 thousand. Situated on primary and secondary arteries throughout a market, poster locations may be specified to conform to ethnic and demographic marketing areas. Figure 19–1 shows a typical 30-sheet poster for Swift's Premium Franks. Note the sparseness of copy. Since posters are often seen from a passing car, copy is generally restricted to package identification and/or brief copy point.

Painted Bulletins. The second major type of outdoor advertising is the painted bulletin. Instead of being printed on paper and mounted on a sign as in the case of posters, painted bulletins are painted directly on movable steel panels which are then mounted on the sign structure. While the size of painted bulletins may vary, the most common size is 14 by 48 feet, substantially larger than a 30-sheet poster which is about 9.5 by 21.5 feet.

Painted bulletins are commonly illuminated and may include protrusions that extend beyond the top, bottom, or sides; they may also contain some form of animation. They may be mounted in a single location or rotated from one location to another on a monthly or bimonthly basis in order to increase coverage. Because of their cost, which may exceed a thousand dollars a month for a single bulletin, they are generally found only in high traffic areas. Figure 19–2 shows a painted bulletin for Montgomery Ward.

Spectaculars. Spectaculars, as the work implies, are the most conspicuous of outdoor signs both in terms

Figure 19–1. 30-Sheet poster

of size and construction. There is no standard size since they are individually designed and constructed, and the cost of the space and construction are negotiated. Prices range from $25 thousand to several hundred thousand dollars a year, and the most elaborate may include flashing lights, animation, simulated waterfalls, simulated explosions, or virtually anything else that can be conceived. The best known single location for spectaculars is the Times Square area of New York City where the spectaculars on display are viewed by millions of people each year. Figure 19–3 shows a spectacular for the Bulova Accutron.

Outdoor Advertising Showings

Historically, outdoor advertising was measured in terms of *showings.* The base unit was a 100 showing, but this designation did not refer to the number of panels used since a 100 showing in a small community might consist of a single panel, whereas a 100 showing in a large metropolitan area might require several hundred panels. Instead, a 100 showing in a particular market consisted of whatever number of boards was necessary to reach approximately 90 percent of the adult population during a 28-day period, with an

Figure 19–2.   Painted bulletin

Figure 19-3. Bulova Accutron spectacular. The picture and numerals are constantly changing. (U.P.I. photo)

average frequency of a little over once a day. A 50 showing, which consisted of about half as many panels, would normally reach about 85 percent of the adult population with an average frequency of once every other day. Since there is considerable duplication among people who drive a great deal, net reach will be significantly less than theoretical reach. However, there are no good estimates of net reach because the standard method of measurement is a traffic count, which does not make it possible to estimate duplication.

In 1973, the OAAA replaced the term *showing* with the term *gross rating points*. A 100 gross rating points (the approximate equivalent of a 100 showing) theoretically provides a daily effective circulation equal to the population of the market. Both terms (*showings* and *gross rating points*) are currently in use, but gross rating points are in the ascendancy. In the following discussion, I will continue to use the term *showing* for convenience, recognizing that the term *gross rating points* could also be used without a substantial change of meaning.

Showings are normally sold in multiples of 25, so that advertisers may buy 25, 50, 75, 100, 125, and so forth. Some outdoor plants offer only 50 and 100 showings. Others sell fractional showings (odd amounts of panels in quantities of less than a 25 showing). Generally, a 150 showing is considered sufficient to saturate a market.

Buying Outdoor Advertising

Posters are generally bought in terms of a showing of a particular size, a certain proportion of which will be illuminated. The cost of a 100 showing will depend on the size of the market and the number of panels required. The minimum length of a purchase is one month. Table 19-1 shows the costs and other relevant data for 100 and 50 showings or gross rating points for various groupings of the top 100 markets in the United States.

Unlike posters, painted bulletins are bought separately on the basis of a traffic-flow map showing the location of the sites in relation to the main arteries and traffic routes of the market. The cost of a particular bulletin will depend upon the amount of traffic exposed to it which, in turn, will depend upon its location and position. Table 19-2 shows the average cost per month per painted bulletin for various groups of the top 50 markets. Bulletins are generally purchased for twelve months.

Spectaculars, of course, are negotiated on an individual basis. Because of the costs of construction, they are generally contracted for three to five years, with an option for renewal.

Outdoor Advertising Circulation

Circulation in outdoor advertising refers to the number of people who may pass a given location and have

Table 19-1.   30-sheet poster costs in top 100 markets.

Markets	# of Panels	100 Gross Rating Points % Illuminated	Monthly Cost
1-10	2,730	72	$ 445,459
1-20	4,282	69	665,594
1-30	5,339	69	796,628
1-40	6,220	68	904,773
1-50	7,000	67	991,377
1-60	7,788	65	1,078,818
1-70	8,476	64	1,152,446
1-80	9,014	63	1,212,320
1-90	9,486	62	1,265,210
1-100	9,927	61	1,302,562
		50 Gross Rating Points	
1-10	1,498	71	247,144
1-20	2,318	68	357,064
1-30	2,885	68	430,494
1-40	3,367	66	448,740
1-50	3,805	65	536,278
1-60	4,245	63	584,137
1-70	4,637	61	625,535
1-80	4,926	61	657,814
1-90	5,202	61	688,314
1-100	5,467	59	711,318

SOURCE: NOAB rates of record, December, 1975

a reasonable chance of seeing the advertising. By convention, this number is measured as half the pedestrians, half the automobiles, and one-fourth of the surface transportation passengers who pass the sign. The primary source for such data is the Traffic Audit Bureau, which is composed of members of the advertising industry. The Traffic Audit Bureau serves the same function as that of the Audit Bureau of circulation for print media; it audits and validates the circulation figures claimed by plant operators.

Strengths and Weaknesses of Outdoor Advertising

Outdoor advertising is truly a mass media, although it can be tailored to reach ethnic and demographic groups through selective placement in major markets. Since it is a local medium, it is geographically flexible and may also be used seasonally for periods as short as one month. On a cost-per-thousand basis, it is relatively inexpensive.

It also has severe shortcomings. Since the viewers of outdoor advertising are generally moving, there are limitations on the amount of copy that can be employed. For the most part, product identification and a short slogan is about all it can accommodate. In addition, its audience figures are ambiguous, and meaningful duplication figures as well as circulation by age groups are nonexistent. While outdoor advertising may be used as either a primary or supplementary medium, it is most often used in the latter fashion. One advertising industry spokesperson complained that advertisers are not sure how to use outdoor advertising and need help from the outdoor industry in assessing its value.[6]

TRANSIT ADVERTISING

Transit advertising consists of paper posters placed inside or on transit vehicles, and in transit stations. While there are about 380 markets in the United States in which transit advertising is available, there are only seven markets that have extensive rapid transit systems and which have station platforms on which advertising can be displayed. These cities are

Table 19-2.   Rotating Painted Bulletin costs within top 50 markets

Markets	Average monthly cost per bulletin
1-10	$1,194
11-20	951
21-30	793
31-40	741
41-50	622

SOURCE: *BBDO Audience Coverage and Cost Guide*, 1976, p. 42.

6. "Marketers want more outdoor data, Crain says," p. 78.

Boston, Chicago, Cleveland, New York, Philadelphia, San Francisco, and Washington D.C. Partly because of its limited availability, transit advertising only attracts expenditures of about $40 million a year. However, in the major markets where it is available, it is a healthy and growing medium. Under the impact of the energy crisis and the apparent need for more public transportation, the industry will probably continue to grow.

Types of Transit Advertising

There are a number of forms of transit advertising. The most common types are *car cards, exterior displays,* and *station posters.*

Car Cards. Car cards are used as interior displays in overhead racks and other locations in subway trains, buses, commuter trains, and other rapid transit systems. The standard car card size is 11 inches high, with widths of 28, 42, and 56 inches. "Square" cards,

measuring 21 by 22 inches are also used at the ends of rail transit vehicles, and miscellaneous sizes are available for special positions, such as over doors. An example of a car card is shown in figure 19–4.

Exterior Displays. Exterior displays are water proof posters appearing on the outside of buses and other transit vehicles. There are a number of standardized sizes. The most popular has a height of 21 inches and a width of 44 to 88 inches. Figure 19–5 shows a number of such signs, and the ways in which they are most often displayed.

The Bus-O-Rama, an illuminated, roof-top panel measuring about 22 by 145 inches is available in some markets.

Station Posters. Station posters, which are similar to outdoor posters, although smaller in size, are displayed on and in stations of subways, rapid transit systems, and suburban railroads. Although similar to outdoor posters, they are sold by the same firms sell-

Figure 19–4. Car card

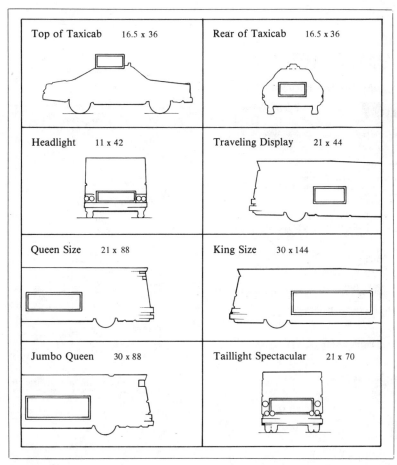

Figure 19–5. Exterior displays

ing car cards because of their locations. The most common sizes for station posters are one sheet (46" by 30"), and two-sheet (46" by 60"). Since waiting passengers have more time to read advertising copy than do drivers of cars, station posters often carry more copy than do the larger, outdoor posters.

Other Forms of Transit Advertising.   In addition to these common forms of transit advertising, there are also floor exhibits, diorama displays, and clock spectaculars located in train and airline terminals. Such displays are usually custom designed for advertisers and are similar to outdoor advertising spectaculars, although on a smaller scale.

Still another form of transit advertising occasionally used is the *merchandising bus*. Such buses are usually chartered by advertisers in connection with sales meetings and/or major promotional efforts. The outside of the bus is covered with advertising messages. In addition, the interior of the bus contains special displays and exhibits. Merchandising buses are sometimes placed in shopping centers in order to take advantage of the high traffic in such areas.

Buying Transit Advertising

There are approximately 70 transit advertising companies serving some 380 markets. These companies are referred to as *operators* and function in a manner similar to outdoor advertising plants. The Transit Advertising Association (TIAA) is the national association for the industry. Its primary functions are to establish and maintain standards and to promote the use of the medium. Mutual Transit Sales, a subsidiary of one of the major transit companies, represents many of the transit operators in selling transit space to national advertisers and advertising agencies.

Although Standard Rate and Data Service has discontinued publication of a transit advertising directory, presumably because lack of demand by agencies and advertisers made it unprofitable, figure 19–6 shows a former SRDS listing for Metro Transit Advertising in Boston, Massachusetts. Note that inside cards, outside cards, and station posters are sold under different rate schedules. Contracts may be for as little as one month, and different size showings can be purchased. For example, in buying inside cards, an advertiser may buy a *full run*, meaning that a card will

MASSACHUSETTS

BOSTON Metro Market

TAA   CERTIFIED *TAA* CIRCULATION

Massachusetts Bay Transportation Authority.
Operated by Metro Transit Advertising, a Metromedia
Co., 72 Sobin Park, Boston, Mass. 02210. Phone
617-268-9590.

1. PERSONNEL
Manager—Robert A. Storella.
Sales Manager—John Waitekus.

2. REPRESENTATIVES/BRANCH OFFICES
Mutual Transit Sales.
  New York, N. Y. 10017—485 Lexington Ave. Phone
  212-682-9100.
  Chicago, Ill. 60611—410 N. Michigan Ave. Phone
  312-467-5200.
  Detroit, Mich. 48235—18080 Jas. Couzens Hwy.
  Phone 313-861-7000.
  Philadelphia, Pa. 19103—135 S. 19th St. Phone
  215-561-5950.
  Los Angeles, Calif. 90028—5752 Sunset Blvd. Phone
  213-467-3117.
  San Francisco, Calif. 94111—230 California St.
  Phone 415-781-2872.

3. AREAS SERVED
All of Suffolk, Middlesex, Essex, Norfolk and part of
Plymouth Counties.

4. AGENCY AND CASH DISCOUNT
Agencies 15%; cash discount 0%. Terms: Cash. Contracts are sold on a rate as earned basis up to 12 month period.

5. ADVERTISING RATES
Eff 2/1/78.
Rec'd 1/12/78.

Outside Rates
Showing Values:
  400 Units—100 Showing.
  300 Units— 75 Showing.
  200 Units— 50 Showing.
  100 Units— 25 Showing.

KING SIZE POSTERS
30″ x 144″:

Units:	(*)	1 mo.	3 mos.	6 mos.	12 mos.
400	400	28,080.	26,680.	25,280.	22,440.
300	300	21,060.	20,010.	18,960.	16,830.
200	200	14,040.	13,340.	12,640.	11,220.
100	100	7,020.	6,670.	6,320.	5,610.
Unit rate (less than 100)		80.00	80.00	80.00	80.00

QUEEN SIZE POSTERS
30″ x 88″:

Units:	(*)	1 mo.	3 mos.	6 mos.	12 mos.
400	400	20,400.	19,400.	18,360.	16,320.
300	300	15,300.	14,550.	13,770.	12,240.
200	200	10,200.	9,700.	9,180.	8,160.
100	100	5,100.	4,850.	4,590.	4,080.
Unit rate (less than 100)		65.00	65.00	65.00	65.00

TAILLIGHT SPECTACULARS
21″ x 72″:

Units:	(*)	1 mo.	3 mos.	6 mos.	12 mos.
400	300	17,880.	16,960.	16,080.	14,280.
300	225	13,410.	12,720.	12,060.	10,710.
200	150	8,940.	8,480.	8,040.	7,140.
100	75	4,470.	4,240.	4,020.	3,570.
Unit rate (less than 100)		55.00	55.00	55.00	55.00

Inside Rates
Service Values:
  Full service—1600.
  Half service—800.
  Quarter service—400.

11″ x 28″:

Cards:	(*)	1 mo.	3 mos.	6 mos.	12 mos.
1600	800	7,910.	7,510.	7,120.	6,330.
800	400	4,280.	4,060.	3,740.	3,440.
400	200	2,140.	2,030.	1,870.	1,720.
Unit rate (less than 400)		7.00	7.00	7.00	7.00

11″ x 56″:

Cards:	(*)	1 mo.	3 mos.	6 mos.	12 mos.
1600	800	10,850.	10,310.	9,760.	8,680.
800	400	5,700.	5,420.	5,120.	4,560.
400	200	2,850.	2,710.	2,560.	2,280.
Unit rate (less than 400)		10.00	10.00	10.00	10.00

22″ x 21″:

Cards:	(*)	1 mo.	3 mos.	6 mos.	12 mos.
800	400	6,830.	6,490.	6,130.	5,450.
400	200	3,420.	3,250.	3,070.	2,730.
Unit rate (less than 400)		10.00	10.00	10.00	10.00

Rates for intensities other than those shown are available.
(*) Gross Rating Points.

MOODS IN MOTION
(All inside cards)

Buses:		3-12 mos.
400		19,400.
300		14,550.
200		9,700.

STATION POSTERS
MAINLINE PLATFORM POSTERS
46″ x 60″ (2 sheet):

Units	(*)	1 mo.	3 mos.	6 mos.	12 mos.
150	150	5,890.	5,600.	5,310.	4,710.
100	100	4,070.	3,860.	3,660.	3,260.
75	75	3,070.	2,950.	2,790.	2,480.
50	50	2,040.	1,940.	1,890.	1,630.
Unit rate (less than 50)		80.	80.	80.	80.

58″ x 144″ (6 sheet):

Units	(*)	1 mo.	3 mos.	6 mos.	12 mos.
75	75	5,930.	5,630.	5,330.	4,730.
50	50	4,010.	3,810.	3,610.	3,210.
25	25	2,030.	1,930.	1,830.	1,630.
Unit rate (less than 25)		100.00	100.00	100.00	100.00

(*) Gross Rating Points.

CLOCK TRANSPARENCY SPECTACULARS
Standard clock installation average price 210.00 a month, 12 month basis depending on circulation of station desired.
All ads subject to approval of advertising company and Massachusetts Bay Transportation Authority.

6. DISCOUNTS
Discounts of 5% for 3 months, 10% for 6 months and 20% for 12 months are applicable to all space (with the exception of Moods In Motion) and are figured in the rate schedule. All discounts are applied as earned with no rebates. Inside and outside space and different kinds of displays are not combinable for purpose of earning discounts. A minimum No. 25 showing will constitute a rate holder for outside space, a minimum quarter service for inside space. Moods In Motion is not discounted.

7. RESTRICTIONS
Political advertising must be paid 30 days in advance of contract starting date. Copy must include wording Paid Political Advertising.

8. MECHANICAL REQUIREMENTS
Production Specifications for all space are issued to advertisers upon signing a contract or can be requested from any Metro Transit Advertising office.
Shipping Information
Shipping dates: Moods In Motion production must be shipped prepaid for arrival at least 30 days before scheduled installation date; all other production, 15 days.
Ship to: Metro Transit Advertising, 72 Sobin Park, Boston, Mass. 02210.

9. MONTHLY ESTIMATED RIDES
TAA—3/31/77
Monthly rides (12 month average)...............46,035,311

Figure 19-6. (By permission of Standard Rate & Data Service)

be placed in every train-car or bus in the market, or a *fractional* run.

Circulation of Transit Advertising

The circulation for car cards is based on the number of fares that are collected. Transit operators submit sworn statements each year, reporting the average number of passengers carried each month. Attempts have been made to measure the exposure of exterior displays by using electronically controlled cameras to count the eyes exposed to the moving vehicle, but the value of this measure is highly questionable.

Strengths and Weaknesses of Transit Advertising

Transit advertising is selective only in a geographic sense. Since it is carried by some 70,000 vehicles in densely populated areas, it has a potential for broad reach in these markets. Also, since transit riders repeat their trips frequently, it offers high frequency among this group. Its cost-per-thousand is extremely low, with inside cards having a cost-per-thousand of less than twenty-five cents, and external signs costing less than ten cents per thousand viewers.[7]

On the negative side, transit advertising is limited to urban areas, and there is little validated information on its effectiveness. Essentially, it is a supplementary medium for national advertisers, although it may be used as the primary medium for local firms.

DIRECTORY ADVERTISING

Directories are a useful form of advertising for consumer product companies with limited distribution, and for industrial firms which market industrial supplies and equipment. Directory advertising may consist merely of the name of a firm or a product, along with an address and/or telephone number, or it may consist of display advertising. There are an infinite number of local, regional, and national directories, ranging from industrial buying guides to the classified (yellow) pages of the telephone book. From the standpoint of consumer use, the best known directory is the yellow pages.

Yellow Page Advertising

Most consumers have recourse to the yellow pages of the telephone directory at one time or another. Whether searching for a plumber or for a local outlet for a national brand, the admonition, "Let your fingers do the walking in the yellow pages," is a part of the

national consciousness. Yellow pages often constitute the only advertising for local merchants, but for national advertisers, it is a supplemental medium used to facilitate the location of products and/or to provide consumers with an address and telephone number (usually toll free) of a central or regional office which they can call for service complaints or information.

There are 6 thousand classified telephone directories in the United States, and some 8 thousand companies use yellow page advertising as a part of their national advertising effort.[8] Advertisers can buy listings or display space in up to 4 thousand markets through a single source, the National Yellow Page Service. The remaining 2,000 directories must be bought locally.

The cost of directory listings vary, depending upon the size of the ad and the size of the market in which it appears. A two-line, bold-face listing in the top 100 markets costs about $30 thousand; a quarter of a column (1/16 page) display ad in these same markets costs about $180 thousand.

A study conducted by Audits and Surveys, Inc. explored the extent to which the yellow pages are used by consumers. Table 19-3, taken from this survey, indicates widespread use of the yellow pages for selected products and services. The high "action" rate following reference to the yellow pages (column 3, table 19-3) indicates that it is a particularly effective medium in reaching people who are ready to buy.

Other Directories

Aside from the yellow pages, the greatest use of directory advertising occurs in firms that manufacture products for the industrial market. Many of these industries are highly specialized, and there are a number of directories designed to meet their specific

Table 19-3. Use of Yellow Pages

Product or service	Number of adults using per year (1,000's)	Average number of references per user	% of references followed up with action
Appliances Major	8,000	2.0	94%
Auto Parts & Supplies	17,000	6.8	87
Building Materials	13,000	8.4	88
Home Furnishings	9,000	3.2	91
Insurance	17,000	5.2	87
Office Machines	6,000	5.1	75
Paints and Wallpaper	9,000	3.1	91
TV, Radio, Hi-Fi	9,000	2.2	85
Travel	23,000	4.2	92

SOURCE: *Yellow Pages National Usage Study*, Audits & Surveys, Inc., June, 1969.

7. *Transit Advertising Rate and Data* (Skokie, Illinois: Standard Rate and Data Service, 1977).

8. Dorothy Cohen, *Advertising* (New York: John Wiley & Sons, Inc., 1972), p. 603.

needs. For example, media advertise extensively in the *Standard Rate and Data Service* directories because they are the basic sources of media information used by advertising agencies. The *Thomas Register of American Manufacturers* is widely used by a variety of industrial manufacturers, as are more selective directories such as *Post's Paper Mill Directory,* the *Data Processing Yearbook,* and many others. The primary question for the advertiser in using directory advertising is whether the value of the directory in reaching a particular target audience is worth its cost. Often, this determination is difficult to make because of limited, published information on the advertising readership of most of the directories that are in existence.

DIRECT ADVERTISING

Direct advertising is distinguished from other media in that there are no ready-made media vehicles that the advertiser may use. Instead, the advertiser must develop the entire advertising effort—the vehicle for reaching the desired audience, as well as the advertising copy itself.

Types of Direct Advertising

The Direct Mail Advertising Association has suggested a three-fold classification of direct advertising based on two criteria: (1) the way in which the advertising is delivered, and (2) the intent or purpose of the advertiser.

Direct Mail. Individual advertisements, either in display or letter form, are mailed directly to customers or potential customers. The purpose of the advertisement may be to inform the customer of the availability of a product, to deliver a coupon or an actual sample of the product, or to pave the way for a salesperson's call at a later date. Used in this way, direct mail is a supplement to other media, a part of a sales promotion program, or a way of increasing the frequency of contact with selected customers.

Mail Order. Advertising sent through the mail, the purpose of which is to persuade the recipient to order something by return mail, is referred to as *mail order advertising.* Widely used by hobby and other specialty manufacturers, mail order advertising may involve shipping catalogues containing hundreds of items to selected customers. Unlike *direct mail* advertising, *mail order* is the ultimate selling tool of its users and is frequently their only contact with customers.

Unmailed, Direct Advertising. This form of direct advertising is not sent through the postal system. Instead, it is delivered directly to consumers either at home, in stores or in shopping centers, or placed in parked cars, and so forth. It may consist of a handbill for a local merchant, but it is also frequently used as a device for distributing product samples that are clumsy to send through the mail.

Mail order Advertising is a huge, specialized business, the scope of which is beyond the purpose of this text. Our primary concern is with *direct mail* and *unmailed* forms of direct advertising. Direct mail advertising is widely used by industrial marketers whose customers are restricted to a relatively small number of manufacturing concerns. Both direct mail and unmailed forms of direct advertising are widely used by manufacturers of retail-distributed products, generally as a part of major sales promotion programs.

Direct Mail Lists

The key to successful direct mail advertising is the development of a list of prime prospects. Department stores often use their list of charge account customers for their mailings. In addition to lists of past customers, direct mail lists are available from a number of commercial sources. These lists range from quite general to highly specialized groups of people. An advertisement that was distributed to the occupant of every household, or every third household in a particular market would represent a general (or nonspecialized) method of distribution. A somewhat more specialized approach would be one in which the mailing was directed to upper-income neighborhoods. A high degree of specialization can be attained by restricting distribution to special groups with predetermined characteristics. For example, marketing professors, presidents of corporations, licensed optometrists, owners of late model sports cars, medical doctors, and builders.

Advertisers often compile their own lists, although it is an expensive and time consuming operation. Advertisers most often buy lists from firms that specialize in their compilation. Standard Rate and Data Service, in its *Direct Mail List Rates* directory, offers an extensive description of the mailing lists that are available. This description includes: (1) the cost of the list, (2) the source of the list, to help the advertiser assess its quality, (3) how the list is maintained, (4) whether the list owner will permit the advertiser to test the list by mailing to a sample of the names it contains, and (5) other services offered by the list owner, which sometimes includes printing, stuffing, addressing, and mailing. Figure 19–7 shows a page of direct mail listings from the sports section of SRDS. Note both the sources and specificity of the lists.

Direct Advertising Costs

Direct advertising costs vary so greatly that few generalizations can be drawn. Of course, the components making up the costs can be identified.

The Cost of the List. Although it is impossible to generalize about the costs of compiling one's own list, purchased lists generally range from about $25 to $45 per thousand names.

The Cost of the Advertising Material Used. Since the material delivered may range from a single page letter to a product sample, no generalizations can be made about material costs.

Mechanical Costs for Stuffing, Addressing, and Mailing. While these costs will depend on the nature of the material being sent, the hourly rates are minimal because it isn't exactly skilled work. There are com-

Figure 19–7. Direct mail lists

mercial companies that will handle these mechanics of the mailing for a fee.

The Cost of Delivery. Whether the material is mailed or delivered in some other way, the cost of delivery can be substantial.

Because there is little published information on the effectiveness of direct advertising (with the exception of coupons and samples) most advertisers who use these methods extensively compile data from their own experiences. Nonetheless, evidence suggests that direct mail advertising material is well read. For example, the director of the United States Postal Services Market Research Department has estimated that 80 percent of direct mail recipients read the material they receive. Actual readership, however, is strongly influenced by the nature of the recipient and by the content of the mailing. An industrial advertiser sending current product information to a select list of customers probably approximates 100 percent readership. And, lists tailored to special interest groups undoubtedly receive greater readership than material sent to more generalized audiences. The secret of success in direct advertising is linked closely with the quality of the list used and the attractiveness of the material delivered.

Strengths and Weaknesses of Direct Advertising

The Direct Mail Advertising Association advances the following advantages of direct advertising.

1. It can be directed to specific individuals or markets with greater control than any other medium.
2. It can be made personal to the point of being absolutely confidential.
3. It is a single advertiser's individual message and is not in competition with other advertising and/or editorial material.
4. It does not have the limitations on space and format as do other mediums of advertising.
5. It permits greater flexibility in materials and processes of production than does any other medium of advertising.
6. It provides a means for introducing novelty and realism into the interpretation of the advertiser's story.
7. It can be produced according to the needs of the advertiser's own immediate schedule.
8. It can be controlled for specific jobs of research, reaching small groups, testing ideas, appeals, reactions.
9. It can be dispatched for accurate and in some cases exact timing, both as to departure of the pieces as well as to their receipt.

10. It provides more thorough means for the reader to get or buy through action devices not possible of employment by other media. [9]

Offsetting these obvious advantages is the problem of cost. On a cost-per-thousand basis, direct advertising is high. And, while it offers a great deal of selectivity, it is unaffordable for most mass marketing. For this reason, advertisers of retail distributed products use direct advertising sparingly and usually only in connection with major promotions.

PROGRAM ADVERTISING

Many advertisers reach target audiences through display advertisements scheduled in programs of public events, such as plays, concerts, the opera, and sporting events. Although this medium is primarily used by local restaurants, cocktail lounges, and bars to suggest a place to go for dinner or a snack, it is also used to some extent by national advertisers of beer, distilled spirits, fashions, furnishings, and other products. By selecting programs carefully, the advertiser can often reach selected audiences. Symphonic concerts, plays, and opera, for example, attract upper-income, better educated, and sophisticated consumers.

Program advertising is not a highly organized medium and often must be purchased on a catch-as catch-can basis, particularly in the case of infrequent special events such as police circuses, ice follies, and traveling entertainment groups. In New York City, however, advertisers can reach most playgoers through *Playbill,* an established minimagazine tailored to the programs of the participating theaters. Similar opportunities exist in other metropolitan areas large enough to have an extensive theatrical season.

The cost-per-thousand for program advertising is usually high, and since the medium is not systematically measured, it is often difficult to verify circulation or to find meaningful data on reach, frequency, and duplication.

FILM ADVERTISING

Films are used in a variety of ways by advertisers, ranging from minute movies shown in commercial theaters to sponsored films on television. Films are also used in sales presentations and by club groups to fill out the program time of their meetings. Whether films should

---

9. "Advantages of Direct Advertising," *Direct Mail Manual* (New York: Direct Mail Advertising Association, Inc.), Manual file: 1201.

be considered as an expense of the advertising, sales, or public relations department depends on how they are used. A film used only for a sales presentation is clearly a sales expense. A film deliberately produced for public relations purposes is a public relations expense. Other uses of films are more ambiguous. If we adhere to a strict definition of advertising as *paid media,* it is probable that a large but unknown proportion of film usage falls outside of this definition.

Nonetheless, films are a form of communications widely used by major companies. It has been estimated that there are some 150 thousand short films in use.[10] A ten-minute, animated Disney cartoon for children that dramatizes ways of preventing colds is sponsored by Kleenex tissues; the Kendell Company sponsors a film titled *Athletic Injuries—Their Prevention and Care;* and Elanco, a major manufacturer of vetinarian medicines, has developed a film to help teach veterinarians appropriate pet-side manners.

One form of film usage that clearly falls in the realm of advertising is the "minute movie," or theater commercial. These films, ranging in length from one to several minutes, are used in some 12 thousand regular and drive-in theaters. To be acceptable to theaters, the longer films should be entertaining and noncommercial in the TV sense, with the sponsor's product shown naturally, but unobtrusively. More recently, organizations such as Screenvision and Cinemavision have been scheduling regular TV-type spots in theaters. Many theater owners have welcomed this use of commercials as a way of offsetting rising operating costs. However, as pointed out in the example at the beginning of the chapter, movie patrons are beginning to object, and the FTC has warned theaters that they must inform patrons that such advertising is being shown.

It is difficult to assess the value of movie theater advertising because of a dearth of information about its effectiveness. Cost-per-thousand for Screenvision is $12.00; for Cinemavision, it is $8.75.[11] On the surface, it would appear to be a good medium for reaching teenagers and young adults who make up the bulk of movie audiences. It should also provide relatively high frequency because people who are "hooked" on movies tend to go often.

EXHIBIT ADVERTISING

Exhibit advertising, with some exceptions, is primarily an industrial medium. The exceptions include such things as annual boating and sports shows in major cities; world, state, and county fairs; and special display sites such as Disneyland and Busch Gardens (a private amusement park operated by Anheuser-Busch). However, by far the greatest use of exhibit advertising is in the industrial and trade fields.

Trade exhibits offer advertisers an opportunity to display and demonstrate their products for key buyers. Exhibits are particularly useful for highly technical products and for bulky equipment that sales personnel cannot easily carry. They are also widely used for other types of products. For example, all of the major college textbook publishers have exhibition booths at the professional meetings of the American Marketing Association, the Academy of Management, Medical associations, Chemical conventions, and so forth. In fact, these exhibits often constitute one of the major promotional activities of publishers. Further, the conventions of retail, wholesale, and industrial associations usually have an exhibition hall where suppliers display their wares.

As pointed out at the beginning of the chapter, over 50,000 exhibitors use over 4,000 trade shows in more than a hundred cities each year as a method of advertising their products. For example, the National Premium Show, where speciality and point-of-purchase suppliers display premiums and other speciality advertising devices, is a "must" by major advertisers and advertising agencies.

The major costs in exhibit advertising include: (1) space rental, (2) exhibit design and construction, (3) personnel to man the exhibit, and (4) miscellaneous expenses such as transportation, installation, and furniture. The total cost for a particular exhibit may be quite low or relatively high, depending upon the discretion of the advertiser. And, while circulation can be measured in terms of the number of people attending the show or stopping at the exhibit for information it is often difficult to assess the value of the exhibit, or to project this data to future shows.

The primary values of exhibit advertising lie in: (1) its selectivity—(only interested prospects attend), (2) the opportunity for demonstration, and (3) enabling salespeople to contact new customers, make appointments, and, sometimes, take orders. Often, manufacturers will time the introduction of new items and models to coincide with major trade shows. This is particularly true in the furniture and fashion fields.

The weaknesses of exhibit advertising are that it is expensive and often difficult to justify in terms of measured results. This latter point, of course, is also true of advertising in general, even where there is a plethora of statistics on reach, frequency, and duplication.

10. Otto Kleppner, *Advertising Procedure,* 6th ed. (Englewood Cliffs, New Jersey: Prentice-Hall, Inc., 1973), p. 279.
11. "Patrons vote no on theater ads: FTC office orders a warning," p. 1.

SPECIALTY ADVERTISING

Specialty advertising is a bucket of worms, albeit an expensive one since it accounts for about a billion dollars a year in advertising monies.[12] It is basically a reminder medium, consisting of items from swizzle sticks to clocks, which bear the name of the advertiser and often a brief sales message. Specialty advertising items are usually, but not always, given free to potential customers and anyone else that happens to be in the neighborhood. There is no limit to the items that can be used for specialty advertising. It is only necessary that the item be affordable and have a printable surface.

The cost of advertising specialties depends on the item used and the quantity purchased. There are three types of organizations operating within the industry: *suppliers, distributors,* and *direct-selling houses. Suppliers* either manufacture, import, or convert items for sales through distributors. *Distributors* develop ideas for advertising specialties, locate suppliers who can produce them, and sell them to advertisers. *Direct-selling houses* combine these two operations into one organization. The trade association for the industry is the Specialty Advertising Association International (IAAI). Most major advertising agencies and many client organizations have some one on their staffs who has an expert knowledge of and maintains active contacts with the various organizations that supply specialty items.

The primary advantage of specialty advertising is that it offers a relatively inexpensive form of reminder advertising that, because of the relatively permanent nature of the item used, has a long advertising life. A calendar, for example, imprinted with the advertiser's name, may be visibly displayed for a year in a buyer's office or home. Book matches, while having a much shorter life than calendars, offer a potential exposure every time a match is struck; ball point pens have a life of several weeks or months; and an expensive executive gift—such as a desk set—may occupy a central position on a customer's desk for several years.

On the negative side, specialty advertising seldom offers an opportunity to deliver a persuasive product story. It is, essentially, reminder advertising and can be easily ignored. There is no measure of its effectiveness, and when specialty advertising is used as an executive gift, it often raises the question of bribery. For example, a gift of a hundred or two-hundred dollar desk set or an expensive set of pony glasses is in questionable ethical taste, and many companies forbid their employees to accept such gifts.

POINT-OF-PURCHASE ADVERTISING

Most consumer products are sold through retail outlets. As a consequence, the last chance an advertiser has to influence consumers before the purchase is made is within the store itself. This influence may be exerted through a variety of on-premise devices—window signs, store banners, shelf-talkers, counter cards, end-aisle displays, gondolas, and permanent display racks.

The term *point-of-purchase display* is a broad one referring to any visual device, other than normal shelf stocking, used in a store to call attention to a particular product or group of products. An in-store display may or may not include a price inducement. It may range from a simple *shelf-talker* (a paper strip attached to the shelf calling attention to a brand) to elaborate gondolas (special displays of merchandise and advertising material occupying a position in the aisle of the store). The use of point-of-purchase material has grown dramatically in recent years until, today, in-store displays represent a $2.5 billion industry.[13]

It is difficult to separate point-of-purchase advertising from special displays of the product itself since much of the use of this material is in connection with sales promotion activities. One important distinction that can be made, however, is the distinction between *temporary* and *permanent* in-store advertising material.

Temporary in-store advertising material is generally printed on paper or cardboard, is keyed to a short-term consumer promotion (a contest, a price-off promotion, a tie-in promotion with another product, and so forth), and is designed to be thrown away after the promotion has run its course. *Permanent* in-store advertising, on the other hand, usually consists of a permanent display rack such as that used by L'eggs hosiery (see figure 19–8) in grocery stores, a special display case for items such as pen and pencil sets, or display cards for small items. These display cards, identified by the advertiser's brand name, contain a dozen or more separate items that the consumer detaches when he makes his purchase. Permanent in-store material is often made of wood, plastic, glass, or metal and may contain back-lighted panels displaying product features.

Since point-of-purchase (p.o.p.) material is non-commissionable media, advertising agencies which design and supervise the production of such material generally do so on a fee or hourly basis, although they

12. Specialty Advertising Association, International, 1973.

13. "P-O-P volume up in 1975," *Advertising Age* (March 15, 1976): 4.

Figure 19–8.

often also receive a negotiated commission for supervising the printing by outside production houses. In addition to advertising agencies, there are a number of point-of-purchase houses that specialize in the development of in-store material.

In this chapter, we have touched on a few forms of other media. There are many that have not been mentioned, and new ones arise everyday. Skywriting, baskart advertising (advertising on the push-baskets in supermarkets), shopping bag advertising, flourescent signs over bars which identify brands, and so forth. Wherever there is space for advertising to appear, and no law against it, someone will eventually try to sell it for advertising purposes. If souls could be embossed in gold as they ascended into heaven or descended into the nether regions, some clown would try to sell advertising space on them, and some advertiser would probably buy it.

SUMMARY

The chapter is devoted to a variety of miscellaneous media that are variously referred to as *minor* media, *secondary* media, *supplementary* media, and *unmea-*

sured media. Because of the diversity of the media included in this group, and because of the wide variations in the extent of their use, none of these terms is really a good description of the media involved.

Outdoor advertising is generally considered the dominant "out of home" medium. Although it is extensively used, only about 5 percent of all outdoor advertising is a part of the organized outdoor industry. The basic unit in the outdoor advertising industry is the plant operator who, on a city-by-city basis, is an independent business firm that owns or leases sites, erects structures for signs, sells space, erects the advertising posters, and maintains the advertising after it is erected. There are several forms of outdoor advertising, each with its own advantages and disadvantages.

Transit advertising, which consist of paper posters placed inside or on transit vehicles and in transit stations, is available in some 380 markets, although there are only seven United States cities that have extensive transit systems.

Other forms of advertising are: directories, direct advertising (direct mail, mail order, and unmailed direct advertising), program advertising, films, exhibits, specialities, and point-of-purchase advertising.

Each of these forms of advertising has unique values which, under the appropriate conditions, may be useful to an advertiser. Each also has shortcomings that limit its use. One of the major shortcomings of the minor media is the lack of data on the readership and effectiveness of the various media included within the classification.

QUESTIONS

1. Identify the major forms of outdoor advertising and describe each.
2. What are the major strengths and weaknesses of outdoor advertising?
3. What are the strengths and weaknesses of transit advertising?
4. Distinguish between the various forms of direct advertising. Which of these forms is a national manufacturer of packaged goods most likely to use?
5. Explain how direct mail advertising might be used by: (a) a local clothing store, (b) a manufacturer of technical industrial machinery, and (c) a marketer of packaged goods sold through grocery stores.
6. Why is it difficult to draw generalizations about the cost of direct advertising?
7. What are the primary advantages and disadvantages of exhibit advertising?
8. What is meant by the term *point-of-purchase* advertising? Identify some examples of this form of advertising.
9. What is the strategy behind using executive gifts as a part of an advertising and promotion program? What are the ethical problems involved?
10. Why are the terms *minor, secondary, supplementary,* and *unmeasured* media each inappropriate when applied to the various media discussed in this chapter?

PROBLEM

As a media buyer, you have been asked to estimate the costs for a 100 showing and a 50 showing for outdoor advertising in Chicago, St. Louis, Cleveland, Kansas City, and Cincinnati. In addition to estimating the total costs for these markets, indicate the closing date for a twelve month schedule beginning January 1. The client, a regional bottler of a line of soft drinks, is not sure whether he should be using this medium in addition to the radio schedules he is using to reach young people, and he has asked you to evaluate outdoor for this purpose.

Sales Promotion—
Strategies and Plans

In chapter 3, it was pointed out that the term "sales promotion" is used to designate those selling activities that fall outside the areas of major media advertising and publicity. Thus, sales promotion activities include temporary point-of-sale material keyed to particular promotions, sampling, coupons, price-off labels, store demonstrations, trade incentives of various sorts, and sales force incentive programs.

Some of the activities may not appear in the marketing plan, "per se". For example, incentives for the sales force are often an integral part of the sales compensation program, are budgeted by the sales department, and are detailed in the "sales plan" rather than in the marketing plan. Such incentives should always be coordinated with the objectives and strategies sections of the marketing plan. To clarify this point, let us take an example.

Let us assume that for a particular product marketing strategy calls for increasing distribution on a large package size from 30 percent to 65 percent all commodity distribution. The sales promotion section of the marketing plan details a stocking allowance on all initial orders, as well as trade advertising and consumer coupons on the large package size. The sales plan, on the other

hand, might set up a point system for sales force compensation which, in addition to giving points for meeting or exceeding quota, would give points for gaining distribution on the large package size. Sales force bonuses would be based on the total number of points earned, regardless of their source. This sales force incentive program, then, would be budgeted in the sales plan, not in the marketing plan. In addition, the sales plan might specify that a certain percent of the sales force's time be devoted to "selling the promotion" for two or three months prior to the coupon distribution. the point is that a well-conceived and executed marketing program leaves little to chance because it coordinates all aspects of the company's activities.

As a practical matter, some of the advertising media we have referred to in the preceding chapter are considered as sales promotion media, not advertising media. Thus, specialty advertising, exhibits, and direct advertising (direct mail as well as unmailed, direct advertising) are found in the sales promotion section of the marketing plan more often than in the media section.

Finally, major media advertising is often used in support of sales promotion activities. Where this occurs, costs for major media are generally-charged to the advertising budget, while other costs—allowances, coupons, mailings, point of purchase material, and so forth—are charged to the sales promotion budget. Although this is conventional practice, individual advertisers may depart from it and charge all, or part, of the major media support to the sales promotion budget.

In chapter 20, we will examine the role of sales promotion and indicate some of the major promotional devices that are commonly used. Whenever media (such as direct advertising, exhibits, specialties, and so forth) enter into the discussion, they will be considered as sales promotion rather than advertising expenditures.

20

The Role of Sales Promotion

60 Billion Coupons?

Yes, 60 billion coupons! That's the estimate of cents-off coupons distributed in the United States in 1977—approximately 280 coupons for every man, woman and child in the country. According to A.C. Nielsen, the use of cents-off coupons has grown from 20.3 billion in 1972 to over 60 billion in 1977. And this growth has given rise to problems—problems of coupon clutter and misredemption.[1]

Major advertisers are becoming concerned over coupon clutter, fearing that the blizzard of coupons blanketing the nation will lead to a reduction in their effectiveness. They are beginning to question whether some of their "coupon money" should be shifted to advertising as a more effective way of using company resources in promoting their products. And then there is misredemption.

Whenever money is involved in large quantities, there will be thievery. And, while no one knows how many coupons are misredeemed, estimates range as high as 33 percent.[2] While there are many ways to cheat on coupons, misredemption can be classified as *casual* or *systematic.* In *casual* misredemption, the retailer, valuing convenience more than integrity, will rebate the coupon value to consumers without requiring them to purchase the product for which the coupon was issued. The retailer then forwards the redeemed coupons to the appropriate manufacturers and collects the coupon value plus a bonus for "handling." The only one that suffers financially is the manufacturer. Casual misredemption probably accounts for most of the misredemption that occurs.

In systematic misredemption, one or more retailers along with fellow conspirators devise a wholesale method for defrauding manufacturers. One such conspiracy in Sioux City, Iowa, operated in the following way. Members of the conspiracy ring paid consumers between $4 and $20 a pound for coupons clipped from magazines and newspapers. According to court testimony, as many as 100 persons would gather at a warehouse on Sundays to sell their clipped coupons. The

---

1. Louis J. Haugh, "New marketing woe; it's coupon clutter," *Advertising Age* (December 26, 1977): 1 ff.

2. Louis J. Haugh, "Misredemption now pegged at 33%," *Advertising Age* (May 30, 1977): 1 ff.

retail members of the conspiracy forwarded the coupons to the appropriate manufacturers, and collected their loot.[3] In this particular instance, eight men were found guilty in a federal district court of bilking national advertisers of at least $350 thousand and were given fines and prison sentences.

Promotion Workshop

Each year since 1969, *Advertising Age* has sponsored a promotion workshop for members of the advertising industry. The tab for participating for two days is $395, and all interested parties are invited. The following body copy is taken from an advertisement announcing the promotion work shop.

> The 9th annual Promotion Workshop shows you how to make your advertising dollars work harder through promotion that extends and amplifies your media program.
>
> You see a wide variety of promotion tools and services and how they're used most effectively at different levels—internally, to the trade and to the ultimate business or retail customer.
>
> You increase your skills at utilizing a broad range of promotion tools and services—direct mail, premiums and incentives, catalogues, trade shows, coupons, point-of-purchase and much, much more.
>
> Your course leaders are the people responsible for today's outstanding promotion programs. So roll up your sleeves and get to work with them.
>
> Learn how to develop programs that get results—the marketing situation . . . program objectives . . . strategy . . . implementation . . . costs . . . results. You learn the pitfalls to avoid. The importance of timing. The very secrets of success.[4]

The point is that sales promotion is a big business, and learning to promote well is an important part of marketing.

Promotion Agencies Just a Dream

The following quotation was taken from "Promotion hotline," a regular feature in *Advertising Age.*

> Although there may be some who will disagree, the concept of a "full service" sales promotion agency, which appeared ready to flower a decade ago, has failed to blossom into a full-fledged partner in the advertising and marketing community.
>
> The advent of a service company that could provide savvy sales promotion ideas and implement ser-

vices for national advertisers, particularly consumer package goods companies is still not here. There are a few exceptions, but they are just that, exceptions. . . .

> There are any number of reasons to explain why the era of sales promotion or marketing services agencies has eluded the hardy brand of practicioners who wanted it to happen. Not the least of these reasons is that there are few, if any, companies which possess or have developed the breadth of knowledge and experience to provide demanding clients with widespread sales promotion counsel and implementation.
>
> Sales promotion is too diversified and, as a result, suppliers have not been in a position to build competent staffs. Consider, if you will, some of the various promotion areas that would be required for a "full-service" sales promotion agency: Sampling, cents-off-coupons, packaging, direct mail, premiums and incentives, point of purchase materials, sales literature, meetings and conventions, trade shows and exhibits. In fact, there are competent suppliers in each and every one of the categories.[5]

The foregoing examples define the parameters of sales promotion. It is big, diverse, complex, and few individuals understand it in its entirety.

AN OVERVIEW OF SALES PROMOTION

Sales promotion includes so many diverse and unmeasured activities that it is not possible to estimate total expenditures in this area. Sixty billion coupons, over $2 billion in point-of-purchase material, contests, sweepstakes, cents-off label promotions, display allowances, advertising allowances, stocking allowances, in-store demonstrations, premiums—this is a partial list of the activities that are normally thought of as sales promotion. Many sales promotion activities are applicable to both consumer and industrial products. Some—such as retail displays—are more applicable to consumer items; others—such as exhibits—are primarily used for industrial, wholesale, and retail trade shows. In this chapter, we will direct our attention to sales promotions used in support of retail distributed consumer products. In doing so, it is recognized that many of the points that are made and some of the activities described are equally applicable to industrial products and to products that are sold directly to consumers, bypassing retail channels. This restriction of our focus on sales promotion is necessary because the field is so diverse that a complete description of it is beyond the scope of this text.

3. Louis J. Haugh, "Promotion Hotline," p. 44 ff. Reprinted with permission from the December 19, 1977 issue of *Advertising Age.* Copyright 1977, by Crain Communications, Inc.
4. Advertisement, *Advertising Age* (May 23, 1977), following page 58.

5. Louis J. Haugh, " 'Full-service' sales promotion agency still just a good idea," pp. 71–72. Reprinted with permission from the May 13, 1977 issue of *Advertising Age.* Copyright 1977 by Crain Communications, Inc.

Definition of Sales Promotion

Most definitions of sales promotion, including the one given in this book, are negative definitions. That is, they define *sales promotion* in terms of what it is not. It is not advertising, although advertising may be used in its support. It is not publicity, although publicity is often a part of a sales promotion program. It is not normal sales activity, although sales promotion is an indispensible tool of the sales force.

One way of gaining insight into the nature of sales promotion is to define some of its salient characteristics. Sales promotion is:

1. A relatively short-term activity.
2. Directed against the sales force, distribution channels, or consumers, or directed against some combination of these groups.
3. Used in order to stimulate some specific action.

Two key thoughts in this definition are *short-term in duration* and designed to *stimulate some specific action.*

An analogy that I have found useful in distinguishing between *advertising* and *sales promotion* is borrowed from the field of armaments.

Advertising is like a shotgun.

Sales promotion is like a rifle.

Advertising is a shotgun in that it scatters its charge against the broad objective of reaching target audiences with a message about the product. Normally, it is not expected to generate immediate action, but to disseminate information, persuade, influence attitudes, and, ultimately, to contribute to sales. In fact, advertising that is designed to generate *immediate* action—such as advertising featuring a price reduction or sale—is referred to as *sales promotion* advertising.

By contrast, sales promotion is a rifle because it zeroes in on a specific objective, and is designed to provoke immediate action. To sample consumers, to induce trial, to deplete inventories, to increase distribution, to gain retail support, to provoke the sales force to focus on a particular activity—these are typical of the objectives of sales promotion.

It follows from this distinction that sales promotion is more *precise* than advertising; both in terms of its target objective and the time span over which it operates. It also follows that, unless a particular sales promotion is aimed at a specific and relatively narrow objective, it will probably be ineffective. This, in fact, is a major cause of failure among sales promotions. Some promotions try to do so many things that they do nothing well.

Sales promotion is *always* a *supplementary* activity. It does not, and cannot replace advertising. Without a solid advertising base to build product recognition and acceptance, promotions tend to fizzle. A brand that is well conceived and carefully positioned may decline in sales because of inadequate advertising support. If it does, an increase in advertising expenditures, supported by strong copy, can reverse the decline and lead to a continuing pattern of growth in market share. This growth can be accelerated by supplementing the advertising with periodic sales promotion activity.

The same brand, without an infusion of advertising can seldom achieve a permanent reversal of a share decline by sales promotion alone. Instead, it only achieves temporary arrests on its journey to oblivion. This point has been demonstrated over and over again through studies of consumer products by companies such as A.C. Nielsen which measure product movement at the retail level. Figure 20–1 shows the typical share of market patterns for the two situations described above. Example 1 demonstrates the effect of advertising *and* consumer promotion on a well-positioned product. Example 2 demonstrates the typical effect of sales promotion alone. The reason for these two patterns is that sales promotion works best on products for which advertising is generating recognition and acceptance. A coupon on a well-known brand is an incentive to buy. The same coupon on an unknown brand is no bargain. To express it another way, the history of a successful brand is characterized by three phenomena:

> Advertising, *which creates* value.
> *Sales promotion,* which induces *trial.*
> The *product itself,* which provides *satisfaction.*

The purpose of the foregoing example is not to discredit promotion as a marketing tool. In some fields, and at certain periods of time, it is exceedingly important. Sales promotion generally plays a larger role in the marketing mix in fields marked by similarity in products as compared to fields in which product differentiation is clear. It generally plays a larger role in the *mature* and *decline* stages of the product life cycle than in the *introductory* and *growth* stages; and it plays a larger role in times of economic recession than in times of affluence.

Types of Sales Promotion

One way of classifying sales promotion devices is in terms of the audiences against whom they are directed. In the following material, we will examine typ-

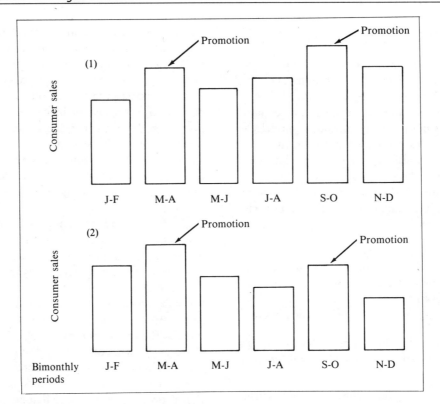

Figure 20–1. Typical sales pattern of (1) a brand supported by advertising and sales promotion, and (2) a brand supported by sales promotion alone.

ical sales promotion activities designed for the sales force, for the trade, and for consumers. However, a combination of devices directed against two or more of these groups is often used. For example, a stocking allowance to encourage retail distribution of a new brand or package size will be accompanied by a consumer coupon to stimulate consumer purchases and thereby consolidate the new distribution gained. Or, a consumer price-off label allowance may be coordinated with a display allowance to the trade in order to make the consumer offer more effective. The selection of a particular sales promotion technique, however, must always be made in terms of the specific problem to be solved.

SALES FORCE PROMOTIONS

Earlier, it was pointed out that sales promotions directed to the sales force are often considered an integral part of the sales force compensation system and, as a consequence, are charged to the sales budget and do not appear in the marketing plan, per se. Since sales compensation, in itself, is a complex and sometimes controversial subject, it will not be treated in detail in this book. Nonetheless, it should be recognized that sales force activities must be coordinated with

marketing objectives and strategies in order to obtain optimum results from the marketing program.

Many companies use some form of commission system—either straight commissions on sales or salary plus commissions—as a basic device for motivating sales people. Such compensation systems, when they are "normal" or standard practice, are *not* considered sales promotion. A short-term sales force incentive, however, in support of a particular marketing strategy (such as gaining distribution on a new product, increasing shelf facings, obtaining displays, or obtaining cooperative advertising support) is properly considered sales promotion. Often, some sort of sales contest will be used in these instances in which salespeople are awarded points for their performance. For example, let us assume that the sales promotion section of the marketing plan calls for a major consumer contest supported by media advertising and in-store product displays with point-of-purchase material describing the contest, its prize structure, and method of entry. In order to assure sales support for the consumer promotion, a separate contest might be structured for the sales force with, say, a hundred points being awarded to individual sales people for each in-store display of fifty or more cases of merchandise that she obtained—fifty points for each twenty-five case display, ten points for each ten case display, and so forth. Prizes would be awarded to the sales people in each sales district or region that accumulated the most points.

The point is that sales promotion directed to members of the sales force should not be neglected if it is considered crucial to the success of a consumer or trade promotion. In fact, it can be argued that the well-conceived sales promotion should contain something for every level in the distribution chain in order to gain their cooperation in making the promotion a success.

PROMOTIONS TO THE TRADE

The ultimate fate of a retail distributed product is in the hands of the retailer because, with the exception of company-owned stores and franchised distribution which together account for an infinitessimal part of retail sales, the retailer determines whether or not a particular brand will be stocked, where it will be stocked, how many shelf facings it will receive, and whether or not it will be given special displays, price features, and retail advertising support.

It has long been recognized that in-store treatment can have a profound effect on the sales of retail distributed brands. In the case of products requiring personal sales support (such as appliances, home furnishings, clothing, cameras, hi-fi equipment), support by retail sales personnel is critical. A retail sales person only has to say, "Our customers have been extremely pleased with brand X, but have had nothing but trouble with brand Y," to relegate brand Y to the black list of unwanted merchandise. Nor, need the behavior of the retail sales person be that blatant. By subtly directing the customer's attention to a particular brand, and extolling that brand's merits, the prospect's choice of brands may be swayed.

In the case of self-service stores (grocery, drug, and variety stores), in-store treatment is a less obvious, but significant, factor in influencing sales. If a particular brand is not stocked or is temporarily out of stock, it cannot be bought, and a substitute may be chosen. A.C. Nielsen, in a survey of 1,173 grocery shoppers, found that, on the average, 58 percent will accept a substitute brand if the one they want is not available.[6]

Aside from brand availability, in-store treatment may also spell the difference between success and failure. *Progressive Grocer* introduces its book, *Display Ideas for Supermarkets,* with the observation:

As any veteran of the food and grocery business knows, the so-called "self-service revolution" owes much of its success to the selling power of displays. For display almost single-handedly has assumed the function of countless sales clerks. Its historic mission has been to uphold the high-volume, low-unit profit principle of mass retailing—to cut operating costs, increase productivity, decrease prices for consumers. . . . The modern grocer builds his sales dramatically with the help of four merchandising tools—namely, special displays, promotional pricing, departmentalization, and storewide promotions.[7]

There is ample evidence from a variety of sources[8] testifying to the value of displays, feature pricing, shelf position, and so forth in generating sales. And, in the face of heavy advertising competition, some authorities believe that in-store treatment may be the single most important variable in determining brand sales and market share.[9]

There are a number of devices used to elicit retail cooperation. Most can be classified in terms of their primary purpose, although each may also have desirable side effects. Thus, a sales promotion designed to obtain special displays may also result in price features or retail advertising support. Major purposes of retail promotions are: (1) to obtain distribution or increase inventories, (2) to gain support of retail sales personnel, (3) to gain special displays and/or price features, and (4) to gain retailer advertising support. Often, these devices are used in combination with one another or in combination with consumer promotions. In any event, the sales promotion plan should specify the primary purpose of the device used and what it is expected to accomplish.

Trade Promotions to Gain Distribution or Increase Inventories.

There are two promotional devices used primarily to gain distribution or increase inventories. One, *stocking allowances,* clearly falls within the realm of sales promotion. The second, *consignment selling,* is borderline. In some fields, consignment selling is a stan-

6. James O. Peckham, Sr., *The Wheel of Marketing* (Chicago: A.C. Nielsen Company, 1973), p. 10.

7. M. Alexander, ed., *Display Ideas for Supermarkets* (New York: Progressive Grocer, 1958), pp. 2–3.
8. *Ibid;* "The Dillon Study," *Progressive Grocer* (October 1960), p. D81; "Improving Sale Item Display: The Display and Merchandising Workshop," *Chain Store Age* (January, 1965), p. 64; *Awareness, Decision, Purchases* (New York: Point-of-Purchase Advertising Institute, 1961), p. 14; *Drugstore Brand Switching and Impulse Buying* (New York: Point-of-Purchase Advertising Institute, 1963), p. 11; "Shelf Merchandising Strategy: A Key to Increased Sales," *Progressive Grocer,* (March, 1964), p. 126.
9. H.S. Gorschman, "New Dimensions in Unhidden Persuasion," *Journal of the Academy of Marketing Science* [*Fall, 1973*]: 110–18.

dard operating procedure; in other fields, it is infrequently used and so qualifies as a sales promotion technique.

Stocking Allowances. Stocking allowances are the most frequently used sales promotion device, the primary purpose of which is to gain distribution. Under a stocking allowance a retailer will be given an allowance for each case on initial orders or on all orders for a specified period of time, such as one month. The ethical justification for a stocking allowance for new distribution is that it compensates the retailer for the expenses incurred in adding a new item to inventories. Practically speaking, it is a legal bribe that has become hallowed by use and thoroughly institutionalized as an acceptable and ethical practice. The use of stocking allowances to increase the inventories of brands already stocked is called *loading.* Loading may be used by manufacturers to increase dealer inventories because of out-of-stock problems (retailers' normal orders are insufficient to keep up with consumer demand) or to increase inventories prior to a consumer deal of some kind that is expected to accelerate sales. Stocking allowances are widely used in package goods marketing, particularly in the food and drug fields.

Several modifications of stocking allowances are often used. The most common is the "one free with . . . " offer. That is, one package free for each six bought; or, for larger retailers, one case free with the purchase of six cases. This approach is widely used in drug stores, particularly for items that are carried only seasonally. Each year, prior to the season it is customary to make a "one free with . . . " offer to encourage early ordering.

A second modification that is sometimes used is *leasing* store space. This approach is most likely to be used when trying to expand product distribution into nontraditional outlets. For example, a manufacturer of fancy chocolates might lease space in a supermarket for a display stand carrying its brand. This tactic relieves the supermarket of the risk of stocking a new product and guarantees an income from the venture. If the venture proves successful, fancy chocolates may ultimately be incorporated as a normal food store item, and the leasing arrangement will be terminated. *Leased departments,* an expansion of the "lease" idea, have been used in department stores, notably by Russell Stover candies.

Consignment Selling. In consignment selling, the manufacturer retains ownership of the product while giving possession of it to retailers so that they can sell it to consumers. Thus, the manufacturer absorbs the full cost of carrying the inventory, and the dealer pays for the goods as they are sold. The Hanes Corporation used consignment selling to induce supermarkets and drugstores to handle its L'eggs brand of pantyhose.[10] A single display rack of Leggs can generate $1300 a year in profits to the retailer since stocking and inventory control are performed by the manufacturer. Consignment selling is also used as a standard selling practice for some big ticket items, particularly to industrial distributors. When it is used as a device to obtain new distribution, however, it may be considered as a sales promotion tactic.

Trade Promotions to Gain Support of Retail Sales Personnel

Retail sales personnel have a minimal role in the selling of self-service products. However, in many other fields (cars, appliances, furniture, carpeting, electronics, clothing, fabrics, proprietary drugs, and so on) retail salespeople are extremely important in consummating the final sale. There are four broad sales promotion devices sometimes used to enlist retail sales personnel support: *retail training, contests, push money,* and *merchandising the advertising.*

Retail Training. In this approach, sales seminars are held for retail sales people. In these seminars, technical information about the product is given, as well as suggestions on how to approach customers, how to sell related items, how to close a sale, and so forth. Since retail salespeople like to sell merchandise they are knowledgeable about, and since they are often appreciative of the sales training they have been given, such efforts may pay off handsomely.

Contests. Contests designed for retail store owners and/or their employees are often used to gain retail support. Such contests may take a variety of forms. For example, the Frigidaire Division of General Motors undertook a major promotional effort to regain a major share of the appliance industry after a slump of several years. Prominent in its plans were dealer-support programs (dealer incentives, volume rebates, sales literature, and even a minitheater for in-store movies). Among the dealer incentives were a series of minivacations for retail dealers and their husbands or wives. It was estimated that about one hundred people in each region (fifty dealer couples) would be eligible for trips earned through points from Frigidaire's on-going "Sell 'n' Share" promotion. In addition to the minivacations, dealers could earn points redeem-

10. *Business Week* (March 25, 1972): 96–100 .

able in merchandise, including General Motors cars.[11] Admiral Corporation, in 1952, sent fifty dealers and their wives to witness the coronation of the Queen of England as part of a dealer incentive program. The promotion was considered so successful in enlisting dealer support for Admiral's products that it became a key factor in the company's marketing program. During the past twenty years, over 20 thousand dealers and their wives have traveled to virtually every major tourist attraction and world capital on the globe. Themes used to attract dealer attention and enlist their participation in the travel-incentive program have included "London Getaway," "Rendezvous in Rome," "Holiday in Mallorca," "Fiesta in Mexico," and "Tour de Paris."[12]

Push Money. Push money (PM) involves paying retail sales people commissions to "push" a particular brand. PMs are sometimes used in selling cosmetics and other personal care items, proprietary medicines, as well as other products where consumer knowledge is weak and recommendations are welcome.

Merchandising the Advertising. To "merchandise the advertising" is to sell the advertising and sales promotion program to channel intermediaries, particularly the retail trade, in order to generate enthusiasm and gain support. Annual sales meetings scheduled by a manufacturer for its sales force usually devote a significant portion of the meeting to outlining the advertising and promotion plans for the forthcoming year. At the conclusion of these meetings, salespeople are often provided with *merchandising kits* (a summary of planned activities) to show to channel members in order to engender enthusiasm for the firm's advertising and promotion activities. Plates 20–1 and 20–2 show two pieces of material from such a kit used by Bristol-Myers to merchandise Tickle deodorant. (See insert following p. 378.) Plate 20–1 is a storyboard for a prototype commercial. Plate 20–2 is a "merchandising" piece for a 15¢ coupon. In addition, the kit contained samples of print advertising as well as details of the media schedule.

Trade Promotions to Gain Special Displays and/or Price Features

One of the most effective devices for influencing product movement, particularly in self-service stores, is the special display. The term *special display* refers to any visual device, other than normal shelf stocking, used in the store to call attention to a particular product or group of products. A special display may or may not include a price inducement; it may range from a simple shelf talker to elaborate gondolas.

The effectiveness of special displays in moving merchandising is well supported by research. One study, carried out in Super Value stores over a period of twelve weeks, tested the effects of approximately 1,500 separate displays. The study found that, on the average, an item given special display will sell five and one-half times as much as will be sold from the normal shelf position.[13] These findings have been confirmed by the Dillon study, which found that the average display boosted sales by 536 percent over normal shelf movement.[14] Still another study reports that 5 percent of all supermarket sales are the results of displays.[15] If this figure is projected to total grocery volume, it would indicate that over $4 billion worth of merchandise is sold from grocery displays each year.

However, products differ widely in terms of their responsiveness to special displays. The Super Value study, for example, found increases as high as 3,453 percent for candy and as low as 36 percent for paper towels. Display effectiveness for a particular product will depend upon: (1) the product field, (2) the type and size of display used, (3) whether or not the display includes a price inducement, and (4) the type of point of purchase material used with the product display. For example, point-of-purchase material that is tied in with the advertising is generally thought to be more effective than that which is unrelated to advertising.

There is no shortage of studies testifying to the effectiveness of special displays in moving merchandise. It is little wonder, then, that sales promotions designed to obtain displays is a major preoccupation of consumer goods marketers.

The primary methods used in obtaining special displays of the product, particularly in self-service stores, are *display allowances, display cards and stands,* and *nonbranded promotions.*

Display Allowances. A manufacturer using a display allowance offers retailers a payment (perhaps 25¢ or 50¢ a case) for each case placed on special display. For simplicity in administration, display allowances are often based on fixed quantities. For example: $2.50 for a 10 case display; $6.25 for a 25 case display;

11. S. Ayling, "Merchandising Helps Turn Frigidaire Around," *Promotion* (April 29, 1974): 22.
12. .R. Gransee, "Admiral Finds Travel Motivates, Builds Goodwill, and Has Glamour," *Promotion* (March 4, 1974), Section 2, Business Meetings Selector, p. 2.
13. M. Alexander, (ed.) *Display Ideas,* p. 35.
14. "The Dillon Study," *Progressive Grocer* (October, 1960), p. D81.
15. "Improving Sale Item Display: The Display and Merchandising Workshop," *Chain Store Age* (January 1965): 64.

$12.50 for a 50 case display; $25 for a hundred case display. Manufacturers usually provide free point-of-purchase material for use on the display; this material may range from posters and banners to easily assembled structures made of metal or wood and cardboard. Display allowances and display structures are frequently used in conjunction with major consumer promotions, such as coupons and contests.

Display Cards or Stands. Another device for obtaining in-store displays is a brand-identified display card or stand for stocking merchandise. A display card of key rings, for example, might take the form of a *counter card* that can be mounted near the cash register and would have a number of key rings affixed to it; the customer would make a selection by removing a key ring from the card. The L'eggs display stand (figure 20–2) is an example of a display stand used in drug and food stores. Another example is the one used to display sunglasses.

Nonbranded Promotions. Nonbranded promotions, sometimes called *storewide promotions,* consist of a wide variety of nonidentified promotional material offered by an advertiser to enable the retailers to decor-

ate their stores. The material usually consists of window signs, store banners, display cards, shelf-talkers, price stickers, and other decorative material that is usually themed for an occasion such as Thanksgiving, Christmas, Valentine's Day, back-to-school, new store openings, and so forth. Included with the nonbranded material will be brand identified point-of-purchase pieces for the brand or brands of the advertiser offering the material. The basic philosophy underlying the use of nonbranded promotions is reciprocity. The advertiser provides the material free; as an expression of appreciation, the retailer gives special displays to the advertiser's brands.

Trade Promotions to Gain Advertising Support

Retail advertising support of a national brand appears to be an excellent way to extend national advertising dollars and to localize a brand's advertising. It extends advertising dollars because the rates for retail advertising are generally significantly lower than national rates and because the cost of the ad is sometimes shared by the retailer. Advertising is localized because it appears in the local media and is identified with the store or stores carrying the brand. There are two basic devices used by national advertisers to gain retail advertising support: *advertising allowances* and *cooperative advertising.* Both of these devices are among the most widely used and most severely abused forms of sales promotion.

Advertising Allowances. An advertising allowance is similar to a display allowance in that the retail organization is given a case allowance for advertising purposes. Sometimes the allowance is offered on a continuing basis; in other instances, it is offered only on orders placed during a specified period of time. The retailer agrees to use the allowance for advertising; she verifies her activity by sending the advertiser (1) tear sheets of the retail advertising containing the advertiser's brand along with (2) an apportioned cost statement indicating the amount spent.

Advertising allowances can be effective when the retailer accumulates the allowances received so that significant space can be devoted to the brand *and* when the sponsoring brand is given a price feature. Usually, that's not what happens. What happens most often is that the retailer will give the brand a column inch or less in a full-page newspaper advertisement or a mention in a radio or television spot *without* a price feature. In newspaper ads, these casual mentions are referred to as *obituaries* in the advertising industry as a reflection of the low esteem in which they are held.

Figure 20–2.

Particularly in the food and drug trade, advertising allowances are often more trouble than they are worth and represent, at best, a form of legal blackmail by retailers. *If* they are carefully policed by the advertiser, and *if* advertising mats of a minimum size are supplied with the requirement that the mat be used to qualify for the allowance, and *if* a price feature is given or required, *then* advertising allowances can be worthwhile.

The absolute worst form of advertising allowance is the *continuing allowance*. It is almost impossible to keep the advertising support given under this arrangement from becoming casual, and if the advertiser withdraws the allowance, she runs the risk of offending the retail organization and, perhaps, losing distribution. The moral in regard to advertising allowances is that, if they are used, (1) they should be used only on orders received during a specified period of time, (2) minimum criteria for the ads should be agreed upon, (3) and the effort should be carefully policed.

Cooperative Advertising. Cooperative advertising is most generally used on big ticket items. Often, it represents the major advertising effort of the manufacturer. Used properly, and carefully policed, it can be extremely effective. Used carelessly, it is a waste of company resources.

Under a cooperative advertising agreement, the manufacturer agrees to pay a portion of the cost (typically 50 percent) of the advertising for its brand run in local media under the name of the cooperating retailer. The annual obligation of the manufacturer is specified, usually based on an estimate of sales that will be made through the retailer organization, and payment is made upon receipt of a tear sheet and a copy of the invoice from the media. For example, a retailer runs a full-page ad in the local newspaper on the manufacturer's brand; the cost of the advertisement is $1800 at local rates. Upon receipt of a tear sheet and copy of the invoice, the manufacturer rebates half of the total cost ($900) to the retailer in the form of a check or credit memorandum. Also, the manufacturer usually provides the mats or other advertising material required by the medium used.

This arrangement has advantages for both the manufacturer and the retail store. The manufacturer obtains local advertising that is identified with a local retailer, gains the advantage of local rates, is only obligated for half of the advertising space costs, and retains control over what is said in the advertisement. The retail organization, on the other hand, obtains advertising at half its normal cost, is provided with professionally prepared advertising copy, and is identified with a prestigious national brand. The advantages of

cooperative advertising are acknowledged by estimates that over $3 billion dollars annually is spent in this fashion.[16]

There are disadvantages to cooperative advertising, however. A great deal of paper work is necessary in order to implement and police the program. Retailers through lethargy or doubts about the values of advertising must be carefully supervised to assure their participation, and tear sheets must be checked to see that advertising is run according to specifications. When broadcast advertising is used, the checking problem is even more difficult since verification requires that station logs be checked or the actual broadcast monitored. Since these procedures are expensive, a more common practice is to obtain an affidavit from an executive of the broadcast station certifying that the commercial actually ran. Such affidavits are widely used but subject to error or fraud. A retailer may conspire with the media to submit an invoice that reflects a higher rate than was actually paid, or fail to follow up with in-store support in accordance with the cooperative agreement. And then there is the problem of waste circulation. As pointed out earlier, local newspapers and television are basically mass media and provide little selectivity for the advertiser.

Cooperative advertising does have value for the manufacturer who uses selective or exclusive distribution. It has less value for the brand that is widely distributed. When cooperative advertising is used for convenience products such as detergents or other grocery store items, it is usually simply a device to give the retailer a price discount, with no expectation that the advertising itself will contribute any appreciable value.

CONSUMER PROMOTIONS

Consumer promotions are generally used for two primary purposes: (1) to attract new customers, and (2) to increase the purchases of existing customers. Inherent in these two purposes, however, are two other functions that consumer promotions often serve. First, they create an aura of *excitement* around the brand, calling attention to it in fresh and unusual ways. Second, they may serve to *deplete inventories* that have become excessive and stimulate retailers to reorder or to order in larger than usual quantities. Further, in the case of new product introductions, consumer promotions are widely used as a forcing device to get retailers to stock the product. The assumption is that if

16. John S. Wright, Daniel S. Warner, Willis L. Winter, Jr., Sherilyn K. Zeigler, *Advertising* (New York: McGraw-Hill Book Company, 1977), p. 621.

customers start demanding the product, retailers will be forced to stock it in order to maintain customer good will and patronage.

Consumer promotions are often used in conjuction with related, trade promotions. For example, a consumer contest or coupon distribution will often be backed up by display material, display allowances, stocking allowances, or even cooperative advertising.

Consumer Promotions to Sample New Customers

No attempt will be made to identify all of the consumer promotions or combinations of promotions that may be used to attract new customers. The type of promotion used is limited only by the budget and imagination of the marketer. Time-worn promotions are constantly being refurbished by the addition of new wrinkles, and I doubt that any promotional device is really new. Underneath its cosmetics, one will generally find a tried and true promotional technique. At the heart of most effective consumer promotions designed to attract new customers are five basic approaches: (1) coupons and price-off label offers, (2) sampling, (3) demonstrations, (4) premiums, and (5) contests and sweepstakes.

Coupons and Price-off Offers

One of the more popular devices for attracting new customers is coupons. Earlier, it was pointed out that 60 billion coupons a year are distributed in the United States. If price-off label offers are added to the coupons, the number of consumer deals represented by these two devices defies imagination.

Basically, coupons designed to attract new customers differ in terms of face value, breadth of distribution, method of delivery, and method of redemption. When New Purina Dog Chow was test marketed in Little Rock, Arkansas, a coupon redeemable for a two-pound box of the product was mailed to every other household in the Little Rock metropolitan area.

Generally, a coupon should be for at least 10 to 15 percent of the normal product price to attract consumer attention, and coupons of less than 10¢ are generally unattractive. Table 20–1 shows the estimated costs for delivering 25 million coupons by a variety of delivery methods. The average face value of the coupons used in these calculations was 14¢; in addition, 5¢ per coupon was paid to retailers for handling, and a 1¢ charge has been included for internal processing. No allowance was made for misredemption, although it was estimated at 20% If misredemption is as high as 33 percent, as some recent industry sources contend, the effectiveness of the programs would be reduced

even further. The cost per coupon redeemed ranges from a low of 23.3¢ to a high of 75.5¢.

There are other methods of delivering coupons. One is the in-package coupon, redeemable on the next purchase. This method of delivery is not particularly good for attracting new users because a coupon good on the next purchase may have little incentive value for the consumer who has doubts about how well she will like the first purchase. As a sales promotion device, this approach is more effective in generating additional purchases by current users. A variation of the in-package coupon that is used by marketers who have multiple products is *cross-couponing*. For example, a coupon in a package of Betty Crocker Hamburger Helper is redeemable on a box of Betty Crocker Cake Mix.

There are also variations in the way in which coupons are redeemed. Normally, coupons are redeemable at the checkout counter of the retailer. An alternative requires that the consumer mail the coupon along with a label from the product directly to the manufacturer. The manufacturer then rebates the face value of the coupon to the consumer. This technique may decrease misredemption somewhat, but it is an extremely weak promotional device because few consumers will bother to mail the coupon in unless its value is exceedingly high. And, if the coupon value is high enough to overcome consumer inertia, the cost of the couponing effort may become exorbitant, and imaginative methods of misredemption will be invented.

Price-off label is a substitute device for couponing that eliminates some of the handling problems associated with coupon redemption and reduces, but does not eliminate cheating. Price-off label offers are generally limited to a certain production quantity, such as a one month supply at retail. The manufacturer either: (1) prints the price-off offer directly on the package or (2) prints it on a removable "sleeve" or band that encircles the package. In either case, additional packaging costs are incurred. The deal merchandise is then sold to retailers at a reduced cost to maintain retailer margins. When the offer is printed on a removable sleeve or band, cheating occurs because unscrupulous retailers will remove the band and sell the packages at the normal shelf price. Greed is a powerful motivator.

Price-off label offers are usually more expensive than coupons because the manufacturer loses income on the face value of the price reduction on all packages carrying the offer, whereas average coupon redemption generally runs less than 10 percent, depending, of course, on the face value of the coupon and its method of delivery. In addition, marketers are often

Table 20-1. Cost per coupon redeemed based upon redemption rates

Circulation method	Cost per M printing/-delivery	Average redemption	Distribution cost (1)	Total number of redemptions (2)	Redemption costs (3)	Total program costs	Cost per coupon redeemed
DIRECT MAIL							
Co-op	$14	11.7%	$ 350,000	2,925,000	$585,000	$ 935,000	31.9ᶜ
Solo	90	16.2 (e)	2,250.000	4,050,000	810,000	3,060,000	75.5ᶜ
MAGAZINE							
Solo	6	3.5	150,000	875,000	175,000	325,000	37ᶜ
Page plus coupon	12	9.1	300,000	2,275,000	455,000	755,000	33.2ᶜ
NEWSPAPER							
600-line r.o.p.	3.75	2.4	93,750	600,000	120,000	213,750	35.6ᶜ
1,000-line r.o.p.	6.25	2.8 (e)	156,250	700,000	140,000	296,250	42.3ᶜ
Co-op r.o.p.							
Coupon only	1	3	25,000	750,000	150,000	175,000	23.3ᶜ
With copy	2	4.5 (e)	50,000	1,125,000	225,000	275,000	24.4ᶜ
Supplements							
Solo	6	3.1	150,000	775,000	155,000	305,000	39.3ᶜ
Free-standing inserts							
Coupon only	2.25	5.4	56,250	1,350,000	270,00	326,250	24.1ᶜ
With copy	3.50	6.4 (e)	87,500	1,600,000	320,000	407,500	25.4ᶜ

(1) Distribution cost based on circulation of 25,000,000; some programs have more, others less distribution.
(2) No allowance made for misredemption, estimated by some industry sources at 20%.
(3) Average cost based on 14ᶜ face value plus 5c handling charge and 1ᶜ internal handling charge.
SOURCE: Redemption rates based on A. C. Nielsen Co. figures where available or industry sources; distribution costs based on published rates and industry estimates.
(e) Estimated.
SOURCE: *Advertising Age* (Oct. 25, 1976), p. 112.

reluctant to use a price-off label offer during a *new product introduction* because the retail value of the product has not yet been established. As a consequence, coupons, rather than price-off label offers are the preferred incentive for new product introductions.

Sampling. Consumer sampling is a direct device for reaching new customers. In this method, a sample of the product (usually a miniature package) is distributed to consumers at home, in retail stores, on shopping center parking lots, or in other high traffic locations. Sampling is expensive, and costs are dependent upon the size of the sample, the number distributed, and the method of distribution. Sampling can be a highly effective device *if* the product being sampled is discernably superior to competitive brands on some relevant dimension. Because of the costs involved, sampling is generally restricted to new product introductions and major consumer promotions.

Demonstration. Demonstration is a form of sampling that is widely used on a variety of products ranging from food items to automobiles. Although product demonstrations may be made at the home or at the place of purchase, they are most frequently made at the place of purchase because of the economy of hav-

ing a central demonstration point. In the case of automobiles, a demonstration ride is a conventional selling technique. Most department stores will from time to time have in-store demonstrations of carpet sweepers, micro-wave ovens, sewing machines, and so forth. Both department and drug stores will often have in-store demonstrators dabbing new fragrances on passers-by. Food stores often have demonstrators handing out small bits of food.

Demonstrations are expensive since they require the salary of a demonstrator in each store in which they are used as well as the cost of the product involved. For this reason, demonstrations are usually restricted to high volume outlets and peak shopping periods.

Premiums. Premiums of all kinds are used to attract new customers. In-pack premiums, near-pack premiums (where the premium is stocked in the store *near* the product), mail-in premiums, trading stamps, combination offers (buy a package of razor blades and get a razor free or at a reduced price), and premiums for opening a new bank account are only a few of the methods used as incentives for new customers.

Many marketers feel that premiums are often unimaginative and over used. For example, Louis J. Haugh, a promotion authority, observes:

Why so many banks and other financial institutions persist in turning their quarterly quest for new savings deposits into bug eye advertising featuring multiple premiums defies common sense.

Some members of this financial community use such unimaginative advertising with its panoply of electronic appliances and other gimcracks that even the defense that such ads are successful in pulling in new savings and new accounts can hardly hold water.

All too often, banks festoon their lobbies with displays of the products used in the premium offer, running the very real risk, it would seem, of confusing someone who may think he or she has walked into a department store rather than a bank.[17]

Despite abuses (and everything that works for one marketer is abused by another), premiums remain a major incentive, both for attracting new customers and rewarding loyal ones.

Contests and Sweepstakes. Contests differ from sweepstakes in that the consumer is required to do something that is judged, and prizes are awarded to the winners. Consumers may be asked to name a product, compose or complete a limerick, write an essay, think up a slogan, guess a number (how many beans are in a jar, for an unimaginative example), or almost anything else. Another form of contest is to have participants prepare something from the manufacturer's product and submit it for judging. An outstanding example of this approach is the Pillsbury Bake-Off that has been run annually since 1949. Heavily supported by advertising, the contest, attracts some 250 thousand women a year who submit their favorite recipe made from Pillsbury flour. Each year, one hundred winners are flown to New York where the final judging is done at the Waldorf Astoria. This particular contest has had some outstanding payoffs for Pillsbury. For example, Bundt Cake, a prepared cake mix that has earned Pillsbury several millions of dollars in profit since its introduction in the early 1970s, was the winning recipe in one of the bake-offs.

The attractiveness of a contest depends both on the magnitude of the prize structure and the complexity of the task. Often consumers avoid contests because the requirements are too great, or the rules too exacting. There are also professional contest entrants who sometimes make a sizable (but unknown) proportion of the entrants, and some consumers avoid contests be-

cause they believe that these professional contenders win most of the prizes.

Sweepstakes avoid the skill element of contests by awarding prizes on the basis of chance. Entrants' names are pooled, and the winners are selected at random. The number of people likely to enter a sweepstakes is much higher than for contests because it requires less effort. On the negative side, of course, it also requires less personal involvement.

Participation in a sweepstakes sometimes requires that the consumer purchase one unit of the sponsor's product and send a label with the entry. However, lottery laws in some states prohibit this requirement because it involves a payment (purchase of the product) and is therefore interpreted as gambling. To circumvent lottery laws, many sweepstakes either require no qualification for entry or permit entrants to submit a facsimile of the label or to print the brand name on the entry blank.

The success of a sweepstake depends upon the prize structure, the number of winners, and the amount of advertising weight devoted to it. Publishers' Clearing House, for example, in its annual drive for magazine subscriptions, offers a $100 thousand house as first prize, plus a vacation home, cars, and a galaxy of other prizes as consolation. On the other hand, Pepsi-Cola ran a sweepstakes in the mid-1970s which offered 65,000 prizes, ranging from $1 to $50 worth of groceries.

While the foregoing consumer promotions have as their primary purpose the acquisition of new customers, few of them pay for themselves on this basis alone. Important collateral values include the retention of existing customers, the combatting of competitive promotions, the creation of excitement around the brand, and the stimulation of both the sales force and trade.

Consumer Promotions Designed to Increase Purchases of Current Customers

While some of the sales promotion techniques used to gain new customers are also used to increase the purchases of existing patrons, they are usually modified when the latter objective is the primary purpose of the promotion. For example, a blanket mailing of coupons or the use of magazine distribution will have as its primary purpose the acquisition of new customers. On the other hand, an in-pack coupon good on the next purchase is more appropriate for generating loy-

17. Louis J. Haugh, "Banks going premium crazy, but promos lack imagination," *Advertising Age* (December 19, 1977).

alty and repeat purchase by current customers. Similarly, a one-time premium offer may be effective for attracting new customers, while a continuing premium offer (a set of dishes or silverware, one piece with each purchase) is intended, primarily, to retain the loyalty of existing buyers.

Some brands are known as *premium* brands because continuing premiums constitute their major promotional effort. For example, Bonus, a Procter & Gamble detergent, contains a premium in every box (a dish towel, a piece of dinnerware, or some other premium) and is positioned to appeal to those consumers for whom premiums are a primary motivation for purchase. Similarly, Raleigh cigarettes offers a coupon on every package; these coupons are saved and exchanged for a variety of merchandise—bridge tables, lawn chairs, small appliances, household furnishings, sports equipment, and personal items—selected from a premium catalogue.

In addition to these devices, there are two other sales promotion techniques commonly used to increase purchase among present customers: (1) two-for-one offers and (2) multiple packs. In the two-for-one offer, two packages will be banded together and sold for the price of one or at a substantial discount from the normal price. In multiple-packs, products are sold in special packaged multiples of 3, 4, 6, etc. as well as in individual packages. Soft drinks, beer, fruit juices, antacid tablets as well as other products are sold in this way. A standard brewing industry sales promotion is the "Pick a pair of six-packs" promotion, widely used in the height of the beer-drinking season.

While these approaches may also attract new customers, their primary intent is for people who have already tried the brand and are familiar with it. Customers unfamiliar with the brand are less likely to commit themselves to multiple purchases on their first trial.

SUMMARY COMMENT ON SALES PROMOTION

In the discussion of sales promotion, sales promotion methods have been classified and discussed in terms of their *primary* objective. This has been done to emphasize the point that sales promotions are relatively short-term, limited-objective marketing devices. The primary functions of sales promotion are to solve

particular marketing problems, to take advantage of specific opportunities, to deplete inventories, to encourage stocking, and so forth—tasks that require activities above and beyond the normal advertising program. And, while sales promotions are an essential part of consumer marketing, care must be exercised that they are not used too frequently because to do so dulls their effectiveness, diminishes their excitement, and (in the case of price promotions) depreciates the value of the brand in consumers' minds. Sales promotions are, after all, a *supplementary* marketing activity, not the major effort of most advertisers.

SUMMARY

Sales promotion is so big, diverse, and complex that few individuals understand it thoroughly. Each year, it includes over 60 billion coupons, $2 billion in point-of-purchase materials, contests, sweepstakes, cents-off coupons, display allowances, stocking allowances, in-store demonstrations, and an untold number of premiums.

Sales promotion has three salient characteristics: (1) it is a relatively short-term activity; (2) it may be directed against the sales force, distribution channels, consumers, or some combination of these groups; and (3) it is used to stimulate some specific action. In this latter respect, it differs from advertising in that it is designed to provoke some immediate action as opposed to advertising's role of disseminating information, persuading, and influencing attitudes. Sales promotion is a supplementary marketing activity and does not replace advertising.

Sales promotion directed to the trade is designed to encourage some particular form of sales activity and is often used in conjunction with trade or consumer promotions.

Sales promotions directed against the channels of distribution are usually designed to: (1) gain distribution or increase inventories, (2) gain support of retail personnel, (3) obtain special displays and/or price features, or (4) encourage retail advertising support.

Consumer promotions are usually used to (1) sample new customers and (2) increase purchasers of existing customers.

Although sales promotion is an essential marketing activity, care should be exercised in not relying on it so heavily that other, more basic marketing activities are neglected.

QUESTIONS

1. Explain the distinction drawn between advertising and sales promotion.
2. Why, according to the text, have full-service sales promotion agencies failed to develop?
3. Identify the basic groups that are the target of sales promotion. Are any of these groups more important than the others? Why or why not?
4. Identify and explain the major sales promotion devices designed to gain distribution and increase inventories.
5. Explain what is meant by *consignment selling*. Under what conditions may consignment selling be considered as a sales promotion device?
6. Identify and explain the major sales promotion techniques designed to elicit support of retail sales personnel.
7. Identify and explain the major sales promotion devices used to gain displays and/or price features.
8. Evaluate the use of advertising allowances.
9. Explain what is meant by cooperative advertising, and identify some of the major problems associated with it.
10. Identify and explain the various forms of sales promotion used to sample new customers.

PROBLEM

You are a member of the sales promotion department of an advertising agency. One of your clients is the maker of a brand of toothpaste that has recently experienced share losses because of flavor improvements of a leading competitor. Your client has recently completed a formula modification that has significantly improved the flavor of your product as measured by consumer tests. The sales promotion strategy for the forthcoming year states:

1. In view of the product flavor improvement, primary emphasis will be placed on a consumer coupon promotion, coupled with a display allowance.
2. A $.20 consumer coupon will be used since company experience has shown this coupon value to be the most efficient in generating redemption.
3. It shall be a point of strategy to sample 1,500,000 households with the improved product.
4. The coupon effort shall not cost more than $.55 per sampled household, and it is a point of strategy to minimize duplication among coupon recipients.
5. The couponing effort will be supported by a display allowance to encourage in-store displays, with emphasis given to displays of twenty-five cases or more.
6. The promotion period will extend from September 1 through October 31 to avoid the decrease in effectiveness characteristic of summer promotions for dental care products, and so as to avoid conflict with the Thanksgiving-Christmas holiday season.

You have been asked to recommend a specific sales promotion plan and to prepare a budget for the sales promotion effort.

You have past figures on cost-per-thousand for printing and delivering various types of coupons, as well as the redemption rates for each method of coupon distribution. (Use the figures from table 20–1 for these two variables).

You estimate that misredemption will be 25 percent, so that, to sample 1,500,000 households with the product, you will have to make an allowance for misredemption. Coupon costs will include a $0.20 coupon plus $0.05 for handling by retailers and $0.01 for internal handling.

In estimating display costs, you know there are 50 thousand class A stores. If you offer $15 for a twenty-five case display, you estimate, on the basis of past experience, that 15 percent of these stores will cooperate. There are also 250 thousand class B stores. Here you estimate that an offer of $5 for a ten case display will obtain cooperation from about 5 percent of these stores.

Prepare your recommendation and budget.

Special Objectives—
Strategies and Plans

In chapter 3, it was pointed out that the "other objectives and strategies" section of the marketing plan for an established product normally deals with such topics as product, packaging, pricing, distribution, and publicity. These variables are an integral part of the marketing plan for a "new" product, but for an established product they exist as givens "unless" unanticipated developments in the market place require that they be examined.

In the actual plan of presentation followed in this text, certain of these variables—namely, product, packaging, pricing, and distribution—were moved forward in the discussion because they are so crucial to the basic marketing effort. Other variables—such as publicity, market testing, marketing research, and so forth—have not yet been discussed as "elements" of the marketing plan, per se, because they are indeed optional, and may or not be included in a

given plan, depending on the competitive situation and perceived marketing trends.

In this section of the book, chapter 21 will deal briefly with some of these variables. Specifically, it will be addressed to the objectives and strategies for publicity, test marketing, and marketing research. In addition, a portion of the chapter will be devoted to corporate advertising.

Normally, of course, corporate advertising has no place in a "product" marketing plan. It is an entirely different subject. In a sense, however, the corporation is a product in itself, and any request for corporate advertising funds should be justified through a separate planning document. A corporate advertising plan, however, has a great deal in common with a product marketing plan. So, in chapter 21, a brief discussion will be devoted to adapting the structure of the product marketing plan to the needs of a corporate advertising program.

21

Publicity, Market Testing, Marketing Research, and Corporate Advertising

Accutron

When Bulova developed the Accutron watch, it was believed the company had made a technological breakthrough. As a consequence, company executives recognized that an intensive consumer educational program was needed to establish the credibility of the company's accomplishment, to lend support to its advertising, and increase the effectiveness of its introduction. Enter product publicity.

Three groups of journalists, who (it was thought) could help create acceptance of the new product were identified. These groups were: (1) shopping column editors of monthly home service and women's publications, (2) editors of technical publications, and (3) general press writers. Since it was recognized that each of these three groups had different lead-time requirements, three separate press briefings were held. The shopping column editors of the monthly magazines, because of their relatively long lead-times, were briefed three months ahead of the public introduction of the accutron; the technical editors, a month ahead of time. Both groups were asked to schedule the release of the information they were given to coincide with the briefing of general news writers on the eve of the introduction. Two hundred

general news writers were invited to a public unveiling of the Accutron in New York. Simultaneous with this event, press conferences were scheduled in thirteen other cities which were connected with the New York affair through closed circuit TV.

Major media in thirty-two markets scheduled for advertising, as well as other key cities, were contacted by the company and provided with information about and photographs of the product. In total, 272 editors in sixty-two cities were contacted. The interest stimulated by Bulova's intensive product publicity program gave additional momentum to the actual product introduction and, in part, was responsible for its success.[1]

A Good Steward

A major consumer products company, both emulated and feared by its competitors, owes at least a part of its success to its almost Biblical emphasis on stewardship. Its product managers are thought of and sometimes referred to as *stewards* of the brands assigned to them, and a "good steward" always sets part of his

---

1. John F. Budd, Jr., *An Executive Primer in Public Relations* (Philadelphia: Chilton Book Company, 1969).

budget aside for learning more about his product and its responsiveness to changes in marketing strategy. Good stewardship often takes the form of market testing, and most marketing plans make provision for some sort of marketing test—a business building test to determine the effect of increased spending on market share; a media test to observe the effect of a shift in media on consumer awareness; a promotion test to determine the appeal of a new premium; an advertising test to evaluate a new copy approach; a package test to assess the influence of a package change; a pricing test to gain knowledge of the price elasticity of a brand. Not all of these tests appear in a single marketing plan, of course. One is often sufficient. In the aggregate and over a period of time, however, a remarkable amount of market testing is done. Nor are large amounts of money spent on most tests since the tests are restricted to a few, limited geographic areas. Not all tests are successful; many fail. Not all of the tests are even valid because of inability to control all of the variables that affect test results. But it is this ceaseless probing, this constant search for marketing opportunities through testing that keeps the company aware of both the strengths and limitations of its marketing programs and keeps competitors off balance. When a test succeeds, the findings are incorporated in the next year's marketing plan, and the scope of the test is expanded to a larger geographic area for verification. The concept of market testing is firmly entrenched in the company's marketing philosophy and made manifest in its marketing strategies.

Who Buys Evaporated Milk?

The Pet Milk Company, along with Carnation, dominated the evaporated milk industry. The company possessed a great deal of information on evaporated milk users, and on the ways in which the product was used. This information had been accumulated over the years from local surveys, from government statistics, from media studies, from the Evaporated Milk Association, and from national surveys and consumer dairy studies that had been conducted by mail.

It was generally recognized that, in terms of social class, evaporated milk was heavily consumed by the *middle majority* (the lower-middle and the upper-lower social classes which include approximately 60 to 70 percent of the U.S. population). It was also known that per capita consumption of evaporated milk was above average among blacks and those of Spanish-American descent. Acting on this information, marketing plans were devised and advertising and promotion were planned with these target audiences in mind. It was also recognized, however, that most of

the information on hand was somewhat imprecise and that estimates of per capita consumption by various ethnic and socioeconomic groups varied widely.

As long as the evaporated milk market was growing, this lack of precision did not present a major obstacle in the eyes of management. Each year, sales and profits increased, and there appeared to be little cause for concern.

Then industry growth "topped out," and the market began a slow decline. Marketing became more competitive; the cost of competition increased; and sales did not respond accordingly. The need for more precise marketing information on target audiences became more pressing.

A new marketing research director employed by Pet proposed a major national, personal-interview survey based on an area probability sample. He argued that much of the past information on users had been gathered by mail survey techniques which, characteristically, under sample low income and poorly educated consumers—precisely the group that was believed to be large consumers of evaporated milk. Pet's product manager on evaporated milk was persuaded, and company management was sympathetic. As a consequence, a national, personal-interview consumer survey recommendation appeared in the "other objectives and strategies" section of the annual marketing plan for evaporated milk. The need for the research was established in the marketing review section, which emphasized the ambiguity of existing data. Funds for the survey were budgeted in the objectives section of the plan, and the following statement appeared in the marketing strategy section: "A key strategy during the next twelve months will be to develop more precise information on evaporated milk usage. This information will be gathered through a national, area probability, personal-interview survey of consumers. It is the judgement of the brand group that such data is essential to increase the efficiency of our future marketing activities."

The foregoing examples of publicity, market testing, and marketing research are typical of the *optional* activities that may be included in the other objectives and strategies section of the marketing plan. They are optional in the sense that whether or not they appear as a part of a particular marketing plan depends upon the marketing situation and the judgment of the marketing planner.

PUBLICITY

Publicity is a somewhat ambiguous term that is used in a variety of ways. For example, Norman A. Hart, in a book titled *Industrial Publicity*, said:

TICKLE ANTI-PERSPIRANT
TICKLE "TESTIMONIAL I"

Length: 30 SECONDS

Comm'l No.: BMTI 7343

(1ST WOMAN LAUGHS)

ANNCR: (VO) This is a testimonial for Tickle...

(2ND WOMAN LAUGHS) The anti-persprant with the big wide ball.

(3RD WOMAN LAUGHS) It's so effective at helping stop perspiration...

(4TH WOMAN LAUGHS) ...so effective at helping stop odor...

(5TH WOMAN LAUGHS) ...it's given people a unique way of saying it works for them.

(6TH WOMAN LAUGHS) How do we know? If Tickle wasn't working, who'd be laughing?

Staying drier is nicer...

with a little Tickle. (SFX: LAUGHING

Plate 20-1. A storyboard for a prototype Tickle commercial from a merchandizing kit. (© 1977 Bristol-Myers). Reproduced by permission of the copyright owner, Bristol-Myers Company.

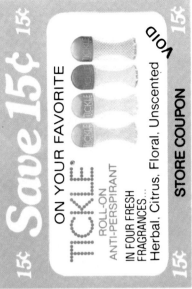
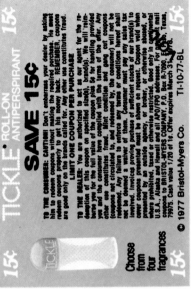

Remember, Sunday inserts deliver the fastest redemption of any coupon vehicle. And, BLAIR INSERTS are supported by radio—with Brand mention—using top stations penetrating all markets.

So don't be caught short...stock and display extra cases during this promotion.

TICKLE® ROLL-ON

Appearing in

BLAIR INSERTS

On Sunday, October 9, 1977

26 MILLION COUPONS CIRCULATED

Reproduced by permission of the copyright owner, Bristol-Myers Company.

Plate 20-2. A merchandising piece for Tickle (© 1977 Bristol-Myers).

The term *publicity* here is used in an all-embracing sense of publicising anything for any purpose. It thus includes activities which contribute to selling and are known as sales promotion. . . .

Under the heading *sales promotion* are included all the various 'channels of persuasion' such as advertising, direct mail, exhibitions, and so on.[2]

In contrast, Rolf Gompertz in *Promotion and Publicity Handbook for Broadcasters* has said:

But whatever publicity is, it is *not* advertising and it is *not* promotion. It is important to make this distinction and to keep it in mind.

Much confusion arises among the general public—not to mention among some clients—over this difference and the failure to make that distinction. The difference between advertising and publicity is quite simple: advertising is *paid for* space (or air time), while publicity is *free* space (or air time).

You can *control* what goes into an ad (or a commercial). You *cannot control* editorial content or editorial space. (You can influence it by the information you make available and the professional service you render, but you *cannot* control the way this information is used. You cannot even guarantee that it will be used.)[3]

This latter definition is the one that is generally accepted by the advertising industry and the one that is used in this text. In chapter 3, publicity was defined in the following way:

Publicity is a form of promotion. It differs from advertising in that it is not paid for at standard rates, and the sponsor is not identified. Usually, publicity appears—unidentified as such—in the editorial or news columns of printed media, or in the non-commercial portion of radio or television programs.[4]

Two key points are implied by this definition and made explicit in the quotation from Mr. Gompertz that preceeds it: (1) publicity is *free*, and (2) the advertiser does not *control* it. Both of these points deserve further comment.

The fact that media do not charge for publicity does not mean that it involves no cost. On the contrary, plans have to be made and coordinated; personnel have to be assigned to the activity; press releases have to be prepared; and press conferences are often elaborately staged. Further, when a press conference is given in behalf of a product, product samples as well

as product literature are often distributed to those attending. As a consequence, a budget must be established for a well-organized publicity program, and the budget should be a part of the marketing plan because it does represent a *cost* for promoting the product.

The second point is that the advertiser has *no control* over the way in which publicity will be used or whether it will be used at all. At best, the advertiser can try to influence what will be said by releasing favorable information. But sometimes even the best of publicity programs backfires. For example, I was involved with a publicity disaster for a consumer product of a major client. As a part of a product publicity program, a series of press conferences were scheduled for newspaper writers in the cities where the product was being introduced. The press conferences were well staged and included a free dinner and a brief presentation by company executives on the product and its values. One popular columnist of a major metropolitan newspaper, either because of an antibusiness bent or because it was his day to be offended, took exception to the press conference and wrote a satirical column that ridiculed the client company, its executives, and the product. While I personally regretted the incident, I thought the column was humorous. Client executives, however, were deeply offended and vacillated between suing for slander and having the columnist tarred and feathered. Ultimately, after some heated and interminable meetings, discretion won out, and it was decided to ignore the incident. Although this example does not represent a common occurance, such things do happen. Normally, the worst outcome of a publicity program is that press releases are ignored and the effort is largely wasted.

In view of these limitations of publicity, the question naturally arises, "Why bother with it?" Many companies do not bother. They prefer to devote their efforts to advertising and sales promotion activities over which they have greater control. There are other companies, however, that use product publicity extensively, primarily for the following reasons:

Publicity Is Free. The greatest value of product publicity derives from the fact that it is not paid for in the normal sense of payment. As a consequence, its appearance implies independent editorial validity of product claims. Generally, the public trusts media (certainly more than it trusts advertising) and the product benefits from this trust.

Advertising Is Expensive. Few clients could afford to pay for the media space and time that results from a successful product publicity campaign. And, in the competitive world of marketing, products need all of the support they can get.

2. Norman A. Hart, *Industrial Publicity* (New York: John Wiley & Sons, 1971), p. 3.
3. Rolf Gompertz, *Promotion and Publicity Handbook for Broadcasters* (Blue Ridge Summit, Pennsylvania: Tab Books, 1977), p. 13.
4. S.W. Dunn and A.M. Barban, *Advertising: Its Role in Modern Marketing* (Hinsdale, Illinois: The Dryden Press, 1974), p. 9.

There Is a Demand by Media for Information on Products. It is one of the services they provide their readers or viewers. In fact, both newspapers and magazines often have a "product corner," a column devoted to consumer products. It is desirable for an advertiser to take advantage of this demand. If he doesn't, there is the strong possibility that his competitor will.

The Basic Ingredient of Publicity

The basic ingredient of successful publicity is *news.* Publicity releases that are truly newsworthy have a high incidence of use. The major problem with publicity releases that are not used is that they are not newsworthy. It's almost as simple as that. This suggests that product publicity is generally more effective for a new product than for an established one, and this is generally true. On the other hand, there are news opportunities for established products. The fact that a particular brand of reconstituted citrus drink is used by astronauts in their extraterrestrial perambulations because of its high nutritional content is news. The selection of a particular brand of trucks for construction work on the Alaskan pipeline because of its ruggedness and starting dependability is news. Preference for a particular brand of tires or sparkplugs by the winner of the Indianapolis 500 because of its performance under trying conditions is news. The manufacturers of outboard motors spend fortunes entering boats powered by their motors in national and international outboard races because the fact that the winning boat was powered by a Mercury motor or an Evinrude motor is news (it is widely believed in the outboard motor industry that share of market is related to share of wins).

The facts surrounding many established products contain elements of news. And, while news is only one of the techniques of advertising, it is *the* technique of product publicity.

Staffing for Product Publicity

Some companies maintain their own public relations departments, which are responsible for product publicity and which work closely with the marketing department. Seldom is product publicity a direct function of the marketing department itself, although in some instances it may be. Similarly, some advertising agencies have a public relations department staffed with experts, which can serve the publicity needs of their clients; this is not a common practice.

Often, both advertisers and advertising agencies rely on specialized public relations agencies, which charge for their counsel and time on a fee basis, with the size of the fee depending on the scope and duration of the services required.

Planning Product Publicity

Not all product publicity releases are preplanned. Sometimes they arise spontaneously and erratically, depending on the environment. An unanticipated opportunity for product publicity will arise, and the company will take advantage of it on an ad hoc basis.

Our primary concern, however, is the systematic use of product publicity as a part of the marketing plan. When used in this way, references to product publicity will appear in various parts of the marketing plan.

Problems and Opportunities. The problems and opportunities section of the marketing plan for a particular product might carry the following statement: "The development of a new circuitry and display mechanism for our model 3062 pocket computer, which extends the life of the battery from 30 to 2,000 hours, appears to be a newsworthy technological advance that should be featured in our advertising and promotion during the forthcoming fiscal period."

Marketing Strategy. The marketing strategy section of the plan might state: "Because of the newsworthyness of the extended battery life of model 3062, product publicity will be used to capitalize on this development. Particular attention should be devoted to: (a) retail buyers of pocket computers in major department stores, (b) technical journals, (c) product columns in newspapers and magazines, and (d) general news writers.

Objectives and Strategy. An objectives and strategy section for product publicity would be prepared by appropriate specialists. This section would include:

1. A brief statement of the purpose and rationale for publicity program.
2. An identification of the specific audiences to be reached.
3. A description of the publicity activities that will be undertaken and the timing of each.
4. A statement of how product publicity will be coordinated with the advertising and sales promotion programs.
5. An estimate of the costs of the publicity program.
6. Finally, and this point is highly desirable, although it is not essential and is sometimes neglected, there should be a statement as to how the effectiveness of the publicity program will be evaluated.

MARKET TESTING

Some form of market testing is often a part of the marketing plan. It can be argued, of course, that some form of market testing should *always* be a part of the marketing plan. This argument can be made because no marketer ever knows all that could or should be known about his product and its responsiveness to a change in marketing variables. A thorough analysis in the marketing review section of the marketing plan will usually raise questions, the answers to which will remain obscure until they are subjected to investigation. Further, market tests can be used to explore the potential of a new premium or sales promotion device before risking national exposure and possible failure. And, the search for new premiums and promotions is an endless task. Almost anyone who has worked extensively in this area has had the experience of a promotion that failed, or has ended up with a warehouse full of premiums that no one wanted, and belatedly wished that a test had been run before committing funds for national exposure.

Of course, there are occasions where market testing is deemed too risky. Concern that a test will tip off competitors who will then sieze the idea and use it, thereby reaping its benefits. There is always this risk. It is one of the prices of systematic marketing. The decision to test or not to test is a question of marketing judgment, and sometimes prudence will dictate not to test. But, all too often, the fear that competitors will sieze an idea that is being tested is simply a rationalization for sloppy thinking.

General Foods sat quietly by while Purina test marketed New Purina Dog Chow, built a multimillion dollar plant to produce the product, exanded the initial test into five markets and then ten markets, and eventually captured leadership in a market that General Foods' product, Gaines, probably should have owned. Their rationalization was that since the chunks in Purina Dog Chow were larger than in the Gaines product it wouldn't really be competitive.[5] Then, Purina sat back and watched General Foods develop Gaines' Burgers and establish a new "moist" category in the dog food market that became a multimillion dollar bonanza.

Betty Crocker and Pillsbury procrastinated while Nebraska Consolidated Mills, a small milling company, took the midwestern cake mix market for Duncan Hines Cake Mix (a brand that was later purchased by Procter and Gamble). Then, they watched

Procter and Gamble introduce Duncan Hines into the eastern part of the country where it became a major brand.

The big three in the American automobile industry dozed in the sun while Volkswagen and other imports got a hammerlock on the small car market and didn't wake up from their nap until profits began to hurt and federal legislation growing out of the energy crises compelled them to trim the size of their cars. These same companies have also lagged in the development of front-wheel drive automobiles while foreign imports were exploiting and benefiting from this feature. And there is nothing new about front-wheel drive. The idea has been a practical alternative for the past thirty years.

The problem appears to be that large companies become victims of their own inertia. They may see something happening in the marketplace, but all too often they decide to watch it and see what develops. When they finally arouse themselves to action, their activities are often delayed by their committment to what they are currently doing, cumbersome internal procedures, and a cautious and conservative management. There is a remarkable reluctance in many companies to "rock the boat."

The point is, of course, that fear of competitive reaction is often overblown and there are important values in making market tests a regular part of the marketing plan. Testing is one of the ways a company prepares for the future. Undoubtedly, there are legitimate instances when prudent judgment will mitigate against testing. Such instances are relatively rare, however, and failure to conduct a market test of some kind for fear of what competitors *might* do is, in my opinion, probably a poor decision.

What to test, how extensively to test, and when to test are often difficult marketing judgments. But marketing professionals are paid to make difficult judgments. And, if one must err, it is generally better to err on the side of testing. After all, a major purpose of *systematic* marketing is to reduce risks. That is precisely what market testing does.

If market testing is a part of the marketing plan, then the basis for it should be laid in the marketing review and the "problems and opportunities" sections of the plan. The marketing strategies section should identify the market test as a strategic decision, and the general structure of the test, along with estimated costs and the basis for evaluation, should appear in a section titled Testing Objectives and Strategies.

One other important facet of testing is the follow-up evaluation of the test results. After a test is completed, someone in the company should prepare a written evaluation of the findings which is (1) distrib-

---

5. Milton P. Brown, Richard N. Cardozo, Scott M. Cunningham, Walter J. Salmon, and Ralph G.M. Sultan, *Problems in Marketing,* 4th ed. (New York: McGraw-Hill Book Company, 1968), p. 728.

uted to concerned executives and (2) placed in a permanent file. When such evaluations are not made in written form, there is danger that a valuable piece of knowledge will be lost. One of the most successful marketers of packaged goods in the United States turns the task of preparing written evaluations over to a junior executive. Company spokesmen say that this practice helps train young executives and generates a permanent file of company experience that can be called up for future reference. They believe this gives them an advantage over competitors who are not so thorough nor systematic in recording the results of their experiences, and, as a consequence, have little accumulated company experience to call on.

MARKETING RESEARCH

While the use of marketing research is often called for in the marketing plan, it seldom appears as a major objective or point of strategy in and of itself. Most frequently, it appears as an adjunct to other objectives and strategies. For example, the section on copy stragegy might contain the statement: "The effectiveness of the new copy in registering the 'high protein' theme will be measured by recall tests through the use of a 'dummy' magazine prior to its commercial use." Or, "The new copy will be evaluated by attitude tests prior to use to provide assurance that the 'high protein' theme is effective in improving consumer attitudes toward the product." The research itself, then, would be described in a separate document. Or, in the case of a market test for a new premium, the objectives and strategies section for the market test might contain the statement: "The new premium will be subjected to in-store testing in at least three markets. Research procedures for the test will be described in a separate document." The estimated budget for the research would then appear in the appropriate section of the marketing plan (in the copy section for the first example given and in the market testing section for the second) and a "lump sum" for all research would be shown in the budget summary.

Occasionally, however, as in the Pet example given at the beginning of the chapter, a major research expenditure will be isolated and referred to in the *marketing objectives* and *marketing strategy* sections of the marketing plan. In these instances, the research proposal itself will be given a special section. This normally occurs when a major research project is required to obtain data for future marketing purposes.

Business Week, in an article titled "Why Business Is Spending Millions to Learn How Customers Behave," points out that, over time, research questions often accumulate to the point that a major research endeavor is required to find the answers.[6] At this point, a major research project finds its way into the marketing plan.

Let us assume that a company manufacturing a food or drug store item decides to subscribe to the A.C. Nielsen Service, the annual cost of which may easily run from $70 thousand to $100 thousand. This strategic decision would certainly appear in the marketing strategies section of the marketing plan, and a section of *Research Objectives and Strategies* would then be included to briefly describe the rationale behind this decision and to define the kinds of information that would be obtained from the investment. In subsequent years, however, as long as the company continued to purchase the A.C. Nielsen data, the only reference that would need to be made to it would be a budget item in the budget summary because the same strategy is being continued. Should a decision be made to discontinue the service at a later date, the marketing plan in which this decision becomes effective would acknowledge this strategy change in the marketing strategy section, and a special marketing research section would be included to explain why the company's basic research strategy had been modified. In this way, the historic file of marketing plans would provide a complete record of the company's thinking and decisions in regard to the use of the A.C. Nielsen service.

When a research project is of such importance that it is described in a separate section of the marketing plan, this section should contain

1. The objectives of the research, along with its rationale.
2. A brief description of the information to be obtained, and an indication of how it will benefit future activities of the brand.
3. A summary description of the research methodology. (If a more detailed description is desirable, it should be relegated to a separate, back-up document.)
4. An estimate of the cost of the project, and a completion date.

CORPORATE ADVERTISING

A clear distinction needs to be made between *brand* or *product* advertising on the one hand, and *corporate* or *institutional* advertising on the other. The difference is one of *primary* focus.

6. "Why Business Is Spending Millions to Learn How Customers Behave," *Business Week* (April 18, 1964): 90 ff.

Brand or product advertising That advertising undertaken in support of the objectives of a *particular* brand. Its ultimate purpose is to influence consumer attitudes about the brand and to increase the probability of brand purchase.

Corporate or institutional advertising Advertising undertaken in support of the objectives of a company. Its purpose is to provide information and influence attitudes concerning the company itself. True, favorable attitudes toward a company probably will help sales of the company's brands. But the *focus* of corporate advertising is on some aspect of the company itself—*not* on individual company brands.

Corporate advertising may be undertaken for a variety of reasons and directed toward a number of diverse publics. The purpose of such advertising may be financial, political, recruitment, public relations, and so forth. A survey conducted by the Association of National Advertisers provides a summary of some general objectives of corporate advertising as viewed by companies which utilize it. These objectives include the following six items.

1. Enhance or maintain the company's reputation or goodwill among specific public or business audiences.
2. Establish or maintain a level of awareness of the company's name and nature of business.
3. Provide a unified and supportive marketing approach (umbrella) for a combination of present and future products and services.
4. Educate the audience on subjects of importance to the company's future (for example, profits, free enterprise, economics).
5. Establish the company's concern for environmental or social issues.
6. Bring about a change in specific attitudes of the audiences toward the company or its products.[7]

The foregoing objectives sound impressive. Although corporate advertising can have value, the truth is that many corporate ads are poorly conceived, badly executed, and largely a waste of company resources. Historically, corporate advertising has been considered by many in the advertising industry as a "bad joke." Too frequently, such advertising has been used, not because there was an objective need for it, but because it was an ego trip for the chairman of the board, the president, and the board of directors of the company—it didn't do much damage, and it made them feel important.

The Problem of Corporate Advertising

Advertising Age recently ran the following editorial on the problems that surround corporate advertising.

There seems to be a widespread recognition that businesses need to use "corporate" ads to communicate their problems and views to the public. If only we knew how to do it.

There was a time when much "corporate advertising" was primarily an ego trip—an opportunity for management to reassure investors and peers, who were already true believers. It was also apparent that the message wasn't getting through to the outside world.

Interviews with the press do not necessarily solve the problem either. "Corporate advertising," used effectively, can help because it gets the message to the right audience in the words management wishes to use.

If this kind of communication is important, then it is also important that it be effective. Alexander Kroll, president of Young and Rubicam U.S.A., fears some corporate ads actually frighten people by projecting the image of business as "rugged, unstoppable, all powerful."

He praises companies like Gulf and ARCO, which deliberately use copy that leaves room for feedback and admits to "warts" on the corporate face.

At the Assn. of National Advertisers meeting a few days ago, Prof. Irving Kristol, who is among the distinguished economists writing regularly for the *Wall Street Journal*, embraced what appears to be the opposite view. He favors clear, candid, issue-oriented ads like those used by Mobil. Critics of those Mobil ads miss the point, he says. The ads aren't aimed at "who reads newspapers, but who writes them," and he says they are beginning to pay off. Prof. Kristol has his caveats. U.S. Steel's current campaign, "We're involved," seems to admit that before they ran the ads they weren't involved, he told ANA.

Backlash is the big danger. Frantic ads in newspapers, magazines and tv concerning a subsidy bill by maritime interests—management and labor working together—may actually have helped bring defeat by encouraging those who say the industry is already too heavily dependent on federal subsidies. Prof. Kristol deplores ads which plead poverty without providing really serious education. "It's bad for the system when major corporations go around whimpering and whining and apologizing all the time," he says.

In corporate advertising, as in other forms of advertising, there are geniuses and charlatans. We'd like to think Mr. Kroll and Prof. Kristol have provided clues which help to distinguish one from the other. But just as we think we can identify the "geniuses," a "charlatan" racks up a success. Which is one of the reasons the debate over what to say in corporate ads goes on . . . and on . . . and on.[8]

7. Harry L. Darling, *Current Company Objectives and Practices in the Use of Corporate Advertising* (New York: Association of National Advertisers, Inc., 1975), pp. 6–7.

8. "Which corporate ads work?" p. 16. Reprinted with permission from the November 7, 1977 issue of *Advertising Age.* Copyright 1977 by Crain Communications, Inc.

And that's the problem. *When* should one use corporate advertising and *what* should one say?

In today's complex economy, major economic and social issues often arise that may have a profound effect upon individual companies or industries or on the basic concepts that underly business in its entirety—concepts such as profit, risk, competition, growth, investment, supply, and demand. Far too often, these issues are raised by those with antibusiness sentiments, and the news coverage that these issues receive is hopelessly one sided. Faced with these situations, there is a temptation to use corporate advertising to communicate corporate values and points of view to the corporation's publics. This temptation is both understandable and defensible. And, when companies understand *what* they want to say, *why* they want to say it, and *when they say it honestly* corporate advertising is a legitimate vehicle for expressing company beliefs.

Too frequently, though, companies do not know precisely what they want to say and why they should be saying it. And, too frequently, companies are not wholly honest in their corporate communications. It is these ads that will probably be ineffective, and most likely backfire.

Earlier in the text, I quoted a sign that Bill Spencer, while creative director of the Gardner Advertising Company, kept posted in his office. It read:

Advertising can survive many imperfections as long as it says what it has to say clearly and distinctly, always keeping in mind the audience for whom it is intended.

This admonition applies to corporate advertising as well as to brand advertising.

Corporate advertising, if it is to be effective, needs to be as thoroughly planned as any brand advertising campaign. It needs a communications plan, just as a brand needs a marketing plan. The marketing plan used as an outline for this book can easily be adapted to the needs of a corporate advertising campaign. This has been done in the following material.

The Corporate Advertising Plan

The justification for a corporate advertising plan is rooted in the overall objectives and strategies of the corporation. The need for the plan will arise from the situation in which the corporation finds itself. As a consequence, the corporate advertising plan will differ in some respects from a product marketing plan. Its basic purposes are the same however, namely: (1) to identify problems and opportunities, (2) to specify objectives and strategies, (3) to develop a specific program, and (4) to provide for the program's evaluation.

Like a product marketing plan, the corporate advertising plan should be objective, reasoned, and systematic. Its persuasiveness should arise from its real strengths—knowledge, logic, incisiveness, imagination—not from the irresponsible enthusiasm of one-sided argument. The format for a corporate advertising plan is outlined in figure 21–1.

In all other aspects (form, tone, appearance, etc.) the corporate advertising plan should follow the same guidelines that have been laid down for product marketing plans.

This procedure will not *guarantee* a successful corporate advertising program. However, it will enable the company to avoid the ill-considered and poorly thought through corporate advertising programs that have been major problems in the past.

SUMMARY

This chapter has dealt with subjects that are normally considered optional in the design of the marketing plan. Specifically, it dealt with product publicity, market testing, and marketing research as objects of marketing strategy.

Product publicity differs from advertising in two major respects. Advertising is *paid* space or time whereas publicity is *free* space or time; the advertiser has no control over publicity, although he may attempt to influence it through the information he releases and the services he performs. The secret of effective product publicity is *news*. For this reason, we normally associate publicity with new products, although many established products have newsworthy features.

Some form of test marketing is often a part of the marketing plan because it is through test marketing that companies gain information about proposed activities and reduce the risk of wasting company resources through the commission of major marketing blunders. Many companies are reluctant to test market for fear that they will tip off competition concerning their future activities. I think that such fears are generally exaggerated.

Marketing research normally appears in the marketing plan as an adjunct to other marketing activities. On some occasions, however, the need for research accumulates to the point that a major research project is required to gather information that will facilitate future marketing activities. When this occurs, marketing research itself becomes an object of marketing strategy, and a section of the marketing plan should be devoted to this subject.

Much corporate advertising is poorly conceived and executed and requires more careful planning than it is normally given. Although corporate advertising has no place in the product marketing plan as such, the product marketing plan offers the basic structure for a systematic approach to corporate advertising.

1. *REVIEW OF ADVERTISING OPPORTUNITIES*

   This section is equivalent to the marketing review section of the product marketing plan and consists, essentially, of a survey and summarization of all pertinent facts concerning the company, its competition, and its environment. Normally, this section will include such factors as:

   a. The strengths and weaknesses of the company and competition as they pertain to the need for or reason for corporate advertising.

   b. A review of important developments or changes within the company, its industry, its environment, or its audiences that the company wishes to influence through advertising.

   c. A review of any research data pertaining to the audience groups that the company wishes to reach with its advertising, particularly as this data reflects audience knowledge of and attitudes toward the company and its competition.

2. *PROBLEMS AND OPPORTUNITIES*

   This section highlights those key facts, assumptions, and conclusions drawn from the review section that help shape and direct the overall plan. It includes such things as:

   a. why corporate advertising should be undertaken,

   b. to whom it should be directed,

   c. how it can help the company achieve its objectives,

   d. identification of any special problems and/or opportunities.

3. *ADVERTISING OBJECTIVES*

   The advertising objectives section takes the place of the marketing objectives section of the product marketing plan. Here, corporate objectives must be clearly specified, and an advertising budget established.

4. *ADVERTISING STRATGEGY*

   Same as for the product marketing plan.

5. *COPY STRATEGY*

   Same as for the product marketing plan.

6. *COPY PLAN*

   Same as for the product marketing plan.

7. *MEDIA STRATEGY*

   Same as for the product marketing plan.

8. *MEDIA PLAN*

   Same as for the product marketing plan.

9. *EVALUATION STRATEGY AND PLAN*

   Every corporate advertising plan should contain a section on how the advertising program will be evaluated in terms of the extent to which it has accomplished its objectives.

   This will involve a program of research that may include (a) special consumer research among the audiences to which the advertising is directed, (b) research among company sales and management personnel, if pertinent, and (c) use of commercial advertising research services such as Starch and Readex.

   Audience research that is designed to measure changes in the attitudes and beliefs of the target audience relevant to the corporate campaign is particularly important for corporate advertising. This is so because, unlike a product plan, one does not have concrete sales results against which to compare the plans accomplishments.

Figure 21-1.

QUESTIONS

1. What are the primary characteristics that distinguish product publicity from product advertising?
2. What are the primary arguments of those who use product publicity as a regular part of their marketing programs?
3. Outline the information that should be covered in a product publicity plan.
4. Companies often avoid test marketing for fear that competition will learn about their future activities from their tests and take steps to counteract these activities. Discuss this dilemma.
5. Under what conditions does marketing research become an object of marketing strategy?
6. When marketing research is an object of marketing strategy rather than an adjunct to it, what topics should be dealt with under the marketing research section of the marketing plan?
7. How does corporate advertising differ from product advertising?
8. Identify the major objectives for which corporate advertising is frequently undertaken.
9. Why, according to the text, is much corporate advertising ineffective?
10. How does the corporate advertising plan differ from a product marketing plan?

PROBLEM

You are the public relations director of an old-line farm tractor company that is a leader in its field. Despite its marketing leadership and increased sales resulting from a growing market, market share has dropped almost five points in the last three years. This has occurred because the company has not kept pace with competitors in terms of product development. Recognizing that the line was in danger of becoming noncompetitive, management had launched a major product improvement program and plans to introduce a "new generation" of farm tractors next year.

Rob Cohen, the marketing director, has asked for a meeting with you. When you and Rob get together, he opens the meeting by saying: "You know we plan to introduce our new generation of tractors at dealer meetings in January. Advertising will start with four-page inserts in the leading farm magazines in February. So far, we have kept the project under wraps because we didn't want competitors to be aware of what we were doing. But I think we are going to need a strong product publicity effort to accompany our introduction. Would you outline a program of product publicity, and have it ready for preliminary discussion in a couple of weeks. If we could get our basic plans wrapped up by May or June, that will give us about six months to work out the details. At this point, don't worry about costs. We'll deal with that problem when we come to it. This operation is too important to the company to worry about nickels and dimes. We need to know what we should be doing in terms of an effective public relations program."

In preparing for this assignment, you first start by identifying the audiences you will need to reach. Basically, you know that you will want to contact the following groups: (1) editors of major national and large regional farm magazines, (2) farm editors for local radio and television stations, (3) farm editors of rural and small town newspapers, (4) agricultural equipment magazines. One problem is the fact that many of the local radio stations and small town and rural newspapers serve regional interests. You figure that there are at least eight regions with different interests: Northeast, Central Atlantic, Southeast, Upper Midwest, Midwest, Southwest, California, and Northwest.

You know you can bring farm editors from national and major regional publications into company headquarters for an unveiling, but you will have to make arrangements for the local media. You also know that radio and newspaper farm editors are often highly competitive, and you certainly want to avoid offending any group.

Assignment

Given this information, outline a product publicity strategy including the type of activities that will be involved and a time schedule.

Measurement and Restrictions

Thus far, we have dealt with advertising and other marketing activities within the framework of the marketing plan. This has been done for three reasons:

1. To emphasize the point that effective advertising can only be developed within the framework of sound marketing considerations.
2. To point up the interdependence of the various part of the marketing plan.
3. To provide the student with a model of how a proper marketing plan should be written.

In this section, we will step outside of the marketing plan to examine two areas that are of utmost importance to marketing and advertising. In chapter 22 we will examine the question of how the results of the marketing plan and, more particularly, of advertising should be measured. In chapter 23 we will examine some of the legal restrictions that surround advertising and the possibility of even greater restrictions in the future.

These two areas have received a great deal of attention in the past few years and they will probably receive even more in the future.

22

Measuring Advertising Effectiveness

CLIO Awards

Each year, CLIO sponsors an annual film festival in which awards are given for the best radio and television commercials submitted for judging. Reels of these commercials are then prepared and made available for rental by the CLIO Educational Division for use by schools and other interested groups. Awards are also given for several classifications of techniques—Editing, Optical Effects, and Graphics; Animation Design; Cinematography; Film Direction; Musical Scores and Jingles; and Use of Humor.

Presumably, those chosen are the brightest and best of national and international broadcast productions. And, perhaps they are. Certainly, the CLIO reels contain many excellent commercials. But, are they the best? Who knows? The winners are selected by a panel of judges, but hard evidence of effectiveness in the market place is notably lacking when selections are made.

Insight and Inspiration

You can't afford to miss this special once-a-year opportunity to gain insight and inspiration. Harry

McMahan's informed commentary is drawn from years of experience nobody else in the business can equal.[1]

Thus an advertisement announced Harry McMahan's annual *100 best commericals* show which, each year, is presented in seven major markets—Boston, New York, Los Angeles, San Francisco, Chicago, Atlanta, and Dallas. Over the years, more than 15 thousand advertising practitioners have viewed one or more of the 100 best showings. In making his annual selections, McMahan views some 14 thousand commercials—national, regional, and local—in markets across the United States. The recent trend, according to McMahan, is toward more stars, more cartoons, and more jingles.[2]

Are these really the 100 best commercials produced during each year? Nobody knows. McMahan says they are, and he has probably written and seen as many commercials as anyone in the business. Other experienced advertising practitioners will undoubtedly disagree with many of his selections and have

---

1. "77's 100 best commercials," *Advertising Age* (January 30, 1978): 67. An advertisement.
2. "McMahan's '100 Best' commercials of 1977," *Advertising Age* (January 30, 1978): 43 ff.

their own favorite candidates that they believe should have been included in his list.

Successful Advertising Campaigns

In 1967, the United States Trade Center for Scandinavia held an exhibit in Stockholm, Sweden, that featured advertising from successful U.S. advertising campaigns. A booklet was prepared that contained descriptions of 135 successful advertising campaigns created by 40 U.S. advertising agencies, along with the criteria of success used to evaluate each campaign. Steuart Henderson Britt, a marketing professor and former director of research for a major advertising agency, concluded after examining the data that

> In the majority of the 135 campaigns analyzed here, the agencies did *not* prove or demonstrate the success of the campaigns which they had themselves publicly stated were successes.
>
> There is even a further implication. That is that most of the advertising agencies did not state (and possibly did not know) what the objectives for determining success were for a particular campaign, and consequently they could not possibly demonstrate whether a "successful" campaign was actually a success.
>
> Advertising may consist of doing something right or of doing something wrong. But do most advertisers and advertising agencies actually know just what that "something" is?[3]

While the campaigns to which Dr. Britt refers were presented in the late 1960s, the situation hasn't really changed in the past decade. What constitutes a successful advertising campaign is still an enigma, even to those closest to the field.

The three foregoing examples characterize the state of advertising evaluation—a state that hasn't changed all that much since advertising became a national preoccupation. This is true despite the fact that some $37 billion a year is spent on advertising, despite the fact that volumes have been written on advertising evaluation, and despite the fact that untold research dollars have been applied to its measurement. Perhaps the current situation is best summed up by the following quotation:

> Today, the money spent on advertising resembles tribute laid on the altar of some savage and arbitrary god.
>
> If you don't advertise, you're dead. If you do, you still may be. The unknowable deity must be appeased. But it's costing too much. Advertisers are rebelling.

They can't stop advertising: they don't want to. But they want to know what they are getting for their money.

So the time of the researcher is at hand. Formulas, concepts, systems of measurement are being invoked. But the answers are confusing, often irrelevant. What should be measured—"exposure," "readership," "awareness," what else? And how? Through a box attached to the TV set, or a personal interview, or by measuring dilation and contraction of the pupils?

If the v-p of sales or marketing could measure anything he wanted, chances are he would say: Measure advertising's relationship to sales and profit. Tell me how much it costs.[4]

Generally speaking, when a question cannot be answered, there is a good chance that the wrong question is being asked. Corporate executives and marketing practitioners alike keep asking for an ultimate, absolute answer to the question of advertising. Perhaps the reason the answer is so elusive is that there is no absolute answer—only a relative one. As I have pointed out earlier, advertising does not stand alone. It is firmly embedded in a matrix of other marketing activities—influenced by the media in which it appears, mitigated or enhanced by what competitors are doing, and dependent on what often appears to be the whims of consumers. An advertising campaign that was an outstanding success one year may be a complete failure the next year because a major competitor markedly improved its product. A new advertising technique that commanded widespread attention when it was first used may quickly become obsolete and routine as it is copied by countless imitators trying to capitalize on its success. Indeed, the field of advertising is like quicksilver: it is constantly moving and changing; it is hard to hold on to and examine. Certainly, there are some constants in the mix—honesty, clarity of expression, a product concept that is appealing to consumers, and a creative presentation that lifts the product above competition and gives it visibility. But there are variables, too. Shifting consumer values and concerns, the state of the economy, the product itself, packaging, pricing, distribution, sales promotion, advertising weight, reach, and frequency, the activities of competitors—all of these influence the outcome of marketing programs. It is little wonder that the effect of advertising on sales is obscure; it is little wonder that the answer to the question, "How much should advertising cost," is elusive.

Despite the difficulties inherent in measuring the effects of advertising, pressure continues to mount to cast some light on its contribution to the marketing

3. Steuart Henderson Britt, "Are So-Called Successful Advertising Campaigns Really Successful?" in S.H. Britt and H.W. Boyd, eds., *Marketing Management and Administrative Action* (New York: McGraw-Hill Book Co., 1973): 553–64.

4. A.J. Vogl, "Advertising Research," *Sales Management*, XCI, No. 10 (November 1, 1963): 40. Reprinted with permission from *Sales Management, the Magazine of Marketing*.

effort. This point is emphasized by the following quotation from a publication sponsored by the Association of National Advertisiers.

> The great debate over whether or not advertising can be measured has been going on as long as most advertising men can remember. Some claim it cannot be done, so why try. Others say that if as much time were spent in researching advertising as is wasted in debating whether or not it can be done, we would be twice as far as we are now. As is usually the case, semantic difficulties and emotional involvement account for the 180-degree difference in opinion. Clarifying these differences is necessary to progress.
>
> A big stumbling block is the word "measurement." Those who expect to find a formula which will accurately relate advertising efforts and short-term sales results will, with a few rare exceptions, be disappointed. But the answer to the question, "Can advertising be *evaluated*?" is unreaservedly "Yes." Every business function *must* be evaluated in terms of the contribution it makes to the profit and growth of the enterprise, on the one hand, and the costs incurred, on the other hand. A business cannot survive without some means of appraising benefits in relation to costs.
>
> The principle of placing dollars at risk in anticipation of a gain is fundamental in the American incentive enterprise system. Obviously this principle must apply to advertising as it does to very other function of the business. The evaluation of advertising effectiveness, both before it appears, and after it appears, is an inescapable business function. The only debatable question—and herein lies a time-worn controversy—is whether this process of evaluation is carried out objectively or subjectively, systematically or haphazardly. [5]

This quotation contains the key to the problem of advertising evaluation. *Advertising will be evaluated.* The proper question is: "Should this evaluation be carried out subjectively or objectively, systematically or haphazardly?"

I doubt that *complete* objectivity can be attained in advertising evaluation; our evaluation tools are simply not that precise. However, insofar as is possible, objective criteria should enter into and be a part of the evaluation process. Further, we can be *systematic* rather than haphazard in our approach to advertising. And to do so means that we *begin* our evaluation with the marketing plan, not with advertising, per se.

EVALUATING THE MARKETING PLAN

It is not difficult to evaluate the effectiveness of a particular marketing plan. Either it achieves its objec-

tives within the cost constraints imposed or it does not. If the objectives call for the sale of 10,250,000 cases with a marketing expenditure of $6 million within a given fiscal year and sales approximate or exceed this level, the marketing plan was successful. If sales fall significantly below the expected level, the plan is a failure.

The difficulty lies, not in determining whether the marketing plan in its entirety succeeds or fails. The difficulty lies in determining the specific contribution that each element of the plan—the product, package, price, distribution, advertising, and so forth—make to its success or failure. Let's take an example.

A cake mix manufacturer test marketed a new type of cake mix. The product concept called for a cake mix image rooted in early American traditions—a low, heavy, rich cake like grandmother used to make. All elements of the marketing plan were, quite properly, designed around this concept. However, in the process of execution, no one was really happy with the package design. It was not that the package design was inappropriate. Rather, the general feeling of both the client and agency was that the package could be better. Too many inputs from too many individuals and too many committees had, in the judgment of the marketing group, routinized the design and dulled its communication potential. Nonetheless, under the pressure of deadlines and concern about competitive activity in developing a similar product, a decision was made to go ahead with test marketing, *but to revise* the package before expanding nationally, should the test market be successful.

The test market was highly successful. Sales exceeded the expectations of both the client and agency. Everyone was jubilant. But now they had a problem. They were afraid to modify the package before expansion because they did not know how much the test market version of the package contributed to the product's success.

In the case of a marketing plan that fails to achieve its objectives, the problem is compounded. What element or elements failed to perform adequately? Were the objectives unrealistic? Did the problem lie in the product concept? The product itself? Pricing? Distribution? Advertising? Or in some other element of the marketing plan?

At this point, a major analysis must be undertaken. Each element of the marketing plan must be carefully scrutinized in order to assess its strengths and weaknesses. Sometimes, certain elements may be easily exculpated. For example, if the product performs adequately in well-designed tests against leading competitive products, then the problem does not lie there. If high levels of distribution were achieved, then this

---

5. Russel H. Colley, ed., *Practical Guides and Modern Practices for Better Advertising Management: Evaluating Advertising Effectiveness,* **VII** (New York: Association of National Advertisers, Inc., 1959), p. 1.

variable can be eliminated. However, each element must be investigated against some criterion of performance. Since the primary concern of this text is advertising, no attempt will be made to develop and discuss performance criteria for all elements of the marketing plan, other than to note that it is often a difficult task and that specific performance objectives must be set before meaningful evaluations can be made. Instead, we will focus on advertising itself. How should advertising be evaluated?

EVALUATING ADVERTISING

Advertising often represents the single largest expense item in the marketing budget. This is particularly true for proprietary drugs and personal care items where advertising and sales promotion may represent 40 percent of company sales for leading brands. For other consumer products, the advertising to sales ratio may be lower, but it still represents a significant sum. When the 100 leading advertisers spend almost $8 billion in advertising, advertising's effectiveness must be a major concern.

Strangely enough, advertising is probably as little understood by its users as by its detractors. Why else would there be so much disagreement among advertising professionals as to what constitutes good advertising? Why else would it be possible for the same company to run a brilliant campaign one year and follow it up with one that is mediocre or worse? Still, major company resources are directed into advertising, and it is the responsibility of marketing and advertising management to see that such expenditures are made wisely.

Advertising research is the primary instrument that managers have to provide some assurance that advertising monies are being used well. Few major companies will invest significant funds in a television or print campaign that has not been thoroughly tested. And, while advertising research techniques may be far from perfect, they can be helpful, although not infallible.

Generally speaking, advertising research can be subdivided into three major areas, each of which is a field of investigation in its own right. These major areas are *budget* research, *audience* research, and *copy* research.

1. *Budget research* is concerned with how much money should be allocated for advertising.
2. *Audience research* is concerned with advertising weight, reach, frequency, efficiency, and the effectiveness of different media and different combina-

tions of media in reaching target audiences.
3. *Copy research* deals with what is said and how it is said in the media that are employed.

These three areas are interrelated and interdependent. For example, the effectiveness of what is said may depend upon the media used. And media effectiveness may be influenced by the available budget. For our purposes, we will isolate copy research and direct our attention to this aspect of advertising evaluation.

PROBLEMS IN COPY RESEARCH

Copy research is beset with problems of definition, measurement, and interpretation. Perhaps the most difficult problem in copy research, however, is determining the objectives against which advertising should be measured. While the *ultimate* goal of advertising may be to increase sales, advertising may contribute to this goal in a variety of ways. On the one hand, there is the direct mail advertiser who succeeds or fails to the extent that advertising does or does not generate immediate sales. On the other, is the president of a large life insurance company who says

> Advertising does not sell life insurance. Only agents can sell a policy. Advertising can simply make the prospect more interested in the idea of investing in insurance and more receptive to our agents than to the agents of our competitors.[6]

Most advertisers of consumer goods fall somewhere in between these two extremes in terms of what advertising is expected to do. For the most part, the marketer who attempts to evaluate advertising in terms of its short-term effect on sales or share of market faces a formidable task. There are a number of reasons why sales or market share are misleading criteria of the effectiveness of a particular advertisement or advertising campaign.

Advertising Does Not Work Alone. Advertising is a part of a total marketing effort. A product that is poorly positioned, overpriced, inadequately distributed, badly packaged, or inferior to competition may suffer sales declines even though the advertising itself is well conceived and professionally executed. If sales are stagnant or declining, advertising may be the scapegoat even though some other part of the marketing mix is the real culprit.

---

6. H.D. Wolfe, J.K. Brown, and G.C. Thompson, *Measuring Advertising Results,* Studies in Business Policy **102,** The National Industrial Conference Board (1962), p. 7.

Sales Response Does Not Always Parallel Advertising Expenditure. Often, in response to advertising, sales may build slowly at first, and then accelerate. Thus, there is often a lag between the appearance of advertising and the sales response generated by that advertising. The length of the lag itself may be a variable, both because of the product being advertised and the advertising appeals employed. A lag between advertising and sales response is expected with most products, but it may be particularly acute for big ticket items and for other items that are infrequently purchased.

Advertising May Be Subject to Threshold Effects. The response to advertising may be the result of the cumulative effects of an advertising campaign as opposed to being a response to a single advertisement or commercial. A $500 thousand campaign may have no apparent effect, whereas a $750 thousand expenditure for the same product may break through the consumer's barrier of awareness and pay for itself many times over.

Advertisers May Find It Difficult To Associate Changes with a Specific Medium. Sales response may result from the combination of media, or it may be possible that one medium generated the bulk of the sales response, while the other contributed relatively little.

Uncontrollable Variables May Obscure the Relationship between Advertising and Sales. Competitive activity and other marketing variables may cause sales not to reflect the effectiveness of the advertising. For example, let us assume that a tire advertiser ran a brilliant campaign for snow tires. Yet, the winter in which the campaign ran was a mild one, and sales were down significantly. Advertising can be blamed for many things, but not for the weather.

Since short-term sales results may be neither a sensitive nor valid measure of advertising effectiveness, it seems obvious that we need turn to other bases for evaluation.

In chapter 11, it was argued that the basic purpose of advertising is persuasive communication—that any effect advertising has must be dependent upon what it communicates to consumers. In this same chapter, several hierarchy of effects models were presented. These models are all communications models and, while they differ in minor details, they visualize the advertising tasks of creating *awareness, acceptance, preference* and *intention to buy* and *of provoking the sale.* Only the last of these tasks—provoking the sale—demands specific action from the consumer. All

of the rest are purely communication measures; they communicate something to the consumer.

The ideal measure of advertising effectiveness is an *action* measure, but such measures are often too insensitive or too contaminated by other marketing activities to be useful. As a consequence, most measures of advertising effectiveness must depend upon communication measures—measures of awareness, acceptance, preference, and intention to buy. Even here, there is danger of contamination from other marketing activities. For example, awareness of a product may arise because a package is seen in a retail outlet, not because of exposure to advertising. Nonetheless, measuring advertising in terms of its communication accomplishments is often the only practical way of assessing its contribution. It is against this background that the following discussion of copy research must be considered.[7]

COPY TESTING

For the advertising practioner, copy testing may perform two basic functions: (1) measuring the effectiveness of an advertisement or an advertising campaign in achieving some predetermined objectives, and (2) providing diagnostic material that can be used in developing or improving an advertising effort. The ideal copy test would be one that fulfilled both functions. There are no practical testing devices that perform both functions equally well. Sales response, the ultimate goal of marketing effectiveness, generates no diagnostic information for improving advertising. Attitude and communications tests, often rich in diagnostic data, provide no real measure of sales response. The basic conflict here is that between quantitative and qualitative data. Advertising effectiveness is measured by numbers, while diagnostic data may not be amenable to quantitative forms. As a consequence, marketing managers normally employ both kinds of testing—qualitative, or diagnostic, testing to help the advertising staff develop advertisements and effectiveness tests to measure the performance of the finished product.

There are essentially three stages in which research can be used in developing advertising copy: a preliminary stage in which concepts may be tested and elements of the proposed ad assessed, a pretesting stage in which the advertisement or commercial is tested in rough or finished form, and a posttesting phase in

7. The following discussion on copy testing, with minor modifications, has been taken from: Kenneth E. Runyon, *Consumer Behavior and the Practices of Marketing* (Columbus, Ohio: Charles E. Merrill Publishing Co., 1977), pp. 432–42.

which the effects of an advertisement or commercial are measured after having appeared in media.

Preliminary Testing

Preliminary testing often starts with a hypothesis that has emerged from an analysis of consumer behavior or from an examination of alternative product dimensions that could be used as bases for a product appeal. For example, in an attempt to develop a new brand of coffee to counteract a competitive brand being introduced in some of its key markets, General Foods exposed consumers to a series of descriptive words such as *rich, dark, fullbodied, full-flavored* in order to determine which combination of words aroused the greatest interest.[8] A detergent advertiser might characterize a detergent as one that "gets clothes whiter" or "makes colors brighter" or "gets clothes cleaner" in an effort to find out which claim elicits the most positive response from consumers. A variety of research techniques, ranging from simple preference to extended interviews, projective techniques, or physiological measures may be used at this stage of testing. The object of the test is to obtain a measure of the ability of the claim or theme to arouse consumer interest.

Discrete elements of a final advertisement may also be tested at this stage. In a television commercial, a model may be tested in terms of her appeal as a product spokesperson; the video portion of a television commercial may be tested to see how well it tells the basic product story without the benefit of the audio portion; or a particular demonstration of a product feature may be checked for its effectiveness in communicating the product benefit. In print advertising, headlines, illustrations, or format may be tested for communication value, memorability, interest, or ability to attract attention.

For many kinds of products, a split run may be used to test the relative effectiveness of a headline or advertising format. In such a split-run test, two or more advertisements that are similar except for one element (such as headline, illustration, or format) will be prepared. Each advertisement will contain a "hidden" coupon offer, such as a free sample or a cents-off deal buried in the body copy. The different advertisements will be inserted in alternate copies of a newspaper or magazine. Presumably, the advertisement that pulls the greatest coupon response is the most effective.

8. M.P. Brown, R.N. Cardoza, S.M. Cunningham, W.J. Salmon, R.G.M. Sultan, *Problems in Marketing* (New York: McGraw-Hill Book Co., 1968), pp. 439–66.

Pretesting of Complete Advertisements

Complete advertisements are pretested in a variety of forms, ranging from rough layouts to finished art for print advertisements and from still photographs with superimposed audio to finished commercials for broadcast. Many pretests involve a potpourri of measures, including measures of attention value, interest, comprehension of message, recall of the advertisement in total or of specific sales points, and attitude change. There is no simple way of cataloguing the types of tests used, since flexible research designs permit one to combine a variety of measures in any given test. In addition, tests are often structured in such a way that the advertisement or commercial simply serves as the focal point for extended interviews with individuals or with groups. The structure of the test depends wholly on the kinds of information that are sought.

Aside from specific measures of interest, attention value, and comprehension of message, overall effectiveness is often measured by attitude tests and recall tests.

Attitude Tests. The theory underlying attitude measures of effectiveness is that the purpose of advertising is to create product preference. Such tests use some form of attitude scaling, either by comparing product preference before and after exposure to advertising or by measuring preference on some absolute scale.

Recall Tests. Recall tests operate from a different philosophical base. Rooted in the psychological phenomenon of selective perception, recall tests hypothesize that consumers will remember those products and sales points that are psychologically relevant (important) to them. High recall is thereby equated with commercial excellence, although neither logic nor evidence provides assurance that what is psychologically relevant is necessarily positive. For example, a consumer exposed to an automotive advertisement may recall that the advertised product is powered by a 360 horsepower V-8 engine, not because she is charmed by having "360 horses" under the hood, but because she is grossly offended at what is perceived as a wasteful and irresponsible use of production facilities and fossil energy.

While both attitude and recall tests are extensively used in estimating advertising effectiveness, neither is supported by unassailable evidence of experimental validity, although both have a great deal going for them logically. Within recent years, attitude measures have gained in popularity, although in many cases the two measures are combined in various ways in a single test. The primary reason for combining the two measures is that attitude tests of effectiveness often provide insufficient diagnostic information to give direction for modifying the advertising approach. The recall technique, although a rich source of diagnostic data, has been criticized because it does not always distinguish between *favorable* and *unfavorable* recall.

Pretest Procedures. Many advertising pretests are conducted with small, nonrepresentative samples of consumers, selected on a judgment or convenience basis. As a consequence, it is not possible to assess the sampling error involved, nor to make statistical judgments on the validity of the data. Pretest sampling practices are usually defended on the basis that they are not intended to yield precise findings, but are only meant to provide general assurance that the advertising is appropriate. The legitimacy of this defense is questionable, but in an industry where personal judgment generally takes precedence over statistics, expediency is often the rule rather than the exception, and rationalization is frequently accepted as a substitute for wisdom. There is no simple way of cataloguing or classifying the pretest procedures that are used, yet there are certain testing approaches that should be mentioned because of their conceptual base or their widespread use. For convenience, these approaches may be identified as: (1) laboratory tests, (2) portfolio tests, (3) simulated media tests, and (4) limited media tests. These designations are somewhat arbitrary, and some of the specific techniques used could be included in more than one category. In general, though, the tests are classified in terms of the artificiality of the test situation, with laboratory tests being the most artificial, portfolio tests next, and limited media tests the least artificial.

We will discuss each of these general approaches below.

Laboratory Tests. The designation *laboratory tests* includes those tests that involve a laboratory setting and special equipment. Many kinds of equipment are used. Some of the most common instruments are (1) pupillometers, designed to measure the change in the size of the pupil of the eye in response to a stimulus as well as its pattern of fixation when exposed to a complex stimulus, (2) tachistoscopes, special projectors used to control the duration of a visual stimulus, (3) psychogalvinometers, which measure the electrical conductivity of the skin and are central components of the battery of instruments that are collectively called a *lie detector*. These devices are most often used

to assess interest and emotional response to advertisements, although they may be used simply as a point of departure for extended interviews or some other information-gathering approach.

One interesting application of operant conditioning theory in a laboratory setting has resulted in a *behavioral* measure of commercial effectiveness. This application is based on the finding that reinforcement (reward) of a response will increase the probability that the response will be repeated. Many laboratory experiments with animals measure the strength of a reinforcing device by the number of responses that a subject will emit in order to receive the reinforcement. ARBOR (Associates for Research in Behavior) has developed equipment in which the brightness of a television commercial and the clarity of the audio portion are controlled by the viewer by pumping foot pedals. The faster the viewer pumps, the clearer the picture. Interest in a commercial is guaged by how hard the subject is willing to work (frequency of emitted responses) to see and/or hear it.[9]

Since it is sometimes difficult to get subjects to come to a laboratory, a number of commercial research organizations have installed laboratories in motorized vans so that laboratories may be taken to the consumer. The van is driven to the parking lot of a shopping center, or some other place where consumers are plentiful, and tests are conducted on the spot. The test sample in this case is, of course, a convenience sample, with all of its shortcomings.

Portfolio Tests. Portfolio tests are usually used to pretest print advertisements, although a modification of the approach has been adapted for television commercials. Normally, a number of advertisements (usually five to ten) are assembled into a portfolio which is given the subject to peruse. One or more of the advertisements will be test advertisements, while the remainder will be controls. Advertisement position in the portfolio is usually controlled since position is known to affect recall. After the subject has leafed through the portfolio and closes it, some intervening activity such as a series of questions on the socioeconomic characteristics of the respondents is undertaken to provide a diversion and induce the forgetting process. Then the subject is asked a series of recall questions about the portfolio material. Attitude information can also be gathered through questions on preferences, beliefs, and values held in regard to the product or brand and its attributes.

9. P.E. Nathan and W.H. Wallace, "An Operant Behavioral Measure of TV Commercial Effectiveness," *Journal of Advertising Research* 5 (December, 1965): 13–20.

In the television version of the portfolio test, several commercials are presented via a portable projector that is brought into the home or is available in a van or laboratory.

Simulated Media Tests. In this approach, the researcher attempts to simulate a normal media situation without actually using commercial media. The two best-known techniques in this classification are the *proven name registration* test for print media and the *competitive preference* measure for commercials.

In the proven name registration procedure, advertisements are added to a dummy magazine that also contains a normal quota of editorial material. Under the guise of obtaining consumer responses to a proposed new media venture, the magazine is placed in the home where it is left for several days to give the subjects a chance to read it. Then, through a series of aided and unaided recall questions, interviewers determine which advertisements are remembered and what is remembered about them. The technique, orginally devised by Gallup-Robinson, is a recall technique, and advertising effectiveness is measured in terms of the percent of the sample that can prove they recall a particular advertisement by remembering something specific about it. Young and Rubicam, a major advertising agency, developed its own testing service along these lines, using its own version of a dummy magazine.

The competitive preference approach was orginally developed by Horace Schwerin, who invited subjects to a theater, ostensibly to preview the pilot show for a new television series. Commercials to be tested are embedded in the format of the show, as they are in a regular TV program. Under the guise of giving away a year's supply of products in the product fields being tested, consumer preferences for specific brands are obtained before and after the program is shown and the commercials seen. An effective commercial is one that causes consumers to change their brand preferences after seeing the commercials. Obviously, the more people who change preference in the desired direction, the better the commercial. The competitive preference method, as opposed to the "proven name registration" technique is an attitude test, since it relies on brand preference rather than on recall for its measure of effectiveness.

Limited Media Tests. The essential characteristic of all limited media tests is that a commercial or advertisement is tested under normal conditions in a limited geographic area before major funds are committed to it. Media tests can take a number of forms. A split-run copy test in a metropolitan newspaper is one form of a media test. A test market is another. In a split-run test, the criterion of effectiveness is usually the response to a hidden offer. In a test market, the criterion of effectiveness may range from measures of awareness to sales response as measured by store audits or consumer panels.

One form of media testing that is widely used for television commercials is one in which a commercial is scheduled in the late movie in a major metropolitan area and telephone interviews are used the next day to elicit recall information. Traditionally, this method has been used by Procter & Gamble as well as other major advertisers.

Another highly sophisticated form of television testing is offered by AdTel, a commercial research organization that maintains a dual cable CATV system and two balanced consumer purchase diary panels in each of several markets. By virtue of the dual cable hook-up, AdTel can funnel different commercials into the homes of each of its two consumer panels in a given market. Commercial effectiveness can be evaluated either in terms of sales response as measured by the consumer diaries, or from follow up interviews designed to obtain recall and/or attitude data.[10]

Posttesting

Posttesting is an extension of limited media testing and is not really testing at all, but a final evaluation. Many research and marketing personnel make no distinction between *testing* and *evaluation*. However, from the standpoint of accountability for business performance, the distinction is crucial. Testing is what is done *before* committing major company resources to a program. The purpose of testing is to provide empirical support for judgments, reduce risk, and eliminate or modify questionable material. Evaluation is made *after* company resources have been committed for a campaign. Its purpose is to determine if company objectives have been achieved. For the marketing or advertising manager, this is the moment of truth.

Both testing and evaluation are the responsibility of the marketing manager, although it is true that some companies hire an outside consultant to make a periodic audit of various marketing activities. The wise marketing manager will make program evaluations personally, however, and make sure that these assessments are communicated to higher management

10. AdTel advertisement, *Advertising Age* (July 15, 1974): 31–33.

along with recommendations for future improvement in those areas where improvement may be needed.

Evaluation, if it is to make sense, must be made against some predetermined objectives or criteria. Without predetermined objectives, meaningful evaluation is not possible. While many specific objectives can be set for advertising, the measurement of these objectives (however diverse) can usually be accomodated by four types of measurements: (1) measures of awareness, (2) measures of recall, (3) measures of attitude, and (4) measures of action.

Awareness Measures. Some marketing and advertising people are highly critical of measures of awareness, feeling that they are too superficial to provide an adequate criterion of advertising effectiveness. Others believe that such measures are invaluable in assessing certain marketing tasks. In introducing a new brand into test markets, for example, measures of awareness are crucial. The interpretation of an unsuccessful test market in which few people were aware of the brand would be quite different from the interpretation of an unsuccessful test market where virtually everyone had heard of the product but refused to buy it. Generally, awareness is an appropriate measure when a new product is being marketed, when a new company symbol or trademeark is being introduced, when a new use for a product is being promoted, or when advertising has been given the specific role of communicating a particular claim upon which the entire product concept hinges. For example, if a bourbon is being positioned or repositioned as the "bourbon for sophisticated people," then awareness of this position would provide an evaluation of how well advertising was doing its job in the overall program.

It is true that awareness is a relatively superficial measure and that its value is probably limited to a few specific applications, such as those mentioned. Also, for an established product it is virtually impossible to separate awareness that has resulted from advertising and awareness that has risen from other sources. Finally, there is always the question of the quality of the awareness. For these reasons, measures of awareness are seldom used alone, although the Starch magazine readership service does use a *recognition* technique that, at best, is a weak awareness measure.

There are a number of questioning techniques for measuring awareness, ranging from "Have you heard of Folger's coffee?" to "What brands of coffee have you heard of?" Obviously, it is much easier for a brand to qualify on the first question than on the second. Marketing research people disagree on how much aid should be given subjects in eliciting aware-

ness. Some argue that only "unaided" questions should be used, while others insist that "aided" questions are preferable because, in the buying situation product stocks and perhaps point-of-sale material facilitate consumer recognition of products of which they are dimly aware.[11] The rigor of the awareness test used depends largely on the predilection of the marketing or advertising manager and her research associates.

As the amount of aid given the subject is reduced, the awareness question blends almost imperceptibly into the recall question, and we find ourselves involved in our second type of measure—measures of recall.

Recall Measures. The purpose of recall tests in regard to advertising or an advertising campaign is to find out what consumers can remember about the advertising. As in the case of awareness tests, there is disagreement among researchers about how much aid should be given subjects in eliciting recollections. At worst, recall tests are nothing more than difficult awareness tests. At best, they can be used analytically in evaluating appeals. For example, the Pet Milk Company elicited advertising recall from users of liquid diet foods. It then cross-tabulated this information with brand-preference data obtained from the same subjects. The cross tabulation revealed that certain advertising claims appeared to be related to usage, whereas other claims seemed to have no such relationship.

Recall measures are particularly useful when the objective of the advertising campaign is to communicate a certain claim or implant a particular image in the minds of consumers. For example, in the detergent market, a certain amount of market segmentation is based on primary product claims. Companies such as Procter & Gamble and Lever Brothers market several brands that compete both against each other and against the brands of competitive companies. Procter & Gamble markets Tide, Cheer, Bold, Gain, Dash, Oxydol, Duz, Salvo, Era, and Bonus in the heavy-duty laundry detergent category. Marketing management carefully designates the particular cleaning function (product position) that each brand will fulfill. Each brand has a copy strategy. This strategy is a succinct statement of how the product will be represented to consumers. Consider: Tide gets clothes

11. Krugman, for example, argues that unaided recall measures severely underestimate the consumer's ability to remember and be influenced by commercials. H.E. Krugman, "What Makes Advertising Effective," *Harvard Business Review* **53** (March-April, 1975): 96–103.

cleaner ("Tide's in. . . . Dirt's out"); Cheer is the all-temperature detergent; Bold powers out dirt and powers in brightness; Gain tackles tough laundry problems; Dash has concentrated cleaning power; Oxydol bleaches as it washes; Duz is the heavy-duty detergent; Salvo is the convenient tablet detergent; Era tackles greasy dirt; and Bonus is the premium brand with a gift inside the box.

The point is that recall tests can be used effectively in determining whether the advertising of each brand is indeed positioning the brand in the consumers' minds as intended.

Recall measures, of course, are not applicable to all marketing objectives. They do not reflect attitude change; nor do they necessarily relate to sales, either in the short term or long run. Neither are recall measures problem free from the standpoint of execution and interpretation. They appear simple, but consumers become confused and cannot always recall what they know under the pressure of the interview. Scanty recall from a respondent may contain persuasive selling points, while large amounts of recall may be superficial and of little value. Like other research techniques, recall measures can provide useful data for advertising evaluation if thoughtfully used and carefully executed.

Attitude Measures. Attitude tests develop qualitatively different data than do awareness and recall surveys. Awareness and recall studies reflect consumer learning. Attitude tests reveal the effect of this learning on the perceptual organization of the learner.

Presumably, a consumer who holds a more favorable attitude toward brand A than brand B will buy brand A—provided no other overriding considerations influence the choice, such as lack of product availability or a large price differential in favor of brand B. It is this chain of logic that leads many advertisers to evaluate their advertising programs on the basis of their effectiveness in creating favorable attitudes, often expressed as measures of "brand preference" or "intention to buy." In fact, attitude measures hold such a hallowed place in the minds of many marketing practitioners that few marketers attempt to evaluate advertising without including some attitude questions in the study design. Sometimes, the attitude-scaling devices used are simplistic; at other times they utilize sophisticated psychological and mathematical designs. Whichever the case may be, attitude measurement is widely used.

Not only are attitude measures widely used to evaluate advertising effectiveness, they are also a meaningful measure. The reasons attitude measures can be meaningful measures are (1) psychologically, they are

a step closer to purchase than mere awareness of a product, or the ability to recollect product attributes, and (2) normally, attitude measurement represents the last point at which advertising can be isolated from other variables in the marketing mix with a reasonable degree of confidence. Once we get to the purchase itself, it is usually difficult to assess advertising's contribution.

Nonetheless, attitudes are at best substitute measures for sales effectiveness. If it is at all possible, the marketing or advertising manager should seek hard evidence that advertising is, in fact, producing sales.

Action Measures. Ultimately, product advertising is expected to produce sales. This is true whether the immediate goal of the advertising is to generate inquiries, produce sales leads to be followed up by salespeople, stimulate immediate sales response, increase store traffic, or instill consumer goodwill.

Sometimes sales response is easy to associate with an advertising message. This is uniquely true of direct-mail advertising, which succeeds or fails in direct proportion to the number of orders that result from its appearance. It is also true of much of the advertising used by retail outlets that feature a sale on certain days for a specific item or group of items. It is also somewhat true of a major consumer promotion run by a manufacturer (usually covering a one- or two-month period) which features a coupon, a price pack, or a combination deal.

Direct sales results are more difficult to trace to display advertising, which is designed to inform consumers about a product or its attributes with the expectation that, at some future date, purchases will be made. Wolfe, Brown, and Thompson emphasize this point.

> Product qualities, selling effort, brand prestige, dealer loyalty, consumer inertia, product distribution, size and location of displays, discount policies, delivery and other seller services, transportation allowances, reciprocal buying—these and other factors consciously or unconsciously influence the buyer in making his purchase decisions. To isolate advertising from these factors is often difficult if not impossible to accomplish.[12]

Even where it is possible to relate advertising to sales, there is often the question of whether the sale that is made is a *new* sale or a substitute for a sale that would have been made anyway. This is particularly worrisome in the case of promotional advertising that involves some sales incentive, such as a coupon or price-off label. Characteristically, consumer sales following a promotion period drop below the level of

---

12. Wolfe et al., *Measuring Advertising Results,* p. 159.

sales preceding the promotion, suggesting that the promotion itself "robbed" sales from future periods. Also, for the manufacturer of consumer goods, an increase in recorded sales may simply reflect a build-up of retailer inventories without creating a corresponding increase in purchases by the ultimate consumer. Such inventory build ups often signal a drop in future orders.

All of this means that careful record keeping, thoughtful analysis, and audits of both consumer sales and channel inventories are necessary before reasonably sound conclusions can be drawn concerning advertising effects. The best results are often obtained by identifying a sample of consumers who have been exposed to a firm's advertising, and a sample which has not, and taking a measure of brand use from each group. Such measures can be made either through specially designed surveys or from the purchase-diary records of continuing consumer panels, such as those maintained by Audits and Surveys, Inc. Even in these instances, though, clear conclusions often cannot be reached because of the secondary effects of advertising. That is, an individual may not have personally seen the advertising for a product but may have been influenced to buy the product by someone who has seen it.

SELECTING A TESTING PROCEDURE

Since there are many specific research techniques and a number of study designs, the alternatives for testing are almost limitless. In the face of this diversity, the key questions are (1) whether to test at all, and (2) what to test.

To Test or Not to Test

Cornelius Dubois has suggested that, before choosing a testing method, a marketer should consider whether to use any method at all.

> Do not test everything—not by any means. One does not need numbers to reject an ad that is in bad taste or too strident, irrelvant, or tinged with the unethical. Some things are too small to test with the instruments available to us. Some are too big and basic to test; some are too nebulous to test, and some are so obvious that they do no require testing.
>
> Copy testing has both its real uses and its real imperfections. It can help us uncover the flaws and weaknesses that might spoil a good ad yet fail to reveal, in the test situation, the strength that a good ad will have in the marketplace.[13]

The rumor mills of advertising are full of horror stories about highly successful campaigns that succeeded because the advertiser ignored negative copy tests and ran the advertisement anyway. It is widely rumored, for example, that the Avis "We're Only No. 2" campaign bombed out in pretesting,[14] that the Ajax "White Knight" was a pretest mediocrity, and it is by no means certain that "Charlie" would have become a leading seller among perfumes had it been subjected to the obstacles of advertising research rather than owing its existence to the inspiration of Charles Revson.

The question of testing or not testing advertising is certainly a relevant one. Most major advertisers do test advertisements and commercials behind which they plan to put substantial resources, although they do not always abide by the test results. Sometimes they will ignore negative research findings if, on the basis of creative judgment, they strongly believe the advertising should be used. Ultimately, the question of testing or not testing can only be resolved by the marketing or advertising manager in terms of such criteria as the magnitude of the expenditures involved, personal belief in the adequacy of the advertising in question, and willingness to take risks. All of these criteria are subjective and, despite the advances of decision theory, do not lend themselves to computerized solutions.

What to Test

The second question, what to test, is even more provocative than the question of whether to test at all. It is more provocative because it leads to more alternatives, and also because it raises the basic question of what advertising is expected to accomplish.

In the earlier discussion of advertising testing, we recognized that advertising may be tested at various stages. At one extreme, we can test an advertising concept for its promise; at the other extreme, we can test a completed advertisement for its effectiveness against some predetermined objective. Advertising practitioners differ in their orientation toward testing in this regard. Arthur Pearson, who was director of marketing services for Clairol in the mid-1970s, believed that the principle role of copy testing is to decide whether to run a particular piece of advertising or not. On the other hand, Larry Light, senior vice-president and research director for a major advertising agency during the same period, argued less for

13. Cornelius Dubois, "Copy Testing," in *Handbook of Marketing Research,* R. Ferber, ed. (New York: McGraw-Hill Book Co., 1974), pp. 4–132.

14. L.G. Ernst, "703 Reasons Why Creative People Don't Trust Research," *Advertising Age* (February 10, 1975): 35.

win-lose tests of finished advertisements than for a "disciplined copy development system" that emphasizes the use of advertising research at the preproduction level of writing advertising strategies.[15] While both postions may have merit, the present sophistication of advertising research lends itself to the more tentative application inherent in the second approach than it does to the win-lose philosophy of the first.

The question of what to test raises another question, "What is advertising supposed to do?" If the advertising is expected to generate measurable sales increases, tests of awareness or recall are poor subsitutes. If, on the other hand, the advertising is intended to communicate a certain product attribute to consumers, recall tests may be appropriate.

Before marketing managers can possibly evaluate an advertisement or advertising campaign, they must set forth the specific objectives that the advertising is intended to accomplish. If advertising objectives are not clearly spelled out, rational evaluation is impossible. If they are clearly spelled out, evaluation is only difficult.

Sometimes it may not be possible to isolate the effects of advertising from other marketing activities, particularly when the ultimate goal of advertising is to increase sales. Under such conditions, marketing and advertising managers may have to forsake the evaluation of advertising alone for an evaluation of the entire marketing program. Alternatively, they may choose to evaluate the advertising on the basis of substitute goals, such as its ability to generate awareness or to create favorable attitudes among an identifiable group of consumers. This is a matter of choice, and different choices will be made by different managers.

However, advertising is generally such a major part of the marketing effort for consumer products and demands such a substantial share of company resources as an investment that effective marketing and advertising managers find it necessary to come to terms with some form of advertising measurement that is acceptable both to them and their management. And, the more systematic the measurement program, the more adequate it becomes in helping develop effective advertising.

15. "Copy testing is still a nebulous area," *Advertising Age* (December 1, 1975): 54.

SUMMARY

Evaluation is a key part of the marketing effort. It is not difficult to evaluate the success or failure of a marketing plan in its entirety, since the essential criterion is whether or not it achieves the projected sales goal within the constraints of available funds. What is difficult to ascertain is the extent to which individual elements of the marketing plan contribute to its success or failure. In the case of a plan that fails to achieve its objectives, the problem becomes one of determining where the problem lies.

The focus of the chapter is on advertising evaluation. There are three kinds of advertising research—budget research, audience research, and copy research. Although these three forms of research are closely interrelated, copy research is isolated for consideration in this chapter.

There are a number of problems in relating advertising to sales. In most cases, short-term sales results are inadequate as a basis for evaluating advertising effectiveness. As a consequence, the most valid measure of advertising, in most cases, is a measure of its communication value.

Copy testing has three stages of development—the preliminary level where concepts are tested and the elements of the advertisement assessed, the pretesting stage in which complete advertisements or commercials are tested prior to use, and a posttesting stage in which the effects of advertising are measured after company funds have been placed behind it. Qualitatively, posttesting differs from the other stages in that preliminary testing and pretesting are undertaken to develop advertising and to reduce risk; posttesting, on the other hand, occurs after advertising funds have been committed and is a final evaluation.

The actual testing procedures employed depend upon what the advertisement is supposed to do and the predilection of those authorizing the test.

Different philosophies of copy testing exist within the advertising industry. For some, copy testing should be an integral part of copy development and be used to provide guidance and direction. For others, testing should be used in the final stage to determine whether or not a particular ad or commercial should be used. In view of the limitations surrounding copy testing methods, the first approach may be the wisest.

QUESTIONS

1. How does one evaluate the effectiveness of a marketing plan? Why is it easier to evaluate the effectiveness of a marketing plan than to evaluate advertising effectiveness?
2. Identify and explain the three major areas of advertising research.
3. Identify the reasons that short-term sales or marketing share changes may be misleading measures of advertising effectiveness.
4. What are the two basic functions of copy testing? Why are different testing measures required for these two functions?
5. Explain what is meant by *pretesting*. Give examples.
6. What are the different philosophies underlying *attitude* tests versus *recall* tests?
7. Explain what is meant by a *simulated* media test, and give examples of such tests.
8. How does posttesting differ from preliminary testing and pretesting? Why is this difference important?
9. Some research practitioners argue that aided recall questions are a better measure of advertising effectiveness than unaided questions. What is the basis for this argument?
10. Why is the question "what to test" such an important one in advertising research?

PROBLEM

You are the marketing research director of a company that markets a line of kitchen appliances—refrigerators, ranges, washers, dryers, and so forth. All of these items are sold under the name of Kitchen-Helpers. While the advertising budgets for the individual appliances differ in size, the total company expenditure for consumer advertising exceeds $30 million.

A new advertising director has just joined the company, and one of her major priorities is to establish a system for evaluating company advertising, most of which appears in print media—women's magazines and the shelter books.

She has asked you to come to her office to discuss the question of advertising measurement. She opens the conversation with the following comment: "I'm surprised that a company as well known as Kitchen-Helpers has never had a formal program of advertis-

ing measurement. We've done a lot of market research on who our target markets are and on their buying practices, but, in looking through our records, I find that we haven't the slightest idea how good our advertising is or how effective our advertising programs have been. I know there is a lot of controversy about advertising research, but I also am convinced that we are going to have to start using some. I'd like you to give the matter some thought during the next couple of days, and then let's get together again and kick around some ideas."

Assignment

Prepare yourself for this meeting by reviewing the kinds of research that might be done, and which of them you think would be most helpful; list the reasons for your decisions.

23

Legal Restrictions and The Future of Advertising

Public Attitudes

The following quotation is taken from a statement of Secretary of Commerce Juanita M. Kreps before the State, Justice, Commerce, and Judiciary Subcommittee of the House Committee on Appropriations.

The public view is that corporations could do much more to protect and serve the public interest. In a 1975 Peter Hart poll, 49 percent agreed that "big business is the source of most of what's wrong in the country today." A 1977 Harris Survey reported that consumers believe they are consistently shortchanged on product quality, safety, repairs, and guarantees; that manufacturers do not really care about the consumer; and that business is responsible for a decline in the quality of life in America. Only last week, a CBS-New York Times poll reported that half the public believes that the energy crises, far from being real, was manufactured to increase prices and profits of the oil companies.

Given these attitudes, it is not surprising that in the last 15 years Congress has enacted—by conservative count—more than 150 major pieces of legislation regulating or restricting business activities as they affect society. Federal standards and regulations are an emphatic manifestation of public concern with business social performance.[1]

Malcolm Hereford's Cows

Malcolm Hereford's Cows is a line of sweet-tasting, milk-type alcoholic drinks marketed by Heublein, Inc. The target markets for the brand are middle-aged women and blacks, and Heublein's market research indicates that it is precisely these groups that consume the product. Betty Furness, a long-time consumer advocate, decided that the brand was really a "very seductive" appeal to twelve- to fourteen-year-olds.

To support her theory, Furness conducted an experiment on her NBC-TV "Today" show in which she interviewed young high school pupils on teenage drinking habits and then invited the pupils to sample

---

1. "Statement of Secretary of Commerce Juanita M. Kreps before The State, Justice, Commerce and Judiciary Subcommittee of The House Committee on Appropriations, January 23, 1978," United States Department of Commerce, Office of the Secretary, Washington D.C., 20230, p. 2

the Heublein product. The kids liked it, so Furness concluded that Heublein was really attempting to exploit children by marketing a good tasting, alcoholic potable.

In the ensuing hullaballoo, Heublein noted that Furness had violated state laws by serving drinks to minors and demanded that NBC take strong disciplinary action. There is no evidence that NBC (which exists because of advertising revenues) even heard the demand. The moral, as pointed out by *Advertising Age* is that " . . . even the high-minded, in fervent pursuit of their goals, can be tempted to rationalize the indefensible."[2]

FTC versus Aspirin

The analgesic industry has long been a target of the Federal Trade Commission for their therapeutic claims. Leading contenders in the field—Aspirin, Bufferin, Anacin, and Excedrin—each claimed that they were the fastest, the safest, or the most effective. For example, Bayer Aspirin has been touted as the pain reliever most frequently recommended by doctors; St. Joseph Aspirin, for its safety; Anacin, as giving the fastest relief; Bufferin, as relieving headaches while preventing the upset stomach often associated with taking aspirin; and Excedrin as the remedy for "big" headaches. In short, each competitor claimed to be better than the others in some respect.

The FTC insisted that these products could not be "best" simultaneously and sponsored a clinical study in an attempt to gain conclusive evidence on the relative efficacy of the products in question. Notwithstanding the fact that the FTC study was poorly conceived and badly designed, it concluded that there were no "significant" differences in the pain-relieving abilities of the brands tested.

Bayer Aspirin seized upon the government's findings and began using advertising phrases such as: " . . . government supported medical team" whose findings were " . . . reported in the highly authoritative *Journal of the American Medical Association* . . . had found Bayer Aspirin equal to the higher-priced pain reliever." In addition, based on these same clinical findings, Bayer advertising claimed that Bayer was as gentle as a sugar pill and was as gentle on the stomach as any analgesic containing more than one ingredient. It should be noted at this point that all of

these claims were absolutely true in accordance with FTC-sponsored clinical research.

The FTC issued a complaint against the makers of Bayer Aspirin asking for a temporary injunction restraining the company from making these claims. The Federal Court denied the injunction, ruling that the claims did not misrepresent the government's findings.[3]

This is the climate in which marketing functions. Under these conditions, it is a modern miracle that it functions at all. In the first instance cited above, big business is blamed by consumers for a decline in the quality of life and for the energy shortage, with no recognition given to the facts that an explosive, worldwide population growth and consumer demands for an ever-increasing standard of material goods may really be the root of the problem. In the second example, a television personality launches an unjustified attack on a segment of business. And, in the third case, a government regulatory agency—the FTC— applies a double standard to its own research. The FTC wants to use its clinical findings against the industry, but is unwilling to have members of this industry use the same findings in its defense.

This is not to say that marketers are blameless. Consider the following noteworthy cases.

The Drug Research Corporation advertised Regimen tablets as being capable of bringing about large losses in body weight in humans without the reduction of food intake. A federal court found the advertiser guilty of false advertising, of faked laboratory reports, and of the use of television models who resorted to drastic dieting rather than using Regimen as claimed.

A Dr. Samuel Massengell packaged sulfanilamide in a liquid form and sold it as a patent medicine called Elixir Sulfanilamide. The product had not been properly tested for toxicity, and it ultimately caused seventy-three deaths in seven states before the Food and Drug Administration seized the remaining supplies.

Rapid Shave produced a television commercial that purported to show the moisterizing effects of the brand by applying it to sandpaper and then removing the sand with one stroke of a razor. Actually, sandpaper was not used in the demonstration. Instead, loose sand was spread on plexiglas to simulate sandpaper.

---

2. "The Furness fiasco," *Advertising Age* (February 6, 1978): 16.

3. "The FTC and Aspirin Advertising—'Headaches for All,'" in Edward C. Bursk and Stephen A. Grayser, *Advanced Cases in Marketing Management* (Englewood Cliffs, New Jersey: Prentice-Hall, Inc., 1968), pp. 184–91.

Campbell's Soup placed marbles in the bottom of a bowl of soup that was used in a television demonstration. The marbles caused the vegetables in the soup to rise to the top where they could be seen, giving the impression that the product contained more vegetables than it actually did. The Campbell defense was that, if marbles were not used, the vegetables sank to the bottom, giving the impression that the bowl contained less vegetables than it actually did.

Profile bread advertising claimed that each slice contained fewer calories than competitive breads without bothering to point out that the slices were also thinner than the slices of competitive products. The FTC required the company to devote 25 percent of its advertising for a year to correct the erroneous "low calory" impression that had been created.

Sears attracted consumers to its stores by advertising an attractive sewing machine for $58. According to an FTC complaint, sales people disparaged the item by such statements as: "(1) the advertised sewing machines are noisy and are not guaranteed for as long a period of time as the firm's more expensive models; (2) certain of them will not sew straight stitch, zig zag stitch, or in reverse; (3) none of the advertised sewing machines is available for sale and, if ordered, there will be long delays in delivery."[4]

Many other examples can be cited. In some cases, advertising is the culprit; in some, other marketing practices have been singled out. In some cases, the intent to deceive is apparent; in others, it is moot. Advertisers have won some cases in courts; others have been won by the government. The point is that marketers themselves have contributed to the woes of the industry and must bear some fault for consumer distrust and government intervention into the marketing process.

THE IMPORTANCE OF ADVERTISING

Business became subject to special legislation regulating its activities with the passage of the Sherman Antitrust Act in 1890. Subsequent legislation has extended government concern to the complete range of marketing activities—products, pricing, selling practices, sales promotion, and advertising. A number of government regulatory agencies have been established to monitor marketing practices, and special-interest

---

4. *In re Sears, Roebuck & Co.*, CCH 20,652 (July 1974); BNA ATRR no. 672 (July 16, 1974) A–20. Quoted material from *Journal of Marketing* (January 1975): 101.

consumer groups have been increasingly active in recent years. In 1962, President Kennedy enunciated certain consumer rights—the right to safety; the right to be informed; the right to choose; and the right to be heard—that have had far-reaching implications for marketing and advertising. There has been a persistent and controversial movement to establish a Department of Consumer Affairs at the cabinet level of the federal government.

As the most visible feature of marketing in the lives of most consumers, advertising often bears the brunt of consumer criticism and government activity. This is not to say that legislation governing other marketing practices has been neglected. Indeed, the Robinson-Patman Act of 1936, dealing as it does with a wide range of competitive activities, is often a central concern of United States marketers. But advertising is the part of marketing that most people see. For this reason, it is the real and alleged sins of advertising that most often catch our attention. These sins give us conversational tidbits with which to regale our friends and neighbors. They serve as a focus for frustrations when the climax of an exciting television show is interrupted for a commercial announcement or when the product that is supposed to solve all of our problems doesn't live up to our expectations.

There is still another reason for focusing our attention on advertising, however, and that is its importance in the entire competitive process. Over $35 billion a year is spent on advertising. It is a major vehicle for reaching consumers and persuading them to buy. Without the communication economies of advertising, mass marketing in a nation of almost 220 million consumers is unthinkable. And, from the standpoint of the advertising practitioner, legislation and regulatory commissions are often seen as a major threat to advertising creativity.

CHARGES AGAINST ADVERTISING

Economists, legislators, and consumers groups alike have often singled out advertising as the subject of their vituperation. Generally, charges against advertising have taken three tacks:

1. Advertising is a barrier to competition. That is, high advertising expenditures by entrenched brands prevent new brands from entering their markets.
2. Advertising is exploitive in that it coerces and/or persuades consumers to buy products they do not need.

3. Advertising offends and deceives consumers because advertising claims are often in poor taste, exaggerated, misleading, and downright false.

Together, these charges have placed the industry on the defensive, generated innumerable legislative restrictions, and given birth to a variety of regulatory agencies. Some of the resulting controls surrounding advertising are undoubtedly desirable and in the interest of both the general public and the advertising industry itself. Some are more questionable in nature. And some, in my opinion, represent harrassment.

The basic purpose of this chapter is to describe some of the agencies and legislation that exert control over advertising. Before doing so, however, let us look briefly at the three major charges against the industry.

Advertising as a Barrier to Competition

The charge that advertising acts as a barrier to competition is based on the assertion that the cost of advertising a new product is prohibitive for any but the giants of an industry. Thus, it is argued that the advertising superiority of entrenched firms enables them to block new competitors from entering the market, thereby fostering monopolies, high prices, and excessive profits.

If this charge were valid, one would expect to find: (1) little brand switching from well-established brands to newly introduced ones, (2) a positive correlation between advertising intensity and the concentration of sales for consumer product industries (for example, advertising expenditures would be high in those industries dominated by a few major companies and correspondingly lower in fields characterized by many competitors.), and (3) little evidence of new brands encroaching on the sales of the brands of entrenched companies.

Little Brand Switching.   Brand switching is a way of life in many, if not most, consumer fields. Richard Posner, testifying before a congressional subcommittee on monopoly, pointed out

No proof has yet been offered that it is easier for the first advertiser to win a consumer's patronage than it is for a second advertiser to shift it to him. The fact that the soap companies are constantly bringing out new brands suggests a taste for novelty on the part of the consumer that does not square with the theory of the first advertiser's advantage.[5]

Soaps are not the only industry in which new products and brands appear to titillate the interest of consumers. Witness the personal care industry, cereals, automobiles, fashions, household appliances, proprietary drugs, and any number of other consumer industries that are characterized by an unceasing parade of new products and brands. In truth, consumers are alert to new offerings in most product fields, and it is through advertising that these brands have an opportunity for consumer exposure.

Correlation between Advertising and Sales.   The expectation of a positive correlation between the intensity of advertising and the concentration of sales in consumer goods industries has been deposed by University of Chicago economist Lester G. Telser, who undertook a study of the concentration of industry-advertising relationships. On the basis of his analysis, he concluded

Changes in concentration and advertising intensity ought to move in the same direction according to the hypothesis that advertising lessens competition. The data for the period 1947–1957 show, if anything, the opposite relation—an inverse association between changes in advertising intensity and changes in concentration. The weakness of the hypothesis claiming a positive association between advertising and monopoly is shown by another fact. Industries that produce industrial goods hardly advertise and yet may be highly concentrated. Thus, if all manufacturing industries were examined to determine the relations between advertising intensity and the concentration of sales among the leading firms, no systematic pattern would emerge.[6]

Little Success of New Brands.   The expectation that there would be little evidence of new brands encroaching on the sales of entrenched companies is negated by the inroads made on the markets of General Motors, Ford, and Chrysler by imports; the effect of Timex on Bulova; Sony's invasion of the television market; Tylenol's entry into the analgesic market; Miller's displacement of Schlitz as the number two brewery in the beer field; Polaroid's success in Kodak's domain; Wilkinson's coup against Gillett and Schick; and dozens of other examples that could be given.

Economist Jules Bachman, in a book titled *Advertising and Competition,* concludes that entry into new markets is easier when advertising can be used[7] and

5. Richard Posner, quoted in U.S. Congress Subcommittee on Monopoly of the Senate Select Committee on Small Business, *Role of the Giant Corporations,* part I-A, July, 1969, p. 923.

6. L.G. Telser, "Some Aspects of the Economics of Advertising," *Journal of Business* (April, 1968), as reproduced in *Advertising's Role in Society,* John S. Wright and John E. Mertes, eds. (St. Paul, Minnesota: West Publishing Co., 1974), pp. 38–39.

7. Jules Bachman, *Advertising and Competition* (New York: New York University Press, 1967), p. 157.

according to *Fortune* magazine, research by economist Harold Demsetz and others has " . . . pretty well disposed of the myth that advertising is a source of monopoly power."[8]

In summary, the weight of systematic research indicates that advertising is not a barrier to entry into new fields. Rather, as Bachman so succinctly suggests, it makes entry possible.

Advertising as Exploitive

The exploitation criticism of advertising is more subjective than the barrier to entry charge and consequently more difficult to deal with. Critics who take this road suggest that advertising is manipulative and that it coerces people into buying products they do not want. The critics also imply that the use of persuasion by marketers is unethical. These writers say that advertising's " . . . prime if not only function is to provide useful information, and not to carry a 'persuasive' or 'coercive' message."[9] One problem with this point of view is that it is incredibly naïve and fails to recognize that the distinction between "information" and "persuasion" is hard to define. For example, the U.S. government's National Goals Research Staff has made the following observation:

In the traditional view, the product is seen as basically a commodity serving a single well-defined purpose, and information is that which tells the consumer about how that purpose is served and which warns him about dangers that might be risked in using the product. The preferred choice process is seen as rational in the common-sense use of that term. If, however, the product is seen in the modern marketer's view as serving many needs, some of them quite subtle, the process of choice is viewed as too complex to be described by any simple notion of rationality. Thus, anything that influences a consumer's choice might be considered as information. In this latter view, the association of a product with a favorable mood (e.g., depicting a food as creating a harmonious family atmosphere or a toiletry as attracting the opposite sex) is seen as informative, just as is technical information.[10]

Arguments against persuasion can also become ludicrous, as Burck indicates in his discussion of criticisms of door-to-door salespeople

Just take a look, the critics say, at manuals and training courses for salesmen. They are taught how to greet the customer in a positive way, how to find out what she is thinking about, how to ask her for advice, how to induce her to say something that the salesman can later use to his advantage, how to anticipate her objections, and how to ask for the order without seeming to ask for it. Anyone who knows how to get along with people, of course, behaves in this way almost instinctively. In the last analysis, politeness, charm, and good looks themselves can be deceptive.[11]

If persuasion is unethical, then advertising stands guilty as charged because advertising *is* persuasion. However, persuasion is not a device used only in advertising. It is firmly ingrained in religious, legal, interpersonal, political, and commercial settings.[12] It hardly seems reasonable to criticize advertising for being persuasive while condoning and even encouraging persuasive behavior in many other areas of our lives. To suggest that persuasion is moral and nonexploitive in some areas, and immoral and exploitive in others requires a further definition of a system of morality where such seeming contradictions are so easily reconciled.

The problem still remains, however. Those who see persuasion as manipulative and immoral will continue to be critical of advertising and pull every persuasive and manipulative stop in their repertoire to convince others of the validity of their position. Those who recognize that persuasion is a legitimate and necessary function in interpersonal and commercial relations will be undisturbed by the charge.

Advertising Offends and Deceives Consumers

This charge against advertising probably has more substance than either of the other two. Some advertising is clearly in poor taste. Some advertising is dishonest. The intentional use of poor taste in advertising is inexcusable, and deliberate dishonesty is both illegal and morally indefensible. The fact that both continue to exist, even though practiced by a minority of advertisers, is a blemish on the industry.

Even these charges, however, are often highly subjective. It is virtually impossible to say anything without offending some individual or some group. Thus, as pointed out earlier, vociferous protests by fundamental religious groups caused General Motors to withdraw its sponsorship of "Jesus of Nazareth," a sensitive portrayal of the life of Christ. A comedian's

8. A.F. Ehrbar, "Martin Fieldstein's Electric-Blue Economic Prescriptions," *Fortune* (February 27, 1978): 54.
9. G. Burck, "High Pressure Consumerism at the Salesman's Door," *Fortune* (July, 1972): 70 ff.
10. National Goals Research Staff, *Toward Balanced Growth: Quantity with Quality* (Washington, D.C.: Superintendent of Documents, Government Printing Office, 1970), p. 139.
11. G. Burck, "High Pressure Consumerism at the Salesman's Door," p. 92.
12. S.A. Greyser, "Advertising: Attacks and Counters," *Harvard Business Review* **50** (March-April, 1972): 22 ff.

burlesque of the "old south," circa 1850, resulted in the cancellation of several carloads of the sponsor's product by offended southern merchants who were still fighting the civil war, and a leading diet product replaced a campaign showing product users resisting tempting foods such as cakes, peanuts, and potato chips because of angry protests by segments of the baked goods and snacks industry. Further, during a period, such as we are now experiencing, in which traditional cultural values concerning sex, religion, ethnic groups, women's rights, and so forth are undergoing rapid change, it is often difficult to avoid offending the taste of someone.

Similarly, the distinction between *deception* and product *puffery* is not always easily drawn. The automobile advertisement that claims that a particular car will give 30 miles per gallon in city driving whereas objective tests show that it only delivers 15 miles per gallon is clearly guilty of deception. However, the same advertisement that claims the same automobile is the "epitomy of luxury and beauty" is only expressing a subjective opinion because there are no objective standards for luxury and beauty. Regulatory agencies and the courts have, historically, recognized the legitimacy of a certain amount of product puffery, while ruling against deception. The Campbell soup commercial referred to earlier falls into a grey area between deception and puffery. When the company put marbles in the bottom of the bowl so that the vegetables could be seen, it was undoubtedly exaggerating the volume of vegetable that the soup contained. On the other hand, when it did not use marbles, the vegetables (which are present in substantial quantity) sank to the bottom and became invisible. Is this deception or puffery? In this particular case, the FTC ruled that it was deception, and most people would agree with this ruling. On the other hand, a charge that Dry Ban deodorant misrepresented its product by claiming that it was a dry spray, not wet when applied to the body, left no residue, and was superior to competing products for these reasons was overruled, even though the product is not all that dry. The FTC commissioners ruled that the ads represented the product's dryness only as compared to a leading competitive spray and did not claim *absolute* dryness. Thus, product puffery won the day.

Many consumers do not distinguish between misrepresentation and puffery when asked their opinion of advertising's truthfulness. Yet, in terms of their response to advertising, they exhibit more confidence than their survey answers indicate. For example, *U.S. News and World Report* recently published a massive report on consumers' opinions of various business, political, and professional institutions. One finding of the report was that only 7 percent of the respondents

gave business a good grade on truth in advertising. *Advertising Age* pointed out that "clearly this level of skepticism is unrelated to fact."[13]

Most major advertisers go to considerable lengths (more than consumers realize) to prevent the use of poor taste and misrepresentation in advertising, but often their efforts are frustrated by fly-by-night operators and the public's willingness to believe the worst. It is this climate that has caused the advertising industry, regulatory agencies, and legislative bodies to focus on the problem of advertising misrepresentation. In the following material, we will examine the various agencies, and some of the FTC policies that have been adopted to keep advertising honest.

REGULATORY AGENCIES

There are a number of regulatory agencies established to monitor advertising. Some of these agencies are established by legislation; others are inspired by industry groups. The effectiveness of the various agencies generally depends upon the extent to which they have and use sanctions against offenders. For example, because the FTC is a federal agency, it has the weight of the federal government behind it and often seeks legal injunctions to enforce its rulings. On the other hand, many industry-organized, regulatory groups are relatively weak. In the following material, a number of the better-known regulatory agencies will be identified and briefly discussed.

Federal Regulatory Agencies

There are several federal regulatory agencies that have an impact on advertising and marketing. The *Securities and Exchange Commission* (SEC) has control over all advertising of public offerings of stocks and bonds, and it is a criminal offense to advertise a security under SEC jurisdiction without having it registered under the SEC (except for certian legal exemptions relating to small offerings). The *Alcohol Tax Unit of the U.S. Treasurey Department* has jurisdiction over a number of practices relating to the sale and advertising of distilled spirits; these regulations include packaging, labeling, and advertising. The *U.S. Postal Department* has authority to stop the delivery of mail (including magazines) from firms using the mails to defraud and to stop the dissemination of obscene materials.

Three federal agencies with the most overall impact on advertising are the *Federal Trade Commission*

13. "Why business rates low," *Advertising Age* (February 20, 1978): p. 12.

(*FTC*), the *Federal Communications Commission* (*FCC*), and the *Food and Drug Administration* (*FDA*).

The Federal Trade Commission. The FTC was initially established in 1914 as a friend of the court to provide technical counsel to the courts in cases involving "restraint of trade" arising from the Sherman Antitrust Act of 1890 and to investigate complaints related to this issue. Subsequent legislation strengthened and broadened the powers of the FTC, extending its jurisdiction into pricing, packaging, selling practices, sales promotion, and advertising. The FTC was also given the authority to initiate actions "in the public interest," in addition to its authority to investigate complaints brought before it by others. Among its responsibilities is the policing of false advertising. False advertising is interpreted as advertising that misleads through untrue assertions, through implication (even though individual assertions may be true), or through the ommission of material facts. Obviously, such a broad definition of *misleading advertising* often calls for highly subjective judgments on the part of the FTC. It is the subjectivity of many of these judgments that fuels the controversy over regulation in the advertising industry.

For example, in the Wonder Bread case the commission held that the advertising claim "Helps build strong bodies 12 ways" was misleading because it was not unique; other "enriched" breads could make the same claim. In this instance, the commission's ruling was reversed by the federal court system when challenged by the Continental Baking Company, the marketer of Wonder Bread. In the case of Cranapple, the FTC charged that the advertising phrase "more food value" was misleading because, technically, *food value* means calories, a fact not recognized by most consumers. In this case, the offending company expiated its guilt by running corrective advertising designed to explain the meaning of *food value* and to confess that it really means calories.

In carrying out its responsibilities, the commission undertakes an investigation of questionable practices and, if the situation warrants, issues a complaint against the offending advertiser. These complaints are often settled by negotiation. In some cases, a cease and desist order (an order to stop an unlawful practice) will be issued by the FTC and accepted by the advertiser. In other instances, the advertiser will enter into a consent decree (an agreement to stop the practice in question without agreeing to its illegality). If the advertiser wishes to contest the FTC's complaint, a hearing is held before a trial examiner who is a member of the commission's staff. The findings of the trial examiner are considered by the full commission,

which rules upon them and issues orders for remedial action. The decision of the full commission can be appealed by the advertiser through the federal court system—Circuit Courts of Appeal and the Supreme Court.

The most common remedy resulting from FTC hearings is a cease and desist order prohibiting further use of the offending advertising. More recently, the FTC has turned to corrective advertising, requiring the offending company to devote a certain proportion of its advertising funds for a given period of time (one year, for example) explaining to consumers that previous advertising may have been misleading. In rare cases, charges can be brought against responsible individuals, and fines and jail terms can be imposed.

The Federal Communications Commission (FCC). In addition to the FTC, the FCC exerts control over broadcast advertising through its authority to license radio and television stations. The FCC has imposed a number of restrictions on products that may be advertised on broadcast media and on the content of advertising. Prior to the congressional ban on broadcast advertising by cigarette advertisers, the FCC required television stations to schedule antismoking advertising, even though many stations were opposed to running such commercials.

Although the FCC has the power to use its licensing authority to control program and advertising content, it has been reluctant to do so. It has preferred to refer specific complaints and general concerns to other agencies such as the FTC for investigation and action. Nonetheless, the FCC has disapproved (on moral and ethical grounds) advertising by physicians, the clergy, those offering advice on marriage and family matters, lotteries, contraceptive devices, and hard liquor.[14] Yet disapproval does not necessarily include prohibition, although it carries weight and encourages caution on the part of the station licensees.

The Food and Drug Administration (FDA). Since the passage of the Pure Food and Drug Act and the Meat Inspection Act in 1906, the federal government has shown an increasing concern over labels and packaging. Today, the FDA regulates labels, packaging, and other materials that accompany the package for foods, drugs, therapeutic devices, and cosmetics. It is authorized to require warnings and cautions on labels, when appropriate, and has developed detailed rules regulating cents-off and other sales promotions utilizing the package label. With the passage of the

14. Dorothy Cohen, *Advertising* (New York: John Wiley & Sons, 1972): 199.

"truth in packaging" bill in 1966, the authority of the FDA was broadened to include such areas as the use of appropriate words to describe a particular package size (Which is less misleading: large, family, or giant size?), the size and location of type used to indicate the volume or weight of a package, slack-fill (failure to fill the package), and standardization of package sizes.

State and Local Regulation

In addition to federal agencies, advertising is also regulated at the state and local level through a multiplicity of state and local laws and enforcement agencies.

State Regulation.   All states, with the exception of Arkansas, Delaware, Mississippi, and New Mexico, have state laws designed to prevent fraudulent and dishonest advertising. Most state laws are based on a *Printer's Ink* model statute that was prepared by this now defunct advertising trade publication in 1911. The original statutes were directed primarily toward print advertising but have been revised to include broadcast. In addition, many states have established consumer protection agencies in recent years.

State statutes are often poorly enforced because of lack of personnel; in addition, since many state statutes involve criminal rather than civil law, local authorities are often reluctant to enforce them and thereby brand violators as criminals. The problem is made more difficult because interpretations of what is misleading in a particular state may differ from those of other states and from federal practices. Thus, it is quite possible for an advertiser to comply with forty-nine states and the U.S. government, but offend the statutes of the fiftieth state. This is particularly true in product fields such as distilled spirits where local prohibition groups may have forced through highly restrictive legislation. Nonetheless, the existence of state statutes and the possibility that they will be enforced in a particular case, complicates the life of national advertisers and serves as a constraint on their activities.

Local Regulation.   Below the state level, many counties and cities have also enacted laws governing advertising and marketing and, in some cases, have established consumer protection agencies to enforce them. Generally, such action is taken to offer protection against unfair and deceptive practices by local merchants since the federal government is primarily concerned with national and regional advertisers. Local regulation is more characteristic of large population centers, such as New York City, than of less populous areas. New York City, for example, has established a department of consumer affairs and given it teeth through a consumer protection act that covers a wide range of deceptive selling and advertising practices. It has been estimated that over fifty cities and twenty counties have organized consumer protection agencies,[15] and it is probable that this number will increase in the future.

Self-Regulation by Media

Advertising media have the prerogative of rejecting advertising that does not meet the standards of honesty and good taste that individual media have established for the conduct of their business. For example, *Good Housekeeping* follows a practice of testing all products scheduled for advertising in its pages. If the advertising claims used are at variance with the tests, the advertising is not accepted. Brands that are accepted for advertising are entitled to use the *Good Housekeeping* "Seal of Approval" on their labels and in other advertising. *Reader's Digest* does not accept tobacco advertising, and the *New Yorker* refuses ads for feminine hygiene products. Since 1969, *Sunset* magazine has refused advertising for products containing dangerous insecticides, although prior to that time *Sunset* carried more insecticide advertising than any other nonfarm publication. Such decisions are at the discretion of the media, and it is generally recognized that as media become more financially secure they also become more discriminating in terms of the advertising material they will accept.

Similarly, both network and individual stations in the broadcast industry screen commercials for acceptability, although standards may vary widely at the local level, and the thoroughness of the screening process is often suspect. The *Radio Code* and the *Television Code* of the National Association of Broadcasters serve as standards for the industry, and the major networks maintain a continuity department that screens all commercials before they are aired. Relatively strict network standards require that advertisers provide substantiation for claims made about their products.

The National Association of Broadcasters may withdraw its "Seal of Good Practice" or expell stations that fail to conform to the code. However, only about 65 percent of U.S. stations are members of the association, and sanctions are not strictly enforced except under conditions of blatant and persistent violation.

Other groups, such as the Direct Mail Advertising Association and the Outdoor Advertising Association,

15. "Consumers Battle at the Grass Roots," *Business Week* (February 26, 1972): 86–88.

also have "Standards of Ethical Practices" that members are expected to observe. However, supervision is weak; sanctions are limited; and conformance is largely determined by the ethics of the individual firm.

Self-Regulation by Agencies and Advertisers

Both advertising agencies and advertiser organizations promulgate ethical standards of practices. Thus, the American Advertising Federation, the American Association of Advertising Agencies, the Association of National Advertisers, and a number of individual industry organizations have established codes of conduct to which individual members presumably subscribe. Perhaps the most effective of the industry efforts are those of the Better Business Bureau and the National Advertising Review Board.

Better Business Bureau. The Better Business Bureau concept grew out of a "truth in advertising" campaign developed by the American Advertising Federation in 1911. Today, over 240 bureaus operate at both the local and national level to protect consumers against deceptive advertising and selling practices. These bureaus—made up of advertisers, advertising agencies, and media—receive complaints, investigate questionable practices, and maintain files on violators (the files are open to the public). While the bureaus have no legal authority, they often work with local law enforcement officials in prosecuting perpetrators of fraud and misrepresentation. According to one source, bureaus handle over 2.5 million complaints annually and investigate over 40 thousand advertisements for possible violation of truth and accuracy.[16]

National Advertising Review Board. Historically, the National Association of Better Business Bureaus directed some of its attention to national advertising, while local bureaus attended to complaints at the local level. In order to increase the effectiveness of the national organization, a reorganization was undertaken in the early 1970s, and the *Council of Better Business Bureaus* was formed. This new organization (together with the Association of National Advertisers, the American Association of Advertising Agencies, and the American Advertising Federation) set up a policy-making group known as the *National Advertising Review Council.* Under the direction of this council, two regulatory divisions were established: (1) the *National Advertising Division (NAD),* an investigatory body; and (2) the *National Advertising Review Board*

(NARB), an appeals body for NAD decisions. Both divisions are staffed by advertising professionals. Figure 23–1 diagrams the relationship between the NAD and NARB.

The authority of the NAD and NARB is severely limited. They cannot (1) order an advertiser to stop running an ad, (2) levy fines, (3) require corrective advertising, or (4) impose any other legal sanctions. What they can do is (1) bring the moral weight of the industry to bear on practices that are judged injurious to advertising and (2) refer cases to the FTC when offenders do not cooperate. The value of the NARB is indicated by the following statement of an FTC official: "NARB helps relieve us (FTC) of much of the burden in the regulatory area."[17]

Summary of Regulatory Agencies

The advertising industry has a long history of attempts at regulation—some industry inspired and some emanating from the government. Self-regulation has generally met with limited success, requiring ever greater government intervention.

The failure of self-regulation stems, essentially, from two sources: (1) the lack of legal sanctions, and (2) disagreement within the industry as to what constitutes deceptive and misleading advertising in the particular case. It is unfortunate, but true, that the critical judgment of industry members is often dulled by the pressures of competition, and the advertiser who is first to complain about deceptive practices of competitors is much less rigorous in her judgments when it is her own advertising that is under scrutiny. Under these conditions, an increasing trend toward government regulation is probably inevitable.

E.B. Weiss, a knowledgeable and vocal observer of advertising, has concluded that advertising will eventually become a regulated industry, very much like railroads, utilities, and banks.[18] This conclusion gains support from the *U.S. News and World Report* survey referred to earlier. When consumers were asked to rate the performance of thirty-one industries, the four industries receiving the highest ratings were airlines, banks, savings and loan companies, and telephone companies—all regulated industries. And, since it is the consumer who will ultimately influence the extent to which government regulation is imposed on advertising, this survey may well foretell the future.

TRENDS IN ADVERTISING REGULATION

Legislation regulating marketing and advertising is often stated in ambiguous terms giving administrative

---

16. Otto Kleppner, *Advertising Procedure,* 6th ed. (Englewood Cliffs, New Jersey: Prentice-Hall, Inc., 1973), p. 687.

17. *Advertising Age* (June 6, 1975), p. 66.
18. E.B. Weiss, "51 New Advertising Marketing Regulations Offer Lively Future," *Advertising Age* (October 25, 1971).

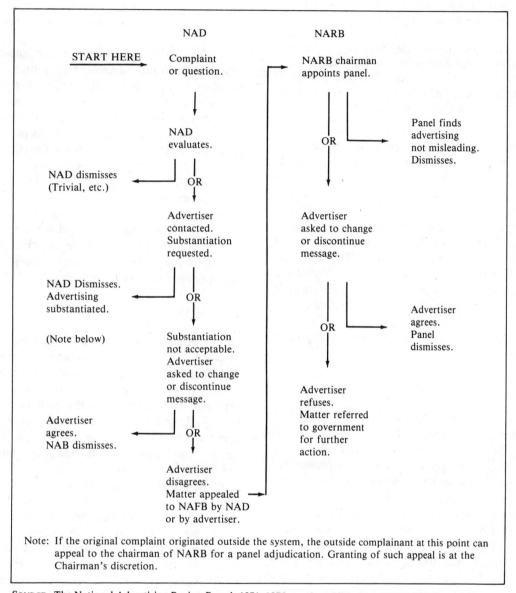

NAD

NARB

START HERE ⟶ Complaint or question.

NARB chairman appoints panel.

NAD evaluates.

Panel finds advertising not misleading. Dismisses.

NAD dismisses (Trivial, etc.) ⟵ OR

Advertiser contacted. Substantiation requested.

Advertiser asked to change or discontinue message.

NAD Dismisses. Advertising substantiated.

(Note below) ⟵ OR

Advertiser agrees. Panel dismisses.

Substantiation not acceptable. Advertiser asked to change or discontinue message.

Advertiser agrees. NAB dismisses. ⟵ OR

Advertiser refuses. Matter referred to government for further action.

Advertiser disagrees. Matter appealed to NAFB by NAD or by advertiser.

Note: If the original complaint originated outside the system, the outside complainant at this point can appeal to the chairman of NARB for a panel adjudication. Granting of such appeal is at the Chairman's discretion.

SOURCE: The National Advertising Review Board: 1971–1975, p. 12, published by NARB, 1975.

Figure 23–1.   Diagram of steps followed by NAD and NARB in dealing with complaints filed against an advertiser.

agencies such as the FTC the task of developing more precise guidelines and interpretations. Thus, the Supreme Court has observed that "Precision of expression is not an outstanding characteristic of the Robinson-Patman Act,"[19] and Lowell Mason, a former FTC commissioner, has said: "Nowhere is institutional whim more apparent and more deadly than in the choice of defendants the FTC sues under the Robinson-Patman Act."[20]

Similar charges might be made against Section 15 of the Wheeler-Lea Act, which defines false advertising in the following way:

The term "false advertisement" means an advertisement, other than labeling, which is misleading in a ma-

19. 346 U.S. 6173 Supreme Court 1017.

20. "Robinson-Patman Act: It Demands a Closer Look Now," *Printer's Ink* (October 20, 1961): 24.

terial respect; and in determining whether any advertisement is misleading there shall be taken into account (among other things) not only representations made or suggested by statement, word, design, device, sound, or any combination thereof, but also the extent to which the advertisement fails to reveal facts material in the light of such representations or material with respect to consequences which may result from the use of the commodity to which the advertisement relates under the conditions prescribed in said advertisement or under conditions as are customary or usual.

Under this definition, false advertising is almost anything the FTC, FTC staff, complainants, or competitors decide is false advertising. As a consequence, the FTC has an extremely broad mandate in determining the truth or falsity of an ad. This fact is manifested by some of the charges that the agency has brought against advertisers. Further, under pressure from consumer groups and as a natural expansion of its functions, FTC interpretations of false and misleading advertising tend to become broader with the passage of time. This is in keeping with Parkinson's Law: Tasks will be increased to fill the time allotted to them. In the following material, we will identify some of the trends that appear to be emerging in regard to advertising.

Material Falsity versus False Impressions

Initially, under the Wheeler-Lea Act, advertising had to contain a literal untruth to be held false. However, over time, judicial interpretations have extended the act to include the "creation of false impressions," even though individual statements may be *literally* true. For example, the commission contested a claim by Chevron gasoline that an ingredient, F–310, helps reduce pollution. The FTC argued that, while F–310 did indeed reduce pollution, the total amount of pollution reduction was not significant and therefore could not be claimed in the advertising.[21] Other examples of the trend are the Profile Bread and Cran-apple cases mentioned earlier.

Burden of Proof

There has also been a trend to shift the burden of proof in cases of false and misleading advertising from the FTC to the advertiser. In effect, this changes the tradition-honored doctrine of innocent until proven guilty to guilty until proven innocent. In one instance, the FTC filed a complaint against Pfizer's Unburn, a burn remedy, demanding that Pfizer produce evidence to support its product claim (rather than

requiring the commission to produce evidence that the claims were false). Although this specific charge was dismissed by the full commission, the FTC ruled in the dismissal that it is unlawful for an advertiser to make a product claim unless there is a reasonable basis for it.[22]

In 1971, the FTC initiated an ad substantiation program requiring advertisers to submit, upon demand by the commission, data supporting past or current advertising. A number of advertisers in a variety of fields have been required to submit such information. Recently, as a consequence of this program, FTC fined the STP Corporation $500 thousand and required $200 thousand in corrective advertising for violating an FTC consent order. The FTC charged that STP's advertising claim that its use would decrease oil consumption by 20 percent was based on faulty tests. A company spokesperson pointed out that: "Nowhere (in the FTC complaint) is there any challenge to the efficacy of the product. It's merely a question of some defective tests done years ago."[23]

Limits of Puffery

Subjective claims such as "amazing," "unsurpassed," "beautiful," "better," and so forth are referred to as *puffery*. Puffery has generally been considered beyond the scope of FTC authority because such statements represent personal opinions that cannot be measured by objective tests. One observer, however, has noted that the FTC has never fully accepted puffery as a legitimate advertising tool and has grown more intolerant of it in recent years.[24]

While puffery has not yet been banned, it has become an object of scrutiny by the FTC. The head of the FTC's Bureau of Consumer Protection has suggested that puffery is permissible when (1) the claim is immaterial; (2) the exaggeration is insubstantial; and (3) the exaggeration is of a type that cannot be measured.[25] Considering the American penchant for measuring everything, regardless of whether the measures are valid, these guidelines seem as subjective as puffery itself.

Full Disclosure

There has been a spate of legislation in recent years requiring full disclosure. The philosophy behind this

21. John Revett, "Standard Oil, FTC Face Off over F-310," *Advertising Age* (April 3, 1972): p. 8 ff.

22. Stanley E. Cohen, "Enforcer Petofsky explains FTC's new get tough policy," *Advertising Age* (January 18, 1971): 14.

23. "Corrective ads for STP publicize settlement costs to business execs," *Advertising Age* (February 13, 1978): p. 1 ff.

24. Ivan L. Preston, "Puffery in advertising," *Advertising Age* (February 14, 1972): 39–40.

25. Stanley E. Cohen, "TV revolutionized FTC's limits of permissible puffery," *Advertising Age* (March 24, 1971): p. 121.

legislation is that consumer must be given sufficient information about products in order to make an informed judgment. Under this reasoning, advertisers are expected not only to provide information of the positive attributes of their products but also on the negative features when these features may constitute a health, safety, or more recently, an economic hazard. For example, drug manufacturers are required to report on the side effects and contraindications of their products. For a number of years, cigarette manufacturers have had to include a health warning on their packages. The "Truth in Lending" law requires that the actual amounts and interest rates for installment loans and credit be publicized. Automobile manufacturers must include a suggested list price on new automobiles. Flammable fabrics must be clearly labeled as such, and a number of other legislative acts require a fuller disclosure of product information than has traditionally been offered in advertising and on labels.

Much of this legislation is clearly desirable. Advertisers' concern for the future, however, is that administrative agency interpretations of "full disclosure" will exceed good judgment. It has been suggested that a government that insists on protecting consumers from the consequences of their own folly will create a nation of fools. There is concern in some quarters that the federal government is well on its way to this consequence.

Unique Claims

Traditionally, advertising has thrived on unique claims. The U.S.P. (unique selling proposition) theory of advertising holds that marketing success depends upon the use of unique product claims, whether these claims are truly unique or simply preempted. The FTC has argued that uniqueness must be real in order to avoid being misleading. The landmark case in this area is the Wonder Bread example used earlier in which uniqueness is implied by the claim "Helps Build Strong Bodies 12 Ways." The FTC charged that since this same claim could be made by any producer of an enriched bread Wonder Bread was guilty of deceptive advertising. FTC's challenge was not sustained by the courts, but one can expect that it will keep on trying.

Emotional Claims

Much advertising is based on the social and psychological benefits that will accrue from using a product. Implications of beauty, confidence, social success, prestige, masculinity, femininity, and so forth are the advertising bases of most personal care items as well as a variety of other highly visible products. Many be-

lieve that the FTC would like to broaden the concept of false advertising to include these implied psychological benefits, although no such complaints have been filed thus far.

Nutritional Claims

Claims of nutritional benefits came under fire from the FTC in the mid-1970s; the cereal and confection industries bore the brunt of the attack. For example, the FTC forced Carnation to change its advertising for Instant Breakfast because the company was exaggerating the nutritional claims of its product. Cereal companies have been challenged for their nutritional claims; the FTC has contended that much of the nutritional value of ready-to-eat cereals comes from the milk that is poured over the cereal, not from the cereal itself. Milky Way candy advertising was cited for emphasizing the milk content of the product; Hostess cupcakes, for focusing on the iron and vitamin content of this delicacy; and Hi-C, both because of the product's name and because of the claim that Hi-C is the "sensible drink."

These are only a few of the nutritional cases initiated by the FTC. Advertisers who make nutritional claims should be well buttressed with nutritional and irrefutable facts supporting their copy.

Corrective Advertising

One rapidly growing practice of the FTC is to require corrective advertising from companies who are unsuccessful in defending themselves against its charges. This practice has emerged because the commission felt that existing penalties were too light and were insufficient to deter advertisers from making false and misleading statements. How far the doctrine of corrective advertising can be extended before it invokes a legislative rebuke under pressure from business interests is an open question. Certainly, the use of sanctions more severe than those provided by the original legislation is a bold extension of administrative authority.

Comparative Ads

The FTC has taken a strong position in favor of comparative advertising. This stand on the part of FTC is of particular interest because comparative advertising is a highly controversial issue among advertisers and advertising agencies. Although comparative advertising has been used sporadically in the past (usually comparing the advertised product with brand X) its modern-day use emphasizes the naming of competitive brands in the comparison. Schick Flexamatic electric shaver ushered in the modern trend in 1972 with the claim that Schick was superior to Norelco, Ronson, and Remington.[26] Subsequently, comparative advertising has become rampant in other fields, notably foods, antiperspirants, automobiles, and analgesics.

Opponents of comparative advertising argue that it creates confusion and publicizes competitive brand names and that, more often than not, the consumer who remembers the comparison forgets which brand was best. The president of the Council of Better Business Bureaus has blasted comparative advertising "as damaging to ad creditability and a negative value in business conduct."[27]

Advertisers who approve of comparative advertising argue that it encourages a flow of facts and enables consumers to make informed judgments. Frankly, there is little hard evidence to support either point of view. On balance, the little-known brand probably benefits by comparing itself to a well-known competitor, gaining acceptance and stature from the association. On the other hand, its use by the leader in a field probably is more detrimental than helpful. Occasionally, comparative advertising does produce some amusing copy, as exemplified by the following Coca-Cola commercial run in response to Pepsi-Cola's comparative taste-tests which demonstrate that consumers prefer Pepsi to Coke.

The Coke TV spot shows an interviewer with his back to the camera asking a respondent to "first try 'S', sir, then 'L'."
Respondent: "Come from a big city, don't you, boy?"
Interviewer: "Yes, I do."
Respondent: "Thought so. You got one of those skinny little big city mouths. Now look here. Let me tell you something. You can't tell nothing from no test like this. Give me that bottle of Coke. I'll show you how we drink them down here. We don't sit around in no fancy bar taking little bitty sips and wearing skinny britches and pointy lizard shoes. You can't come down here flim-flamming honest people. You got to watch what you do down here, boy."
Announcer: "There's more to Coke. Coke adds life."

Advertising to Children

During the 1970s, various consumer groups became agitated over advertising to children. Their basic argument was that children are unable to distinguish between fact and fancy and between truth and exag-

geration and that they must be protected from the onslaughts by predatory advertisers and from the irresponsible persuasiveness of their commercials. They further argued that when parents refused children's requests for products seen in advertising the child-parent relationship was injured. Opponents of this point of view generally respond that (1) if parents don't want their children to see commercials they should turn off the set or that (2) one of the time-honored functions of parents is to protect their own children by saying no occasionally.

Nonetheless, in 1978, the FTC's staff proposed major strictures on children's TV ads. The proposed rule urged by FTC's Bureau of Consumer Protection would

1. Ban all advertising from TV shows seen by substantial audiences of children under 8 because they are too young to understand the selling intent of the message.
2. Ban advertising of sugary foods that pose a dental health risk from TV shows seen by significant numbers of children between ages 8 and 11.
3. Allow continued TV advertising of less hazardous sugared foods to the 8- and 11-year-old group, but only if individual food advertisers found "balancing" nutritional and/or health disclosures.[28]

A curious question raised by these guidelines is: Will FTC commissioners sit in family living rooms to prevent children under 8 from watching inappropriate TV commercials?

At the time of this writing, the final disposition of these recommendations has not been made. If they are adopted, they may or may not reduce children's exposure to television advertising. They will probably decrease the number of professionally produced children's TV shows, however, because there is little profit in producing shows that can't carry advertising. But, that may be a good thing in itself since audience studies indicate that children spend more time watching TV than they spend in school.

Monopoly Effects

A final regulatory trend to be noted is concern over the monopolistic effects of advertising. Despite substantial evidence to the contrary, the FTC continues to subscribe to the "barrier to entry" charge against advertising. One major target of the FTC is the cereal industry.

Specific charges have been filed against Kellogg,

26. "Weston: Comparative ads spur flow of facts," *Advertising Age* (November 4, 1977): p. 6.
27. *Ibid.*
28. "Report by FTC's staff recommends major strictures on children's tv ads," *Advertising Age* (February 27, 1978): 1 ff.

General Mills, General Foods, and Quaker Oats. The charges in the FTC complaint against these companies are many and complex, but the essence of the advertising charges are that the "... practices of proliferating brands, differentiating similar products, and promoting trademarks through extensive advertising result in high barriers to entry into the RTE (ready-to-eat) cereal market."[29]

In 1978, after six years of litigation, 200 trial days, and 29 thousand pages of transcript, the FTC dropped its charges against Quaker Oats, although it is continuing its prosecution of the other defendants. According to *Fortune* magazine, the government's case is "... a muddle of untested economic theory, garbled fact, and contradictory testimony."[30]

In another major case of the 1950s, Procter and Gamble acquired the assets of the Clorox Chemical Company. The FTC forced P&G to divest itself of its Clorox holdings under section 7 of the Clayton Antitrust Act, contending that the effect of the acquisition "... may be to substantially lessen competition, or tend to create a monopoly" in the household-bleach industry. A central argument in the FTC case was that P&G's advertising strength could be used to monopolize the bleach market and to prevent any other company from becoming an effective competitor.[31]

SUMMARY STATEMENT ON ADVERTISING REGULATION

In the preceding pages, we have reviewed the major regulatory agencies, as well as some of the trends in the regulation of advertising. It is apparent that legislative and administrative decisions regarding advertising have become increasingly restrictive and show promise of becoming even more so in the future.

They are probably inevitable for a number of reasons including the following:

1. Advertisers and advertising agencies seem incapable of policing themselves. Difference of opinion in terms of what constitutes deceptive advertising and a reluctance to censor others for fear that others will censor them often mutes criticism.
2. The sheer volume of advertising has become such that it is inevitable that some portion of the industry—through greed, poor judgment, or both—will violate canons of honesty and good taste.
3. In large companies top management often loses touch with some of its corporate activities, and control of these activities is exercised by lower echelon managers whose personal ambitions for success often dull their critical judgment.
4. As product fields become more crowded and competitive, there is a temptation to use deceptive and exaggerated claims as an easy substitute for imagination and product innovation.
5. The constant pressure for corporate profits at a time when costs are being driven up by inflation and prices are being driven down by competition often leads to the substitution of shoddy material and a lowering of quality control standards.
6. There is a growing consumer discontent with many of our institutions. Advertising is one of these institutions.

All of these reasons, and perhaps others, suggest further restraints on advertising activity.

This is unfortunate because the marketing system, fueled by a constant flow of new products and abetted by advertising, has contributed to an unprecedented abundance of goods, wide consumer choice, and a high level of material affluence. It is probable that further restraints on marketing and advertising will blunt this process and deprive it of much of its vitality.

What is the answer? In the broad sense, there is none. We are merely observing a process that is leading toward some unknown conclusion. For the individual firm, the foreseeable future is not that uncertain. Sound marketing practices, systematic planning, respect for the consumer, imaginative innovation, basic integrity, and honest and creative advertising offer an opportunity for the individual company to earn consumer confidence and to achieve marketing success, as indeed a large number of companies have done.

This is the challenge for those who are now preparing themselves for careers in marketing and advertising. This book has been written in the hope that it will aid you in meeting this challenge by providing you with a broad framework and a general procedure for integrating advertising into the marketing effort and using it in a constructive fashion. For those in whom the contents of this book strike a responsive chord and who are planning careers in the business field, I offer an old Irish benediction: "May the wind be always at your back—and may the Lord hold you in the palm of his hand."

SUMMARY

The present climate of marketing is one of widespread criticism. The general public, consumer advocates,

29. Nancy Gibes, "Kellogg calls FTC order devastating," *Advertising Age* (January 31, 1972): 8.
30. Walter Kiechel III, "The Soggy Case Against the Cereal Industry," *Fortune* (April 10, 1978): 49.
31. *Journal of Marketing* (April, 1964): 82.

legislative bodies, and regulatory agencies are often highly vocal in their criticism of advertising and marketing practices. While some of these criticisms are undoubtedly deserved, many are not.

Advertising, because of its visibility, often bears the brunt of much of the criticism directed toward business, even though it is not always guilty of the charges made against it. Generally, most criticism of advertising takes one or more of the following tacks: (1) advertising is a barrier to competition; (2) advertising is exploitive; (3) advertising offends and deceives consumers.

A number of regulatory groups at the national, state, local and industry level have promulgated standards regulating advertising. Self-regulatory industry groups have been relatively ineffective because they lack sanctions against transgressors. The bulk of advertising regulation springs from federal regulatory bodies.

Although the trends in advertising regulation are inevitable, they may also be unfortunate because their ultimate effect may be to dull the edge of competition from which a marketing economy derives much of its vitality.

QUESTIONS

1. Identify the major charges made against advertising by its critics.
2. Evaluate the charge that advertising is a "barrier to competition."
3. Distinguish between *deception* and *puffery* in advertising.
4. Which of the various regulatory bodies—federal, state, and industry—are least effective in regulating advertising? Why is this so?
5. Distinguish between a cease and desist order and a consent decree.
6. Who are the founders of the NAD and the NARB? What is the relationship of these two agencies?
7. Discuss the area of *material falsity* versus *false impression* in advertising. What is the trend in this area by the FTC?
8. Evaluate the use of comparative advertising. What is the FTC's position on this practice?
9. Describe the most recent proposal by the FTC staff concerning advertising to children. Do you think this proposal should be adopted? Why, or why not?
10. The chapter suggests several reasons that increased control of advertising is probably inevitable. What are they? Do you believe that additional control is desirable? Why, or why not?

PROBLEM

Fran Blair, manager of the consumer relations department, was meeting with Ron King, the company's marketing director.

"Ron," Fran said, "I'm getting concerned about our most recent advertising campaign and some of the complaint letters we have been getting."

"What about them?" Ron asked. "They can't be too serious since the most recent Nielsen report shows we've gained five share points in the last six months."

Fran answered: "I see two problems. First, the commercials say that the low phosphate content of our detergent helps reduce pollution. Second, we say it is better for getting out greasy dirt than competitive products."

"It does have a lower phosphate content," Ron said. "That statement's wholly true."

Fran shook her head. "Ron, it's not enough lower to make any difference, and you know it as well as I do."

"Don't worry about it," Ron answered. "Copy tests show that it is one of the strongest statements in our copy, and it's absolutely true."

"What about the superiority claim?" Fran asked. "We don't have any research to support that claim."

"Fran, you worry too much. That's just product puffery, and there is nothing wrong with that."

Assignment

1. How do you evaluate Fran's concerns?
2. If her concerns are justified, what federal agency might bring charges?
3. What are the possible consequences if charges are filed?

4. What recourse would the company have if deceptive advertising charges were brought against them?
5. In Ron King's position, what would your response be to Fran's concerns?

APPENDIX 1

A Sample Marketing Plan

The following marketing plan is for a fictitious product—Golden Grain Grits—which has been devised to illustrate the way in which a marketing plan should be written, and the subject areas with which it typically deals.

Throughout the plan, references are made to exhibits that are not a part of the main body of the plan but which represent detailed analyses from which data appearing in the plan itself have been abstracted and summarized. These detailed exhibits have not been reproduced in this appendix. They serve to emphasize the kinds of backup data to which the reader of a marketing plan may refer if she wants a more detailed understanding of the data presented.

The plan itself is a summarization of relevant findings that have been developed from extensive analyses of all data that might have a bearing on marketing objectives and strategies.

MARKET REVIEW

The following section summarizes key trends and developments in the canned grits market during the past twelve months. Except as otherwise noted, data on retail distribution and sales is drawn from the A.C. Nielsen Food Index.

1. Market Growth

   Total industry retail sales of canned grits products through grocery outlets reached 9.9 million cases during the year ending March 31, 1977, up 5.3 percent from the previous year. Based on the relatively uniform rate of growth during the past five years, it is estimated that the total market during Fiscal 1977–78 will reach 10.4 million cases.

Fiscal	Industry Retail Sales (1000's Cases)	Increase vs. previous year
1973–74	8,523.4	5.0%
1974–75	8,975.1	5.3%
1975–76	9,396.9	4.7%
1976–77	9,894.9	5.3%
1977–78 (est.)	10,399.5	5.1%

2. Regional Variations in Market Development

   Growth of the market continued to be uniform in all regions (exhibit 1) with the result that two regions (S.E. & S.W.) continue to account for over 60 percent of all sales.

Regions	1000's Cases Fiscal 1976-77	% of Cases	% of Population	Consumer Index U.S. Average = 100
N.E.	791.6	8%	22%	36
S.W.	3,166.3	32	20	160
S.E.	2,968.5	30	18	167
N.C.	1,979.0	20	28	71
PAC.	989.5	10	12	83
U.S. TOTAL	9,894.9	100%	100%	100

3. Shipments

   Golden Grain sales for Fiscal 1976–77 are currently estimated at 2,632,000 cases. While this represents an increase of 29,000 cases over last year, it is almost 100,000 cases below our 1976–77 objective of 2,730,000 cases. Failure to meet the case objective is attributed primarily to two factors: (a) trade loading during the final quarter of last year which adversely affected first quarter sales and (b) failure to achieve projected market share of 27.6 (estimated performance, 26.6 percent).

	Quarters				
	1st	2nd	3rd	4th	Total
Est. '76–77 (1000's cs.)	695.0	663.0	681.0	691.0	2,730.0
Actual (1000's cs.)	645.0	651.5	660.0	675.5	2,632.0
Difference (1000,s. cs.)	−50.0	−11.5	−21.0	−15.5	−98.0

4. Competitive Shares

   a. National.   Examination of national share data for Fiscal 1976–77 compared to last year reveals three significant points: (1) Golden Grain's market share has decreased over one share point; (2) Chef's Choice exhibited a significant increase in market share; and (3) the long-term share growth of the All Other group appears to have been arrested.

	Brand Share—Total U.S.			1976-77 Percent Point Change
	1974-75	1975-76	1976-77*	
Golden Grain	27.2	27.7	26.6	−1.1
Chef's Choice	35.0	32.5	35.0	+2.5
Martin's	14.3	15.3	14.5	−0.8
All Other	23.5	24.5	24.0	−0.5
Total	100.0%	100.0%	100.0%	

*Based on 8 months Nielsen data.

b. Regional.   Golden Grain's national share loss can be traced entirely to the Southeastern Region where it experienced a share decline of 4.0 percentage points. This loss is the result of a sharp gain made by Chef's Choice at the expense of all brands.

Regional Share Comparisons for
Golden Grain and Chef's Choice

	1976-77		Share Change vs. Previous Year	
Regions	Golden Grain	Chef's Choice	Golden Grain	Chef's Choice
N.E.	21.0%	32.5%	+0.2	—
S.W.	23.4	34.3	+0.5	−0.2
S.E.	30.2	38.1	−4.0	+5.3
N.C.	24.5	35.1	+0.9	+0.1
PAC.	28.7	37.6	+1.0	−0.4
Total	27.6%	35.0%	−1.2	+2.5

(See Exhibit #4 for detailed analysis of regional brand share trends for all brands)

c. Chain vs. Independent.   Golden Grain's market share continues to lag Chef's Choice in chain stores to a greater extent than it does in independent outlets. This difference in performance is attributable to two factors: (1) distribution weaknesses in chains compared to Chef's Choice and (2) lower sales per store stocking than Chef's Choice in chains compared to independents.

	Chain Outlets		Indep. Outlets	
	Golden Grain	Chef's Choice	Golden Grain	Chef's Choice
Brand Share	24.0%	37.1%	29.0%	32.9%
All Commodity Distribution	75%	85%	76%	78%
Sales Per Month Per Store Stocking	125	175	73	72

5. Distribution.

Regional examination of distribution for Golden Grain and competitive brands indicates: (1) no major changes during the past year and (2) relatively uniform distribution by region. (See Exhibit 5 for detailed distribution analysis.)

6. Competitive Advertising and Promotion.

a. Expenditures.   Both Chef's Choice and Martin's continue to outspend Golden Grain on a per case basis, and Chef's Choice consumer advertising remains the dominant force in the market. Significant competitive developments during the year have included:

(1) Chef's Choice's return in September to the use of daytime network television and increased advertising and promotion activity in the Southeastern Region directed primarily to Blacks.

(2) Martin's shift in media emphasis from national magazines to local spot television concentrated in the top 50 U.S. markets.

Estimated competitive expenditures are summarized below in comparison to Golden Grain.

Estimated Direct Expenditures

January-December 1976 ($1000's)

	Media	Promotion	Total	Est. expenditures per case (retail)
Golden Grain	$1,520.0	$380.0	$1,900.0	$0.72
Chef's Choice	2,200.0	500.0	2,700.0	0.80
Martin's	1,000.0	400.0	1,400.0	1.04

   b. <u>Copy Evaluation</u>. Three measurements of Golden Grain's 1976–77 advertising were employed during the past year.

     (1) Theater tests of one of a pool of three commercials resulted in a competitive perference score of 14.8. This is significantly higher than our previous theater average (9.7) and the average of all competitive commercials tested (8.2).

     (2) Although portfolio tests of our current magazine campaign indicated that it was on a par with last year's effort, subsequent Starch ratings have shown that it is significantly below the current Chef's Choice campaign in terms of both Noted and Seen-Associated scores.

   c. <u>Promotional Activities</u>. Promotion activity in the market continued to be characterized by periodic advertising allowances and intensive use of unbranded display material.

    The only significant developments were (1) the appearance of price-packs employed by Martin's nationally during the Fall (results not yet available, (2) the use by Chef's Choice of heavily advertised mystery shopper promotions in Black areas of the Southeastern Region.

7. Product Evaluation and Development.

   a. <u>Competitive Product Tests</u>. A blind product test conducted by Golden Grain's Marketing Research Department in October indicated that Chef's Choice has improved its product texture and flavor.

    The present Chef's Choice product has apparently overcome disadvantages that it has had in these areas and is fully competitive with Golden Grain in terms of consumer preference.

   b. <u>Product Research</u>. R&D personnel have reported a temporary setback in their development of an improved product containing vitamin additives. Six-month storage tests of several alternative formulas are now being initiated in an attempt to improve product stability.

    Even if current storage tests are successful, manufacturing considerations will preclude introduction of an improved product before 1980.

8. Special Activities.

   a. <u>Product Usage</u>. A special research study undertaken by the Clay Andrews Co. reveals that: (1) Black per-capita consumption of grits is substantially greater than was previously estimated (almost double the consumption of white families), and (2) there has been a sharp increase in multiple unit purchases since the previous study in 1974.

% of Total Transactions:	1974 Study	1977 Study
1 can	50%	36%
2 cans	35	32
3 or more cans	15	32
All transactions	100%	100%

% of Total Unit Volume (All Brands):		
1 can	27%	21%
2 cans	45	27
3 or more cans	28	52
Total Units	100%	100%

   b. <u>Advertising Research</u>. An advertising penetration study conducted in September to establish a benchmark for advertising awareness revealed the following:

	% of Housewives Using Grits	
Brand	Claimed Aware of Advertising	Recalled 1 or More Sales Points
Golden Grain	30.4%	15.3%
Chef's Choice	40.3	17.2
Martin's	15.0	3.1

CONCLUSIONS—PROBLEMS AND OPPORTUNITIES

Based on the foregoing marketing review, the brand group has drawn the following conclusions pertinent to 1977–78 advertising:

1. Market Growth.   The continued strength of the grits market reaffirms our belief that the company should continue its aggressive advertising and promotion activity in order to achieve the long-range goal of brand leadership.
2. Media Strategy.   Our 1976–77 media strategy involving national magazines and spot television in selected markets appears to have been successful in achieving effective message penetration.
3. Advertising Copy.   The encouraging performance of our television commercials reaffirms our confidence in our copy strategy. However, the disappointing Starch performance of our print advertising indicates a need to strengthen the execution of the print effort.
4. Black market.   Two factors contribute to the conclusion that special emphasis should be given to the Black market: (1) new research data showing high per capita consumption of grits by Blacks, and (2) share gains by Chef's Choice in the Southeast Region apparently achieved through stepped-up advertising and promotion activity directed to Blacks.
5. Chain Outlets.   There is a continued need to find effective devices for increasing our distribution and sales per store stocking in chain outlets.
6. Rate of Expenditure.   The elimination of Golden Grain's product advantage resulting from Chef's Choice's recent product improvement increases the burden that will have to be borne by advertising and promotion and decreases our confidence that we can continue to make share gains if we continue to be outspent by competition on both a total and cost-per-case basis.
7. Packaging.   Research findings that indicate an increase in multiple unit purchases by consumers suggest an opportunity for increasing our market share through the introduction of a multiple-pack or a larger package size.

GENERAL MARKETING OBJECTIVES

Proposed strategies and plans for Fiscal 1977–78 are based on the following basic marketing objectives.

1. To attain the following case volume and market share, with a total expenditure of $2,580,000 for advertising and sales promotion:

			Est. Actual Proposed Change:	
	Fiscal 1976–77	Fiscal 1977–78	1977–78 vs. 1976–77
Industry Sales (cases)	9,894,900	10,399,500	+5.1%
Golden Grain Sales	2,632,000	2,870,000	+9.0%
Golden Grain Market Share	26.6%	27.6%	+1.0 points
Expenditures (adv./pro)	$1,900,000	$2,580,000	+36%
Expenditures per case	$.72	$0.90	+25%
Golden Grain Expenditures as % of Chef's Choice Estimated Expenditures	70%	90%*	

(Note: Sales and share figures may not correspond exactly due to inventory changes and minor errors in Nielsen volume estimates.)

* Assumes Chef's Choice will increase expenditures 5 percent, holding case rate constant and yielding a budget of approximately $2,830,000.

2. To develop and test market both a multiple unit package and a large package size in order to ascertain the relative effectiveness of these two approaches in increasing market share—with the long range objective of adding to the product line during Fiscal 1978-79.

GENERAL MARKETING STRATEGY

Recommended activities designed to achieve the foregoing objectives are based on these major points of general marketing strategy:

1. Total planned expenditures for advertising and promotion during Fiscal 1977-78 will be increased substantially versus this year in recognition of: (a) the competitive threat posed by Chef's Choice product improvement and dominant advertising weight, and (b) the objective of reversing Golden Grain's recent competitive setback by achieving volume and market share gains during 1977-78.

2. The augmented total marketing budget for 1977-78 will be allocated generally as follows:
   a. Five percent of the total budget (130,000) will be held in unallocated general reserve against the possibility that the volume objective cannot be met. A special recommendation for the disposition of this reserve will be submitted to management before November 1, 1977.
   b. An additional sum, not to exceed 5 percent of the total budget ($130,000), will be set aside to defray the costs of test marketing and researching consumer acceptance of the multiple-unit and larger packages.
   c. The remaining budget will be allocated between advertising and sales promotion in the ratio of approximately 80 percent/20 percent, implying that
      (1) Primary emphasis will continue to be placed on consumer advertising as a basic selling technique designed to influence brand preference among current users as well to contribute to further growth in the grits market.
      (2) Secondary emphasis will be given to sales promotion techniques capable of achieving temporary, periodic competitive advantages within the existing market.

3. Consistent with recent practice, total marketing support will be distributed to
   a. Provide effective minimum sustaining advertising and promotion support in *all* areas of the country.
   b. Concentrate media weight in the Southeast and Southwest Sales Regions, where per-capita brand and total industry sales are heavily concentrated. In view of the heavy inroads made by Chef's Choice in the Southeast Region, 1977-78 plans will place increased emphasis on this area.
   c. Concentrate promotion support insofar as practical (1) against chain outlets and (2) so as to capitalize seasonally on the October-March peak in consumer movement and the established trade pattern of "loading" during September.

4. In recognition of new information bearing on the importance and responsiveness of the Black market, increased emphasis will be placed during 1977-78 on special supplementary advertising and promotion activities directed specifically to the Black consumer.

5. In view of the apparent success of our current media and copy strategies, these basic strategies will be followed in 1977-78, with the recognition that
   a. Increased advertising funds will permit both an increase in our broad national effort as well as a concentration of pressure in key markets.
   b. New print copy must be developed and tested to strengthen execution of the current copy strategy.

ADVERTISING OBJECTIVES

1. To direct advertising to housewives as the primary purchase group and place primary emphasis on
   a. Current users of grits, estimated to be 25 percent of total U.S. households, heavily concentrated in the two Southern Regions where breadth of usage reaches 50 percent of all families.
   b. Those socioeconomic groups that include the bulk of heavy users. That is, Blacks; families in which the head of the household is under 40 years of age; larger, urban families; and families with average to slightly below average incomes.

2. To increase advertising penetration levels as shown below and as measured by a new penetration study to be conducted approximately January, 1978 (16 months after the previous study).

	Awareness Level	% Recalling One or More Sales Points
From (September, 1976)	30.4%	15.3%
To (January, 1978)	33.0%	16.5%

The objectives which appear above are based solely on judgment, since data is lacking that would provide a reliable basis for forecasting annual rates of change in advertising penetration.
3. To encourage retail grocery trade cooperation—especially within chain outlets—by communicating Golden Grain brand strength to dealer personnel in buying, merchandising, and store management roles.

ADVERTISING STRATEGY
Key strategic considerations governing the use of advertising:
1. Advertising support will be sustained throughout the year, but will
   a. Be reduced during June-August in recognition of reduced retail sales and media efficiency.
   b. Provide peak support during two periods of major promotional activity (September-October and February-March).
2. Advertising expenditures in support of the two major promotions will not exceed $400,000 (20 percent of total media budget).
3. The basic copy unit for print advertising will be a full-color page. This conclusion reflects both
   a. Media requirements for continuity and brand reach, and
   b. Creative requirements for dominant space and appealing product-use illustrations.
4. Recognizing the need to achieve maximum consumer pressure in view of aggressive competitive activity, advertising production expense will be limited to a maximum of 3 percent of the total advertising budget through the reuse of existing television commercials and the production of not more than four new print ads.

COPY STRATEGY
1. Consumer Copy
   a. Golden Grain will be sold primarily on the basis of its superior creaminess and flavor.
   b. Copy presentation will identify the product with appealing Southern traditions and institutions (Detailed rationale for the foregoing conclusions is provided in Appendix 7).
   c. The mood of the copy will be dignified but friendly, emphasizing the gracious traditions that are associated with Southern living.
   d. Copy will recognize that grits are a staple food that may properly be served at any meal or on any occasion.
2. Trade Copy
   a. Golden Grain will be presented to the trade in terms of its high dollar volume and its superior opportunity for profits.
   b. This representation is possible because of Golden Grain's strong market position, its growing consumer franchise, its relatively high unit profit, and its responsiveness to display.
   c. The copy tone will be responsible, straightforward, and businesslike.
   d. Golden Grain Grits is a food staple which, because of its compatibility with a wide variety of foods, offers ample opportunity for tie-in promotions.

COPY PLAN
1. Television copy.   TV copy, executed last year in the form of a pool of three 30-second commercials is characterized chiefly by the following:
   a. Both creaminess and flavor claims are employed. Emphasis is given to the creaminess claim, which is supported by a video comparison of the particle sizes of Golden Grain (extra fine) and an unidentified "leading brand" (coarse).
   b. Important use is made of extreme close-up shots of the product in usage situations in association with appetizing Southern specialties such as ham, yams, and black-eyed peas.
   c. The introduction and concluding 10-seconds of each commercial employ the grits jingle sung by an off-camera chorus.
   d. Product usage situations include family dining occasions characterized by graciousness and family participation.
   e. User families are depicted as younger families with children in the 6–12 age group.
   f. All package close-ups open with a view of the product itself and pull back to reveal the entire front panel.
2. Consumer print copy.   New print copy is currently under development. A revised print copy plan will be submitted on or about February 1, 1977.

3. Trade print copy.   Trade print copy represents an extension of the 1976–77 campaign and is characterized by
   a. Pictorial emphasis on the product selling from mass display.
   b. Statistics from the Dillon Study demonstrating the profit importance of grits.
   c. The use of various headlines that dramatize the sales increases obtained by actual retailers when they displayed Golden Grain Grits.

MEDIA STRATEGY

Recomended media plans were developed within the framework of these basic points of media strategy:
1. National consumer magazines will be employed as the product's basic medium primarily on the basis of: (a) their national coverage, (b) their ability to concentrate messages among younger housewives, and (c) their unique strength as a vehicle for both the dissemination of recipes and the appetizing portrayal of the product itself.
2. Local spot television will be employed on a regional basis as an important supplementary medium designed to (a) complement the coverage achieved with consumer magazines, and (b) permit the brand to apply increased media weight in sales regions where potential is greatest. Spot television is selected in preference to other local and regional media primarily on the basis of its cost efficiency, broad reach, ability to extend message reach into middle and lower-middle income groups, and its strength as a fully-dimensional copy vehicle.
3. Black radio will be employed in selected markets to provide selective, supplemental coverage of Blacks in recognition that the basic consumer magazine program will not achieve broad reach among this high-potential group.
4. The relative emphasis to be placed on each of the three consumer media will be determined primarily on the following two points of strategy:
   a. Total media expenditures per case of Golden Grain retail sales will be approximately the same in each region, except that additional weight will be applied in the Southeast Region to counter Chef's Choice's aggressive effort there.
   b. Total media expenditures per case will be relatively greater in markets that include substantial concentrations of Black population.
5. Significant strategic conclusions regarding the use of each recommended medium include:
   a. Consumer Magazines:
      (1) A minimum of six insertions will be run in each magazine used to insure adequate frequency of impressions and provide continuity of support throughout the year.
      (2) Preferred position space (basic unit: one page, four colors) will be used where available at attractive rates to increase readership of each ad.
   b. Spot Television:
      (1) Thirty-second daytime and late evening commercials will be purchased in order to reach housewives with the greatest possible efficiency.
      (2) Spot television will be purchased in separate waves of support during the year in order to maintain competitively effective short term levels of reach and frequency and to concentrate support during the peak months of consumer sales.

MEDIA PLAN

The principal features of the media plan (see budget summary) are
1. The use of eight consumer magazines. Five of these publications have been employed during the past two years and are considered the primary coverage group (nine insertions each). True Story and Modern Romances have been added to the list this year to extend coverage of "blue-collar" housewives (see Exhibit 8 for analysis of magazine coverage by income and occupational subgroup). Ebony has also been added this year to increase coverage of Blacks. The three new publications are scheduled to receive only six insertions each (all insertions are full-page, four-color units).
2. The plan also provides for the use of spot television in 30 markets. The proposed market list (Exhibit 9) includes all major markets in the Southeast and Southwest regions. These 30 markets will provide coverage of an estimated 80 percent of all households in the Southeast and Southwest regions.
3. Each spot television market will receive 60 to 100 gross rating points weekly for a total of twenty-six weeks, which will be divided as follows into four waves of spot activity:

Wave No.	No. Weeks	Weekly GRP	Period
1	6	60	4/1-5/15
2	8	100	9/1-10/30
3	4	60	11/1-12/1
4	8	100	2/1-3/30

It is estimated that the proposed levels of spot television weight will develop reach and frequency as follows during each four-week period of activity:

	60 GRP	100 GRP
Reach (% TV homes covered)	40%	60%
Average Frequency	6.0	6.6

4. The plan also provides for 30 weeks of spot radio activity on 26 Black stations in 21 markets (Exhibit 10 provides market list, estimated costs and a brief rationale for the market selection). These 21 markets together provide coverage of an estimated 64 percent of total U.S. Black population.

SALES PROMOTION STRATEGY

Within the broad framework of its role in providing strong, periodic sales stimulus, it is proposed that the specific objectives of Golden Grain's 1977–78 promotion program continue to be to stimulate product trial and repurchase by (1) gaining trade support in the forms of in-store display and price features by retailers, and (b) communicating appealing new product usage ideas to consumers via both point-of-purchase materials and general consumer advertising integrated with the promotion effort.

Basic strategy for achieving these objectives will provide that

1. Primary emphasis will continue to be placed on direct trade incentives in the form of merchandising allowances. This recommendation is in keeping with the generally favorable results achieved by similar promotions during the past two years.
2. Departing from recent practice, merchandising allowance support will take the form of contractual payments to retailers for in-store displays complying with substantial, but reasonable minimum quantities of product (that is, $5 payment for a ten-case display; $15 for a twenty-five-case display). The specific purpose of this approach will be to stimulate cooperation on the part of chain and large independent outlets.
3. All major promotions involving merchandising allowances will be designed to capitalize on the special opportunities to tie in with other manufacturers in order to (a) reduce investment requirements for point-of-purchase materials, and (b) extend sales force coverage by utilizing personnel of the cooperating manufacturer, and (c) extend consumer advertising support.
4. Total basic national promotional weight will be concentrated in two tie in merchandising allowance efforts during the year. These major efforts will be timed to capitalize on the seasonal peak in consumer movement and the established pattern of trade loading during September-October and February-March.
5. In recognition of the special opportunity for promoting the product among Blacks in the Southeast Region, a supplementary effort will be initiated regionally during the year on a trail basis. Strategy governing this effort will provide for:
   (a) Adoption of the proven "pay day" promotion format based on cash payments to Black families who have the product on hand when called upon by a representative of the company.
   (b) The use of aggressive local media advertising to support this promotion. Local spot radio will be devoted entirely to this program during the promotion period.

SALES PROMOTION PLAN

The basic sales promotion plan (see budget summary) provides for:

1. Two major, tie-in promotions, one during September-October, and the other during February-March. (See Exhibit 12 for basis of allowance cost estimates.)
2. A regional (Southeast Region) Black promotion to be initiated in September (the earliest possible date for the availability of materials) and to continue throughout the fiscal year. (See Exhibit 13 for assumptions and estimated costs.)

SPECIAL ACTIVITIES—NEW PACKAGE TESTING

General marketing objectives and strategy provide that test marketing will be employed during 1977–78 to evaluate two new packaging concepts: (1) a larger size can, and (2) a multi-can package.

Basic points of strategy affecting the development and testing of these new packages are as follows:

1. The two package concepts will be developed and test marketed independently. Although it may subsequently prove desirable to gain market experience with both new packages in a single area, testing during the 1977–78 period will be conducted independently to (a) allow each project to progress at its own rate and (b) limit the number of variables to be evaluated under controlled conditions.

2. Basic strategy provides that each package will be introduced in limited test areas representing 1–3 percent of total U.S. population for a period of at least six months. Further, the program(s) of introductory support for each new package will be developed on the basis of a national effort, which will then be translated to the test areas.

3. The basic technique for evaluating test market results will be the measurement of brand market share by means of retail store panel audits. Field checks and sales reports will be employed as secondary measurements of distribution, pricing, and trade attitude.

4. Study of various alternatives for executing the two packaging concepts leads to these conclusions:
   a. That the large-size can should be 16-ounces because:
      (1) a 16-ounce can will meet the needs of larger families (16 ounces will provide 5 to 7 servings).
      (2) a 16-ounce can could probably be priced to retail in the favorable 43 to 45¢ range and permit special promotional pricing of 39¢ with trade cooperation.
   b. The multican package should contain three 8-ounce cans banded together to retail at 59¢ versus an average of 63¢ for three 8-ounce cans purchased separately.

5. It will be a basic point of marketing strategy to limit the investment involved in introducing one or both of the new packages to not more than $70,000 during any one fiscal year and to conduct all special activities in behalf of the new packages on the basis of a one-year theoretical payout. This implies that new funds may be requested if a volume increase can be projected.

6. Basic strategy will also provide that national expansion will be executed in a series of two to four steps covering a period of not more than 18 months and not less than 9 months. A minimum of 9 months is recommended to insure adequate time for appraisal of results in the first expansion area.

7. Label design work for the new packages will proceed on the assumption that it is strategically sound to relate the new labels very closely to the existing label for the 8-ounce can. However, it will be an important objective in the final test plan to use marketing research to make sure that the recommended label designs are free from confusing elements.

Specific objectives and plans and estimated expenditures will be submitted separately (by June 15, 1977) when complete data is available regarding (a) delivery schedules for the new packages, (b) costs and margins, and (c) consumer acceptance of the new packages in panel placement tests.

GOLDEN GRAIN:
SUMMARY OF PROPOSED ADVERTISING AND SALES PROMOTION
ADVERTISING

1. Consumer Magazines

   6–9 4-color pages in each of 8 magazines; total exposure of 84.5 million. Estimated net
   unduplicated coverage of 56% of U.S. households: $940,000

9 Pages 4C	6 Pages 4C
LH Journal	Ebony
Good Housekeeping	True Story
Redbook	Modern Romances
Family Circle	(exhibit 11 provides detail)

2. Spot Television

   60–100 Gross Rating Points weekly for 26 weeks in 30 markets in the SE and SW Regions
   (exhibit 19).   710,000

3. Spot Radio

   15–20 60-second commercials weekly for 30 weeks on estimated 26 radio stations in 21
   markets (exhibit 10).   173,000

4. Production, Preparation, Use

Magazines:	Prepare 4-color pages	$15,000
TV:	Est. talent fees & misc.	8,000
Radio:	Production and est. talent fees for pool of 6 commercials	4,000
	Total Advertising	$1,850,000

1. Major tie-in promotion based on 50¢/case display allowance; national magazine support. 200,000
2. February-March: Repeat Fall tie-in promotion: 200,000
3. "Pay Day" Black promotion—SE Region   40,000
4. Promotion materials   30,000

   Total Promotion   470,000

RESERVES

1. For test marketing 2 new packages   130,000
2. General reserves (5% of budget)   130,000

   Total Reserves   260,000
   Grand Total $2,580,000

Checklist of Facts on Product Marketing

The following checklist may be helpful in preparing the market review section of the marketing plan. It may also be helpful to creative groups as they seek out information about the products or services for which they are preparing advertising. Its purpose is to provide a relatively exhaustive list of questions that help identify the truly significant facts of the marketing situation.

The list contains questions that are not pertinent to *all* products. For example, questions on styles or models are not relevant to a food product. Nor are all of the questions relevant to the normal marketing plan. For example, questions on profitability, cost of goods, and so forth may not be pertinent in a particular case. Nonetheless, these are relevant questions that must be dealt with at some point in the planning process. Also, the list tends to overemphasize the importance of historical data as opposed to data that illuminates the current situation.

Basically, this list is intended to serve as a reminder of the wide range of factors that need to be considered in developing a successful marketing effort. As such, the list provides an example of the art of asking questions.

---

1. SOURCE: Herbert West, *Advertising Agency Magazine* May 10, 1957).

SECTION I—The Size, Scope, and Share of Market

A. *Sales History*

1. What is the sales history of all manufacturers of this product in dollars?
2. In units?
3. In percentage share of the market in dollars?
4. In units?
5. Same data on consumer purchases?
6. How do geographical differences affect the share of the market held by various manufacturers?
7. City size differences?
8. Price differences?
9. Seasonal differences?
10. Racial differences?

B. *Market Potential*

11. What is the trend in the sales history of the total market per 1,000 population?
12. What is the trend of the total market, as a percentage of the Gross National Product?
13. What is the trend in use by consumers of related products?

A. 14. What is the trend in use by consumers of products which produce a need for this product?
15. What is the trend in use by consumers of products which eliminate the need for this product?
16. What statements have been made by responsible men in this field about the future potential for this product?
17. What is the manufacturing potential of all principal manufacturers?
18. What new manufacturers are expected to enter this field?
19. How do geographical differences affect the market for this product?
20. Seasonal differences?

C. *Pricing History*

21. What is the pricing history of the most popular unit of sale charged by major manufacturers to their distribution channels?
22. Charged by the distribution channels to the consumer?
23. Same data on other units, manufacturers to distribution channels?
24. Distribution channels to consumers?
25. What are the reasons for the principal fluctuations in pricing?

SECTION II—Sales, Costs and Gross Profits on Our Product

A. *Sales*

26. What is the sales history of our product in manufacturers' dollars by different sizes or models?
27. In units?

28. What is the history of introduction of the product and the sequence of marketing steps which led to its present distribution?
29. What is our sales history, in dollars by sales districts?
30. In units?
31. What is our sales history by sales districts, in units per 1000 population?

B. *Cost History*

32. What is the cost history of our product in total cost of goods delivered?
33. In selling expense?
34. In advertising expense?
35. In administrative expense?
36. In all other expense?

C. *Gross Profit*

37. What is the cost history of our product in total cost of goods delivered?
38. In selling expense?
39. In percentage of net sales?
40. What is known about the profits of other manufacturers in this field?

SECTION III—The Distribution Channels

A. *Identification of Principal Channels*

41. What is the sales history in dollars handled by each type of distribution channel for our product?
42. In units?
43. In dollars, for our competitors?
44. In units, for our competitors?
45. What distribution do we have in each type of outlet, by districts?

B. *Buying Habits and Attitudes of Principal Channels*

46. What is the attitude of the principal distribution channels toward these aspects of our product versus competitors?
47. Price?
48. Availability?
49. Credit?
50. Purchase deals?
51. Assortments?
52. Styling?
53. Packaging?
54. Turnover?
55. What are the purchase habits of our principal channels in terms of the time they buy our product?
56. The quantity?
57. The assortment?
58. What shelf frontage is given our product versus our competitors?
59. What are the inventories of our product currently held by each of our principal channels?

60. What is the out-of-stock situation in each channel?
61. What information is available on net profits enjoyed by each of our principle channels of distribution?
62. What variations exist in the volume handled by different channels because of geographical differences?
63. Population differences?
64. Differences of sizes or models?

C. *Our Selling Policies and Practices*

65. How do our sales practices differ from competitors on these points:
66. Percent of accounts covered?
67. Frequency of call?
68. Length of call?
69. Quality and Training of [people]
70. Method of selling?
71. How do our sales policies differ from our competitors on these points: Damaged goods?
72. Display allowances?
73. Advertising allowances?
74. PM's (Push money or promotion money)?
75. Fair trade?
76. Free samples?
77. Discounts to employees?
78. Retail clerk training?
79. What do the [people] in distribution channels like most about our sales policies and practices?
80. Dislike most?
81. Like most about our competitors?
82. Dislike most?

D. *Pressure Promotions*

83. What is the history of pressure promotions we have used with the distribution channels?
84. Which type of promotions have been most effective?
85. Which least effective?
86. What pressure promotions have our competitors used with the distribution channels?
87. How effective have their pressure promotions been?
88. What do the people in the distribution channel like or dislike about our pressure promotions?
89. About our competitors' pressure promotions?
90. Which type of distribution channel has been the most cooperative on pressure promotions?
91. Which the least?

E. *Trade Advertising, Literature, and Exhibits*

92. How does our strategy on trade advertising differ from our principal competitors'?
93. What have been the objectives of our trade advertising?
94. What evidence is available to show whether these objectives have been met?
95. What is the history of our trade advertising in dollars spent?

96. In media selection?
97. In copy theme?
98. In size of space?
99. In frequency?
100. As a percent of net sales?
101. What types of sales literature have we furnished the distribution channels?
102. What are the objectives of this literature?
103. What evidence is available that these objectives have been met?
104. Which types have been most effective?
105. Which least effective?
106. How does our strategy on sales literature differ from our competitors?
107. What do the [people] in the distribution channels like and dislike about our sales literature?
108. Our competitors?
109. What is the history of our trade exhibit and convention participation?
110. How does our strategy on participation in trade exhibits and conventions differ from our competitors?
111. How effective has this strategy been?
112. What do the people in the distribution channels like and dislike about our participation in trade exhibits and conventions?

F. *Point-of-Sale Display*

113. What types of point-of-sale displays have we used in the last five years?
114. Which type was most effective?
115. Which least effective?
116. Which type is preferred by people in the distribution channels, and why?
117. Which of our competitors' point-of-sale displays have been effective?

SECTION IV—The Consumer or End User

A. *Identification of Person Making Buying Decision*

118. Who makes the buying decision for our product—classified by age?
119. Sex?
120. Income level?
121. Education?
122. Geographical locations?
123. Urban versus rural?
124. Race?
125. Religion?
126. Occupation?
127. Marital status?
128. Size of family?
129. Home ownership?
130. Car ownership?
131. TV ownership?

B. *Consumer Attitudes*

132. What is consumer attitude on our product versus our competitors' on these points: Quality?
133. Maintenance?
134. Price?
135. Availability?
136. Selection?
137. Styling?
138. Packaging?
139. Guarantee?
140. Ease of use?
141. Benefits of use?
142. Length of useful life?
143. What personality does our product have in the consumer's mind?
144. How many potential consumers are there for our product?
145. To what extent are potential consumers informed of our product?
146. How many potential consumers have tried our product?
147. How many have stopped using our product?
148. Why?
149. Same data on competitors' products?
150. How many have switched from our brand to a competitor's?
151. From a competitor's to our brand?
152. How many consumers now use our product?
153. What influenced them to try it?
154. What do they like most about it?
155. What least?
156. Same data on competitors?
157. How does folklore, tradition, social ritual and prejudice affect consumers' attitudes toward our product?

C. *Consumer Purchase Habits*

158. What are consumers' purchasing habits for our product, by season?
159. By months?
160. By weeks of the year?
161. By day of week?
162. By price level?
163. By type of outlet?
164. By frequency of purchase?
165. By method of purchase (case or credit)?
166. By full price versus discount?
167. By sizes or models?

D. *Consumer Use Habits*

168. What are the major uses for our product, in order of popularity?
169. Under what conditions is our product used?
170. How frequently?
171. By whom in the family?
172. Where is it kept?
173. What is average rate of consumption of a standard unit of our product?

174. What consumer differences affect this rate of consumption?
175. What personal characteristics identify our largest consumer?
176. How is our product misused?
177. What is the extent of misuse of the product?
178. What new uses does our product have other than those we promote?
179. To what extent are these other uses practiced?
180. How does the consumer judge when the useful life of our product has ended?

E. *Our Advertising History*

181. What is the history of our advertising expenditures in dollars?
182. Per unit?
183. As a percent of sales?
184. Per 1,000 population?
185. By geographic region in relation to sales?
186. By sales districts in relation to sales?
187. By city size in relation to sales?
188. By media?
189. By seasons?
190. By months?
191. What is the history of competitive advertising expenditures in total dollars?
192. As a percent of estimated sales?
193. By geographic region?
194. By media?
195. How does competitive advertising differ from ours in timing?
196. In size of space?
197. In frequency?
198. What is the most important single impression to deliver with our advertising?
199. Second most important impression?
200. Third?
201. Fourth?
202. What is the copy strategy used on our product for the past five years?
203. What are the reasons for major changes?
204. What basic copy themes have been used on our product?
205. Why were they changed?
206. What copy strategy has been used by our competitors?
207. What research results are available on the effectiveness of our copy: Starch?
208. Nielsen?
209. Surveys?
210. Market tests?
211. Hidden offer tests?
212. Gallup-Robinson?
213. Other tests?
214. What media strategy have we used for the last five years and why?
215. What major changes have been made in media strategy and why?

216. What measurements are available of the effectiveness of the media we have used?
217. How has our budget percentage in each of the following media compared with our competitors: Newspapers?
218. Newspaper supplements?
219. Magazines?
220. Television?
221. Radio?
222. Business papers?
223. Outdoor?
224. Car cards?
225. Other media?
226. What trends are evident in media which might affect our advertising?
227. What has been the media strategy of our competitors for the last five years?

F. *Publicity and Other Educational Influences*

228. What devices have been used to influence consumers other than advertising and point-of-sale material: Publicity?
229. Donation of prizes?
230. Educational films?
231. Stockholder mailings?
232. Sampling?
234. House-to-house?
235. Leaflet throw-aways?
236. Dealer envelope stuffers?
237. Consumer parties?
238. What has been our strategy in the use of these devices over the last five years?
239. What are the reasons for changes, if any, in this strategy?
240. How has our strategy with these devices differed from our competitors?
241. What evidence is available on the effectiveness of of these devices?

SECTION V—The Product

A. *Story of the Product*

242. When was the product developed?
243. By whom?
244. Why?
245. How was it developed?
246. What improvements have been made in the product since it was introduced?

247. When was it introduced?
248. When were different sizes and models introduced?
249. Why?
250. Same data on competitive products?
251. How long has the current label been in use?
252. What are the reasons for the various elements on the label?
253. How long has the current package been in use?
254. What are the reasons for the various elements of package?

B. *Comparison with Competition*

255. What are the principal differences between our product and competitors?
256. What evidence is available on the quality and performance of our product versus competitors' from: Production Department?
257. Research Department?
258. Engineering?
259. Designers?
260. Quality control laboratory?
261. Independent testing organizations?
262. Consumer research groups?
263. Consumer surveys?
264. What is the product's outstanding advantage over competitive products?
265. What information is available on competitive plans to overcome this advantage?
266. What are the product's shortcomings in relation to competition?
267. What plans are being made to overcome them?

C. *Product Research*

268. What research is being conducted on our product to improve its quality?
269. Improve design?
270. Lower its price?
271. Make it easier to use?
272. Lengthen its useful life?
273. Make the label more attractive?
274. More useful?
275. Make the package more attractive?
276. More convenient?
277. Reusable?
278. Improve servicing of the product?
279. What information is available on areas of product research being explored by competitors?

APPENDIX 3

Media Cost and Coverage Data

United States
Population Statistics

The population of the United States in 1978 was estimated at over 218 million by the Bureau of the Census. The 25- to 34-year-old segment continued to grow in size. And, in 1978, accounted for roughly 15% of the total population.

Household income in the United States is increasing. According to the latest estimates, 50% of all males 18+ and 40% of all females have incomes $15,000 or above.

Much of the cause of household income growth is related to working women. In 1978, approximately 37 million women were working.

All population data found in the following tables are BBDO estimates based on the *Current Population Reports* published by the U.S. Bureau of the Census and Simmons media studies.

I. Totals

	Number	Distribution
	(000)	%
Children 2-11 years	32,946	16
Teens 12-17 years	24,113	11
Women 18+ years	80,969	38
Men 18+ years	74,142	35
	212,170*	100

II. Non-Adults by Age

A. Children

2-5 years	12,110	37
6-11 years	20,834	63
	32,944	100

	Number	Distribution
B. Teens (12-17 years)	(000)	%
Females	11,823	49
Males	12,292	51
	24,115	100

*Excludes children under 2

III. Adults by Selected Demographics

A. Age

	Women		Men	
	(000)	%	(000)	%
18-24	14,384	18	14,595	20
25-34	17,074	21	16,874	22
35-49	18,291	23	17,450	24
50-64	17,014	21	15,488	21
65+	14,207	17	9,735	13
	80,970	100	74,142	100

B. Household Income

	Total Males		Total Females	
	(000)	%	(000)	%
Under $5,000	7,341	9.9	15,222	18.8
$5,000-$9,999	12,530	16.9	16,761	20.7
$10,000-$14,999	16,904	22.8	16,842	20.8
$15,000-$24,999	23,206	31.3	20,890	25.8
$25,000-$34,999	8,304	11.2	6,882	8.5
$35,000+	5,857	7.9	4,372	5.4
	74,142	100	80,969	100

C. Occupation

	Total Employed			
	Women 18+		Men 18+	
	(000)	%	(000)	%
Professional/Technical	6,283	17	8,823	16
Managerial/Administrative	2,209	6	8,081	15
Clerical/Sales	15,282	41	6,969	12
Craftsman/Foreman	594	2	12,011	22
Other employed	12,480	34	19,573	35
	36,848	100	55,457	100

D. Education

	Women (000)	%	Men (000)	%
College graduate or more	8,582	11	12,308	17
1-3 years college	11,741	15	12,011	16
1-4 years high school	46,800	58	36,997	50
Elementary school or less	13,846	16	12,826	17
	80,969	100	74,142	100

E. Working Women

	Number of Women 18+ (000)	%
18-24	8,825	24
25-34	9,184	25
35-44	6,803	18
45-54	6,670	18
55-64	4,308	12
65+	1,058	3
	36,848	100

Note: Includes women who work one hour or more per week

Television
General Dimensions

I. TV Penetration

(Fall 1977)

TV Home Penetration	98%
TV Home	72.9 million
Color TV (% Total TV)	78%
Multi-Set (%Total TV)	46%
CATV (% Total TV)	15.5%*

* Represents Fall '76

Source: BBDO Estimates

II. TV Billings

	$(Mil)	% Tot.
Network	3,455	45%
National Spot	2,260	30
Local Spot	1,915	25
Total	7,630	100%

Source: TVB

III. Cumulative Reach Levels

	Per Day	Per Week	Per Month
Women (18+)			
Weekday Daytime	46%	63%	75%
Early Evening	57	79	85
Prime Time	68	89	95+
Late Evening	35	70	80
Early & Late Evening	65	85	95
All Time Periods	78	91	95+
Men (18+)			
Weekday Daytime	20	40	50
Early Evening	50	72	80
Prime Time	63	88	95+
Late Evening	30	65	80
Early & Late Evening	60	85	90+
All Time Periods	73	89	95+
Working Women			
Weekday Daytime	26	45	56
Early Evening	50	75	82
Prime Time	65	88	95+
Late Evening	29	63	78
Early & Late Evening	61	86	90+
All Time Periods	75	91	95+

	Per Day	Per Week	Per Month
Teens (12-17)			
Weekday Daytime	30%	55%	70%
Weekend Daytime	42	55	80
Early Evening	52	76	95
Prime Time	58	86	95
Late Evening	15	60	75+
All Time Periods	68	90	95+
Children (6-11)			
Weekend Daytime	70	80	95+
Weekday Daytime	40	70	90+
Early Evening	70	91	95+
Prime Time	70	94	95+
Late Evening	5	30	45
All Time Periods	83	96	95+
Children (2-5)			
Weekend Daytime	75	85	95+
Weekday Daytime	60	85	95
Early Evening	74	90	95
Prime Time	59	87	95+
Late Evening	5	20	30
All Time Periods	84	94	95+

Source: BBDO Estimates Feb. '77

IV. Distribution of Viewing by Quintiles

	I Heaviest 20%	II Next 20%	III Next 20%	IV Next 20%	V Lightest 20%
Women (18+)					
Mon-Fri Day	56	28	13	3	—
Early Evening	51	29	14	6	—
Prime Time	37	27	20	13	3
Late Evening	59	27	11	3	—
All Viewing	42	26	18	11	3
Men (18+)					
Mon-Fri Day	88	12	—	—	—
Early Evening	55	27	13	5	—
Prime Time	39	28	20	11	2
Late Evening	53	27	15	5	—
All Viewing	42	26	18	11	3

Source: BBDO Estimates

Note: This table reads as follows: The 20% of women who view the heaviest accounts for 42% of the female audience in an average TV time period. The same 20%, however, does 56% of all weekday daytime viewing, but only 37% of all prime-time viewing, etc.

V. Average Viewing Levels by Time of Day
(Per Quarter Hour)

	% Homes Tuned In	% People Viewing Women	Men	Teens	Child
Monday-Friday					
7 AM-10 AM	13.0%	7.4%	3.8%	4.5%	11.6%
10 AM-1 PM	21.1	14.9	5.9	9.4	10.6
1 PM-4:30 PM	27.6	20.4	7.2	12.1	12.8
4:30 PM-7:30 PM	41.6	26.7	21.4	23.8	31.8
10 AM-4:30 PM	24.7	17.9	6.6	10.9	11.8
7:30 PM-8 PM	51.6	37.9	32.4	27.0	35.8
All Evenings					
8 PM-11 PM	56.6	43.7	40.0	34.9	30.8
11 PM-11:30 PM	43.5	32.2	31.2	19.3	8.2
11:30 PM-1 AM	25.6	16.9	16.5	11.5	3.6
Saturday					
7 AM-1 PM	18.3	5.9	5.4	12.7	33.3
1 PM-4:30 PM	26.0	13.6	16.2	16.3	16.8
4:30 PM-7:30 PM	37.9	23.7	26.8	19.6	19.6
Sunday					
7 AM-1 PM	14.3	6.9	7.0	8.0	15.4
1 PM-4:30 PM	30.9	17.0	23.5	17.7	14.5
4:30 PM-7:30 PM	42.3	28.1	32.5	22.6	23.5

VI. Demographic Indices

A. Women

| | Weekday Daytime | Viewing by All Women = 100* | | | |
		Early Evening	Prime Time	Late Night	All Dayparts
By Age					
18-24	103	89	91	95	94
25-34	83	77	98	97	91
35-54	91	93	103	108	98
55+	119	130	104	96	112
By Household Income					
$15,000+	79	85	93	93	87
$10-15,000	102	97	103	111	104
Under $10,000	129	122	109	105	116
By Employment Status					
Work	46	79	93	96	81
Not Employed	129	112	103	101	110
By Size of Household					
1-2	100	118	104	102	106
3-4	101	93	101	97	98
5+	97	77	89	100	90

* Thus compared to the viewing rate for all women in daytime, those 55+ are 19% above, etc.

B. Men

| | Weekday Daytime | Viewing by All Men = 100* | | | |
		Early Evening	Prime Time	Late Night	All Dayparts
By Age					
18-24	76	73	80	83	78
25-34	73	80	103	112	97
35-54	75	88	98	101	94
55+	173	153	115	99	124
By Household Income					
$15,000+	61	79	91	90	86
$10-15,000	88	90	103	115	100
Under $10,000	193	152	117	112	130
Selected Upper Demo's:					
$15,000+, with non-adults	48	63	89	88	78
$15,000+; HOH POM	43	66	82	82	76
$15,000+; HOH 1+ Yrs. Coll.	57	74	89	98	84
HOH 4+ Yrs. Coll.	61	71	83	98	79

* Thus, compared to the viewing rate for all men in the early evening hours, men are 30% above average, etc.
Note: HOH—Head of House
POM—Professional, owners, and managers
Source: BBDO Est. Nov, 1977

VII. Viewer Attention Levels
By Program Type

	% at Full Attention	
	Total Men	Total Women
Weekday Daytime	72	66
"Today Show"	57	38
Serials	73	72
Quiz/Game	73	64
Early Evening News	71	59
Prime Time	79	74
Mysteries	79	72
Movies	82	75
Variety	67	68
Drama	79	72
Sit. Comedy	77	75
Late Night	78	72
"Tonight Show"	65	65
"Late Nite Movies"	80	66

Source: BBDO estimates based on Simmons.

VIII. Seasonal Viewing Patterns

| | % Homes Tuned in per ¼ Hr. | | | |
	Nov.	Feb.	May	July
M-F 7 AM-10 AM	14%	15%	12%	11%
M-F 10 AM-4:30 PM	24	28	22	25
M-F 4:30 PM-7:30 PM	46	50	37	34
All Eve. 7:30-8 PM	59	63	45	38
All Eve. 8PM-11 PM	61	64	54	46
All Eve. 11 PM-1 AM	30	32	29	29

IX. Standard Reach Tables

| Gross Rtg. Pts. (4 Wks.) | Women | | | Men | |
	Day	Fringe	Prime	Fringe	Prime
100	39	48	58	46	56
150	46	57	68	59	67
200	52	67	76	67	74
250	55	70	80	72	79
300	58	74	84	76	83
350	60	77	86	79	85
400	62	80	88	81	87

Network Television

This section deals with network television, its seasonal and yearly audience levels and current cost dimensions.

The following tables detail the costs and audience relationships for standard program types in network TV. Although, for purposes of brevity, we have restricted ourselves to "top-line" comparisons, i.e., Total Households, Women, Men, Teens and Children, each of the program categories has inherent demographic appeals (by age, income, location, etc.) which should be considered when making planning or buying decisions.

Costs are shown for 30-second units but a broad range can exist even within program types. So although we have chosen to provide a single cost which represents a "typical" statistic for the category, the user must view these data with caution, relying upon them for a general indication of efficiency rather than as a specific measurement.

I. Prime Time

A) Regular Entertainment

		Households	Women	Men	Teens	Children	Cost per 30"
ANNUAL AVERAGE	Avg. Rating	17.2%	13.0	12.0	10.9	9.7	
	CPM 30"	$3.61	4.58	5.51	17.28	14.36	$45,000
1st Qtr. 1978	Avg. Rating	20.1%	15.6	14.2	13.2	12.5	
	CPM 30"	$2.80	3.41	4.17	12.74	9.84	$41,000
2nd Qtr. 1978	Avg. Rating	15.9%	11.4	10.6	9.8	9.2	
	CPM 30"	$4.06	5.35	6.41	19.67	15.33	$47,000
3rd Qtr. 1978	Avg. Rating	13.3%	9.7	8.9	9.0	6.9	
	CPM 30"	$3.71	4.82	5.84	16.41	15.65	$36,000
4th Qtr. 1978	Avg. Rating	19.6%	15.1	14.1	11.4	10.3	
	CPM 30"	$3.85	4.72	5.63	20.28	16.61	$56,000

B) Specials

		Households	Women	Men	Teens	Children	Cost per 30"
Awards, Pageants	Avg. Rating	18.8%	18.0	13.6	14.7	7.7	
	CPM 30"	$4.79	4.73	6.97	18.45	25.83	$66,000
Child, Animated	Avg. Rating	19.1%	13.0	10.3	16.1	35.5	
	CPM 30"	$4.32	6.01	8.44	15.44	5.13	$60,500
Documentary— General	Avg. Rating	13.8%	10.3	9.7	7.4	9.0	
	CPM 30"	$5.14	6.52	7.71	28.87	17.41	$52,000
Documentary—News	Avg. Rating	11.3%	9.5	8.9	3.9	2.4	
	CPM 30"	$3.62	4.08	4.85	31.60	37.69	$30,000
Drama	Avg. Rating	18.4%	16.0	13.3	11.0	8.0	
	CPM 30"	$4.45	4.84	6.48	22.41	22.61	$60,000

		House-holds	Women	Men	Teens	Chil-dren	Cost per 30"
Movie Specials	Avg. Rating	23.6%	20.5	18.9	13.1	7.6	$71,500
	CPM 30"	$4.14	4.51	5.44	22.42	28.35	
Variety	Avg. Rating	19.7%	17.3	14.2	11.6	11.7	$66,000
	CPM 30"	$4.57	4.93	6.68	23.37	17.00	

II. Daytime (Mon.-Fri.)

			House-holds	Women	Men	Teens	Chil-dren	Cost per 30"
A)	Annual Average	Avg. Rating	6.8%	5.4	1.8	2.7	2.8	$ 9,300
		CPM 30"	$1.87	2.22	7.43	14.16	10.02	
B)	Serials	Avg. Rating	7.2%	6.2	1.5	2.2	1.5	$11,900
		CPM 30"	$2.26	2.48	11.41	22.24	23.94	
C)	Game Shows	Avg. Rating	5.9%	4.2	1.6	2.8	2.5	$ 7,100
		CPM 30"	$1.64	2.18	6.38	10.41	8.56	
D)	Situation Comedies	Avg. Rating	6.0%	3.7	2.0	3.9	3.7	$ 9,300
		CPM 30"	$2.12	3.25	6.69	9.80	7.58	
E)	Today	Avg. Rating	4.3%	3.6	2.0	0.7	0.7	$ 8,600
		CPM 30"	$2.73	3.09	6.18	50.59	37.07	
F)	CBS Morning News	Avg. Rating	2.1%	1.3	0.8	0.1	0.8	$ 2,000
		CPM 30"	$1.30	1.99	3.59	83.33	7.55	
G)	Good Morning, America	Avg. Rating	3.2%	2.4	0.9	0.8	0.7	$ 4,200
		CPM 30"	$1.79	2.26	6.71	21.54	18.10	

III. Fringe (Annual Average)

			House-holds	Women	Men	Teens	Chil-dren	Cost per 30"
A)	Early News	Avg. Rating	11.3%	8.5	7.9	2.9	3.4	$24,000
		CPM 30"	$2.90	3.65	4.37	34.00	21.28	
B)	Late Weekend News	Avg. Rating	6.9%	4.8	4.9	2.7	1.3	$13,000
		CPM 30"	$2.57	3.50	3.81	19.79	30.16	
C)	Tonight Show	Avg. Rating	8.0%	5.6	5.0	2.7	0.6	$19,000
		CPM 30"	$3.24	4.38	5.46	28.92	95.47	
D)	Late CBS Movie	Avg. Rating	6.0%	3.6	3.7	2.1	0.6	$13,000
		CPM 30"	$2.96	4.66	5.05	25.44	65.33	
E)	ABC Late Movies							
	Police Story (Monday)	Avg. Rating	5.4%	3.4	3.3	1.9	0.6	$14,000
		CPM 30"	$3.54	5.32	6.10	30.24	70.35	
	Movie of the Week (Tues.)	Avg. Rating	5.5%	3.5	3.2	2.2	0.7	$14,000
		CPM 30"	$3.47	5.17	6.29	26.12	60.34	
	Police Story (Wednesday)	Avg. Rating	6.5%	4.3	3.7	3.3	1.0	$14,000
		CPM 30"	$2.94	4.21	5.44	17.43	42.17	
	Starsky & Hutch (Thurs.)	Avg. Rating	6.6%	4.8	3.7	2.3	0.5	$14,000
		CPM 30"	$2.90	3.77	5.44	25.00	84.34	
	Baretta (Fri.)	Avg. Rating	6.5%	4.0	3.6	4.8	2.0	$14,000
		CPM 30"	$2.94	4.52	5.59	11.99	21.12	
F)	Midnight Special	Avg. Rating	3.9%	1.9	2.0	3.5	0.5	$ 8,000
		CPM 30"	$2.80	5.44	5.75	9.39	48.48	
G)	Tomorrow	Avg. Rating	2.7%	1.6	1.5	0.5	—	$ 2,900
		CPM 30"	$1.47	2.34	2.78	2.38	—	
H)	Saturday Night	Avg. Rating	7.4%	4.5	6.0	7.3	0.8	$22,000
		CPM 30"	$4.06	6.31	5.27	1.23	83.02	
I)	Weekend	Avg. Rating	6.0%	4.3	4.4	3.2	2.4	$17,000
		CPM 30"	$3.86	5.11	5.55	2.18	2.13	

IV. Children

			House-holds	Teens	Children Total	2-5	6-11	Cost per 30"
A)	Sat. & Sun. AM	Avg. Rating	5.1%	3.8	10.7	10.9	10.5	$ 8,300
		CPM 30"	$2.11	8.97	2.34	6.18	3.79	
B)	Mon.-Fri. Capt. Kangaroo	Avg. Rating	3.4%	1.0	5.8	9.7	3.4	$ 2,500
		CPM 30"	$1.00	10.29	1.30	2.09	3.53	

V. Sports (Average by Type)

		House-Holds	Women	Men	Teens	Chil-dren	Cost per 30"
A) Baseball							
Saturdays	Avg. Rating	6.6%	2.6	5.7	2.5	1.6	$17,500
	CPM 30"	$3.64	8.73	4.43	28.71	32.82	
Monday Nights	Avg. Rating	12.4%	5.4	11.4	6.4	3.3	$29,000
	CPM 30"	$3.21	6.97	3.68	18.59	26.37	
All-Star Game	Avg. Rating	24.5%	13.4	22.7	15.7	5.1	$75,000
	CPM 30"	$4.12	7.13	4.68	19.72	44.93	
Playoffs	Avg. Rating	17.7%	10.4	15.5	5.4	5.2	$45,000
	CPM 30"	$3.42	5.51	4.11	34.39	26.44	
World Series	Avg. Rating	29.0%	17.0	25.6	10.7	7.9	$85,000
	CPM 30"	$3.94	6.37	4.70	32.79	32.87	
B) Basketball-College							
NCAA Regular Season	Avg. Rating	6.3%	2.9	5.8	3.8	1.8	$17,500
	CPM 30"	$3.81	7.83	4.36	18.89	29.17	
NCAA Playoffs	Avg. Rating	8.4%	3.2	8.3	3.0	1.7	$24,000
	CPM 30"	$3.92	9.73	4.18	32.81	42.36	
NCAA Championship	Avg. Rating	19.7%	11.2	19.3	11.8	6.9	$57,500
	CPM 30"	$4.00	6.66	4.30	19.99	25.00	
C) Basketball-Professional							
NBA Regular Season	Avg. Rating	7.4%	3.6	7.1	3.3	2.1	$18,500
	CPM 30"	$3.43	6.67	3.76	22.76	26.43	
All-Star Game	Avg. Rating	8.7%	4.4	7.3	6.0	5.9	$26,000
	CPM 30"	$4.10	7.67	5.15	17.77	13.22	
Playoffs	Avg. Rating	7.2%	2.9	6.8	3.1	1.0	$22,000
	CPM 30"	$4.19	9.84	4.67	29.11	66.00	
Championship	Avg. Rating	11.3%	4.5	10.5	8.7	4.1	$42,000
	CPM 30"	$5.10	12.11	5.78	19.80	30.73	
D) Football-College							
Regular Saturdays	Avg. Rating	13.3%	5.2	12.5	5.6	4.7	$39,000
	CPM 30"	$3.95	9.55	4.42	28.74	25.35	
Bowl Games	Avg. Rating	19.2%	10.2	19.8	8.2	8.0	$49,000
	CPM 30"	$3.43	6.12	3.51	24.66	18.71	
E) Football-Professional							
Pre-Season	Avg. Rating	9.3%	4.3	8.9	4.5	2.8	$30,000
	CPM 30"	$4.34	8.89	4.77	27.51	32.74	
Regular Season	Avg. Rating	14.8%	6.3	14.3	6.0	3.5	$48,000
	CPM 30"	$4.37	9.70	4.75	33.02	41.90	
Monday Nights	Avg. Rating	21.2%	8.9	20.1	9.6	4.0	$85,000
	CPM 30"	$5.40	12.16	5.99	36.54	64.93	
Playoffs	Avg. Rating	25.7%	9.4	26.4	11.4	6.7	$83,700
	CPM 30"	$4.38	11.34	4.49	30.30	38.17	
Championship	Avg. Rating	32.8%	15.5	30.0	14.5	10.6	$98,000
	CPM 30"	$4.02	8.03	4.63	27.89	28.25	
Super Bowl	Avg. Rating	45.0%	25.9	47.4	26.1	16.0	$175,000
	CPM 30"	$5.23	8.61	5.23	27.67	33.42	
F) Other Sports							
Auto Racing	Avg. Rating	10.4%	6.4	8.4	5.5	4.6	$30,000
	CPM 30"	$3.96	6.08	5.16	22.37	19.57	
Bowling	Avg. Rating	7.1%	4.1	5.1	2.7	2.0	$14,000
	CPM 30"	$2.70	4.43	3.97	21.27	21.00	

		House-Holds	Women	Men	Teens	Chil-dren	Cost per 30"
Golf	Avg. Rating	6.0%	3.3	5.5	1.9	1.5	$21,000
	CPM 30"	$4.80	8.26	5.52	45.33	42.00	
Tennis	Avg. Rating	4.0%	2.1	2.8	1.8	1.6	$12,500
	CPM 30"	$4.29	7.72	6.45	28.48	23.44	

G) Sport Series

		House-Holds	Women	Men	Teens	Chil-dren	Cost per 30"
ABC Wide World of Sports	Avg. Rating	8.8%	4.6	6.8	5.3	3.4	$21,000
	CPM 30"	$3.27	5.92	4.46	16.25	18.53	
American Sportsman	Avg. Rating	4.6%	2.4	2.9	1.8	2.5	$15,000
	CPM 30"	$4.47	8.11	7.47	34.39	18.00	
Superstars	Avg. Rating	10.5%	6.5	8.3	7.8	6.6	$26,000
	CPM 30"	$3.40	5.19	4.53	13.67	11.82	
CBS Sports Spectacular	Avg. Rating	6.2%	3.3	4.4	3.6	2.9	$15,000
	CPM 30"	$3.32	5.90	4.93	17.09	15.52	

III. Conversion Factors to Generate Cost per Points for Selected Viewer Group

	M-F Day	Early Fringe	Prime	Late Fringe	Early & Late News
Men 18+	500%	182%	155%	133%	143%
Men 18-49	500	222	156	133	167
Women 18+	125	143	127	133	125
Women 18-49	167	182	140	133	143
Adults 18+	194	159	139	133	133
Adults 18-49	244	199	147	133	153

Radio

I. Total U.S. Radio Audience by Daypart (Average ¼ Hr. Basis)

	People Using Radio		
Daypart	Women	Men	Teens
Monday-Friday			
6 AM-10 AM	28%	25%	18%
10AM-3 PM	23'	21	9
3 PM-7 PM	20	20	22
7PM-Midnight	11	11	17
6AM-Midnight	20	19	16
Saturday			
6 AM-10 AM	19%	16%	12%
10 AM-3 PM	24	18	22
3 PM-7 PM	17	15	19
7 PM-Midnight	9	10	16
Sunday			
6 AM-10 AM	14%	11%	10%
10 AM-3 PM	20	17	20
3 PM-7 PM	13	13	18
7 PM-Midnight	8	9	14
Saturday-Sunday			
6 AM-Midnight	15%	17%	18%

Source: BBDO Estimates

II. Radio Reach Potentials by Daypart (All Stations Combined)

	Daily Reach			Weekly Reach		
	Women	Men	Teens	Women	Men	Teens
M-F 6 AM-10 AM	66%	68%	67%	85%	86%	90%
M-F 10 AM-3 PM	48	46	34	75	73	66
M-F 3 PM-7 PM	49	52	60	77	80	92
M-F 7 PM-Midnight	31	33	54	61	64	90
M-F 6 AM-Midnight	82	84	90	93	95	99

Source: BBDO Estimates

III. Network Radio Costs

Network	# of Affiliates	6-10AM 3-7 PM	10-3 PM	7-12M
MBS*	780	1,230	1,150	600
NBN	83	500	500	500
MBN	93	500	500	500
CBS	275	1,550	1,230	535
NBC	247	1,500	1,100	450
ABC-C*	382	2,100	1,400	700
ABC-I*	497	1,400	1,700	430
ABC-FM*	205	900	700	750
ABC-E*	467	1,600	1,800	500

Note: 60-second units are approximately 170% of :30 rate
  *60-second units are approximately 200% of :30 rate

Spot Television

This section deals with spot television, that is, commercials placed individually through local-market stations as opposed to a single overall network purchase. The most common dayparts and their time-period definitions are listed below:

Daytime —Monday thru Friday—9:00 AM- 5:00 PM, NYT*
Early Fringe —Monday thru Sunday—5:00 PM- 7:30 PM, NYT*
Prime —Monday thru Saturday—8:00 PM-11:00 PM, NYT*
Sunday—7:00 PM-11:00 PM, NYT*
Late Fringe —Monday thru Sunday—11:30 PM- 1:00 AM, NYT*
* Central Time Zone begins one hour earlier.

I. TV Market Coverage and Costs
Network Stations Average

Cost Per 30-Second Rating Point (ADI: TV Home Ratings)

Markets	% U.S.	M-F Day	Early Fringe	Prime	Late Fringe	Early & Late News
1-10	33%	$ 434	$ 589	$1,246	$ 814	$ 946
1-20	46	602	811	1,766	1,124	1,156
1-30	54	739	962	2,157	1,366	1,260
1-40	61	824	1,071	2,327	1,495	1,316
1-50	67	938	1,163	2,516	1,591	1,398
1-60	72	1,004	1,269	2,674	1,706	1,445
1-70	77	1,061	1,318	2,780	1,770	1,489
1-80	81	1,107	1,390	2,857	1,843	1,531
1-90	84	1,153	1,441	3,025	1,913	1,582
1-100	86	1,217	1,496	3,082	1,974	1,616

Note: Spot television costs are subject to wide variations depending on demand at any point in time. Consult your media department for current data.

II. Average Rating Levels
(ADI: TV Home Ratings)

	M-F Day	Early Fringe	Prime	Late Fringe	Early & Late News
Top 10 Markets	3.0%	6.0%	18.0%	3.0%	6.0%
Top 25 Markets	4.0	7.5	18.0	3.0	8.0
Top 50 Markets	4.0	8.5	18.0	4.0	9.0
Top 100 Markets	5.0	9.5	18.0	4.0	9.0
Total U.S.	5.0	10.0	18.0	4.0	10.0

IV. Spot Radio Costs (60 Second)

These estimates represent the average cost per rating point for one 60-second announcement on the top three stations in each market. It should be noted that spot rates are negotiable and actual schedules may cost less than indicated.

a. Cost per Rating Point (Metro Area Ratings)

Markets	Men 18-49	Women 18-49	Teens 12-17
1-10	$ 639	$ 582	$332
1-20	946	855	481
1-30	1,180	1,062	621
1-40	1,392	1,260	732
1-50	1,542	1,393	819
1-60	1,670	1,503	904
1-70	1,795	1,603	970
1-80	1,891	1,681	1,032
1-90	1,985	1,755	1,081
1-100	2,066	1,829	1,124

* Source: 1977 ARB, BBDO Estimates

All Cost per Point information based on the following rotations:

Men 18-49:	70% Drive Times, 30% Weekends
Women 18-49:	70% 6AM-7PM, 30% Weekends
Teens:	70% 3PM-12MD, 30% Weekends

b. Average Metro Area Ratings by Market Group
(For stations used in Cost per Point analysis)

Markets	Men 18-49	Women 18-49	Teens 12-17
1-10	2.0	2.0	5.0
1-50	2.5	3.0	6.0
1-100	3.5	3.5	6.0

Consumer Magazines

The following section contains information pertaining to advertising costs and audiences for selected publications.

Table I indicates the one-time four-color and black-and-white page costs for each publication, except where other units are appropriate. The latest available SRDS listings, as well as information obtained directly from the publications, were used as the sources for all data in these tables.

The on-sale date indicates the approximate time that a magazine may be purchased at a store or newsstand and often precedes the cover date—in the case of weekly publications by up to seven days, and monthlies by up to three weeks.

The closing date indicates the lead time needed by the publication to accept advertising.

SPECIAL NOTE:

The inclusion or exclusion of a particular publication in this section should not be construed as either an endorsement or censure by BBDO. For quick and easy reference, we have listed all of the selected publications in alphabetical order.

I. Page Costs, Rate Base, and On-Sale Dates

Magazines	Rate Base	Effective Date	Page 4-Color	Page B & W	On-Sale Date	Closing Date (Weeks Prior to Cover Date) 4-Color
A.D.	320	6/1/77	$ 2,500	$ 2,100	3rd wk.	8
Air Group One	1,000	10/1/77	20,678	16,542	1st	6
Aloft (National Airlines)	220	11/77	3,950	3,140	1st odd mos.	7
Ambassador (TWA)	301	1/78	6,600	5,800	1st	6
American Baby	1,000	1/78	16,925	12,240	20th	8
American Girl	630	1/78	6,745	4,650	25th	6

Magazines	Rate Base	Effective Date	Page 4-Color	Page B & W	On-Sale Date	Closing Date (Weeks Prior to Cover Date) 4-Color
American Legion	2,670	1/76	$12,426	$ 8,570	1st	10
American Way (American Airlines)	280	1/78	6,615	6,160	1st	7
Apartment Life	800	1/78	12,000	8,500	1st pre. mo.	10
Argosy	150	2/77	2,600	1,700	20th	9
Atlantic, The	325	10/77	6,260	4,100	3rd wk.	8
Baby Care	500	Spring'78	6,900	5,180	Qtrly.	6
Baby Talk	800	6/77	9,605	7,119	20th	8
Barron's	218	1/2/78	(1)	5,496	Mon.	5 days
Better Homes & Gardens	8,000	2/78	46,850	38,735	10th-20th	14
Black Enterprise	230	10/77	8,310	6,500	1st	7
Boating	197	3/78	5,295	3,840	4th wk.	9
Bon Appetit	800	4/78	9,800	6,600	1st	8
Book Digest	1,000	3/78	12,500	9,000	14th	12
Boys' Life	1,550	4/77(4)	10,500	7,500	25th	13
Bride's Magazine	293	2/78	9,750	7,850	4th wk.	12
Business Today	200	6/76	3,200	2,850	Semiannual	5
Business Week	780	1/1/78	21,300	14,200	Thurs.	5
Car Craft	300	1/78	4,920	3,075	20th	9
Car & Driver	725	1/78	15,990	12,870	20th	8
Catholic Digest	525	5/77	2,676	2,112	12th	10
Christian Science Monitor, The	170	12/31/76	4,620	2,040	Mon.-Fri.	2 days
Christian Herald	265	2/78	2,470	2,245	15th	7
Clipper (Pan American World Airways)	210	1/78	4,950	3,715	1st	6
Co-Ed	1,000	1/78	8,931	5,910	20th	9
Columbia	1,000	7/76	3,528(2)	3,206	1st	9
Commentary	56	1/78	2,080	1,150	1st	5
Cosmopolitan	1,800	1/78	18,595	13,820	25th	9
Country Gentleman	200	Fall'77	2,714	1,764	Qtrly.	8
Cue	272	9/1/77	6,400	4,500	Mon.	4
Delta Sky (Delta Airlines)	200	1/78	6,370	4,780	1st	6
Dun's Review	225	1/78	6,535	4,825	1st wk.	5
East/West Network (Domestic)	1,168	1/78	28,480	21,364	1st	6
Ebony	1,350	1/78	16,443	10,638	4th wk.	9
Elks Magazine	1,600	1/78	7,450	4,900	25th	6
Episcopalian, The	270	6/77	2,400	1,800	4th wk.	5
Essence	600	1/78	7,870	5,245	3rd wk.	10
Esquire	650	1/78	13,400	8,950	17th-24th	15
Family Circle	8,350	3/1/78	49,750	41,600	(3)	13
Family Health	1,000	9/76	11,200	8,000	20th	9
Farm Journal	1,400	1/78	27,520	19,575	16th-24th	7
Field & Stream	2,000	2/78	20,500	13,750	24th	8
Flying	412	1/78	11,100	7,650	30th	7
Flying Colors (Braniff)	166	1/78	3,800	3,100	1st	4
Forbes	660	1/9/78	15,500	10,210	1st and 15th	6
Fortune	625	1/78	20,670	13,600	16th and 30th	6
Glamour	1,700	1/78	15,300	10,875	1st	9
Golf	700	1/78	12,770	8,510	20th	9
Golf Digest	910	1/78	16,795	11,195	15th	7
Good Housekeeping	5,000	1/78	36,835	29,350	20th	10
Gourmet	650	7/77	11,500	6,500	1st	7
Grit	1,250	1/77	9,375	7,500	Sun.	6
Guns & Ammo	425	1/78	5,785	3,615	19th	9
Harper's	300	10/77	6,260	4,100	3rd wk.	8
Harper's Bazaar	500	8/77	10,550	7,300	1st	9
Harvard Business Review	185	1/78	5,010	3,645	1st	5
High Fidelity	322	10/77	9,895	7,970	20th	8
Hot Rod	800	1/78	12,480	7,800	4th wk.	7
House & Garden	1,000	1/78	16,360	11,100	20th	9
House Beautiful	800	1/78	13,300	9,080	20th	9
Hunting	150	1/78	3,000	1,875	20th	10
Hustler	2,500	9/77	16,250	11,250	1st	13
Industry Week	250	1/78	6,537	4,842	Mon.	4
Jack & Jill	600	6/71	4,400	3,300	2nd wk.	12
Jet	700	1/78	6,305	3,826	Thurs.	4
Kiwanis	273	1/75	2,400	1,450	25th	7
Ladies' Home Journal	6,000	2/78	36,180	28,590	17th	9
Lady's Circle	350	2/78	1,700	1,375	25th	12
Lion, The	687	10/76	4,232	2,997	25th	6
Lutheran, The	580	1/1/78	3,480	2,380	1st & 3rd Weds.	5
Mademoiselle	800	1/78	8,950	6,120	29th	9
Mainliner (United Airlines)	365	1/78	10,005	7,505	1st	6
McCall's	6,500	2/78	41,600	32,825	22nd	10
Mechanix Illustrated	1,650	2/78	15,990	11,300	20th-25th	10
Modern Bride	317	Spring'78	9,805	7,905	4th wk.	8
Modern Photography	600	1/78	17,108	13,134	1st	6
Modern Romances	200	2/78	1,845	1,280	4th-8th	11
Money	750	1/1/78	13,555	8,665	25th	5
Mother's Manual	900	10/77	12,600	9,250	1st	8
Motion Picture	150	11/77	1,645	1,145	4th	12
Motor Boating & Sailing	125	8/77	3,360	2,260	1st	7

(1) Hi-Fi and Specta Color available.
(2) Two colors only.
(3) Published 14 times per year—approximately every 26 days.
(4) Anticipated 2nd half rate increase not included.

Magazines	Rate Base	Effective Date	Page 4-Color	Page B & W	On-Sale Date	Closing Date (Weeks Prior to Cover Date) 4-Color
Ms.	500	9/76	$ 7,620	$ 5,550	last wk.	8
Motor Trend	750	1/78	14,705	9,190	4th wk.	9
National Enquirer	5,200	10/19/77	N.A.	10,500(5)	Tue.	6
National Geographic	8,650	1/78	67,665	49,390	1st	9
National Jewish Monthly, The	192	2/1/78	1,300	2,100	1st	5
National Lampoon	630	10/20/77	7,590	5,165	1st	8
Nation's Business	1,130	9/77	15,220	10,500	1st	5
Natural History	425	10/77	7,100	4,730	20th	7
Newsweek	2,900	1/2/78	41,590	26,660	Mon.	5
New Dawn	174	2/77	2,000	1,450	1st	9
New Times	350	6/24/77	6,985	4,375	Mon.	4
New West	290	1/31/78	8,480	4,560	Mon.	4
New Women	900	11/77	8,000	6,000	1st	13
New York	375	1/31/78	9,440	6,050	Mon.	5
New York Times Magazine	1,480	10/2/77	11,605	7,825	Sun.	7
New Yorker, The	470	1/2/78	10,900	7,000	Mon.	6
Oui	1,100	1/26/77	11,900	7,560	1st	11
Outdoor Life	1,700	1/78	16,370	11,520	25th	8
Parents' Magazine & Better Family Living	1,500	2/78	17,460	13,640	25th	9
Passages (Northwest Airlines)	150	1/78	4,245	2,968	1st	6
Penthouse	4,500	7/77	31,085	20,700	8th-14th	12
People	2,200	1/9/78	18,950	14,875	Mon.	7
Photoplay	1,250	11/77	8,600	5,935	4th-8th	12
Playbill (NY)	1,040	1/78	14,874	9,887	1st	7
Playboy	4,500	10/77	36,675	26,190	1st	12
Playgirl	750	1/78	7,850	5,888	10th	12
Players	200	10/76	2,200	1,400	2nd wk.	12
Popular Mechanics	1,600	1/78	15,900	11,280	4th wk.	8
Popular Photography	815	10/77	20,510	16,145	30th	7
Popular Science	1,800	1/78	16,655	11,740	1st	8
Presbyterian Survey	119	11/1/75	1,311	833	1st wk.	4
Professional Group, The	500	4/77	11,500	9,575	1st	6
Progressive Farmer	900	1/78	15,210	10,780	20th	6
Promenade	200	4/78	7,590	5,940	Semi-Ann.	6
Psychology Today	1,175	1/78	19,090	13,225	20th	7
Reader's Digest	17,750	1/78	69,610	57,920	25th	9
Redbook	4,400	2/78	29,525	22,220	20th-24th	9
Redbook's Young Mother	3,595	2/78	39,720	30,590	1st	12
Review (Eastern Airlines)	300	1/78	7,860	5,895	1st	6
Road & Track	550	10/77	10,775	7,150	18th	10
Rolling Stone	600	11/77	10,875	7,020	Tues.	7
Rotarian, The	450	8/78	3,925	2,775	18th	7
Sail	160	1/78	4,800	3,360	1st	6
Salt Water Sportsman	111	8/76	1,675	1,100	25th	6
Saturday Evening Post	450	9/77	7,118	4,745	10th-20th	9
Saturday Review	511	2/19/77	7,940	5,770	Thurs.	6
Scholastic Magazines Jr.-Sr. High School Market	3,900	9/77	25,205	17,550	Thurs.	7
Sr. High School Market	2,900	9/77	17,755	12,360	Thurs.	7
Scientific American	575	1/78	13,950	9,300	1st	7
Scouting	1,000	9/75	7,450	4,750	20th	12
Sea/Rudder	180	8/77	4,165	2,975	1st	6
Seventeen	1,450	2/78	13,000	9,000	1st	9
Signature	725	8/77	6,160	5,100	1st	7
Ski	444	9/77	9,995	7,070	20th	10
Skiing	475	9/77	11,200	7,925	20th	9
Skin Diver	165	1/78	3,900	2,515	4th wk.	10
Smithsonian	1,500	3/77	22,500	15,000	1st	7
Southern Living	1,400	1/78	15,390	10,880	15th	10
Sphere	600	1/78	8,125	6,740	3rd	9
Sport	1,300	2/78	14,000	9,590	20th	9
Sporting News	338	1/1/78	4,398	3,423	Sat.	3
Sports Afield	500	5/77	7,000	5,000	25th	9
Sports Illustrated	2,250	1/2/78	37,235	23,870	Wed.	7
Successful Farming	750	1/78	14,890	10,780	15th	6
Sunset	1,210	1/78	14,891	10,669	25th	9
Talk (Formerly Girl Talk)	250	5/77	7,800	6,200	27th	6
Teen	900	1/78	8,580	5,535	12th	11
Tennis	425	1/78	8,415	5,610	20th	7
Time	4,250	1/2/78	58,755	37,665	Mon.	7
Town & Country	158	8/77	5,900	4,525	1st	8
Travel/Holiday	750	1/78	6,600	4,600	20th	8
Travel & Leisure	800	9/77	11,070	8,400	22nd	7
True Confessions	350	11/77	2,755	1,900	4th-8th	11
True Story	2,000	8/77	13,580	9,375	4th-8th	11
TV Guide	18,300	4/1/78	61,000	51,300	Weds.	7
US	800	3/7/78	6,730	5,280	Tue.	
U.S. News & World Report	2,000	1/9/78	28,800	18,250	Mon.	6
V.F.W. Magazine	1,800	1/1/78	7,540	5,980	1st	7
Viva	500	5/75	4,000	2,670	2nd Tues.	12
Vogue	800	8/77	11,800	8,100	1st	9
Wall Street Journal(5)	1,485	1/9/78	N.A.	8,897	Mon.-Fri.	2 days
Western's World (Western Airlines)	250	1/78	4,250	3,350	1st	6

(5) Published in standard-size newspaper format. Rate shown is ¼ page unit, which is approximately equal in area to a 7" × 10" magazine page.

Magazines	Rate Base	Effective Date	Page 4-Color	Page B & W	On-Sale Date	Closing Date (Weeks Prior to Cover Date) 4-Color
Where	223	11/1/77	$10,690	$ 9,295	Sat.	19 days
Woman's Day	8,000	3/1/78	47,500	39,680	(3)	13
Working Woman	200	1/78	2,800	1,960	18th	8
World Tennis	325	1/78	6,375	4,250	25th	7
Yachting	124	8/77	4,070	2,730	1st	6

II. Average Issue Adult Audience

The table below utilizes W. R. Simmons 1976/77 female and male readers-per-copy estimates to project coterminous U.S. (48-state) magazine audience and coverage.

Circulation numbers shown below were taken from the publication rate cards available at time of printing and are adjusted to a 48-state basis.

Magazines	48 State Circ. (000)	Women %U.S. Cov.*	Women Audience (000)	Women RPC	Men %U.S. Cov.*	Men Audience (000)	Men RPC
American Baby	1,000	2.1	1,620	1.62	.4	260	.26
Barron's	232	.4	278	1.20	1.1	773	3.33
Better Homes & Gardens	8,000	23.1	18,000	2.25	9.1	6,480	.81
Business Week	704	1.0	767	1.09	4.3	3,084	4.38
Car & Driver	674	.7	539	.80	3.7	2,642	3.92
Cosmopolitan	1,638	7.6	5,946	3.63	2.5	1,753	1.07
Esquire	990	1.8	1,396	1.41	4.1	2,891	2.92
Family Circle	7,766	22.6	17,551	2.26	4.1	2,951	.38
Family Weekly	10,851	13.1	10,200	.94	11.7	8,355	.77
Field & Stream	2,010	3.6	2,794	1.39	10.3	7,316	3.64
Forbes	670	.6	476	.71	1.8	1,306	1.95
Fortune	570	.5	428	.75	1.8	1,300	2.28
Glamour	1,632	7.8	6,038	3.70	.9	636	.39
Golf	631	.6	492	.78	2.0	1,458	2.31
Golf Digest	826	.7	578	.70	2.2	1,561	1.89
Good Housekeeping	4,800	20.2	15,696	3.27	4.8	3,408	.71
Harper's/Atlantic/Natural History (Gross)	1,076	2.0	1,528	1.42	2.5	1,797	1.67
House & Garden	970	6.9	5,335	5.50	2.5	1,814	1.87
House Beautiful	784	6.0	4,641	5.92	1.6	1,145	1.46
Ladies' Home Journal	5,880	17.3	13,465	2.29	3.3	2,352	.40
Mademoiselle	768	3.1	2,404	3.13	.3	215	.28
McCall's	6,435	21.7	16,860	2.62	4.7	3,346	.52
Mechanix Illustrated	1,440	1.3	979	.68	6.3	4,464	3.10
Money	825	1.0	767	.93	2.0	1,452	1.76
Ms.	495	2.3	1,772	3.58	.6	416	.84
National Enquirer	4,325	9.2	7,180	1.66	7.5	5,363	1.24
National Geographic	7,093	12.1	9,434	1.33	16.2	11,562	1.63
Newsweek	2,871	9.3	7,235	2.52	14.1	10,049	3.50
New York	383	1.1	831	2.17	1.1	762	1.99
New Yorker	447	1.7	1,323	2.96	2.4	1,712	3.83
New York Times (Daily)	795	1.0	755	.95	2.0	1,391	1.75
New York Times Magazine	1,379	2.7	2,124	1.54	2.8	2,013	1.46
Oui	913	.8	612	.67	4.2	2,958	3.24
Outdoor Life	1,722	2.4	1,860	1.08	7.4	5,269	3.06
Parade	19,647	24.0	18,665	.95	25.4	18,075	.92
Parents'	1,470	4.6	3,602	2.45	1.1	750	.51
Penthouse	3,690	2.3	1,808	.49	11.3	8,044	2.18
People	2,068	10.7	8,396	4.06	8.4	5,977	2.89
Playboy	4,005	3.9	3,044	.76	14.5	10,333	2.58
Popular Mechanics	1,536	1.6	1,244	.81	7.2	5,130	3.34
Popular Science	1,674	1.2	954	.57	5.7	4,085	2.44
Psychology Today	1,163	3.3	2,605	2.24	3.0	2,105	1.81
Reader's Digest	18,283	29.6	23,037	1.26	26.4	18,831	1.03
Redbook	4,312	13.2	10,306	2.39	2.8	1,984	.46
Road & Track	440	.5	370	.84	4.8	3,436	7.81
Saturday Review	520	.7	536	1.03	1.2	832	1.60
Scientific American	454	.6	504	1.11	1.7	1,185	2.61
Sport	1,300	1.0	806	.62	5.0	3,536	2.72
Sports Afield	495	.7	510	1.03	2.6	1,856	3.75
Sports Illustrated	2,250	3.7	2,903	1.29	12.9	9,158	4.07
Sunday	21,470	30.9	24,046	1.12	31.9	22,758	1.06
Talk	548	10.6	8,220	15.00	—	—	—
Time	4,378	11.4	8,844	2.02	15.5	11,033	2.52
TV Guide	19,080	30.6	23,850	1.25	27.3	19,462	1.02
U.S. News & World Report	2,000	3.9	3,080	1.54	7.1	5,080	2.54
Viva	345	1.1	856	2.48	1.3	894	2.59
Vogue	728	5.2	4,026	5.53	.6	393	.54

* Current 48 state population provided by W. R. Simmons: 77,825,000 females 18+ and 71,232,000 males 18+.

Magazines	48 State Circ.	Women % U.S. Cov.*	Women Audience	Women RPC	Men % U.S. Cov.*	Men Audience	Men RPC
	(000)		(000)			(000)	
Wall St. Journal	1,451	1.9	1,509	1.04	4.7	3,337	2.30
Women's Day	7,440	21.2	16,517	2.22	2.2	1,562	.21
Ziff Davis (Gross)	3,552	5.4	4,191	1.18	18.2	12,965	3.65

* Current 48 state population provided by W.R. Simmons: 77,825,000 females 18+ and 71,232,000 males 18+.

III. Total Audience Formation

Standard total audience research measures the number of readers of a magazine at the end of that magazine's issue life. For example, a weekly requires five weeks from its on-sale date to be read by all of its measurable readers; a typical monthly takes about 11 weeks. However, from the day it first reaches the newsstand, a magazine builds its audience. The timing of this accumulation can be helpful in the scheduling of insertions and in the determination of reach potentials.

The following table is presented to illustrate the total audience formation of a typical weekly and a typical monthly from the first week of their issue life through to the last. Please note that TV Guide is shown separately. Because of the currency of its information, it gathers its total audience more rapidly than do other weekly publications.

Percent of Audience Reached by the End of Various Weeks

	Week 1	Week 2	Week 3	Week 4	Week 8	Week 12
Typical Weekly*	60	80	92	98	100	—
Typical Monthly	40	60	65	70	89	100
TV Guide	90	97	100	—	—	—

* Excluding TV Guide.

To read: After the first week in the issue life of a typical weekly, 60% of its total audience has been accumulated; by the end of eight weeks 100% has been accumulated.

Newspapers

Newspaper advertising accounts for approximately 30% of the total ad revenue, with local advertisers responsible for most of the dollars spent. As in the past, national rates are higher than those paid by the local merchant, since the latter derives few benefits from circulation outside the retail trading zone. Typically, the rate differential between national and local is approximately 50%, but this may vary according to the size of the ad.

I. Total Circulation of U.S. Newspapers

	No. of Papers*	Circulation
		(000)
Morning	346	25,858
Evening	1,435	35,119
Sunday	650	51,565

* Totals by editions, not papers.
Source: Editor & Publisher Yearbook, 1977

II. Total Circulation and B/W Rates for Selected Daily Newspapers in the Top 50 Markets in Rank Order

Market/Newspaper	Ed.	Total Circ. (000)	Open Line Rate	Cost Per Page
New York, N.Y.-N.J.				
News	M	1,912	$10.05	$12,060
Post	E	503	4.70	5,640
Times	M	867	5.68	13,632
Los Angeles-Long Beach, California				
Times	M	1,019	$4.40	$9,120
Herald Examiner	E	338	2.91	6,205
Long Beach Independent Press Telegram	M/E	145	1.11	2,673
Chicago, Illinois				
Sun-Times; News	M/E	926	6.45	7,646
Tribune	D	757	4.70	11,858
Philadelphia, Pa.—N.J.				
Inquirer; News	M/E	644	5.90	10,490
Bulletin	E	556	4.75	8,298
Detroit, Michigan				
News	E	644	3.50	9,319
Free Press	M	620	3.45	8,064
Boston, Massachusetts				
Globe	M/E	460	3.10	7,992
Herald American	M	293	2.58	6,696
San Francisco-Oakland, California				
Chronicle, Examiner	M/E	625	4.24	10,210
Oakland Tribune	E	167	1.20	2,890
Washington, D.C.				
Post	M	555	4.00	11,124
Star	E	375	2.80	7,231
Dallas-Fort Worth, Texas				
Dallas Times Herald	E	235	1.41	3,820
Dallas News	M	272	1.45	3,915
Ft. Worth Star-Telegram	M/E	222	1.20	3,251
Nassau-Suffolk, New York				
Newsday	E	479	3.57	3,570
Houston, Texas				
Chronicle	E	315	1.82	4,865
Post	M	300	1.77	4,683
Pittsburgh, Pennsylvania				
Press, Post-Gazette	M/E	457	3.35	7,812
St. Louis, Missouri				
Post-Dispatch	E	262	1.89	5,050
Globe-Democrat	M	270	1.70	4,428
Baltimore, Maryland				
Sun	M/E	349	2.20	5,940
News American	E	174	1.70	4,590
Minneapolis-St. Paul, Minn.				
Minneapolis Star, Tribune	M/E	474	3.77	6,468
St. Paul Dispatch, Pioneer Press	M/E	223	2.06	3,182
Newark, New Jersey				
Star Ledger	M	408	2.30	6,152
Elizabeth Journal	E	53	.67	1,613
Morristown Record	E/E	49	.75	1,323
Bridgewater Courier News	E	59	.56	1,517
Cleveland, Ohio				
Press	E	323	1.83	5,188
Plain Dealer	M	381	2.00	5,400
Atlanta, Georgia				
Journal, Constitution	M/E	434	2.20	5,298
Anaheim-Santa Ana-Garden Grove, California				
Register, Bulletin, Star-Progress	M/E/E/E	223	1.36	3,275
Costa Mesa Orange Coast Pilot	E	46	.48	1,152
San Diego, California				
Union, Tribune	M/E	320	2.09	5,033
Tampa-St. Petersburg, Fla.				
St. Petersburg Times, Independent	M/E	250	1.33	3,203
Tampa Tribune, Times	M/E	203	1.25	3,544
Miami, Florida				
Herald, News	M/E	513	4.79	8,963
Seattle, Wash.				
Times	E	237	2.14	4,045
Post-Intelligencer	M	186	1.54	3,450
Denver, Colorado				
Post	E	251	1.34	3,655
Rocky Mountain News	M	246	1.30	1,560
Milwaukee, Wisconsin				
Journal, Sentinel	M/E	507	2.55	6,120
Kansas City, Missouri				
Star, Times	M/E	638	3.14	5,859
Cincinnati, Ohio				
Post	E	199	1.25	3,005
Enquirer	M	192	1.20	2,920
Buffalo, New York				
News	E	280	1.55	3,819
Riverside-San Bernardino-Ontario, California				
Riverside Press, Enterprise	M/E	92	.73	1,758
San Bernardino Sun, Telegram	M	78	.70	1,680
Pomona-Ontario Report, Progress-Bulletin	E/E	69	.65	1,565
Phoenix, Arizona				
Republic, Gazette	M/E	352	1.75	4,741
San Jose, California				
Mercury, News	M/E	208	1.40	3,371
Palo Alto News Tribune	E/E	64	.77	1,854

Market/Newspaper	Ed.	Total Circ. (000)	Open Line Rate	Cost Per Page
Portland, Oregon				
Oregonian, Oregon Journal	M/E	342	$1.88	$4,985
Indianapolis, Indiana				
Star, News	M/E	375	2.20	5,307
New Orleans, Louisiana				
Times-Picayune, States-Item	M/E	329	1.65	4,293
Columbus, Ohio				
Dispatch, Citizen-Journal	M/E	305	1.40	3,969
Hartford-New Britain, Connecticut				
Courant	M	206	1.00	2,400
New Britain Herald	E	35	.36	867
Fort Lauderdale-Hollywood, Florida				
Fort Lauderdale News, Pompano Beach Sun-Sentinel	M/E	138	1.00	1,890
Hollywood Sun-Tattler	E	43	.37	1,049
Rochester, New York				
Democrat & Chronicle, Times-Union	M/E	258	2.18	4,682
Sacramento, California				
Bee	E	179	1.15	2,496
Union	M	93	.85	1,836
San Antonio, Texas				
Express, News	M/E	157	1.01	2,709
Light	E	128	.95	2,574
Louisville, Kentucky				
Courier-Journal, Times	M/E	375	2.22	3,996
Providence, R.I.				
Bulletin, Journal	M/E	209	1.67	4,509
Albany-Schenectady-Troy, New York				
Albany Times-Union, Knickerbocker News	M/E	140	1.25	3,386
Schenectady Gazette	M	64	.45	1,109
Troy Times Record	E	46	.41	1,010
Dayton, Ohio				
News, Journal Herald	M/E	296	2.15	6,095
Memphis, Tennessee				
Commercial Appeal, Press-Scimitar	M/E	315	2.00	5,273
Oklahoma City, Oklahoma				
Oklahoman, Times	M/E	263	2.00	5,418
Birmingham, Alabama				
News, Post-Herald	M/E	258	1.44	3,770
Bridgeport-Stamford-Norwalk-Danbury, Connecticut				
Bridgeport Post, Telegram	M/E	91	.68	1,714
Stamford Advocate	E	31	.48	855
Danbury News-Times	E	38	.44	792
Norwalk Hour	E	22	.36	650
Greensboro-Winston-Salem, N.C.				
Winston-Salem Journal, Twin City Sentinel	M/E	112	.96	2,396
Greensboro News, Record	M/E	109	.91	2,465
Toledo, Ohio				
Blade	E	171	1.00	2,778

III. Cost of Page B/W Ads in Papers Needed to Obtain 60% Gross Metro Coverage in Top 100 Markets

Markets	No. of Papers	% Gross Metro Coverage	Gross Metro Circulation (000)	Line Rate	Page B&W
New York	3	56	2,078	$20.43	$31,332
Los Angeles/Long Beach	3	43	1,159	8.42	17,998
Chicago	2	63	1,507	11.15	19,504
Philadelphia	2	68	1,093	10.65	18,788
Detroit	2	72	1,062	6.95	17,383
Boston	2	49	646	5.68	14,688
San Francisco/Oakland	2	48	586	5.44	13,100
Washington, D. C.	2	79	826	6.80	18,355
Dallas/Ft. Worth	3	71	629	4.06	10,986
Nassau/Suffolk	1	56	452	3.57	3,570
Houston	2	66	530	3.59	9,548
Pittsburgh	1	52	417	3.35	7,812
St. Louis	2	59	463	3.59	9,478
Baltimore	2	71	502	3.90	10,530
Minneapolis-St. Paul	2	78	534	5.83	9,650
Newark	4	63	411	4.28	10,605
Cleveland	2	92	613	3.83	10,588
Atlanta	1	55	339	2.20	5,298
Anaheim-Santa Ana-Garden Grove	2	41	253	1.84	4,427
San Diego	1	52	306	2.09	5,033
Tampa/St. Petersburg	2	64	367	2.58	6,747
Miami	1	59	325	4.79	8,963
Seattle	2	64	343	3.68	7,495
Denver	2	77	395	2.64	5,215
Milwaukee	1	85	409	2.55	6,120

Markets	No. of Papers	% Gross Metro Coverage	Gross Metro Circulation (000)	Line Rate	Page B&W
Kansas City	1	108	506	$3.14	$5,859
Cincinnati	2	74	344	2.45	5,925
Buffalo	1	57	260	1.55	3,819
Riverside-San Bernardino-Ontario	3	45	204	2.08	5,003
Phoenix	1	65	285	1.75	4,741
San Jose	2	53	218	2.17	5,225
Portland	1	62	255	1.88	4,985
Indianapolis	1	80	312	2.20	5,307
New Orleans	1	74	276	1.65	4,293
Columbus, O.	1	75	273	1.40	3,969
Hartford-New Britain	2	56	198	1.36	3,267
Ft. Lauderdale-Hollywood	2	49	172	1.37	2,939
Rochester	1	75	249	2.18	4,682
Sacramento	2	70	226	2.00	4,332
San Antonio	2	80	246	1.96	5,283
Louisville	1	88	262	2.22	3,996
Providence	1	66	192	1.67	4,509
Albany-Schenectady-Troy	3	81	229	2.11	5,505
Dayton	1	81	229	2.15	6,095
Memphis	1	80	225	2.00	5,273
Oklahoma City	1	64	180	2.00	5,418
Birmingham	1	69	191	1.44	3,770
Bridgeport-Stamford-Norwalk-Danbury	4	60	164	1.96	4,011
Greensboro/Winston-Salem	2	65	174	1.87	4,861
Toledo	1	59	155	1.00	2,778
New Haven-Waterbury	2	68	178	1.52	3,366
Nashville	1	64	168	1.51	3,624
Salt Lake City	1	55	134	1.06	2,872
Norfolk-Portsmouth-Virginia Beach	1	83	202	1.61	3,900
Jacksonville	1	72	172	1.58	3,805
Northeast Pennsylvania	2	52	119	1.18	2,836
Allentown	1	50	110	.77	1,386
Akron	1	68	150	1.48	2,797
Tulsa	1	71	155	1.53	2,763
Syracuse	1	83	180	1.35	3,300
Worcester	1	64	137	1.39	3,323
Jersey City	2	50	107	1.07	2,824
Honolulu	1	81	171	1.08	2,684
Orlando	1	57	119	1.69	4,070
Charlotte	1	68	137	2.30	4,347
Richmond	1	92	185	1.60	3,840
Gary-Hammond	2	65	130	1.42	3,742
Springfield	1	70	140	1.05	2,863
Omaha	1	72	138	1.45	3,492
West Palm Beach	1	49	91	.96	1,814
Grand Rapids	1	60	110	.97	1,793
New Brunswick-Perth Amboy	2	54	100	1.10	3,020
Youngstown	1	51	92	.55	1,386
Greenville-Spartanburg	2	70	126	1.52	3,817
Wilmington	1	66	114	1.35	2,435
Flint	1	59	100	.90	1,663
New Bedford-Fall River	3	56	92	1.16	1,160
Tucson	1	68	111	.90	2,438
Fresno	1	61	97	.85	1,992
Raleigh	1	50	79	1.25	3,150
Paterson-Clifton-Passaic	2	56	88	1.67	3,888
Long Beach-Asbury Park	2	55	76	1.02	2,652
Knoxville	1	71	109	.72	2,041
Harrisburg	1	66	101	.72	1,950
Oxnard-Ventura	3	53	76	1.07	2,544
Tacoma	1	64	92	.75	2,032
Lansing	1	48	69	.64	1,783
Johnson City-Kingsport-Bristol	3	61	84	.96	2,352
Canton	1	49	67	.52	1,441
Chattanooga	2	71	97	.92	2,216
Wichita	1	95	129	1.60	2,995
Austin	1	63	85	.89	2,411
Albuquerque	1	67	88	.76	1,830
Little Rock	2	75	97	1.70	4,121
Davenport-Rock Island-Moline	2	82	106	1.13	2,721
Mobile	1	71	91	.77	1,909
Baton Rouge	1	69	88	.99	1,770
El Paso	1	60	76	.70	1,806
Fort Wayne	1	84	104	.75	2,093
Peoria	1	69	86	.68	1,637

Note: Morning and evening newspaper combinations are counted as one.

Source: SM Survey of Buying Power, 1977
ANM Circulation, '77/'78
SRDS September, 1977
Prepared by Newspaper Advertising Bureau, December, 1977

IV. ROP Color Premiums (Top 100 Markets)

	1,000 Lines	Full Page
Black and one color	35%	17%
Black and two colors	50%	24%
Black and three colors	62%	29%

Source: Newspaper Advertising Bureau

V. Total Newspaper Coverage

	Women		Men	
	Average Weekday	Average Sunday/ Weekend	Average Weekday	Average Sunday/ Weekend
Read any paper	70%	68%	72%	69%
Read 1 paper	54	54	52	53
Read 2 papers	16	14	20	16

Source: BBDO Estimates based on Simmons

VI. Women/Men Costs per Thousand for Daily and Sunday Newspapers in Top 100 Markets

		Women	Men
Daily	—Page B/W	$13.80	$14.46
	—1,000 Lines B/W	6.06	6.35
Sunday	—Page B/W	12.45	13.05
	—1,000 Lines B/W	5.51	5.78

Source: BBDO Estimates based upon 60% coverage

VII. Average Audience Delivery by Age and Income (Women/Men Base = 100)

	Average Weekday		Average Sunday/Weekend	
	Women	Men	Women	Men
TOTAL	100	100	100	100
BY AGE				
18-24	85	88	95	95
25-34	91	96	99	99
35-49	109	104	107	103
50+	106	107	99	102
BY HOUSEHOLD INCOME				
Under $8,000	86	81	81	74
Under $10,000	88	84	85	77
$10-$14,999	101	100	103	99
$15,000-24,999	113	111	116	117
$25,000 and over	116	112	119	120

Source: BBDO Estimates based on Simmons

Sunday Supplements

Sunday supplements are magazine-type publications which are distributed within the weekend editions of carrier newspapers.

"Tuesday" and "Tuesday at Home" are monthly black-oriented publications, available market by market on a regional or nation-wide basis. "Sunday," a locally edited supplement, may be purchased alone or in any combination of affiliated carrier papers in 43 cities including 7 two-paper markets.

Since supplements have almost no pass-along audience, their "primary audience" represents virtually their entire "total audience." Approximately two adults, one woman and one man, read each issue along with a more difficult to define complement of teens and children. Since minute variations in reader-per-copy levels which may occur from one survey to another are not really significant, we have excluded readership and efficiency comparisons.

Number of Papers and Circulation per Issue

	Number of Carrier Newspapers	U.S. Circulation	Effective Date	Page 4-Color	Page B&W
		(000)			
Family Weekly	332	11,400	1/78	$ 65,430	$ 57,450
Parade	118	20,323	1/78	125,050	101,735

	Number of Carrier Newspapers	U.S. Circulation	Effective Date	Page 4-Color	Page B&W
		(000)			
Sunday	50	22,478	1/78	$160,850	$134,573
Tuesday/Tuesday at Home	21	1,700	10/76	14,450	12,750

Source: SRDS and publications

Sunday Comics and Comic Books

All major newspapers, with the exception of The New York Times, carry a weekend comic section. The two largest Sunday comic syndicators, Metro and Puck, include about 200 newspapers between them. The Metro Total Network consists of the Basic Network (large cities) and the Metro Selective Members (smaller markets). Puck is also comprised of two distinct and exclusive networks: the National Network (large cities) and the American Network (smaller markets).

I. Sunday Comics

NUMBER OF PAPERS, CIRCULATION AND COSTS

	No. of U.S. Papers	Effective Date	Total Circulation	Page 4-Color	1/2 Page 4-Color	1/3 Page 4-Color
			(000)			
METRO						
Basic Network	57	1/78	20,369	$147,499	$ 96,565	$74,853
Total Network	81	1/78	21,934	163,665	106,351	82,126
PUCK						
National Network	58	1/78	14,122	119,372	69,652*	52,972**
American Network	65	1/78	4,253	40,423	22,326	16,189

* Full page in tabloid
** ⅔ page in tabloid

Source: SRDS and publications

II. Comic Books

NUMBER OF COMICS, CIRCULATION AND COSTS

	No. of Titles	Total Circulation	Page 4-Color	Page B & W
		(000)		
Archie Comic Group	17	6,000	$ 8,400	$ 8,400
Charlton Comics Group	13	2,250	2,700	2,700
DC Comics Group	20	8,270	16,445	16,445
Gold Key Comics Group	38	3,500	4,950	3,690
Harvey Comics Group	28	3,920	6,600	6,600
Marvel Comic Group	16	12,000	16,365	16,365

Source: SRDS and publications

Out-of-Home Visual Media

I. General

The category of Out-of-Home Media includes numerous media forms which have a common feature: They expose a visual advertising message to a mobile audience away from its place of residence.

II. Thirty-Sheet Poster Costs
Within Top 100 S.M.S.A.'s

The unit of sale for this medium is daily "Gross Rating Points." Rates are generally listed for multiples of 25 GRP's, but other levels are often available upon request. GRP's are quoted on the basis of the market as defined by the plant operator's geographic area of service, rather than broadcast Areas of Dominant Influence (ADI's.)

Posters are bought on a monthly basis with discounts usually applicable for an annual schedule. In an average market, 100 GRP's will reach approximately 90% of the adult population during a 28-day period with an average frequency of a little over once a day. A level of 50 GRP's requires about half as many panels and will reach 85% every other day.

Thirty-sheet panels have an overall size of 12.5'H X 25'W and a copy display area of approximately 235 square feet. They are available in all major marketing areas throughout the continental United States, except Alaska. Located on primary and secondary arteries throughout the market, they can be used to provide high reach and frequency. Locations may be chosen to conform with ethnic and demographic marketing areas.

100 Gross Rating Points

Markets	# of Panels	% Illuminated	Monthly Cost
1-10	2,741	74	$ 557,979
1-20	4,389	71	830,210
1-30	5,519	71	1,013,924
1-40	6,436	70	1,150,251
1-50	7,256	68	1,264,048
1-60	8,000	66	1,358,486
1-70	8,660	65	1,443,714
1-80	9,165	64	1,511,928
1-90	9,562	63	1,564,376
1-100	10,046	62	1,616,651

50 Gross Rating Points

Markets	# of Panels	% Illuminated	Monthly Cost
1-10	1,505	73	305,996
1-20	2,361	69	445,962
1-30	2,947	69	540,059
1-40	3,450	68	613,058
1-50	3,897	66	673,542
1-60	4,329	64	726,954
1-70	4,692	62	773,786
1-80	4,940	62	809,352
1-90	5,152	61	837,169
1-100,	5,439	59	868,643

Source: NOAB rates of record, January, 1978

III. Rotating Painted Bulletin Costs
Within Top 50 S.M.S.A.'s

14'H x 48'W bleed painted bulletins located on major arterials are rotated either monthly or every other month throughout the Metro Area to provide complete market coverage. Average unit costs only are given. Bulletins are generally purchased for 12 months, but may be bought efficiently in 12-month increments.

Markets	Average Monthly Cost per Bulletin
1-10	$1,368
11-20	1,108
21-30	926
31-40	922
41-50	709

Source: NOAB rates of record, January, 1978

IV. Exterior Bus Displays

Posters are displayed in frames mounted on the exterior sides, fronts and backs of buses and streetcars traveling on most major arterials serving a market area.

Transit advertising is available in many sizes. However, all cost data and sign requirements outlined in this section are limited to king-size posters (30"H X 144"W), the most commonly used format.

Typically, a #100 showing provides enough signs to reach 85% of the population an average of 15 times in a 30-day period. A #50 showing provides slightly less reach with half the frequency in a 30-day period.

#100 Showing—Top 100 ADI's

Markets	# King-Size Posters	Monthly Cost
1- 10	4,827	$274,913
1- 20	6,097	344,366
1- 30	6,731	379,123
1- 40	7,163	401,003
1- 50	7,670	428,264
1- 60	7,997	443,179
1- 70	8,387	462,184
1- 80	8,535	470,256
1- 90	8,709	479,106
1-100	8,774	482,206

Source: Batchelder Co., Mutual Transit Sales and Winston Network estimates.

V. Interior Transit Vehicle Displays

Interior cards are available in municipal rapid-transit vehicles in most of the larger markets. The following availability and cost data are based on a monthly full run for 11"H X 28"W "rack" position cards within all municipal transit vehicles operating in each market.

Markets	No. Monthly Rides (Millions)	No. of Vehicles	Monthly Cost
1- 10	441	32,231	$ 86,476
1- 20	498	38,053	97,977
1- 30	533	41,143	104,998
1- 40	546	42,768	108,979
1- 50	554	44,198	111,934
1- 60	560	45,165	113,906
1- 70	561	46,253	116,256
1- 80	562	46,595	117,118
1- 90	564	47,057	118,078
1-100	565	47,268	118,425

Source: Batchelder Co., Mutual Transit Sales, and Winston Network estimates.

VI. Station Posters

Seven markets have extensive rapid-transit systems that are either underground, elevated, or both. In each case, advertising is available on station platforms in the form of poster panels. There is a variety of shapes and sizes; therefore, the following data will be restricted to the most common units—2-sheets, 46"H X 60"W; 1-sheet, 46"H X 30"W.

Market	Full Coverage or Equivalent		
	# Panels	2 Sheets	1 Sheet
Boston	150	$ 5,614	—
Chicago	400	6,127	$ 3,063
Cleveland	60	1,418	—
New York	1,200	24,304	14,177
Philadelphia	120	3,422	—
San Francisco	48	1,831	—
Washington, D. C.	50	3,000	—

Source: Mutual Transit Sales and TDI Div. of Winston Network.

VII. 8-Sheet Poster Costs Within Top 100 Markets

8-Sheet Posters measure 6' high by 12' wide, with physical proportions and appearance identical to 30-sheet units.

Junior Panels, as they are sometimes called, are attached to the walls of retail outlets in city and suburban shopping areas, or may be free-standing. They are at eye level near the line of traffic flow and are of optimum size to expose messages to pedestrians, plus automotive traffic in congested areas.

"Eights" can be used for general market coverage, or to target into specific in-market ethnic groups, such as concentrations of black or Spanish-speaking people. They can be geared to the retail level —trading areas of supermarkets, package-liquor stores, neighborhood and major shopping centers, etc.

#50 Showing—Top 100 SMSA's

Markets	Number of Panels	Space Cost
1-10	1,074	$ 52,077
1-20	1,639	77,355
1-30	1,999	93,146
1-40	2,209	102,560

Markets	Number of Panels	Space Cost
1-50	2,503	$115,430
1-60	2,658	121,661
1-70	2,813	127,821
1-80	2,970	133,858
1-90	3,113	140,239
1-100	3,258	145,742

Note: Above figures are based on a #50 Showing of 8-Sheets, General Coverage, for one month, in the top 100 Markets as determined by BBDO.

Source: Outdoor Representatives Co., Junior Panel Outdoor Advertising Assn.

VIII. Three-Sheet Poster Costs

3-sheet posters (83½"H x 41"W paper size) are available in sixty major markets. Posters are placed in shopping areas on or near supermarkets, liquor stores and other retail outlets. Their special characteristics include ethnic and demographic selectivity. Individual panels cost $25.00 monthly, subject to continuity discount.

King-size panels (85½"H x 88"W) are also available in fifteen major markets. The annual unit cost is $40.00. Short rates may be negotiated as space becomes available.

Source: Criterion Advertising Co.

Food Store Trade Media

Publication	No. Issues/ Year	Circ.	Audit Source	Page B&W	Closing Date
Food Products					
Chain Store Age Supermarkets	12	96,220	ABC	3,990	1st prec. mo.
Food Engineering	12	44,360	BPA	1,580	1st prec. mo.
Food Processing	12	56,096	BPA	1,520	1st prec. mo.
Frozen Food Age	12	17,803	BPA	1,085	5th prec. mo.
Progressive Grocer	12	82,905	BPA	4,240	1st prec. mo.
Quick Frozen Foods	12	20,873	BPA	975	5th prec. mo.
Supermarketing	12	80,165	BPA	4,025	1st prec. mo.
Supermarket News	52	56,258	ABC	3,595	5 days prec.

GLOSSARY

A

AAAA (4A's) American Association of Advertising Agencies. A national organization of leading advertising agencies.

AAF American Advertising Federation. A national association of advertisers, advertising agencies, media, and allied businesses organized to promote and defend effective advertising.

ABC Audit Bureau of Circulation. An organization sponsored by publishers, agencies, and advertisers to audit and validate circulation figures of magazines and newspapers.

ABP American Business Press. An organization of trade, industrial, and business papers formed by the merger of the Associated Business Publications and the National Business Publications groups.

account An advertiser. Used to refer to a client of an advertising agency.

account executive/supervisor A member of an advertising agency who is responsible for liaison with one or more accounts. Responsible for the supervision of marketing and advertising work done by the agency.

account service The department in an advertising agency to which account executives and account supervisors belong.

adjacency A broadcast time period immediately preceeding or following a scheduled program.

advertising Any paid form of nonpersonal presentation and promotion of ideas, goods, and services by an identified sponsor.

advertising agency A business organization rendering advertising services to clients.

advertising specialty A form of advertising. Products bearing the name of an advertiser and given as gifts to prospective customers.

affiliate A broadcast station that enters into an agreement to carry programs provided by a network.

agate line A unit of measure of print advertising space, one column wide (regardless of column width) and one-fourteenth of an inch deep.

aided recall A research technique used to measure the communications effectiveness of advertising in which the respondent is given aid in the form of an advertisement, brand name, or some other device to facilitate recall.

all commodity distribution A measure of retail distribution expressed as a percentage of total retail sales of a particular outlet type. For example, *30 percent all commodity distribution* in food stores means that a product has distribution in food stores accounting for 30 percent of all food store sales.

alternate sponsorship A form of program sponsorship in which two or more sponsors assume responsibility for a program and share commercial time.

AM Amplitude modulation. A method of transmitting radio signals by varying the amplitude or size of the electromagnetic wave as opposed to varying its frequency. *See* FM (frequency modulation).

AMA American Marketing Association. A professional association of academic and business people devoted to furthering the development of marketing.

ANA Association of National Advertisers. A national association of advertisers dominated by larger manufacturers.

animation Giving movement to static objects for attention value or effect. Used in filmed cartoons and in point-of-purchase displays or outdoor boards by adding moving parts.

ARB American Research Bureau. A broadcast rating service for TV and radio. Uses both a viewer diary method and an electronic recording and tabulating system known as *Arbitron*.

Arbitron *See* ARB.

ARBOR Association for Research in Behavior. An independent research organization that measures commercials and conducts other marketing research.

audience The total number of people who are able to receive an advertising message delivered by a medium or combination of media.

audio Sound portion of a TV commercial or program. See *video*.

availability A broadcast time period that has not been sold and is therefore available for purchase.

average frequency The number of times the average member of an audience is exposed to an advertising message within a given period of time, usually four weeks.

average issue circulation The average delivered circulation for all issues of a publication. Obtained by dividing the total annual circulation by the number of issues.

bait advertising An unethical practice in which a product is advertised at a highly attractive price in order to lure customers to the retail outlet where they find it difficult or impossible to buy the product at the advertised price.

BBB Better Business Bureau. Local organizations supported by advertisers, advertising agencies, media and other businesses to discourage false and misleading advertising and marketing practices.

B of A Bureau of Advertising, American Publishers Association. An organization that promotes the use of newspapers as an advertising medium.

billboard (1) The television presentation of the name of the sponsor at the beginning and close of a program. (2) A popular name for an outdoor sign.

billing The amount of money charged to clients by advertising agencies, including media costs, production costs, and service fees.

bleed Printing to the edge of the page, leaving no margin.

block type A general type face also known as *sans serif*. Characterized by vertical strokes of uniform thickness and the absence of cross strokes (serifs) at the bottom and top of the characters.

body copy The text of an ad, excluding headline, subheads, illustration, and logotype.

boldface Type in which the strokes are heavier than other designs of the same type family.

boutique A limited service type of advertising agency that usually performs only a creative service for a fee.

BPA Business Publications Audit of Circulation. An organization that audits business publications, primarily controlled circulation publications.

brand A name, term, sign, symbol, or design, or a combination of them that is intended to identify the goods or services of one seller or a group of sellers and to differentiate them from those of competitors.

broker A manufacturer's agent who receives commissions for sales to channel members. Does not normally take title to merchandise sold.

brand image The picture or likeness of the brand that exists in consumers' minds.

brand share The share of market held by a brand.

CATV Community Antenna Television System. A system for extending television coverage through the use of coaxial cable to subscribers in remote areas. Popularly known as *cable TV*.

campaign An advertising effort on behalf of a particular product or service that extends for a specified period of time.

caps A term used in typography. Refers to capital or uppercase letters in contrast to small or lowercase letters.

caption Explanatory text accompanying an illustration.

center spread A single sheet of paper that forms the two facing pages in the center of a publication or brochure.

chain break An interruption in network broadcasting to permit local station identification. Also a commercial broadcast during this interruption.

channel The frequency in the broadcast spectrum assigned to a station for its transmission.

circulation The number of copies of a publication distributed. In broadcast, it is the average number of listeners or viewers during a particular time period.

city zone That portion of a newspaper's coverage area that includes the corporate city plus adjacent areas that have the characteristics of the city.

classified advertising Advertising arranged according to the product or service advertised. The advertisements are limited in size and use of illustrations.

class magazines A term used to refer to magazines that reach upper socio-income groups.

clear-channel station A radio station with interference-free broadcasting rights on a particular frequency, and with broadcasting power up to 50,000 watts. Also referred to as *Class A stations*.

client   An advertiser with whom agencies and/or media do business.

closing date   The date by which advertising materials must be delivered to a medium in order to appear at a particular time.

coaxial cable   A special cable used to transmit telephone, telegraph, and television signals.

collateral material   An advertising term used to refer to noncommisionable media used in connection with an advertising campaign.

color separation   Used in connection with four-color advertising. In the printing process, the advertisement is decomposed into its primary color components.

column inch   A unit of publication space, one column wide and one inch deep.

combination rate   A discounted rate for advertising in two or more publications under the same ownership.

company forecast   An aggregate forecast for all products sold by a company.

comparison advertising   Advertising that compares two or more brands in terms of one or more product attributes. Also referred to as *comparative advertising.*

composing stick   A small, adjustable metal box used in assembling type in hand composition.

composition   Setting type and/or assembling it with engravings.

comprehensive   A layout, accurate in terms of size, color, and location of elements, to show how the final ad will appear.

conspicuous consumption   A term coined by the economist Thorstein Veblen that refers to the purchase of goods and services to enhance social prestige.

consumer orientation   A key element in the marketing concept in which goods and services are designed in terms of consumers' interests.

continuity   Repetition of the same basic theme. *Continuity* in media refers to the regularity with which advertising for a particular product appears in a particular medium throughout the marketing period.

continuous tone   A screened photographic image that contains gradiations of color or of black and white.

cooperative advertising   Retail advertising in which the cost is shared by the retailer and a national advertiser.

copy   Broadly speaking, any material to be included in an advertisement. In a narrow sense, it refers to verbal material only.

copy plan   A part of the marketing plan that consists of a summary statement of the essential elements to be included in an advertisement or commercial. The copy plan is usually written after a prototype ad or commercial has been developed and serves as a guide for other advertisements or commercials in the same campaign.

copyright   A legal term referring to protection granted an individual or company against reprinting—use of an original production without express consent.

copy strategy   A part of the marketing plan consisting of summary statements about how a product or service will be presented in advertising.

copy testing   Measuring the effectiveness of an advertisement or an element of an advertisement against some predetermined objective.

cost plus   A system for compensating advertising agencies for work done based on internal costs, out-of-pocket expenditures plus an agreed upon percentage of these costs to cover overhead and profit.

corporate advertising   Advertising designed to communicate corporate values as opposed to advertising done in support of a particular product or service.

corrective advertising   A punitive sanction employed by the FTC in which advertisers are required to run advertising specifically designed to correct false or misleading impressions created by previous advertising.

cost per thousand   The cost to an advertiser for delivering an advertising message to a thousand viewers, readers, or listeners. It is used as a basis for comparing the efficiency of alternative media.

counter card   Point-of-purchase material designed for display on a counter or near the cash register of a retail outlet.

cover   The front of a publication is referred to as the first cover; the inside of the front page is the second cover; the inside of the back page is the third cover; and the back page is the fourth cover. Extra rates are often charged for cover positions.

coverage   The percent of households or individuals exposed to a specific advertising medium in a designated area.

CU   Close-up. A term used in television production.

cume   The total audience reached by a succession of advertising messages within a defined period.

cursive type   A general group of type faces that resemble handwriting. Also referred to as *script.*

cylinder press   A printing press with a rotating cylinder under which a flat bed containing type or plates slides back and forth.

dagmar   A model for measuring the communication effectiveness of advertising. Conceptualizes the effects of advertising as four steps: awareness, comprehension, conviction, and action.

deal   Any of a variety of price incentives used to move merchandise. Examples are a cents-off-label, two for the price of one.

dealer   A retailer.

dealer tie in   A national advertiser's promotion in which dealers participate.

delayed broadcast   A repeat broadcast of a program by tape or film. Routinely used by networks to compensate for time zone differences between the east and west coasts.

design   The organization of the elements in a print advertisement.

direct lithography   A form of lithographic printing in which the printing plates are in direct contact with the printing surface. It is distinguished from off-set lithography in which the plate image is transferred to an intermediate surface (blanket) for printing. *See* Lithography.

directory advertising Advertising in published directories such as the Yellow Pages, or other business and industrial directories of firms.

display advertising Print advertising using illustrations, typography, colors, and design to attract attention, in contrast to classified advertising.

dissolve A technique used in television production for changing scenes. One scene is brought into sharp focus as the previous scene fades out.

dolly To move a camera in or out of scenes to gain a different camera angle or perspective.

down-and-under A direction given in radio and TV production to reduce the sound level of music or other sound effects so that it will not interfere with the dialogue to follow.

drive time The peak period for radio listenership when people are driving to and from work. Normally, 7–10 A.M., and 3–7 P.M.

duplication Multiple exposure of the same people to an advertising message.

economic profit That profit above the profit required to meet the basic objectives of a firm. The concept of economic profit is often used in marketing budgeting.

ECU Extreme close-up. A very close camera shot to show maximum detail.

electrotype A duplicate of another plate made by the electrotype process.

em A typographical measure based on the square of a body of any given type face, and derived from the letter M which is as wide as it is high. By convention, the term usually refers to the 12-point em, which is equal to 1/16 of an inch.

en Half the width of an em.

engraving An original printing plate. Also a process for reproducing a design for printing by etching metal plates.

fact sheet A page of product selling features used by broadcast personalities and announcers in ad libbing a live commercial.

fade A broadcast direction. To *fade in* is to gradually increase the intensity of sound or image. To *fade out* is to gradually decrease the intensity.

family of type A single design of a type face in a range of sizes and variations, such as Caslon Bold, Caslon Bold Italic, Caslon Old Style.

FCC Federal Communications Commission. The Federal authority authorized to license radio and television stations and to assign frequencies.

FDA Food and Drug Administration. The Federal agency authorized to enforce Food, Drug, and Cosmetic legis-

lation. Also regulates packaging, labeling, and advertising in these industries.

fee systems A method of compensating advertising agencies in which the client pays the agency an agreed-upon fee for its work.

field intensity The measurement of the coverage area of a broadcast station in terms of its signal strength. Field intensity contour maps indicate station coverage patterns.

finished layout A layout made to look as much like the finished ad as possible. Used primarily in sales presentations of the advertising campaign.

flat bed A printing press for letterpress printing containing a flat metal bed on which forms of type are locked for printing.

flat rate A uniform charge of space or time with no discounts for volume or frequency.

flight In broadcast, the concentration of commercials in a relatively short time period.

FM Frequency modulation. A method of modulating tone in broadcast by frequency of waves, rather than by their amplitude. More limited coverage than AM, but less affected by static.

font A complete assortment of type characters of one style and size.

format The size, shape, style, and appearance of a book or publication. In broadcast, the structure of a program.

four-color process A photoengraving process for reproducing color illustrations by a set of plates—one for each of the primary colors and one for black.

frequency The number of times an advertising message is delivered within a specified period of time.

frequency discount A discount in advertising rates based on the number of ads or commercials used within a specified period of time.

fringe time The hours directly before and after prime time. Also may be specified as early fringe or late fringe.

FTC Federal Trade Commission. A Federal agency concerned with the regulation of monopolies, unfair methods of competition, and fraudulent and misleading advertising.

full-service agency An advertising agency offering a wide range of marketing and advertising services.

Gallup-Robinson A research organization, best known for its copy testing services.

general advertising National or nonlocal advertising in newspapers.

generic product (1) The essential benefit a consumer expects to get from a product. For example, the woman buyng lipstick is not buying a set of chemicals and physical attributes; she is buying beauty. (2) Descriptive of an entire group or class of products (for example, aspirin or cake mix).

gestalt A German word meaning pattern or configuration. It refers to the overall impression created by a stimulus (an advertisement, for example). Also a school of psychology known for its work in perception.

Gothic A term sometimes used to refer to *block type.*

GNP Gross National Product. The aggregate value of all goods and services produced by a country.

gravure A printing process that transfers images to paper from ink in depressions in the plate, as opposed to *letterpress* which prints from raised surfaces. Also known as *intaglio.*

guaranteed circulation A minimum circulation level guaranteed by magazines. If circulation drops below this level, the advertiser receives a prorata rebate.

gutter The two inside margins of facing pages in a newspaper or magazine.

half run In transit advertising, a half run is a car card placed in every other car of the transit system. Also referred to as a *half showing.*

half showing *See* half run.

halftone A photoengraving plate produced by photographing through a glass screen that breaks up the subject into small dots of varying size and thus makes possible the printing of gradation of shades or tones.

hand composition Type set by hand as opposed to machine composition.

head-on position An outdoor advertising location directly facing traffic, as opposed to an angled or parallel position.

heaviside layer A layer of ions that encircles the earth. At night it bounces AM transmissions back to earth, extending the range of AM stations. It does not affect FM transmissions, however.

hi-fi color A device used to obtain high fidelity color reproduction in newspaper advertising. An ad, consisting of a continuous design, is preprinted on one side of a roll of paper, leaving the other side blank for the newspaper's use. Since the ad is continuous, the roll may be cut at any point to form newspaper pages without damaging the effect of the advertisement.

high-assay models A computer model used in media selection that selects media sequentially.

house agency An advertising agency controlled by a single advertiser. Also referred to as an *in-house agency.*

house organ A company magazine issued regularly for its employees, dealers, prospects and other groups.

ID Identification announcement. A broadcast term for a brief commercial between programs. The announcement is usually 8 seconds, thus allowing only enough time for the identification of the product.

impact The degree to which an advertising message or medium affects the audience exposed to it.

insert (1) A special page or pages preprinted by the advertiser and forwarded to a publisher who binds it in the publication. (2) A coupon or advertising message inserted in a package, often referred to as a *package insert.*

insertion order Instructions from an advertiser or advertising agency authorizing a publisher to print an advertisement of a specified size on a given date at an agreed price.

institutional advertising *See* corporate advertising.

intaglio *See* gravure.

intensive distribution Widespread distribution of a consumer product in which many retail outlets are used, as opposed to selective distribution where few retail outlets are used.

island display A store display centered in the aisle or other open area.

island position A newspaper advertisement surrounded by editorial matter.

jingle Words set to music and used in a commercial.

judgment sampling A research sample selected on the basis of judgment as opposed to a random or probability sample. Widely used in advertising research.

justify type Arranging type so that the letters are evenly spaced, and the lines are the same length.

keyline A layout in which all elements are keyed to their exact position and size, including type specification. Used as a blueprint in producing a final ad.

kinescope Film of a live commercial or program made by photographing the television tube image.

king-size poster An outside transit display placed on the side of a vehicle. Size: 30" x 144."

Lanham Act The Federal Trademark Act of 1946, which governs the registration of trademarks and other identifying symbols used in interstate commerce.

layout (1) The process of laying out the elements of an advertisement. (2) The results of this process which show where the various elements of the ad will be placed.

leading Pronounced "ledding." The insertion of metal strips or leads between lines or type to increase readability and improve appearance.

letterpress A method of printing in which the image is transferred to the paper from a raised surface.

linage Any amount of advertising space measured in agate lines.

line cut (plate) A photoengraving made without the use of a screen and which produces only solid lines or masses without intermediate shades or tones.

line drawing A drawing made with a brush or pen with whatever shading that exists produced by variations in the size and spacing of the lines.

linotype A machine that sets type mechanically, casting the type one line at a time.

lip sync. In television, the synchronization of a speaker's lip movements with a separately recorded audio track.

lithography The process of printing from a flat surface on which the ink is retained by a greasy deposit. There are two forms of lithography: (1) direct lithography in which the plate prints directly on the receiving surface, and (2) offset lithography in which the printing plate image is transferred to an intermediate surface (blanket), which does the actual printing.

live program The broadcasting of a message without pre-recording it.

local advertising Advertising that is placed by a local business, as opposed to a national or regional firm.

log In broadcasting, a detailed record of every program and commercial aired by the station, kept chronologically and required by law.

logotype (logo) A trademark or trade name expressed in the form of distinctive lettering or design and used to identify the advertiser.

loss leader A product offered at cost or below cost to attract store traffic.

Ludlow A typesetting process that is a combination of hand setting and machine casting.

machine composition Setting type mechanically or by machine as opposed to hand setting.

mail order advertising Advertising designed to produce orders by mail without the use of retail outlet.

make good The repeating of an advertisement by a publisher or station without payment in compensation for an ad or commercial that was omitted or which did not meet reasonable standards of reproduction.

margin The difference between the selling price and the cost of goods sold for a business firm.

market A generic definition is a group of people with purchasing power who are willing to spend in order to meet their needs.

marketing The performance of business activities that direct the flow of goods and services from producer to consumer or user.

marketing concept An approach to marketing that embodies three concepts: (1) consumer orientation, (2) internal organization of the firm in the service of the consumer, and (3) profit.

marketing mix The manipulation of marketing variables—product, package, price, distribution, channels, personal selling, advertising, and sales promotion—into a suitable marketing program for the firm.

marketing plan A written document that serves as a blueprint for the marketing program.

market profile A demographic and psychographic description of the target market for a product.

market review A part of the marketing plan that reviews the current marketing situation and lays the basis for future planning.

market segmentation A marketing strategy in which the total market for product is divided into homogeneous subsets, so that each subset may be addressed in the most appropriate manner.

market share A brand's share of the market, expressed as a percentage.

market skimming A pricing strategy for a new product in which a relatively high price is charged in order to recover investment quickly.

markup The difference between the selling price of a product and its cost. May be expressed in terms of a percentage, or in terms of dollars and cents.

mass communication The delivery of a large number of identical messages simultaneously.

master print In television, the final, approved print of a commercial from which duplicates are made for distribution to stations.

matrix (mat) A mold of paper pulp, plastic, or similar substance made from type or plates. Molten lead poured in this mold forms a replica of the original plate known as a *stereotype.*

maximil rate A newspaper's milline rate based on its highest rate.

mechanical An assembly of pictures and proofs of type pasted in a desired arrangement, to be photographed by a camera and made into a printing plate.

media Vehicles that carry advertising messages, such as radio, television, magazine, newspapers.

MEDIAC A computer model used for the selection of media. Characterized by the ability to handle a variety of variables.

media plan A part of the marketing plan that details the media that will be employed in a marketing program.

Media Records, Inc. An organization that compiles and sells on a subscription basis records of the space used by advertisers.

media strategy A part of the marketing plan that specifies how media will be used to accomplish marketing objectives.

merchandising (1) Traditionally applied to retailing, the selection, pricing and display of merchandise. (2) In advertising, a synonym for sales promotion.

merchandising the advertising The promotion of consumer advertising to the sales force and to distribution channels.

milline rate A basic unit of comparison for newspaper costs. Computed by dividing the agate line rate by the circulation and multiplying by one million.

minimil A newspaper's milline rate computed on the basis of its lowest rate.

modular advertising agency A full-service agency that sells its services on a piecemeal basis. Sometimes called an *a la carte* agency.

monotype A machine method of composing type in which individual letters are separately molded and automatically assembled into lines.

motivation research An umbrella term applying to a variety of research techniques, mostly borrowed from the social sciences, that attempt to ascertain why consumers purchase the products they do.

MRCA A marketing research firm that gathers consumer purchase information through a mail diary and sells the results to advertisers on a subscription basis.

NAB National Association of Broadcasters. An organization of radio and television stations and networks.

NAD National Advertising Division of the Council of Better Business Bureaus. Investigates complaints of false and misleading advertising by national advertisers as part of the industry's self-regulation procedure. Refers disagreements to the NARB for adjudication.

NARB National Advertising Review Board of the Council of Better Business Bureaus. The final arbiter of complaints investigated by the NAD. If unable to resolve differences with advertisers, NARB may refer the complaints to the FTC.

narrative commercial A type of radio commercial, tells a story using a narrative format.

network In broadcasting, a group of stations affiliated by contract and usually interconnected for the simultaneous broadcasting of programs.

Nielsen Food and Drug Index A national research organization that audits consumer purchases through panels of food and drug stores and sells the results to advertisers on a subscription basis.

Nielsen Ratings Provides audience ratings for television in individual markets (Nielsen Station Index, NSI) and for network programming through the Nielsen Television Index (NTI).

NOAB National Outdoor Advertising Bureau. A cooperative organization for placement and inspection of outdoor advertising owned and used by advertising agencies. Disbanded in 1977.

noted (noting) *See* Starch.

OAAA Outdoor Advertising Association of America. An association of plant operators having standard outdoor advertising facilities.

off camera In television, action or sound outside camera range and not visible to the audience.

off mike In broadcasting, sound away from microphone. In contrast to *on mike.*

offset A lithographic printing process in which the image from the plate is transferred to an intermediate surface (blanket), which does the actual printing.

one-time rate The rate paid by an advertiser who does not use enough space to qualify for a discount.

open rate In print, the highest advertising rate from which all discounts are computed.

ornamental type A class of typeface characterized by embellishments or decorative forms. Difficult to read and used to create special effects.

outdoor advertising Signs placed along highways that meet the standards established by OAAA.

overprinting Printing headline or body copy over the illustration. A controversial practice in advertising.

package insert *See* insert.

page proof A proof of an ad in page form as it will finally appear.

painted bulletin An outdoor advertising sign that is painted on movable panels, in contrast to one printed on paper.

pan In television, to move the camera across a scene.

participation A commercial within a program as opposed to one scheduled between programs.

pass-along readership Readership of publications by individuals who are not members of the purchasing family.

paste-up A layout in which all elements are combined in their proper places for reproduction as a single engraving.

penetration The extent to which an advertisement reaches a particular audience. Usually expressed as a percent of the total audience.

penetration pricing A pricing strategy in which prices are set relatively low in order to expand the market and to obtain a major share.

personality commercial A commercial that gains its strength from the use of a well-known personality.

photocomposition A method of setting type by a photographic process. Also referred to as *cold type.*

photoengraving A relief printing plate made by a photochemical process. Also the process itself.

pica A unit of measurement for type and printed materials. Six picas equal one inch.

picture-headline format A format for print advertising utilizing a dominant illustration on the upper portion of the page with a headline under it.

plant operator In outdoor advertising, the businessperson who leases, erects, maintains, and sells space on outdoor signs.

plate The metal or plastic from which impressions are made by any of the various printing operations.

platen The part of a printing press that holds the paper and presses it against the plate or type.

point A unit of vertical type measurement. Equal to 1/72 of an inch.

P.O.P. Point-of-purchase advertising. Any displays or advertising materials used in a retail store.

positioning *See* product position.

poster An advertising message printed on large sheets of paper and pasted on panels.

preemption In broadcast, the appropriation of time from a scheduled program or commercial in order to broadcast another program or commercial.

preferred position   Any advertising position within a publication for which the advertiser must pay a premium price.

preprint   A reproduction of an advertisement prior to publication.

press run   The number of copies printed for a particular job.

primary colors   In printing, red, yellow and blue.

primary demand   Demand for a type of product without regard for a particular demand.

prime time   A continuous period of time of not less than three hours per broadcast day as designated by the station. Usually, 7:00 P.M. to 11:00 P.M., E.S.T., and 6:00 P.M. to 10:00 P.M., C.S.T.

private label (brand)   Goods produced for exclusive labeling by distributors or retailers. Sometimes referred to as *distributor brands* as opposed to *producer brands.*

probability sampling   A statistical method of sampling in which every unit in the universe has an equal and known probability of being selected.

producer   In broadcast, the person responsible for producing a program or commercial.

product concept   A description of a product in terms of its physical and psychological attributes. The product concept serves as a basis for developing the product itself, as well as the product package, name, pricing, advertising, and so forth.

product differentiation   A marketing strategy in which a product is differentiated from competitive products either through minor product modifications, through appeals, or a combination of these two approaches.

product-life cycle   A concept that suggests that the life of a product can be divided into stages: an introductory stage; a growth stage; a maturity stage; and a decline stage. Each stage requires a different marketing approach.

product manager   The individual in the client organization who is charged with the responsibility for marketing a particular product.

product position   The location of a product in a product space. This position determines how the product will be presented to consumers in terms of its physical and psychological attributes.

product space   An abstract space bounded by relevant product attributes. Used as a logical device for defining a product in terms of consumers' needs.

production department   The department reponsible for the production of advertisements and commercials.

progressive proofs   A set of engraver's proofs used in four-color advertising. These proofs show each color plate separately and in combination.

projective techniques   Research techniques used in motivational research. Based on the tendency of individuals to perceive the enviroinment in terms of personal need-value systems.

psychographics   A way of classifying consumers based on their activities and interests.

publicity   A story or information about a product or company published or broadcast as editorial material and without cost to the company.

publisher's statement   A statement of circulation issued by a publisher.

puffery   Exaggeration of a product's attributes in advertising. As long as this exaggeration is in qualitative areas where it is a matter of opinion, puffery is not illegal.

Pulse   A research organization that reports on radio and television audiences as well as conducting other marketing research studies.

queen-size poster   An outside transit advertising display piece placed on the sides of vehicles. Size: 30" X 88." See *King-size poster.*

quota sampling   A method of sampling in which respondents are chosen to fill demographic quotas. For example, a certain number in each age, occupation, and income group. Inferior to a probability sample in terms of representativeness of the total population.

RAB   Radio Advertising Bureau. An organization of radio representatives, stations, and networks to promote radio as an advertising medium.

RADAR   A market research organization that has done extensive research on radio audiences.

random sampling   A form of probability sampling in which each member of the universe has an equal and known chance of being selected.

rate card   A card issued by an advertising medium listing its rates, mechanical requirements, and other information needed by an advertiser.

rating point   (1) In TV, one percent of all TV households in a defined geographic area. (2) In radio, one percent of all households in a defined geographic area.

reach   The number of different households or members of a target market exposed to one or more advertising messages during a specified period of time, usually four weeks.

readership   The number of people exposed to a specific advertisement, publication, or editorial in a given publication.

read most   *See* Starch.

reading notices   Newspaper advertisements set in editorial style and identified by the word *advertising*. Charged at higher rates than other advertising.

recall tests   A method of testing advertising in which respondents are given clues (such as the product category) to aid their recall of specific advertisements or products.

reference group (person)   A group or individual with which an individual wants to be associated and whose beliefs, attitudes, values, and behaviors the person will seek to emulate.

recognition test   A test of advertising in which respondents are shown an advertisement and asked whether they have seen it and, if so, how much of it they read. This is the method used by the Starch readership studies.

rep   Representative. A designation given to a salesperson of media or other suppliers.

reprint   A copy of an advertisement or editorial after it has been published.

repro proof   Reproduction proof. A proof of type used for photographic reproduction by the various printing processes.

retail advertising   Advertising designed to attract people to a retail outlet to purchase merchandise.

retail trading zone   An area surrounding a central city whose residents patronize stores in the central city.

retouching   Correcting or improving photographs or other artwork prior to photoengraving.

reverse type   Using white type on a dark background as opposed to black type on a white background. Research indicates that it tends to reduce readership.

Robinson-Patman Act   Amended the Clayton Act in 1936. Deals with unlawful competition, price discrimination, brokerage allowances, and promotional practices.

ROI   Return on investment. A financial measure used by business to evaluate investment opportunities.

roman type   A general type group distinguished by a variation in the weight of the strokes and the inclusion of serifs.

rotation plan   In outdoor advertising, painted bulletins are rotated from one location to another at regular intervals, usually on a monthly basis.

rotary press   A method of printing employing only cylinders. Used in high-speed newspaper presses.

rotogravure   *See* gravure.

rough   The first step in developing layouts. Also referred to as a *rough layout.*

run of paper (ROP)   Any location in the publication convenient to publisher, in contrast to preferred position.

rushes   In television, the first, uncorrected and unedited film obtained in shooting commercials.

S

SAG   Screen Actors Guild.

sales promotion   Any supplemental sales activity, excluding personal selling, advertising, and publicity. Includes such things as displays, coupons, contests, sweepstakes, price-off-label.

sales promotion advertising   (1) Advertising in support of sales promotion activity. (2) Advertising products at reduced prices to attract customers.

sans serif   A type face that has no cross strokes or serifs at the top and bottom of characters.

saturation campaign   A media pattern of intensive frequency over a relatively short period of time.

schedule   A listing of proposed advertisements and/or commercials by media, with dates, amount or space or time, specific publications and/or stations, etc.

screening   (1) A special viewing of a program or commercial for advertisers, agencies, or other special groups. (2) A method of printing. See *silk screen.*

script   In television, a description of the video along with the accompanying audio, used in the preparation of a storyboard, or in lieu of it. In radio, the audio portion, along with a description of the effects to be created.

script type   *See* cursive type.

secondary coverage   The geographic area in which the reception of a radio station is fair, but subject to variation.

selective demand   Demand for a particular brand of a product, in contrast to primary demand, which is demand for the general product type.

selective distribution   A distribution strategy in which distribution is restricted to a relatively small number of retail outlets in order to gain more control over the conditions of sale. *See* intensive distribution.

self-mailer   A direct mail piece that can be mailed without a wrapper or envelope.

serifs   The short cross strokes at the tops and bottoms of type characters.

serigraphy   *See* silk screen.

sets in use   In television, refers to the percent of total TV households in a defined geographic area with their sets turned on at a specific time.

set solid   Lines of type set without leading.

SFX   Sound effects. A direction used in television and radio scripts.

share of audience   In broadcasting, the percentage of homes with sets in use turned to a particular program.

short rate   The higher rate an advertiser must pay for failing to use the amount of space or time specified in the contract.

shoulder   That part of a unit of type that extends above and below the type character, and which does not print.

signature   (1) The advertiser's name in an advertisement; (2) a musical passage that identifies a radio or television program, or a commercial; (3) a single sheet of paper folded and ready for stitching for a book, usually four pages or a multiple of four pages.

silk screen   A printing process operating on a stencil principle in which a stenciled design is applied to a screen of silk or other material, and ink is forced through the mesh of the screen to the paper beneath it. Also known as *serigraphy.*

simulation   Used in computerized media selection. A process for introducing media data into a computer for the purpose of imitating the effects of a media schedule.

simulcast   A program broadcast simultaneously over radio and television, or over AM and FM radio.

slug   (1) a unit of type; (2) a notation placed on copy to identify it temporarily, and not to be reproduced in final printing.

specialty   *See* advertising specialty.

spectacolor   A sophisticated form of hi-fi color in which newspaper advertising is preprinted with registration points to fit the newspaper page so that a continuous design is not necessary.

spectacular   (1) A large outdoor sign, electrified and usually animated. (2) In broadcasting, a special, irregularly scheduled program, usually an hour or more in length.

split run The use of two or more advertisements of the same size in alternate copies of a newspaper or magazine. Often used for testing purposes, or to feature different products in regional issues of a magazine.

sponsor An advertiser who pays for talent and time for a radio or television broadcast. Unlike a participation, the sponsor assumes financial responsibility for the production of the program.

spot announcement (SPOT) (1) A broad term used for a radio or television commercial. (2) Technically, a commercial bought from an independent station. In order to distinguish the different kinds of *spot,* the terms *local spot, participating spot,* or *national spot* are sometimes used.

spread Two facing pages in a publication. Also called a double-truck.

square serif A form of type face that embodies features of both roman and block type. Like roman, it has serifs; like block, the strokes are of uniform thickness.

SRDS Standard Rate and Data Service. An organization that publishes current information on advertising rates, mechanical requirements, closing dates and other related information for a variety of media.

Starch A research organization that conducts studies of magazine readership using a recognition technique. Starch provides three measures of readership: (1) *noted* —the percent of respondents who claim they saw the ad in the publication being studied; (2) *seen-associated* —the percent of respondents who claim that they associated the advertisement with the advertiser; (3) *read most*—the percentage of respondents who read half or more of the copy.

station break Designated time between network programs, or within programs set aside for local station identification.

station rep An individual or organization who sells time on local stations.

stereotype A duplicate printing plate cast from a matrix.

stop motion A photographic technique for animating inanimate objects.

storyboard A series of drawings used to represent the action in a television commercial. Used for getting advertiser approval, for obtaining estimates on production costs, and as a blueprint for production.

super (Superimposition) In television, the imposition of one image over another, usually used for names, slogans, or key sales points.

supplement A special feature section in a magazine format distributed in newspapers, usually on Sunday. Also referred to as *Sunday supplement* or *Sunday magazine.*

Survey of Buying Power An annual publication of Sales Management magazine that contains population, income, and retail data broken down by region, state, county, and metropolitan county areas. It is a basic market reference, sometimes referred to as the *bible* of marketing.

TAA Transit Advertising Association. An organization of firms selling transit advertising.

TAB Traffic Audit Bureau. A firm that provides uniform, objective data on outdoor advertising circulation.

tabloid A newspaper, about half the page size of standard newspapers.

tape In broadcasting, audiotape or videotape used to record programs or commercials.

target market A population group believed to hold the greatest sales opportunity for a product and against whom marketing efforts are directed.

tear sheet A page containing an advertisement, removed from a publication and sent to an advertiser for checking purposes.

theme The central idea of an advertisement, a program, or a sales promotion.

thirty sheet Designation for a size of outdoor poster. Contains about 25 percent more advertising space than a 24-sheet poster.

thumbnail A rough layout in miniature form.

time buyer An advertising agency employee who is responsible for buying broadcast time.

trade advertising Advertising directed to the channels of distribution.

trade character An animated cartoon or character used to identify an advertiser or product, such as Reddy Kilowat or Speedy Alka-Seltzer.

trademark Any symbol or word used to identify the maker or origin of a product.

trade name The name under which a firm does business.

traffic department The department in an advertising agency that schedules work through the agency and makes sure that the work is completed on schedule.

transit advertising A form of out-of-home media appearing in and on transit vehicles and in transit stations.

Trendex A research organization engaged in marketing and audience research for various media.

type family A group of typefaces of the same basic design, but varying in the weight of strokes, width of characters, and so forth.

type groups Broad groups of type with similar characteristics. See *bold, roman, cursive,* and *ornamental.*

UHF Ultra High Frequency. Television channels 14 to 83, operating on frequencies from 470 Mc to 890 Mc.

unaided recall A research technique in which respondents answer question without any memory aids.

UPC Universal Product Code. A computerized system for identifying and pricing products for use in checkout counters.

uppercase Capital letters.

VHF   Very High Frequency. Television channels 2 through 13.

video   The visual portion of a television program or commercial.

videotape   An electronic unit that simultaneously records audio and video on the same tape and permits immediate playback.

visualization   The process of picturing in the mind what an advertisement will look like.

VO   Voice over. In television, the use of narration without the narrator appearing on the screen.

waste circulation   That part of the circulation of a medium that does not reach logical prospects for a product, or circulation in areas in which the product does not have distribution.

weight of type   The relative blackness of a type face.

Wheeler-Lee Act   An amendment to the Federal Trade Commission Act intended to protect consumers against unfair trade practices and false and deceptive advertising. Enacted in 1938.

WIPE   In television, a rapid transition technique for replacing one scene with another.

zinc etching   A photoengraving in zinc.

zoom   A television term used to describe the effect of having the subject suddenly grow larger (zoom in) or smaller (zoom out).

Author Index

May, Elaine, 277
Mayer, Martin, 187, 215
Miracle, Gordon E., 176
Moran, William T., 306
Morgens, Howard, 138
Morris, R.T., 169
Mortimer, Charles A., 127
Moskowitz, Milton, 67

Nathan, P.E., 395
Newman, J.W., 92
Nichols, Mike, 277
Norins, Hanley, 276
Norman, Norman B., 215
Norris, James S., 209, 285
Norris, Vincent, 189

O'Brien, Niel, 285
O'Connor, John W., 185
O'Gara, James V., 23
Ogilvy, David, 20, 21, 187, 190, 195, 229, 253
O'Meara, John T., Jr., 139
Ornstein, Robert E., 18
Oxenfeldt, Alfred R., 69, 170

Packard, Vance, 93
Paepcke, Walter, 239
Palda, Kristian S., 197
Patton, Richard B., 87
Payne, S.L., 111, 113
Pearson, Arthur, 399
Peckham, James O., Sr., 365
Pirsig, Robert M., 17
Plisken, Robert, 239, 242
Posner, Richard, 405
Preston, Ivan L., 412

Quera, Leon, 254

Reeves, Rosser, 3, 187, 190, 208, 254
Revett, John, 412
Revson, Charles, 153, 399
Richardson, Larry, 173
Ries, Al, 17, 153
Robinson, Claude, 211
Roman, Kenneth, 253
Rosebrook, Jack, 209
Rosenberg, M.J., 93

Ross, Wallace A., 278
Roth, Paul, 331
Rubicam, Raymond, 230
Rugg, D., 113

St. Georges, Joseph, 305
Salatich, William G., 40
Salmon, Walter J., 381, 394
Sandage, C.H., 189
Scheuing, Eberhard E., 139
Schoner, B., 112
Schwab, Victor O., 191
Scripps, Charles E., 218
Seiden, Hank, 282
Shapiro, I., 107
Sherif, Carolyn W., 170
Sherif, Muzafer, 137
Sloan, Alfred P., 11
Sloan, Alfred P., Jr., 41
Smith, Adam, 6, 7
Smith, G.H., 81, 104, 116
Smith, W.R., 10
Spencer, Bill, 194, 384
Stanley, Thomas B., 240
Starch, Daniel, 240
Steiner, G.A., 86, 196
Stone, Jack R., 86
Sultan, Ralph G.M., 381, 394
Swan, J.E., 138
Sweeney, Kevin, 277

Talley, Walter J., Jr., 147
Tanner, J.C., 100
Telser, L.G., 405
Thomajan, Zareh Garbed, 223
Thompson, G.C ., 197, 392
Toffler, Alvin, 86
Tombaugh, Tom N., 83
Treasure, John , 195
Trout, Jack, 17, 155
Tull, D.S., 169
Twedt, D.W., 102
Tyler, William D., 185, 187

Uhl, K.P., 112

Van Buren, Abigail, 192
Vanderwicken, Peter, 93
Vogl, A.J., 390

Subject Index

Diagram of the Marketing Plan

The marketing plan in the modern, sophisticated company is the basic control document that underlies the execution of the final communications program for a particular product. The plan outlines the specific objectives and strategies to be employed for each element of the program. Its purpose is to coordinate all aspects of the company's marketing activities relative to that product.

The flow of the marketing plan, which is essentially the flow of this book, is illustrated below. Each step in the process logically leads to the next. The whole process starts with a market review (Part III of the book) and culminates in an evaluation of the program's success (Part IX of the book). This evaluation becomes a central part of the next market review, which begins the marketing plan for the next time period.

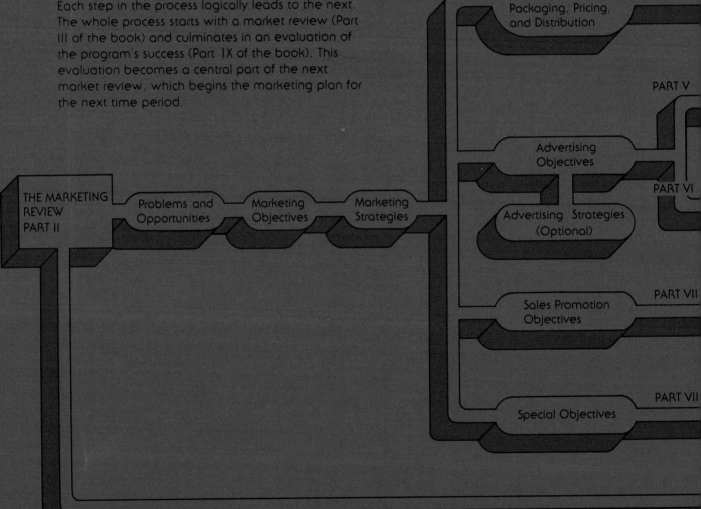

THE MARKETING REVIEW PART II → Problems and Opportunities → Marketing Objectives → Marketing Strategies

Objectives for Product, Name, Brand, Packaging, Pricing, and Distribution — PART IV

Advertising Objectives — PART V

Advertising Strategies (Optional) — PART VI

Sales Promotion Objectives — PART VII

Special Objectives — PART VII